The Great Pyramid

The Great Pyramid's eerily precise architecture has for centuries both
astounded and puzzled archaeologists and has given rise to numerous
modern fantasies concerning the so-called 'Mystery of the Pyramids'.
Sweeping away an accretion of myth and bafflement, John Romer
describes for the first time exactly how the Great Pyramid was
designed and built. He argues that the pyramid-makers worked from
a single plan whose existence has long been doubted and even denied
by scholars. Moreover, the Great Pyramid's unique architecture is
integral to the processes of its manufacture, and at the time the
Pyramid was built the tasks of construction and design had not been
placed into our modern separate compartments, each one overseen by
its appropriate professionals. By placing this seminal building back
into its genuine contemporary context, this book underlines the
extraordinary talents and the originality of the ancient Egyptians
of the time of King Khufu.

To Mr. L. M.

from Gisa, 1776

I Have laid before you, Sir, the ancient and modern enquiries on the subject of the great pyramid, to which I have added such observations as occurred to me from the presence of the objects; I hope they will give you a satisfactory idea of it, and save you the trouble of reading a number of volumes, the attentive perusal of which might only augment your doubts, as long as you do not go yourself to examine it more minutely on the spot. I will own to you, Sir, that after meditating on the descriptions which have appeared of these ancient monuments, I found it impossible to adopt any fixed opinion and I remained in a painful uncertainty. The truth I sought after was hid in the obscurity of many different opinions, that the more I studied, the less I was informed. I flatter myself, however, to have discovered it since at the foot of the pyramid, in the gloomy recesses of its interior, and on its lofty summit; the torch of reflexion has always guided my footsteps: may it also have directed my pen, and produced conviction in your mind; for in matters of science, to doubt, is to be in torment.

Claude Étienne Savary, Letters from Egypt, London 1786

The Great Pyramid
Ancient Egypt Revisited

JOHN ROMER

CAMBRIDGE
UNIVERSITY PRESS

CAMBRIDGE UNIVERSITY PRESS
Cambridge, New York, Melbourne, Madrid, Cape Town, Singapore, São Paulo

Cambridge University Press
The Edinburgh Building, Cambridge CB2 8RU, UK

Published in the United States of America by Cambridge University Press, New York

www.cambridge.org
Information on this title: www.cambridge.org/9780521871662

First published 2007

Printed in the United Kingdom at the University Press, Cambridge

A catalogue record for this book is available from the British Library

ISBN 978-0-521-87166-2 hardback

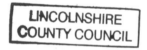

For Beth

Contents

Illustrations

Prologue The Valley of the Kings

No man knows the meaning of ANYTHING in any paper until he knows what interests control it. Curiosity in this domain is limited to an élite. It is almost un-english to mention any such topic.

Ezra Pound's Guide to Kulchur[1]

So, Mr Pound. Thirty years ago, I was living in Egyptian Thebes and entirely captivated by the Valley of the Kings. What had so fascinated me was that most of its great tombs had been made by a few families of craftsmen working side by side for centuries, yet every one was different. You could see ancient people making living choices. Walking through the tombs that they had made was like taking a trip back into part of the ancient mind.

One windy evening as the branches of the palm trees rattled in the darkness outside the windows of my studio, I drew out the plans of some of those royal tombs on slips of tracing paper so that, by placing them one over the other, I could compare the changes in their architecture. Even as I watched the shapes of various tomb plans twist this way and that down through the centuries, something unexpected happened. Despite their differences, I could see an underlying constancy in their design, a strict set of rules that had been most carefully applied from one tomb to the next. It was profoundly moving.

I had rediscovered something of the essence of those tombs, and for a while I alone in all the living world shared that information with the ancient people who had planned and made them. Later, I discovered that the application of those rules had developed and expanded, tomb by tomb, in a way that was so regular, so logical, that I could predict the arrangement and shapes of parts of the later tombs by measuring up the plans of earlier ones and making some simple calculations.[2] So although at first those ancient monuments had seemed so full of individuality, in reality each one was a subtle variation on its predecessor; the Royal Valley, a great fugue.

And once again, within these last few years, as I worked with the plans of ancient Egypt's early pyramids, I have experienced the same thrill of discovery many times. That same eerie dialogue as, once again, I stumbled through the thoughts of ancient tomb designers. This time, however, I was working with the product of the geniuses who had planned and built one of the greatest monuments on our planet: the Great Pyramid of Giza.

I'd started my pyramidological perambulations innocently enough, with a ruler, a pair of compasses and a plan, trying to work out how on earth the ancient Egyptians had managed to set a mysterious block of limestone that lies in one of the Great Pyramid's interior corridors exactly at the height at which the area of the base of the pyramid above the block is precisely half of the area of the base of the entire pyramid (see fig. 1, and ch. 3 below). And then perhaps, once I had solved that strange conundrum, I would discover why these ancient people had set such specific mathematics within the tomb of pharaoh.

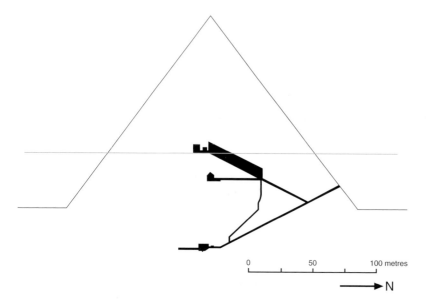

Fig. 1 A section through the Great Pyramid. The grey line is drawn at the level at which the area of the base of the Pyramid above the line is half the area of the base of the whole Pyramid.

The first thing that I discovered was that, unlike the royal tombs of Thebes, the combination of the Great Pyramid's colossal size and extraordinary precision – for the accuracy of its architecture can be measured on occasion within fractions of an inch – easily defeats the efforts of a modern draftsman. That the width of a line upon a scale plan of the Great Pyramid will cover several feet of solid stone at the Pyramid itself so that any such plan printed on the pages of a book cannot prove that the Great Pyramid's architecture is related to the passage of the sun and stars, to Pythagoras' Theorem or a map of the Cairo subway system or a ticket to the moon. And so I turned to other methods. From the beginning and in common with many other people through the ages, I sensed that, like the royal tombs of Thebes, the architecture of this Pyramid, both its dark interior and its celebrated silhouette, was held in a cat's-cradle of geometric harmonies and contained a kind of hidden logic.

Three years and several pyramids later, I discovered what that logic was. And in those ancient patterns, I rediscovered something of the pyramid-makers' purposes and ambition, and something of their wisdom, too.

Now I am well aware that my claim to have uncovered some of the Great Pyramid's innermost secrets after four and a half millennia appears to verge on the bizarre. From the first day I started working on the Great Pyramid, whose measurements alone induce a sense of unreality, my investigations took on a somewhat Quixotic air. If only then, to reassure my readers and myself, my first task when I set out to write this book was to discover why no one else had done this work before me; why the archaeological study of ancient Egypt's most celebrated monument, and most especially its interior, had been neglected for so long. And why, despite all the books and articles – amazon dot com presently lists two hundred works upon the pyramids – the most accurate descriptions of Egypt's most celebrated monument are more than a century old. How such a failure of scholarship and imagination had occurred and why, as a scholar-reviewer recently observed: 'Modern Egyptologists have largely given up on the pyramids.'[3]

My story is founded on three main premises. First, that the builders of the Great Pyramid worked from a single construction plan, a plan whose existence has long been doubted and even denied by many scholars, but one that I have now recovered; a plan whose ambitions for the body and the spirit of the dead king had been developed from those of earlier royal tombs. Second, that the daily effort involved in building the Great Pyramid was similar to that which has been recently calculated for the construction of the so-called Red Pyramid, which was built a few decades before it. Third, that the processes of the Great Pyramid's construction were integral to its design; that, at the time that this Pyramid was built, the modern processes of architectural construction and design had not yet been placed into their separate compartments, and that subtle harmonies held within its architecture are the product of the methods of its manufacture; of its craftsmen and their specific use of their materials.

This then, for the first time, is an account of the design and construction of the Great Pyramid of Giza based upon its rediscovered ancient plan and a near-contemporary timetable of pyramid construction.

Nor is this account based upon yet another theory of pyramid construction and design. As well as being the most accurately surveyed building in the modern world, the Great Pyramid is also one of the most accurate the human race has ever made; some of the elements of its architecture are yet precise to within fractions of an inch. The ancient symmetries and patterns that it contains exist in cold hard blocks of stone, in tens of tons. The real challenge, then, was not simply to expose a plan within the Great Pyramid's architecture, but to establish how and why the plan was made.

To rediscover the how and why of the Great Pyramid, a product of a pre-literary age,[4] we must attempt to feel inside its craftsmen's finger tips, to move inside their minds, to understand their largest and most mysterious creation. It is a voyage back into the shapes and forms and textures of early ancient Egypt, a voyage in which mathematics, geometry and modern plans are but the means to an end, to be employed as one would a modern grammar book to penetrate the purposes and meanings of processes that have been lost and whose sole surviving traces are held within the Pyramid itself and the landscapes in which it was created.

Part One, 'Visions of the Pyramid', introduces the Great Pyramid and describes how our present knowledge of it was built up; an egyptological misadventure in which the simultaneous establishment of both academic egyptology and pyramidology prompted a rivalry that has served to stifle pyramid studies and at the same time create the best part of the Great Pyramid's so-called 'mysteries'. It also introduces the two new sources of information that are the motors of the book: a reconstruction of the Great Pyramid's building timetable and an outline account of a previously unobserved underlying plan within its architecture, the traces of an elegant and sophisticated system by which the Great Pyramid, the largest stone block building in the world, was built by a nation of Bronze Age farmers with a population of the size of Manchester or San Francisco.

Part Two concerns the people who made the Great Pyramid and is divided into two sections. 'The ghosts in the cemetery' discusses the vulgar representations of ancient Egyptians that have come to haunt the Giza Plateau and deform discussion of how and why such great pyramids were made. It is therefore as much concerned with present misconceptions of the king for whom the Pyramid was made, with his subjects and their titles and professions, as it is with the Pyramid itself. The second section, 'The people on the Plateau', considers the surviving traces of the pyramid-makers themselves. It deals in epitaphs and portraits, in quarrymen and chisel-cuts. Here then, the book's substance echoes its subtitle. For the creation of this unique Pyramid cannot be explained by recourse to that woolly entity now known collectively as 'ancient Egypt'.

Part Three, 'The land and the Pyramid', describes the exploitation and the mobilisation of the ancient land of Egypt in the drive to build the Pyramid. Information gained in recent surveys right across the ancient kingdom offers a fresh understanding of how the materials of the Great Pyramid were obtained and moved.

Part Three also deals with the physical and metaphysical impact of Egypt's landscapes upon the culture of the pyramid-makers: the river and the rocks, the minerals and the earth that sustained the Pyramid's makers and their state and informed their sensibilities.

Part Four, 'The great inheritance', describes the historical origins of the Great Pyramid's design and specifications and the traditional arrangements for the burial of the king. It shows how the materials extracted and transported from the length and breadth of Egypt were manipulated in a series of aesthetic and technical developments, a process more akin to craft work than Western processes of architectural design, that culminated in the Great Pyramid's construction.

It is often said that the establishment of ancient Egypt, the world's first nation state, was based on the development of writing and of national government, a progress said to have been 'accompanied by advances' in Egyptian art and architecture.[5] The evidence of the early pyramids, however, is that a great part of this revolution was played out in their construction and design. In this respect, the Great Pyramid was not just a building project, an architectural display, but is the physical residue of the process of the creation of the Egyptian state, a process set underway in previous centuries, as the royal tomb and stone block architecture had been developed.

Part Five, 'Planning the Pyramid', describes how the Great Pyramid was sited, located and designed. In this, I have derived much fresh material both from modern surveys and from little-known features on the Giza Plateau whose ancient purposes came to light during my analysis of the Great Pyramid's plan.

Part Six, 'Building the Pyramid', outlines the processes of the Pyramid's construction, year on year. Based upon a time frame derived from the imperatives of the Great Pyramid's construction, this method brings enormous dividends to an understanding of how the Pyramid was built.

The climax of this epic labour, the entombment of the king, was the last act in the national ritual of making this Great Pyramid. It was also the moment where stone and time and royal destiny became as one. Not only then had the Great Pyramid's unique geometry served it as its own theodolite during the long years of its construction, but in the final stages of its ancient functions that same geometry had also served quite literally as a definition of the route to royal burial: the royal destiny.

'After Khufu', a two-part coda, briefly outlines the huge effect of the Great Pyramid on later periods: this pyramid, it would appear, not only defined the fate of the king for whom it had been built but also holds the novel notion of a resurrection in its stones.

Apparatus

A great deal in this book is new and I am well aware that without the appropriate facts and footnotes to back up its arguments it will register inconsequentially, as yet more pyramidological speculation. At the same time I have tried to make my text accessible to all who are interested in the Great Pyramid, rather than just to that narrow circle of professionals, the archaeologists and egyptologists, who for the most part are not interested in it at all.

Primary references to specific antiquities and excavations are usually given in the endnotes to the text. Many of my observations, however, cover swathes of scholarly material and full citations are impracticable. In these instances, the general references that I have cited are of recent publications and have been chosen because their bibliographies will serve to lead the curious back through the main lines of previous research. I might add that I wrote with a handful of excellent general reference books by my side, including Mark Lehner's *The Complete Pyramids*, Rainer Stadelmann's *Die ägyptischen Pyramiden* and the Highway Code of ancient Egyptian building books from which one departs at one's peril, Dieter Arnold's *Building in Egypt*.[6]

My prime reference, however, was Petrie's *Pyramids and Temples of Gizeh*, the classic nineteenth-century tome that holds the results of the last full survey of the Great Pyramid. Whenever that survey has been tested, its measurements have been found quite accurate, and Petrie after all was but checking and correcting a mass of earlier data that had itself been gathered with unusual, not to say fanatic, care.[7] For reasons of consistency therefore, I have usually preferred Petrie's measurements as given in that work rather than mixing those figures with the results of later but more partial surveys.[8] I have also on occasion mined the recent exhibition catalogue *Egyptian Art in the Age of the Pyramids*, a splendid example of what Glyn Daniel has called 'haute vulgarisation', as a sort of 'Gombrich' of contemporary academic opinion concerning the period in which the Great Pyramid was built; it also has the added advantages of splendid maps and photographs, lavish references and up-to-date bibliographies.[9] It is for these specific reasons that I refer so frequently to it in my text, and I hope that the catalogue's numerous contributors will not take offence at my occasional re-examination of their words.

Those familiar with Mark Lehner's fine book upon aspects of the monuments and topography of the eastern side of the Great Pyramid, *The Pyramid Tomb* etc., may detect both similarities and divergences in our two treatments of this area.[10] Although I came to the detail of his survey after I had already formed the outline of my understanding of the geometry underlying the Great Pyramid's plan, several of Lehner's observations allowed me to expand my results. And for that I am extremely grateful.

Finally, a few paragraphs concerning specific aspects of the text.

All distances have been calculated using latitude and longitude as given in Baines and Málek's *Atlas of Ancient Egypt*, with shipping distances given at an extra 10 per cent, excepting those which necessitated a passage around the so-called Kena Bend in Upper Egypt, to which 40 per cent has been added.[11] As no one can be entirely sure of the ancient course of the Nile, closer calculation seems hardly practical. Employing data gathered from the work of Jeffreys and Tavares, however, I have estimated that, at the time of the Great Pyramid's construction (c. 80 BC), the Nile's stream at the latitude of Giza ran about 1½ miles (2½ km) west of its present course.[12]

In similar fashion, the year dates that are presently accepted for the reigns in which the Great Pyramid and the other early pyramids were built are provisional and will almost certainly remain so; fortunately, the arguments of this book are not dependent upon chronological exactitude. For the lengths of the reigns of the early kings of

Egypt, I have generally followed von Beckerath's *Chronologie des pharaonischen Ägypten*, although I have modified some of those figures, using more recent information.[13] I have also extended the length of the reign of Khufu's father Sneferu by six years as Rainer Stadelmann the excavator of his Red Pyramid has proposed and, following the new date for the Great Pyramid's foundation proposed in Kate Spence's elegant paper upon its stellar orientation,[14] I have reset von Beckerath's absolute chronology (see Appendix 1).[15] At the risk of disappointing devotees of chronology, I have not chased the consequences of these date-shifts throughout the following half-millennium; a reluctance founded, I admit, on the desire to keep less-impassioned readers awake and reading, and fortified by the belief that my readjustment does not question currently accepted patterns of chronology.[16]

For like reasons, all ancient names have been given in a single form of common usage.[17] So, King Khufu's name appears here only in that form and not in its variants. Once again, this simplification has been made in the interests of narrative; neither would the themes of my book be enhanced by its further discussion.[18] Place names too are given in a single form of common usage, the majority taken from Baines and Málek's Egyptian Atlas.[19]

For reasons of style, I have capitalised the word pyramid where it is used as an abbreviation of the Great Pyramid. All other uses of the word, except where it is employed as a proper noun, are given in lower case. I have also employed the modern term 'Giza Plateau' for the rocky outcrop on which the Great Pyramid sits, and I have capitalised the common names of the architectural elements inside the Great Pyramid: the Grand Gallery, the Queen's Chamber, etc., whose locations are indicated in figure 11 – although to avoid confusion I have described the uppermost room, which its early explorers dubbed the 'King's Chamber', as the burial chamber.[20] By themselves, of course, none of these modern labels define the ancient purposes of the architecture they describe.

Similarly, although I am well aware that the royal title 'pharaoh' was first employed in ancient Egyptian literature in later dynasties than Khufu's, I have occasionally dubbed King Khufu as a 'pharaoh'. The word after all has a millennial history of its own within the English language – Piers Plowman's 'Pharaones tyme' denoting all the days of ancient Egypt – and it seemed a shame to sacrifice such a splendid biblical term to academia.[21] Its use here may also serve to remind the reader that the word 'king' which is more generally used to denote ancient rulers such as Khufu is loaded with equally unwonted connotations, as many ludicrous 'reconstructions' of ancient Egypt in the modern media unwittingly demonstrate.

I have also employed the word 'spirit' – a broad term, though not at all ambiguous – to denote the non-physical aspects of the Egyptian dead. No texts from Khufu's time or that of earlier reigns provide an ancient alternative, whilst the Oxford Dictionary's definition of spirit as 'the animating or vital principle in man (and animals); that which gives life to the physical organism, in contrast to its purely material elements' provides an apposite alternative to such common egyptological terms as 'ba' and 'ka' which are only to be found in texts of a far later date than the Great Pyramid, and are not in general English usage.

The use of such jargon, moreover, often serves to create another of those endless circular discussions – the egyptological equivalent of claiming the writings of Bernard Berenson to have been the inspiration of the Renaissance – where there is never anything new under the Egyptian sun and everything is 'explained' by reference to something else. To do that would be to deprive the Great Pyramid of its originality, and its makers of their humanity. I have therefore avoided general discussion on 'how the pyramids were made' and dealt principally in facts found upon the Giza Plateau and other early sites with direct connection to the Great Pyramid itself.

For similar reasons, I have confined discussion of ancient Egyptian mathematics and geometry to endnotes. The Great Pyramid, after all, was built in what can now be described as a 'pre-literary Age', and such mathematical texts as have survived from later periods of Egypt's history – basically school books – do not begin to approach the sophistication of the Great Pyramid's design. Neither could the accurate physical replication of such subtle maths as the Great Pyramid contains have been accomplished at the time of its construction: such an extraordinary labour would have required the employment of equipment that has only been available in the last few centuries. And in that conundrum lies a great part of this Pyramid's fascination.

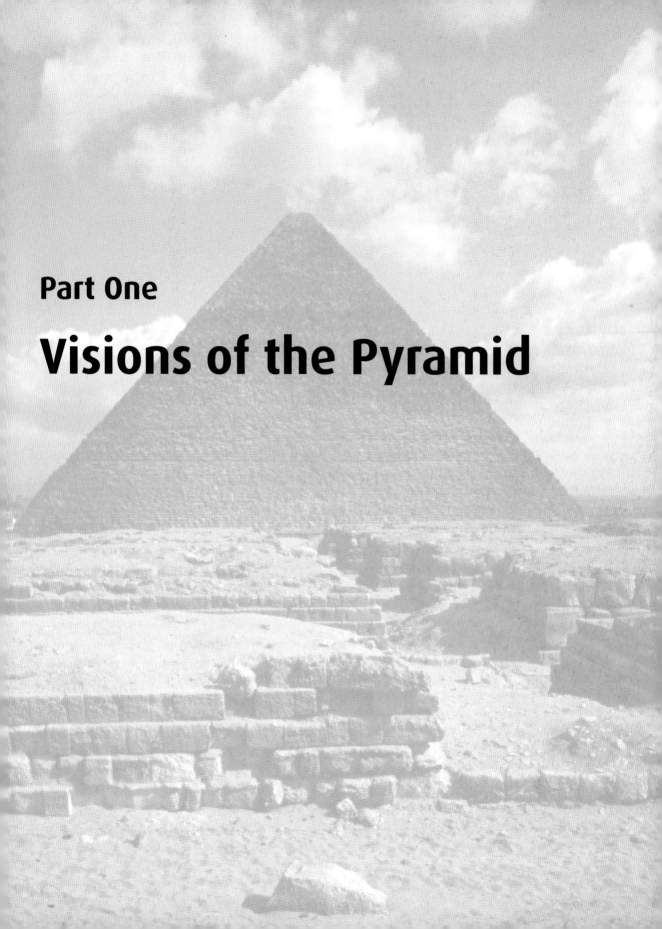

Part One

Visions of the Pyramid

1 Introduction

I made a Voyage to Grand Cairo, on purpose to take the Measure of a Pyramid.

Joseph Addison in The Spectator, 1, March 1711

At first it seems to be a ragged thing, a shimmering tent hovering over Cairo's western suburbs. Then as you approach, you realise that the Great Pyramid is the foremost of a row of three, lined up behind each other on the Giza Plateau, along the desert's edge.

Built for the Pharaoh Khafre, the second pyramid in the line seems to be the equal of the first but it is blurred by sand and stone decay; the third, a granitous jewel made for the Pharaoh Menkaure the son of Khafre, is but half the others' size. The Great Pyramid then, the foremost, holds the eye. Built within a century or so of the invention of stone block architecture, it is the largest and most accurate stone building in the world, made with such exactitude and aligned with such precision to the movements of the stars that only modern optical surveying equipment has detected any errors in its ancient stones.[1]

This Pyramid has shimmered in the world's imagination since the days of its creation. To Europe and the West it was an archetypal symbol of forgotten wisdoms standing at the edge of the known world, a thing so ancient and so perfect that it seemed, like God Himself, to measure out both time and space.[2] 'The notion or idea of

Fig. 2 A view of the Giza Plateau from the south showing, from right to left, the pyramids of Khufu, Khafre and Menkaure.

God', wrote the Cambridge alchemist Henry More in 1653, 'is no more arbitrarious or fictitious than the notion of a cube or tetraedrum or any other of the regular bodies in Geometry.'[3] So when his friend Isaac Newton attempted to find a numerical model of the universe it was quite natural that he should have first compared the 'dimensions of the Greatest Pyramid', obtained from a travelling Oxford professor, with the biblical account of Solomon's Temple at Jerusalem 'to make history suite with Nature, with Astronomy . . . and with itself', a pyramidal progress that had its culmination decades later in the *Principia Mathematica*.[4]

The Egyptians on the other hand, Christians and Muslims both, although they believed the omnipresent Pyramid to be the largest and the oldest work of humankind, had long shunned such pagan things. Only the Arab dictum that 'Everything fears time, but time fears the pyramids' betrays something akin to the awe more easily expressed from a distance in the West.[5] Thanks to this pious reticence – even the Bible never mentions pyramids – the Great Pyramid and most of Giza's other ancient monuments still stand up straight and sharp and true, despite the superficial depredations of medieval stone robbers. For millennia, however, the only written history of the mysterious structure was to be found in the writings of ancient Greek and Roman tourists, and the remnants of the alchemical and hermetic literatures of ancient Alexandria.[6]

High up on its plateau, the Pyramid itself obtains an eerie air, all explanation of its ancient point and purposes obscured by the facts

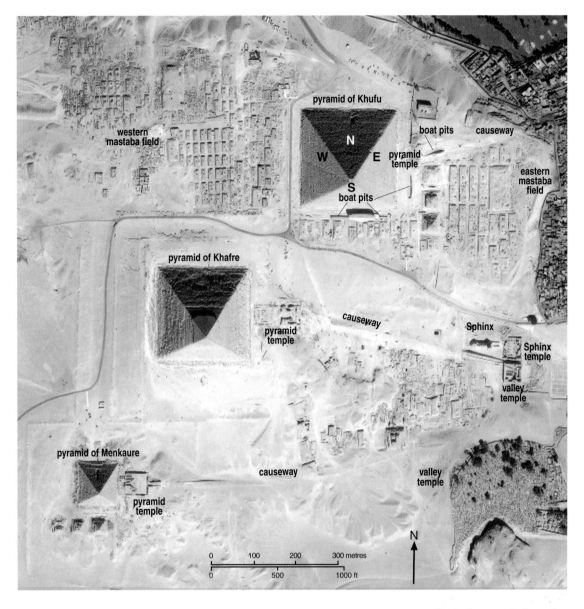

Fig. 3 A general plan of the monuments upon the Giza Plateau.

and fancies that have swirled up around it through the ages like waste paper in a desert updraft. At sunrise sometimes, when the old iron survey post upon its summit casts its thin shadow high into the mist, it seems as if it were hitched to heaven by a spinning thread. Later in the day, rippling inside a mirage of warm air, it trembles as if it were alive, as if its 5 million tons of stone were floating just above the ground. And on moonless nights, when the floodlights have been dulled, all that remains is a barely perceptible warmth upon the cheek coming from the daytime heat that is held within its stones; that, and a great black triangle that blots out half the stars within the sky.

That this strange old building was made four and a half millennia ago in the reign of Khufu, king of Egypt, called Cheops by the Greeks, has been established beyond all reasonable doubt. Long-sealed chambers deep inside the Pyramid still hold the scribblings of some of the royal work gangs, and they name Khufu as their king.[7] Standard tests on fragments of reed and charcoal extracted from the mortar set between the Pyramid's stones have dated their origins to the middle of the third millennium BC, when Khufu ruled, while yet more recent work has shown that the Great Pyramid was orientated so accurately to the stars that it holds its birthday in its stones, a stellar alignment having pinned down the setting of its baselines to around 2478 BC.[8] And all around King Khufu's Pyramid, in the cemeteries and temples, are hieroglyphic texts naming members of his family and court, which two centuries of egyptological research have used to build an outline of their lives and times.[9] Further research has identified and ordered the reigns of other kings who built great pyramids before and after Khufu's, whilst a plethora of later texts, as well as the fragmentary human remains that have occasionally been found in other royal pyramids, confirm that most of Egypt's pyramids were built to serve as tombs, as the sarcophagus that lies in the Great Pyramid's uppermost chamber would attest.[10] 'We must recur, therefore', as de Volney put it in the 1780s, 'to the ancient opinion, antiquated as it may seem, that the pyramids are tombs.'[11]

Those then are the facts that presently underpin the foundations of all true histories of the Great Pyramid of Giza. There is, however, no contemporary literature, no written record, that deals with the building of this Pyramid or celebrates its makers. Nor is there any record of the intellectual milieu of Khufu's reign which, in common with that of the surrounding centuries, remains utterly unknown: as the egyptologist Jan Assmann recently observed, the spiritual climate of that period 'can only be guessed at'.[12] Nor is there any direct evidence of

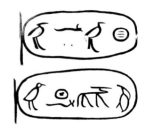

Fig. 4 Nineteenth-century copies of graffiti, found deep inside the Great Pyramid and written on its building blocks, showing two different versions of one of King Khufu's several names. (Fig. 196 shows the positions of these same graffiti upon the building blocks.)

Fig. 5 The Great Pyramid seen from its western cemetery. These lines of tombs are some of the eighty or so stone-block mastabas that were built beside the Pyramid during Khufu's lifetime. They accommodated, so their inscriptions tell, members of his family and household, and officers of his court.

Fig. 6 A great part of the Plateau on which Giza's three great pyramids were built is buried under enormous amounts of stone chippings and debris, some of which contains hearth stones, ash and pottery: strata composed of the disturbed remains of ancient workshops and accommodations.

the physical means of the Pyramid's construction: as Dieter Arnold, the doyen of ancient Egyptian architectural studies, has pithily observed, all modern theories as to how its great stones were raised up into their positions are 'in vain since no traces of any [construction] ramp survived'.[13]

Boundless and bare, only the Great Pyramid's stones remain, the residue of an extraordinary achievement and the perfect litmus test for everything that we have thought, or might yet think, about the past.

2 Making the mystery

They possess extraordinary astronomical instruments of perfect construction and instruments for measuring altitudes of wondrous, amazing, and precious construction. And they have telescopes for looking at the stars and measuring their scopes and sizes.

From Al-Jabarti's Chronicle of the French occupation of Egypt, 1795[1]

Great thoughts stir within me at the sight of ruins. Everything gradually crumbles and vanishes. Only the world remains. Only time endures. And how old the world is!

Diderot[2]

The modern mystery of the Great Pyramid was born in the autumn of 1798, three months after the French invasion of Egypt and some 4300 years after King Khufu's astronomers laid out its baselines on the soft stone of the Giza Plateau.

Breaking out of the Citadel of Cairo, the Green Zone of its day, Napoleon and fifty of his officers and men and a handful of the Parisian scholars who had accompanied the French Army into Egypt crossed the great river to the fortified city of Giza on its western bank, where they entered the deserted palace of the Egyptian military commander, Murad Bey, who had fled south to Upper Egypt. And after a night passed on velvet sofas in gardens scented with jasmine and

orange blossom, they sailed through the reeds of the Nile's rising flood to the pyramids of Giza, at nine o'clock in the morning on the 2nd of Fructidor in year 6 of the French Republic.[3]

Contrary to his later hagiographers – 'Soldats! Songez que du haut de ces pyramides, quarante siècles vous contemplent' – Napoleon was not impressed by Egypt's ancient monuments. He did not climb up the Great Pyramid to its summit that day, neither did he enter the dark web of corridors, that airless, filthy journey to the royal burial chamber from which, as another military man of the day recounts, we emerged 'dusty, dirty; faces covered with perspiration from the heat, and blacked by the smoke of torches, we looked as I have seen men look in battle'.[4]

Despite their Commander-in-Chief, the scholars who had pressed for an excursion to the Giza pyramids from their first days in Cairo were inspired. Fuelled by *eau-de-vie*, portly chemists and revolutionary economists puffed their way up to the Pyramid's summit, eminent mathematicians calculated the amount of stone required and the cost of its manufacture in contemporary France, the cartographers of the École des Ingénieurs-Géographes laid plans to make great maps of Egypt and, all the while, the expedition's artists sketched out their progress. This then was the start of the West's stocktaking of this most ancient civilisation, the beginning of that process by which ancient Egypt was inducted into the halls of academia.

Fig. 7 Napoleon's inquisitive savants examine ancient Egypt's legendary Sphinx, and the Great Pyramid looms above them all.

A well-known engraving tells the story in a single image; in the shadow of the Sphinx, a group of scholars in breeches and white stockings and tricorn hats measure the antiquities with a precision not seen on the Giza Plateau since the days of pharaoh: and finally, the secrets of the ancient East are brought into public gaze.[5]

In the months after that first trip, in the aftermath of an insurrection, as the French hold on Egypt increased, most of the 150 savants and scholars who accompanied Napoleon to Egypt followed in his footsteps to the Giza Plateau. Although it is unlikely that Edmé François Jomard, a fresh-faced twenty-year-old engineering student from the Paris Schools, had accompanied his Emperor on that first trip, it is certain that he spent much time beside the pyramids of Giza, often in the company of the Expedition's senior geographers, the engineers Coutelle and le Père, a hundred French dragoons standing as their guard. In December 1799, working with plumb bobs and measuring cords, he supervised the digging out of part of the Great Pyramid's foundations.

Jomard had spent much of the previous year in Upper Egypt with several of his friends and classmates from the Parisian military engineering schools working at Napoleon's command to measure and record its ancient monuments. Yet Jomard's watercolours are rather different from those of his fellows.[6] Whilst the other draftsmen tended towards traditional topographical descriptions and delineated the ancient monuments with a mechanical precision, Jomard's pictures show a lightness, a theatricality even, in which the ancient monuments appear like the back-drops of an opera; the sky soars, the stars twinkle and all is magic in this new-found ancient land. 'Great thoughts stir within me at the sight of ruins', as the encyclopaedic Diderot had recently exclaimed.[7]

Jomard's passion for the Great Pyramid was also born of one of Napoleon's express commands, which had sent Coutelle and le Père to map the relative levels of the Red Sea and the Mediterranean with an eye to making a canal across the Isthmus of Suez. Because they decided to tie their plans' co-ordinates to the Great Pyramid's northeastern corner, young Jomard, it seems, was charged to dig into the sand and rock that covered the lower sections of the Pyramid to determine its original size. After considerable effort, and having cleared some 50 feet of sand and chippings that lay upon the Pyramid, the debris left from the medieval quarrymen who had quarried out its casing stones, Jomard hit the bedrock of the plateau beside the Pyramid. Twenty feet out from the corner of the Pyramid itself at the two ends of its northern face, Jomard's men uncovered two

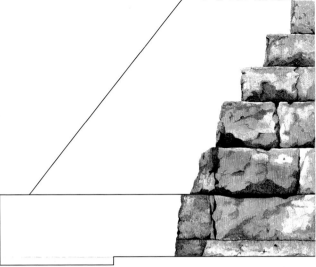

Fig. 8 The Napoleonic expedition's careful record of the socket that Jomard uncovered at the Great Pyramid's north-eastern corner. Unfortunately, the reconstruction of the missing stonework – shown in heavy line – is incorrect; it is but the first of many such erroneous restorations of the Pyramid's original dimensions.

rectangular excavations in the flat rock of the Plateau, two carefully levelled cloisons whose outer corners reflected the rough surviving corner stones of the Pyramid itself. To Jomard, it appeared that these two fine sockets had once held the original corner stones of the Great Pyramid which had long since been stripped away. After taking bearings on their line and discovering, to his amazement, that they were in perfect alignment with the cardinal points, Jomard then used the measurement between the new-found sockets in combination with the angle of the rising Pyramid, to calculate the first reconstruction of the Great Pyramid's original dimensions (fig. 8).[8]

As Jomard worked his calculations up into plans, the literature of ancient Greece and Rome rose up to haunt his mathematics, especially those reports that described the length of the Pyramid's apothem – that is, the line from its apex to the mid-point of its base-lines – as being the same length as the ancient Greek unit of measurement known as the stade, a unit which the classical authors recorded was the equivalent of 600 Greek feet, or one eighth of a Roman mile.[9] Now, Jomard found, his measurements and calculations confirmed those ancient words. And, all at once, he saw that the vanished surfaces of the Great Pyramid had once held the measuring units of ancient Greece and Rome and Egypt in their stones; at 185 m, the apophthegm, he calculated, was a whole number of units in modern measurement as well!

Such unlikely equivalencies held especial resonance for Jomard and his companions. The metre unit, the standard measure of the French in Egypt, was a comparatively recent French invention taken up by the revolutionaries as a replacement to the venerable, if unfashionable, *pied de roi*. And as Jomard well knew, the procedure by which the size of the metre unit – a product of the division of the theoretical circumference of the earth – had been obtained was taken directly from classical literature, which also told how a similar procedure had been used in antiquity to fix the length of the Greek stade.[10]

To Jomard and the French geographers, therefore, it suddenly appeared that, just as great Newton had imagined, the Giza Pyramid was a universal mediator, a measure of the earth itself, of nature and nature's laws, set up in that antique land in which the ancient Greeks believed both wisdom and geometry were born. Digging deep into the desert sand, young Jomard had recovered universal truths!

In February 1801, however, a less hurried survey by Coutelle and le Père along with a further clearance of the mounds that lay against the Pyramid enabled more exact measurements of the Pyramid, corrections that greatly dampened their enthusiasm for Jomard's theories. Jomard, however, remained enchanted and, writing over several decades, he produced a series of increasingly imaginative excursions that have since become the bedrock of esoteric speculation on the Great Pyramid's significance and meaning: that it was precisely set on the meridian of Egypt and that its angles measured out the shape of the living land; that its interior corridors and rooms served as an astronomical observation post; that the granite burial chamber and sarcophagus held within them units of size and volume and proportion that were the very measure of the world: that, above all else, the Great Pyramid of Giza was filled with messages and meanings, and stood quite apart from all the other ruins of antiquity. Jomard, in short, was the world's first pyramidologist.

Back home in Paris, Bonaparte's oriental adventure, that grandest of Grand Tours, was memorialised in the volumes of the *Description de l'Égypte*, which was subsidised by Napoleon himself. A Domesday Book compiled in the Age of Reason and quantifying all of Egypt, natural and cultural, old and new, the first edition consisted of fourteen elephantine folios accompanied by nine 800-page imperial quartos and wisely offered with its own mahogany bookcase with a built-in lectern, especially designed in Paris' best egyptianising manner by Edmé François Jomard.[11]

One of the greatest publishing ventures of all time – by themselves, the enormous pages of the *Description* were a triumph of paper making whilst the 3000 plates that they carried are unrivalled as examples of copper plate engraving – the *Description* took longer to publish than it had taken Khufu's craftsmen to built his Pyramid at Giza.[12] Within those tomes the science of egyptology was born, their hefty boards containing images of all the standing ruins of those pyramids and tombs and temples which Napoleon's scholars had surveyed and measured on site in Egypt, and all of them planned and pictured, and even occasionally restored to life, with the addition of ethereal bands of ancient priests and princes, to make a vision of a living ancient Egypt.

For more than thirty years, Jomard served as both an editor and a writer for the *Description de l'Égypte*, becoming in the process a powerful force inside the French establishment, part of the clique of *égyptologues* who had suffered the joys and rigours of Napoleon's Egyptian campaign and who were now considered to be the world's authorities on that strategically situated kingdom. As well as overseeing the complicated task of publishing the *Description*'s sumptuous plate volumes, Jomard also contributed a series of elegant commentaries upon ancient Egyptian monuments up and down the land, some essays on Egyptian metrics and his pioneering decipherment of the hieroglyphic system of ancient Egyptian numerals. Two further articles were dedicated to speculations on the pyramids and were focussed on the largest and finest pyramid of them all: the Great Pyramid at Giza.[13] Thus the first modern pyramidologist was also one of the founders of modern egyptology.

Several of the *Description*'s plates show the Great Pyramid in the last years of its millennial innocence, the limestone plateau and its

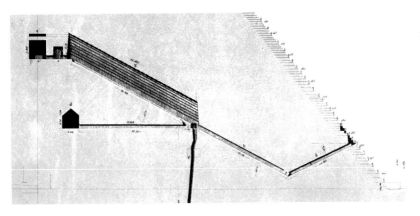

Fig. 9 Part of the *Description*'s elegant plan of the Great Pyramid, with each of its courses numbered and measured. It appears, however, that the savants were unable to gain access to several sections of the Pyramid's interior, whilst their mistaken reconstruction of the Pyramid's exterior dimensions has sent their plan askew: in reality, the Pyramid's centre line runs through the vault of the lower chamber in the plan and through the high step at the ending of the gallery above.

pyramids deep in desert sand, untouched by archaeology or exploration. Alongside several landscapes situating the pyramids and Sphinx are splendid maps of Giza and the surrounding area and fields and a superb cross-section of the valley of the Nile from the Giza Plateau through Cairo to the eastern cliffs; this the work of Coutelle and le Père. Here too are the first accurately scaled drawings of the Great Pyramid's unique interior and two elaborate perspectives, the darkness filled with wondering savants and scrambling Arabs, showing that unique vault known now as the Grand Gallery that leads to Khufu's burial chamber, that slot-like corridor deep inside the Pyramid that is unlike any other in the world and certainly, as Jomard's commentary asserts, one of the greatest architectural works of any ancient people.[14] The Great Pyramid, Jomard's commentary continues, is perfect, timeless and ethereal. Using levels, measuring cords and plumb bobs, these rationalists had discovered that the ancestors of the people whose land they had invaded had built more accurately than the greatest architects of modern France, and they had been unfashionably amazed.

For the first time, Jomard says, a proper understanding of these ancient marvels is within our grasp – his special ambition was to decipher the meaning of the thousands of hieroglyphic texts that the savants had so painstakingly recorded; even the Greek and Roman tourists had not penetrated such mysteries. 'At the beginning of this century', he continues, 'we discovered – and are still discovering daily – characteristic features of the ancient Egyptian civilisation about which all the early writers have remained absolutely silent'.[15] They may well have seen the monuments in a better state of preservation than today, he notes, and when the religion was still active, but for that very reason it had been 'impossible for them to enter the interior of the sanctuaries and study them'.

Fig. 10 The Grand Gallery. Rendered in the *Description* as an aquatint, Cécile's two atmospheric drawings yet remain the most informative images of this unphotogenic marvel. They show the Gallery from both its top and bottom, and in the same instant of time. In the left-hand image, the savants, portfolios in hand, are engaged in mapping the tiny ancient tunnel whose entrance is at the ladder's very top. The right-hand image shows the hands of a man grasping a rope as he begins a descent into the deep shaft that runs down from the side wall of the bottom of the Gallery.

Ten years after the French retreat from Egypt, the deluge of European interest in all things Egyptian that the invasion had provoked found splendid culmination in the discoveries of Jean-François Champollion, a French scholar who, despite the tenacious opposition of Jomard and his friends, had succeeded in obtaining a general acceptance of his method of deciphering Egyptian hieroglyphics.[16] Quite suddenly, the gist of the tomb and temple texts that the older *égyptologues* had so carefully recorded but never understood, the names and prayers upon the mummy cases and the statues, all of those ancient labels and inscriptions and papyri, could be read out aloud.

The magic world that the *Description* had brought so beautifully to life had lasted but for a single decade. As Jean Starobinski has remarked: 'When men reached the stage of deciphering the names of the forgotten gods, of unearthing ancient vases, it was the end of the ambiguous poetry of the ruins.'[17] As far as the Great Pyramid is concerned, it signalled the beginning of a split in our understanding of that great monument that has obscured its point and purposes down to this day.

A man of the Age of Reason, Jomard of course would never have considered the Great Pyramid to be the work of alchemists or a Divine Creator as previous generations had imagined, but a man-made mystery, an ancient architectural cipher that, with the right key, could be opened to reveal its true purposes. Ancient Egypt, he declared, could be rescued from the realm of the imagination and the uncomprehending writings of the Greeks and Romans. And yet, although the *Description*'s splendid maps and plans are decorated with the trappings of Western science, Jomard's appreciation of Egypt and its Great Pyramid was still founded, like Newton's before him, upon courtly European tradition and ultimately the remnants of that alchemical and hermetic literature of Greco-Roman Alexandria that set out to explain the mysteries of old Egypt.[18] In 1803 indeed, for the coronation of Napoleon, Jomard acknowledged this inheritance in the pattern he designed to decorate the Imperial coronation robe, which filled the ancient hieroglyph of an oval rope that denotes a pharaoh's name, and which the French savants had called a *cartouche*, with the pretty hieroglyphs of a star and a bee. At that time, some twenty years before Champollion's decipherment, the original meaning of those two signs was not understood, Jomard deriving their significance from the hermetic texts.[19] On that December day, therefore, in Notre Dame, and to their great delight one might imagine, only Jomard and a few of his fellow *égyptologues* would have understood the meaning of the signs so elegantly stitched in golden thread on Napoleon's velvet cloak: 'divus rex', 'the divine king'.

Champollion, on the other hand, was a real revolutionary; indeed, he would be haunted throughout his life by his youthful affiliations with Jacobins and anti-royalists. And, although his fascination with ancient Egypt had been awakened as a young man by meeting with Jean Baptiste Fourier, a friend of Jomard's who had written the grand historical introduction to the *Description de l'Égypte* and accompanied Napoleon on that first trip to Giza, his progress to the decipherment had been greatly hampered by the old hermetic ways of thinking. Indeed, he had succeeded in deciphering the hieroglyphs only after abandoning such preconceptions and concentrating on the internal evidence of the hieroglyphs themselves which, to everyone's surprise, were part-based on an alphabetic system.

As one would expect, Champollion's sense of history was founded not in the European tradition of divine providence and the divinity of kings, but in the application of rules of politics and economics. Once he had deciphered the hieroglyphs therefore, Champollion started to reassemble the histories of the Egyptian pharaohs and to discover something of the way of life within their various dynasties, a monumental pioneering work that was rewarded with the world's first chair of egyptology at the Collège de France. Champollion's decipherment, therefore, had effectively transformed the magical world of the plates and drawings of the *Description de l'Égypte*, that ambiguous mix of ruin, science and tradition, into an academic industry.

For the continued study of the Great Pyramid, however, the effect of this would be disastrous. The Pyramid was dumb. There were no ancient hieroglyphs engraved upon its stones, nor was there a single ancient Egyptian text that so much as mentioned the processes of the Great Pyramid's manufacture or so much as hinted at its ancient purposes. Not surprisingly, therefore, on his one and only expedition to the land of Egypt, the great Champollion found less of interest in the Great Pyramid than did the tourists who at that same time were visiting Egypt and its monuments in ever-increasing numbers. 'There is little to do here', Champollion wrote to his brother from his camp at Giza on 8 October 1828; 'as soon as the artists have copied a few domestic scenes from a tomb beside the Second Pyramid, I will return to the boats'.[20]

It is as if Champollion had sensed that the silent Pyramid, the greatest symbol of a land of symbols, was itself a part of that mystic wisdom, that same tradition which had inspired the bitter attacks that Champollion had suffered from Jomard and the other *égyptologues* when the young scientist had scattered their visions and memories for ever. To this day many of Champollion's successors seem to regard the Great Pyramid as a monument to megalomania or primitive irrationality or, indeed, 'a tedious and foolish ostentation of the wealth of kings', as the elder Pliny had remarked some eighteen centuries before.[21]

Despite the silence of its stones the Great Pyramid's sheer celebrity ensured that all of the adventurers who sailed to Egypt in the wake of Napoleon's invasion also followed in his footsteps to the Giza Plateau to marvel at the greatest single relic of antiquity. And some of them, dynamiters, cranks and consuls, hydraulic engineers, old soldiers and primordial archaeologists, rummaged in the sands around the Pyramid and measured up its strange interior.

A rich and pious man, Colonel Howard Vyse of the 15th Hussars and the 2nd Life Guards, first visited the Giza pyramids in his retirement in 1836 and was entirely fascinated by the 'grandeur and simple majesty of their forms'. Specifically, Vyse tells us, he was interested in discovering the purposes of their interior passages and chambers and establishing whether they had been used as astronomical observatories as was commonly supposed.[22] A veteran of Wellington's Peninsula Campaign, Vyse set about the Great Pyramid in military fashion, working with a few fellow countrymen, mostly residents of Cairo, and engaging surveyors and engineers and excavators of various nationalities along with a considerable local workforce to trench the desert and blast away offending obstacles with quantities of English gunpowder.[23] Under the Colonel's regime, the Great Pyramid and those of its companions then visible were probed and mapped and measured. At the Great Pyramid in particular, massive excavations cleaned huge quantities of sand and chippings from both its northern and southern faces.[24] And to Vyse's great surprise, in May 1837, at the very bottom of the northern face and in its centre, they came across some buried blocks of highly finished limestone: the pitiful remains, as he and his staff immediately realised, of the Pyramid's original casing stones, most of which had been stripped away by medieval masons and used as building stone (fig. 11). A few of these blocks were still set in their original positions along part of the baseline of the Pyramid and they were standing on a limestone pavement that was itself 'well laid, and beautifully finished . . . worked with even greater exactness, and to the most perfect level'.[25] The casing blocks, Vyse was informed by one of his surveyors, measured 8 feet 3 inches at their widest point and were some 4 feet 11 inches high, and their outer surface, which was most beautifully polished, was cut at the angle of the rising Pyramid, which had been 51° 50'.

May 1837 was a busy month for Khufu's Pyramid. At the same time that the remains of its outer casing were being uncovered on its northern face, its interior was being sapped and probed with explosives and steel rods, a frightening process that eventually opened up a series of low chambers, of entresols that had been sealed since Khufu's day, above the granite burial chamber and which held upon their walls the hasty texts that name some of Khufu's work gangs.[26] Here then at last, inside the Pyramid, was something that would interest the followers of Champollion. Post-haste, Vyse sent copies of the ancient scribblings to Dr Samuel Birch, one of the Keepers of Oriental Antiquities of the British Museum, who, after wrestling with the ill-drawn inscriptions as best he could, confirmed the possibility that, just as the ancient Greeks had written that the Pyramid was made by the pharaoh Khufu, so the stones uncovered at the Pyramid's very heart bore that self-same name. Published between 1840 and 1842, Vyse's account of the 'operations', as he called his work at Giza, included drawings of the Pyramid's new-found inscriptions, along with plans of the Giza Plateau and its pyramids that were more accurate and complete than those of any other monument in Egypt. Finally, the Great Pyramid had entered scientific history.[27]

Even as Mr Frazer of Regent Street was engaged in publishing the Colonel's three grand quartos, another and yet more ambitious expedition was beginning its work in Egypt. Set up in direct competition to the French, lavishly subsidised by the king of Prussia and led by Doctor Richard Lepsius of the University of Berlin, its aim was to gather paper records of the ancient kingdom of the highest scientific quality, and enormous quantities of genuine antiquities as well. A remarkable scholar in his early thirties, Lepsius had already proved and extended Champollion's pioneering labours and, to the chagrin of the French, would soon assume his mantle as Europe's leading egyptologist.[28]

In light and elegant prose reminiscent of Champollion or of Goethe himself, Lepsius' diary, written 'at the foot of the Great Pyramid', records his expedition's work within the cemeteries that lie around the Giza pyramids; months spent mapping the architecture of 130 of these tombs and in gathering together, for the first time, the hieroglyphic memorials of Khufu's family and court: 'nearly all these tombs', writes Lepsius, 'were erected during or shortly after the building of the Great Pyramid, and therefore present us with an inestimable series of dates . . . The subjects on the walls are usually representations of scenes from the life of the departed persons . . . The numerous inscriptions describe or name those scenes, or they set forth the often widely-extended

Fig. 11 Francis Arundale's lithograph of the excavation of part of the Great
Pyramid's original baseline is a rare record of the most important discovery
ever made at Khufu's Pyramid. The angle and positions of these fine-cut
casing stones, brought to light in the course of Colonel Vyse's investigations,
would eventually lead to the accurate reconstruction of the Pyramid's
original dimensions.

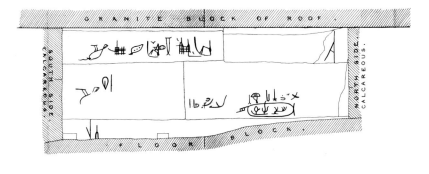

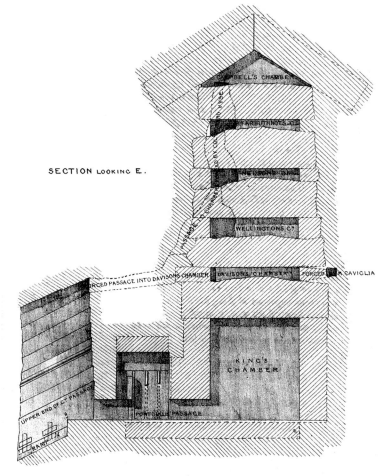

SECTION LOOKING E.

GREAT PYRAMID.

KING'S CHAMBER AND CHAMBERS OF CONSTRUCTION.

Scale of   5   10   20 Feet

Published by J.Fraser, Regent St. 1840.

Fig. 12 Vyse's published drawing of some of the graffiti that decorate the walls of 'Lady Arbuthnot's chamber', the penultimate of the four low entresols that stand above the Great Pyramid's burial chamber. The gallant colonel named the chamber after the wife of a visitor to his encampment who had helped to make the drawings of the graffiti.

Fig. 13 Vyse's published drawing of the four chambers that he opened up inside the Great Pyramid. The lively cross section marks the beginning of the conventions that are still used to describe the Great Pyramid's interior today; although it is clearly impossible to measure most of these granite blocks without demolishing a large part of the Pyramid's stonework, such images as this are so widely used that many people imagine them to be literally true.

family of the departed, and all his offices and titles, so that I could almost write a Court and State Directory of the time of King Cheops'.[29] Here, then, Lepsius is starting to create the air and ambit in which the Great Pyramid still stands: his work, indeed, is fundamental to modern academic studies of the period.

Just as Jomard's and Champollion's generations had done before, Lepsius published the product of his Egyptian researches in a series of huge weighty volumes, *Denkmaeler aus Aegypten und Aethiopien*, subsidised by the progressive Prussian king in the manner of Napoleon and dedicated under a magnificent black eagle to *Seiner Majestät*.[30] Here then, a splendid series of airy lithographs show Giza's pyramids still standing in a broad clean landscape, their accompanying tombs buried in gentle desert sand, the three grand pyramids, archaic and majestic. There is a new map of Giza too, showing the positions of the pyramids, the topography of the Plateau, and the positions of the tombs that Lepsius has investigated, and a mass of sharply elegant steel engravings of tomb plans and their carefully copied-out inscriptions: the hieroglyphic keys to Khufu's kingdom.

In the knowledge, perhaps, that Colonel Howard Vyse had recently expended considerable time and effort in mapping and exploring the Great Pyramid, the Prussian expedition, like Champollion's before it, did not trouble to replan its architecture. Unlike the surrounding cemeteries, after all, the Pyramid had no sculptures, texts or decorations, no architectural forms at all beyond those of the basic quarry block; little, then, to whet nineteenth-century taste. Confirming Birch's first impressions, Lepsius simply made an accurate record of the precious scribblings of King Khufu's work gangs that Vyse's gunpowder had blasted into the light a few years earlier.[31]

The grand old Pyramid, however, served the expedition in other ways; Lepsius' diary informs us that they celebrated the Christmas of 1842 by placing a flaming beacon and their national flag upon its summit and planting a Christmas palm-tree, complete with burning candles and dangling presents, inside the royal sarcophagus. 'Dark has been thy night, Oh Egypt, but the flame of new-born science guilds [*sic*] thy ancient name', as an American guest at these 'ever merry celebrations' remarked.[32]

A few months later, before his expedition left for Upper Egypt and Nubia, Lepsius had eleven columns of the best hieroglyphs inscribed on one of the enormous blocks of limestone that surround the present entrance to the Great Pyramid's interior.[33] A panegyric in honour of the king of Prussia's birthday, they are the only hieroglyphics engraved on Khufu's Pyramid:

Thus speak the servants of the King, whose name is the Sun and Rock of Prussia, Lepsius the scribe, Erbkam the architect, the brothers Weidenbach the painters, Frey the painter, Franke the former, Bonomi the sculptor, Wild the architect: Hail to the Eagle, Shelterer of the Cross, the King, the Sun and Rock of Prussia, the son of the Sun, freer of the land, Frederick William the Fourth, the Philopator, his country's father, the gracious, the favourite of wisdom and history, the guardian of the Rhine stream, chosen by Germany, the giver of life. May the highest God grant the King and his wife, the Queen Elisabeth, the life-rich one, the Philometor, her country's mother, the gracious, a fresh-springing life on earth for long, and a blessed habitation in Heaven for ever. In the year of our Saviour 1842, in the tenth month, and the fifteenth day, on the seven and fortieth birthday of His Majesty, on the pyramid of King Cheops; in the third year, the fifth month, the ninth day of the Government of his Majesty; in the year 3161 from the commencement of the Sothis period under King Menophthes.[34]

So the old Pyramid had been provided with the hieroglyphs it had always lacked, and on his return to Berlin the courtly wheel turned full circle and Lepsius was awarded several further titles of his own.

Despite the amazing achievements of the nineteenth-century expeditions and the establishment of academic egyptology that followed their publications, all that the early guidebooks to Egypt offered in explanation of the Great Pyramid – and by Lepsius' day they were already selling in their thousands – were comparisons of its size with other famous buildings, most popularly St Peter's in Rome, and quotations from the literature of the ancient Greeks and Romans.[35] And this it was, this gaping hole in the scholarly accounts of ancient Egypt, that a quarter-century on led to the Astronomer Royal of Scotland, one Charles Piazzi Smyth, undertaking his own small expedition to the Giza Plateau.

Piazzi Smyth arrived at Giza by a long and winding road, a journey that had started thirty years earlier when he was little more than a grammar school boy and had travelled to South Africa to assist the world-renowned astronomer Sir John Herschel in his survey of the southern hemisphere in his observatory on the Cape of Good Hope. At that same time, the great astronomer had been asked by Howard Vyse if current theories that the Great Pyramid had been a stellar observatory and that its corridors and shafts were sited on specific stars could have been based on astronomical fact; specifically, if Ursa Minor, the polar star that was thought to have been visible from the bottom of the Pyramid's descending corridor at certain times of the year, had been in that same place in Khufu's day. In his usual kindly fashion, Sir John had replied that it most certainly had not; that Ursa Minor would have been in quite another location 4000 years before, which was the estimated age of the Great Pyramid at that time, adding for good measure that 'no other astronomical relation can be drawn from the . . . angles and dimensions of the passages', nothing, indeed, appeared to be 'connected with any astronomical fact, and was probably adopted for architectural reasons'.[36] Unlike Herschel, many scientists of the day regarded the Great Pyramid just as Newton had done before them, not as a work of architecture but as a natural phenomenon.

As the nineteenth century progressed, a wide variety of scientific skills were brought to bear on the Great Pyramid, some of them by engineers engaged in projects of similar dimensions to the Great Pyramid itself. To these empire builders, it was inconceivable that the finished Pyramid could not have served some kind of active economic function. Several astronomers, indeed, claimed the Great Pyramid to have been an astronomical observatory despite John Herschel's comments, a gigantic version of the Moghul observatories of British India. Others asserted that it had been designed so that its shadow would serve as a cultic calendar in the manner of the Roman obelisks, a theory nebulously supported by reported assertions of local villagers who lived beside the Giza Plateau that they counted the approach of the Vernal Equinox by observing the tip of the Great Pyramid's winter shadow as it stretched a mile and more across their fields.[37]

In that most opulent age of nonconformity, many of these pyramidological theorists were pious folk whose ultimate source of reference was the King James Bible, which in the nineteenth century still included Archbishop Ussher's seventeenth-century dates that had set the Creation of the world at 4004 BC, and numbered each and every printed Bible verse in the system introduced by its Renaissance editors.[38] Trawling its variously published plans with rapt attention and using these dates and verse numbers as their guides, some of the pyramidologists now used the measurements of the Great Pyramid's internal architecture to divine all manner of prophecies and prognostications,[39] searching for anything that could link the Pyramid to a fraction of the Earth's diameter or weight, or the Greenwich Meridian or the movements of the sun and stars, or mathematical and musical sequences or the numbers of the verses of the Book of Revelation or anything, anything, for goodness sake, that would supply the unearthly monument with a role more elevated than that of a marker for a pagan grave.

Naturally enough, to such ardent researchers, the histories of the egyptologists, of Champollion and Lepsius and all the rest, were an irrelevance or even an irreverence: an attitude exemplified in the title of John Taylor's highly influential work of 1864: *The Great Pyramid: Why Was It Built? Who Built It?* And naturally enough, in their turn, the egyptologists utterly ignored the pyramidologists.

In 1865, a gathering cloud of pyramidological speculation culminated with the Egyptian expedition of Piazzi Smyth:[40] ironically enough, that same expedition also marks the beginning of the period of the Great Pyramid's most intense examination, for such theories depend upon mathematical coincidences and require high levels of precision in the maps and measurements of the Pyramid itself. Whatever one may think of the claims of these early pyramidologists, one should respect the high seriousness which attended their inspections of the Pyramid; for their energy and enterprise and for the photographs they took, and for the care they took with their measurements and plans at a time when the profession of archaeology had not begun to do such work.

The immediate motive for Piazzi Smyth's Egyptian expedition had been the resolution of the discrepancies between several recent surveys of the Great Pyramid, which were hampering the pyramidologists' fireside cogitations. His ambition was to make a definitive survey of the Great Pyramid in all its parts, to establish its original dimensions inside and out, once and for all.[41]

A pious and independent man and entirely tantalised by the harvest of mathematics and revelation that the Great Pyramid appeared to promise, Piazzi Smyth passed three months upon the Giza Plateau accompanied by his long-suffering wife whose ghostly image, luridly illuminated by magnesium flares, appears stern-faced and buttoned up in dusty taffeta in many of his photographs. Employing a variety of especially designed equipment, ingenious orchestrations of mahogany and brass, cords, candles and the finest optics of the day, they solemnly surveyed the Great Pyramid, inch by inch, within and without, and in so doing, initiated a tradition that has seen the Great Pyramid more carefully measured and surveyed than any other building on the planet.[42]

Rummaging through the drifting sand that the local villagers had excavated yet again from all around the Pyramid, Smyth, like his predecessors, marvelled at the exactitude of the surviving casing stones, and then his passion for precision led him to re-excavate and remeasure the two corner sockets that Coutelle and le Père had surveyed as well as the two other sockets to the south. To Piazzi Smyth, it seemed as if he were uncovering the fragments of a great machine which, in

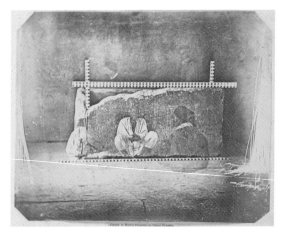

Fig. 14 The flare of burning magnesium splashing all around them, the ghostly images of Charles and Jesse Piazzi Smyth, and in all probability the ubiquitous 'Ali Gabry, haunt the first known photograph of Khufu's burial chamber and sarcophagus. A pioneering photographer in his own right, Smyth made the wet collodion negative from which this albumen print was made in 1865.

Fig. 15 Piazzi Smyth's photograph of the cleaning and resurveying of the socket at the Great Pyramid's north-eastern corner discovered by the French savants, who had previously recorded it in the *Description de l'Egypte* (fig. 8). However, Smyth identified these corner sockets with verses from the King James Bible, where God asks Job: 'Where wast thou when I laid the foundations of the earth? . . . Whereupon are the sockets therefore made to sink? Who laid the cornerstone thereof?' (Job 38:4 and 8). The standing figure is a certain Mr Inglis, one of two Scottish engineers who had been holidaying in Egypt whom Smyth persuaded to help with his work. They uncovered and measured all four of the Pyramid's corner sockets.

his finished drawings, he would attempt to reconstruct as if the Pyramid were new.

Such paper reconstruction was not required inside the Pyramid. Though the Smyths had found the long dark climb to the burial chamber exhausting and unpleasant, heavy with dust and bats and rustling with impressive spiders, after the Khedive of Egypt had ordered them to be especially cleaned the corridors and chambers, although heavily glazed in effervescent salts, had preserved most of their original surfaces. And still today, although now carefully cleaned and kitted out for tourism, these rooms and corridors are like no others in the world: three smooth dark chambers joined by a vein-like net of small square corridors that, at the slippery slope of 2:1, are as steep as escalators yet so low you cannot stand in them. With the exception of the Grand Gallery, that single great sloping corridor that

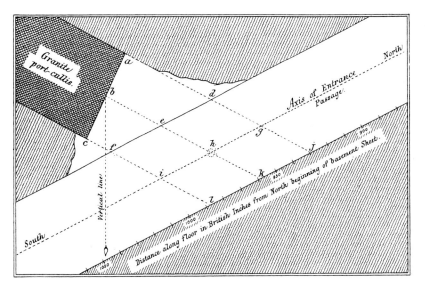

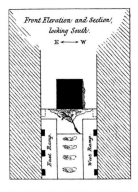

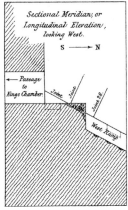

Fig. 16 Smyth's plan of the junction – the so-called Prism Point – between the Ascending and Descending Corridors inside the Great Pyramid. Accurate to fractions of an inch, the drawing shows the care and attention which Piazzi Smyth lavished on the Pyramid's interior; such care, indeed, that the Pyramid's subsequent surveyors have incorporated them into their work.

soars up through the middle of the Pyramid, this interior was hardly made for grand processions. Nonetheless, to the generations of Piazzi Smyth when similar shapes were being built in factories and deep beneath the Western cities of the day, the Pyramid's interior appeared as lucid and precise in its design as the shafts and sluices of a power station.

As it turned out, what Smyth found at Giza fulfilled his wildest dreams. After correcting Vyse's earlier observations and taking bearings from all four corner sockets, his recalculations of the Pyramid's full height confirmed that, just as the ancient Greeks had written, when new and perfect it had indeed held the magical proportions of the circle squared within its stones: that relationship in which the height of a pyramid is equal to the radius of a circle whose diameter is equal to the length of the pyramid's four sides! And that, in turn, gave Piazzi Smyth a value for pi that was within 0.0001 of modern calculations! For many of the nineteenth-century pyramidologists, such magical geometry was by itself firm evidence of divine intervention on the Giza Plateau.

Back home in Edinburgh, further calculations suggested further revelations to Piazzi Smyth. If, for example, the Great Pyramid's reconstructed height was divided into 233 equal units, then the

Fig. 17 Piazzi Smyth's modest drawings of the Great Step, the stone block at the top of the Grand Gallery that marks the level in the Great Pyramid at which the area of the base of the Pyramid above the line is half the area of the base of the whole Pyramid (cf. fig. 1 above).

lengths of the Great Pyramid's four baselines would each measure 366 of these same-sized units; the number of days in the ancient Egyptian year! Not only, then, did the Great Pyramid appear to contain the measures of the world within it as Jomard and many other pyramidologists supposed, but the rhythms of time as well!

The problem with such delirious mathematics, and Piazzi Smyth spun more webs with them than Bruce's spider, was that although he had appeared to have confirmed that the Great Pyramid was saturated with numerical concordances, he could not imagine what ends they may have served. Certainly, he reasoned, such sublime perfections could hardly have been engineered by savage idol worshippers such as the pharaoh Khufu and his subjects. Who then had made this mighty monument? Why was it made so beautifully? Why had it been made at all?

To which Piazzi Smyth could only answer, God only knows; or, as he more reverently expressed the same sentiment in the language of the day, no one in this world could possibly divine the mysterious ways of the Author of All Wisdom or fathom His Divine Revelations.[43]

3 Surveying Giza

Now that we are furnished, for the first time, with an accurate knowledge of the ancient dimensions of the Pyramids, we can enter on an examination of the theories which have been formed, and test them by the real facts.

W. M. Flinders Petrie[1]

Just fifteen years after Piazzi Smyth's sojourn in Egypt, in 1880, one William Matthew Flinders Petrie travelled from London to Cairo to take again the measure of King Khufu's Pyramid.[2] A friend and follower of Piazzi Smyth, Petrie's father had planned to travel to Egypt together with the Astronomer Royal in order to survey the Pyramid but had not found the time to do so. After the astronomer had published his results, however, both Petries, father and son alike, had seen the need for a more accurate and extensive survey of the Great Pyramid than their old friend had managed to accomplish; they had collected and adapted some of Europe's most sophisticated surveying instruments especially for that purpose and, after three years of preparation, young Petrie was embarked for Egypt and the Giza Plateau.

The problem was that, although devoted to his Pyramid, Piazzi Smyth was neither a surveyor nor an archaeologist. At Giza too he had found the daily round both hard and disconcerting. Young Petrie, on the other hand, who was descended from a famous line of empire builders and explorers, was already an accomplished if precocious antiquarian and an experienced archaeological surveyor to boot. As a boy, he had collected coins for the British Museum's collections. As a young man he had single-handedly surveyed many of England's finest Bronze Age monuments, and to this day his first book, *Inductive Metrology*, is considered a standard work upon the detection of units of measurement in ancient monuments.[3] By the time he arrived in Egypt then, at the age of twenty-seven, Flinders Petrie was well on the way to becoming one of the most astute observers of ancient crafts-manship who has ever lived. And, quite unlike Piazzi Smyth, he quickly came to relish life upon the Giza Plateau; a famous photo-graph shows the confident young man standing barefoot by the doorway of a tomb, relaxedly enjoying both the desert and the company of the villagers who had come to work for him. In Petrie then, the Great Pyramid had found its measure, and at the same time, at the Pyramid, Petrie found his life's vocation.

On his first day on the Giza Plateau, Petrie had been met by a local guide, whose services had been recommended to him by several pyra-midological researchers. 'Ali Gabry had seen them all. As a boy, in the 1830s he had joined the local villagers clearing sand for Howard Vyse. From then on, between working as a guide to tourists, he served most expeditions to the pyramids, providing their accommodations in the manner of the early tourists to the Giza Plateau, who were advised by Murray's Hand-Book that

the principal requisites in a visit to the pyramids are a stock of provisions, some *goollehs* or water bottles, a supply of candles, a lanthorn, mats, and carpet; and, if the traveller intends passing the night there, a mattrass and bedding, and a broom for sweeping out the tomb, where he is to take up his abode. A fly-flap is also necessary, and, in hot weather, a mosquito curtain. If he wishes to visit the rooms discovered by Colonel Howard Vyse over the King's Chamber [= burial chamber], he must take a rope-ladder, or a wooden ladder in short pieces, to enable it to be carried into the upper passage.[4]

By the time that Petrie came to Giza – he had indeed made his own rope ladder to visit Vyse's chambers – 'Ali had taken over these ancient accommodations, keeping a series of rock-cut tombs under lock and key expressly for the use of the pyramidologists and their supplies and staff. In this manner he had helped the Piazzi Smyths; in many of their photographs 'Ali and other members of his family appear, patiently awaiting orders. A few years later, he had similarly aided Mr Waynman Dixon, an English engineer who had gone to

Egypt with his brother John to help package Cleopatra's Needle in a barge of iron for shipping off to London, but, in answering the written requests of Petrie's father, had uncovered two small previously unknown shafts inside the Great Pyramid.[5] Again, in 1874, 'Ali had helped the astronomer David Gill set up the iron survey post that still stands on the top of the Great Pyramid; this the uncelebrated memorial of a long-forgotten expedition sent out by the Royal Geographical Society to observe the Transit of Venus.[6] And all of these great pyramidographers had given the Petries their advice on Giza; Gill had even given the young man the unpublished results of his survey of the Giza Plateau.[7]

Throughout two long winter seasons, through sandstorms, revolution and invasion, from 1880 to 1883, whilst gangs of workmen cleared away the ever-drifting sand and 'Ali's family shielded his precious instruments from the midday sun, Flinders Petrie checked, corrected and extended the work of the Piazzi Smyths and all the earlier surveys of the Giza Plateau.[8] And just as it had done with all his predecessors, the smooth accuracy of the Pyramid's great stones simply overwhelmed him. The cut of the surviving casing blocks, he enthused, is 'equal to opticians' work of the present day, but on a scale of acres'.[9] The joints between these same vast blocks, he measured, were on average just 1/50th of an inch wide and 'to place such stones in exact contact would be careful work; but to do so with cement in the joint seems almost impossible'.[10]

Along with the demands of pyramidology, the ancient exactitude of the Pyramid itself prompted an extraordinary care in Petrie, a

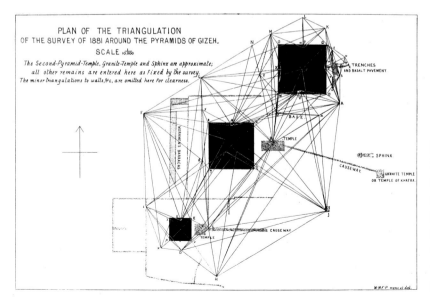

Fig. 18 Catching the Giza Pyramids in the web of a nineteenth-century survey: in 1881 Petrie produced a plan of the Great Pyramid that is virtually as accurate as the most modern surveys (see further Appendix 2).

competition with the ancient stones: 'If we want to understand what kind of precision the ancients aimed at, our errors in examining their work must be so small as to be insignificant by the sizes of their errors.'[11] Petrie's aim, then, was to outdo the pyramid-makers, in which enterprise, according to his estimation, he succeeded in all but one location; that is, the centre line of the descending corridor which 'shows in this particular we have not yet got within the builder's accuracy; readings to 1/100th inch, or to 1′ on the longer distances, are now required'.[12] Petrie, indeed, measured and surveyed the main axis of the architecture of the Pyramid with such extraordinary skill that, along with the earlier and more detailed plans of Piazzi Smyth, his survey stands to this day as the basis of all modern plans and computer graphics of this most ancient monument.[13] And that is exactly as it should be, for, as most surveyors would acknowledge, it is better to use the results of a single complete survey than the piecemeal measurements of half a dozen different enterprises.

As far as the Great Pyramid's exterior was concerned, Petrie found errors that none of its previous measurers had seen, establishing that the ancient builders had laid the Pyramid's surviving casing stones within 5 seconds of arc of true north, an extraordinary precision for a building of any period of history and of the same order of resolution that in 1973 NASA was proudly employing to map the sun from Skylab.[14] Following a series of soundings along the Pyramid's four baselines, Petrie also established that when newly built the Pyramid's four sides should have formed a theoretical square of 755 feet 8¾ inches (230.346 m) and that, in reality, the fine stone of its casing had deviated from that absolute perfection by a little less than 2 inches, a calculation that a century on (for the Pyramid's old stones still encourage such precision in its surveyors) advances in surveying equipment have tightened by less than half an inch and 1.5 seconds of arc.[15]

As far as pyramidology was concerned, however, the outlook was grim, for in his reconstruction of the Pyramid's original dimensions, Petrie found that Piazzi Smyth had followed Coutelle's work in the *Description* (pp. 20ff) in the belief that the four sockets cut into the living rock that lay outside the Pyramid's surviving stone work demarcated its original dimensions. After detecting more of Vyse's casing stones on all four sides of the Pyramid, Petrie proved that it was the lines of these angled stones and not the outlying sockets that marked the Pyramid's full size and that in consequence Piazzi Smyth's measurements had a fatal in-built 6 feet error.[16] That by itself alone put paid to many pyramidological propositions.

General summary of the positions inside the Great Pyramid :

	Horizontally.			Vertically.
	From N. Base.	From Centre.	E. from Centre.	Above Pavement.
Beginning of entrance	524·1 ± ·3	N. 4010·0 ± ·3	mid. 287·0 ± ·8	+ 668·2 ± ·1
S. end of entrance passage	4228· ± 2·	N. 306· ± 2·	mid. 286·4 ± 1·	− 1181· ± 1·
S. end of N. subterranean passage	4574· ± 2·	S. 49· ± 2·	mid. 286·3 ± 1·	− 1178· ± 1·
Subterranean Chamber, centre ...	4737· ± 2·	S. 203· ± 2·	mid. 25·9 ± 2·	− 1056· ± 2· roof
N. end of S. subterranean passage	4900· ± 2·	S. 366· ± 2·	mid. 284·9 ± 1·	− 1219· ± 1·5
S. end ,, ,, ,,	5546· ± 3·	S. 1012· ± 3·	mid. 277·1	− 1213· ± 2·
Beginning Ascending ,,	1517·8 ± ·3	N. 3016·3 ± ·3	mid. 286·6 ± ·8	+ 179·9 ± ·2
End of ,, ,,	2907·3 ± ·8	N. 1626·8 ± ·8	mid. 287· ± 1·5	+ 852·6 ± ·3
Queen's Chamber, N.E. corner ...	4402·1 ± ·8	N. 102·0 ± ·8	side 308· ± 3·	+ 834·4 ± ·4
,, ,, mid. W. roof...	4533·8 ± ·8	N. ·3 ± ·8	side 72· ± 3·	+ 1078·7 ± ·6 roof
Gallery, virtual S. end, floor	4595·8 ± ·9	S. 61·7 ± ·9	mid. 284·4 ± 3·	+ 1689·0 ± ·5
Gallery, top of step face............	4534·5 ± ·9	S. ·4 ± ·9	mid. 284·4 ± 3·	+ 1694·1 ± ·7
Antechamber, N. end, floor	4647·8 ± ·9	S. 113·7 ± ·9	same ?	+ 1692·6 ± ·6
,, S. ,, roof	4763·9 ± ·9	S 229·8 ± ·9	same ?	+ 1841·5 ± ·6 roof
King's Chamber, floor	4865·0 ± ·9	S. 330·9 ± ·9	mid. same ?	+ 1692·8 ± ·6
,, ,, N.E. wall base	4864·7 ± .9	S. 330·6 ± ·9	side 305·0 ± 3·	+ 1688·5 ± ·6
,, ,, roof..............				+ 1921·6 ± ·6
				to 1923·7 ± ·6

Fig. 19 Petrie's table of spot measurements taken inside the Great Pyramid. Along with his other measurements and observations, this small table has served as the foundation of all later surveys of the Great Pyramid's interior.

Under Petrie's expert eye, parts of all previous surveys – not only of the Pyramid's exterior but of much of the intricate detail of its interior as well – were proven to have been based on either ill-judged archaeology or mistaken measurement; errors that by themselves destroyed most of the pyramidologists' pet theories. 'Well Sir!' one benighted enthusiast had exclaimed after Petrie had shown him around his work at Giza, 'I feel as if I have been at a funeral.'[17]

Published in 1883, the year of his thirtieth birthday, a handsome buckram quarto containing the results of Petrie's epic survey brought the Great Pyramid right back down to earth. After a sixty-page description of his survey and its results and some comparisons with other pyramids, Petrie expanded into a chapter entitled 'Theories Compared with Facts' beginning with these words: 'Now that we are furnished, for the first time, with an accurate knowledge of the ancient dimensions of the Pyramids, we can enter on an examination of the theories which have been formed, and test them by the real facts of the case.' There followed a devastating examination of the theories of Jomard, Piazzi Smyth and other pyramidologists:

the theory of the wall-height being 1/50 of the Pyramid base is quite beyond possibility . . .

Another theory is that the chamber contains ten million 'Pyramid inches' . . .

the date of the Exodus, & C are of still less exactitude . . .

Now, of all these objections to the Tombic theory . . .

Another theory, which is quite impossible . . .

One by one, past and present theories were carefully stated and precisely checked against his survey and most of them, in their turn, were found to be a trick of numbers or mismeasurement.

At the same time Petrie found nothing that disproved the pyramidologists' assumption that the Great Pyramid had been built according to a master plan. Indeed, he describes the Pyramid's architecture as being filled with extraordinary mathematical harmonies and concordances: those same strange symmetries that had so haunted the pyramidologists. Petrie not only noted, for example, that the proportions of the reconstructed pyramid approximated to pi – which others have since elaborated to include those twin delights of Renaissance and pyramidological mathematicians, the Golden Section and the Fibonacci Series[18] – but for good measure even confirmed Jomard's original pyramidological observation (see p. 22), noting that 'the stadium theory fits remarkably closely to the facts'.[19]

As far as the Pyramid's interior was concerned, Petrie's survey also confirmed the bizarre assertion that a huge block of fine white limestone which stands at the top of the Grand Gallery, and which the pyramidologists had long since dubbed as the 'Great Step', had been set precisely at the point on the Pyramid's vertical axis where the area of the base of the pyramid above the step is exactly half the area of the base of the entire Pyramid.[20] Petrie went even further, showing that the Great Step, a key point in the elaborate geometry that runs right through the architecture of the Pyramid's interior, was also linked precisely to the main axis of the Pyramid and thus, through the four cardinal points, to the stars of the night sky.[21]

Petrie well knew that even these extraordinary observations would offer little consolation to the pyramidologists, and this perhaps is why he discusses their various claims dispassionately and without mentioning their authors' names. At the same time, his fierce rationality did not shrink from producing, as he says, 'the ugly little fact which killed the beautiful theory'. Nonetheless, it must have been a sad task for a man whose family had long been friendly with Piazzi Smyth's and whose father, still a firm believer 'in the symbolic meaning of the Pyramid in regards to Christ's life', had done so much to help him on his way to Egypt.[22]

The English scientific establishment harboured no such sentiments; the Royal Society, which earlier had shunned the pyramidological speculations of Piazzi Smyth who had resigned in consequence, granted Petrie £100 towards the publication of *The Pyramids and Temples of Gizeh*, which had grown well beyond the confines of an architectural survey to include some archaeological studies and some shrewdly speculative essays on the methods of the ancient pyramid-builders. In the academic world where study of the Great Pyramid, the sole survivor of the classical Seven Wonders, had suffered long neglect, the book was very well received: 'services . . . rendered to history and to science', as one reviewer put it.[23] And it was widely popular as well, selling out within a month or so.

Surprisingly perhaps, Piazzi Smyth was amiably bemused by Petrie's publication, innocently observing that earthquakes and poor workmanship might well account for the discrepancies between his own work and that of the 'smart young scientist', and that he saw no need whatever to change his earlier assertions.[24] And, of course, he's been proved absolutely right; in the long run, Petrie's survey has provided more grist to the magic mill, which thanks to his work now claims itself to be 'scientific' too!

As for Petrie, the Giza Survey proved to be the turning point of his life, drawing him into half a century of classic excavation all over ancient Egypt, a passionate labour that recovered entire epochs of previously unknown history and introduced some of the methods of contemporary European archaeology into the Middle East. At the same time as he was embarking on his new-found vocation, Petrie edited a second edition of *Pyramids and Temples*, halving its original length and generally omitting what he somewhat ingenuously describes in a new preface as 'a quantity of matter which was only of technical interest'.[25] In reality this drastic exercise saw him abruptly turning his back upon the very interests that had taken him to Giza in the first place. No more pyramidology for Petrie. In the second edition, all comparisons of Pyramid fact with pyramidological theory have entirely disappeared, along with a chapter on that perennial pyramidological concern, the length of the ancient Egyptian measure of the cubit – this in all probability in deference to a celebrated treatise on this same subject by Professor Richard Lepsius of Berlin University, who was considered to be the greatest living egyptologist.

This edit, then, was Petrie's tacit acceptance of a common attitude in his newly adopted profession towards the pyramidologists: that of contemptuous and exasperated silence, a strategy that has led many of their modern-day successors to the belief – would it were that simple! – that the academic establishment is withholding rediscovered ancient wisdoms from them; hence for example, the Legend of the Lavatory, which tells of a secret tunnel running from the facilities at the Government Offices at Giza to hidden chambers beneath the Great Pyramid.[26] The real motive, however, is often rather simpler; dialogue in this democracy of ignorance where fact and theory, inaccuracy and inclination are given equal weight, is Sisyphean. As Petrie himself concluded, 'It is useless to state the real truth of the matter, it has no effect on those who are subject to this type of hallucination.

They can but be left with the flat earth believers and other such people.'[27]

As far as the future study of the Great Pyramid was concerned, yet more important than Petrie's attitude to pyramidology was that his drastic précis of *Pyramids and Temples*, his cutting twenty-two chapters down to nine and, with it, his commentary upon the Pyramid's remarkable mathematics, was the beginning of a process by which any discussion of the Great Pyramid's architecture beyond a bland enumeration of its rooms and corridors would be treated with the same blank silence as pyramidology itself. Today, especially since Petrie's slim second edition is more common than the first, most egyptologists are entirely unaware of the geometric harmonies that he so carefully recorded at the Pyramid.[28] Yet as we shall see, they are the key to a better understanding of this extraordinary monument.

4 Excavating Giza

Throughout the surveys of Jomard, of Howard Vyse, Piazzi Smyth and Petrie, most of the monuments up on the Giza Plateau had lain buried underneath a beautiful quilt of windblown sand which, though Doctor Lepsius had briefly pulled it back, had quickly enfolded the site again on his departure. Just as the first photographs of the Great Pyramid show,[1] despite the Europeans' rush to dig up all of ancient Egypt's major sites, the best part of the Pyramid's surrounding monuments were inaccessible. With the exception of a temple beside the Sphinx the entire Plateau was relatively undisturbed.

The problem was that digging out the monuments upon the high Plateau was hard and dangerous; even Petrie in his soundings by the Pyramid had 'narrow escapes from tons of stuff suddenly slipping in'.[2] The Giza tombs, moreover, were large and regular and lay in rows and had relatively little decoration, and the spare contents of their burials had been largely broken. Compared with other Egyptian sites therefore, most collectors considered Giza's cemeteries not worth the effort of their excavation, especially as the modern taste for the archaic in antique art was hardly born. Once the great museums had gathered up sufficient samples of the 'arts of the Pyramid Age' from keyhole digs, the sands had blown back once again across the tombs

and buried them.[3] When Petrie had arrived in 1880, the Giza Plateau had been so neglected by the archaeologists that the best map available had been the monumental delineation of Lepsius' Prussians, made forty years before.

In 1902, however, a group of archaeologists, American, Italian and German, met one day at the Mena House, a pretty Turkish hunting lodge that stood a little to the north of the Great Pyramid and which had been transformed during the nineteenth-century tourist boom into one of the world's great hotels.[4] And there, on the hotel's wooden veranda, with the Great Pyramid looming up behind, the Plateau and its pyramids and tombs and temples were divided up between them, as the day diary of the American archaeologist George Reisner records:

Everybody wanted a portion of the great Western Cemetery [beside the Great Pyramid]. It was divided in three strips East–West. Three bits of paper were marked 1, 2, and 3 and put in a hat. Mrs. Reisner drew the papers and presented one to each of us. The southern strip fell to the Italians, the middle to the Germans and the northern strip to me. Then we proceeded to divide the pyramids. I perceived that the Italians were interested in the First Pyramid [Khufu's] and the Germans in the Second [Khafre's]. I kept my mouth shut and let them wrangle. When they had adjusted the line between the First and Second Pyramid the Italians thinking that I might insist on a ballot resigned

Fig. 20 Published in the first of the great folios issued by the Prussian expedition, this splendid view shows the Great Pyramid with it baselines and the pyramids and tombs that lie around it buried deep in sand and rubble. Ernst Weidenbach, one of the expedition's artists, took his view from the top of Khafre's pyramid, whose shadow cuts into the picture's foreground. The lakes and pools upon the Nile's plain beyond tell us that he worked as the inundation was receding; Lepsius' diary (Lepsius 1852) suggests that was early in the winter of 1842–3.

to me the northern part of the area east of the First Pyramid, if I would accept the Third Pyramid [Menkaure]. I was perfectly willing to have the Third Pyramid but of course accepted his offer.[5]

Joined later by Egyptian expeditions, the greater part of which were led by the redoubtable Selim Hassan, the large-scale scientific excavation of the Giza Plateau continued on and off for more than forty years.[6] This then is why that gentle shrouded plain so beautifully lithographed by Lepsius' watercolourists is a disturbed and complex place today, wasted by wind and archaeology, crusted with tarmac

Fig. 21 Produced for the tourist trade of the 1890s, this photograph shows an Egyptian guide standing in the great trench that Vyse's men had excavated some sixty years before, when part of the Great Pyramid's casing stones visible at the bottom of this photograph had been discovered (see fig. 11 above). The gap in the blocks above the guide and to his left is the excavation known as 'Ma'mun's Hole' after an early Caliph and legendary pyramid explorer. The 'Hole' now forms the Pyramid's modern entrance. Lepsius' hieroglyphic inscription lies yet higher up, underneath the white stain at the centre of another ancient excavation.

roads and tumbled tombs, which after decades of cleaning and conservation are splendidly transforming once again.[7] Most of our
present knowledge of the Great Pyramid and its makers was born of
this indiscreet unveiling. All the great row tombs standing back to
back to the east and west of the Great Pyramid, those tombs that
Lepsius had reported were the resting places of King Khufu's courtiers
and family, those low massive stone block structures that represent
extra years of working for the pyramid-makers, have been cleaned and
cleared and mapped and planned and photographed, along with mile
upon mile of later and generally smaller monuments that lie open
now, in measured rows and random clusters, all around the pyramids.

The haul of statues, bones and hieroglyphs from these tremendous
excavations was, of course, terrific. And the shelf upon shelf of solid
scientific volumes that record the archaeologists' slow progress
through the Giza cemeteries, especially the publications that record
the inscriptions and the rare and splendid works of art discovered,
now form the backbone of the academic study of King Khufu's life
and times.[8] So powerful has been the influence of these excavations
that until quite recently most research projects concerned with the
Great Pyramid were paper excavations conducted in academic
archives and museums far from the Giza Plateau. As for the Great
Pyramid, just as Champollion had augured, its lack of formal inscriptions, allied now to Petrie's survey, left it a silent onlooker in this
grand adventure, relegated to a minor role in what had essentially

Fig. 22 German
archaeologists working
in the Great Pyramid's
western cemeteries in the
1920s. The huge stone
monument from which
the line of workmen are
carrying loads of debris
is the tomb of a certain
Kasudja, who lived in the
century after Khufu, yet
built his tomb close to his
Pyramid. The man in the
white jacket is Herman
Junker, who led the
German excavations on
the Giza Plateau over
fifteen years and who
published the results of
his labours during the
following twenty-five, in
twelve large volumes.

Fig. 23 The Great Pyramid's western cemeteries photographed by Mohammedani Ibrahim, one of Reisner's staff photographers, in January 1915, when the American expedition had already cleared the better part of their concession in this area.

Fig. 24 Taken before the First World War, the photograph shows the Great Pyramid's western cemeteries emerging from the desert and the archaeologists' tips of sand and rubble running down from the Plateau's north-western edge. The building in the foreground is the Mena House Hotel – see p. 48 and p. 468 note 4. Watered by a well spring at the foot of the Plateau, its nursery garden, a small oasis in the Giza deserts, served the hotel's restaurants.

become a study of the language and arts of the courts of Khufu and his successors. Nor did any of the cemeteries' inscriptions, mostly epigraphs and titularies memorialising the people buried in its tombs, offer any explanation of the Pyramid's purposes or design, nor did they so much as mention its construction. Given that no literary texts are known from any earlier periods of Egyptian history than King Khufu's reign – the oldest known versions of any Egyptian literary text having been written out some two and a half centuries after the Great Pyramid was finished – the excavation of King Khufu's cemeteries had served to underline the fact that the design and construction of the Great Pyramid was undertaken in what still, today, may be considered as a pre-literary age.

Following the excavation of King Khufu's cemeteries, all practical archaeological explanations of how the Great Pyramid had been designed and built came to centre on the theories of a triumvirate of archaeologists.[9] First, always and inevitably quoted, were Petrie's published observations from his Giza survey, although after the excavation of the cemeteries these were usually augmented by the observations of two near-contemporary field workers; Ludwig Borchardt, a pioneering architectural archaeologist educated in Berlin by protégés of Professor Lepsius, and George Andrew Reisner, a ruthlessly efficient and similarly educated American who for more than forty years had excavated and explicated Giza's monuments as if they too were elements in a Berlin grammar book.[10]

Not one of Giza's archaeologists had followed Petrie's footsteps on the Giza Plateau. A century ahead of his time, Petrie's fascination with the processes and residue of ancient daily life had led him to explore and excavate the Plateau for evidence of the pyramid-builders' workshops and dwellings; until Cairo University's excavations of the 1970s the only material available was Petrie's own account of his exploratory digs.[11] In the 1880s, however, archaeological reporting was hardly up to modern standards and Petrie too had chosen to interpret his revolutionary fieldwork through the literature of the ancient Greeks and Romans, those slave-owning Iron Age tourists who were as far removed in time and in mentality from Khufu's pyramid-makers as they are from us today. Nonetheless, from his theoretical timetable of the Great Pyramid's construction to his estimations of the size of the ancient workforce, Petrie's persuasive mix of practicality and classical reference remained the standard description of how the Great Pyramid had been built for the best part of a century.[12]

Along with Petrie's broad outline, Reisner's careful archaeology and detailed analyses of stone working and tomb design helped to situate the Great Pyramid amidst the other monuments of Khufu's time, mostly, that is, the tombs and pyramids of his family and courtiers which displayed many of the techniques of stone working visible upon the Pyramid itself.[13] It was the Berliner Borchardt, however, who most influenced modern studies of the Great Pyramid and, in so doing, dealt it a blow from which it is still recovering. In 1922, after enlisting the officers of the Geographic Survey of Egypt to confirm Petrie's survey of the Great Pyramid's exterior,[14] Borchardt broke the egyptologists' traditional silence on the subject of pyramidology and published an extended version of a Berlin lecture, a fiery denunciation entitled 'Against Numerical Mysticism at the Great Pyramid of Giza'[15] that, simply by providing a sample of the ridicule that numerical speculation could provoke in academic circles, effectively ensured that discussion of the Great Pyramid's architectural harmonies has been an academic no-go area ever since.[16]

One might rather sympathise with Dr Borchardt. After the gritty experience of excavating half-buried monuments for more than twenty years, after pioneering the archaeological examination of pyramids and their temples and their methods of construction, after painstakingly re-establishing their original forms – his splendid drawings and their accompanying explanations are basic to this subject to this day – Borchardt was widely recognised as the world's leading authority on pyramid engineering and design. At the same time, however, partly engendered by the surge of spiritualism that grew up around the First World War, some fifty volumes of varied pyramidological speculations on the Great Pyramid had appeared.[17] Written by a wide variety of armchair adepts, they regarded Dr Borchardt and his like just as their predecessors had regarded Champollion and Lepsius, as boorish materialists and quite irrelevant to their search for 'higher wisdom'. It must have been very annoying, especially for a man who had a reputation for not suffering fools gladly.[18]

At the same time as he was battling the pyramidologists, Borchardt was also developing a radical theory of his own concerning the Great Pyramid, one based upon an old proposal of Richard Lepsius' that Petrie had summarily dismissed: the so-called 'accretion theory', which maintained that the great Egyptian pyramids had been built onion-style, layer upon layer, so that each pharaoh would have had a near-completed pyramid ready for him, even if his death came unexpectedly.[19] That Khufu's Pyramid had indeed been built in three such stages of accretion, Borchardt now claimed, could be seen in the detail of its interior architecture. He proposed at the same time, that each of the Great Pyramid's three interior chambers, the rock-cut Subterranean Chamber, the so-called Queen's Chamber high above it made of fine-cut limestone blocks and the granite King's Chamber above them both, had been built one after the other as the Pyramid's bulk grew larger with the passing years, with each in its turn designed to serve as Khufu's burial chamber, and with the King's Chamber and its sarcophagus serving as the third and final crypt.[20]

Here, then, is specific reason for Borchardt's surprising attack upon the pyramidologists. Intent as he was on proving that the Great Pyramid's construction had been a nip and tuck affair, the long-held assumption that its architecture held a single mathematically harmonious design, let alone that this design may possess some kind of metaphysical rationale, would have been anathema to him. The very idea that the ancient Egyptians of Khufu's day had been sufficiently cultivated to conceive such architectural complexity ran contrary to contemporary academic opinion; without texts or architectural decoration, the Great Pyramid appeared to them to be a very early marker on the road to civilisation, one of Borchardt's senior colleagues at Berlin tagging the age as one of crude if 'fully developed fetishism' and a handbook of the Berlin Imperial Museums characterising early Egyptian religion as the legacy of a race of 'naked, half savage peasants'.[21] For the most part then, Borchardt's contemporaries assumed, in the spirit of his time, that the Great Pyramid's makers had been filled with a primitive urge to build a great tumulus for their dead king and that its construction had been a quasi-evolutionary process in which its internal architecture had just grown like Topsy.[22]

At all events, Borchardt's novel three-stage theory of the Great Pyramid's construction quickly convinced his fellow professionals[23] and, welded to Petrie's general observations upon pyramid construction, it became the standard academic explanation of how the Great Pyramid had been made and why its architecture had assumed the forms it did. Indeed, the theory is still widely held today.[24] For seventy years Borchardt's double-barrelled blast of scorn and scholarship, attacking alternative views on pyramid design whilst promoting his own, effectively gagged all further discussion. One effect has been that the work of poor old Piazzi Smyth, whose photographs of the Pyramid alone are a precious archaeological record and whose three Giza volumes, as Petrie states in the preface to his survey, are 'required for the measurements and description of the interior of the Great Pyramid', is only ever mentioned in academic works in terms of derision: not pyramidologists now, but pyramididiots. And even I. E. S.

Edwards, that most gentlemanly of commentators, concludes the later editions of his *magnum opus, The Pyramids of Egypt*, that essential pocket book for generations of enthusiasts, with a swipe at Piazzi Smyth,[25] and even those rare egyptologists who have questioned Borchardt's three-stage theory since the 1990s barely mention the rare subtleties of the Great Pyramid's interior architecture or their relationship with the Pyramid's exterior.[26]

As well as encouraging pyramidological paranoia amongst egyptologists, the practical consequence of Borchardt's writings has been to shift the focus of study away from considerations of the Pyramid's architecture to the hypothetical mechanics of its construction, as if the heart of this phenomenal enterprise could be explained by showing how its stones were gathered up and laid in rows.[27] Apart from the sporadic attempts of various groups of physicists to sound out the Great Pyramid for hidden corridors and chambers – essentially hi-tech pyramidological procedures in the best nineteenth-century tradition – the complex architecture of its interior has been ignored by archaeologists who have mostly concerned themselves with the accuracy of the Pyramid's baselines, which, as Petrie's survey had shown a century ago, is no more or less precise than the architecture of the Pyramid's interior.[28] The Great Step for example, that marvel of construction at the portal of King Khufu's burial chamber, is not so much as listed in the index of any modern archaeological work upon the pyramids. Indeed, with the splendid exception of the Great Pyramid's extensive conservation by the Egyptian authorities, egyptologists have 'largely given up on the pyramids' as our reviewer has already noticed (p. 3 above), a neglect that may even be greeted on occasion with professional approval: 'It is truly refreshing to read a study [of the pyramids] that devotes only two and a half pages out of 144 to the Great Pyramid!'[29]

Given the silence of the archaeologists, it is hardly surprising that pyramidology has gone from strength to strength; that today there are four times more books published on the Great Pyramid than there were in Borchardt's time. And consequently the successors of those earnest nineteenth-century nonconformists with a dozen different rulers in their pockets and the Holy Bible as their plan now have enormous followings, and the centre of pyramidological publishing has moved from Dunstable in Bedfordshire to Fifth Avenue, New York.

Yet modern pyramidology has less to offer now than it did in the days of Piazzi Smyth. Although it regularly encourages us to abandon the small amount of scientific information on the Great Pyramid about which we may be sure – that it was built some 4500 years

Fig. 25 Nothing daunted by the archaeologists' arrival, Smyth's successors continued to check and measure the Great Pyramid itself. Photographed by his brother Morton in the winter of 1910, the Glaswegian nonconformist John Edgar is measuring the portal between the Descending Corridor and the Subterranean Chamber, the lowest elements of the Pyramid's internal architecture.

Followers of C. T. Russell, the founder of the movement popularly known as 'Jehovah's Witnesses', the Edgar brothers published three volumes of biblically inspired commentary upon the Great Pyramid's Divine Plan, which they illustrated with a unique sequence of fine photographs.

ago in the reign of King Khufu – it never bothers to replace those hard-won facts with anything but unproven theories. Just as Jomard tried so hard in his day to stop the discoveries of Champollion, so, like a disreputable theology, pyramidology spends most of its time attacking its apostates and addressing true believers.[30] Although they often like to dress like Indiana Jones, pyramidologists should never be confused with archaeologists. And certainly they offer no true explanation of the real mysteries of the Giza Plateau.

How, then, to make sense of this great Pyramid? Today, there are a host of brand new tools available. A sea-change has been taking place within Egyptian archaeology. Modern excavation no longer consists of shovelling quantities of sand and 'rubbish' away from buried monuments in the manner of Colonel Howard Vyse. Since the 1980s and the US/Egyptian surveys led by Mark Lehner and Zahi Hawass, archaeology at Giza and the Great Pyramid has been conducted with the awareness that the landscape of the Plateau holds more within it than fine architecture; that a complex ancient environment is buried in its sand;[31] that it holds the traces of a builders' yard of vast dimensions and, perhaps, the pavilions of courtiers and kings, the homes of labourers and craftsmen and the levelled survey lines on which the Great Pyramid was set, and even perhaps the merest outlines of the ramps up which its blocks were hauled into position.[32]

At the same time too, other archaeologists have recovered detailed plans of most of the Great Pyramid's predecessors – those pioneering pyramids that provided Khufu's workforce with their skills and the Great Pyramid with its proportions and design.[33] With great good fortune, one of these archaeologists also uncovered ancient records that allow a realistic calculation of the time that the Great Pyramid took to build; an estimation that for the first time is based not on modern guesswork or experience or ancient gossip, but on real work rates recorded during the construction of a near-contemporary pyramid.[34] At last then, we can start to reconstruct how the Great Pyramid's makers went about their daily work and something also of their ambitions.[35] Add these new facts to information gleaned from surveys and excavations of ancient roads and boats and mines and quarries throughout Egypt, and you can build a picture of pyramid-making in the days of Khufu that has not been seen for almost five millennia.

Nor is this merely modern science simply decorating old histories with the spurious 'clues' and 'breakthroughs' of pop documentaries. Many modern egyptologists now dig to recover traces of genuine ancient life rather than to uncover yet more representations of 'ancient Egypt' as it is portrayed in ancient works of art and literature. The traditional vision of 'ancient Egyptian daily life', therefore, is swiftly disappearing along with the stale old nineteenth-century image of Egypt of the Pharaohs, and a fresh and largely unknown ancient culture is beginning to take its place.[36]

What then might be the role of the Great Pyramid in this renaissance? Just as it would be frivolous to continue to discourse upon the Pyramid's massive forms in eighteenth-century terms in the manner of the pyramidologists, so it is equally inappropriate to claim in the manner of many nineteenth- and twentieth-century egyptologists that Khufu's personality is somehow expressed in the hard labour of its manufacture and the formality of the spare inscriptions of the time. Better now to view King Khufu's Pyramid as a formal work of art, as part of that elaborate presentation, that millennial project, that intricate and highly formal portrait which to our very great delight has been so well preserved, in which the ancient Egyptians represented certain aspects of their world in wood and paint and stone. To view this Pyramid, therefore, as a precise and costly exercise whose highly finished surfaces aimed ultimately at some form of communication.

If then, we wish to discover what the pyramid-makers were doing, what they may have been intending to communicate, we should start by taking the Pyramid at face value and analyse its formal qualities of workmanship and architecture. For those it was that guided both its shape and its construction, that held the aspirations and ambitions of its designers and controlled the timetable of its manufacture. First then, for a better understanding of this Pyramid, it is necessary to recover its ancient master plan.

5 The Pyramid's plan

The side of the pyramid is . . . as wide as the Thames at Westminster; yet the errors of the sides are less than a little finger's breadth in length and in angle. If a brass rod were used for measuring, less than seven degrees warmer or cooler would cause as much error as the pyramid builders made in carrying out their enormous work. The courses were laid out so truly that they are true to the thickness of a sheet of paper in a length of twenty feet.

Flinders Petrie[1]

The smooth perfections of the Pyramid's great stones have long suggested to many of its visitors that it was built according to a single plan and this has always been the pyramidologists' assumption. No archaeologist, not even Petrie or Borchardt, its two most assiduous investigators, has managed to uncover such a master plan within its architecture; and that, perhaps, is why Borchardt's theory of the Great Pyramid's piecemeal construction was so readily accepted by egyptologists, and for so long.

Yet the complex symmetries that Petrie found in the Great Pyramid are real enough: the Great Step, for example (see p. 2, above), shows that the upper sections of the Pyramid's architecture were precisely related to its lowest sections, built long years before. And that alone suggests the existence of some kind of

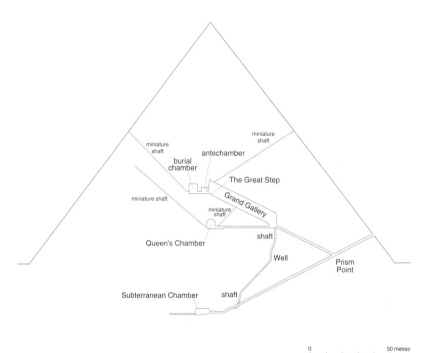

miniature shaft

miniature shaft

antechamber

burial chamber

The Great Step

miniature shaft

Grand Gallery

miniature shaft

Queen's Chamber

shaft

Well

Prism Point

Subterranean Chamber

shaft

0   50 metres

→ N

Fig. 26 Cross section and plan of the Great Pyramid with the names of the elements of its interior architecture employed in this book.

The Ascending Corridor rises from the Prism Point, passes through the Grand Gallery and stops at the rise of the Great Step.

The Descending Corridor runs down from the entrance and passes through the Prism Point before ending at the Subterranean Chamber.

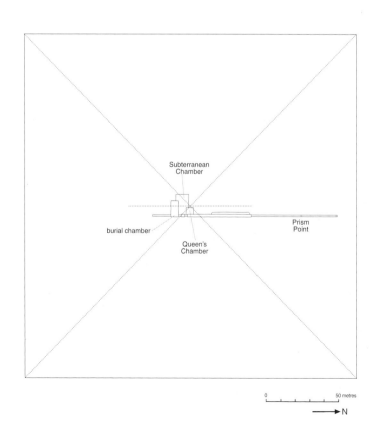

Subterranean Chamber

burial chamber

Queen's Chamber

Prism Point

0   50 metres

→ N

ancient overarching scheme. How then may we discover what it was?

First, perhaps, by establishing the parameters of the search. Like all other ancient buildings, the Great Pyramid contains sufficient ambiguities within its architectural plans to fit it out with any number of brave theories whilst those same ambiguities may also lead the doubters of those same brave theories to flush out the baby with the bath water and observe in the manner of Marilyn Monroe's well-known comment upon one of her most assiduous biographers that he was 'inaccurate': that although its individual parts are beautifully made and virtually perfect in their form and measurements, there was never a master plan for the Great Pyramid or alternatively, indeed, that its modern surveyors are not to be trusted. Even Dieter Arnold precedes his observation that the interior architecture of the Great Pyramid and of Khafre's too is yet more accurately oriented to north than the exterior, with the caveat 'if Petrie's measurements are correct', although all subsequent checks upon his work at Giza have confirmed their consistency and accuracy.[2]

How then, with all of this, can one hope to find the pattern of a long-lost plan within this battered Pyramid? The destruction of its exterior for example, that inadvertent rasterisation which has given it its present jagged silhouette, permits as many modern measuring points as does a set of fractals. Even the Pyramid's apex, the marker of its original height, is lost, along with several of its supporting courses. Nor should we assume that Khufu's pyramid-makers possessed the necessary skills to build as accurately high up on the Pyramid's exterior as they did along its baselines (see below, pp. 402ff) and that what was once built conformed precisely to an ancient abstract plan. Cracking and displacement too, earthquakes and subsidence, have certainly caused slight movements in the architecture of the Pyramid's interior. How then can we separate the ruined present from a perfect past and determine which points in this time-blunted Pyramid still hold the elements of its original design?

Happily enough, many sections of the Pyramid's standing stones are built to tolerances far tighter than those demanded of most modern buildings. So, although modern restorations of the Pyramid's exterior are based upon a series of assumptions and founded upon but a few surviving surfaces at the bottom of the Pyramid, we may reasonably assume that they represent part of a genuinely ancient design, especially as the abstract dimensions with which this restoration provides us are precisely reflected in the architecture of the Pyramid's interior, as Petrie's survey clearly demonstrates (see ch. 3

above). We may assume, therefore, that in the absolute perfection of its plan the Pyramid would have measured exactly 755 feet 8.76 inches (230.391 m) along its baselines and have risen at an angle of 51° 50′ to a height of 481 feet 3.96 inches (146.709 m).[3]

Other potential hazards in our investigation are related to the Pyramid's sheer size. As Petrie and Borchardt both observed, the Great Pyramid is so enormous that simply by the addition or subtraction of 'a hairsbreadth' you can count out its architecture in round numbers of any unit of measurement that you might wish to use, from Mexican parsangs to Atlantean and Egyptian cubits, or the Pyramid Inches of Piazzi Smyth or, indeed, the numbered verses of the Book of Revelation.[4] In searching for traces of the Pyramid's true plan therefore, symmetry alone – harmonies of angle, form and size that are as accurate as the best working tolerances of its surviving architecture – can be the only sign of genuine intention.

Another hazard related to the Pyramid's sheer size is the simple fact that, as I have already observed (p. 3), scale drawings of the Pyramid's architecture have built-in limitations of their own. Petrie's published plan of the Great Pyramid, for example, is reproduced at such a small scale that the width of a single pencil line represents a black hole in the architecture of some 6 feet (1.8 m) at the Pyramid itself, a handy place in which to find a million 'hairsbreadths'. Scale drawings, then, can only serve as the roughest of rough diagrams for this exquisite architecture which, as the numbers of Petrie's survey show, can be accurate in their dimensions to within an inch or so of absolute perfection: that is, they hold an accuracy of 0.02 per cent in some 755 feet! Only direct comparisons of measurements taken at the Pyramid therefore can prove the existence of an ancient pattern in this architecture: in practical terms, then, only a comparison of Petrie's surveyed measurements, the last major survey of the Great Pyramid in it entirety, can enable us to rediscover its ancient plan.[5]

If, for example, the Great Step had been set a few feet up or down from its present position, the precise qualities that Petrie describes – that the area of the Pyramid above the Great Step is exactly half the area of the base of the whole Pyramid (see p. 44 above) – would not be true. Petrie's spot measurements, however, show that the pyramid-makers aligned the Great Step to that theoretical point with an astonishing precision: with a 6 inch (15.2 cm) difference between theoretical perfection and the hard rock of the Pyramid: a building error of 0.1 per cent, which is similar to that between the physical lengths of the Pyramid's four baselines.[6]

There is more, however, to this Great Step than its remarkable placement on the Pyramid's vertical axis. For Petrie's measurements also show that it was set with an equal horizontal precision; that the plane of the Great Step's rise along its northern edge is just 6 inches from the Pyramid's theoretical east–west axis (see fig. 233), that is, just 0.16 per cent short of mathematical perfection! Such unnerving three-dimensional alignments, and Petrie recorded many of them, cannot be accidental. Weighing tons, and cut from a fine limestone especially shipped to the Great Pyramid for use in just such locations where high levels of precision were attained, such key blocks as the Great Step required large gangs of workmen and a great deal of finesse to set in position. These fine-placed stones mark genuine intentions.

Fig. 27 The Great Step at the summit of the Grand Gallery, the bottom of which is set on the level in the Pyramid at which the area of the base of the Pyramid above is exactly half the area of the base of the entire Pyramid. Morton Edgar's photograph shows that the Step appears to have been considerably eroded since its appearance in the *Description*, a century earlier (cf. fig. 10).

Though the Pyramid's interior was still encumbered by centuries of grime at the time of the Edgar brothers' researches, their photographs show its architecture with great clarity and without the tourist facilities which render modern visits so convenient, yet modern photographs confusing.

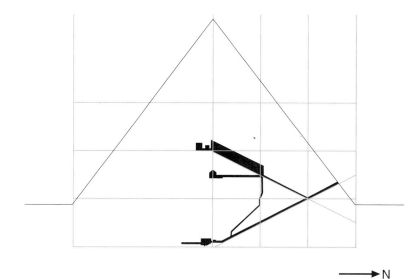

Fig. 28 The six-square grid that underlies the internal architecture of the Great Pyramid.

N

Now Khufu's pyramid-makers could only have placed the Great Step into position when some two-thirds of the Pyramid's stones were already in position, years after the beginning of construction. Given that it is most precisely placed both in relation to the Pyramid's intended height and to the length of its baselines, some kind of long-term architectural planning must have been an integral part of the making of this Pyramid from the beginning of the work. That some of the architectural elements of the Pyramid's interior such as the Great Step have been so precisely linked to the dimensions of its exterior must lead us to the belief that, just as the nineteenth-century pyramidologists had assumed, the Great Pyramid was constructed to some kind of overarching plan; that it holds a unity within its architecture, mapping out King Khufu's destiny in blocks of stone.

To modern eyes, the framework of this grand design is best seen on a cross-section of the Pyramid cut from south to north (fig. 28) in which the plan of the Pyramid's interior, in common with so many ancient Egyptian designs, can be seen to have been set upon a grid of squares.[7] Right away it is apparent that the floor lines of the Pyramid's corridors form a regular symmetrical design within this grid. And that the fifth division of the grid marks the point where the line of the Pyramid's entrance corridor divides symmetrically into equal parts, one passage striking down to the Subterranean Chamber, the other upwards to the Great Step atop the grid's first square. I have named this key juncture in the plan the Prism Point.

It is a simple plan, and it is unique. Little like it had appeared before King Khufu's time and only parts of it would ever appear in later pyramids.

Fig. 29 In this unique photograph of the Prism Point, the Edgar brothers' camera looks down the Pyramid's Entrance Corridor, through a wrought iron grill towards the Subterranean Chamber. Caught fast in the lower section of the Ascending Corridor above (cf. fig. 26 above), one of the granite plugging blocks appears to hang suspended in the air. The man sitting underneath, Judah, one of the Edgar brothers' servants, rests on a pile of debris long since cleared away, which obscured the exact location at the Prism Point that corresponds to the crossing of two of the lines of the Pyramid's six-square grid (see Appendix 4).

There yet remains, however, a serious obstacle in this amiable progress of uncovering the pattern in the Pyramid, and one that has undermined all previous attempts to find it. For the designers of King Khufu's Pyramid did not employ this six-squared grid consistently. As figure 28 shows, only selected parts of the Pyramid's interior are fixed upon it, other elements of its plan having no immediate connection with it. Yet it was not mere capriciousness that fixed the positions of those other elements of this design, but the consistent use of what might be called the Great Pyramid's double helix. For the Pyramid's architecture is governed not by a single grid of squares but by two staggered grids of equal size set on the same vertical planes, the upper being the one described above, the lower being set some 15 feet (4.6 m) beneath it at the level of the Pyramid's baselines.[8]

That this double grid is a genuine abstract principle of the Pyramid's design is shown by the fact that at 51° 50′ the very angle of its rise is linked precisely to the lower of these two six-square grids, for the Pyramid's exact angle may be obtained by simply adding 20, 40 and 60 Egyptian cubits to the squares of this lower grid, as shown in figure 30.[9]

That the Pyramid's fine-placed stones mark the underlying presence of these two grids is yet further shown by the very height of some of the stone courses of which the Great Pyramid is constructed, for they hold the levels of the squares of both the upper and the lower grids within them (see fig. 179, and further p. 367 below). In this extraordinary design, therefore, plan and elevation, section and volume are all operating together.

As to its ancient purposes, in a world where labour, logistics and the architectural plan were undivided aspects of a single reality, its practical application is best explained within the context of the Pyramid's construction and the deposition of the king. Here, suffice it to say that it was an aid both to building and to burial.

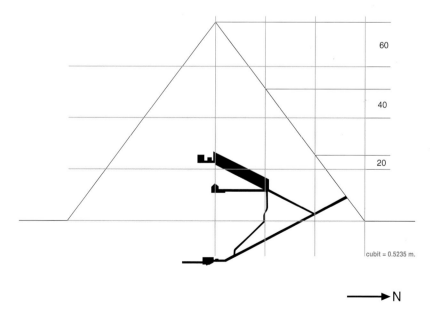

60

40

20

cubit = 0.5235 m.

→ N

Fig. 30 The Great Pyramid's second grid – the other half of the double helix of its design – showing how the addition of 20, 40 and 60 cubit co-ordinates to three squares of a grid set on the Pyramid's base will produce the angle of its rise.

Already, within this rediscovered scheme, we start to touch upon the edges of a way of thought that it is no longer possible to appreciate instinctively; a world in which modern 'common sense' may have been not at all common, and common sensibilities entirely different. Just as we no longer assume, as did the ancient Greeks and Romans, that the Great Pyramid was built by slaves, so neither should we assume today that Khufu's pyramid-makers employed 'primitive' equivalents of modern building plans and systems to make their pyramids. My diagrams of the Pyramid's plan, for instance, are set upon a modern type of drawing, specifically a cross-section, which was only named as such two centuries ago.[10] So whilst these modern tools provide us with a useful window through which to view the ancient Pyramid's design we must always bear in mind that its ancient builders worked without such plans, just as they also worked without the surveying equipment that enables such drawings, along with their accompanying specifications, to be realised as they are today.[11]

The discovery of this ancient pattern in our modern plans, therefore, is but a shadow of a lost reality. The challenge is to set that modern abstraction into the gritty context of the Pyramid's construction, to rediscover its reality by following the hands and the ambitions of those who made this most ancient building and learn, just for a short while, to think like an Egyptian.

6 The Pyramid's timetable

we do not have to explain everything in order to explain something

David Lewis-Williams 2002[1]

Like beads upon an abacus, the rows of horizontal blocks that make up the Great Pyramid encourage calculation. From the ancient Greeks to Flinders Petrie, everybody did it. Count out the blocks of stone and work out their combined weight – which is usually taken at about 5½ million tons – then divide that number by the maximum time the Pyramid could have taken to build – which, in lieu of any written records, is usually taken to be the length of Khufu's estimated rule – and you may quickly establish the theoretical monthly, daily, hourly, rates of work required to build the Great Pyramid of Giza. Then, after further enquiry and experiment, you can estimate the numbers of people required to perform such an outrageous task and then, if you compare the figures of this hypothetical workforce with statistics of Egypt's population in King Khufu's day, you can even estimate what the Great Pyramid had cost the ancient state.

Such bald figures, however, are far too broad to summon up the shadows of the past. Traditionally then, when asked for an account of how the Great Pyramid was built, most archaeologists sucked on their pipes and read their Petrie and added some of their own experiences

Fig. 31 A detail of the Great Pyramid's west face. A single larger course, the thirty-fifth, stands out amidst the rest.

of moving stones about in Egypt to the basic maths, before concluding with excerpts from such lively writers as Herodotus of Halicarnassus, who flourished in the fifth century BC:

Till the death of Sneferu, the priests said, Egypt was excellently governed, and flourished greatly; but after him Khufu succeeded to the throne, and plunged into all manner of wickedness. He closed the temples, and forbade the Egyptians to offer sacrifice, compelling them instead to labour, one and all . . . Some were required to drag blocks of stone down to the Nile from the quarries in the Arabian range of hills; others received the blocks after they had been conveyed in boats across the river . . . A hundred thousand men laboured constantly, and were relieved every three months by a fresh lot . . . The pyramid itself was twenty years in building. It is a square, eight hundred feet each way, and the height the same, built entirely of polished stone, fitted together with the utmost care. The stones of which it is composed are none of them less than thirty feet in length . . . There is an inscription in Egyptian characters on the pyramid which records the quantity of radishes, onions, and garlick consumed by the labourers who constructed it; and I perfectly well remember that the interpreter who read the writing to me said that the money expended in this way was 1600 talents of silver. If this then is a true record, what a vast sum must have been spent on the iron tools used in the work . . . The wickedness of Khufu reached to such a pitch that, when he had spent all his treasures and wanted more, he sent his daughter to the stews, with orders to procure him a certain sum – how much I cannot say, for I was not told.

Herodotus Book II, 124–6[2]

Despite such dragomanic tales or, indeed, precisely because of their apparent artlessness, such ancient estimations might at first glance appear to have advantage over those of modern times. After all, these old Greek gentlemen had visited ancient Egypt whilst it yet lived and had chatted to priests working close by the Great Pyramid who seemed to know a thing or two; their texts too had first informed the West that the Great Pyramid was built by an ancient king called Khufu and that should count for something. And yet, these same Greeks had regarded the Great Pyramid as nothing but the giddy memorial of a legendary oriental despot whose very shade they regarded with an instinctive apprehension:[3] our word 'pyramid', indeed, appears to have been derived from the Greek 'pyramis', a term used in ancient Levantine bazaars to describe a tiny pointed loaf of bread and employed at Giza apparently as an apotropaic sarcasm to cut the alien monuments down to size.[4] All in all then, it is worth remembering that Herodotus' visit to the Pyramids took place some two millennia after Khufu's death, when building technologies, social circumstances and national ambitions had all greatly changed.[5]

Until quite recently such antique observations were the only beads that could be set upon the abacus of the Pyramid's theoretical statistics. As far as determining the length of time that the Pyramid had taken to construct, upon which depended all calculation of the work rates, they were no real use at all. And without that vital outline figure, all estimations of the size of the pyramid-makers' workforce could be little more than guesswork.

Following the line of least resistance, most modern estimates of the pace of the Great Pyramid's construction simply followed the calculations of the chronological historians who until quite recently gave Khufu twenty-three years of rule, and used this figure as the maximum time available for building.[6] Clearly, unless the Egyptians had secretly practised ritual murder, the pyramid-makers could hardly have predicted the length of Khufu's reign, which cannot therefore reflect the real time it took to build his Pyramid. At the same time too, it is difficult to imagine that the construction of such an enormous and sophisticated monument was begun on the serendipitous assumption that one fine day the job might be completed. We may assume, therefore, that from the beginning of their work the pyramid-makers planned to finish the Great Pyramid within King Khufu's lifetime. What then did they consider practical and possible for the pharaoh and his Pyramid: what in short, were their plans, their timetables, their ambitions?

One thing is certain. Whether the Great Pyramid was finished in five or fifty years, its builders were faced with the task of moving enormous quantities of stone about and fast. Given the brutal fact that more than 5 million tons of rock were cut and carried up onto the cliff of the Giza Plateau to form the bulk of the Great Pyramid, the crudest of mathematics shows that this by itself was a monstrous architectural progress. Working at a single continuous rate, for example, with a ten-hour day, three hundred days a year, one and one third tons of stone had to be set in place upon the Pyramid during every minute of every working day for the Pyramid to have been finished within the twenty-three-year period traditionally allotted to King Khufu's reign:[7] a bald abstraction that in itself suggests that a revolution had taken place upon the Giza Plateau, part of a transformation within the world's first nation state in which farmers had been turned into masons, whilst the rest of the population made food enough to feed them all. This then is a hint of an extraordinary revolution that could appear yet more remarkable if the Great Pyramid's authentic building rates were recovered. Long before the coming of Herodotus, however, all record of this remarkable adventure seems to have been lost. And that is why most of the tales about the building of this Pyramid tell more about the slave societies of ancient Greece and Rome, or latterly, the technologies of the industrial and colonising West, than they do of the realities of life in Khufu's Egypt.

In the 1980s whilst excavating around the so-called Red Pyramid, the third great pyramid to be built in the reign of Khufu's father Sneferu, Rainer Stadelmann of the German Archaeological Institute uncovered a mass of ancient graffiti.[8] Scratched and scribbled on some of the pyramid's building blocks, most of these brief texts were hieroglyphic check marks relating, it appeared, to the delivery or the positioning of the blocks of quarried stones. Three, however, were unique. Although similar in style to some of the graffiti that yet remain inside the Great Pyramid, they did not record the prayerful names of work gangs, but the years, one may presume, in Sneferu's reign in which the blocks on which the texts were written had been put into position on the rising Pyramid.[9]

These rare graffiti then, one of which was drawn on a foundation stone, the others on blocks lying close to their original positions higher up the pyramid, provide genuine data about the rate of pyramid building in the last decades before Khufu came to the throne of Egypt.[10] They also record the progress of a pyramid that is very similar in its construction to the Great Pyramid and, though just two-thirds of its volume, is still one of the largest that the Egyptians ever built. Given the regular geometric form of pyramids as well, even this small sample of genuine work rates provides sufficient data for reconstructing the speed at which the entire pyramid could have been built. And that in turn offers a rare injection of reality into the hoary hypothetics of how long it took to build the Great Pyramid of Giza.

From start to finish, so its graffiti tell, Sneferu's Red Pyramid was built in just ten years and seven months, a time span far shorter than

Fig. 32 Three of the Red Pyramid's building graffiti. The graffito on the left, which appears to record the date of its foundation, was found on a block by the pyramid's south-west cornerstone and has been known for many years. The other two, however, were excavated in 1982. Found at around the levels of the pyramid's twelfth and sixteenth courses, they record different dates: 'information for determining the speed with which . . . [the pyramid was] constructed' (Krauss 1996, p. 49).

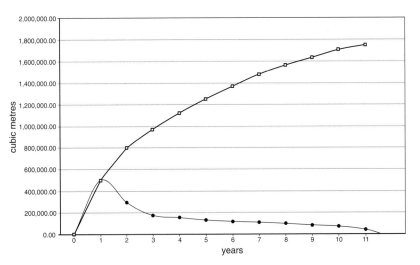

Fig. 33 Graph showing the rate at which the Red Pyramid was constructed, based upon the evidence of its building graffiti. The upper line charts the accumulating volume of stone laid over the years of the pyramid's construction; the lower line, the yearly amounts of stone required (data derived from Appendix 5 below).

earlier estimates of such building works.[11] Nor do the surprises end there. For the three graffiti and some ingenious mathematics also indicate that the rate at which the Red Pyramid had risen into the air was constant; a very high initial build rate of more than 30 feet (9.45 m) a year dropping down through following years before a final spurt as the pyramid builders approached the apex (fig. 33). And although at first glance this might seem unremarkable, in reality it tells us that something extraordinary was happening at the work site during this pyramid's construction.

Given that pyramids rise up to a sharp and single point, one would anticipate that, with a labour force of a single size working at a constant rate, the annual build rate would increase exponentially as the pyramid narrowed and approached its apex. At the same time, the dramatically decreasing area available to the workforce as the pyramid tapered into the sky would have increasingly denied them the physical access they required; at the ending of the work there would only have been room for very small numbers of workmen. The shape of the Great Pyramid alone, therefore, suggests that its construction did not engage a workforce of a single size from start to finish as the ancient Greeks and many other theorists seem to have assumed.

Combine those simple geometric facts with the Red Pyramid's graffiti that tell of a relatively constant rate of rise and the mathematics inescapably demands that, for that pyramid to have been finished in the time available, the volume of stone set in place each day at the beginning of the work would have had to have been many times the amount required in the last years of its construction.[12] And that in turn shows us that the first year of building at the Red Pyramid witnessed an explosion of effort during which more than a quarter of the pyramid's entire bulk, around a million tons of limestone, was cut and hauled and set precisely in position. And even though that titanic workload slackened off after the first furious year of building, demand for stone during the next eighteen months or so was hardly less intense. By the ending of the first three years of work half of all the stone required for the Red Pyramid's completion would have had to have been set in place, a calculation borne out by the condition of several other early pyramids that were left unfinished, so it would appear, when their short-lived pharaohs had died: pyramids that, despite the few years available for their construction, had at least a quarter of their bulk and the great part of their interiors completed.[13]

Here then are the first steps towards an understanding of how the Great Pyramid was built: transposing the work rates from the Red Pyramid to Khufu's workforce on the Giza Plateau would provide not only the first rational estimation of the overall length of time the Great Pyramid took to build, but a set of broad parameters for varying workloads during the different phases of its construction.

Now of course there is no proof that in reality the pyramid-builders' work rates remained the same during the successive reigns of Sneferu and Khufu. The Red Pyramid figures, however, represent the genuine work rates at the last major royal pyramid to have been built before the Great Pyramid, one closer in its construction to the Great Pyramid than any other pyramid and built in all likelihood whilst Khufu was a prince, by part of the self-same force of pyramid-makers that he presumably would inherit from his father. The Red Pyramid's graffiti, therefore, offer a genuine and realistic scenario for the building of the Great Pyramid.

Although such work rates might first appear extravagant and impracticable, the graffiti prove that the pace that they record was within the capability of Khufu's pyramid-makers.[14] And, of course, if Khufu's administration had employed a yet larger workforce than the one his father had engaged for the Red Pyramid, its progress would have been even faster; at present there is no way to tell. These newly established figures, however, are well beyond the vague guesses of earlier generations and provide the only known ancient parameters for such an enterprise. They offer us a place to start from and some-thing to adjust if more information should become available. Above all, they provide a genuine taste of ancient dust and energy and ambi-tion.[15]

Transposing the Red Pyramid building rates to the Plateau of Giza (fig. 34 and Appendix 5), we discover that it would have taken

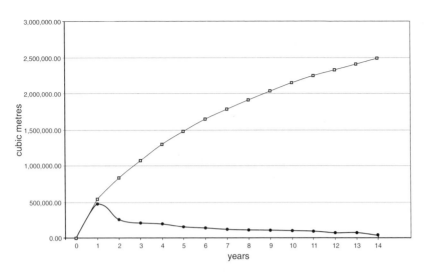

Fig. 34 A building timetable for the Great Pyramid based upon the premise that the annual building rates were the same as those established for the Red Pyramid (cf. fig. 33). The upper line charts the accumulating volume of stone laid over the years of the Great Pyramid's construction; the lower line the yearly amounts of stone required.

fourteen years to build the Great Pyramid at Giza. And all at once we catch a glimpse of how this Pyramid was made; for once a genuine contemporary time frame is set into place, all the other statistics that can be derived from the Great Pyramid's standing stones can be slotted into place. And, once again, the results are as fascinating as they are unexpected.

Under this regime, for example, during the first frantic year of working, the Great Pyramid would have risen some 44 feet (13.25 m) from its baselines and around 470,000 of the Pyramid's 2½ ton blocks of stone – almost a quarter of its entire bulk – would have been cut, hauled and set into their places.[16] Assuming that the same number of pyramid-builders worked at the same rates on both the Red Pyramid and the Great Pyramid, around 21,000 people would have been required for this first phase of working at the Giza Plateau; but during the next eighteen months this number would have almost halved, a fall that would be sustained throughout the remainder of the work (fig. 234).[17]

As well as this grand gathering there were many thousands of people employed upon the Pyramid's construction at this same time working at sites all over Egypt, gathering materials, manpower and provisions, and packing them off to Khufu's rising Pyramid. Building materials were shipped from up and down the Nile, barges bringing granite from Aswan on Egypt's southern border and fine limestone from quarries just across the river from the Giza Plateau, whilst desert caravans, long lines of men and donkeys, carried copper from desert mines and smelters, and gypsum too, along with a variety of other materials from smaller mines and quarries.[18]

Overall, the Red Pyramid's building regime shows that the Great Pyramid would have employed a nation-wide workforce of some 26,000 people during the first year of its building, a figure that would have dropped dramatically at first and then steadily year after year, to fewer than 4000 individuals as it approached completion.[19] At first glance then, this might appear to supply a more modest picture of the project than has previously been supposed; fewer people working for less time. It also offers a welcome corrective to the old visions of peasant masses labouring under whips and brute coercion, and moves us towards an attitude of respect both for the craftsmen who built the Pyramid and for the people who planned, organised and supplied their work.

At the same time, these estimates also assume extremely heavy annual workloads: a routine of ten hours each day for 300 days of each and every year.[20] To guard national prosperity stone setting rates at such great pyramids as Khufu's had to be kept high, the pace dramatic. Although at first glance, with the best estimate of the ancient Egyptian population during Khufu's reign standing at around 1.6 million, the numbers directly involved in pyramid building may appear to be but a drop in the national ocean, yet if work had been conducted at a gentler pace, if there were more holidays or shorter days so that the stone setting rates were halved, the results could have been catastrophic.[21] For if the Great Pyramid was to be kept rising at the same rate as the Red Pyramid, such a halving in work rates would have necessitated a virtual doubling of the workforce. And that in turn would have meant that the furious work rates of the first year would have required the labour of more than 20 per cent of the adult male population of Egypt which, along with their simultaneous removal from the food-producing economy, would have had an effect approaching that of a national plague.[22] In a world of such modest expectations as the Bronze Age when the difference between prosperity and hardship of the general population was often set upon a knife's edge, even a loss of 10.88 per cent of the male workforce to Giza and the Pyramid as my statistics indicate, would probably have been unsupportable for more than a few harvests at a time.[23] These savage work rates then would have served to reduce the economic consequences on Egypt's population of erecting such great pyramids.

A degree of hardship nonetheless appears to have afflicted all Egyptians during the time that these great pyramids were constructed. As Reisner's excavations at Nag' el-Deir have underlined, provincial cemeteries that had accommodated fine burials in earlier periods hold relatively impoverished ones from the age of the great

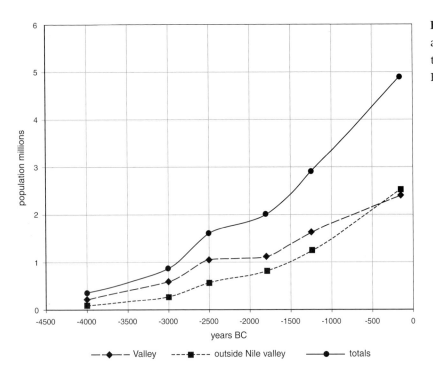

Fig. 35 The population of ancient Egypt from 4000 to 0 BC (data derived from Butzer 1976, p. 83).

pyramids, a posthumous privation that appears to have ceased once that pyramid building on such an enormous scale stopped.[24] Confirming this impression, graphs of population estimates for ancient Egypt show a unique dip in ancient Egypt's normally rising population levels during that same period of time, a dip that ends when the age of building the enormous early pyramids is over. The Egyptians, then, paid heavily for King Khufu's Pyramid. At the beginning of the work especially, with a great part of the population and the nation's wealth and wisdom working furiously together on the Giza Plateau, it must have caused a national paroxysm. No wonder that the name of one of his work gangs – 'May the White Crown of Khufu strengthen the sailing!' – seems like a prayer asking for a good wind to speed the royal stone barges.[25] Just as the Great Pyramid's architecture laid out King Khufu's destiny in blocks of stone, so the labour of its construction had linked his fate directly to that of the people of his kingdom. This Pyramid, then, was more than just a tomb, more than a monument to mark a royal grave.

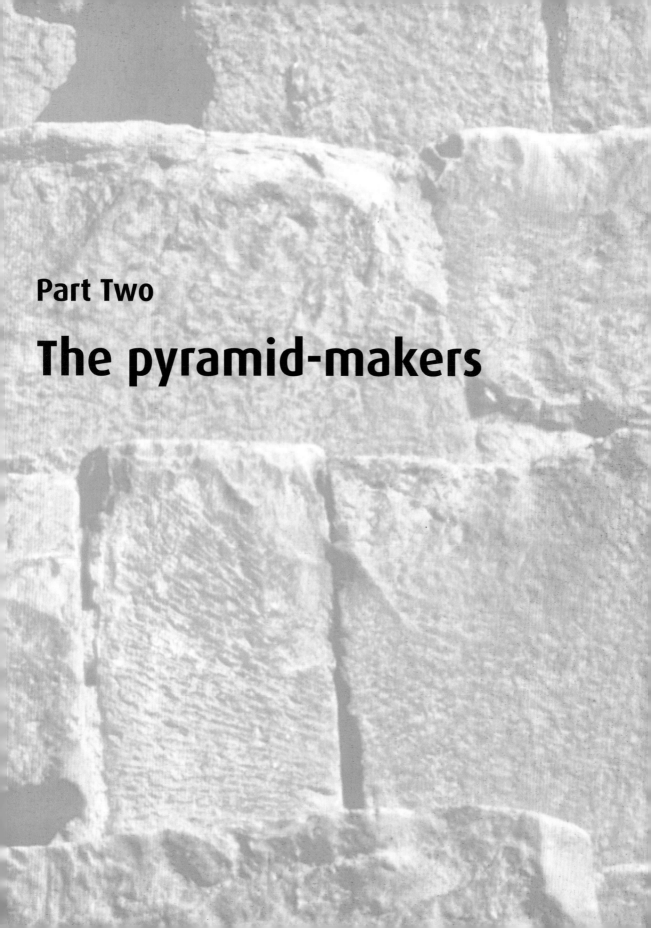

Part Two

The pyramid-makers

SECTION ONE

The ghosts in the cemetery

7 At the court of the king

Saddle the camels, we ride for Luxor tonight!

King Khufu in Warner Brothers' 1955 production of The Land of the Pharaohs[1]

There is but one indisputable sculpture of the fabled pharaoh for whom the Great Pyramid was made; a work so small that it could sit within the hollow of your hand, yet so monumental in its execution that, as photographs of it sometimes pretend, it could be 10 feet tall.[2] Cut from a tusk of ivory, this 2 inch (5.5 cm) Khufu was found by Flinders Petrie in 1903, along with an assortment of similar bits and pieces, in the waterlogged ruin of a provincial temple.[3] It is not well preserved. Half of its surface has been lost, and its shiny shoulders are darkly stained with those inky blots that archaeologists call dendrites. What remains shows us a man with a large solid-looking head set on a short neck supported by the same powerful body that the royal sculptors gave to the other kings of his dynasty. His right hand clasps a model threshing flail, a regal sceptre; his left lies gently down along the royal thigh, as in the statues of much older kings. He wears a pleated linen kilt and a close-fitting crown. And on the battered throne beside the king's right leg, inside the squared hieroglyph that signifies a royal palace, two hieroglyphs spell out King Khufu's name.[4]

Fig. 36 The statue of the king: the sole surviving image of the Pharaoh Khufu, found by Flinders Petrie at Abydos. 'Though the face was only three-eighths of an inch high, like the tip of a little finger, it bore the most amazing portrait' (Petrie 1933, p. 182).

Despite the ivory's decay, the statue seems as if it were alive. The full forms of its face echo and complement each another; the flat arc of the chin, the crown's low curve, the nicely balanced features larger even than a film star's. This, then, is not a copy from the life but a sculpture that has been most carefully designed: in a living person, for example, the distance from the bridge of the nose to the chin is usually a quarter of the distance from the chin to the belt; in archaic Greek sculpture, the same proportion is around five to one;[5] in Khufu's sculpture, however, it is three to one, giving it an enormous face as is entirely suitable for a work of such diminutive size. The features too, although they are but a quarter of an inch in height, are designed in a similarly careful manner. In comparison with the monarchs of the following generations, the ivory face is rounder and flatter; the mouth set low and straight and wide, the nose, although exaggerated by abrasion, drawn flat and broad, the ears, large and archaic; the eyes, wide-spaced, wide-open, in the manner of the artists of his ancestors.

There are several other royal sculptures that share this same distinctive face, in alabaster, limestone and red granite. None of them, however, is of the superb quality one would expect from the royal sculptors of King Khufu's dynasty and one of them at least has the dreary qualities of a fake.[6] And all are broken and anonymous. Despite his mighty Pyramid, King Khufu is elusive. Considering that the longest known royal documents of his reign are a few inscriptions in his mines and quarries and that these contain but brief and fairly standard phrases, you could say that he has all but disappeared.

Standing at the foot of the Great Pyramid, however, viewing it simply as the residue of a titanic process as if it were a slag heap in Belgium or South Wales, it is self-evident that, whatever historians have had to say about Khufu's character or marital status or his adventures in trade and arms, the most significant single event of his reign – or arguably of all of ancient Egypt's history – was the construction of this extraordinary Pyramid. This Pyramid, after all, was the climactic product of an age that had undergone a revolution; a transformation in which riverside communities of Bronze Age farmers had been brought together in a powerfully centralised system of construction and supply. Everything about this unique monument speaks of change and dynamism; even the communities that built the early pyramids, essentially state-supported municipalities governed by the state's ambition to build pyramids, were entirely novel. And at just this same time, whilst this century-long adventure of pyramid building was underway, a great part of those distinctive styles of painting and sculpture, architecture and relief that we now recognise as being 'ancient Egyptian' were being brought to their maturity.[7]

So this extraordinary age whose culmination was the making of King Khufu's Pyramid was also the beginning of what is popularly known as 'ancient Egypt': that vision which encompasses everything from a distinctive visual style to religious belief and the offices of state.[8] There is, however, very little evidence that our present version of this 'ancient Egypt', that often vulgar parody based upon the great grand histories of the last two centuries, reflects in any meaningful way the living society that built the first great pyramids. To recover something of that lost reality we must set the usual suspects into a more open-ended context.

It is not difficult, in fact, to free the Great Pyramid's creators from this fake Egyptian bondage, for in reality the people of that time are utterly unknown. Even Khufu still hovers on the outer edge of real history: despite his millennial celebrity, we know little more of him than his names, an approximation of the length of time he ruled and the bare fact that the Great Pyramid was built to be his tomb. Not a word of Khufu's has survived, no trace of personality, not a single hard stone sculpture with his name; only minor images set beside the brief texts of the mines and quarries, ciphers showing pharaoh sitting on a throne or clubbing Egypt's enemies.[9] Other than his Pyramid, there is very little left of Khufu.

Given this grand hiatus, traditional egyptologists have juggled the scanty evidence and managed as best they can, as these extracts from a recent history show:

Sneferu's successor, Khufu, is mentioned in Herodotus as Cheops, the Greek form of his name. In hieroglyphs he is called Khufu, an abbreviation of Khnum khuef wi (May the God Khnum Protect Me); the reading of his Horus name, transcribed as Medjedu, is only conjectural. Modern historians think the prince must have been about forty when he assumed power. The Turin Canon [compiled some thirteen centuries after Khufu] gives twenty-three years as the length of his reign, but Herodotus gives fifty and Manetho sixty-three . . .

Among the scant details known concerning his reign is the fact that expeditions were conducted outside the Nile Valley to Sinai in quest of turquoise and copper; to the deserts of Nubia . . . and to Lebanon for cedar logs. Vases bearing Khufu's cartouche have been found at Byblos . . .

The crowning achievement of Khufu's reign is the celebrated pyramid at Giza, called the Great Pyramid . . . Admired throughout the centuries, it remains the focus of endless speculation and mystical-fantastical interpretations by those dedicated to the study of pyramids.

Khufu himself has been detested as harsh and cruel in Egyptian folk memory ever since the First Intermediate Period, when the authority of the central power came into question. He had a large family, with many wives and more than twelve children. Prince Kawa'b, the eldest son of his first wife, Meret-ites, died before his father. His second son . . .

When Khufu died, the royal succession was so hotly contested that work was abruptly interrupted on the mastabas [tombs] of many royal princes. Out of these palace intrigues, Djedefre emerged the victor, but he was considered an usurper according to some traditions and thus . . .[10]

So King Khufu's unknown kingdom, that distant, dynamic and ambitious age, is assimilated into the cosy sort of history that we were taught at school; the sort that Hollywood embellishes and TV travesties; the bare rump of that grand heroic vision born in ancient Greece and Rome.

Now the thing about the ancient Greeks of course is that they loved to tell a good story, just as we still like to hear one. In similar fashion, the nineteenth-century West, the West of Walter Scott and Victor Hugo, took up that antique taste for history as grand dramatic narrative and added contemporary ideas of destiny and progress to make a new past for the Age of Industry. Despite von Ranke's celebrated assertion, made in the same decade as Champollion's decipherment, that as a modern historian he was no longer interested in the 'task of judging the past, of instructing the present for the benefit of ages to come',[11] the novelists and poets, the painters and the historians of the age did exactly that, carefully manufacturing a vision of the past in which things like pyramids were seen as markers in a material and intellectual progress; a grand morality play that like all such dramas lent itself quite naturally to casts of heroes, visionaries and villains.

This is where those epithets and titles that Lepsius and his successors had dug out of the Giza cemeteries came in so handy; or, at least, the various translations of the elegant hieroglyphics in the great tombs that stand around King Khufu's Pyramid as if they were a royal court in ordered session.[12] Flesh out those texts with information gathered from more loquacious eras of Egyptian history, combine that information with the lively portraits recovered from the Giza cemeteries and you can quickly conjure up familiar images of 'ancient Egypt'; of a courtly aristocracy ruled by a strong king from a throne of ivory. Stand in the ponderous shadows of these same tombs, declaim those same translations and all the cemeteries' streets will fill with personalities:

Kawa'b. King's eldest son of his body, hereditary prince, Chief lector-
    priest, and wife Hetep-heres.

Kaem'ah, King's son, Overseer of the work gangs of Upper Egypt,
    Greatest of the Ten of Upper Egypt.
Wepemnefert, King's son, Prophet of Heket, heka priest of Mehyt.
Yunu, King's son, overseer of the work gangs of Upper Egypt, Greatest
    of the Ten of Upper Egypt.
Khufukha'ef, King's son of his body, Chief Justice and Vizier and wife
    Nefertkau.
Khentka, King's son of his body, Sole companion.
Duaenhor, King's son of his body, Companion of his father.
Mertiotes, King's daughter of his body.
Meres'ankh, King's daughter of his body.
Khufunakht, Royal acquaintance.
Nufer, Royal acquaintance.
Sethiheknet, Royal acquaintance.
Kanufer, Overseer of commissions, Director of bowmen.
Iny, Director of cattle-herdsmen and the pastures.[13]

Is this then a real taste of Khufu's kingdom; does it display the order
of his court and government; or is it but a mirage, conjured up by
translators and historians?

In common with many other emerging disciplines of the nineteenth century, many of the terms of these translations have their
origins in the processes by which the languages of early modern
Europe were stretched to accommodate the new industrial society.
From the sale rooms, for example, the egyptologists adopted such
terms such 'faience','porcelain','terracotta' and 'niello' as equivalents
of ancient Egyptian techniques and materials. And just as
astronomers had adopted the friendly word 'companion' to designate
a class of star, so egyptologists also adopted that same term to denote
a common epithet of the inscriptions that accompany male burials in
some ancient Egyptian cemeteries.[14]

Since those early days several of these terms have been dropped
whilst others have taken on lives of their own with meanings well
beyond the simple words that they employ. The use of the term 'companion' for example, or 'friend' as it is sometimes called, has not
changed since the times of the decipherment, yet, in another of those
orientalising sexualisations that Edward Said perceptively identified,
the nineteenth-century term 'acquaintance', which was adopted for a
title borne by some of the women of King Khufu's cemeteries, is often
rendered nowadays as 'concubine'![15]

All this, of course, is part of the same vocabulary, the same dream
world, that so enlivens the ancient Egypt of Verdi's slave-princess

Aida. And both of course are products of the same era; the age of the fustian European courts that patronised Champollion and subsidised Professor Lepsius, who in their turn attended at the divans of the Khedives of Egypt which were served by the egyptologist Auguste Mariette, who in his turn provided the literary inspiration for Verdi's egyptianising opera.[16]

> Glory to Egypt, and to Isis,
> who protects its sacred soil.
> To the king who rules the Delta
> we raise our festive songs!
>
> Dance Egyptian maidens
> and sing your mystic praises,
> As the bright stars of night
> Dance around the sun.

Aida, Act II, scene 2

Thus speak the servants of the King, whose name is the Sun and Rock of Prussia, Lepsius the scribe, Erbkam the architect, the brothers Weidenbach . . . Hail to the Eagle, Shelterer of the Cross, the King, the Sun and Rock of Prussia, the son of the Sun, freer of the land. Frederick William the Fourth, the Philopator, his country's father . . .[17]   Richard Lepsius

For the Victorians, such rolling phrases set into the translations of the ancient hieroglyphs would certainly have aided the comfortable conviction that when they visited the ruins of Khufu's cemeteries with their Murray's Hand-Book and viewed, say, the tomb of a King's Son or an Overseer, they understood the workings of that ancient kingdom as well as any other in their Empire. At the same time too, there are hints in the sonority of such translations of a connection between the court of pharaoh and those of the King James Bible which served to reinforce the common belief that anyone could instinctively appreciate how power and precedence operated in such distant kingdoms – that they were quite similar to contemporary courts and universities. So, when a recent commentary assures us that 'Any Old Kingdom pharaoh could state, with more justification than Louis XIV, "the state is me" ', nothing could seem more reason-able.[18] All we are being asked to do, after all, is to go down again to Pharaoh Land, as Yankees at an ersatz Court.

This is not to deny, of course, that the little figure on his throne of ivory was not a kind of a king, nor that our instinctive reactions to the manners of his household would lead us wildly astray should we ever have the good fortune to attend it. We would, however, be entering a world where our instincts and our understanding of more recent ceremonial might quickly render us perplexed or frightened. Yet even then, perhaps, another part of our inheritance might serve as comfort: that old arrogance, born of European romanticism, that holds that there is but one fixed order, one set of accomplishments and sins in all humanity and that with just a little patience we can understand any other human culture. But you may be sure that, just as Prince Khufu never danced at Cinderella's ball, so there are today, and always have been, courts and cultures all around the world that organise themselves in ways quite different from those of the modern West and are inhabited by people with reactions and ways of thinking that, to our eyes, are very difficult to understand.

8 The adventures of the vizier

As tyme requireth, [he is] a man of merveylous myrth & pastymes and somtyme of sad gravite: as who say, a man for all seasons.

Whittinton's Vulgaria *(1520)*[1]

In one of those marvellously theatrical events for which archaeology is so famous, excavators digging in the morning shadow of King Khufu's Pyramid were confronted with an unexpected sight as they cleared the drifted sand from the shattered façade of an enormous tomb and peered into a small rough hole in its neat-cut blocks of stone; for there before them was one of the very finest of Egyptian sculptures, a vivid life-sized seated figure cut from limestone, bearing an inscription of a man called Hemiunu.[2]

Hemiunu, member of the elite, high official, vizier, king's seal bearer, attendant to Nekhen, and spokesperson of every resident of Pe, priest of Bastet, priest of Shesmetet, priest of the Ram of Mendes, Keeper of the Apis Bull, Keeper of the White Bull, whom his lord Loves, elder of the palace, high priest of Thoth, whom his lord loves, courtier, Overseer of Royal Scribes, priest of the Panther Goddess, Director of Music of the South and North, Overseer of All Construction Projects of the King, king's son of his own body, Hemiunu.[3]

Surely then, whatever the shortcomings of translation, this Hemiunu was pharaoh's right-hand man: head of government and music, a great priest, a director of building works and, as his sumptuous and well-positioned tomb suggests, a regular Pooh Bah, and one of Khufu's cherished sons to boot. Even the statue's noble head and ample corporation, a strong and active youth overtaken by the just rewards of a successful middle age, underline the same impression. This then, it appeared, was the very image of an ancient Egyptian building magnate, a pre-industrial Brunel: the man who made the Great Pyramid of Giza.

Once again, things may not have been as they appear today. Consider for example, the apparently no-nonsense epithet 'King's son of his own body', a common-enough translation of a not infrequent appellation of males buried in King Khufu's cemeteries and a powerful message to modern Westerners, whose culture is traditionally based upon inheritance through the male line. Another inscription, however, from another cemetery made in the reign of Khufu's father, tells us that this same Hemiunu was the 'son' of Khufu's father Sneferu and, therefore, Khufu's cousin![4] Together then what these two texts really tell us is that the epithet held a different meaning from its formal English usage.[5] In many other cultures too, of course, such terms are often used as social conventions rather than descriptions of an individual's DNA, and this, it seems, may well have been the case in Hemiunu's time as well.

Several other of Hemiunu's impressive oriental titles – the terms 'vizier' or 'elder of the palace', for example – still seem to suggest that this Hemiunu was powerful enough to have built the Great Pyramid for Khufu, especially when he is described as 'Overseer of All Construction Projects of the King'. None of these phrases, however, holds the specific meanings that they would imply. The term vizier for example, an early Arabic word for a porter or a carrier, was used by Ottoman Turks to describe a wide variety of state appointments from that of a provincial governor to a senior minister in Istanbul. Ever since the nineteenth century, however, when Egypt was in the orbit of the Turkish court and egyptologists attended the divans of Alexandria and Cairo to obtain permission for their work, the loose term 'vizier' was employed as a translation of a set of hieroglyphs which have more recently been characterised as signifying 'the greatest of all Egyptian officials . . . [at the] peak of the civil service hierarchy'.[6] So the relationship of Hemiunu's hieroglyphic titulary to that of oriental viziers is vague indeed. And vaguer still is its relationship to the pyramid-makers.

Fig. 37 Revealed by Herman Junker and his excavators on 12 March 1912, the head of Hemiunu's statue peers blindly out of the tomb. Unknown robbers had cut the hole into the tomb's façade to locate the rooms of its interior, and attacked the statue's head with chisels and removed its eyes, which had been inset with gold.

Fig. 38 The body of Hemiunu's statue in his tomb, one of the largest monuments in Khufu's cemeteries (cf. fig. 40). The craftsmanship employed on some of the stone work of the tomb of this 'Overseer of All Construction Projects of the King' is as fine as that of the Great Pyramid itself.

Fig. 39 Thoroughly restored for his debut in the modern world: the powerful head of the vizier Hemiunu.

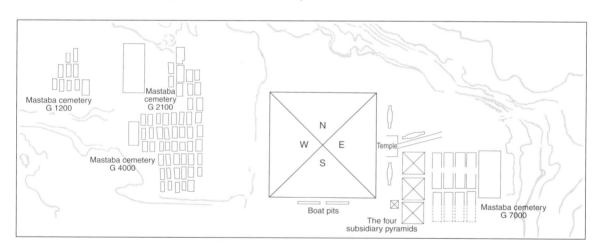

Fig. 40 A map of the monuments on the Giza Plateau that were built in the time of Khufu.

'Cemetery G 7000', to the east of the Great Pyramid, appears to contain the tombs of some of Khufu's extended family. It underwent a series of enlargements. The three cemeteries to the west of the Pyramid appear to contain the mastabas of court officials; the largest tomb in 'Cemetery G 4000' is that of 'vizier' Hemiunu; the occupant of the enormous mastaba in 'Cemetery G 2100', however, is unknown.

Three of the subsidiary pyramids housed the burials of Khufu's queens; the fourth and smallest is generally believed to have served some kind of ritual function. The 'boat pits' housed full-sized Nile boats. Three more open pits are indicated on the Pyramid's east side. The 'Pyramid Temple' was joined to a causeway that ran down from the eastern cliff top into the Nile Valley.

Similarly, the phrase 'Overseer of All Construction Projects of the King', which other less fastidious translations often render along with other apparently similar titles as 'architect', implying that Hemiunu was the individual who designed the Great Pyramid of Giza, is of equal ambiguity.[7] Brushing aside the happy thought that there is something of the air of a New Yorker cartoon in the notion of an ancient Egyptian working in the manner of Michelangelo or Le Corbusier – 'Not a single point *agaain*, Chief Architect?' – the *Oxford English Dictionary*'s definition of an architect as 'a skilled professor of the art of building, whose business it is to prepare the plans of edifices' is hardly relevant to the processes of building and design in Khufu's day, as we shall see: indeed, the *Dictionary* further informs us, the use of the term 'architect' to describe an individual designer is but a few centuries old, born around the same time as the modern definition of an 'artist'.[8]

Neither can literal translations of these ancient titularies throw clear light upon their contemporary meanings; adopting the same principles today would have Sir Winston Churchill supervising the Queen of England's bath time.

How, then, should we take these traditional translations? Certainly with mindfulness of the nineteenth century's fondness for biblical sonority and luxurious orientalism and with the added proviso, too, that many of these epithets may not describe family affiliations or job descriptions at all, but may in fact have been, as was the custom in later times, 'offices of the necropolis' – that is, that they are simply honorifics to be set upon a grave.[9] There must remain as well some doubt as to whether these epithets may properly be termed titles in the modern sense at all: 'titles', that is, which can be ordered and analysed in the manner of the nineteenth-century codifications of contemporary courts, as, for example, Victoria's courtiers and pedigrees and protocols were compiled and sorted in Burke's precise and monumental *Dictionary of the Peerage and Baronetage*.[10] And certainly, the notion that King Khufu's cemetery texts can provide a similar reconstruction of his living court, let alone the offices of the pyramid-makers' administration, must remain an open question – especially when it is recalled that the order and ceremonial of the British court was itself in grave confusion in the decades before Sir Bernard Burke began his careful labours![11]

There are other pitfalls too in such traditional approaches to King Khufu's times. The sheer size and opulence of Hemiunu's funerary arrangements, for example, are apt to give a false impression of the status of the man, especially as the physical position of his tomb within the cemetery appears to command a group of smaller tombs whose owners sport less impressive titles, and so naturally aids an impression of subservience within the living court.[12] Yet Hemiunu's tomb is not the largest monument in King Khufu's cemeteries. The other great tombs, however, entirely lack the 'personality' of Hemiunu's monument with its rich cache of titularies and fine art, for when their excavators dug them out, most of them were found to be plundered and anonymous. Whatever facts we may marshal from these monuments, therefore, they are all ultimately dependent on a spin of chance: the haphazard harvest of two centuries of rummaging through the scanty wreckage of a very distant age. In its present context the first thing Hemiunu's tomb and all the others can tell us of King Khufu's life and times is that our present understanding of that distant age is fragile and indistinct. And that we need, therefore, to make more open-ended histories.

Some things, however, are certain. Just as we should guard against setting Khufu and his courtiers and their titles in an unchanging oriental Camelot or a dominion of the British Empire, so too the old myth that the Great Pyramid was built by a rural labour force tyrannically snatched from distant villages and whipped to work by a bureaucracy governed by talented noblemen can no longer serve as an automatic explanation of how this Pyramid was made. Many alternatives to such unthinking images have been described by anthropologists and historians in a wide variety of contexts and there is not the slightest evidence to bear out such colonialist metaphors.[13] In the light of the wide range of abilities displayed by the Great Pyramid's creators, then, we might begin with the assumption that its makers were intelligent, inventive and surprising people, and that the great old Egypt of the Pharaohs that the West has cultivated for so long, with its slaves and whips, its harems and its oriental court intrigues, should take its proper place in nineteenth-century social history, just as should their modern-day successors: those narratives that still assume that the Great Pyramid's construction was controlled by production managers juggling deadlines and worrying about overspend, or 'practicality' as it is sometimes called; with bands of surveyors using primitive equivalents of modern tools, and engineers living on-site in mud-brick Portakabins and keeping the Pyramid's plans upon papyrus rolls, and foremen running gangs of mindless labourers as if they were the antediluvian equivalents of a fleet of dumper trucks.[14] If we do not ditch such sorry visions, we will discover very little of the making of King Khufu's Pyramid and merely conjure up sad pastiches of our own preoccupations.

9 The new Egyptians

There yet remain some instant and immediate points of contact with the people of King Khufu's cemeteries: more than two dozen unique images, lively life-sized individual sculptured heads.

Like the startled images on the little strips of paper that roll out of passport photo booths, these chalky portraits have an unexpected air about them. Most of them were found in sand-filled chambers deep beneath the tombs and yet darker than a photo booth. Unfocussed yet

Fig. 41 The first of the mysterious so-called 'reserve heads' to be found at Giza, still lying as it was discovered in 1904, upon the half-excavated sand that had long filled the burial chamber of the tomb of Kanufer, Giza Mastaba 1203.

Fig. 42 Photographed in a splendid row in one of the storerooms of Reisner's expedition, these eight 'reserve heads', a quarter of all the known examples, were excavated by his expedition from a line of tombs in Cemetery 4000 (see fig. 40) during the season of 1913.

alert, their wide-open eyes gaze as if waiting for the strobe to flash once more, an ancient moment that has left us with a very lively range of faces, some of them, like so many of the rare products of King Khufu's reign, amongst the very finest objects of Egyptian art. Once more, we are on the edge of mystery. For not one of these ancient individual heads that so touch our imagination so much as bears a name. Hampered by modern ideas of what constitutes masculine and feminine features on a face, it is difficult now even to guess their sex, let alone the roles the people of these portraits may or may not have played in the running of King Khufu's kingdom.[1]

Most of these heads were found close by the burial chambers that lie beneath the great block tombs and it is tempting to claim these sculptures as portraits either of the owners of these tombs or of members of their family circle, just as their excavators usually assumed. Some archaeologists further suggested that these lively works were *Ersatzkopf*, sculptured heads made to serve as substitutes for someone buried in the tomb. Generally concurring with this notion, English-speaking archaeologists called them 'Reserve Heads',[2] implying that just as the rare examples of mummification from the Giza cemeteries reveal that the nobles' corpses were wrapped in fine linens and remodelled on occasion in gypsum plaster so as to hold the living body's form and hide the processes of its decomposition, so these portrait heads were another aspect of this sculptural image bank designed to serve as habitations for the spirits of the dead.

Whatever their purposes each separate head presents an individual image and most of them show a precise provision for their exhibition and display, having been carefully designed and cut to stand up on their own, upon their necks, without support. In fact, these sculptures are extremely well presented, the form of each one scrupulously established with the same bland and almost skin-like finish that Egyptian craftsmen had employed upon bowls and statues for the previous thousand years and more. But on these heads that gentle surface is enlivened by the addition of precise cuts drawn swiftly into the soft stone with a flat sharp chisel in a line hovering, as in a good portrait it must, between dignity and caricature, to fix the line of eyes and mouths and ears and noses.

Now a portrait, to paraphrase John Singer Sargent, is a picture of someone with a little something wrong with the mouth,[3] an observation that holds true for these images from the Giza tombs as well. For as if to correct that 'little something wrong', at least one of these heads has been hastily reworked after it had received what was to have been its final finish.[4] This overriding care for visual exactitude evidences some kind of dialogue, either between the sculptor and his own work or between the sculptor and other individuals.[5] Hidden away inside the Giza tombs, of course, such fussy alterations, along with the sculptors' emphasis upon the age and individuality of their subjects, give the impression of genuinely private pleasures; of the shared activity of a group of sculptors and their clients. How well then such tractable and attractive pieces fit the traditions of good old-fashioned Western connoisseurship: indeed this bright descriptive sculpture invites such speculation: 'Is her figure less than Greek, is her mouth a little weak?' 'Does A look like B?' 'Is this a portrait of an "Asiatic", a "Nubian" or a "native"?'[6]

The trick, and it was widely used at Giza, was to finish each sculpture with a distinctive set of facial features, but to place those attributes upon the same simplified sculptural forms, the same basic manikin, over and over again so that the individuality of each and every sculpture was emphasised inside a single common type. So even when the cemetery portraits appear individual to the point of idiosyncrasy as in the case of that tremendous fleshy life-sized full-length seated sculpture of Hemiunu with its body set in rolls of fat and the hooked nose and gold-lined eyes of the portrait head above, the same underlying figure type is used so that the fat hangs from Hemiunu's handsome frame in a way that a modern portrait artist might well consider to be unrealistic, for its sagging forms are set over a stereotypical straight strong body of the time. The 'Reserve Heads' too hold similar combinations of individuality and archetype, temporality and perfection, a mix that in later ages appeared highly flattering to its subjects, as Sir Peter Lely and Sir Joshua Reynolds well understood.

Forensic examination of an archaeological harvest of shining nut-brown skulls from Khufu's cemetery informs us of a different past. In life, King Khufu's courtiers had bad teeth, inflamed sinuses, dandruff and arthritis and many of them shared hereditary illnesses and died at a young age. Few of their surviving bones, however, show signs of trauma or of malnutrition or of having undertaken hard physical labour, which would suggest, along with the elaborate nature of their

Fig. 43 Found in 1906 during the excavation of the tomb of Nefer (Giza Mastaba 2110), this head shows extensive evidence of hasty alteration with a broad, flat chisel. That the sculpture's roughly reworked nose shares its distinctive profile with the reliefs of Nefer on the walls of his tomb's small offering chapel suggests that the aim of these alterations was to produce a continuity within the images within the tomb: a continuity also, of 'portraiture'? (see further Smith 1949, p. 29, no. 22, and pl. 48 d and e; also Smith 1960, pp. 36–7, and p. 475 note 2 above).

tombs, that they were neither pyramid-builders nor working farmers.[7] This then is a sample of the physical reality of some of the inhabitants of Khufu's Giza cemeteries. In their wide-eyed elegance the 'Reserve Heads' seem to present images of how some of these privileged people wanted to appear and, judging by their continuing popularity, how too we still wish to see them.[8]

Yet these chalky heads are not merely flattering portraits of the aristocratic dead. Nor are they necessarily portraits in the modern sense at all. Like the diverse images of Christian saints, many of the other images found in the Giza graves, although named and labelled as the same person, may have entirely different physiognomies.[9] Whether these anonymous 'Reserve Heads' are real likenesses we may never know. What we can see in them, in their immediacy, is that they betray a special fascination with a passing moment, an overwhelming sense of living changing time that was also a part of the reality of life in a regime that day by day, year on year, was building a great pyramid which, one day, they would finish.

Here then is a contradiction. On the one hand, the Great Pyramid and its accompanying cemeteries show a grand preoccupation with permanence and order; indeed, the rhythms and repetitions of those monumental buildings appear well suited to an agrarian population accustomed to ordering the Nile-side landscape in regular and fruitful patterns. On the other hand, both the state administration and the pyramid-builders were caught up in a dynamic that no ancient agrarian society had ever known before, a monstrous timetable generated not by the passing seasons of the year or by the progression of the sun and stars but by the finite earthly imperatives of making this enormous building.

Rather than moving within the cyclic space of earlier agrarian societies, this building programme by itself must have engendered something close to a modern sense of history within the offices of Khufu's state; something of time measured out as a succession of unique achievements and events. And that perhaps is why the people of the Reserve Heads seem to walk a narrow line between the ageless images of their ancestors and the 'real time' of the Great Pyramid's building timetable. Along with the Pyramid's logistics, these portraits evidence a new dynamic emerging in Egyptian society.[10]

And that alone, whatever the significance of the titles that those nobles may have held, shows that a wind of change was blowing on the Giza Plateau, an emerging sense of individual human history, freshening the studios of the sculptors of the royal court. At all events, the momentary smile that flits across the stony lips of several of these portraits seems to hold within it something of the tension between permanence and change, between the monumental and the here and now, in which so much of the modern fascination with this most ancient culture has its real roots.

10 The social contract

> . . . he who dares to undertake the making of a people's institutions ought to feel
> himself capable, so to speak, of changing human nature, of transforming each
> individual . . . he must in a word, take away from man his own resources and give
> him instead new ones alien to him.
>
> *J.-J. Rousseau*[1]

As they worked their way along the streets of tombs in Khufu's cemeteries, opening the chapels, digging out the graves, the archaeologists
brought to light a unique group of small stone stelae, many of them
excavated close to the same tombs in which the Reserve Heads had
been found.[2]

The proportions of a visiting-card and around 2 feet long (about 60
cm × 38 cm), these stelae were cut in the most exquisite low relief,
their fine white limestone over-painted in exact and flowing lines
with clear calm colours. All of them bear the same set of traditional
images; on the left-hand side, the owner of a tomb in Khufu's cemetery sits upon a chair in a pose typical of many earlier statues and
reliefs: that is, with one arm held across the waist or chest, the other
outstretched, leading the eye down to a table stacked up with loaves
of bread,[3] the rest of the space being filled with lines of text and tabu-
lated lists all written out in the very finest hieroglyphics. Although all

these stelae are similar, they are never repetitious. Each one is a beautiful variation on the others; together they are a masterclass in elegant design.

Named as 'Slab Stelae' by the American archaeologists, there are some eighteen known examples.[4] Many were broken up, their pieces scattered through the tombs. Some were found in their original positions, set up facing Khufu's Pyramid at the southern ends of some of the great stone row tombs, amidst the ruins of little chapels built after the burial to shelter the place where offerings were laid. By good fortune several had been hidden from view, the builders of these chapels having on occasion set similarly sized plain slabs right up against the bright reliefs.[5] So when the archaeologists pulled aside these facing stones several of the stelae were as fresh as ever. Set right at the focus of their tombs and scrupulously protected, we may assume that in Khufu's time these painted jewels were highly treasured.

Much as the svelte images of these tomb owners, each one drawn before their offering tables, seem fresh and elegant, the archaic origin of their design and the burden of their accompanying inscriptions are powerful witnesses of a continuity of ritual and belief

Fig. 44 This limestone stela, naming one 'Wepemnefert', is one of the finest of the so-called 'slab stelae', a body of work containing some of the most exquisite examples of ancient Egyptian writing and relief to have survived.

Fig. 45 and Fig. 46 below. Wepemnefert's slab stela as found and photographed by Reisner in 1905. Having been carefully hidden in the east wall of the largest mastaba of Cemetery 2100 since the time of Khufu, the stela was in pristine condition.

extending back to the beginnings of Egyptian history, long before the existence of a state (see further ch. 24 below), when people offered provisions at the grave in the apparent belief that the dead remained dependent upon the goods and trappings of the living world.[6] The elegant hieroglyphs of the Slab Stelae, however, elaborate this long tradition, telling us that at these tombs pharaoh himself has granted a royal donation to the individual pictured on the stela, a royal gift of all the objects named and numbered in their lists: everything from jars of beer and cuts of meat and heaps of bread and grain-filled granaries and figs and onions, to the fine linens and cosmetics used in burial rituals and mummification, all carefully quantified in quality and number and listed in a grid of lines that is as regular and well designed as the streets that divide the great block tombs of Khufu's cemeteries. These slabs outline a system of ration and supply from pharaoh to some of the individuals buried in the royal cemeteries and they inform us too, in a now-traditional translation, that these goods are 'a boon that the king gives': a favour disposed by pharaoh to the individual named and pictured on the stela.[7] At royal command, therefore, the Giza cemeteries are transformed into a Bengòdi, a Cockaigne, a rustic paradise in which Khufu and his courtiers are bound together in a carefully constructed zone of art and obligation, a single space between the cornucopia of real food placed in the little chapels and the stony images and lists so artfully engraved upon the stelae: a space that holds the living and the dead.

Although these texts never promise to supply food so that the recipients will be free to work upon the king's behalf, some such sentiment must surely have existed between Khufu and the thousands of people who came to Giza to erect his Pyramid; like the spirits of his noble dead, his living workforce must also have been provisioned from outside.[8] And they too may have understood that their provisions were part of a compact between them and the king, and that the task in which they were engaged – that of making a space upon the earth to hold his tomb – held out a promise similar to that of the Slab Stelae: that, mediated by the king and through their labour, they too might share a kind of afterlife, a funerary feudalism. Such implications of reciprocity may help account for the apparent fervour of this enormous workforce, for the unstinting integrity of their work which shows a care beyond that of normal human enterprise. Seen in this light, the Pyramid's block by block integrity, the grinding process of careful and continuous duplication of its construction in the manner of a religious ritual, appears as a part of a system of communication, a process that ratifies the state.

Khufu's, however, is an age without contemporary explanation: no surviving literature, no theology, only cemeteries made of stone, some beauteous images, the traces of often enigmatic actions and the unearthly precisions of the king's Great Pyramid. As counterweight to the common vision of Khufu and his court as bustling builders and politicos, by echoing the fact that the remaining monuments of Khufu's predecessors invariably portrayed the king in acts of ritual, we may just as well propose that Khufu, the man upon the ivory throne, lived the life of a shaman or a pope, or indeed a Chinese emperor: that he and his ranks of entombed courtiers had lived together inside the white walls of a great enclosure, and passed their lives in endless rounds of rite and ritual.[9] As to whether Khufu or the 'Vizier' Hemiunu, or any of those queens and courtiers whose tombs now lie in measured rows beside the royal Pyramid, sat year on year enthroned on Giza's windy plateau controlling the intricacies of the Great Pyramid's construction, we may never know.

On the other hand, the presence of the pyramid-makers, those thousands who hauled and shaped its building stone, is far more tangible than that of Khufu and his courtiers. Millions of their careful chisel-marks still flicker over the great stones they cut and shaped – the marks of living hands at work – and there are many further traces too of the connected labours of surveying and design.[10] And in the stone quarry to the south of the Great Pyramid the ancient chisel-cuts that stripe the cliffs still measure out in the line of their arc the spans of individual arms and shoulders and, in the disjunction of these patterns, their hourly progress at the rock face. Deep trenches in this quarry held the very shadows of the quarrymen who cut them; people slim enough to fit inside such narrow slots and wield a chisel

Fig. 47 Produced by driving a pointed chisel in short hard arcs, working down and across the wall from right to left, the vigorous chisellings of one of Khufu's quarrymen still decorate the quarry face. These same distinctive cuts may also be seen in other locations on the Giza Plateau: in the Great Pyramid's Subterranean Chamber for example (fig. 52), which was excavated from the natural limestone of the Plateau, and on the rock that held the Pyramid's now-vanished causeway (fig. 48).

Fig. 48 The underpass that ran beneath the Great Pyramid's now-vanished causeway. Some of the chisel-marks of Khufu's quarrymen can be seen at the side of its entrance.

could not have stood much over 5 feet tall. For the most part these pyramid-makers were a tough and wiry lot and similar to the populations that live throughout the Mediterranean and the Middle East and who until the advent of machinery still worked stone by hand.

As well as this multitude of marks and shadows, there is a single element of architecture on the Giza Plateau that, if it was not designed expressly for the pyramid-makers, would certainly have helped them on their daily round. It dates from the latter years of Khufu's reign after a huge stone causeway was built to run up from the plain below, over the cliff, to a temple on the east side of the Pyramid.[11] This causeway had effectively divided the area between the Pyramid and the cliff in two separate halves,[12] so that anyone who wished to walk from one end of the Pyramid's east side to the other would have been forced to turn westwards into the desert for a half-mile trip around the other three sides of the Pyramid. In Khufu's time, to solve this problem, an underpass was cut beneath the causeway.[13] Barely wider than a man and too low to accommodate a rider on a donkey, it must nevertheless have been a great convenience. Certainly, whoever it was in the administration that ordered its construction – for this subway is a square and well-made cutting rather than a rounded rough-cut hole – it provided a unique concession to the living in a landscape built to accommodate the dead. Still today, although the causeway up above has all but disappeared, the intimacy of the little passage makes it one of those rare places on the Giza Plateau where you can share the same space, the very air, with the living people who made King Khufu's Pyramid, left their marks upon the Plateau and then simply disappeared.

SECTION TWO
The People on the Plateau

11 Working the stone

The greater part of the Egyptian pyramids is only an aggregation of Nummulites.

Figuier's Ocean World, *1868*[1]

King Khufu's quarrymen cut some 5½ million tons of limestone for his Pyramid, an enterprise of such extravagance that on the Giza Plateau alone it has left a hole that is a quarter of a mile across and a hundred feet in depth.[2] Having quarried, hauled and set far more than that in the previous half-century, Khufu's Egyptians were well accustomed to such copious labour.[3] We can therefore assume that the nucleus of the workforce that went to Giza to start work on his Pyramid was already handling its tools and materials with skill and confidence, as an examination of the base of the Great Pyramid still shows.

Amongst their first tasks upon the Giza Plateau, just as it had been at royal tombs since the beginning of the Egyptian state four centuries earlier, was the excavation of a funerary chamber in the living rock.[4] At Giza, and for the first time, this traditional subterranean apartment was never finished. The modest corridor that gives access to it was finished, however, and by itself it is a masterpiece of stone working.[5]

A little over waist high and cutting almost 230 feet (70 m) into the living rock, this steeply angled corridor affords bizarre accommodation to its visitors. And yet it is a perfect statement of the pyramid-makers' ambitions for the work ahead; the corridor's precision, its minute perfection, take your breath away. As Petrie noted in his survey, this 3½ feet wide (1.1 m) corridor was the single element in the Pyramid where his instruments were unable to match the accuracy of Khufu's pyramid-makers: in the entire length of its descent, his survey found, the corridor never deviates from true by more than a quarter of an inch (6.35 mm), its four beautifully finished faces, the walls, the floor, the ceiling, stamping four dead straight lines down through the living rock at an angle of 26° 31' 23" precisely.[6] As well as this, Petrie noted, the corridor is as carefully aligned to north as the Great Pyramid's much-measured baselines or as any other of the main elements of the Pyramid's internal architecture.[7] As fresh today as when it was made some forty-five centuries ago, this eerie master-

Fig. 49 John Edgar sitting in the portal to the Subterranean Chamber, at the ending of the Descending Corridor.

work, a point of reference for the pyramid that was to be built above it, brings you face to face with the ancient realities of pyramid making and also with the especial qualities of Giza's Pyramid Plateau, the living rock on which the Great Pyramid would stand and from which, when quarried block by block, such prodigies of craftsmanship were coaxed.

The natural stone through which this perfect corridor was cut is a bright white limestone prettily banded on occasion with 50-million-year-old fossils from a vanished ocean.[8] Like all Egyptian limestones, when it is first split from its matrix it has a texture like human skin, is warm to the touch and so soft that you may mark it with your fingernail as if it were a schoolroom chalk. But this freshly opened stone soon dries a little in the desert air and shrinks and hardens, making it sharper-edged, lighter and less creamy, and more brittle and far more resistant to wear and scratches.

Easy to work and quick to temper, these Egyptian limestones are a splendid architectural material and they are also very plentiful: a fundamental element of the Egyptian landscape, they are the primary component of the high frame of cliffs that run southwards from Giza some 475 miles down each side of the Nile to the city of Esna in Upper Egypt, where this eroded antediluvian sea bed gives way to equally ancient beaches of low dramatic sandstones. It is to be expected, then, that this gentle, luminous and ubiquitous rock that ancient Egyptian scribes called simply the 'white stone' was the pharaohs' favourite building material from the time of the first pyramids down through fifteen centuries.[9] To date, some ninety-odd ancient quarries have been located in the Nile-side cliffs and in the nearby deserts, and doubtless there are dozens more yet to be discovered, still buried underneath the sand.[10]

Until quite recently, Egyptian quarrymen worked and used this limestone in similar if more modest ways to their ancient ancestors. They knew the earthy, slightly salty smell that it obtains when it is first cleaved from the living rock and they understood the grain within the stone, that horizontal stratification obtained when it had been laid down at the bottom of a prehistoric sea, and they exploited the stone's tendency to cleave with that grain or at right angles to it, so that they could quarry quickly and conveniently into seemingly impenetrable cliffs.[11] So even though the perfect little corridor beneath the Pyramid is so narrow that only one mason at a time could have worked at the rock face, its excavation would not have taken very long. Indeed, the continuous process of checking and maintaining its exact angle and proportion would certainly have absorbed more time and energy than the simple task of tunnelling through the rock.

It is strange, after stumbling down that long and perfectly inconvenient corridor, finally to straighten up in the dark space at its ending beneath the centre of the Pyramid. Some 46 feet (14 m) long and half as wide, this is the largest of the Pyramid's three rooms. It is also deep in dust and frozen in its incompletion, as if its ancient quarrymen have just left off their work. Here then is a model of the means by which the Great Pyramid was made.

Laying out such rock-cut rooms was of itself a curious art, like pitching a tent within the living rock. Unlike its access corridor, whose size and angle of descent could have been continuously measured and checked with plumb bobs, cords and angled wooden forms, the shape of this chamber had first to be established by tunnelling small passages similar to those that miners cut in seams of coal, out from the ending of the perfect corridor to the four points within the rock where the corners of the room were planned to be.[12] These then, the chamber's corners, would be carefully established with a vertical line cut precisely in the rock and a crawl-space cut horizontally to join the corners all together at the level of the chamber's ceiling. All that then remained was to extend the level of the chamber floor outwards from the doorway at the bottom of the corridor, and to begin the process of removing the living rock that filled the body of the room.

The chisel-marks within the chamber suggest that, just as in the pharaohs' later building projects, two gangs of quarrymen worked there side by side.[13] As you would expect of Khufu's pyramid-makers, their labours were conducted in a highly ordered way: they excavated what was, in effect, a giant stairway running right across the room, up from the level of the floor in a few great steps to the crawl-space underneath the ceiling (see fig. 52). Then, the quarrying proceeded by cutting back this staircase step by step.[14] That the work was left unfinished means that today about a third of the chamber's interior is still engaged to the living rock, with parts of the pyramid-makers' 'staircase' still running up from the floor beside the doorway in steps as jagged as a mouth of broken teeth.[15]

This is a good model of the fundamental processes by which the stone blocks of the Great Pyramid itself were quarried and delivered – the Subterranean Chamber taking the place of the Pyramid's great quarries and the Descending Corridor standing in the role of the service ramps by which the quarry blocks were hauled up eventually, by means of angled ramps, on to the rising Pyramid.

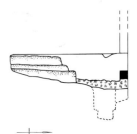

Fig. 50 The technique employed to quarry the Great Pyramid's Subterranean Chamber – the so-called 'staircase' method – was used by quarrymen and tomb-makers of all periods of ancient Egyptian history.

Figs. 51 and 52. The Edgar Brothers' photographs of the Pyramid's Subterranean Chamber, the largest room in the Great Pyramid, showing that work on its creation was proceeding in typical ancient Egyptian fashion, with the full dimensions of the room established at the level of its ceiling before the full volume of its interior was quarried out. This, then, is a work in progress; the rubble in these photographs, however, was as much a product of Vyse's excavation into the Chamber's floor as of King Khufu's quarrymen. It has since been cleared away.

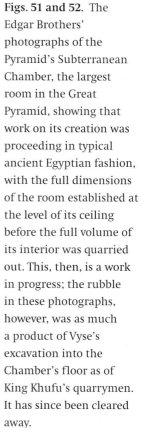

There are of course, huge differences of scale. In the airless Subterranean Chamber, Khufu's quarrymen worked in warm dust and semi-darkness; outside on the Giza Plateau, they laboured amidst the glare of fresh-cut limestone under the Egyptian sun in an open quarry. And in the chamber underneath the Pyramid, the size of the quarry steps and thus the blocks that they removed from them were dictated by the dimensions of the little corridor up which the quarried stones were taken to the surface; nothing was quarried in that dark room therefore, that two or three men could not have carried out between them. In Khufu's desert quarries, on the other hand, the sky was literally the limit; that and the ability of the hauling gangs to handle the huge blocks that the quarrymen had cut out of the cliffs.

As to the tools the pyramid-makers used to perform such prodigies, like most things connected with the Great Pyramid of Giza, they are entirely lost to us. Their marks, however, are still visible inside the Pyramid and on the quarry blocks of its exterior and also in the nearby quarry. And these show that the pyramid-makers employed two basic types of cutting tool whose marks are equivalent to those produced by the two chisel types still used by stone workers today, who commonly refer to them as 'flats' and 'points'.[16]

As its name suggests, a modern 'point' is a stout chisel with a narrow sharply tapered cutting edge that leaves a characteristic v-shaped gouge in the stone as the point is hammered across its surface, a gouge that is punctuated at the bottom of the cut, by the individual blows upon the chisel that sent it on its way.[17] Just as the marks of the pyramid-makers' chisels still clearly show, the progress of an ancient point through limestone can be relatively rapid, which surely is why the Giza quarrymen used heavy points and much impacted force for detaching fresh blocks from their quarries and also for the processes of squaring up and smoothing out the stone. This hard labour requires as much sensitivity and skill as it does muscle, for if the soft metal chisels that were available to the pyramid-makers were not to be bent or blunted at the first blow and the surface of the stone left splintered and irregular, the path of the cut, that is, the progress of the point into and across the stone, had to be coaxed to cut with its grain. Both on the Pyramid's laid blocks and in the quarries you can see the deep-gouged points of Khufu's masons running diagonally with the limestone's grain in successive parallel lines just two or three inches apart, roughing out and flattening the surface of the stone.

The gentler marks of the pyramid-makers' flat-ended chisels on the other hand, which are exactly like the marks of little modern 'flats', can be seen running lightly over the rough-cut surfaces that the points have left behind them, spreading out like ink blots, shallow cuts half an inch or so in width, gently trimming the tops of the ridges left by the points and fining down the surface. Wherever an extra touch of precision was required to fit the individual block into the Pyramid, these modest marks crowd over the surfaces of the Great Pyramid's great stones, the patient little cuts, a testimony to the extravagant care that the pyramid-makers lavished on every one of these huge stones. Here then, the care and slowness that the use of such humble implements enforces combined with the pyramid-makers' sensitivity to limestone to produce an overall continuous precision.

Both points and flats of course required some kind of hammer to drive their cutting edges through the stone; but none have been found upon the Pyramid. Wooden mallets, however, are often found in excavations of other ancient Egyptian stone-working sites from virtually all periods of ancient Egyptian history, many of which are similar in their form to the so-called 'balloon-headed' mallets still used by Western wood-carvers to this day.[18] A wide variety of splendid models and graphic scenes from all ages of ancient Egyptian history show their ancient equivalents in use in a variety of workshops.[19] Most intriguingly, these same scenes also tell us a great deal about the ancient craftsmen's attitudes to limestone, for they show several of the same tools – mallets, chisels and the little open-toothed saws that the Egyptian craftsmen favoured – being used by both stone masons and carpenters alike to cut both wood and limestone.[20] Fresh limestone being of similar hardness to fine-quality timber, and with both having distinctive grains, they were often cut and shaped with similar tools. Hard-stone sculptors, on the other hand, employed entirely different techniques:[21] shaping their work for the most part with a variety of hand-held stones, which were employed to pulverise, abrade and polish, and it would certainly have been entirely futile to attack such intransigent material with the soft metal chisels of King Khufu's time (see further p. 165 below). Although modern text books tend to divide

Fig. 53 Look carefully into this photograph and you will see the marks of flat and pointed chisels: the traces of Khufu's pyramid-makers at their work. The radial patterns of these markings indicate the position of individual craftsmen working their way across the surface of the block.

ancient Egyptian materials and processes into the separate categories of wood and stone working, it is not a division that reflects the working attitudes and sensitivities of ancient Egypt's craftsmen.

Curiously enough, although the pyramid-makers lived in what is now popularly called the 'Bronze Age', the tools that have survived from ancient Egypt are not for the most part made from that most useful alloy but from one of its naturally occurring components, copper, which despite the traces of other chemicals and metals that might be present in it, is a far softer material.[22] For modern sculptors the enforced use of softer chisels would be a crippling deprivation.[23] The Bronze Age, however, was not a less efficient Iron Age with softer and more bendy chisels. The pyramid-makers related to their tools and their materials quite differently from modern masons. They did not, for example, strike their chisels with as much force as they could muster as a mason working with iron or steel tools might do, for that as we have seen would simply blunt and bend the chisel. With expert handling and, perhaps, the chisel's tip cold-hammered to a natural temper to make it a little harder, a copper chisel can cut soft stone effectively.[24] The lines of a quarryman's cut across the Giza limestone show not the brute progress of a tungsten point powering through the stone but usually the angled cut of a point or often that of a near quarter-inch flat chisel which was used as a point and rocked from side to side at every hammer blow,[25] a technique that would have spread the chisel's wear, just as many surviving ancient chisels would appear to show.[26] And certainly, by striking the limestone firmly with copper chisels and patiently working with the stone's own grain, the pyramid-makers shaped the limestone with greater intelligence and far more finesse than modern workers operating power tools, as the myriad cuts that they have left upon the blocks of the Great Pyramid still testify.

Even though the soft Egyptian limestone was generous to these Bronze Age masons, it would still have devoured the substance of their chisels at a considerable rate, the side of a copper point some-times leaving a visible smudge of shining metal upon the limestone chipping just below the point of strike.[27] And in the days of Khufu, copper, which was difficult to mine and smelt, was by definition a precious metal (see pp. 166ff below). The use of copper chisels to flatten surfaces of limestone in order to dress the surface of the stone may well have been accompanied by the use of a flint with a cutting edge flaked like a flat chisel and set in a short-handled tool to allow a useful swing, a working rhythm, and some precision too. Such tools had been used at the very beginning of stone architecture in Egypt,[28] and probably at the Great Pyramid as well, though the mark of these flat flints is often difficult to separate from those of a copper tool. The scarcity of flaked flint within the surviving building residue at Giza, however, suggests that the use of flint cutting tools was not as widespread as at other sites, where large quantities of knappings have been found.[29]

The roughing out of limestone blocks with copper points may also have been accompanied by the use of large hard-stone hammers sometimes tied to wooden hafts to increase the force of impact, these designed to pound and shatter – quite literally to 'bash' – the softer limestone somewhat in the manner employed by the hard-stone sculptors.[30] Such a brute attack upon a limestone face leaves irregular and less distinctive marks than copper chisels and the use of such stone pounders is thus difficult to detect. Giza's pyramid-makers, however, did use rounded hard-stone pounders, as the widely scattered, well-worked remnants of thousands of such stones that are still found upon the Giza Plateau clearly testify.[31]

There is an essential difference between hitting limestone with a stone and with a sharpened copper chisel, for the bruising blows of stones do not encourage limestone to flake and split as does a blow from a sharpened edge aimed to take precise advantage of the grain.[32] Limestone, moreover, is not easily pulverised and rendered into dust like harder stones; the blunt blows of a stone pick or hammer simply stun its surface, transforming the gentle rock into white compacted powder and causing random superficial cracks beneath so that when the pulverised limestone dust eventually falls away, it leaves a surface similar to one caused by fire or by explosive.[33] So although stone hammers may have been used occasionally to bash away unwanted protuberances and rough out the surface of the blocks, they would have been of little use to Khufu's master craftsmen.

In that beautiful descending corridor deep beneath the Giza Plateau, where the swing of the stone cutter's arm was cramped by lack of space yet accuracy was absolutely paramount, only a steady stream of resharpened copper chisels would have served to keep the corridor moving downwards through the rock. Such ancient Egyptian mallets as have survived would certainly have provided an effective and well-balanced weight to drive those chisels and offered excellent insulation from the continual shock of the blows as well, so that King Khufu's master masons could have coaxed their soft-pointed chisels through limestone over many hours. We may imagine, then, a solitary mason for there is but room for one at that small rock face, a master craftsman feeling his way through the softly splitting rock, following its every crack and fissure, levering away the flakes of limestone, then slowly cutting out the corridor's four corners and finishing finally the flatness of its walls with hundreds of small cuts each one of them angled so as to produce that roughened finish that is unique to ancient Egypt. Here then, in the warm darkness of this awkward little corridor, we start to meet the makers of King Khufu's Pyramid.

12 The Giza quarry

By the standards of other ancient Egyptian quarries which soar sometimes like arched cathedrals, the remains of Khufu's quarry on the
Giza Plateau are unremarkable and mostly still buried beneath millennia of drifting sand and rubble. Best characterised as an open-cast
quarry 'when a vein is worked open to the day',[1] in the last years of
Khufu's reign it would have appeared as a wide white bite into the
gentle golden slope that lies a quarter of a mile to the south of the
Great Pyramid, forming the side of a sandy valley that runs eastwards, down into the river's plain (see fig. 54).[2] Such desert washes,
which are typical features of the edges of the floodplain, often expose
low seams of the underlying limestone and lent themselves perfectly
to Bronze Age quarrying.[3] With narrow seams of softer limestone conveniently banding the strata of the Plateau, and millennial movement
and decay naturally producing vertical faults within the rock beds,
such landscapes by themselves conveniently chopped the limestone
strata into enormous square-sided blocks that greatly aided the
pyramid-makers in their extraction of the stone.[4] Here then, Khufu's
quarrymen cut a wide grid of trenches into the slope, following wherever they could its natural rock faults. Then, starting low down in the
sandy valley, they cut a series of quarry 'staircases' along the edges of
their excavated grid in their usual manner, and following whenever

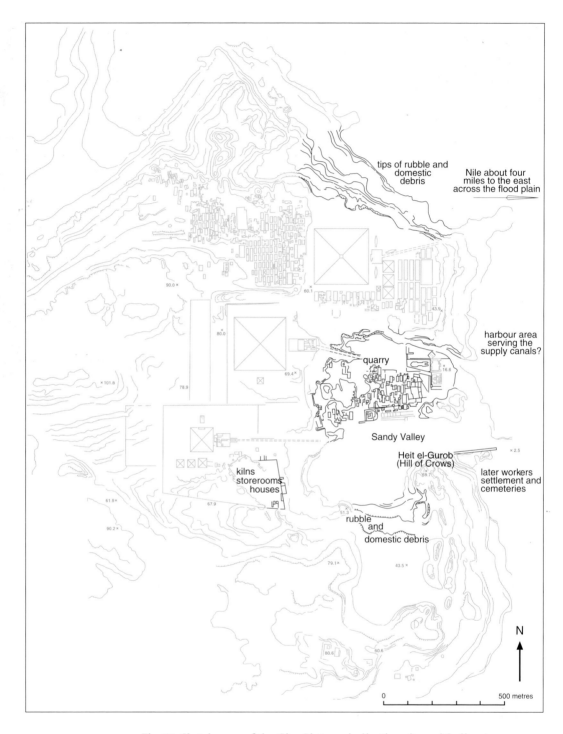

Labels on map:
tips of rubble and domestic debris

Nile about four miles to the east across the flood plain

harbour area serving the supply canals?

quarry

Sandy Valley

Heit el-Gurob (Hill of Crows)

later workers settlement and cemeteries

kilns storerooms houses

rubble and domestic debris

N

0   500 metres

Fig. 54 Sketch map of the Giza Plateau, indicating sites with direct connection to Khufu and the Great Pyramid, adapted from Lehner 1985a, fig. 2, Lehner 1985b, fig. 9 and Hawass 1996b, fig 1.

Fig. 55 The Giza Plateau and its quarry from the south. The Great Pyramid's quarry fills the entire middle ground of the photograph, the long dark shadows under Khafre's pyramid marking its western edge. Inside this busy textured area, the lines of the quarrymen's cuttings are still clearly visible. The large monument in the middle ground, a later tomb, was founded on a rectangular knoll of stone abandoned by the quarrymen. Sondages in the early 1980s indicated that a main route up from the quarry to King Khufu's Pyramid lay in the shadowed area behind the later tomb, in the quarry's north-western corner (cf. Lehner 1985a, fig. 3B 10 and 11).

they were able the lines of the softer horizontal seams, took out their building blocks step by step. The quarry thus grew ever larger throughout King Khufu's reign, its rock faces moving out and up the slope towards the Pyramid to form the huge wide crater that at the finish of the work would serve as a convenient site in which to tip the debris of the Pyramid's construction; and this so successfully that its first purpose as a quarry was completely lost to view until the present century (see further p. 206 below).

Fitfully dug about by Lepsius in his search for noble tombs yet still so choked with dumps of ancient rubble that in Petrie's day that great field archaeologist had no notion of its full extent, parts of Khufu's quarry were cleared in the 1920s–30s in the general excavation programme on the Giza Plateau. And at that time yet more tombs were excavated and surveyed as well: the memorials of mortuary priests, queens and princes.[5] Some of the finest of these tombs had been made for people who lived in the reign of Khafre, Khufu's successor in pyramid building on the Giza Plateau, which shows that a great part of this quarry must have fallen out of use by Khafre's time:[6] that parts of King Khafre's mortuary architecture actually stand on other sections of the quarry underlines this fact.[7] Although no inscriptions have survived that tell us so, this great wide quarry must therefore date from before the time of Khafre and the building of Giza's second royal pyramid. And certainly, as it is the only quarry in the area that could have possibly supplied the quantity and quality of stone from which the bulk of the Great Pyramid is made, it is reasonable to assume that this is indeed King Khufu's Giza quarry.[8]

The confident chisel-lines of Khufu's quarrymen still run beside the doorways of those later tombs which sometimes cut right through them; the line of pointed chisel-cuts, flattening, smoothing and shaping the rock face in the anticipation of extracting more blocks from the same rock face. Rows of the quarrymen's trenches, too, still lie behind these ancient quarry faces, half-buried now in limestone chip and drifting sand, grid-like trenches cut parallel and at right angles to the quarry faces and running back into the gentle rise of the limestone plateau; trenches 10 and 20 feet in depth and just wide enough to walk through, they outline the main direction of future quarrying.[9] Had the work not stopped, Khufu's quarrymen would have continued by subdividing this enormous outline grid and by removing stone blocks section by section, step by step, in the time-honoured way. Smoothed and trenched, the rock faces yet await their undercutting and finally the levering away of the excavated blocks to tumble down onto the quarry floor. And then, for their removal from the area of the rock face, we may imagine that these tumbled blocks were manoeuvred on logs or sledges, or even on rounded balls of hard black stone, before their journey up the long ramps of the Pyramid.[10]

There are still some half-extracted blocks inside the quarry, partially attached to the living rock, and these show that on occasion units up to 30 feet in length and weighing around 200 tons were extracted in one piece; that blocks of just 30 tons and more occur within the rising Pyramid suggests that these enormous stones were split again down upon the quarry floor.[11] Typically the pyramid-workers cut and hauled and laid blocks upon the Great Pyramid that weighed around 2½ tons each. Right from the beginning of the work

Fig. 56 Part of the west face of the Giza Quarry. The natural bedding of the stone in hard and soft layers, visible now owing to erosion, would have greatly aided its quarrying. The black rectangles at the base of the rock face are the doorways of later tombs. That many of these rock tombs date from the time of Khafre, whose pyramid looms in the background of this photograph, shows that the greater part of this quarry had already fallen out of use by the time that pyramid was built.

the lower courses of the Pyramid, which were cut into the natural rock of the plateau, are approximately of the same size as the courses of stone blocks that tower above them: blocks that are typically some 4¼ feet long, some 4¼ feet deep and around 2¼ feet high. Bearing in mind that the pyramid-makers have set many blocks of hard stone in the Great Pyramid that are some forty times heavier than this right into the centre of the Pyramid and with extraordinary facility, and that on other occasions they also built with blocks weighing far less than the standard 2½ ton size, it is clear that the specifications of the basic building blocks which stand out so clearly in the stone courses of the rising Pyramid were the product not of necessity, nor of accident, nor of habit, but of most careful choice.

As Petrie has observed, the size of this standard block would have enabled six stone cutters to work upon it simultaneously; two at its ends and two pairs working shoulder to shoulder along its two longer sides.[12] Thus a team of, say, ten men could have worked on one block all together, sculpting, finishing and checking at the same time. In similar fashion, modern experimentation has shown that ten men of Khufu's time could also move one of these 2½ ton blocks without much difficulty, although it is difficult to imagine that they could have kept at such hard labour continuously for a full working day.[13] Indeed, although there is insufficient information from the reign of Khufu in itself, records from the other Giza pyramids suggest that pyramid work gangs were ordered in units of ten and twenty individuals.[14] Twenty-man gangs would provide a more rational work group for block shaping and hauling, a number that would not only allow for absentees and for gang members engaged in related work tasks such as water distribution, but would also enable a shift system to operate within this small community, keeping the pace of the work constant and individuals free from exhaustion, a vital consideration in work of such long duration as building a gigantic pyramid.[15]

This ideal standard block size with accompanying gangs of twenty workmen provides a handy theoretical ruler with which to start to reconstruct a practical account of the pyramid's construction. In similar fashion, the adoption of this standard block would also have simplified the ancient processes of pyramid construction, enabling swift and simple estimations of the numbers of people and provisions required throughout the years of its manufacture; as we shall see (pp. 277–8 below), it may even have had an influence upon the Great Pyramid's design.

At first glance, as with many things connected with the Great Pyramid, the practical logistics of the work within King Khufu's quarry seem to be overwhelming. In less than fourteen years, more than 5 million tons of cut stone blocks were hauled up out of that quarry and set up on the Great Pyramid: a theoretical total of around 2,080,000 standard 2½ ton blocks.[16] As we have already seen (fig. 33 above), it appears that workloads were very much higher at the beginning of the work than at its ending. It follows, then, that working the notional ten-hour day for 300 days each year (see p. 75 above), in those first few years during which half the Pyramid was built, more than 12,000 souls would have been required to labour in the Giza quarry, a colossal number in itself, quite apart from those working on the Pyramid.[17]

Such things will not be made again. A great part of the reason why the Great Pyramid appears to be stuck somehow in time, to be set

Fig. 57 Part of the Great Pyramid's north-western angle. The Giza quarrymen's expert choice of stone still shows today in that there is little erosion of the Pyramid's core blocks. The unusually wide layer of stone is course thirty-five, which was laid around the third year of the Pyramid's construction.

halfway between a natural cliff and a work of architecture, is precisely because the blocks that the pyramid-makers brought up from the Giza quarry were mostly set upon the Pyramid with their grain placed horizontally, just as it had lain within the living rock of the nearby quarry. And so the Pyramid has weathered like a perfect natural cliff. Today modern quarrymen and masons no longer work with the grain within the stone, or plan each chisel-cut to shape the block in accordance to the way that it was first formed, or set it in position according to those same principles. Now, stone is cut mechanically in straight and polished lines, and so the slight variations in its horizontal grain are continuously severed and re-severed along the edges of each and every crisp-cut block, allowing humidity and pollution to creep through its highly polished surfaces so that it will weather unevenly and long before its time. Such modern blocks will not last as long as those that make up Khufu's Pyramid.

Khufu's half-buried quarry, then, is a vivid relic of the making of one of the world's great wonders: a place where you can still taste something of that ancient labour that once filled and formed it, where you can feel the dust, the energy of individual people as they slowly cut and reshaped the desert landscape to make their pyramid. This is a world quite separate from the Great Pyramid's famous silhouette: one that the ancient Egyptians did not deliberately arrange, one held in the marks its makers left upon the rocks, in the urgent lines of the quarrymen's points, the fussy marks of the stone setters' tiny chisels and, most movingly of all perhaps as we shall see, in the fingerprints left in the wet mortar as it was applied to the great granite blocks of Khufu's burial chamber. If, in photographic terms, the Pyramid's architecture may be thought of as a fixed pose, a formal portrait, then this informal past is the equivalent of a pile of torn-up snaps, an odd accumulation of disconnected and anonymous moments in real time collected from the ruins of settlements and towns and harbours, from debris trapped beneath collapsing walls and from the ash of ancient kilns, from Khufu's mines and quarries, from the cracks between the Pyramid's great stones and painted survey points, in things lost or abandoned, or simply thrown away.

13 Fire and the Pyramid

For almost ninety years, no one cared to follow in Petrie's footsteps and search for traces of the pyramid-makers in the Giza sand; for hard evidence of the lives of the people who had worked in its quarries and its stone yards, in the workshops and warehouses required to support such enterprises. Had not Flinders Petrie after all identified and part-excavated the buried remains of a rectangular settlement behind the Pyramid of Khafre, a settlement that he described as 'the workmen's barracks . . . strong and useful, and with about as much elaboration as an Egyptian would put into work that had to last in daily use for one or two generations . . . [to] hold about 4,000 men; and such would not be an unlikely number for the permanent staff of masons and their attendants employed upon a pyramid'[1] Undecorated, unlettered and utterly unprepossessing, such proletarian amenities were of scant interest to traditional egyptologists, so that over the years as other similarly planned and more elaborate settlements were excavated close to other royal pyramids, Petrie's assumptions about the Giza pyramid-makers went unquestioned: just like the British Army garrison in Cairo, it seemed that they had lived regimented lives in standard housing, simply another part of that ordered and unchanging vision of old Egypt cultivated by the earlier generations of egyptologists and by the thousands upon thousands of ancient scenes and sculptures that decorate so many of the surviving monuments.

Then in 1971 archaeologists from the University of Cairo working under the direction of Abdel-Aziz Saleh began to probe the upper sections of the same desert wash in which King Khufu's desert quarry had been cut, excavating down along the ragged outline of a huge wall made of local stones and shale whose ruined top stuck out amongst the ancient mounds of stone chippings and the spoil heaps of earlier excavators (see fig. 58).[2] At first it seemed as if this great wall, which was carefully battered and most finely plastered with a

Fig. 58 Abdel-Aziz Saleh's excavations in the wadi behind the Giza quarry. The top of the great wall that formed the spine of this work (see fig. 59) runs away from the camera, northwards and towards the pyramid of Khafre; the houses on its eastern side are clearly visible; the rough white stones littering the foreground are blocks of alabaster left over from the period when this area served as a masons' workshop.

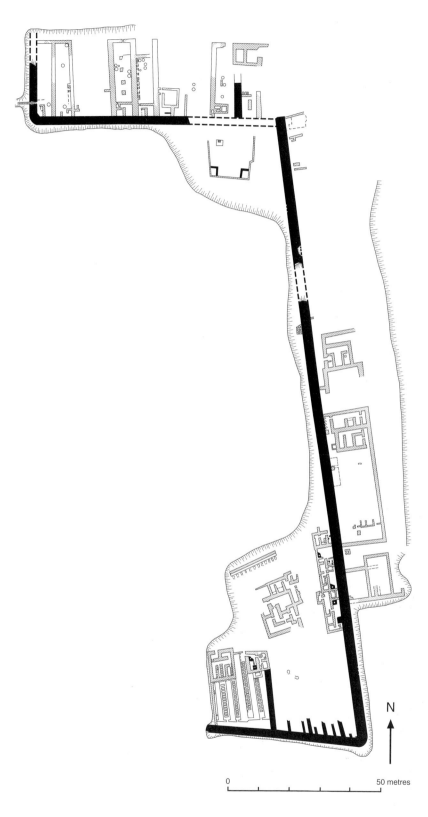

Fig. 59 Plan of Abdel-Aziz Saleh's excavations in the wadi behind the Giza quarry. The massive central wall, built of nicely plastered limestone, is shown in black. The group of long halls attached to its northern section probably served as storerooms or as dormitories; many of the smaller buildings were adapted over time to serve a variety of purposes (see fig. 60). Those that are set inside open courtyards, however, are best identified as houses. After Saleh 1974, fig. 2.

N

0   50 metres

creamy finish, had run straight across the desert valley and served as
a section of a grand enclosure that had been built to surround all of
the Giza pyramids. As they dug it out, however, following it down
through the sandy valley, the excavators discovered that in the course
of just 300 yards the great wall changed directions several times
forming the rough outline of a reversed italic 'E' before disappearing
underneath a mountainous range of excavators' tips. Now the wall
appeared as if it could have been the ruin of a self-contained enclosure.

Built up against this wall both inside and outside the E and made
from the same materials, a wide variety of buildings were uncovered
by Saleh, most of them carefully faced with plaster and occasionally
decorated with coloured paints and dados. Sealed under a deep bank
of ancient masons' chippings, some of these structures still stood 3 or
4 feet high. As had Petrie in the excavation of the 'workmen's barracks', Saleh found nothing in these buried buildings, neither texts
nor pictures nor inscriptions, to fix the date of their construction.
Their isolated position in the desert, however, makes them more
appropriate to the work of making pyramids than any other occupation and, most significantly, the banks of chippings that had buried
and protected them appeared to be the undisturbed products of an
adjacent quarry that had supplied some of the building stone for
Giza's third great pyramid, built for Khufu's grandson, Menkaure.[3]
This then serves to date the wall and its settlements with reasonable
certainty to a time before the work on Menkaure's pyramid began;
that is, to the reign of either Khufu or his son Khafre. Some of the
people of this settlement would therefore probably have seen the
Great Pyramid whilst it was yet being built. The many changes and
adaptations to its architecture also show that the settlement had had
a growth and life span of its own. Its dissolving walls therefore show
something of the texture of the developing daily realities of Giza's
pyramid-makers. Moreover, the architectural vernacular of these
ancient walls and houses is quite timeless: somewhere today in the
Egyptian countryside, an Egyptian farmer is making similar if less
finished accommodations from these same materials. Such simplicity,
such uniformity of design, allows a wide range of interpretation as to
what purposes these buildings may have served; just like the Great
Pyramid, therefore, they are a litmus test of modern attitudes
towards the ancient pyramid-makers.

The largest of the buildings in this desert settlement was a group of
five halls 50 feet (15 m) long. Some of them apparently had rows of
columns in them; all of them had small rooms at their rear separated

from the main hall by a chicane of added walls. Similar in their style and proportions to warehouses and dormitories built in later reigns and dynasties, these appear to have offered the same facilities, with small areas behind the long halls set aside possibly for the use of people who were attached to them.[4] Like many of the other structures at the site, the shapes and thus perhaps the usage of some of these buildings appeared to have been chopped and changed in time, a relatively easy thing to do with an architecture made of mud and water. In an economy without machinery, such a mix of purposes and functions would not have been as inefficient as it might appear.[5]

Further down the outside of the *E*-shaped wall were other buildings that are best identified as individual houses, for some of their larger and more public rooms had a little dais in them such as the Egyptians built to support chairs, and some of their other smaller rooms had similar but longer platforms in them that may well have served the same purpose for beds.[6] Although these rooms are mostly 4 or 5 feet wide and not much longer, more people may well have lived within these tiny homes than we might imagine; with the addition of a few coats of whitewash such modest dwellings sometimes served the same families for centuries, and indeed some of these desert houses show just such signs of redesign and redecoration. One of these buildings had been set within the substantial mud-brick walls of a large courtyard, a typical feature of larger ancient Egyptian houses and of many Egyptian country houses to this day where the enclosure provides privacy for the family, storage for food and supplies, stalls for animals and a play area for children.

More houses, though yet smaller ones, were excavated along the inside of the *E*: two tiny dwellings built together as a single unit divided by a party wall, their interiors individually arranged as if to accommodate two separate households, and each one again with its 'reception' room and chair dais near the entrance and behind it this time, in the relative darkness hard against the massive wall, two large kitchens with storage bins and baking ovens. And on one end of this double housing unit, the excavators found a tiny little cell, a dwelling place in miniature.

These then were typical examples of the millennial accommodations in which the ancient Egyptians lived in towns and villages all up and down the Nile; the modest dwellings in which most people slept and cooked and stored their food; those household ovens, the real furnaces in which the national gold of ancient Egypt's agrarian economy had been millennially refined. Emmer wheat and barley, the two staples of the Near Eastern Neolithic Revolution, had been introduced into Egypt from Palestine several thousand years before the pyramids were built, and from the very beginning the Nile Valley had proved an ideal environment for hand-cropping corn.[7] Just as it would later underpin Rome's bread-and-circuses, so earlier on in history Egypt's fabled grain enabled Egypt's pharaohs to equip their state and build their pyramids from the surpluses of a centralised agrarian economy. As one authority has said, it was 'the most successful plant–people interaction in human history'.[8] And this is how some of its people had lived.

Fifty feet in front of those two small housing units, standing in the open and backed by a long thin wall, the excavators found the remains of a row of twelve more ovens and a 100 feet away from them, tucked into the lee of the great enclosing wall, what appears to have

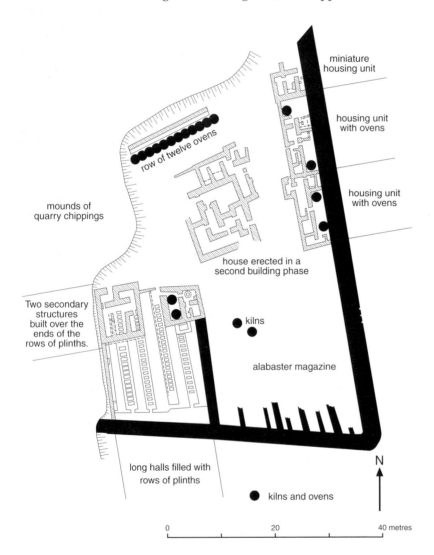

miniature housing unit

housing unit with ovens

housing unit with ovens

row of twelve ovens

mounds of quarry chippings

house erected in a second building phase

Two secondary structures built over the ends of the rows of plinths.

kilns

alabaster magazine

long halls filled with rows of plinths

N

kilns and ovens

0   20   40 metres

Fig. 60 A detail of the southern section of Saleh's excavations (see also figs. 59 and 61). After Saleh 1974, fig. 2.

been the ruin of a Bronze Age factory for grinding wheat, four rows of eighty-odd plinths set side by side in two long halls about the same size as the warehouses, where lines of women could have knelt elbow to elbow, grinding cereal on stone querns in that Neolithic pose that has been so well observed in the decorations and the sculptures of so many ancient tombs.[9] That seems the only rational explanation for these long halls that were originally filled with rows of plinths, for although the quern-stones which would have proved their purpose beyond all doubt have vanished, the carefully made clay troughs built all around their distinctively shaped bases yet remained and had been most carefully modelled as their excavator describes, 'as if to allow small quantities of liquids or otherwise to flow off'.[10] At the ending of each row indeed, these channels are carefully arranged in such a fashion as to allow the collection of the flour.[11] Statistics resurrected from other ancient Egyptian sites show that the twelve-row kilns of this desert bakery could have produced some 1200 large loaves of bread a day.[12] Here then, it appears, are the scant remains of some of the Bronze Age engines that fuelled the building of the Giza pyramids.[13]

Saleh also discovered that over time there had been changes in the operation of this bakery. That in a second phase of building a large

Fig. 61 Looking westwards over Saleh's excavations, towards the pyramid of Menkaure. The rows of mud brick plinths that may have supported wheat-grinding querns are clearly visible, as are the two buildings and the two large kilns that were later built over a part of this establishment, which would appear to have been a flour mill.

square house had been erected in the open space in front of the ovens, and that the corn grinding halls had been transformed into a single rectangular enclosure guarded at one end by two square buildings, one of which housed the ruins of two more ovens whose interiors were still burnt a blushing red from the heat of the ancient fires (see fig. 73, p. 167). Should we assume that pharaoh's bakers built a new and larger desert dwelling for themselves right beside their baking ovens, demolished half their flour mill and built two new, yet larger and thus hotter ovens right next to the remaining corn halls? Alternatively, do these alterations show a basic change of function inside the enclosure?

Just as with the translated titles from the cemeteries and our modern maps of ancient pyramids, it is easy to be circumscribed by contemporary ways of thinking when looking at such ancient and unlettered things. In modern terms ovens are chambers designed to contain heat: bakers use ovens to make bread, potters use ovens called kilns to fire and harden their ceramics, whilst ovens known as furnaces are used to forge and smelt and cast hot metal.

Now hundreds of ancient ovens of a wide variety of shape and size have been found in Egypt and most of them have been readily identified as kilns or furnaces or baking ovens by the debris that surrounded them: by the nearby ruin of a potter's workshop, for example, or the shattered remnants of ceramics spoilt in firing, or alternatively by the mounds of ash and slag left after smelting metal and the distinctive equipment of that process, the stone mortars used for crushing ore, the crucibles for smelting.[14] In similar fashion too, Egyptian bakers often baked their bread in rough ceramic moulds whose littered fragments all around the ruins of some ancient ovens allow us to claim those sites as bakeries.[15]

Here in the Giza desert the excavation was relatively empty of such handy clues, the entire site having been abandoned and its buildings stripped even of their roofs and doors along with most of their contents before being buried under mounds of quarry chippings. And certainly, there was no litter left to tell us what they had been cooking in the ovens. Conceivably, one of the two buildings that had been erected over part of the milling hall could have served as a potters' studio, such as were often situated in just such little rooms.[16] If this were so, the grinding plinths that yet remained might well have served as stands on which the fresh-made pots were set out to dry.[17] Though it may at first appear nonsensical to suggest that the pyramid-makers founded a pottery, an enterprise that requires the constant use of large amounts of water, half a mile up a desert wadi, it cannot be dismissed out of hand. In addition, these two later larger ovens are similar to others which, by the huge amounts of broken and burnt ceramics that still surrounded them, can be identified as pottery kilns.[18]

At this point our modern predilection for giving ancient things precise identities by comparison breaks down entirely and confusion threatens. For three other ovens of exactly similar size and age to these two within the Giza compound were found during the excavation of an Egyptian colony in ancient Nubia where they were employed not as pottery kilns, but as furnaces for smelting local copper ore.[19] So were these two big ovens built upon the Giza milling rooms intended to bake bread, fire pottery or smelt hot metal?

What we know is that ancient copper workers sometimes used similar ovens to fire their pottery and smelt their copper; this has been proven in excavations in the Sinai where copper furnaces have also been used as kilns, the basins of the potters' workshop being built directly on the slag heaps left by the copper smelters.[20] Here, the excavators also observed that some of these same kilns had been used for baking bread and other foods as well![21]

Whereas the modern world separates kilns and furnaces and baking ovens, the ancient Egyptians on occasion maintained no such firm distinctions. Only a few hundred degrees of heat separates firing pottery from melting copper, a difference that prehistoric copper smelters were able to achieve long before the existence of the pharaonic state.[22] We may imagine then that while only highly efficient and well-ventilated furnaces could smelt copper ore, with suitable adaptations to their superstructure these same ovens could be used as kilns for firing pottery and, as they cooled, for a variety of other purposes as well, just as in recent times the heat of a Mediterranean bread oven was used to bake a hierarchy of other foods, from lamb to figs, as it cooled down from the bake. Quite clearly too, Giza's pyramid-makers had need of both kilns and ovens to provide crockery and cooked food for their community, just as they also required copper furnaces, for the work upon the pyramid needed a constant supply of fresh sharp chisels which required worn and split tools to be remelted and recast.[23] This work of recasting not only used furnaces to liquefy the worn-out chisels but required the use of pottery kilns as well, in which the moulds in which the new chisels would have been cast could have been fired.[24]

So just as we have seen that with proper modifications some large ovens can function equally efficiently as ceramic kilns and copper furnaces, so too the neat rows of grindstone plinths might also have served in a third manifestation as supports for the chisel moulds into which the liquid copper was poured! For ancient Egyptian scenes of metal casters at their work always show them performing the delicate and dangerous task of pouring the hot metal standing up, with the casting moulds set up on plinths:[25] just such casting benches, indeed, were found beside the Nubian smelting furnaces.[26] At Giza too the mud-brick grinding plinths would have helped both to disperse the heat of the molten copper and to trap the overspill within the guttering.

There are other examples of such ambiguous ovens built close by early pyramids. At Dahshur, near the Red Pyramid, four such installations have been excavated. And there too, as at Giza, precious little spoiled pottery was found to enable their identification as either ceramic kilns or bakeries. Moreover, as appears to have been the case at Giza, the ovens stand inside a large enclosure, a strong-walled rectangle standing lonely in the desert, a suitable location for the smelting of fine metal.

At Dahshur too, as in Professor Saleh's Giza excavations, there was a total lack of the tell-tale evidence by which copper smelting sites are traditionally identified; no messy mounds of slag nor miscellaneous chemical compounds, no crucibles, no mortars such as have been found in Nubia and Sinai. Here, beside the pyramids, the Egyptians were not smelting copper from mined ore, but simply resmelting and recasting previously refined copper.[27] These ovens would only have been used for what was essentially the equivalent of the second half of the ancient process of copper refining in which mined ore that had already been reduced in a furnace to raw ingots of 'black' copper was reheated and refined into gleaming metal. It is to be expected that beyond some small amounts of copper oxide like those that Saleh found at Giza, none of the bulky and noxious compounds usually associated with smelting furnaces were excavated at either the Giza or the Dahshur ovens.[28] As for the absence of any traces of the metal itself, copper's intrinsic value well explains its absence: like ancient gold mines, the sites of these resmelting plants were emptied of all fragments, sieved of every precious prill.

These may well have been some of the reasons why the pyramid-makers of King Khafre's or King Khufu's times or perhaps the both of them carried large quantities of fuel, water and provisions up into this isolated wadi behind the royal quarry to fire a multitude of ovens.[29] It may also be the reason why families perhaps of guardians and storekeepers appear to have set up house in this lonely arid place;

the purpose may have been the safekeeping of some of the stocks of wheat and fuel and copper needed for the work upon the pyramids. Set well beyond the confines of King Khufu's quarry and guarded by great high walls, this compound held a number of individual buildings that at various times may have served as stores and dormitories and houses, as potteries, bakeries and foundries.

Above all perhaps, the lesson that this ambiguous settlement affords is that just as we no longer believe that Petrie's 'strong and useful . . . workmen's barracks'[30] are to be identified as such in the nineteenth-century manner, so too these newly excavated aspects of the pyramid-makers' Egypt should not be treated as housing 'primitive' versions of present-day technologies. Our lists of elements, our sense of scientific truth, analysis and terminology are alien to most of the cultures who have lived upon this Earth. Certainly those ancient bakers' ovens in the desert, the pottery kilns and copper smelters and all the other installations that King Khufu's pyramid-makers operated, had little in common with the fixed and finite establishments of modern industry. As we have seen, the pyramid-makers' appreciation and manipulation of their materials was organic, skilful and instinctive. Whilst improving the classification of ancient objects in our museums, modern attitudes to ancient culture often run the risk of diminishing our understanding of ancient attitudes to materials and technologies. Pharaoh's farmers, it has been said, could tell where wheat had been grown by the taste of the bread made from it;[31] similarly modern Mediterranean stone masons and potters have an understanding of their materials far in excess of the generalising terms of modern scholarship. Certainly King Khufu's chisel casters worked to an order quite different from the one we perceive within the natural world today; an order that by modern standards, might easily be labelled as 'subjective' or 'instinctive', but an order nonetheless, on its own terms, which was strict and highly structured. To understand King Khufu's Pyramid therefore, its geometry, its extraordinary accuracy, its extreme precision, we must gain a knowledge and appreciation of the world order that its builders understood.

14 Entrepôt and accommodation

Although few things are certain about the making of King Khufu's Pyramid, of this we may be sure: that it was built and shaped with a workforce and materials gathered from all over Egypt and thus, necessity insists, one of the first works undertaken before construction could begin was the excavation of a harbour. The working harbour that was the pyramid-makers' lifeline. A harbour set close to the desert Plateau and connected by canal to the Nile and through that great river to all the valley of the Nile and all the products of that ancient state. That this vital artery has now vanished, leaving the Great Pyramid high and dry upon its Plateau with no obvious contact with the living world below, adds greatly to its present air of disembodiment and silent mystery.

The most convenient location for such a harbour, as the topography of the Giza Plateau shows (see further figs. 54 and 214), is half a mile to the south of the Great Pyramid, at the foot of that broad valley in whose northern slopes King Khufu's pyramid-makers cut their primary limestone quarry, where aeons of primeval floods had disgorged water, sand and gravel from the desert and spread it in a great fan across the river plain,[1] overlooked by the Great Sphinx and framed now by the low line of its accompanying temples. Small probes in these alluvial gravels in the area of the floodlights of the

Giza Sound and Light Show have revealed a sudden drop off in the level of the subterranean rock beneath; an indication, it appears, of the point where Khufu's gangs may well have cut the quays of Giza's oldest harbour.[2]

Such grand hydraulic enterprises do not appear to have been especially burdensome to the pharaonic state. Similarly sized earth-moving enterprises involving the cutting of harbours and canals were undertaken in all eras of pharaonic history.[3] Unlike pyramid building, it was mostly a labour of moving the soft silt deposits of the river's floodplain, which by its very nature was not as difficult as working upon desert tombs or pyramids. In all probability, Khufu's harbour was situated, as were all the other known royal harbours, at the edge of the desert rock where it met the Nile plain and, like the others, it was probably a rectangular excavation with stone-lined quays.

The work of harbour and canal digging in ancient Egypt was usually unsung, yet one of the most ancient surviving scenes of all pharaonic art, made five centuries before the reign of Khufu, shows the king armed with a workman's hoe opening a canal whilst a little servant stands in front of him obligingly holding a basket in the now time-honoured fashion, to accommodate the royal sod.[4] And that essentially is how pharaoh's canals were made: by excavating the earth and sand of the Nile's valley and piling it up beside the cut to make a levee, one person digging with another standing by to gather up the earth for dumping; their tools the basket and the hoe, the elemental hieroglyphs of ancient civilisations and indeed the earthworking equipment of all Egyptian farmers until the middle of the last century.[5] The common notion that these ancient canal and harbour workers were raised and operated as a corvée or a *levée en masse* as they were in more recent times is yet again a nineteenth-century fantasy; we simply do not know how Khufu's labour forces were raised and certainly the surviving images and scenes of similar enterprises in later eras of ancient Egyptian history are drawn with a more humane eye than that of European colonialism.[6]

There are several ingenious reconstructions of the possible routes of Khufu's canal or canal network that gave access to the Giza Plateau from the Nile, some of them based on combinations of archaeology, land survey and soil soundings.[7] In this millennially untroubled land and certainly in the long ages before tractor-driven ploughs and modern irrigation methods rendered the fields completely flat, it is not impossible that the strange-shaped patterning of the quicksilver pools of the annual Nile flood that are visible in many nineteenth-century maps and photographs (see fig. 20) of the plain, the gentle

hillocks, the oxbow lakes and long symmetric channels, are echoes of a topography created in the time of Khufu and his successors and represent the faint residue of the excavation of their harbours and canals.[8]

In the days of Sneferu and Khufu the location of the river was not as it is today nor even as it appears in those early photographs. Recent soundings in the floodplain show that the Nile's course has moved several miles to the east in the last 5000 years. In Khufu's day the green strip of the plain gave way to sand and gravel much sooner than it does today, after millennia of farmers carefully enlarging their fields.[9] Nonetheless, as the first supply barges turned westwards away from the Nile and down the newly cut canal that led to Khufu's harbour, a journey of around 4 miles, they would have sailed across a fertile black-earthed plain greened annually by the Nile's flood, a semi-cultivated oasis of swamps and hilltop villages and chequered pasturelands, with strips of vegetables and arcs of hand-cast wheat rolling in the evening breeze, a stormy sea within their little fields. Large tracts of the river valley were still entirely wild, especially in the middle of Egypt, which with its wide and shallow floodplains was difficult to farm.[10] Even these wildernesses supported grand harvests of wild food, fish, fowl and turtle and a variety of native vegetables. At Giza, however, the plain was more amenable to human habitation

Fig. 62 Taken in the 1880s, Henri Béchard's photograph of the receding inundation records what was essentially the same environment as that which Khufu's barge crews would have known, but which has now completely disappeared. This particular stretch of water, however, was the product of the construction of a levee thrown up in 1869. Marked in this photograph by the line of trees, this earthwork held a modest two-lane highway that ran from Giza City to the Pyramids Plateau: the first version of the modern 'Pyramids Road'.

than those wetlands and had long supported human settlement. With the coming of the pyramid-makers we may assume that it was entirely colonised with farms and settlements.[11] That all was abundance, with sweet fast-ripening crops and grazing cows and goats and hidden backwaters and quiet pools and sparkling lakes flicking with fish and rustling with duck all edged with lines of spiky vetch and sedge and great green fields of reeds, with the added frisson of hidden crocodiles and hippopotami to trample the crops and scare the children.[12] So fertile was this rare paradise in the desert that in the millennium before the Great Pyramid was built there had been a near fourfold increase in its population, so that when Khufu acceded to the throne it stood at about a million people in the Nile Valley and about half that number in the river's delta.[13]

At the ending of this now-lost canal, we may well imagine that King Khufu's brand-new harbour was set inside a walled enclosure, a dry and dusty place piled with supplies that under Egypt's eternally high blue sky required but little shelter from the elements. Certainly in those first days the land beyond – the desert and the Giza Plateau – would have been a wild and barren place before the pyramid-makers built their settlements, with snakes and scorpions and little birds, a few old tombs, and shimmering in the desert to the south three great gleaming pyramids, two of them made by Khufu's father. Here too on this gently rising desert, ostriches and gazelles ran nervously in the sun and lions roared into the night. A thousand years later, and probably until the Romans caught the last of them for their games, these same animals were hunted from the golden chariots of princes, who lived in nearby Memphis, one of the greatest of all ancient Egyptian cities. One of these young men, so a commemorative stela tells us, never forgot 'the excellence of the resting place of King Khufu', whilst another stela set beside it in the shadow of the Sphinx tells us that another of these young huntsmen had taken a midday siesta in this unearthly place and dreamed one day he would be king.[14] Here on the boundary between the parched sand and the living fields, between life and death around King Khufu's newly excavated harbour, some of Giza's first pyramid-makers appear to have set up home.

As if guarding this now-vanished entrepôt, a wall of massive quarry blocks of honeyed limestone runs some 600 feet (200 m) to the south of the area of our hypothetical harbour. Part buried now, but still standing some 30 feet (10 m) in height and with a width, at its great base of almost 40 feet (12 m), this great long wall has but a single broad gate at its centre spanned by a single row of massive quarry blocks, a mighty barrier that appears to have provided a monumental entrance to the white realms of the royal dead upon the Giza Plateau and which may also have marked the perimeter of the harbour area with its stacked supplies and stores.[15] This great wall also served as a protective breakwater, channelling the main flow of the flash floods that washed through the broad desert valley, away from the area of the vanished harbour.[16]

A large and well-planned settlement similar to other developments built near other pyramids was set up in the lee of this great wall and thus conveniently close to our hypothetical harbour.[17] It is still under excavation, but Mark Lehner's team has uncovered the remains of houses, dormitories and storehouses, smelting furnaces, bakeries, potteries and workshops, set neatly on a grid of streets. And all around lay huge mounds of dust and chippings from extensive hard-stone sculpture workshops and scattered shards of the rough moulds in which Egyptian bread was baked, and brewing pots as well, for wheaten beer was another major component of the ancient diet.[18] This settlement, although on a much grander and more formal scale, with accommodations for some 2000 people, appears to have been a supply town with many of the same facilities that Saleh found in his excavations in the desert.[19] Several of the later tombs within the Giza cemeteries yielded small groups of semi-caricaturing statues of people engaged in many of the activities that were undertaken within this well-planned community: women kneading bread and grinding corn on querns, potters at their wheels, brewers making the doughty ancient beer that helped to fuel the building of the pyramids and doubtless leavened many a sore evening in the settlements as well.[20] Later in ancient Egyptian history drunkenness was sometimes regarded as a religious experience; at Giza too one of Menkaure's work gangs was called 'the drunkards', implying at the very least a certain team spirit, whilst simultaneously informing us that the Giza breweries were much appreciated.[21] Just as wine became an essential element of classical culture and is reflected as such in the abundant drinking cups and oenological paraphernalia buried in the tombs, so at Giza too, as later mortuary texts would celebrate, alcohol appears to have been a leading lubricant of the first pyramid age.[22]

Near to this gridded city, on the slope of the rising desert to the west, Egyptian archaeologists are presently excavating the ruin of a cemetery built, presumably, for some of the city's inhabitants: a burying ground containing modest versions of the courtly tombs, and low round burial tumuli made of brick and mud all studded with fragments of granite gleaned from the work upon the nearby pyramids. There are other monuments too, built high and round in the shape of ovens and all of them surrounded by a mêlée of 600 poorer graves.[23] And sometimes, in this most touching landscape, there are tiny model temples made of brick and daub in imitation of the enormous funerary foundations built upon the Giza Plateau.

Rare as these discoveries are, none of the eloquent artefacts can be securely dated to the reign of Khufu; the name of Khafre, Khufu's son and successor at Giza, is the oldest so far found within this pyramid city which appears to have been occupied long after all three of Giza's royal pyramids were finished and would therefore be contemporary with the construction of the largest graves within the nearby cemetery.[24] Similarly, the great stone wall that forms part of the city's northern boundary cannot presently be dated to the reign of Khufu either, though certainly it was built in the same century as the three great Giza pyramids, which was the only time when the local stone was quarried on such a scale. An indication of the wall's date is in the colossal dimensions of its largest stones, some of which weigh upwards of 200 tons and are the same size as the largest quarry blocks marked out in Khufu's nearby quarry. King Khufu's buildings, however, contain no such massive monoliths; but the Giza architecture of both Khafre and Menkaure holds similarly enormous blocks, so it is reasonable to assume that this great wall was made in one of those two reigns, especially as the earliest dated objects found in the adjoining settlement are of those two same kings.[25] Such huge blocks could have been extracted from the lower sections of King Khufu's quarry and slid down along the broad valley and into their present positions in the wall with relative ease; measured cuttings for similarly sized blocks are still to be seen in the living rock of the eastern sections of the quarry, so this work could well have been accomplished at the same time that the graves of some of Khafre's queens and courtiers were being prepared in the quarry's upper sections.[26] Until further information comes to light we should assume that both the great wall and the gridded city set beside it owe their origins to Khafre's reign when the pattern of pyramid making and the requirements of the pyramid-makers on the Giza Plateau had been well established: just like the remains of Khafre's desert workshops that Petrie dubbed 'the workmen's barracks' (see p. 121 above) this gridded city and its wall show an urge to systematise the processes of making pyramids.

Whilst no trace of King Khufu's pyramid-makers seems to have survived within this city, something may well lie underneath its neat orthogonal plan, for in deeper soundings its archaeologists found evidence of older buildings. Ancient Egyptians frequently established

fresh buildings upon the ruins of older structures that had performed the self-same functions in earlier times.[27] Aerial surveys and
exploratory excavations made around Khufu's father's pyramids show
carefully planned housing settlements, so there is no reason to
suppose that some of Khufu's workers did not enjoy similar accommodations.[28] Such careful continuing arrangements for a key workforce would help to explain the close continuity and development of
royal pyramids and court cemeteries throughout the reigns of
Sneferu and Khufu, just as it would also help to explain the continued development of court funerary architecture of later reigns as
well. It would be reasonable to assume that, when Sneferu, Khufu's
father, died and the decision was taken to build the new king's
pyramid at Giza, a part at least of this standing royal workforce was
moved north from Meidum and Dahshur to new settlements close by
the Giza Plateau. To that extent at least, the decision to build Khufu's
and his father's pyramids at such lonely sites may be seen as a part of
the Egyptians' own colonisation of the Nile Valley, a process that continued throughout ancient Egypt's history.[29]

At all events, this gridded city by its massive wall could only have
contained but a small percentage of the pyramid-makers' initial settlements at Giza in the first years of construction when the workforce
was so very large. Nor has the evidence of that pioneering adventure
been completely lost, for some 15 feet beneath the modern levels of
the Nile's plain there lie the scanty ruins of a spread of settlements

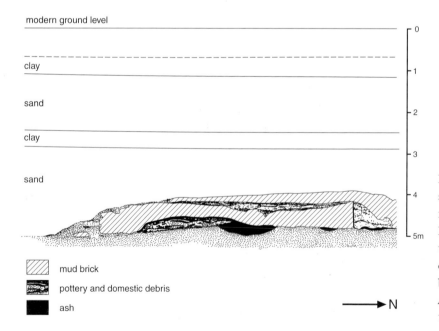

Fig. 63 Section showing
some of the scant
remains of one of the Old
Kingdom settlements
that have recently been
detected lying deep
beneath the Giza Plain.
Adapted from Hawass
1996a.

buried deep in the alluvial silt.[30] Evidence of these dwellings was first located in the cores of exploratory bore holes and in key-hole excavations made in the deep trenches of recent civil engineering projects undertaken as Giza City pushes ever further out across the plain. The fragments of mud brick and Old Kingdom pottery recovered by the rescue archaeologists are hardly suitable material for display in a museum but their careful analysis and the ongoing geophysical exploration in the Giza plain have begun to show the full extent of these ancient settlements whose scant remains lie deep beneath thick deposits of the river's silt: some 250 acres (100 ha) of little bumps and mounds of mud-brick walls and wind-blown sand and pottery and ash lying upon the surface of a long-buried desert (fig. 63). It is reasonable to assume that in the first years of Khufu's reign, when the initial settlement of the area exploded as the workforce rapidly expanded, the Giza plain was rapidly sprinkled with shelters and workshops, habitations and storerooms – thousands of small buildings, perhaps, scattered across the desert and the plain – and as the first rush of pyramid building subsided and the workforce shrank, so Saleh's excavations would suggest, these homes and stores and workshops were abandoned, adapted or enlarged as the pyramid-makers required.

Unfortunately, the chances of finding more of these settlements in the deserts near the Great Pyramid now seems increasingly remote: although the settlements that Saleh found had been stripped out before being buried in the desert, Austrian archaeologists digging for more such dwellings on the south side of the sandy valley of King Khufu's quarry (see fig. 54) found not buried ruins in the desert sand but mounds of building rubble, the debris, it appeared, of settlements that had been cleared away from other sites.[31] Whilst the Austrian excavators found no texts to identify any of the occupants of these demolished homes, they did find the names of Khufu and Khafre amongst the rubble, stamped on plaster sealings that had been used presumably to close the bags and jars that had held imported rations and supplies.[32]

Such rubble has also been found along the other edges of the Pyramid Plateau; vast amounts of similar debris still lie amongst the screes of chip and building rubble that run down the high cliffs to the north of the Great Pyramid whilst yet more extensive rubbish from human habitations darkens the deep strata that still fill large parts of King Khufu's quarry (fig. 93).[33] Such tips appear to be the residue of the landscaping that took place at the ending of the work on each of the three great Giza pyramids (see further pp. 409ff), when their makers demolished their building ramps and cleared away the masons' chippings from the stone workshops whilst at the same time obliterating all traces of their lives and times upon the Giza Plateau. Although it is possible that some of the debris in these locations may date to periods later than the reign of Khufu, their very depth and circumstance indicate, as we have seen, that parts of them at least were laid down at the completion of the Great Pyramid and are the scattered relics of those first days at Giza.

It is strange, today, to see in the exposed seams opened by the archaeologists the relics of these anonymous lives, a past that was never intended to survive, the dust and dirt of mud-brick houses, layered in the limestone chip and mud that was the refuse of the Pyramid's construction. The perfection of their preservation, the intimacy of broken pots and pans, scraps of charcoal, linen and the rest, produces an immediate contact with the distant past, a feeling of commonality that the Great Pyramid itself cannot give us.

15 The living city

Unlike the makers of his Pyramid, King Khufu's only surviving presence on the Giza Plateau is in the monuments they built for him; if a royal palace ever stood beside this pyramid, its position is as lost as any certain knowledge of his role in government. Whatever part the king may or may not have played in his Pyramid's construction, it seems likely that, as the head of state, Khufu would have been physically present on occasion at the site of his kingdom's greatest enterprise. Several short texts have been interpreted as holding references to a building of King Khufu's that once stood at Giza and these may well refer to the enclosure of his palace.[1] At the same time we might also expect that some at least of the craftsmen of the royal court, suppliers to both the living and the dead and the makers of the image and identity of Khufu's state, would have lived and worked at Giza with the royal court. And certainly, we should expect the offices of the Pyramid's administration to have been close to the rising Pyramid: the halls of those who oversaw the work of quarrying, of the supply of copper and the rest, of those concerned with the architecture of the rising Pyramid and all of those facilities that directed the provision and supply of the pyramid-makers' communities; the harbour masters, the fleet controllers and all of those officials and administrators whose task it would have been to enumerate and

supply everything from sacks of grain to the delivery of fuel and
water. One might assume as well, though once again all record has
entirely disappeared, that a great part of the offices of national government may also have been set up at Giza, where the consuming
activity of that state was underway.

Here, at the edge of the Giza Plain, in the soft shade of evergreens,
amidst high palms and sweet-smelling fig and fruit trees, you would
probably have seen some of the houses of the royal administration,
and perhaps a palace for the king and court and rooms for their
attending workshops, all built of mud and brick, and wood and
wattle. Buildings that may well have been built on an *ad hoc* basis and
swept away when the Great Pyramid was finished, or alternatively
whose scanty ruin may still form part of the deep-buried settlements
that lie underneath the modern plain or be piled up somewhere, a
buried mass of sand and rubble, on the desert's edge.[2]

Whilst the accommodations of King Khufu's state may well have
disappeared, there is still a great deal to be said about the life of this
community that grew up on the Giza Plateau. As we will see in
chapter 34, its core population was probably the residue of his
father's workforce, that body of highly practised stone workers who

Fig. 64 Francis Frith's
photograph of the Great
Pyramid records the same
spare group of trees
drawn by Napoleon's
savants sixty years before
(*Description* V, pl. 7). They
marked the edge of the
Nile's ancient water table,
the furthest extent for
any human habitations
that could be sheltered,
as was the common
ancient custom for large
houses, by trees and
vegetation growing
without artificial
irrigation.

after overseeing the emplacement of Sneferu's burial may well have sailed up to Giza to start work upon the pyramid of his son. At an estimated 3000 souls plus their families and retainers this essential body of skilled craftsmen would hardly have been sufficient to achieve the estimated workload of the extraordinary programme of the first year of construction.[3] This small core must have been swiftly followed to the Giza Plateau by a host of recruits: labourers and harbour diggers, ramp builders and quarrymen, stone haulers and water carriers and their families too, and the craftsmen, servants and supporting staff who in the first months of construction would have enabled an estimated population of more than 40,000 people to live and work productively upon the Giza Plateau during the first years of the Great Pyramid's construction.

In the absence of contemporary information, one might assume that this enormous workforce – one of the largest that the ancient world had known – was drawn from Egypt's general population; from the families of the farmers who are assumed to have made up the bulk of ancient Egypt's people. Apart from the small traces that are occasionally excavated from deep beneath the present Giza Plain, the dwellings of much of this first wave have left but little record, a fact that could well stand as a metaphor for our knowledge of the general population of an estimated 1.6 million individuals who lived and farmed the landscapes of the River Nile.[4] For all that survives of this ancient agrarian nation outside the orbit of the court that built the early pyramids are some provincial graves and a hundred or so names and images of people gleaned from Khufu's Giza cemeteries. 'The (extremely fragmentary) sources', Jan Assmann has remarked, '. . . contain no reference whatever to estates or classes, tribes, clans and families, local princes, or magnates, or to centres or concentrations of power.'[5] Virtually nothing remains of the ancient Egypt of King Khufu's day outside the structures of his court and the hot-house community that made his Pyramid.[6]

This was a unique society around the Giza Plateau. Unlike other Bronze Age cities which were manufacturing and marketing centres, Khufu's Giza settlements gave nothing tangible in return to the country that supported them. The extraordinary pace of building during the first frantic years makes it unlikely that pyramid making was timed to the slack seasons of the agricultural year as the classical writers and many egyptologists have imagined. Similarly, other evidence gives the lie to Petrie's story, born of the ancient Greeks, that the Great Pyramid's blocks were shipped to Giza on the waters of the Nile's annual flood;[7] for recent reconstructions of those ancient water levels prove that this inundation, which was at its full height for less than two months of the year, would not have provided sufficient draft for Khufu's stone boats to travel over Egypt's flooded fields.[8] Harbours and canals, therefore, were essential for heavy stone transportation which could then have continued right around the year.

Unlike the usual ancient Egyptian life of farming and hunting, the community upon the Giza Plateau was not bound to the seasons of the agricultural year, its civic focus being entirely fixed upon the single process of making Khufu's Pyramid. Just as the sculptured heads placed within the courtly tombs show an acute interest in a singular identity at an individual moment, so Khufu's pyramid-makers inhabited a unique community whose sense of time had stretched beyond the usual confines of contemporary society.

As these recruits first set foot upon the Giza desert, as they left the lush green and the calm enclosing cliffs that had framed their lives within the river valley, as they walked out on the desert Plateau, these farmers passed from one existence to another. Even the work upon the Pyramid would have been entirely new to them. At the same time as their sense of time and history was transformed by the monstrous imperatives of building this enormous pyramid, cultivators became stone workers, and their hands and feet and bodily musculature would surely all have changed. Here then, they joined a unique community, set away from the rhythms of the fruitful valley which now served only to support them. This in short was a city utterly dependent upon the good order of the state. A city and a community entirely at the service of the king, for only the national state controlled sufficient resources to make a great pyramid of blocks of stone, the monument that was in itself the very definition, the tangible manifestation, of King Khufu's state. These recruits had therefore joined something without parallel in the ancient world.

By necessity Khufu's Giza was a community where most of the pyramid-makers may well have known the royal administrators and even perhaps the king and his courtiers by sight. To that extent at least, Khufu's city would have been similar to that of the small city states common in the rest of the ancient world and unlike the other communities of ancient Egypt who may never have laid eyes upon their pharaoh.

There was, however, a well-defined set of highly visible status symbols operating in this court and pictured in the representations of kings and courtiers. The same flash of finely polished gold that presently sells tickets to international exhibitions enabled the new recruits at Giza to identify the pharaoh and his family. Certainly such regalia would have appeared as exotic to these newcomers as they do to us today. Kings, for example, may be identified by their fine linen, by the sharp silhouettes of their unique head-dresses and the flashing furniture decorated with ebony and gold that seems to have formed part of their cortège.[9] In similar fashion, court officials may have been distinguished by accoutrements hardly less elaborate, their status marked upon occasion, so their sculptures show, by a variety of elegant sticks and batons, and sometimes by a hieroglyphic badge of office worn over the shoulder like a bandoleer, an inky palette and a box for brushes; the tools of every scribe.[10]

Literacy especially was an essential element of pyramid construction; the need for written lists and orders was as fundamental as the standardisation of weights and measures and accounting procedures as neat and precise as the lists the scribes compiled for the sculptured inscriptions set up on the tombs of Khufu's courtiers. Indeed, as writing in itself appears to have developed to enable the listing and counting and labelling of the property of the state[11] so, appropriately enough, the scribes of the Great Pyramid left no narrative of their great adventure on the Giza Plateau or, if they did, no trace of it survives.

By their very nature, the ancient exponents of writing – the state scribes and government officials – would probably have been as inherently conservative as the spare texts from the courtly tombs suggest. In similar fashion, although the Slab Stelae are elaborate codifications of much earlier traditions that arose in more egalitarian communities before the unification of the Egyptian state, little has been discarded from the earlier examples; for the most part they have been codified, expanded, but above all else preserved.[12] Underscoring this impression, the lists of so-called titles in the tombs of Khufu's contemporaries also show that, for the great part, they were hereditary and some of them several centuries old. They also tell us that such positions were limited to males from noble families and that the role of noble women hardly extended beyond the home and court. And this in turn encourages us to imagine that if the living community at Giza bore any relationship to that of the courtly dead, it would have been highly stratified, with little social mobility.[13] That these same inscriptions also indicate that these noble families lived in large and stable units may also have been a reflection of the living community as well.

A somewhat similar social order is also suggested by the Pyramid's theoretical building statistics; after the first explosion of settlement and building at the beginning of King Khufu's reign, the community beside the Giza Plateau was a relatively small and constantly diminishing society. It was, therefore, a socially diverse community in which most people could well have seen and recognised each other on a daily basis.[14] In such societies where there is a broad degree of contact and few organs of opinion beyond daily gossip, there is usually a minimum of social distrust. At the same time, the very angles and orientations of the Pyramid itself, which were maintained with such single-minded precision through years of astonishing endeavour, cry continuity and integrity amongst its makers. So, although the order of their communities need not have been one that we would readily recognise as such today, there would appear to have been a strong system of both control and accord operating inside the Giza settlements. Given their unusual sense of time and order and their extraordinary circumstances, it would appear that in their day the inhabitants of Khufu's pyramid city were utterly unique.

16 Coda: thinking with stone

The contents of a remarkable three-chambered burial vault, closed
since the days of the Giza pyramids and opened in the years before
the First World War, are presently displayed in the Museo Egizio in
Turin. Discovered in the provincial cemetery of an ancient city built
beside the Nile at Gebelein some 350 miles south of Giza, the vault
had held the mummies of four anonymous male Egyptians and was
filled with mostly homely things, many of them possessed of that
unaffected elegance typical of so many products of the first great age
of pyramid building.[1] The sarcophagi, three of which were made from
short rough planks of local woods and bound with rawhide, had all
been plastered in careful imitation of the grand stone boxes of some
of the courtly tombs within the distant Giza cemeteries. Indeed, in
life, the little mummies from Gebelein might themselves have
worked at Giza, for they were accompanied by a stock of well-used
stone-working tools: some stout copper chisels and a balloon-headed
mallet to drive them through the limestone and, coiled up beneath
one of the sarcophagi, a pyramid-maker's most basic machinery –
heavy rope suitable for hauling quarried stone.[2]

Piles of household possessions were laid out around each of the
burials, both fine domestic pottery and utilitarian ceramics, brewing
pots for making beer and moulds for baking bread. There were great

bundles of cloth as well, such as Egyptian women wove, mummy cloths and domestic linens and graceful chests of aromatic cedar wood to store them in. There were pairs of workaday sandals too, made from woven rush and leather, their insides polished and flattened by the feet that had once walked in them. And lying on some plain wooden tables, five loaves of well-baked bread, with shiny husks of grain still flecking their brown-baked surfaces, and each one pinched into the sharp shape of a little pyramid.[3] The entire tomb offers a rare insight into the households of stone-working craftsmen at the time that the first great pyramids of Egypt were being built.

One object stands apart from this unpretentious domesticity. An exquisite pale grey bowl of hard stone taken from a desert quarry, and made so thin that the glow of the Turin sunlight passing through its sides seems to set it floating weightless in the air.[4]

Several similar drinking bowls have been excavated in other provincial cemeteries as well, some of them inscribed with the name of Khufu's father, Sneferu.[5] When found in such simple burial vaults, such unexpected treasures are usually described according to the archaeologist's inclination, as either heirlooms or rewards for stints of royal service. Certainly, long before the age of Sneferu and Khufu, similarly fine bowls and vases made of alabaster and hard volcanic stone, or sometimes even cut from amethysts and porphyries and capped with lids of ivory and gold, appear to have served as the currency of courtly gifts, part of the elaborate traffic of obligation and reward, so it has been suggested, between the nobles and the king.[6]

Such treasures were traditionally taken to the grave; royal Egypt's first great tombs held thousands of them. Centuries later, some of the corridors beneath the first Egyptian pyramid were stacked high with them, their inscriptions telling that many were already centuries old when they had been gathered up and stacked there in the darkness, like eggshells one inside the other, some 30,000 of them, and many of them cut as fine as flowers.[7]

Just as this exotic assemblage was a literal bringing together of different stones gathered from many of Egypt's different landscapes, so right throughout ancient Egyptian history a wide variety of hard and splendid stones were gathered up from all across the kingdom and brought together in the tombs and temples of the state. Sometimes, as in those warm dark corridors underneath the first Egyptian pyramid, these rare collections were entirely hidden; more commonly they were exhibited like gigantic necklaces of multi-coloured stones as the substance, the very blocks, of the royal architecture. Even then, their diverse origins and the extraordinary achievement of their transportation often from remote desert locations were seldom mentioned in the accompanying inscriptions.

Similarly, the pair of famous seated statues that stand together upon the plain of Thebes, the northern one of which is known as the Colossus of Memnon and was said to have uttered sounds each day at dawn, appear to have been cut from the same glittering dull-red stone commonly used by the craftsmen of King Amenhotep III in whose name they were made and in whose temple they once stood.[8] Yet the Vocal Memnon and his fellow were shipped to their present positions from the opposite ends of Egypt; one floated 200 miles downstream from a quartzite quarry near Aswan on Egypt's southern border, the other brought 330 miles upstream to Thebes, from another quartzite quarry at the Gebel Ahmar, close now to the suburbs of modern Cairo.[9]

As if underlining these two highly physical acts – each one of these statues weighs some 700 tons[10] – the sides of the two huge thrones on which the two colossal figures sit bear traditional emblems of Egypt's unification, exquisite hieroglyph-derived images of two figures knotting together the heraldic plants of Upper and Lower Egypt that in turn support the full name and titularies of the king.[11] Such images had their beginnings 1500 years before, in the First Dynasty, and appear in their mature form four centuries later as part of a representation of King Khufu, where the pretty image of the entwined heraldic plants of Upper and Lower Egypt supports his throne, and thus, quite literally sustains the seat of national power.[12]

Such carefully configured semi-hieroglyphic images are usually described as 'symbolic' or 'emblematic', just as in similar fashion the extraordinary undertaking of placing the two geologically diverse colossi side by side upon the Plain of Thebes might also be explained as a 'symbolic' act. Yet the physical achievement of bringing these two gigantic images together after combined voyages of some 500 miles is never mentioned in the statues' texts nor in any other of the copious inscriptions of Amenhotep's reign. Indeed, the diverse origins of the two colossi was long unknown, the sources of their stone only established by petrographic analysis in 1984.[13] Unlike the symbols on their thrones, therefore, the physical gathering together of these two huge stones, these two colossi on the Plain of Thebes – in itself, one of ancient Egypt's greatest engineering feats – was not intended as a visible 'symbol' of national unification. In common with the vases stacked beneath the Step Pyramid they are, quite literally, the residue of complex and elaborate national acts of state that employed hundreds of people in their commission, activities that in themselves in

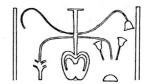

Fig. 65 The entwined plants of Upper and Lower Egypt, a common emblem of the union. From an inscription of King Khufu carved on the face of an alabaster quarry in Middle Egypt.

their own time held the very essence of the power and style of pharaonic government.

Ancient Egyptians often worked in stone rather than political rhetoric or theology. And of course, above all others, the age of Sneferu and Khufu was very rich in cut and quarried and collected stone. It is unnecessary to search for suitable abstractions that the Great Pyramid may or may not have 'symbolised'. Like much to do with ancient Egypt, where even writing was made of concrete images and there were precious few abstractions in the written language, the physical process of making this Great Pyramid was in itself a kind of thinking.

There is perhaps something quintessentially academic in this continual search for 'symbols' to explain King Khufu's Pyramid. There is something too of sheer silliness in the notion that tens of thousands of state-supported craftsmen were consciously engaged in making symbols so abstruse that few people in the next five millennia could agree as to what their meaning may have been. Nonetheless, a powerful tradition has grown up within the West to search out some kind of an overarching intellectual purpose behind the massive presence of the Pyramid. From Piazzi Smyth and Jomard and the hermetic sages of Greek Alexandria who claimed that speech alone links sky and earth, to those eminent Victorians who held that speech above all things was the dividing line between men and beasts, that the invention of writing represented a vital watershed in human evolution, the west has long assumed that action necessarily proceeds from thought and language. As William Camden put it, those that 'lackt wit to express their conceit in speech, did use to depaint it out (as it were) in pictures'.[14]

One of the problems with such assumptions is that they leave us with so few tools with which to comprehend non-literary ages – those crucial periods, for example, in which the fundamental technologies of human life emerged: the domestication of plants and animals, the smelting of metals, the growth of villages and nations. And this is why, as far as the Great Pyramid is concerned, which was one of the ultimate products of the pre-literary world and perhaps its greatest rebus, traditionalists are forced to transpose the prose of later ages into the silent world that made King Khufu's Pyramid.[15]

At the silent Pyramid itself, however, where a great part of the purposes of its design is held within the very methods of its manufacture, there is another very different kind of language; one held in the fine lines of abrasion running over the Pyramid's casing blocks, the marks of a master craftsman feeling for perfection in the stone, in the quarrymen's rough chisellings and the finished stones of its dark interior. Above all else, however, it is held within the ancient landscapes that not only informed the sensibilities of the ancient craftsmen and designers but also supplied the forms and materials of the Pyramid itself. It is these ancient landscapes then, that hold the origins, the inspiration and the means by which this extraordinary monument was made.

Part Three

The land and the Pyramid

17 Prospecting Egypt

In Khufu's reign, deserts that had seen little more of the Egyptians than the occasional expedition prospecting on behalf of sculptors and vase makers for pretty blocks of stone were transformed by the dispatch of large well-organised communities of quarrymen and miners backed by transport networks which supplied the royal building works.[1] The Great Pyramid indeed, and its associated temples, prompted an explosion of prospecting whose product can be seen as a physical summation of the kingdom, of its deserts and its cliffs, its waterways and wadis, their minerals and materials all mined and smelted, quarried and transported, and employed to make this geometric mountain on a desert cliff.

In the 1920s, prehistorians surveying the desert to the east of the Giza Plateau came across a long thin ridge striped with bands of soft white gleaming stone, and all around lay the huts and tools and workshops of its ancient miners. Known now as the Umm el-Sawwan, this is the only ancient gypsum quarry yet found in Egypt.[2] Amidst a broad scattering of dust and powder lay discarded bowls and dishes cut from rock taken from the harder sections of the gypsum matrix; vessels, so their shapes informed the archaeologists, that had been made during the first four Egyptian dynasties.[3] Nor was there any evidence of later activity at the site. As the chemical similarity of this

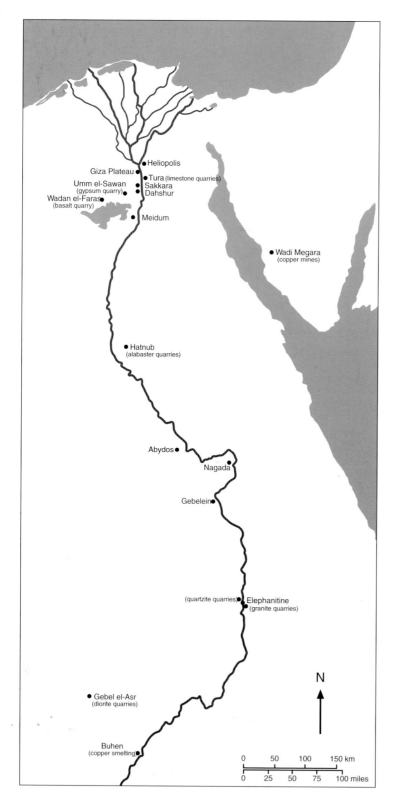

Fig. 66 Map of Egypt and northern Nubia showing the locations of the mines, quarries and settlements described below.

Fig. 67 The Great Pyramid is composed of mortar, limestone and granite: 5.5 million tons of limestone, 8000 tons of granite and a half a million tons of mortar. Further huge amounts of stone were used in the Pyramid's associated buildings, fragments of which – a red granite block and part of a basalt temple pavement – appear in the lower sections of this photograph.

deposit to that used by King Khufu's pyramid-makers suggests, this is a likely and convenient source of the mortar that was used in such huge amounts during the construction of the Great Pyramid.

Soft, crystalline and easily mined, pulverised and bagged, the desert gypsum of Umm el-Sawwan could have been taken to Giza by two separate routes (see fig. 66). Most directly, it may have been carried in caravan along a track that runs a few miles eastwards to join an ancient desert road that runs straight down into the Nile Valley at a point close by two of Sneferu's pyramids from where, presumably, the gypsum could have been embarked for Giza from a harbour connected to those pyramids.[4] More conveniently, a similarly short desert journey south from the desert ridge would have led to a more substantial road, 'the oldest and most pristine example of a purpose-built quarry road in the world', that runs some 7 miles down through the desert to the fabled shores of the desert Lake Moeris.[5] Here, near an ancient quay, archaeologists have found some stone and bowls that had been mined and worked apparently at the Umm el-Sawwan.[6] In Khufu's day, when the lake's levels were much higher than they are today, the desert gypsum could also have been conveniently shipped to Giza and the Great Pyramid from these long-lost quays, along with the diverse products of other desert quarries.[7]

At all events, an estimated 300,000 cubic yards (230,000 m³) of gypsum was baked and slaked and brought to Giza in the reign of Khufu where, after being mixed with water, it was poured, pushed and shovelled into the cracks and crevices between the Great Pyramid's limestone blocks where it may still be seen today.[8] As well as this, that same desert gypsum was used to make the thin plaster that lubricated the passage and final adjustments of the vast blocks that form the Pyramid's interiors, and its fine-cut casing stones as well. The white marks of this looser mix, which was more finely sieved and highly fired than the plaster used for filling the gaps between the quarry blocks, can still be seen in some places in the Pyramid's interior, where it appears to be still dribbling like fresh milk over the great dark stones.[9]

Although the gypsum quarries of the Umm el-Sawwan have yet to be excavated, it would be reasonable to expect that considerable traces of their miners' humble lives and times are yet still buried in that driest of Egyptian deserts.[10] That information by itself would be a valuable addition to our understanding of the Great Pyramid's economy, for all traces of other similar large-scale enterprises that were no less essential to its construction have completely disappeared. There is no known evidence, for example, of fuel gathering;

the collection year on year of the enormous quantities of tinder and wood that were required not only to bake and hydrate the desert gypsum of the Umm el-Sawwan, but also to heat the pyramid-makers' kitchens and pottery kilns and furnaces. Similarly, there are no surviving traces of the harvesting of Egypt's lakes, canals and riversides, the gathering of enormous quantities of papyrus, reed and rush, the sedge and halfa grass that along with palm-tree fibre were the principal materials of the ropes with which the Great Pyramid's blocks were hauled into position.[11] Although celebrated in a dozen hieroglyphs, all traces of their manufactory have disappeared.[12] The very name of pharaoh, however, would be held inside and denoted by a ring of rope, the so-called 'cartouche' hieroglyph, and not surprisingly the cartouche came into use shortly after the Egyptian kings began to build with blocks of stone.[13] That it became the standard way of writing royal names as the early pyramids were being built serves to underline how closely rope, specifically heavy hauling rope, encapsulated an essential link between rope and kingship and the state.

Another of these vanished industries provided the rounded rocks of gneiss and diorite and granite; the hard-stone pounders that were another fundamental tool of pyramid making and which were gathered from the surfaces of the Egyptian deserts and shipped to Giza in enormous quantity. Hundreds if not thousands of them are still to be seen at Giza, studding the sand and the strata of the archaeologists' excavations. Small enough sometimes to fit into a child's hand, though with others weighing 35 lb (15 kg) and more,[14] most of them are still pock-marked by their ancient use, whilst some still support the great stones they may well have helped to shift into position.[15] None of these ubiquitous hard-stone balls are of a stone native to the Giza Plateau: in Khufu's day, however, they were used there in such quantities that it must have seemed as if they surely were.

After these circumstantial evidences of Khufu's desert harvests, it is a pleasure to find contemporary inscriptions actually recording some of these activities: splendidly heraldic evidence indeed, in the quarries of Hat-nub, some 200 miles south of Giza, where high on a bright white cliff of Egyptian alabaster, Khufu's name appears alongside a ghostly image of pharaoh on a throne, and all of this accompanied by the names and titles of a dozen later pharaohs who shared his taste for Hat-nub's honeyed alabaster.[16] It is hardly surprising that, in common with those of other kings, Khufu's workmen mined Hat-nub's distinctive stone, a rock as warm as clotted cream, a soft translucent stone that polishes like granite. Although it had been

Fig. 68 Line drawing of an inscription of King Khufu, elaborately carved in raised relief, on a rock face in the alabaster quarries of Hat-nub.

worked millennia before the beginning of the Egyptian state,[17] alabaster was little used as a building material and never in King Khufu's Pyramid. Nonetheless, some tomb statues and a variety of fine-cut bowls and vases made from alabaster have survived from Khufu's time and in the 1920s, digging close to the east side of the Great Pyramid, Reisner's expedition discovered a burial chamber that held a splendid empty sarcophagus cut from a fine block of translucent alabaster which had been quarried apparently at Hat-nub to serve as the coffin of Khufu's mother.[18] So, the 10 mile long road that leads down to the Nile from Hat-nub's alabaster quarries may well have been laid down in Khufu's reign to aid the passage of such large blocks of fine stone, for the dumper trucks that use this same track today run underneath the cliff which bears King Khufu's name and image.[19]

Another and yet more dramatic occurrence of King Khufu's name set up in a stone quarry was discovered in the desert by some Egyptian Army officers in the 1930s out for a spin and sheltering from an unexpected sandstorm 150 miles south of Egypt's ancient boundary at Aswan. Once the air had cleared, the soldiers found themselves at the centre of the sprawling ruins of an ancient quarry settlement, built all over a desert ridge as yellow as custard and studded with dark plums of rare hard stone.[20] And lying all around, amongst the tumbled huts and stone workings, were hieroglyphic inscriptions celebrating some of the ancient pharaohs, the courtiers and quarrymen, who had mined this desolate and long-forgotten place.[21] First

Fig. 69 Khufu's quarry stela as it had stood in the Nubian desert for almost four and half thousand years, photographed at 'the hunting ground of Khufu' by Rex Engelbach in 1938, before its removal to the Cairo Museum.

amongst these royal names was Khufu's, his great cartouche most beautifully hammered onto a curving 5 foot flake of slim black rock that had been set upright in the desert and supported by two long stones.[22] Underneath the royal name, an elegant if brief inscription informed all travellers that they had come to 'The hunting ground of Khufu'; this presumably a geological hunting ground[23] for the unique stone that is only to be found at this place and the self-same stone, in fact, on which Khufu's inscription had been cut, a dense and mottled greenish gneiss, with the fresh matte bloom of a grape and a strange blue hint of inner iridescence.[24] This then, this remote ridge called the Gebel el-Asr, was the previously unknown source of the beauteous stone from which the famous statues of King Khafre, Khufu's son, were made. During his survey of the Great Pyramid, Petrie had found many chippings of this same stone and concluded that they were the residue of sculptures that had been destroyed;[25] these perhaps the only surviving evidence at Giza of the sojourn of King Khufu's quarry-men in that most lonely place.

The extent to which blocks of such rare stones were valued by the royal artisans is shown by the huge amounts of effort invested to transport the mottled gneiss to Giza. Above all by the 50 mile quarry track, all of it levelled, cleared and marked with cairns and serviced with small wells, that runs east from the Gebel el-Asr through the high desert down to the River Nile. Even then, after this extraordinary haul across a baking desert and embarkation for a 600 mile barge trip on the Nile's stream to Giza and the royal workshops, the precious blocks still had to shoot the rapids of the granite cataract at Aswan, a risky venture only to be undertaken on the river's annual flood at the end of summer.[26]

In sheer effort even the trackway from the Gebel el-Asr is surpassed by the beautifully graded road that was laid down relatively close to the Giza Plateau, a carefully bedded construction paved with limestone and fossil wood and set on occasion in gypsum mortar, which was built to enable the transportation of blocks of basalt from another of King Khufu's desert quarries high on the outcrops called the Widan el-Faras, the 'horse's ears', a pair of dramatic volcanic outcroppings standing 1000 feet above the Western Desert and which are part of that same formation of mountainous ridges that, just 18 miles to the east, hold the gypsum quarries of the Umm el-Sawwan (see pp. 155ff above).[27] So, King Khufu's basalt quarriers may well have shared this splendid desert road running south down through the desert to Lake Moeris with the royal gypsum miners.

This hard, dull, charcoal-coloured basalt had never been used as a standard building stone before King Khufu's time, when it was employed at the great temples connected to the Great Pyramid. These buildings, however, are either ruined or as yet unrecovered, so present estimates of the quantities of basalt used by Khufu's builders are certainly conservative.[28] Even so, it has been estimated that in Khufu's time half of all the basalt ever quarried by the ancient Egyptians, more than 1000 cubic metres of the rock, was brought to Giza from the ancient lava flows of the Western Desert.[29] And just as

Fig. 70 The basalt pavement on the east side of the Great Pyramid, part of a long-vanished temple.

today the residue of these extraordinary labours may still be seen beside the Great Pyramid, where they form a ruined pavement on its eastern side, so too the dark ridges of the Widan el-Faras are crusted with the jagged chippings left by Khufu's miners, mute evidence of their long struggle with this intractable material. And this in an environment which, on a pleasant day in March within the Nile Valley with crops growing high and green, would produce temperatures in shadowed sections of the desert of more than 35°C, and temperatures at the surface on the basalt rock at double that amount.[30]

18 Desert copper

Khufu's quarrymen were fortunate, at least, in that much of the basalt of the Widan el-Faras had naturally split into roughly rectangular blocks which, as they mostly weighed less than a ton, could be prised out from the mountain and sent rolling down the valley to the desert road below where, after a rough pounding down to size with other lumps of hard stone in the usual way, they could be taken off to Giza.[1] Beside King Khufu's Pyramid, however, on the Giza Plateau, this hard-won stone shows clear evidence of cutting with a kind of saw.

Handsaws, as we have seen (p. 109 above), were occasionally used by pyramid-makers to provide a fine flush fit between two blocks of limestone casing stone.[2] Judging from the occasional accompanying encrustations of verdigris and the surviving saw-marks, these had been modest hand-held fine-toothed copper implements similar to

Fig. 71 Robert Moores' reconstruction of Khufu's gigantic copper saw showed it swinging in a bath of water, with a workman pouring quantities of cutting powder, such as emery or quartz dust, down into the cut. The marks of these or similar abrasives are often found on drilled and polished surfaces produced by ancient Egyptian craftsmen (Lucas/Harris 1962, pp. 72ff).

those used by ancient Egyptian carpenters. Basalt, on the other hand, could hardly have been worked with such modest tools, and yet the deep swift cuts that are still visible upon the paving blocks of the Great Pyramid's now-vanished temples clearly betray the operation of a most efficient saw: a saw that has left cuts a quarter of an inch (6 mm) wide and that ran in deep and brutal swathes right through the dense black stone.[3] Such an extraordinary saw must have been a fearsome thing: a straight-swinging blade, its cut betrays, some 15 feet (4.5 m) in length and attached in all probability to a wooden trestle so that it could be pulled briskly back and forth across the stone. The very tip of Khufu's stone-working technologies, this archaic monster of a machine would have required the muscle of a dozen men working in unison to keep this huge blade in motion. Weighing, so it has been estimated, around 300 lb (140 kg), and continuously fed with a lubricant such as vegetable oil and handfuls of cutting sand or emery or pounded quartz, this great long slab of toothed copper cut through the dense dark blocks of desert basalt at a rate of an 1½ inches (40 mm) a minute!

Super-saw apart, the basic tools of Khufu's pyramid-makers, the fundamental means by which their geometric mountain was made to rise so quickly and so straight and true, were masons' chisels. Copper chisels flat and pointed, large and small. Chisels that though soft and weak by modern standards gave the pyramid-makers the edge, the crisp fast cut they needed to finish their work within the lifetime of the king, and at the same time maintain an extraordinary accuracy.

By some miracle, the finest of all ancient Egyptian stone-working chisels known to have survived was found close by the great stela of King Khufu in the gneiss quarries of the Gebel el-Asr, where it had been left in the hot sun on a small flake of rock.[4] Such a chisel, however, is incapable of cutting gneiss; its only use, therefore, on the Gebel el-Asr was either as a crowbar or, as it shows no marks of stress upon its shanks, in shaping the pieces of local limestone that were used in the construction of the road that led down from the quarry to the river. Certainly, the chisel's gently mushroomed head and lightly blunted point showed clear signs of normal ancient use.[5] At all events, the presence in that lonely place of this stout and heavy point specifically designed for roughing out big blocks of limestone tokens the presence at the Gebel el-Asr, along with the hard-stone quarry-men and the stone gatherers and haulers, of one of Khufu's skilled stone-working gangs.

As elegant as a statue and well suited to serve in the manufacture of the world's most extraordinary building, this lone chisel from the

Fig. 72 The copper chisel from the Gebel el-Asr.

desert is a beautiful example of a type of tool whose basic shape has hardly changed down till today. And on its shaft, rough texts appear to name the work gang to whom it was once assigned: 'the southern gang' which, if these rare inscriptions are to be interpreted according to their later usage, was part of the 'Green Division', one of the well-known units of ancient Egypt's generic pyramid-building workforce.[6]

At all events, thousands upon thousands of such chisels must have been cast for the construction of the Great Pyramid and all of them, so present research indicates, cast from copper taken from Egyptian mines.[7] As we have already seen, the handy notion that, once discovered, pure copper quickly gave way to bronze, a tougher alloy made from copper mixed with tin, simply is not true.[8] In this, Khufu's Egyptians displayed a technological conservatism common amongst many ancient cultures.[9] Even at the time when iron from the north was beginning to arrive in Egypt, more implements of pure copper were still placed in Tutankhamun's tomb than those of any other metal, a fact that by itself suggests that for the best part of its existence the ancient Egyptian state harboured no ambitions for its tools other than those that their native copper could provide: that they considered this darkly lustrous metal from their deserts sufficient to their need.

Smelted, cast, resharpened and recast in a variety of shapes, Egyptian copper chisels shaped King Khufu's Pyramid. Right through Egypt's ancient history copper's crisp passage through quarried limestone, and later through the soft sandstone of which the great temples would be built, made it an indispensable commodity for the pharaohs: an equation recognised, so it appears, in Egyptian hieroglyphics which visually link the pyramid with the means of its production; the chisel sign *mr* appearing along with a host of other evocative terms, as a variant of *mr*, 'pyramid'.[10] Several of the rare surviving records of the bureaucracy also indicate the metal's value to the state; royal scribes recount the weighing and counting of copper chisels with obsessive accuracy whilst a general's order written at the beginning of the first millennium BC that tells the royal tomb-makers to recast their stock of copper into spears also underlines its strategic value.[11] No wonder, then, that so few copper chisels have survived: but there is no doubt, as every block of stone on the Great Pyramid still shows, that in the reign of Khufu they existed in their tens of thousands.

A difficult and expensive enterprise at the best of times, copper mining on the scale needed to supply such enormous enterprises would have required the full attention and resources of King Khufu's

Fig. 73 The ruin of one of the large circular kilns excavated by Abdel-Aziz Saleh in 1971–2, in an area to the west of the Giza quarry. The stone and plaster set up around this kiln, whose mud bricks have been burnt bright red in its firing, suggest that it was taken to higher temperatures than those required for baking food or firing ancient pottery; similarly, the remains of its flue show that it could have provided access for forced air pumped from bellows, a typical attribute of ancient copper smelting furnaces. As discussed in chapter 13 above, this kiln could have been employed in the casting and recasting of chisels used at the Great Pyramid.

state. This indeed was a state industry throughout ancient Egyptian history, and it has left tell-tale stains and traces across wide swathes of the Egyptian deserts, in the peninsula of Sinai, in Nubia and in the dry wastes between the Nile and the Red Sea; the residues of an elementary if effective mining and refining industry.[12] And sometimes still, beside the desert copper mines, beside the fire stains and the ruined furnaces and slag heaps, beside the ceramic fragments of crude broken crucibles and tuyères, and the remains of charcoal used to heat the ore to melting point, archaeologists have uncovered dust-dry rows of the copper workers' water jars and kitchen pots buried in the floors of the little huts that sheltered their sojourn in the desert.[13]

It is difficult today to overestimate the role that this dark-shining metal has played in shaping modern-day perceptions of ancient Egypt. To many historians, for example, 'great' pharaohs are those that left the most stone monuments behind them, 'weak' ones simply those that left the least; and a hidden but nevertheless essential factor in the making of such monuments was the availability of copper.[14] Ancient copper has shaped the public face, the standing monuments, of ancient Egypt. To that extent at least, that state's ability to mine and smelt the desert metal may be considered as an invisible index of the prosperity and power of different epochs of the ancient kingdom: and certainly during the Fourth Egyptian Dynasty, the dynasty of Khufu, more stone was cut with copper tools than in all the rest of ancient Egyptian history added up together.[15]

From the evidence of the surviving ancient slagheaps, it has been broadly estimated that throughout the three millennia of ancient Egyptian history, pharaoh's copper mines produced some 10,000 tons of metal, of which 8000 tons were mined in Sinai.[16] Now the splendid chisel found in Khufu's southern quarry weighs some 2 lb 3 oz (0.995 kg); a ton of copper would therefore provide a little over a thousand

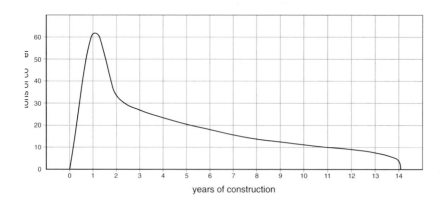

years of construction

Fig. 74 The annual tonnage of copper required to fashion the chisels used during the Great Pyramid's construction, estimated from the amounts of stone required for each year of working, as given in Appendix 5, table 2.

such tools.[17] As we have seen, however (p. 110 above), when working limestone, copper chisels crack and bend and quickly wear away. Allowing King Khufu's hard-worked quarrymen and masons an average of five such chisels for every year of working, we may roughly estimate that some 300,000 of these chisels were required to shape the Great Pyramid of Giza, with a combined weight of 290 tons of copper.[18]

This extraordinarily high use of copper during the century-long reigns of the three greatest pyramid-builders – Sneferu, Khufu and Khafre – and the huge growth in mining and smelting that must have accompanied it, had some remarkable consequences. During the last years of the Great Pyramid's construction, for example, around 8 tons of copper would have been actively employed by its craftsmen; at the beginning of the work, however, that figure would have been multiplied by a factor of eight. Some of the surviving chisels from the earlier phases of the work, therefore, could well have been resmelted to make Khufu's monstrous stone saw, which the building programme indicates could only have been put to sawing basalt pavement blocks after the bulk of construction work upon the Pyramid itself was finished.[19] In all likelihood, however, a great part of the redundant copper was stored just as it would have been after the bulk of the work of Sneferu's pyramids had been completed, so that the intensive work rates undertaken at the beginning of a new pyramid could have been supplied with sufficient copper tools at short notice.

What happened, then, to this store of copper when pyramids of such colossal size were no longer being built, and a dwindling royal workforce no longer required a vast mass of chisels? Whilst no written records remain to tell us, the monuments hold their own histories: after the great pyramids were finished at the ending of King Khufu's dynasty, the use of copper in ancient Egypt greatly changed. Whereas in the reigns of Sneferu and Khufu and Khafre the use of copper chisels was virtually restricted to the royal pyramids and their associated cemeteries, in later reigns sculpted tombs were increasingly built outside the royal cemeteries and in ever larger numbers.[20] During the Fifth and Sixth Dynasties there was an explosion in the manufacture of sculpture and reliefs all over Egypt, and thus an enormously increased availability of copper chisels. And sometimes, as the handiwork betrays, these tools were placed in the hands of inexperienced sculptors, ill educated in the manners of the craftsmen of the royal court.[21] It would appear, therefore, that this trend away from the orbit of the court cemeteries – which was accompanied by an increasingly elaborated vision of an afterlife – was occasioned by an outflowing of a mass of copper from the offices of pyramid making into the more generalised offices of local government; without the widespread availability of fine copper, after all, this multitude of provincial monuments could not have been made.

Whilst the first great pyramids were being built, however, before the state's copper resources were dispersed, it may be reasonably estimated that the bureaucracy of Khufu's dynasty oversaw the mining and smelting of some 950 tons of copper: about a tenth part of the entire copper production throughout ancient Egyptian history.[22] Yet only in the mountains of south-western Sinai, high above their ancient copper workings, was this vast metallurgical enterprise celebrated in inscriptions; in the desolate valley of the Wadi Maghara, King Sneferu's and Khufu's names and images once sat side by side.[23]

These inscriptions were once but a small part of many such advertisements carved on the cliffs of this most lonely place high above the copper miners' settlements; some forty-five similar scenes and masses of inscriptions are inadvertent testimonials to the central role of copper for the creation of the image of their millennial state.[24] And all of them were chiselled into the rich-red desert rock that to a prospector's eye betrays the presence of copper and other useful minerals.[25] Here then, in the dry canyon of the Wadi Maghara, at the place the Egyptians called the 'Terraces of Turquoise' for nodules of that bright blue stone were often found embedded close to the veins of copper ore, were the entrances to some of Egypt's most ancient mine shafts.

A hundred years ago, at the ending of Flinders Petrie's ground-breaking survey of the Sinai, many of these reliefs were cut away and sent to Cairo to save them from destruction at the hands of turquoise miners who had been using explosives to blast the mines and cliffs and in the process, sadly, had destroyed the better part of Khufu's images and inscriptions.[26] Nowadays this unique ancient site exists in the drawings and descriptions of early travellers like the indefatigable Richard Lepsius and a processional of English reverends diligently searching the Sinai for traces of Moses and the Exodus. Rare early photographs too, especially Petrie's fine pictures of the wadi and its surroundings, show something of the lost environment, with the royal inscriptions still standing in that great wide natural amphitheatre that, these early travellers tell, seemed to inhabit another time and place.[27] Even now, it is a splendid place, the surviving evidences of its ancient habitations a moving testimonial in a dangerous desert to the ancient state's millennial need for copper and for copper tools.

Khufu's Sinai inscriptions, so the early records show, were as reticent as all his other texts; little more than royal names with some accompanying epithets. Beside these spare inscriptions, however, were two well-made images of the king himself, drawn beside another of his father Sneferu, three in a row, in the age-old stance of conqueror, their arms and legs outstretched, clubbing on this particular occasion a handful of local people; 'whose faces seem to express satisfaction at the honour of perishing by the royal hand', as one of the old travellers put it, although in reality the heraldic scenes may celebrate the ancient Egyptians' temporary victory over the harsh desert as much as the defeat of a local population.[28]

Neither were these renderings of standard courtly poses merely provincial copies as you might expect, roughly made and far from civilisation. Many of them contained intelligent and innovative elements in their design only seen within the Nile Valley in monuments of far later ages. One of Khufu's smiting scenes, for example, contained the first known example of pharaoh wearing the Double Crown of Upper and Lower Egypt. This same scene also contained the first-known image of the god Thoth, the great numerator and calendar

Fig. 75 An early photograph of Khufu's rock inscriptions in the Wadi Maghara, Sinai, which were destroyed by turquoise miners at the beginning of the last century.

maker, in human form.[29] And all of this, as far as can be seen from the surviving photographs, was cut directly into the reddish sandstone in a robust and vivid manner, whilst underneath and all around these rock-cut images were the entrances to mines, horizontal shafts some 4 to 6 feet high and 100 feet and more in depth, cut deep into the darkness of the dull-red mountain, diligently following the veins of ore and opening on occasion into great high caves supported by unexcavated pillars of the natural rock. In 1869, E. H. Palmer, the most enthusiastic of the early European travellers to the Sinai, explored one of the deepest of these ancient mines, lighting his way with a smoky candle and stringing in the manner of Perseus, a large ball of cord from its entrance to serve as his guide. After walking some 400 feet through pitch darkness and clouds of screeching bats, he came across a wooden pit prop in a small side working; 'and there it stood, dry and brown enough certainly, but as perfect in shape as when it was first set up, perhaps before the Great Pyramid was built'.[30] At its height, in Khufu's day, as many as a thousand men may have worked these mines and smelted copper in these dark-red hills.[31]

Although not as rich as some of the other copper ore deposits in Egypt, the Sinai ores had the advantage of being easier to mine and more amenable to the crushing and sieving required for their reduction in the furnace.[32] So whilst the local turquoise, that most courtly stone used by the pharaonic jewellers centuries before King Khufu's day, seems to have been gathered up directly from these excavations and taken off to Egypt to be worked and polished, some of the copper ore at least was refined right on the spot, in the workmen's villages that run along the bottom of the wadi.[33] Close to Khufu's inscription and marked by a broad scattering of kitchen pottery dating from the time of the great pyramids lie the ruins of 120 small stone houses that, when Flinders Petrie excavated them a century ago, still had wood ash and domestic pottery in them.[34] In nearby settlements as well, along with quantities of flint and hard-stone pounders that could have been used to crush the copper ore, Petrie found hard evidence that the miners had smelted copper ore beside their huts: the modest furnaces and crude clay crucibles that had transformed the dusty ore into ingots of warmly gleaming metal to be carried north and west to Egypt and to the Nile and Giza.[35]

Apart from their constant need for water and provisions, these mining encampments required large amounts of fuel for copper smelting, and this would also have helped to warm the miners in the steely winter nights that are common in the high desert. The environmental analysis of other ancient smelting sites confirms the suspicion that life in Khufu's copper mines would have been not only wretched, consumed by heat and cold and hard work, but also poisonous; analyses of ancient copper slag heaps in deserts to the north of Sinai have found levels of residual heavy metals in the ground so high that they still pollute the sparse vegetation, and thus the local sheep and the health of those who eat their products.[36] Standing in this lonely valley you realise an essential difference between the ancient Egyptians and ourselves; whereas a modern artisan may think of copper as a cheap worldwide commodity and quite unsuitable for heavy work, King Khufu's masons fashioned their Great Pyramid with a rare and shining metal that they had transmuted in desert fire and at great cost, in a distant valley where the veins of ore were streaked and coloured on occasion by deep-blue azurite, by precious turquoise and the green malachite that some ancient Egyptians used as eye decoration.[37]

Twelve miles from the Wadi Maghara, along the mountaintop of the Serabit el-Khadim, stands a pretty temple of the goddess Hathor, Lady of Turquoise, who delighted, we are told, in jewellery and royal motherhood. A thousand years after Sneferu and Khufu, when the mine shafts of the Wadi Maghara had been worked out, Hathor was worshipped here as the deity of copper mines, her temple set up piecemeal at the order of later pyramid-building monarchs whose miners had worked at other sites close by.[38] Some of these kings, and many of their miners too, had set special store by Sneferu, King Khufu's father, whose administration had sent miners to the nearby Maghara centuries before them.[39] Whilst several of these monarchs, so their inscriptions say, were 'beloved of Sneferu', some of their miners and officials used King Sneferu's name as part of their own and boasted that things had not been done so well 'since Sneferu's time'. And they prayed for the protection of that most ancient king who, driven by the need for enormous quantities of chisels for his stone workers, had sent regiments of miners into these lonely mountains so that the first great pyramids could rise up fast and straight and true within the Valley of the Nile.

19 Aswan granite

At Aswan, at the southern end of Egypt, the slow wide Nile is squeezed through a dramatic granite gorge before settling back again into that most amiable river which runs into the Mediterranean. In ancient times, before dams and barrages were built to parcel out the river's

Fig. 76 The First Cataract of the Nile at Aswan, on ancient Egypt's southern border. The ancient town was set straight upon the granite outcrops in the Nile's stream. The granite quarries lie above the river in the desert; however, the ancient Egyptians may well have begun their harvest of the hard red stone by shaping boulders lying at the river's edge.

Fig. 77 An ancient granite quarry high above the river, which was reopened in the nineteenth century.

flood around the year, this granite cataract was a rushing 3 mile stretch of white water and dull-red boulders, of reeds, papyrus and small stony outcrops, the northernmost of which, the Isle of Elephantine, held a frontier town whose pretty ruin nowadays frames the modern town of Aswan that stands upon the river's eastern shore.[1]

In one of the first recorded uses of stone in all Egyptian architecture, some four centuries before King Khufu's Pyramid was built, blocks of Aswan granite had been used to pave a royal tomb.[2] At that same time too, a garrison was maintained at Elephantine; a barracks, a cemetery, some small temples, a palm-shaded palace for the administration and a four-square fortress whose mud-brick walls had been set straight upon the handsome granite boulders that have perhaps provided this island with its eponymous Greek name.[3] From this gorgeous outpost at the gates of central Africa, state officials had maintained an exotic border trade in ebony and ivory and leopard skins, and a courtly traffic too, in pretty blocks of local granites, pink and grey. The decision of Khufu's pyramid-planners, however, to construct the Great Pyramid's burial chamber entirely from colossal slabs of Aswan stone, transformed this frontier town and its granite gorge into the location of a colossal ancient industry whose waste, enormous drifts of dust and chippings, still lie for miles around.

Figs. 78 and 79 Although these cuttings were made a thousand years after the Great Pyramid was built, the techniques of granite working at Aswan had hardly changed, as the blocks in the Great Pyramid still testify. The shallow indentations on the top of the unfinished obelisk (left) are the marks of rows of heavy granite pounders worked day on day, by hand. The neat rows of indentations at the bottom of the trenches show the positions of lines of quarrymen labouring with similar pounders, standing side by side. These are forms and textures that iron and steel tools could never replicate: the rippling, glistening, pitted surface produced by bashing one hard stone against another; the gently wavering line of the edges of the quarried block.

Unlike Egyptian limestone that hardens and rings only after its exposure to the air, Aswan's granite resonates when you hit the matrix with your open palm, the sound seeming to bounce around inside the living rock like echoes in an auditorium. Metallic, tensile, springy, in King Khufu's day granite was the only material apart from imported beams of timber that could span roofs and doorways more than 6 or 7 feet wide. A hundred times harder than limestone, this sharp and shiny stone was shaped and shipped from Aswan at tremendous cost.

Copper chisels have little effect on blocks of Aswan granite, which has a structure like a sugar cube and is as hard as glass. Hitting granite with another piece of granite, however, or with a scrap of yet harder stone such as can be found in the Egyptian deserts, has the same effect as a rock hitting a car windscreen, rendering the shining stone to gritty powder. So the pyramid-makers worked the granite in that way, bruising the rock with heavy hard-stone pounders, slowly dissolving its surface and leaving, in the process, telltale rounded pits in the surface of the living rock where their continuous striking had shattered their way down through the stone.[4] At around an inch an hour, this painfully slow process, this constant hitting on a single spot, had the advantage of allowing a skilled worker with a good eye to exercise great accuracy of cut and slowly, very slowly, sculpt the granite.[5]

This is the elephantine technology that is precisely celebrated in ancient Egypt's granite sculpture. Unlike the limestone sculptor's copper chisels whose quick marks seem on occasion to be drawing in three dimensions, searching for the form within the stone, granite fosters an entirely different sensibility, the broad slow cut of pounding being better suited to describing the forms of a subject's surface rather than its underlying form, a process flattered by the fact that the texture of lightly polished granite, as the pounded stone is rubbed with granite dust or abrasive sand or powdered emery or quartz, reproduces that of human skin.[6] So granite sculptures were often burnished to a soft shine on the top of rounded forms like toes and shoulders, and left abraded in concave grooves that described pleated linen clothing or the furrowed features of a face. And at their ending, such works were often finished with sharp thin lines chiselled precisely along at the edge of broader forms of mouths and eyes and all those other passages in Egyptian sculpture that are so vital in imparting the essential quality of life to images of stone.[7]

Exactly the same process of bashing out, followed by abrasion and polishing, though without a fine finishing cut, also produced the lustrous shine and gently undulating surfaces of the finished faces of the granite building blocks used in Khufu's Pyramid. And as the ancient craftsmen often left the deepest marks of the stone's rough pounding untouched, these small rough pits peppering the faint scratches of the final finish, a dull and slightly textured shine, give the blocks a mottle unlike anything a modern machine can manufacture.

Most of the granite quarried by ancient Egyptians at Aswan was cut out from the granite ridges of the Cataract high above the river, from where the dull-red shafts of stone were slid like fat crocodiles, scrunching down the shallow slopes to the banks of the rushing river for embarkation and the journey north.[8] In those days, as the ancient cuttings in those bleak ravines still show, the quarrymen cut the matrix in a manner somewhat similar to that of limestone quarry workers, although far, far slower, and usually with a series of slow, wide vertical bashed-out cuts that could accommodate row upon row of quarryman through months of pounding.[9] In oven heat and sharp with pounded granite dust, such quarries must have been a purgatory.

As far as anyone can judge within the continuously diminishing landscapes of working quarries, these cuttings on the higher ridges of the granite were undertaken during later reigns than Khufu's. From the gentle marks of water erosion still to be seen on some of the unworked faces of the great long blocks inside the Great Pyramid,[10] it would appear that at the time of the Great Pyramid the Aswan stone gangs had simply squared up and shipped some of the great water-rounded boulders that lay beside the running water of the Cataract;[11] in fact a rough cartouche with Khufu's name can still be seen pecked into the granite of the Island of Sehel, a picturesque pile of rounded boulders and Nile silt to the south of Elephantine, at the very centre of the Cataract.[12] One day perhaps, amongst the thousands of inscriptions that cover the cliffs and boulders of the area and celebrate so many stone-gathering expeditions of the later pharaohs, we may also find a written trace of Khufu's quarrymen: the name of a scribe or supervisor perhaps, tapped lightly onto one of the enormous rounded boulders that stand reflectively along the water's edge.

Sixty of the largest stones shipped from Aswan for the Great Pyramid were used as supporting shafts in the complex of granite architecture that surrounds King Khufu's burial chamber, and these weigh about the same as the largest blocks of limestone used at the Pyramid: that is, around 55 tons each.[13] Even with the relative luxury of hard steel tools, modern stone workers estimate that extracting Aswan granite requires some ten times the workforce needed to quarry limestone,[14] and this figure is borne out by the numbers of people who worked upon extracting blocks of Aswan granite in later periods of pharaonic history.[15] To extract and shape the near 7500 tons of granite that appear to have been used inside the Great Pyramid – roughly the equivalent of 135 of its largest blocks – would have required a workforce at Aswan in Khufu's day of a size that it had never seen before.[16] As well as this vastly increased volume in quarrying at Aswan there was also a burning question concerning the speed of the work to be accomplished, for all the granite known to have been used inside the Great Pyramid had been set in place by the time that three quarters of its bulk was built.[17] Assuming that work in the granite quarries at Aswan proceeded at a constant rate, the granite shipped to Giza for use in the Pyramid's interior would have been shipped at a rate of 940 tons per annum until the eighth year of construction, when granite was no longer used.[18] At Aswan then, in those early years, it is reasonable to estimate that the royal garrison on its island fortress would have overseen a workforce of a hundred souls, engaged on cutting, hauling and shipping this series of enormous granite shafts to Giza.[19] Even after that, indeed, the remnants of Khufu's temples show that the red stone from the south was required for other purposes than pyramids, so that the same high levels of quarrymen working at Aswan may well have continued throughout King Khufu's reign.[20]

It is interesting to reflect that the plans of Khufu's pyramid-makers to use granite on such a scale must have been founded upon relative inexperience, for the stone seems to have been but little used in the reign of his father, Sneferu. Certainly, when Khufu came to the throne, granite building blocks had not been cut and used in any quantity since the time of King Djoser, a century and more before.[21] Nonetheless, the few granite objects cut in Sneferu's time that have survived, a few sarcophagi and statues, suggest that quarrying and collection of the stone had continued at Aswan during his reign, and this in turn suggests that some of the old quarry workings and loading quays could also have been used by Khufu's work gangs. Yet the huge amounts of granite required for the Great Pyramid would probably have meant that these previous arrangements would have been insufficient to the pyramid-makers' needs; that their inventiveness and sheer determination required the enlargement of those awful labours, so that the hard and shining stone from the very end of Egypt could be brought to house the body of the king.

20 Tura limestone

Not all the stone of Khufu's Pyramid was quarried from the Giza Plateau or shipped 400 miles from the south. Its fine white skin and all those parts of its interior built with exceptionally high levels of accuracy were made of blocks of especially fine limestone quarried

Fig. 80 Tura limestone on the Giza Plateau: fragments of the Great Pyramid's northern pavement and casing blocks, discovered by Colonel Howard Vyse (see fig. 11). This relatively soft limestone has sustained much damage by erosion and souvenir seekers. The Edgar brothers' photograph, however, shows the Tura blocks in relatively pristine condition; the solitary figure is a fellow worker, the American Dow Covington, who had undertaken their re-excavation.

from a series of low hills on the east bank of the Nile, in a district caught up now in the sprawling southern suburbs of greater Cairo and known as Tura, some 8 miles upstream from the Giza Plateau.[1] Greyer and somewhat colder in appearance than Giza limestone and with hardly any embedded fossils or other irregularity, Tura stone is milk-pure, even grained and softer and more regular, more serene as stoneworkers say, than the ample limestone of the Giza Plateau.

Each one of the Pyramid's three building stones therefore makes a distinctive contribution to the finished architecture. The local limestone whose generous rough-hewn quarry blocks form the Pyramid's bulk bears the careful marks of the setting masons' small flat finishing chisels in just those places where the craggy blocks have been precisely fitted to their neighbours. The Tura blocks upon the other hand, which were more carefully quarried and finished before their emplacement on the Pyramid, were used for its finished surfaces; for the four now-vanished faces and most of the interior architecture as well. Calm, matte and bland, the final finish of this smoothed limestone is quite different again from that of the surfaces of Aswan granite that glimmer at the centre of King Khufu's tomb.

Having been bashed laboriously down to size by the vertical cut of pounders and polished to a shine with their own dust, these blocks of shining granite seem slightly swollen, rubbery even, giving the impression that like the rocks of the Nile Cataract from which they were cut, they may have been shaped and smoothed by water. The finished surface of the Tura limestone, on the other hand, runs sharp, flat and thin towards each edge. The difference is a quality of time; whereas the precise flatness in the granite blocks was held in the decision to stop pounding at the surface to within the right quarter of an hour, the flatness of the Tura stone is the judgement of a moment, made usually in the course a series of rapid chisel blows across the surface. No wonder that, installed side by side inside the Pyramid, they appear as chalk and cheese.

We live now in mechanically made environments filled with perfectly flat surfaces and we are thus accustomed to such extraordinary levels of anonymous precision within our everyday environment. This was not the case, of course, within the ancient world where even pharaohs lived in palaces of mud brick; where some of the finest domestic pottery of King Khufu's reign, as it had been since far more ancient times, was still curved upon the bottom so that it would maintain its balance on irregular surfaces.[2] King Khufu's pyramidmakers, however, went to extraordinary lengths to achieve near-perfect flatness and precision in their architecture for the dead.

Fig. 81 Blocks of Tura limestone, part of the fine-worked casing blocks of one of the four small Giza pyramids built by Khufu's masons. A soft and even-textured stone, it allowed the swift creation of the smoothest surfaces and the tightest joints.

Without the aid of modern machinery it was a quality that was hard won and by a craftsman's hand. As fine as a lithography stone and fast to work, Tura limestone was a perfect medium in which to achieve such remarkable precision. Of Egypt's many different stones, in Tura limestone the builders of the Great Pyramid could conveniently draw lines and angles of great accuracy with their copper chisels and shape surfaces to extraordinary levels of exactitude, cutting and abrading when the occasion demanded, to within hundredths of an inch.[3] It was Tura limestone, then, that enabled Khufu's masons to produce a building of such perfection as the Great Pyramid of Giza, not only providing the facing of its four faces, but framing, marking and controlling every major element in its construction.

The Tura quarries, for example, provided the stone for the Great Step, that high white block at the very centre of the Pyramid whose placement had so amazed its nineteenth-century surveyors.[4] Tura blocks were also used right through the Pyramid's interior as well as for the external pavements and the huge corner stones that marked out the Pyramid's full size and provided the bench-marks that placed it in precise alignment and orientation. On rare occasions, Tura stone was also used as the substance of the pyramid itself, in some of the vaults of its interiors for example, and for the final critical courses of the pyramid itself, the blocks beneath the apex still showing the distinctive paler white of weathered Tura stone in contrast to the creamy

Fig. 82 The caverns of the Tura quarries show off the warmth and luminosity of their limestone, providing a hint of the colour and appearance of the Great Pyramid when it was freshly made: the antique quarry face in the shadowed area beside the ramp shows evidence of the pyramid-makers' method of cutting stone out block by block, in steps. The great loose mass of stone above, however, is the product of modern blasting.

brown weathering of the blocks of local Giza stone that lie beneath them (see fig. 199). Ultimately of course, the Pyramid's fine white sheath of Tura limestone proved to be the building's downfall, the stone for many a medieval mosque and wall being quarried directly from these fine casing blocks and leaving the Pyramid's core of rougher Giza limestone exposed to centuries of erosion.

In all, Tura's quarries supplied around 220,000 tons of stone to the Great Pyramid.[5] As demand for the fine stone remained fairly constant during the entire course of the Pyramid's construction, we may reasonably assume that the Tura workforce fluctuated at a similar rate to that of Giza's. Thus, the Tura quarries could have seen a permanent workforce of some 300 to 600 quarrymen in the early years, dropping to less than half that number towards the ending of the Great Pyramid's construction, numbers that at the very least may be doubled if the subsidiary supporting workforce, the water carriers, provisioners and chisel sharpeners, are taken into account, a figure that yet excludes those family members and other dependants who would probably have formed part of a permanent community within the Tura quarries.[6] Apart from the officials of the administration and the crews of the boats and barges who shipped the quarried stone to Giza – and it should be borne in mind that some of the blocks

Fig. 83 The evenness, the lack of blemish, of fine Tura limestone that made it a perfect medium for Khufu's finest craftsman also made it a preferred stone for the Great Pyramid's vast vaults, where consistency was a structural necessity. Exposed on the Pyramid's north face, these four great Tura blocks were set above the tiny entrance corridor to disperse the burden of the Pyramid above. Covered by a patina of wind-blown desert clay, part of the golden finish that glazes the best part of the Pyramid's modern exterior, the chiselled square containing Dr Lepsius' hieroglyphics is now barely visible at the vault's top, upon its right-hand side.

shipped from Tura were as massive as the granite beams of Khufu's burial chamber – we may reconstruct a royally subsidised village of around 1000 souls at Tura during the time of the Great Pyramid's construction.[7]

Unlike the Giza Plateau, where, judging by the dates of the tombs cut into the quarry walls, work had largely stopped in the main quarry at the end of Khufu's reign, at Tura, as at all quarries whose stone has remained in continuous demand, the rock faces have been cut and changed down through the ages. Tura indeed, whose very name seems to have descended from the ancient Egyptian, has been worked as a quarry now for at least 5000 years.[8] It is hardly surprising that there are few remaining traces of quarrying at Tura that appear to date from before the middle of the first millennium BC when the ever-increasing use of iron by the quarrymen gave birth to a brisker technology – a change of pace that has recently accelerated once again, with the use of dynamite to feed the nearby concrete manufactories. At the turn of the last century, however, tourists were still able to visit a series of enormous ancient caverns, great low arches cut into the Tura hills, which were regarded as one of the sights of Egypt. 'The quarries of the pyramids', so Baedeker advised, required a day's trip, a guide, a donkey and a candle.[9] In those days, before the last explosion in working Tura stone, it was possible to read inscriptions of pharaohs and officials who had ruled and quarried in later dynasties than Khufu's on Tura's cliffs, as well as the rocky scribblings of visiting Greeks and Romans. Earlier guidebooks than Baedeker's even record elaborate ancient reliefs cut into the quarry face, one image showing oxen pulling blocks of stone set on wooden sledges.[10]

Modern warfare appears to have inadvertently preserved a few at least of Tura's dark interiors, the ancient quarry workings deep inside the limestone hills offering shelter from foreign bombs and spying eyes. In 1940–42, troops of Montgomery's Eighth Army cleared some of these high caverns of their millennial bat guano, and doubtless at this same time of most of the surviving evidence of ancient quarry work.[11] Amongst the finds, although no date was ever ascertained for them, were 2½ inch (7.65 mm) ancient ropes made of twisted papyrus suitable for hauling the largest blocks.[12] It was also reported, although it seems hardly credible today, that pyramid-sized blocks of the fine white stone were found inside these quarries' caverns, lined up and marked and numbered and still sitting on the logs that would have rolled them to the riverside for shipping. After this military clearance, as the quarries were used as depots for top-secret radar, for army workshops, hospital supplies and ammunition, and finally, as Middle Eastern alliances changed, as Soviet missile stores, they are unlikely to have been altered. Outside, however, blasting and quarrying has continued inexorably in the surrounding hills, and this has largely devastated the ancient environment. Today, therefore, all that is apparent to the casual visitor are some rare lines of pointed chisel cuts drawn in the herring-bone patterns that are typical of ancient quarrymen, these usually found at the bottom of new-made cliffs, huge high dynamite-shattered voids that are almost as impressive as the ancient pyramids themselves.[13] And all of this is a quarter of an hour's slow drive down to the docks beside the river, a journey through a landscape so deep in fine-powdered stone that when you leave your car your foot falls as quietly as if it were upon the moon.

In Khufu's day, this soft white land had been a low plateau of gently rolling limestone hills covered in clinking flints. Eastwards, they rolled out and up towards the open desert; westwards, beyond the peasants' careful smallholdings far across the Nile's plain and over the gleaming river, stood the tremendous pyramids of Khufu's forebears, all of whom had also taken stone from these same quarries. In those days, before the quarries had bitten so deeply into that golden landscape, one may imagine Khufu's quarrymen worked far lower down and closer to the canals and quays that had been cut to take this soft white stone away on the obliging river, to Giza and the rising Pyramid.

21 The river

Despite the well-built desert tracks that serviced Khufu's quarries, metalled roads were scarce throughout antiquity; whatever the truth about its much-debated 'invention', the advent of the wheel had little economic impact in the ancient East. Water transport, boats, rafts and barges, was its main mover. And later too, despite Rome's much-sung highways, it still cost merchants more to cart their grain 75 miles along the road from the port of Ostia to Rome than it did to ship those same grain sacks from one end of the Empire to the other.[1] In Khufu's day as well, once the labour of quarrying a block of stone and loading it upon a barge had been accomplished, it mattered relatively little whether the journey was of 10 or 500 miles before the block was disembarked and hauled off to its building site.[2]

The Nile river itself was a main reason why there was never a single centralised metropolis in ancient Egypt; the riverside and its bordering fields, its farms and towns and temples, its palaces and the pyramid-builders' settlements were all part of a homogeneous state spread ribbon-like along its banks.[3] And of course the keys to this narrow kingdom were the boats and barges of the royal court, the fleets of state; and the construction of King Khufu's Pyramid was as dependent on this single artery as was the state itself.

In ancient Egypt, the Nile's omnipresence was an underlying fact of life. In the reign of Khufu too, as the five huge boat pits cut beside his Pyramid still testify, real Nile boats were thought to be a necessary part of pharaoh's burial and afterlife as well. In later ages too, images of boats, of skiffs and rafts and noble yachts, became a commonplace of funerary decorations, the notion of voyaging through the eternal realms one of the most powerful literary images of an afterlife where dying could be described as 'passing through the field of reeds', those Elysian Fields whose earthly equivalents fringed the banks of living Egypt.[4]

Contemporary evidence of the fleet used in the construction of the Great Pyramid is virtually non-existent. All that remains beyond the presence of the Tura stone and Aswan granite is held within the rough-drawn graffiti preserved at the centre of the Pyramid itself, on the blocks that make up the walls of the entresols, those small compartments that lay above King Khufu's burial chamber; those same texts indeed, that witness Khufu's name inside his Pyramid. Broad brushed with red ochre and a watery wash onto blocks of Tura limestone, some of these calligraphic hieroglyphics name three work gangs: 'Khufu is pure!', 'Khufu is bright!' and this – the sole allusion to the role of shipping in building the Great Pyramid – 'May the White Crown of Khufu strengthen the sailing!' Now, all those swift-drawn texts are of a similar size and quality of line and every one of them is contained upon one face of a single block of stone; that many of them are also upside down shows they were written before their blocks were tipped over into their final positions on the Pyramid.[5] These labels were drawn not upon a wall inside a pyramid but on the individual blocks of which these walls were built. The gang name that appears to be a short prayer for a good wind – 'May the White Crown of Khufu strengthen the sailing!' – further suggests that these tags were written whilst their blocks yet lay within the Tura quarries or were awaiting shipment on the eastern quays.

Here, then, are the names of three of the gangs who worked King Khufu's stone. What their texts do not tell us, however, is what task or tasks these gangs performed: were they quarrymen or loading crews or block haulers? And then again, although modern minds may separate such activities, we should not assume that this was also true in Khufu's day. Tura fine limestone, after all, is less than 5 per cent of the total amount of stone used in the Great Pyramid,[6] and work at the Tura quarries could well have been conducted in the manner of stone procurement expeditions to the Egyptian deserts which appear to have been self-contained, prospecting and quarrying the stone, and then delivering it to its final destination.[7] Perhaps the gangs that cut the blocks within the Tura quarries also hauled them down a track onto the loading quays, then took them off the boats beside the Giza Plateau and up onto the rising Pyramid: in truth, we have no record of how any of the work of building the Great Pyramid was organised.

At all events, by incorporating a prayer into their name, by asking for the power of Khufu's majesty to speed the stone boats on their way, the gang's very name, 'May the White Crown of Khufu strengthen the sailing', underlines the essential role of Khufu's fleets in building this great Pyramid. Here, we may imagine, there were squadrons of river boats and barges laden with building stone, materials and provisions, whose crews were versed in the millennial skills of riverine culture, who understood the currents and the winds and who were used to navigating the tricky shoals that moved each year, erratically on the Nile's flood.[8]

When all that is left are the Pyramid's dry stones, it is easy to forget the contemporary impact of this immense and lively industry that carried supplies and stone to Giza. The order of these boats, indeed, was echoed in the very order of the state itself: some of the titles even, in the tombs of Khufu's nobles, appear to derive from the bipartite order of a Nile boat crew, with its captain and two officers controlling two halves of a divided crew.[9] By the time of Khufu's grandson Menkaure, if not the time of Khufu, the entire pyramid-building workforce was similarly organised, the names of many of the work gangs in these two halves adopting such nautical names as 'prow', 'stern','starboard' and the like.[10] Thirteen centuries on, the workforce that made the royal tombs of the Valley of the Kings were still called 'the crew', and they too were divided into two halves: a 'left side' and a 'right side'.[11] Nor was this terminology merely another example of the use of nautical terms to lighten dull officialdom – though this evergreen cliché is also to be found in pharaoh's Egypt[12] – for the word 'side' was itself born of an ancient word designating the two sides of a boat and the two rows of oarsmen who sat 'left' and 'right', facing their two gang masters in the stern.[13]

We may be sure, of course, that this elemental riverine hierarchy was far older than the ancient Egyptian state; images of boats with two rowing crews and a single captain appear on pots and rock drawings a millennium before King Khufu's time.[14] Pyramid building, however, that supreme act of unification, seems to have tested and extended that archaic organising principle. Within a hundred years of the erection of the Great Pyramid, similar bi-partitions were operating within the ranks of the Egyptian priesthood which, like the pyramid-makers' workforces, were organised with terms taken from the order of ships' crews.[15] A little later too, the funerary texts of the Egyptian afterlife that employed the age-old image of a boat journeying through the celestial realms describe the dead king serving as a captain of two gangs, whilst the gods of Upper and Lower Egypt either crew the boat themselves or pull it along canal-fashion, with good stout tow ropes.[16] In similar fashion, the bipartite order of the Nile boats and the pyramid-builders' workforces also came to be reflected in the order of national government, with the two primary divisions of Upper and Lower Egypt being controlled by its own first ministers operating under the command of Captain Pharaoh.[17]

The earthly realities of these great armadas have been entirely lost. Unlike the courtly riverboats that were buried in great pits beside King Khufu's Pyramid – one of which, to international amazement, was excavated virtually intact in the 1950s[18] – not one of the Great Pyramid's stone-transport barges, which at the height of their employment may have required the services of 400 to 500 sailors, is known to have survived.[19] From later centuries, however, boat-building scenes and images of harbours and of ships in the decorations of tomb chapels are not uncommon and these give glimpses of traditional boatyards and a variety of river craft at work, whilst some rare scenes from later royal monuments even show some of the state's stone barges plying the river: low-sailing, square-fronted rugged-looking leviathans piled with huge loads, with their crews scuttling over their enormous decks and small altars set up on their prows to aid the journey.[20] Although the precise dimensions of these enormous boats are not recorded, the weights of the stones that they delivered give genuine account of their drafts and capabilities. Just as many of the imported blocks set in the Great Pyramid, for example, weigh upwards of 55 tons, others quarried and shipped in later ages weigh ten times that and more.[21] Nor should we assume that only one of these enormous blocks was transported at a time: one famous scene shows two pairs of decorated granite columns lashed together to the deck and sailing down to Memphis; another from the time of Hatshepsut pictures two 100 foot (30 m) granite obelisks lying side by side upon a barge set fair for Karnak Temple![22]

Such transports were necessarily enormous, their construction massive.[23] All have disappeared, although some of their timbers have survived, having been employed in much the same way that the wooden frames of broken Elizabethan galleons were occasionally reused in very different contexts.[24] Excavated at the sites of pyramids later than King Khufu's, both frames and planking from dismantled stone barges, great timber baulks, had been laid down like railway sleepers by the ancient builders to form the underpinnings of trackways on which the pyramid's stone blocks were hauled.[25]

Although this rare surviving evidence dates from seven and eight centuries after the Great Pyramid was finished, boat construction seems hardly to have changed for the best part of ancient Egyptian history: these huge barge timbers share their basic design with the more delicate examples recovered from the courtly sailing boat found in one of the Great Pyramid's five boat pits.[26] All these boats, therefore, were made according to a single simple principle of a smooth-bottomed boat without a keel, the cross-section of their hulls being a simple arc of about a third of a diameter of a circle. The lateral strength that such traditionally shaped stone barges would have required was provided, as their reused wooden timbers show, by a massive long straight beam, a so-called keelson, that was set halfway between the deck and the bottom of the boat, and ran from bow to stern. The blocks of building stone were laid upon a massive timber deck, supported by a series of enormous solid transoms made of baulks of jointed timber, set up inside the hull. That these massive transoms also accommodated the central keelson made for a very solid ship.[27]

As was usual with Egyptian wooden boats, the planks and frames of these enormous barges were secured with hardly any nails or pegs, each of their great timbers being lashed to its neighbour with rope similar to that used for stone haulage, although here set carefully into the timbers in deep-cut mortices, a technique that, when the lashings were water-tightened, was capable of sustaining massive loads.[28] That this too was a traditional technique of Egyptian wooden boat construction is emphasised by the term used in later texts to describe the general activity of boat building; for the ancient Egyptians 'sewed' rather than 'built' their boats.[29] These boat-sewers, however, were also expert and ingenious carpenters, shaping each separate piece of wood to exploit its individual qualities in the same way that the stone workers shaped each block according to its grain. Growing in a country whose slight alluvial soil could not support the growth of long straight trees, the native Egyptian wood stocks – acacias, tamarisks, sycamores and jujubes – were gnarled and bent. Such species, however, make hard tough timber and in Khufu's time the Nile Valley supported far larger quantities of them than are to be seen today.[30] The technique of shaping each and every piece of wood according to its individual shape and strength has resulted in the surviving planks of dismembered barges resembling the intricately interlocking pieces of an enormous jigsaw puzzle.

The construction of such massive vessels as Khufu's stone barges would have involved not only the gathering of large amounts of native timber and resources, but extensive foreign trade as well, for in all the ancient East only cedar wood grew to a sufficient size and bulk to form the mighty keelsons and the other long timbers that these stone barges required.[31] And cedars, as every Bible-reader knows, grew in ancient Syria and in the Lebanon. Nor was Solomon the only ancient ruler who used this fabled wood for building. Cedar was the only wood available to ancient Egyptian builders suitable for use as large-scale construction timber and for the long levers that would have enabled stone-setting gangs to move blocks of stone. Two of Sneferu's pyramids indeed still have baulks of ancient cedar supporting parts of their interiors; here, we may imagine, the wood workers used to handling such precious beams could have been drawn from pharaoh's boatyards.[32]

Not surprisingly, the Egyptians had established trade routes to the cedar forests to the north long before the age of Khufu, surviving fragments from some desert graves showing that prehistoric Egyptians had also treasured and traded this darkly aromatic wood, whilst some of the subterranean burial chambers of kings who ruled centuries before Khufu's time were built from enormous baulks of this same imported timber whose desiccate remains still stain the desert cemeteries to this day.[33] This trade, therefore, between ancient Egypt and the Lebanon was millennial and immense.[34] Some 14 tons of this imported timber, so Cheryl Ward has estimated, was required to build the small fleet of funerary boats that has been recently discovered in one of these earliest royal cemeteries of Egypt.[35]

Few traces of this exotic traffic have survived from Khufu's time beyond a rough sketch of a riverboat drawn beside what might be King Khufu's name, upon a cliff in Upper Egypt,[36] and a rare surviving fragment of the state annals from the days of his father, telling of the arrival of forty shiploads of imported cedar, part of which appears to have been used for boats and part for doorframes in King Sneferu's palace.[37] Other than the circumstantial evidence at the Great Pyramid itself – where a variety of marks appear to betray the one-time presence of extensive wooden scaffolding[38] – we know little of the visits of Egyptians to the cedar forests during Khufu's reign beyond the presence of a copper axe-head found in a river bed close to Syrian Byblos, inscribed with the names of Khufu and a boat crew; this perhaps an inadvertent record of a trading mission, for the port of Byblos was used by ancient Egyptians to gain access to the mountain forests of the interior and their famous groves of cedar trees. That fragments of

Fig. 84 The Nile boat recovered and most beautifully restored, found in 1954 in one of the Great Pyramid's five boat pits. No stone transport, but a regal yacht whose elegance shows the sophistication of King Khufu's shipwrights and the skills held within the workforce that maintained and built the fleets of royal transports which supplied the pyramid-makers with material and provisions.

an alabaster jar inscribed with Khufu's name have been found in Byblos' seaside temples, along with pieces of other vases inscribed with the names of earlier and later pharaohs, suggests that these are the debris of Egyptian gifts or offerings, sent with various pharaonic expeditions, to aid their progress to the mountainsides on which the cedar forests grew.[39]

The most eloquent witnesses to this international traffic, however, are the dismantled planks of Khufu's yacht found in one of the Giza boat pits close to the Great Pyramid, the fine carpentry of these cedar beams and planks self-evidently the product of a long tradition of design in this exotic material.[40] Nearly 140 feet (42 m) in length, Khufu's pleasure boat is composed of 650 major elements all lashed together with a mile of rope. At an estimated 40 tons, its displacement demonstrates that even this slender and most courtly vessel, one of the surviving wonders of the ancient world, would have been capable of transporting several of Tura's quarry blocks to Giza. Those great stones, however, would have bruised and split the boat's fine decks, whilst its high-set prow and stern would have rendered it dangerously unstable under such a load. This pleasure yacht also entirely lacks a keelson to provide the necessary strength and lower its centre of gravity. Better then to conjure the living reality of Khufu's stone barges from the ancient images of later dynasties.[41]

One thing is certain about King Khufu's ghostly fleets, as we have already seen; riding low in the water with their titanic loads, such stone barges could never have sailed over Egypt's flooded fields, which were under but a few feet of water. And that is why the pyramid-builders were forced to cut canals from Tura to the Nile, and from the Nile again to the edge of the Giza Plateau, with harbour facilities and handling ramps to manage the loading and unloading of the stone.

Even with this net of waterways and harbours, Nile sailing varied greatly throughout the three seasons of the Egyptian year. In summer, a speedy north wind drove the stone barges quickly up the river to Aswan, from where they could ride back north again to Giza on the strong tide of the rising flood. Winter and spring, however, were comparatively slow times for sailing, when the river's flow was gentler and its winds were less. Then the boat crews would walk the Nile-side footpaths, using long cables to haul the barge against the

Fig. 85 The inundation of the Nile, seen from the Great Pyramid in the early 1920s. Khufu's Giza harbours were probably located in the middle distance of this photograph, close by the waters of the receding inundation. The easiest route for stone haulers bringing blocks up from the valley and the ancient harbours to the Pyramid runs up the side of the sandy valley lying beyond the row of small, as yet unexcavated, pyramids.

current just as the gods would later aid the passage of the dead king's boat through the darkness of the underworld. When the construction of the Great Pyramid was underway, this traffic was particularly intense: nearly 300,000 tons of stone was shipped to Giza in that time, as well as the copious provisions and supplies required to maintain the workers at the Pyramid and the other workers too, the miners and quarrymen employed from one end of Egypt to the other. And all of this was carried on the wide stream of the Nile.

Assuming that the largest of Khufu's stone barges carried but a single 50 ton block with other smaller blocks as complement, the necessary traffic from Aswan sailing north to Giza would have engaged the services of two great vessels for a full six years of building, after which time all the granite presently inside the Pyramid could have been delivered.[42] Tura limestone, on the other hand, was used throughout all stages of the Great Pyramid's construction and in a wide variety of sizes, and thus shipping would have continued throughout the Pyramid's construction.[43] We may therefore estimate that for the full fourteen years of the Great Pyramid's construction some fifty small-sized transports could have been in constant employment carrying loads of 20 tons or so, to and fro from Tura to the rising Pyramid, whilst the two larger vessels that usually served the Aswan quarry could have taken turn occasionally, to ship the great blocks that the smaller vessels could not handle. All in all, this constant river traffic would have employed some 1750 people and would, of course, have entailed considerable support from other trades and professions as well as the maintenance of the sailors' and bargees' settlements.[44] In the manner of all sailors, however, these homes would have been visited erratically – a round trip from the Giza Plateau to Aswan could have been of thirty days' duration. The brisker traffic from Tura on the other hand could have been accomplished in a single day, providing that the supplications of Khufu's work gangs had been answered, and the sails of the cedar stone barges had filled with a generous wind.

22 The Giza ramps

What then awaited these ancient freighters when they arrived at Giza? As we have already seen, most of our reconstructions of the building of the Great Pyramid are but versions of those same elements that the Victorians had juggled so effectively in the exploitation of their empire, with an educated noble caste governing a rural workforce whose presence at the Pyramid was dictated by the demands of the agricultural year, and with 'problems' such as the moving of stone onto the Pyramid fitted out with standardised 'solutions' similar to those that Henry Ford designed for his production lines; an impoverished vision then, of ant-like lines of nameless peasants under the control of an alien administrative caste.

What, in reality, would have greeted the crews of Khufu's stone barges as they hove in to the canals and quays of Giza? By itself alone, the Great Pyramid shows that the era in which it was erected was one of unparalleled innovation in ancient Egyptian history.[1] So, before assuming that the Great Pyramid's construction was but one version of a long line of similar work at similar pyramids, just another banal product of a quasi-eternal government staffed by titles culled from cemeteries, we should re-examine the contemporary evidence. For although there is but precious little information other than the Pyramid itself and the landscape in which it stands, fresh studies of those two elements alone have been sufficient to enable us to break away from such stale visions. In the last few decades indeed, archaeologists have partly solved the mystery of how this Pyramid was built.

The overwhelming imperative, of course, is to explain how such enormous quantities of stone were laid so accurately and in such a relatively short time span. These are the brutal facts: nearly 5½ million tons of rock were quarried and carried up onto the Giza Plateau during the reign of Khufu, a process that, at the same rate of construction as his father's largest pyramid was built, would have been accomplished, as we have seen, in fourteen years.[2] At these rates of working, so the mathematics demand, during the first year of its construction, around five of the Great Pyramid's standard 2½ ton building blocks must have been set in place upon the Pyramid every second minute of each and every working day; that is, with a nominal ten-hour day and working some three hundred days in the year. And all of this, of course, accomplished within the exacting parameters of the Great Pyramid's near-perfect architecture. What awaited those fleets of barges as they docked at Giza was clouds of dust and industry and a kind of careful organisation.

Of this too, we may be sure; the Great Pyramid's builders had at their disposal the same technology of ramps and roads and ropes that the quarry workers had used to move the Pyramid's stone blocks out of the desert quarries, down to the riverside and up onto the royal barges.

Egyptian deserts still hold some of the ramps and trackways that aided the progress of the quarried stone onto the Nile barges.[3] A few rare pictures too, from later ages of Egyptian history, show gangs of men engaged in moving heavy stones and statues, and they are drawn, so modern calculations show, with a fidelity to life.[4] Recent excavations at Giza and at the sites of other pyramids have also uncovered the remains of some of their construction ramps. Made of mud and brick and stone, some of them have been found still in position against the sides of pyramids.[5] Just as the ancient pictures show, the simple machine of muddy rampways generously slicked with water are so efficient that small crews of workmen could move many times their own weight up long sloping ramps; just ten men with skill, strong ropes and a lot of lubricating water could have delivered one of the Pyramid's standard building blocks up onto the rising Pyramid.[6]

It has long been known, of course, that similar ramps were used in major building projects in later periods of ancient Egyptian history as the tomb-paintings have shown; a schoolbook papyrus even provides a ready reckoner by which the volume of such ramps may be calculated, whilst the impressive remains of a well-built ramp are still to be seen standing up against the First Pylon of the Karnak Temple.[7] Following the discoveries of building ramps at pyramids, some of which are older than the Great Pyramid at Giza, it was recognised that the remains of two enormous well-made battered walls that had been excavated in the 1970s, and which stand to the south of the Great Pyramid, had not marked some kind of ancient boundary as had previously been proposed, but were in fact the retaining buttresses of a vast ramp that had been built for the delivery of building blocks to some of the great tombs of Khufu's cemeteries.[8] Filled with assorted building debris – which included some plaster sealings bearing Khufu's name[9] – and with its two rough stone walls held by a cement whose high sand content would have ensured that, although more brittle than contemporary mud brick, the mortar would dry as a hard unyielding cement, such a ramp as this could have carried rock up onto the Great Pyramid itself. A few years ago, indeed, the scanty traces of what appears to be the base of a similar construction were found still in place, at the Pyramid's south-western corner.[10]

At first glance, it may seem unlikely, mysterious even, that such simple means as these mud ramps enabled the construction of one of the Wonders of the World. This, however, is because the modern world has largely lost the lively skills that such structures demanded of their workers. In money economies as well, where mass communal enterprise has been abandoned in favour of mass-produced machinery, such methods appear to be uneconomic and therefore impractical. Until quite recently, as the collections of the great museums of the West so amply testify, gangs of Egyptian farmers who were quite unskilled in such labours moved large ancient sculptures across Egyptian deserts and down through their fields to the Nile for their shipment off to Europe. And although this work was not necessarily conducted in the ancient ways, it was certainly accomplished with the employment of what some wiser Western heads discerned was an extraordinary sense of balance and rhythm, of community and trust in one another, and a deal of ingenuity and prayer. It is no longer necessary, therefore, to resort to the eccentric imaginings of modern theorists; 'you see, with only a cork, a whistle and a gas balloon the Egyptians could have . . .'

That the Great Pyramid's near 2½ million blocks of stone were moved accurately into position in the reign of Khufu is surely beyond dispute. That they were delivered up on the rising Pyramid using the same technology of ramps and trackways that had earlier been

Fig. 86 The two walls of a stone-hauling ramp built on the Great Pyramid's east side. Emptied of its fill by archaeologists, who found plaster sealings bearing Khufu's name within its debris, the ramp's two walls run straight towards the pyramids and mastabas of Khufu's family and courtiers.

Fig. 87 One of the battered walls of the stone-hauling ramp built upon the east side of King Khufu's Pyramid. The tip of Khafre's pyramid appears behind it.

employed to move the same stones out of their quarries is so rational, so simple an explanation, that to propose a different solution without the merest hint of proof seems as unnecessary as attempting to prove that the Industrial Revolution was inspired by Martians.

What awaited the stone barges at the Giza docksides year on year was an extension, a conflated mirror image, of the methods used by Khufu's various quarry masters all over Egypt. And just as they only chose to extract their blocks from locations from which the stone could be taken from the quarry and slid down ramps and roadways to the riverside, so too at Giza the same imperatives dictated the progress of those same blocks in their journey from the quayside up onto the rising Pyramid. Khufu's Giza Plateau was no generic building site, no archaic production line staffed by faceless labourers, but a series of separate and individual workspaces catering for the real-life topography of that Plateau. And this it was, in all its snagging, nagging detail, that forced the stone handlers and ramp makers to devise ingenious routes by which the quarried blocks could be glided smoothly up onto the rising Pyramid on slipways that over the span of the Pyramid's construction had to be continuously modified, demolished and rebuilt to reach the ever-changing, ever-diminishing building site atop the ever-rising Pyramid. The broad answer, therefore, to the question of how the Great Pyramid was built is held within the detail of the ancient landscape in which the Pyramid was set, and in the detail too of the architecture within the rising Pyramid.

Now Giza's three great pyramids, so modern geologists observe, stand upon a single firm foundation, a stone plateau formed by a gentle upturn in one of the great limestone formations in which the prehistoric Nile once cut its valley.[11] Sloping gently south, the Plateau runs down into the same broad valley where Khufu's pyramid-makers sited their largest quarry.[12] Beyond the quarry to the south, the other side of this sandy valley is bordered by a rocky outcrop similar to that on which the Great Pyramid stands; this, another element of the limestone formations that make up the Nile Valley but with a composition far less stable than the Pyramid's Plateau, is made up of spongy shales and varied streaky beds of fossils and brittle limestones that could never have supported a row of mighty pyramids. This outcrop, however, named the Heit el-Gurob, the Hill of Crows, presumably from the soaring flocks that glide around it in eddies of hot air, provides a perfect view of the quarries and the long slope up to the Great Pyramid.[13] From its highest point, a windy headland high above the sandy valley Khufu's builders could have taken in the entire orbit of

Fig. 88 The Heit el-Gurob, the Hill of Crows, whose heights command an overview of the entire Plateau of Giza. Its shales have long been mined by local farmers, who use it as a fertiliser; when soaked in water, these oily, slippery shales would also have provided perfect trackways for Khufu's stone-hauling ramps. The structures underneath the peak are the tombs of a modern cemetery.

their ambitions, from the distant Nile shining in the sun, to the harbour and canals at the bottom of the sandy valley to the crest of the Giza Plateau where they planned a pyramid would stand. From here too, as the Great Pyramid rose before them, they could have planned and controlled its various supply lines as if they were working from a map (see also, figs. 54 and 89).[14]

That, in essence, was a fundamental revelation of a group of archaeologists undertaking a geological survey of Giza during the

Fig. 89 The Giza Plateau from the Heit el-Gurob.

1970s and 1980s as part of a joint Egyptian/American project for the conservation of the Sphinx.[15] For the first time since Petrie's day, the Giza Plateau had been seen in all its detail as a place of process, rather than as plinth for monuments or a happy hunting ground for archaeologists. This it was that changed the traditional question, 'how did such primitive people ever manage to make such a thing?' to 'how can you move big blocks of stone across this piece of land and up onto that Pyramid?'

The identification of the local quarry from which, in all probability, the bulk of the Great Pyramid's stone was taken was of course a second revelation. Although geologists had long known that the greater part of the Great Pyramid's stone was identical to the rock of the Plateau on which it stood,[16] no one had recognised the size of the buried quarry that lay in the sandy wadi south of the Great Pyramid. Now, however, through a series of judicious probings and careful observations, a number of half-buried disparate quarry workings were all seen to be parts of a single quarry, an enormous low and roughly rectangular excavation 100 feet deep, half a mile wide and more than three quarters of a mile long, a hole whose volume, by itself alone, could have supplied all the stone of the Great Pyramid.[17] The quarry wall that was closest to the Great Pyramid even seemed to have sections of what may have been a ramp remaining, part of the route along which the quarried stone had been taken up onto the Pyramid Plateau. At all events, this previously overlooked quarry was a vital clue in a proper understanding of how the Great Pyramid had been built. For once the source of 95 per cent of its building blocks had been identified, the broad outlines of their route up to the Pyramid could be established.

Imagine the scene that greeted the first boats docked at the Giza quays, as building was beginning. High above the wide green valley on the empty Plateau, masons and labourers are engaged in levelling the top of the sloping Plateau to accommodate the Great Pyramid's first courses. To the south, and in the side of the broad sandy valley, another workforce is clearing the desert and opening up the Pyramid's main quarry. Soon, streams of stone barges will arrive whose cargoes will require firm docksides and unloading ramps and a swift access to the ramps and tracks that must be put down to give access to the rising Pyramid. How, then, were the exigencies of stone hauling tailored to the unforgiving 125 foot (38 m) rise up to the Plateau?

From the headland on the Hill of Crows, the Heit el-Gurob, you may see that in the area of the Western Desert behind the site of the intended Pyramid, there is but sand and rock sloping up and away into the shimmering Sahara. No easy means of access there from Nile-side canals nor from Khufu's quarry. By the tenth year of Khufu's reign indeed, when the building ramps would have been reaching high up to the Pyramid and were therefore massive and extended structures,[18] some of the tombs of Khufu's nobles were being built upon this western hillside, and therefore no high ramp could have stood there.[19] To the north and east of the site of the Great Pyramid upon the other hand, sheer limestone cliffs, the Plateau's escarpment, dropped straight down into the lively marshes of the Nile's valley, denying any access to the Pyramid Plateau unless of course an enormous ramp was built along the line of the processional way that was built later in King Khufu's reign to join his Pyramid's two temples.[20] But such a ramp, a titanic undertaking in itself, would only have delivered the stone to the Pyramid's foot, for there is no room here, between the Pyramid and the cliff, in which to fit a ramp of sufficient size to rise up to the top of the Great Pyramid. In any case such a hypothetical stone-hauling ramp could only have served to deliver the stone shipped into the Pyramid's harbour, for these cliffs are a considerable distance from the main quarry to the south.[21] Better, therefore, than hauling the Giza quarry blocks for miles back into the Valley to reach the ending of this hypothetical ramp would have been to have built a single ramp rising from the south, to run directly from the quarry up onto the rising Pyramid. And this ramp too would have been convenient of access for the blocks shipped into the Giza harbour, which stood in all probability somewhere at the ending of the same sandy valley in which the quarry had been cut.

Whether you were employing dumper trucks or gangs of men with ropes, the lie of the land permits but this single route by which all of

Fig. 90 A rampway running out of Khufu's quarry. Until the coming of the archaeologists, this area of the quarry was buried in construction debris that was a product, it appears, of the construction of King Khafre's pyramid, which stands above the quarry and its tombs.

Fig. 91 The grey line of the modern tarmac road that runs down from the Great Pyramid to the Sphinx may partly cover an ancient stone-hauling ramp that, as old photographs from the last century show (cf. fig. 92), was some 20 feet in width and ran up and over the now-demolished edges of the quarry face.

Fig. 92 Taken in 1910, this photograph shows an ancient rampway running up from Khufu's quarry and onto the Plateau. This, in all probability, was one of the routes by which the stone shipped into Giza from Khufu's other quarries was taken up from the harbours at the edges of the cultivation to join the ramps that ran up from the desert quarry.

the Pyramid's stone blocks, those quarried at Giza and those shipped to its harbour, could gain access to the rising Pyramid, and this is from the south. Here, it appears, a series of paths and ramps provided access to the main avenue of ascent onto the Pyramid, a single high ramp that rose up the sandy valley. It is likely then that the modern road that runs up from the line of harbour temples, on past the Sphinx up to the Pyramid Plateau, is built upon part of a stone hauling ramp that ran from the harbour to the Plateau and served for the transportation of imported stone. Once upon the Plateau, in Khufu's day, this subsidiary ramp would then have joined others running from the quarry, all of them serving the central ramp that ran right up onto the rising Pyramid.

It is improbable, given the constantly changing shape of both the Pyramid and its quarry, that there was ever a single set solution to the problem of delivering stone up onto King Khufu's Pyramid. Rather, we should imagine a variety of interlinking ramps and walk-ways that were continuously adapted in their forms and shapes as the quarry was worked out and the Pyramid grew ever higher. For the later years of its construction, however, there was probably a single central ramp built up higher and longer that rested on the Pyramid's south face, a gigantic sloping walkway held, as the surviving examples show, between two rough stone walls cemented with clay mortar and packed with rock and dust and chippings from the ongoing work, and in the same position as the faint traces of the ruined structures found recently at the south-west corner of the Pyramid.[22]

And running up to the base of this vast ramp from all around the valley, an ever-changing network of supply, sucking stone from the Giza quarry and stone and supplies from the harbour down below. And all around the works, white-ribbon pathways ran west and south across the yellow desert, joining the harbour to the quarry and the settlements and workshops and ovens and food stores and pottery kilns and all the other parts of this city in the desert: its palace and the offices of the Pyramid bureaucracy, the dwellings of the gangs and of their masters and the stone-barge captains and their crews, the houses of the workers, the hauling gangs and foremen, the quarry-men and the stone setters who worked each day upon the Pyramid, and of the gypsum burners and copper smiths and the ramp makers and water carriers, and the butchers and bakers and cooks and potters and laundry men and donkey wranglers, and their donkeys, too. And all these smaller ramps and trackways changed angle and direction as the form of the main ramp changed with the rising Pyramid.[23]

As to what has happened to the substance of these multifarious constructions, some of them clearly enormous structures in their own right, and one of them at least built to support multitudes of men hauling millions of tons of rock hundreds of feet into the air – and bigger therefore, in its own right, than most of the other pyramids of Egypt – the answer is contained in the solution of another long-time mystery connected to the Great Pyramid: the location of the Pyramid's major quarry. For when the last stones of the Pyramid were emplaced and the work of fine-finishing its outer casing was completed, the area around the finished Pyramid was landscaped: this building site was cleared and levelled, the residue of dust and chipping from the stone gangs' work upon the Pyramid, the stone-hauling ramps themselves, the pyramid-makers' villages and stores and workshops all were demolished, leaving the fresh new Pyramid, high and white and utterly inaccessible upon a perfect straight horizon.

Vast amounts of debris from this remodelling were tipped off the cliffs to the north of the Pyramid, burying the limestone cliffs in a gigantic scree of rubble, and this was graded horizontally, extending the baseline on which the Pyramid stood. At the same time, Khufu's enormous quarry to the south was filled with this same building rubble, and here too it was graded so carefully, fitted over and around the Plateau's gentle slope, that the best part of the buried quarries remained invisible for four and a half thousand years.

So successful was this titanic clean-up, this redistribution of hundreds of thousands of tons of chip and mud and mortar, that even Petrie's eagle eye was unable to determine what had taken place.[24] Even though he rummaged deep into the great long screes of debris on the north side of the Plateau,[25] even though he describes a buried mass of chippings on the flat plain to the south, he never appreciated the vast scale of the last labours of King Khufu's pyramid-makers, those careful modifications to the natural landscape of the Giza Plateau that left his Pyramid standing on a long and straight horizon.

The great quarry ramp, therefore, had provided the route of its own destruction, its demolishers simply having to carry its rubble as they demolished it, back down into the quarry. Beautifully layered now, by the methodical dumping of this ancient debris, much of this remaining debris still fills parts of King Khufu's quarry, an archaeological treasure trove of minute information awaiting examination.[26] Strata of demolished dwellings, the broken fragments of the pyramid-makers' work and lives; stone pounders and rope and fibres and the ubiquitous shaped flints and pounders; sherds from their pots and bowls and other domestic rubbish too, and indeed their very excrement to tell us what they ate (see fig. 93). And layered over some of this was a great part of that enormous mass of sand and rock and dust and chipping that once packed the space between the buttresses of the Pyramid's building ramps. And threaded through this mass, along with the rough rocks and mortar of the ramp's high walls, are livid streaks of a fine grey band of hard-dried mud, the remains of a khaki-coloured clayey marl that egyptologists and Egyptian farmers now call *taffla*, an element that is not native to the Giza Plateau but was brought there for a single purpose. For when this shaley rock is touched by water, it dissolves into an oily, light and slick and highly slippery mud: a perfect lubrication for sliding Khufu's building stone up onto the rising Pyramid.[27]

These, then, are the broad outlines of the method of the Great Pyramid's construction. The old restorations that blunted the Great Pyramid's familiar silhouette and decorated its stump with geometric and symmetric ramps served by thousands of ant-like robots

Fig. 93 A section through the debris in King Khufu's quarry, cut in the first half of the last century by archaeologists searching for buried tombs. Though heavily eroded, at least three separate strata are visible in this photograph. Some of these appear to hold little but stone-working debris, yet rainwater has washed fragments of domestic pottery out of others, along with worked flint and animal bones, whilst the sooty stones that are still embedded in the cut, some of which have been roughly worked with picks or chisels, suggest that parts of this section are the products of the demolition of ancient hearths and habitations. Though some of this material was deposited centuries after the construction of the Great Pyramid, similar deposits from the time of Khufu have been identified around the Giza Plateau, although few of them have yet been excavated.

working to what are essentially modern engineering specifications, simply re-created what Coleridge in a nicely hermetic turn of phrase once called 'a serpent with its tail caught in its mouth'; a 'great grand self-fulfilling tautology'; a modern answer to a modern question.[28] Self-evidently, Khufu's monument is something more than the residue of mindless labour and a bureaucracy of manufacture and supply.

The necessary near-continuous redesign of the Pyramid's stone ramps as the structure rose into the air is an apt metaphor for this entire project. These early groundbreaking pyramids of which the Great Pyramid was the climax required a regime of continuous invention in almost every aspect of their manufacture[29] – something that is emphasised by the fact that every one of Giza's eleven known pyramids appears to have a different internal structure! At the same time, the Great Pyramid's near-perfection speaks of close management, of an overall architectural control working inch by inch, day by day, year on year on every aspect of its architecture: the very geometry of a pyramid, that most simple form, was an ideal structure over which to exercise such a level of control that today would be dubbed as 'micro management'.[30] Without the use of modern surveying equipment, this control was maintained by eye and touch, and that would have required but a single short line of command. Just as the Great Pyramid was the fruit of a practical tradition of stone block building, and not therefore conceived in the manner of modern architectural or engineering projects, so the modern conception of its construction being supervised by architects and surveyors hardly fits the work in hand. We might, in fact, imagine that large numbers of the workforce were able to bring various levels of inventiveness and skill to their work, and that, far from being as disruptive as this would be in an industrial environment, this process of continuous invention was in fact essential to the phenomenal achievement of building the Great Pyramid.

Part parallel, perhaps, may be found in the construction of enormous, virtually hand-made dams in Mao's China where the workers appear to have operated inside similar frameworks of control. Another example, and often quoted as such, is the building of the European medieval cathedrals, these (so it has often been asserted) having been erected with a mix of prayer and pragmatism and high levels of individual creativity, yet at the same time with an anonymity of creativity that is completely different from later periods of European history.[31] These two visions may stand as antidotes to the usual assumption that the building of the Great Pyramid was a non-creative process, like that of ancient Rome whose labour pool was gathered from diverse cultures with no common cultural heritage. Although the construction of the Great Pyramid was doubtless hard and fast and very dangerous, at the same time the integrity of its architecture holds a level of individual responsibility, a care, beyond that which is usually obtained by tight controls or brute coercion.

23 Coda: the commanding landscape

There is a popular belief that the ancient Egyptians employed extensive artificial irrigation systems. It is not true. Ancient Egypt was supported by a passive system in a bountiful environment. Overflowing at the summer's ending onto the valley's bone-hard soil, the Nile's flood lay like sheets of shining glass upon the withered fields and farmers simply trapped its water behind embankments made of mud. And even though Egypt has no rainfall to sustain the crops the farmers planted in these watery basins, the residual moisture levels in the fields and the valley's natural water table enabled the annual harvest to mature to sweetness beneath a fearful sun months after the floodwater had receded.[1] Apart from those rare times when the annual inundation failed, this valley was a paradise, a Hesperidian oasis as inevitably providential as the progress of the great slow silent river moving through its centre.

Even in the desiccating deserts, beyond the Nile-side fields, nothing seemed to perish. From the moist fertility of its soil to this preserving desert, everything appeared as ordered and immutable. The wildness and inconsistencies of neighbouring landscapes with their inclement and inconsistent climates and the random processes of drought and plenty that were an intrinsic part of them and thus, of the destinies of all who lived there, did not apply to those who dwelt upon the

Fig. 94 The Nile Valley south of Thebes

Nile.[2] All the Egyptians had to do to be sure to receive the boon that their valley measured out so generously was to set their lives according to its rhythms.

When Khufu's workforce sailed on the Nile to Giza, when the stone-barge captains brought their blocks into its harbour, they voyaged in certainty upon the river that was the very measure of their lives. Their years were counted by the appearance of the annual flood; the measure of their prosperity by the flood's extent. And every day was counted out by the bisecting sun rising behind the river's eastern bank and setting behind the western one. Like the shutters of a telescope, the river valley served as a slot through which the Egyptians counted out the yearly patterns of the moon and stars.[3] And these too moved in tandem with the rhythms of their river and their lives.[4]

At night, as Khufu's stone boats moved on the darkly lapping current, the stars mirrored in its great wide stream carried its northward flow up into the very centre of the night where the polar stars encircled the dark point at the centre of the sky.[5] And all these elements together, the earth, the river and the sky, the passage of the sun and moon and the procession of the stars, were fixed markers in this singular natural landscape where polarity, rhythm and regularity, where life and death and land, desert, wind and water, dryness and fertility, were intrinsic and symmetrical.

As a text attributed to Hermes Trismegistos, a god of Greek-Egyptian Alexandria, observes to a student of the older Egyptian ways: 'Do you not know, Aesclepius, that Egypt is an image of heaven, or, to speak more exactly, in Egypt all the operations of the powers which rule and work in heaven have been transferred to earth below? Nay, it should rather be said that the whole Cosmos dwells in this, our land, as in its sanctuary.'[6]

Only Egypt was so ordered in both time and space, and its harmonies most powerfully affected its inhabitants. Made in the First Dynasty of Egyptian kings, a modest drawing shows this order of their valley as a series of symmetric ideograms: two high hieroglyphs frame the sides of the design and support, as do the valley's cliffs, the span of the horizon. And in the space between them stand the hieroglyphs for life and the king, and over and above them all, in his voyage from horizon to horizon, is the image of a falcon perched inside a barge of state, an embodiment of transcendental power associated with the sun.[7] Texts from ages later than that of Khufu's endowed this same strange landscape with powers to transmute all things that came into their perfect valley as if by alchemy, into their intrinsic form.[8] Outside of Egypt, they tell us, even the Nile has no real existence. Its slow and ordered stream begins at Aswan on Egypt's southern border; beyond that point, it is but another random river like all the other rivers of the world. In Egypt everything finds its proper place and form, as if the randomness of all creation has passed through the narrow prism of the Nile's valley and attained perfection in that single place. Outside of Egypt, in that endless chaos of random hills and plains, of deserts and mountains without edge or shape, rivers flowed in many and diverse directions, and birds appeared as shades and spirits, human-headed talking things: 'but as soon as they come to eat plants and nourish themselves in Egypt', one of these later texts informs us, 'they alight under the brightness of the sky and take on their bird form'.[9] Those Egyptians, then, who sailed this unique river knew that from east to west, from the river to the desert cliffs, from Aswan to the Mediterranean, south to north, lay the perfection of the universe and they were at home in it.

As steady as a ticking clock, this narrow valley was also very claustrophobic. By Khufu's time, ancient Egyptian images of native flora and fauna were already as intense and regular as Byzantine icons, drawn in repetitious ways and informed with a millennial familiarity. Just as the valley held within it a powerful and unchanging order, so the ancient Egyptian artists representing the living things within the valley also shunned novelty and change. Rather than represent the creatures of their world as they might randomly appear in daily life, they made ideal images of their forms that were so carefully designed that modern naturalists can classify the birds and fish they represented with little hesitation: the count so far, seventy-two Linnean birds and twenty different species of Nile fish.[10] Extraordinary care was also taken to ensure that images of people were drawn out in similarly iconic ways. Centuries before King Khufu, in the first days of the monarchy, a notional grid was adopted for drawings of the human figure, which, by ensuring that its representation could not be garbled and rendered incomprehensible, effectively contained any drift away from those first-made poses and proportions for almost three millennia.[11] At the same time, there was always a pulse of real life within these images of living things: an underlying force that flows through the images of the Egyptian arts as inevitably as the river flows through Egypt, a subtle cadence that enlivens all of them. Despite the continuous, near-duplication of images in everything from individual hieroglyphs to colossal statues, they appear as meditations on the power of life within the narrow valley.

Unlike those lively images, of course, Khufu's Pyramid is not based on living things. It is a pure abstraction. Yet it was also shaped by sensibilities formed inside that same environment, and owes its architecture and its orientations to those same idiosyncratic people who lived within the ancient landscape of the Egyptian Nile. Just as its rhythms had given Khufu and his Egyptians their unique sense of time and place, so it had also shaped their sense of form and space as well.

Four hundred miles long and on average 2 miles wide, the better part of ancient Egypt was virtually two-dimensional, a strip within a lifeless desert, its landscape set between two lines of framing cliffs and centred along the line of the flowing river, which measured out the nation's life in an annual rhythm such as you might see on an oscilloscope. Yet, as you will see when you turn an oscilloscope onto its side, just as its screen has no real depth, so neither did this valley's landscape.[12]

A practical effect of this strange space on many of its inhabitants, down to this day, is that if you live in rural Egypt and lose sight of the river itself, you may still feel its linearity within you, running like the magnet of an internal compass, south to north. Nor is this hyperbole. Look down from the high cliffs at the valley's edge and you will see that the greater part of the landscape has been shaped by the Nile's stream. Before modern irrigation projects, the fields and tracks and the great part of the valley's topography ran parallel or at right angles to the river. In this naturally centuriated landscape the habituated eye simply searches out this underlying pattern in the sun, the shadows and the fields, turns your sensibilities towards the Nile and informs you of the direction of the river's flow.[13] So strong was this near-instinctive sense of orientation that many older villagers living in the valley describe directions that we would customarily denote as right and left, front and back, with the names of the four cardinal points. And as they change their physical position in relation to the river, so they simply change those four compass points unthink-ingly.[14] In similar fashion, ancient carpenters often wrote the hiero-glyphs denoting the cardinal points on the various elements of collapsible furniture to aid its reconstruction – Ikea on the other hand, preferring the use of arbitrary symbols to the four points of the compass, conceives its customers as being constant elements in an otherwise chaotic universe.

Egypt, however, was unique, the very reverse of the rest of the inhabited world. Egypt's landscape, after all, did not stretch out to far horizons or into boundless space, nor was it erratically confined by a diversity of seashores or haphazard mountains. Indeed, the straight lines of the parallel cliffs along its two long edges reversed the usual earthly landscapes of outflowing space. Facing those two cliffs like two glass mirrors back to back, the river's single line, that polar linearity that ran through earth and sky, not only induced a particular sense of place and orientation in the Egyptians, but led them to duplicate that same strange inward-turning space, the same linear axis, in their representations of the human figure and in their architecture too.

Without a twist or deviation therefore, Egyptian drawings of their fellow humans and their gods – though naturally, drawings of foreigners and gods from less well-ordered landscapes may sometimes break these rules – show the elements of the human torso and the head laid out along the single central line, which within the valley, was the flow of the central river and the flow of life.[15] Similarly, figures sculptured in relief were also drawn in this same way and they too inhabit the valley's same thin space, that narrow envelope in which the engraver may subtly model the illusion of full round forms of the human figure without venturing into the illusion that his images inhabited a three-dimensional space. Outside the narrow valley, after all, was chaos and danger; all of the confusion of random open space without a picture frame to confine or to control it.

Egyptian sculptors also worked within those same conventions, their slow technique of hard-stone cutting being especially suited to this same vision. Work usually began by cutting a rectangular block of stone to proportions designed to contain the sculpture that they planned to make; a space frame to contain the figure. Line drawings, outlines of the sculpture that they wished to make, were then

Fig. 95 Unfinished sculpture from a workshop active a century and more before the reign of Khufu, excavated by the Step Pyramid at Sakkara. The flattened profiles of these life-sized images of King Djoser reflect the outlines painted at the beginning of the work upon the rectangular blocks of stone on which ancient Egyptian sculptors invariably conceived their work. The next stage in the process of these sculptures' finishing would have been to smooth down the sharp edges and work towards a standard lifelike image of the king.

painted upon the five upper sides of the block, all of them drawn symmetrically upon an interrelated series of grids and all employing the same set of proportions used for paintings and reliefs.[16] Then, the stone block was simply cut down to the profiles of those drawings, leaving a chunky three-dimensional figure, little more than a set of interrelated rectangles, which, after its edges had been suitably smoothed and rounded, could then be worked with the same degrees of subtlety as that employed by the relief engravers to make an image of a person or a god.

These sculptures are deceptively different from traditional figurative sculpture of the Western tradition. Although completely three dimensional, they were not designed as free-standing figures to occupy an open space. Just as each one of those five drawings on the grids drawn on the sculptor's block has its own centre line, so, by joining these five profiles in a single solid image, the sculptors unified these separate centres around a single axis at the centre of their sculpture.[17] The result is that their statues hold that same core, that linear compass, that precise experience of form and place that linked the living ancient Egyptians directly to their river and its cosmic rhythms.

This was the world, the space, in which the Great Pyramid was conceived and built.[18] As we have already seen, its makers measured out the size and silhouette of Khufu's Pyramid upon a grid of squares as if it were a sculptor's block. And similarly, just like the drawings and the sculptures, the Pyramid's interior rooms and corridors were ordered on another grid, the elements of their architecture set out one above the other on that same essential centre line. And all of these interior elements are set inside a narrow envelope of space as if it were a sculptural relief. An envelope precisely orientated on the same south–north direction as the river, the valley and the stars.

The architecture of this Pyramid is a product of profoundly different sensibilities from those of ours today. Standard modern drawings of the Great Pyramid, for example, usually place its architecture in a wide open space and, by emphasising its solidity and mass with shadow, even set it at a specific time of day. Modern-day architects alternatively might construct imaginary scaled-down cross-sections of the Pyramid, that cerebral slice through its centre that the ancient Egyptians never knew, nor would have understood. An ancient Egyptian drawing of the Pyramid, on the other hand, makes few demands upon a modern sketch pad for the image is essentially two-dimensional: three joined lines, a simple triangle with its two base lines extended as if to emphasise the Pyramid's horizon.[19]

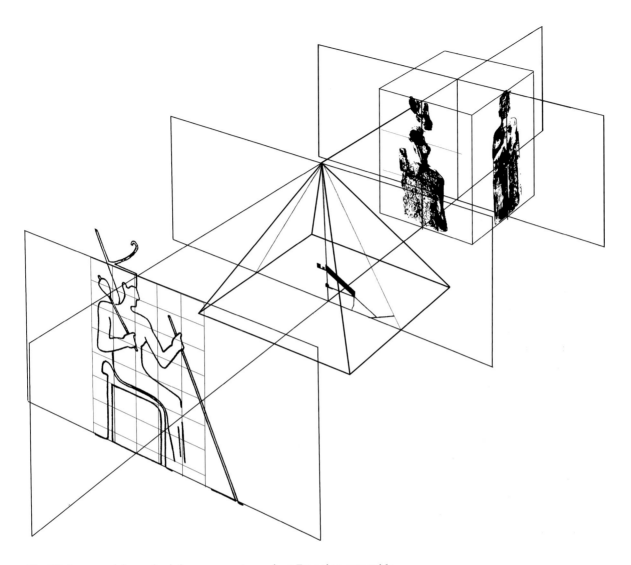

Fig. 96 An organising principle common to ancient Egyptian pyramids, sculptures and drawings.

The Pyramid's interior architecture was set in the manner of a sculpted relief, within a narrow envelope of space. And like a sculpted drawing or relief, it was set upon a grid of squares (fig. 28).

The Pyramid exterior was envisaged as a sculptor's block whose four vertical planes had been pushed together into a single point. And here too, the grid's squares on which the sculptors set their work were also employed as a set of co-ordinates that controlled the rising angle of the Pyramid (fig. 30).

The drawing of Khufu is from the Hat-nub quarries; his sculpture, from Petrie's excavations at Abydos. The outline of this scheme is derived from Giedion 1964, fig. 308; the grid from Robins 1994, fig. 10.6; the sculptor's block set in the manner discussed in Schäfer 1974, pp. 326ff.

Fig. 97 The Giza
pyramids viewed from
the Plateau at Abusir,
7 miles to the south.

By reducing the three dimensions of the Pyramid's baselines to the two dimensions of its central axis and then by pushing the four top edges of the sculptor's block together so that they met upon that centre axis at the apex of the Pyramid, they shaped the three dimensions of its external architecture to reflect the linearity of their transmuting valley. By aligning it precisely to the ideal centre of the river and the sky – to polar north – the pyramid-makers attached the royal tomb to the rhythms of their life and of their universe. As if by alchemy, they had ordered the chaos of death itself, and set the dead king within a perfect model of their universe.

It is very difficult today to imagine a situation when the formal order of the universe could be so readily encompassed. We have lost all such certainty; we are not even sure whether our universe is expanding or contracting. By their sheer rigour and intelligence, however, King Khufu's pyramid-makers contained the lively harmonies that they perceived within their valley within the architecture that they built upon the Giza Plateau. And this, of course, as part of a millennial developing tradition of designing for the dead.

Part Four

The great inheritance

SECTION ONE
The first pyramid

24 The spirit and the tomb

The invention of the pyramid was a simple enough affair and rather
sudden, the first having been erected in the reign of Djoser of the
Third Dynasty of kings, 120 years before the Great Pyramid was
begun.

Even so, the roots of pyramids, that rare attention to the arrangements made for death and burial, reach back even to the first hunter-
gatherers in Egypt, some of whom left a flint axe, Egypt's 'first
attested piece of funerary equipment', beside the face of a man
placed in a shallow desert grave in Upper Egypt.[1] By the fifth millennium BC, some of the settled farming communities within the Nile
Valley were burying their dead with the finest things that they could
make, leaving weapons, tools and jewellery, and sometimes even
models of the boats they used to sail upon the Nile, as if they thought
that the dead had some of the same needs as the living.[2]

By their very presence, such provisions and possessions laid within
the grave tell us that these people believed that some part of the dead
person had not died with the body and yet remained within the
grave: that the dead, therefore, were present in forms other than
their physical remains; in forms that we may describe as spirits.[3]
That the cemeteries of some of those early farming communities
were set in clear view of the houses of the living, and that some of

their children were buried beneath the floors of their houses, further shows us that these communities arranged for the spirits and the corpses of the dead to stay close by the living.

In the last centuries before ancient Egypt's unification under a single king, some of the graves of these farming communities were larger and more elaborate than the others, and their contents too were richer and more diverse, these differences reflecting, so many archaeologists infer, similar social stratifications within the communities that designed and built and filled these tombs.[4] From these more lavish graves, we may assume that both the bodies and the spirits of their occupants were thought to require the trappings and the status that their occupants appear to have enjoyed within the living world, whilst their positions along the fringes of the Nile's fields show that they were buried within view of the communities which in life appear to have afforded them their wealth and status.[5]

After 3000 BC and the unification of these various Nile-side populations, these so-called elite tombs were made far larger and were stuffed with yet more grave goods, some of the grandest of them being established in the manner of a great earthly household, with huge burial apartments and smaller chambers all around them stacked up like the storerooms of a palace, with model granaries and even, on occasion, simulacra of the offices of government built up beside them.[6] Elaborating the fundamental prehistoric belief in a form of life after death, and so it would seem of the possibility of a voyage of the spirit from the tomb, Nile boats were sometimes buried by these tombs, whilst gatherings of more modest graves lined up beside them suggest that some of the retainers and the pets from living households were buried beside these mortuary palaces to accompany their masters in their death.[7] As for the owners of these spirit palaces, they were provided with the finest things that the early

Fig. 98 De Morgan's partial reconstruction of the royal mastaba of Nagada – a splendid example of that part of the archaic royal tomb-building tradition which flourished in the cemetery of Sakkara. Though none of the tops of these great brick structures have survived, it is likely that they resembled those of the palaces of the living kings, whose forms they appear to emulate.

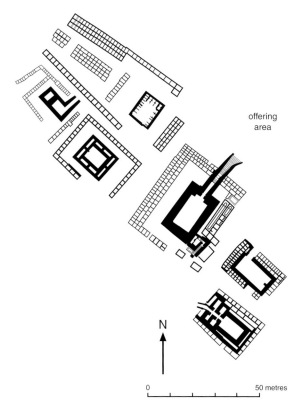

Fig. 99 Six of the royal tombs in the Abydos cemetery surrounded by the cell-like tombs of retainers. The largest of this group, a rectangular crypt accessed by a descending staircase, was the tomb of a king called Den. Although the burial chamber was impressive, a massive brick-lined room with granite slabs upon its floor and a wide ceiling set close to ground level supported by substantial beams of cedar wood, its superstructure was extremely modest and, in consequence, has all but disappeared.

Fig. 100 Petrie's workforce excavating the tomb of King Den at Abydos in 1900. In the 1990s the tomb was re-excavated and conserved by the German Archaeological Institute.

This form of pit and staircase cut into the desert became a universal feature of archaic royal tombs and was maintained to the very ending of the pyramid-building age (cf. figs. 222 and 229). It was the route to royal burial. Uniquely, the Great Pyramid's burial pit would be set inside the Pyramid's own mass rather than in the natural rock of the Egyptian desert.

state could manufacture; with beds and chairs and lavatories and linen and all the produce of the Nile Valley, from fresh meat to honey, and the tools and the utensils used in every activity of Egyptian life. Whilst heavily plundered, the quality and quantity of the wretched fragments that have survived from these great funerary palaces show that these tombs had also held large quantities of treasures which, although not heavy in fine gold, were the artistic equal of anything ever found within the fabled tombs of ancient Egypt. Some of these tombs, indeed, had held such quantities of imported wine and aromatic oils in them that when, after five millennia, Flinders Petrie dug out their ruins, the ancient perfume rose again into the air.[8]

Desiccated and anointed, bandaged, stiffened and bejewelled, those buried in these grand archaic mausolea appear to have been preserved as statue-like cadavers.[9] And at the time of burial, their encoffined bodies were taken down deep stairways into spacious subterranean burial chambers roofed with sturdy beams of cedar wood and hung with decorated mats and wooden panels, enlivened on occasion with glittering strips of beaten gold. Just as the storerooms of these tombs appear to echo those of the palaces of the living, so too these lavish crypts allow a further glimpse into the state apartments, the living throne rooms, of the first two dynasties of pharaohs.[10]

It is especially fascinating to see that the earliest-known examples of Egypt's famous tomb chapels, the first-known architectural evidence of a continuing cult of caring for the dead in ancient Egypt, were set up beside some of these same tombs: the cult marked by a small flat area by a doorway to the storerooms of the tomb with a scattering of pottery left upon it, or in a group of modest mud-brick rooms with stone-paved floors built close to the tomb itself, tiny ritual theatres usually set upon a north–south orientation, where supplies of food and drink were offered to the owner of the tomb over periods of time.[11] That the remains of some of the oldest known statues in the ancient Egyptian style were found in one of these cult buildings underlines the continuity of the prehistoric belief in the continuing presence of the spirit of the dead beside the body and the tomb.[12] That the tens of thousands of funerary statues made in later periods of Egyptian history were usually inscribed with the name of a tomb owner may even suggest that the Egyptian conception of individuality was itself born in these early tombs along with this architectural division between flesh and the spirit, the burial chamber and the offering chapel. And that, in turn, provides a compelling reason for the ancient Egyptians' millennial preoccupation with the preparation of their tombs, for in establishing that careful cult of flesh and spirit, of burial and offering, individual sentience was rendered visible and tangible.[13]

At all events, these early architectural arrangements for the continuation of offering to the dead transformed the prehistoric custom of burying goods and chattels at the time of funeral into a living system of communication with the dead that was capable of operating over extended periods of time, a system in which tombs were no longer memorials and funerary vaults, but half-way houses between the quick and the dead. And naturally, as the food offerings reflected the harvests of the agricultural year, so the rites of their offering were synchronised with the rhythms of the Nile Valley, with the passage of the river and the sun: and the dead, therefore, with the powers who embodied and controlled all life within it.

Like Queen Elizabeth I and Charlemagne, the archaic pharaohs appear to have led peripatetic lives;[14] during the 300-year period of Egypt's first two dynasties of kings, indeed, the two largest royal cemeteries were almost 300 miles apart. Whilst boats buried beside some of these great tombs would have allowed the spirits of the dead the same mobility that they had enjoyed in life, some archaeologists have proposed that these pharaohs had tombs prepared for them in different cemeteries, a custom shared by many ancient Egyptians of later ages.[15] And certainly, the lavish series of regal funerary monuments that were built throughout the land of Egypt at that time would have provided a tangible and commanding demonstration of the reach and richness of the world's first state and of the slow formation of that state's particular identity. Just as the epitome of this ancient kingdom would be the building of the Great Pyramid at Giza and the complex processes of its manufacture, so too the building and stocking of these great archaic tombs would have been a kind of thinking.

The southernmost of these two great archaic burying grounds is set upon a sandy plain in Upper Egypt close to the archaeological site of Abydos; the other, in the desert by the modern village of Sakkara, a few miles upstream from Cairo. And both of these grand cemeteries were close to ancient population centres with enormous and millennial graveyards.[16]

The Abydos burying ground was gathered on a low hill at the centre of a desert wash that ran down from a cleft in the western cliffs to the edges of the most fertile floodplain in Upper Egypt; the same area, so later legend tells, from where the first pharaohs struck north to conquer their neighbours and unite the land of Egypt.[17] Sakkara's great archaic tombs, upon the other hand, were set along the ridge of the western horizon, so that today their ruins look down from their cliff to the Nile's plain and northwards to the pyramids of Giza. At the time of the first dynasties, this splendid row of monuments would have overlooked the nearby royal fortress-palace known as Inebu-hedj – the White Walls – the first known foundation of the Egyptian state which stood, in all probability, beside a lake upon the plain.[18]

At Abydos, the palatial subterranean chambers of the royal tombs were marked upon the surface of the desert by a series of simple if substantial low-walled rectangles filled up with sand.[19] A mile to the

south, however, stood two great rows of high-walled brick-built court-yards, some of them as large as city blocks and built, so the fragmen-tary inscriptions found within them would suggest, as complements to the unassuming graves within the nearby cemetery.[20]

The regal significance of these great desert courtyards was announced at first sight by the elaborate decoration of their exteriors, which were ornamented with the so-called 'Palace Façade' design, a simple pattern made with light and shade produced by a series of ver-tical niches.[21] The very names of the first three dynasties of Egyptian kings, indeed, are identified as royal names precisely by their being set inside a hieroglyph of a rectangle decorated with this same Palace Façade design, the same enclosing rectangle with its design that would be part of the elaborate titulary of every monarch down to the ending of the Egyptian state: the *per'a* – the 'Great House', as this enclosure could be called – being the origin of the word 'pharaoh'.[22] This elaborate archaic decoration, then, was the primary hieroglyphic signification both of the name of the early king and of the royal resi-dence in life and death.

Fig. 101 The mud brick enclosure of King Khasekhemui at Abydos, one of the best preserved of many such enclosures erected by the archaic kings. The royal tombs were cut into a shallow mound lying in the desert plain beyond.

Whilst there are examples of these huge mud-brick enclosures at other sites in Egypt with similarly elaborate façades, precious little evidence has survived in any of them to tell us what they once contained: some huts and halls perhaps, of mud and rush and wattle, slight, temporary, that would have left but little trace.[23] At all events, a dozen splendid burials of Nile boats uncovered close to one of the Abydos enclosures, a row of wooden hulls enclosed in mud-brick walls, each hull some 60 feet (18 m) in length and similar in its design to Khufu's yacht,[24] serve to underline the close connection of these enclosures with the royal graves, for similar 'boat burials' were placed by some of the great Sakkara tombs as well.[25]

For many years, the revelations of the large-scale excavation of the Sakkara tombs made it appear that in their day they had outshone the royal tombs of Abydos, which Petrie had mapped half a century earlier. Nor did the primacy of the Sakkara cemetery appear unreasonable, for although both sets of tombs had similarly grand burial arrangements, the superstructures of the Sakkara monuments had been far more impressive than the low-walled graves of Abydos. Called 'mastabas' by archaeologists after an Arabic word for bench,[26] the Sakkara tombs had been massive mud-brick structures, huge narrow rectangles some 50 yards and more in length and two and three stories high which, like the enormous enclosures at Abydos, had been gloriously furnished with the characteristic niches of the 'Palace Façade', decorated on occasion with bright-coloured geometric patterns and bulls horns set in rows upon a shelf that ran along the bottom of their main façade.[27] Behind these grand exteriors, set over and around their funerary crypts, their excavators found many of the storerooms untouched, still stacked with jars of wine and oil and honey and, as the scattered fragments of more valued deposits mournfully proclaimed, the exquisite remains of many burnt and plundered treasures too. To contemporary Egyptians living on the Memphite plain, these tombs must surely have appeared as massive treasure chambers, the wealth and power of royal Egypt lined up on the horizon. Between Abydos and Sakkara and the other sites where similar mastabas and royal enclosures were occasionally built, the effort to build and fill these lavish mansions of the dead must in itself have been colossal;[28] an extraordinary manifestation of the power and status of their occupants and of the potential of the living state as well.

Long after the Sakkara excavations, archaeologists debated which of these two great cemeteries, Abydos or Sakkara, had physically housed the bodies of the archaic kings, their apparent mixtures of various burial traditions underpinning a great game of archaeological attribution.[29] More recently, excavations at Abydos have tipped scholarly inclinations back again towards the south,[30] though if this were ever proven to be true, it would have great significance for the story of the Great Pyramid. For if the Sakkara mastabas had not been royal monuments at all but the tombs of high officials as is now often suggested, it would show that in the first centuries after Egypt's unification a great part of ancient Egypt's national wealth and the regal iconography of death was still not dedicated to the near-exclusive service of the king, as they would be in Khufu's time. And this in turn would serve to underline the importance of the first great pyramids in the formation of the ancient Egyptian cultural identity, for they would mark the era when the bulk of the nation's resources was first placed at the disposal of the pharaoh.

Whatever the answer to this archaeological conundrum, one fact emerges from the century-long excavation of these archaic cemeteries that directly affects our understanding of Egypt's pyramids, and the Great Pyramid in particular: that is, the slow-growing idea that the noble dead could leave the confines of their graves; that their spirits were no longer confined to the darkness of burial chambers but could travel through the architecture of their tombs to partake of fresh provisions that had been left nearby, or even that they might take to the boats that were occasionally buried by their sides. Unlike their prehistoric ancestors, the spirits of Egypt's early kings were on the move.

25 Mud to stone

Around 2600 BC, Egypt's royal tomb-makers, who for centuries past had built their monuments of sun-dried mud brick, built King Djoser of the Third Egyptian Dynasty an enormous pyramid from blocks of stone. This single historical event was the beginning of the fundamental revolution in the economy and structure of the ancient state that, a century on, enabled the creation of the Great Pyramid of Giza. As one might expect of ancient Egypt, there are no contemporary records to tell us what occurred. But the materials themselves – the mud bricks of the monuments of the earlier kings and the first-used blocks of stone – show that by King Djoser's day Nile mud was fast approaching the end of its architectural potential as the raw material from which the pharaohs' tombs were made.

Simply made and incredibly resilient, as the world's most ancient ruins testify, sun-dried mud brick is humankind's most widely used building material.[1] Brought to Stone Age Egypt in all probability from Palestine with the first farming technologies, the technique of mud-brick manufacture was used in the Nile Valley millennia before the beginnings of the monarchy.[2] Being, as the Egyptian architect Hassan Fathy once described, 'a more lively material than concrete', mud is quite different from modern building materials.[3] Over the years, as mud bricks desiccate, they often shrink and shift and even shuck

their coating of mud plaster, and thus they change their buildings' lines and forms. And later too, as wind and rain and sand distress and abrade its surfaces, mud architecture loses its first fresh finish and takes on again the texture of the earth. To the modern eye, such grey-silty walls with their over-plastering appear as an exotic building medium, and certainly, with their slightly rounded corners and their every surface reflecting the moving hands of those that shaped them, the great archaic monuments of Abydos and Sakkara shared their architectural aesthetic with modern third-world villages and the celebrated cities of the Yemen and West Africa.[4]

The architecture of archaic Egypt's regal tombs, indeed, was precisely shaped by the use of mud and mud brick. Characterised, in the way of scientists, as having 'the lowest-known compressive strength values for materials used in architecture',[5] the batter that is often given mud-brick walls to add to their stability gave the royal tombs their distinctive sloping silhouette, whilst the fact that, without additional support, mud-brick walls can hardly rise above the height of a six-storey building, kept archaic architectural ambition well within that range.[6] By Djoser's day, however, the mud-brick mastabas were being built so large that, had they risen any higher, they would have crumbled under their own weight.[7]

Fig. 102 Archaic mud brick architecture was invariably built to lie in soft and low and dark and massive lines, as the well-preserved walls of King Khasekhemui's enclosure at Abydos still testify.

Fig. 103 Limestone and mud brick used together, the low black bricks lying gently over the sharp white stone of the wall of the burial chamber of Sakkara Mastaba 3506, built in the reign of Den. The bricks are made of Nile silt and have been bedded in a cement of natural desert plaster, which has also been used to set the field stones of the lower sections of the wall. The black mud running down the limestone wall is the residue of mud bricks that have dissolved in local rains since their uncovering in the 1950s: mud brick is highly vulnerable to rain.

There were other problems too. Some of the burial chambers of these great tombs have suffered badly from heavy desert rains. At Abydos, for example, the subterranean walls in the newly built tomb of Djoser's predecessor, King Khasekhemui, had buckled and collapsed; this, it would appear, after the rainwater of a desert storm had increased the standing weight of its superstructure beyond anything that saturated mud brick could sustain, and so the ceiling fell.[8] Earlier tombs within the same cemetery seem to have suffered similar problems.[9] And at Sakkara too, most of the great mastabas had also suffered internal collapse, and not all of this as a result of 'robbers' fires' as is usually assumed, for the traces left by the ancient thieves show that sometimes they had to tunnel through the rubble of the ruined burial chambers to reach their prizes and had even, on occasion, built rough supporting walls inside the burial chambers to guard against their further disintegration.[10] In some of the later Sakkara tombs the subterranean sections of the tomb were made smaller so that the cedar beams that held up their ceilings were no longer laid on mud-brick partition walls, but on ledges carved directly into the living limestone of the desert plateau. Whatever the ritual significance of such changes may have been – and once again, there are no contemporary theologies to provide a commentary – this modification made the burial chambers more secure. Throughout the First Dynasty of kings all the great tombs display a general trend towards greater structural stability; nevertheless, the inherent problems of an architecture made of mud brick and spanned by beams of wood remained.[11]

There is, unfortunately, a century of architecture that is largely missing in this unwitting progress towards the making of the world's first pyramid; at Abydos, there are few known tombs of the Second Dynasty, whilst at Sakkara, which was one of ancient Egypt's grandest and most used cemeteries for several thousand years, the superstructures of the Second Dynasty tombs appear to have been either subsumed into some later monuments or simply swept away, so that all that remains are a few dark labyrinths, elaborate systems of storerooms and burial chambers, cut into rock beneath the desert.[12] Far beyond these empty chambers, running for miles beneath the sand of the Western Desert, are the ruins of a series of enormous rectangles, one of which at least, so recent surveys indicate, was built at the ending of the Second Dynasty in the time of King Khasekhemui. Although these grand enclosures have often been compared to the mud-brick funerary enclosures on the desert plain at Abydos,[13] some of them, including Khasekhemui's which at a third of a mile long is the largest, are built of slabs of local limestone set in straight courses and laid in muddy plaster.[14] These are amongst the first examples of the move from mud to stone in royal funerary architecture and so presage the building of King Djoser's pyramid.[15] Yet there is little chance that much more will be discovered about these great empty courtyards in the near future, for in the high wide desert the expense

Fig. 104 Petrie's photograph of Khasekhemui's burial chamber at the time of its excavation: 'this modest room, the first known-room in all the world to have been built of blocks of quarried stone'.

Fig. 105 Petrie's photograph of a detail of one of the walls of Khasekhemui's burial chamber showing 'the dressing of the stone'.

of excavation is considerable and, as a recent geophysical survey has confirmed, the archaeological rewards seem thin indeed.[16]

Away to the south the German archaeologists who revealed the structural disaster wrought by rainwater in the Abydos tomb of Khasekhemui have also established that the tomb was rebuilt after its first soaking and collapse, the greater part of its elaborately designed mud-brick storerooms being added at this time[17] along with its celebrated burial chamber that a century earlier Flinders Petrie had already hailed as 'the oldest stone construction yet known'.[18] As Petrie described it, this modest room, the first known room in all the world to have been built of blocks of quarried stone, is a relatively thin-walled crypt some 17 feet long by 10 feet wide (5.31 m × 3.16 m), made of regular rectangular blocks of limestone all closely set like bricks in horizontal rows and laid in a mortar of natural desert gypsum. Such blocks, of course, are not soluble in water and have an incomparably greater resistance to compression than mud brick; indeed, King Khasekhemui's replacement burial chamber stands safe and sound and perfect in his desert tomb down till this day.[19]

Limestone, which Egyptian vase-makers had worked so carefully and so prolifically since prehistoric times and which the mud-brick builders had sporadically employed as paving stones and portcullises, as door jambs and as roofing blocks, had provided Khasekhemui's tomb-makers with the means to make a room within the southern desert sand with the stability and strength of one of Sakkara's rock-cut burial chambers. From their chisel-cuts it seems as if the royal masons had conceived their novel task as similar to that of hewing out four walls from an excavation in the living rock, for they worked the blocks of Khasekhemui's stone block burial chamber with small flat chisels in the same way that their fellow craftsmen had finished the walls of the rock-cut burial chambers at Sakkara.[20]

Only the interior facing of Khasekhemui's burial chamber was finished in this distinctive way, the rest of the stone work being left rough-hewn. Egypt's millennial tradition of stone vase making, however, would have ensured that these craftsmen knew that their new-found architectural medium could sustain workmanship as exquisite as that employed on fine stone vases. From the beginning then, stone block building held the possibility of an architecture that, unlike mud brick, would last for ever and one in which even the finest, smallest details would never lose their shape. Not only that. Limestone's superior resistance to compression also offered the royal tomb-makers the possibility of building to previously unattainable heights.

Such was the immediate enthusiasm for this new architectural medium that the superstructure of the tomb of Khasekhemui's immediate successor, that of King Djoser of the Third Egyptian Dynasty, was built right at the centre of the royal cemetery of Sakkara entirely out of blocks of stone.

Building with stone is an entirely different activity from building with mud brick. Much more intractable, stone requires quite different tools from those used to manipulate mud bricks; specifically, chisels made of copper. The tasks of quarrying and shaping stone quarry blocks therefore requires far higher levels of organisation and supply than the parochial tasks of gathering up some local earth and water and moulding bricks of mud. In construction too, whilst stone's potential for accuracy and permanency encourages more care than the swift approximations of mud brick, it also takes more time and labour to set into position. So, building the superstructure of a royal tomb entirely out of blocks of stone required a dramatic and immediate enlargement of the royal workforce as well as the establishment of brand-new reservoirs of skill inside the state, and in a range of non-agrarian technologies. No wonder that the mines of the Wadi

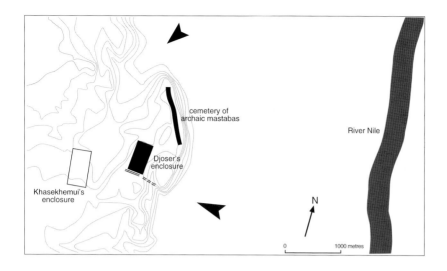

Fig. 106 Map of the Sakkara plain and plateau, showing the two routes available to Djoser's workforce for hauling stone blocks shipped from Tura up onto the plateau of Sakkara.

The northern approach, a long haul up a desert wash, leads to the west side of the Step Pyramid's enclosure. In Djoser's day, the settlement later known as Memphis appears to have lain in the vicinity of the uppermost arrow; it would have been served by canals connected to the Nile. The southern approach may also have been accessed by a canal which is known to have served for the delivery of stone to later pyramid-building projects at Sakkara and came directly to the foot of the plateau. The dotted lines running from the plain onto the plateau indicate the traces of an ancient ramp.

Maghara were established in King Djoser's reign,[21] for the royal workforce had immediate need of large tonnages of copper: Djoser's stone monuments, it may be estimated, requiring some 70 tons of copper for their manufacture, an amount far in excess of anything the human race had ever prospected and procured before.[22] In short, the adoption of stone building would have required a transformation of the traditional offices of an agrarian bureaucracy into a state machine capable of supporting and supplying a brand-new industry.

There was, of course, an enormous and millennial reservoir of practical experience on which the first architectural stone masons could have drawn; stone vase production at the royal court was a large and venerable industry. The first excavators of Khasekhemui's Abydos tomb, for example, had found hundreds of perfect vases yet remaining in its ruins, many of them cut from rare and precious desert stones and many of them too, embellished with bands of beaten gold.

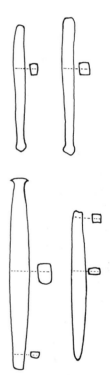

Fig. 107 Copper chisels used by Djoser's masons excavated during the clearance of the Step Pyramid enclosure in the 1930s. All four of these tools had flat cutting edges; the longest, whose tip has been broken off, is almost 8 inches in length.

Even when Petrie re-excavated the tomb in 1899 after most of its contents had been dispersed, he was still able to recover 'between 10,000 and 20,000 pieces of vases of the more valuable stones and much larger quantities as well, of slate and alabaster'.[23] Years later too, archaeologists working in the Sakkara cemeteries recovered fragments of hundreds of hard-stone vases from every one of the great mastabas they excavated.

At the very beginning of the Third Dynasty stone vase production, along with the collection of masses of antique stone vessels, was at its height; a single gallery beside King Djoser's subterranean burial chamber holding some 30,000 fine stone vessels with an estimated weight of some 90 tons.[24] A little over a century later, after stone had been taken up for use in building, the workshops that for centuries had made vases as fine as flowers from the hardest of stones had all but disappeared; in the tomb of Khufu's mother, for example, right beside his Pyramid, Reisner's expedition found just thirty-eight stone vessels, and these carved not from the adamantine desert rocks so popular in earlier times but in the tractable alabaster of the Valley of the Nile.[25] It would appear that in the rush to stone from mud-brick architecture, the court's stone vase-makers had deserted their traditional occupations. Indeed, the work of shaping and moving the more than 600,000 tons of limestone from which Egypt's first stone tomb was built represents an investment of labour roughly equivalent to that required to produce those 30,000 hard-stone vases that lie in one of the corridors underneath his pyramid.[26]

As to the craftsmanship of Djoser's first stone tomb, it is as if the interior walls of Khasekhemui's burial chamber have been turned inside-out and given a finer flatter finish. For though the core of Djoser's building is composed of blocks of local limestone roughly split and cut and laid in muddy mortar, its exterior is made of well-shaped blocks of high-quality limestone shipped to Sakkara, in all probability, from the Tura quarries.[27] Certainly, the workmanship employed upon the finish of this fine white stone is far superior to that of any earlier stone construction; in fact, it is as surely worked and brusquely cut as a roughed-out limestone vase.

0   10 metres

Fig. 108 Reconstruction of the first of the stone tombs that were subsequently embedded in the masonry of Djoser's pyramid. The monument appears to have been square, with all four sides sharing a similar elevation: a form akin to the earlier royal tombs in the Abydos cemetery.

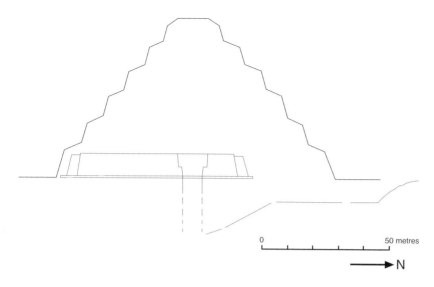

Fig. 109 Fig. 109 Cross section of
the Step Pyramid. Little
is known of the earlier
stone architecture
incorporated into this
familiar silhouette; there
may be more stone
mastabas than are shown
here, and other, smaller,
pyramids. Djoser's burial
arrangements also
underwent similarly
complex processes of
enlargement (see further
chapter 27 below); only
the main outlines of the
final version are shown
here.

As to the architecture of this first stone tomb, it is a low building, a
plain rectangle with battered sides similar in its form to the simple
superstructures of the earlier royal graves at Abydos.[28] Some 28 feet
high and 200 feet square (8.5 m × 63.1 m) at its base, it has been set
on the cardinal points of the compass and a half-mile back behind the
ridge that holds the great archaic mastabas. There are no known
precedents at Sakkara for such a monument, for as we have already
seen none of the superstructures of the tombs of the preceding kings
appear to have survived, a gap in continuity which has prompted the
suggestion, and there is nothing to deny it, that Djoser's tomb-makers
did not make this monument at all, but simply subsumed its form
within their rising pyramid after it had been built by one of his royal
predecessors.[29]

Fig. 110 The Step
Pyramid's south face,
with the embedded lines
of earlier stone mastabas
still visible within the
lowest sections of its
masonry.

Amidst such speculation, it is easy to miss the essential significance of this simple building in the story of the Great Pyramid. Not only does it show you the invention of stone architecture taking place, step by step, before your eyes, but it is also quite literally the foundation on which the world's first pyramid was built. For after the royal stone masons had finished building this first low tomb, they doubled its dimensions by fitting further sets of buttress walls around it like the layers of an onion, and then in a gesture of extraordinary extravagance, they built a pyramid of six great steps over and above it all. And that is how the first pyramid was made.[30]

26 To make a pyramid

It is moving now, to trace the edges of the first stone block building, that defining moment of human history, embedded in the base of Djoser's pyramid.[1] At the same time it is difficult to believe that this building really was the first, for it is so accomplished in its craftsmanship; its facing walls indeed would be highly regarded by any stone mason working today. Nonetheless, the surviving building blocks of its façade have retained the tell-tale proportions, if not the sizes, of contemporary mud bricks, and just like them they are laid in bonded horizontal courses. The aesthetic of the archaic tombs, however, the organic qualities of mud brick, has entirely disappeared. Those languid lines, the shrinkage and erosion that give every yard of a mud-brick building an individual life and movement, are here replaced by crisp-cut stonework that to this day stands sharp and flat and true. Although the foundation course of this first stone tomb, a single row of limestone blocks set directly on the desert rock, still echoes the unassuming mud-brick ledges of the Sakkara mastabas,[2] here the form is drawn in blocks of fine white stone laid and cut so straight and sharp that under the hard Egyptian sun they appear to be a single perfect line of light ruled out upon the desert sand, a line that precisely measures out the quality and size of the building up above. Equally remarkable are the edges of the stone tomb's battered

Fig. 111 The limestone mastabas as they appear today, embedded in the Step Pyramid's south face. The perfect line of their cut stone blocks and the crisply chamfered edges of their façades herald the dramatic ending of a five-century-long tradition of a royal funerary architecture made of Nile mud.

Fig. 112 Detail of a chamfered corner of one of the stone mastabas that were incorporated into the fabric of the Step Pyramid.

walls. As the sun moves with the day, a well-cut chamfer some two inches wide serves to produce a carefully defined straight line along the building's corners, an intermediate half-tone between sun and shade that softens and solidifies the architecture's weight and mass. Decorated and elaborated throughout the following millennia, the same device will help define the form of Egypt's grandest temples and, later on in history, the columns of ancient Greece and Rome as well.

Stone architecture, then, leapt straight from its creators' minds well formed and subtly detailed, a synthesis of millennial architectural experience in mud brick and the expertise of the stone-vase workshops.

Just as remarkable is that Djoser's stone workers planned to build the first pyramid in a single giant leap up into the sky; an unknown architectural journey over and above those first low tombs. For the pyramid's six high steps were not set tentatively one upon the other as a series of separate structures like the three phases of the first low tomb, but were designed and built and bonded from the beginning as a single integrated whole. And at the same time too, the relatively small-sized blocks that had been used to build the different phases of the low tombs, which could have been man-handled by two or three

Fig. 113 Stripped of its various coatings, the east face of the Step Pyramid displays some of the many stages of its invention. Although the blocks of the first stone mastaba (left) rise straight and sharp, they are laid like bricks, in horizontal lines. The slabs of the second mastaba, however, have been stacked up against them at an angle, a technique that employs some of the intrinsic qualities of stone blocks to the benefit of the structure, and one that would be repeated on a grander scale in the foundations of many later pyramids.

people, were replaced by blocks that were some five and even on occasion ten times larger.[3] Neither were these new blocks set like the earlier ones, in imitation of the horizontal bonding of mud brick. Laid end to end and angled down towards the central axis of the pyramid, the rows of huge foundation blocks would have provided extra stability for the pyramid they planned to build on top of them.[4] So, as those tilted slabs of Tura limestone clearly show, the first pyramid was not conceived as a traditional work of mud-brick architecture and then translated into a new material: from its baselines to its apex, the pyramid was envisaged in enormous blocks of quarried stone.

Golden now, wind-varnished, stripped of its fine white outer skin and with its loose and toothy stones half-smothered in drifted sand, this grand old pyramid has hardly moved in nearly five millennia. Solid, still and tranquil as befits a primordial structure, it is difficult to imagine the ferocious energies that were mobilised to build it to its finished height of 200 feet (60 m), a task that, at the later building rates, would have required a labour force about a tenth of the size that a few generations on would be required to build King Khufu's Pyramid at Giza.[5] Here for the first time in human history, thousands of human beings were organised into a single workforce on the plain of Sakkara; one that quarried, cut, carried and laid more than 600,000 tons of stone to build a pyramid. By those lights alone, the construction of King Djoser's pyramid is a major historical event.

What could have prompted the king's builders to set this novel form – a six-stepped pyramid – over and above the traditional design of an earlier archaic tomb? It would be an easy trick, of course, to produce another of Coleridge's serpents and claim that the common pyramidal images conjured up in later ancient Egyptian writings were the 'symbolic' inspiration of this first pyramid; but that would be an explanation similar to explaining the invention of the petrol engine by quoting a few words from a driving manual.[6] Then again, we might generate another of the poet's 'great grand self-fulfilling tautologies', by reviewing the plans of the archaic mud-brick tombs and isolating any vaguely pyramid-looking shapes that they might contain and plot a pseudo-evolutionary progress for the 'birth of the pyramid' from its germination on the plain of Abydos to maturation on the Giza Plateau. Pyramids, however, are not pumpkins, but the work of human beings capable of making choices, and blessed, as Djoser's builders clearly show us, with an incredible capacity for invention and design.

It would be easy too, when words like genius, creativity and copyright are common currency, to propose that Djoser's beautiful stone architecture was the creation of a single talented individual, or at least an elite band of architect-designers. And in January 1926, as excavators cleared around the south-east corner of King Djoser's Pyramid, it seemed that they had discovered the name of just such an individual, engraved in exquisite hieroglyphics upon a broken statue base: 'Seal Bearer of the king of Lower Egypt, first after the king of

Fig. 114 The broken
statue base that once
supported a life-sized
figure of King Djoser,
and still holds this brief
inscription naming
Imhotep as a royal
courtier and priest
and supervisor of the
royal workshops, a
happenstance that has
led to the hailing of this
individual as the
architect and inventor of
the Egyptian pyramid.

Upper Egypt, Administrator of the Grand Palace, hereditary noble,
High Priest of Heliopolis. Imhotep, builder . . . carpenter . . . sculptor
. . . vase maker . . . engraver.'[7]

Was this Imhotep, all at once as his titles might suggest, a brilliant
administrator, a carpenter of royal lineage, a sculptor, an engraver,
the designer of the world's first pyramid and the inventor of stone
block building? Was Imhotep a member of that happy band, along
with Napoleon and Michelangelo, to be placed upon the Hegelian
short list of 'Men of Destiny'?[8] Once again, just as they did with
Khufu's family and courtiers, the terms of the translation invite us
into a Technicolor world.

Yet there is something rather different about this man Imhotep.
Whatever tasks he may or may not have undertaken in his lifetime,
he certainly enjoyed a long-lived fame. A thousand years after he had
died, he was still considered to have been a founder patron of the
scribes and a 'Son of Ptah', the fair-faced god of craftsmen and of
manufactory.[9] Later too in Greco-Roman times, his continuing
celebrity earned him an apotheosis so that he became a little god of
wisdom, a doctor and a scribe so popular that today most museums of
Egyptian art have small bronze figures of Imhotep in this later manifestation, as a slight young man with a tight-fitting cap sitting on a
plain Egyptian throne with a papyrus scroll upon his lap.[10]

Not once, however, throughout Egyptian history, had Imhotep been
described as the inventor of the pyramid. Nor is this to be expected,
for the ancient Egyptians do not appear to have considered what we
today would call works of art or architecture as the creations of individual personalities.[11] It was the Victorians, after all, who gave such

words as 'architect' and 'genius' their modern meanings. Since then, moreover, we have discovered myriad human cultures where concepts of genius and artistic individuality are unknown, and art is not considered as a work of individual creation.[12] So there is little reason to suppose that ancient Egyptian appreciation of the arts was similar to Queen Victoria's, and naming Imhotep as the genius-inventor of the pyramid and stone block building simply dresses up the mystery in nineteenth-century clothes.

The truth is that, as with the Great Pyramid of Giza, beside a clutch of titles, some brief and standard hieroglyphic phrases and a few names of courtiers and queens, we know next to nothing of the living world of Djoser and the makers of his pyramid.[13] There are no inscriptions on Djoser's standing monuments at Sakkara, not a hieroglyph above the ground, other than the appreciative graffiti of later ancient Egyptian scribes, written on the blocks of then-already ancient monuments, praying that King Djoser 'the opener of stone' would be kind to them, and that they too might enjoy 'a full lifetime . . . and a goodly burial after a happy old age, like yourself'.[14] Not much, it may appear, yet by the standards of ancient Egyptian society such spare endorsements are loquacious. As is the fact that in the most detailed list of pharaohs to have survived from ancient times, Djoser's name alone is written not in black like the names of other monarchs, but as in the manner of a check mark added to a scribal list, in a bright red ink.[15] The two names, both Imhotep and his king, held a special place in ancient Egyptian memory; but their roles in the creation of the first pyramid are still open to conjecture.

One unsung yet vital element in the story of how the first pyramid was built is that Djoser appears to have inherited a settled state from Khasekhemui and that, like his predecessor, he was blessed with a long reign.[16] Pyramids after all are not modern buildings, they have no intrinsic value nor is there any profit in their completion; their real 'value', as we have seen (ch. 16 above), being in the very act of building in itself, for here it was that the power of government was made manifest and the machinery of state consolidated and enlarged. Once the quarrymen, bargees and stone masons had been assembled, and Djoser's men were working at Sakkara and the necessary supply lines had been put in place throughout the land, there was no reason why the living processes of building should have stopped when the first-made tomb was finished. Thus the architecture of King Djoser's funerary monuments was continuously enlarged and modified throughout his reign.[17] Such rolling innovations are typical in ancient Egyptian history when the ruling king outlived his initial building programme and the assembled workforce continued to elaborate and enlarge on its original tasks, or even sometimes move on to quite new and different things.[18]

And yet the making of a pyramid could not have been anticipated in the days of mud-brick architecture. Only with the use of blocks of stone, as we have seen (pp. 236ff above), were the royal tomb-makers able to rise to such new heights. Neither was their pyramid the product of a flash of inspiration. Djoser, after all, ruled for twenty years at least,[19] and from the construction of the three 'low' tombs to the erection of the pyramid above them there is a clear arc of constructional continuity which itself is rooted in earlier decades when the burial chamber of Khasekhemui's rain-soaked tomb at Abydos had been rebuilt with blocks of stone. There are further connections too, between those three stone tombs and some of the superstructures of the earlier royal mud-brick tombs at Abydos. Just as the Sakkara stone masons followed the exemplar of Khasekhemui's Abydos burial chamber in their use of blocks of stone, so as they enclosed the first low tomb with further sets of fine stone walls, they had also followed the construction of the archaic tombs at Abydos, whose similarly shaped superstructures had also been enclosed in the manner of an onion, in a succession of walls and tumuli made of brick and sand and matting and mud plaster.[20] Even the location of these first low stone tombs at Sakkara echoed the situation of the Abydos tombs which were also set back from the desert on a gentle rise within a wide and sandy wash.[21] Here then are powerful hints of a venerable architectural tradition linking the first stone tombs to the mud-brick monuments of the royal ancestors.

The definitive break in this progression occurred when Djoser's stone masons stopped mimicking the forms of mud-brick architecture; when experience had shown them that their cut stones would not collapse under their own weight as wet mud brick would do; when they understood that building with stone blocks allowed them to set architectural lines of previously unparalleled accuracy; when they realised that they could draw their stony lines up into the sky with the same precision with which the builders of Djoser's three 'low' stone tombs had drawn the straight lines of their foundation courses flat down upon the desert.

As to any visual impulse that may or may not have led King Djoser's designers to pile tomb on tomb in so extravagant a fashion, once more there is no contemporary evidence beyond the monuments themselves. Could it be that the gathered forms of the three 'low' tombs, which all together would have appeared as a single low sloping structure with three modest steps along its crest, had encouraged Djoser's builders to erect six larger steps above them? Such outrageous changes of size and scale were frequently undertaken by Egyptian craftsmen – a contemporary precedent being the layout of a model courtyard set beside one of the mastabas at Sakkara, the proportions of which were greatly magnified and reproduced by Djoser's craftsmen as part of the funerary complex that was built around his pyramid.[22]

The rising pyramid itself, or at least the practical difficulties of controlling its enlarging form, may well have provoked its division into six equal steps. Exactly the same principle of control by co-ordinates is recorded in the single scrap of constructional design to have survived from Djoser's time: a modest chip of limestone bearing a diagram of five co-ordinates whose numbers demarcate a rising line.[23] And certainly, the following generations of pyramid-makers wrestled mightily with just such problems of control; the Great Pyramid is also based upon a design divided into six equal parts.[24]

As to the specific form of the pyramid's six steps, the angle of their rise is simply the same as the batter of the walls of the three 'low' tombs on which they were built.[25] At the beginning of the work, therefore, the pyramid-builders set another parallel wall, their fourth, against those of the 'low' tombs and extended the area of those earlier monuments to approximately twice the size, a simple ratio of enlargement that would be widely used in some successive pyramids as well (see ch. 30 below). From the beginning of the work, as we have already seen, the angle of the pyramid's massive foundation blocks shows that its builders did not intend to stop at the height of earlier tombs, and neither did they have to. This pyramid was not the product of architectural inspiration in the modern sense at all, but the outcome of a progression in design that took on the intrinsic qualities of a new material – rectangular blocks of quarried stone – which then became its means and inspiration.

At all events, the erection of King Djoser's pyramid set a unique marker into the landscape of the Nile Valley. In the clear air of ancient Egypt, its sharp white shape must have been visible from 20 miles away, from the White Walls of the royal palace known as Inebu-hedj, and from Heliopolis in the north where Djoser's masons had cut and engraved an exquisite series of reliefs on fine white limestone blocks.[26] The pyramid also marked the centre of a millennial spread of graves and cemeteries set in the little deserts that ran along the two edges of the living world, thousands upon thousands of them all along the ending of the river's valley before it debouched into its

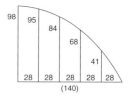

Fig. 115 This modest sketch drawn in red ochre upon a flake of limestone was found in the Step Pyramid's enclosure and is considered to date to Djoser's time. It appears to be a working plan: a unique record of how King Djoser's builders thought.

Assuming that the ancient numbers written between the ostracon's five straight lines (above) had designated Egyptian digits – that is, 1/28th parts of a cubit – the egyptologist Rex Engelbach found that, if the five lines were separated from each other by a single cubit and digit numbers were treated as co-ordinates, they would describe a curve similar to that drawn upon the ostracon: a curve reflected in some of the limestone architecture that had stood close to where the little ostracon was found.

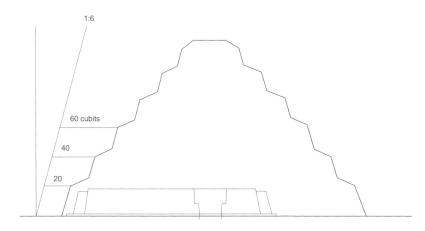

Fig. 116 Jean-Philippe Lauer's diagram showing how the Step Pyramid's angle of rise may be generated by the use of 20 – 40 – 60 cubit co-ordinates. Here, however, the determining angle is not 90° as it is at the Great Pyramid (see fig, 30), but 74°, which is close to the angle of the walls of the mastabas that the pyramid encloses.

Fig. 117 The Step Pyramid as it appears today, on the horizon of Sakkara. In his report upon the excavation of King Djoser's monuments, James Quibell recalled that King Djoser's pyramid was not difficult to climb; that its summit is an oblong platform some 50 feet in length and almost half as wide; and that the air there seemed always to be still, so that in a roaring desert wind butterflies came to rest upon its yellowed stones.

delta.[27] And still today, the Step Pyramid dominates the landscape all around it, from Sakkara's desert cemeteries to the silvered mounds of ancient Memphis and its palm-trees far below, to the quarries of Tura and Ma'sara, away across the river.

Yet it is far from proven that Djoser's pyramid was undertaken to create this visual effect and we cannot know therefore that this powerful presence was part of its intended purposes. We do know, however, that within half a century or so of its completion the Step Pyramid had been widely imitated, not only in other royal mortuary complexes but also in an Egypt-wide series of stone markers, half a dozen small stepped pyramids without any apparent funerary connections, sprinkled down along the Nile Valley to mark the locations of administrative centres and royal residences.[28] Whatever the intentions of its builders may have been, the abstract form of the world's first pyramid had swift and powerful impact.

27 Accommodating Djoser

As you might expect, the designs for Djoser's funerary crypt are as dynamic as the architecture of the pyramid that stands above it. So chopped and changed were the various accommodations made for Djoser's flesh and spirit that they appear today as a jumbled mess of pits and corridors, stairs and tunnels, rooms and chambers, and all of them so dusty, dangerous and extensive that their totality has yet to be explored.

The first plan to accommodate King Djoser's burial appears to have been traditional enough: a shallow staircase cut into the desert rock, running down beneath the north side of the first 'low' tomb in the usual manner of the archaic monuments, accompanied by store-rooms and set directly underneath the centre of the tomb. Much of this, however, was quarried away in later alterations, so its full plan is now lost.[1] As well as these modest excavations the tomb-makers cut a series of nine shafts outside the walls of the first 'low' tomb, set in the usual way of archaic subsidiary burials, in a neat straight row. Unlike any earlier examples these shafts cut straight down a hundred feet (32.50 m) and more, and each one was given a long corridor at its ending, all of them running in parallel towards the centre of the tomb. When archaeologists first entered these dark corridors in the 1920s, they found many treasures from Djoser's time, for the top of these shafts had been twice covered over and quite lost, first by the two enlargements to the 'low' stone tomb and then by the addition of the pyramid itself. Two of the corridors held alabaster sarcophagi, simple cubic blocks of glistening yellow stone; others, scattered body parts and traces of wooden coffins that appear to have belonged to members of King Djoser's family.[2] Yet another contained the famous hoard of 30,000 hard-stone vases, many of them still carefully stacked up and surrounded with fragments of the sacks in which they had been packed up and carried off to lie for four millennia and more in Djoser's funerary domain.[3] This is the first example of a family cemetery placed upon the east side of the royal tomb, just as it would be on the Giza Plateau beside King Khufu's Pyramid.

At the same time as these deep shafts were excavated, another pit was cut right down through the centre of the first 'low' tomb, an enormous excavation some five times wider and almost as deep as the subsidiary shafts, passing down through the first-cut burial chamber. This shaft became the permanent locus of the royal burial,[4] so that even when the Step Pyramid was built over and above it, a cedar scaffold was placed across the mouth of this great pit to support the pyramid above – a task that parts of this same scaffolding still perform today.[5]

King Djoser's builders set up a unique burial chamber at the bottom of this huge shaft, gathering thirty ponderous shafts of rose-red granite into the form of a huge stone box with a cubicle at its centre just 10 feet long and 5½ feet wide (2.96 m ×1.65 m), to hold the body of the king. Ten colossal blocks weighing 12 tons each make up the chamber's floor, nine more its roof, with access to the tiny central burial vault obtained through its roof by means of a circular hole that, after the burial, was neatly corked with a tapered 3 ton granite plug.[6] Smaller than any of the burial chambers of his royal predecessors, this eccentric free-standing arrangement set up on little stacks of limestone blocks at the bottom of the burial shaft, is more like a coffin than a crypt.

Whatever the tomb-makers may have imagined they were making – and they changed the surroundings of this granite box several times – this burying chamber was as extraordinary a conception as the pyramid that they were building up above it. The kings of Egypt had not used granite on such a scale for generations, and even then, whilst the blocks had been plentiful enough and handsome, they had been relatively thinly cut and mostly used for flooring.[7] King Djoser's chamber, however, is of a different order; these measured shafts of stone shipped from the cataract at Aswan display the same sense of

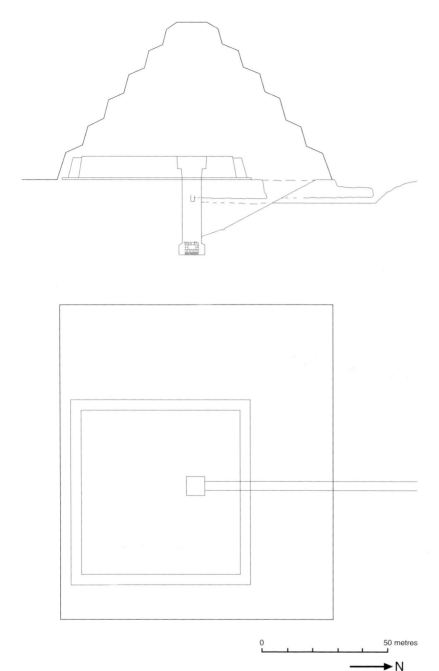

0   50 metres

N

Fig. 118 King Djoser's burial chamber. As with the pyramid itself, present information is insufficient to allow a complete understanding of the changes to its design; however, these always followed the traditional plan established in the archaic tombs, in which a stairway running from the north gave access to a burial pit. Here, however, the step by step enlargement of the superstructure's footprint caused the entrance stairway to be made ever longer, and thus deeper, whilst at the same time the floor of the burial pit was lowered. The unique granite crypt set up inside the enormous final pit, however, was a remarkable innovation, many of whose features would be taken up again at the Great Pyramid.

pure design in blocks of quarried stone, of a newly developing three-dimensional abstract architecture, as do the Tura foundation blocks of the pyramid itself.

All around this granite box, the tomb-makers cut out an entanglement of corridors that over the following millennia would be elaborated and co-joined by gangs of robbers and restorers; some 3 miles of

Fig. 119 A box of granite set on plinths of limestone, Djoser's massive burial chamber was closed with a 2 ton granite plug, notched, as this photograph shows, to accommodate the huge ropes by which it was lowered into position. Like the granite blocks of the Great Pyramid's burial chamber, there are placement graffiti marked upon every block of this funerary crypt, showing that this too was designed and built for reassembly as a free-standing structure.

Fig. 120 The dramatic shaft that holds King Djoser's burial crypt. The visible changes and alterations in its architecture reflect the changes to the superstructure of the tomb.

Fig. 121 The so-called 'blue rooms', a part of the subterranean pseudo-palace built beneath the South Tomb in King Djoser's mortuary complex. Named for the beautiful rare tiles that once covered the better part of their walls, they were a near-duplication of similar suites built underneath the Step Pyramid.

them have so far been explored. Part of this dark labyrinth was designed for the living rather than the dead, Djoser's masons having to excavate a long deep trench, a gross enlargement of the original short descending staircase, so that the royal burial party could gain access to the deep granite grave after the pyramid had been built. On the other hand, all around the central burial shaft there was extraordinary accommodation for the spirit of the dead king, doorways in each of its four walls giving access to nets of corridors that spread out in all directions. Three of these complexes appear to have served the traditional functions of magazines for the provisions and utensils. The fourth doorway, which faces east, the sunrise and the living valley of the Nile, led onto an exquisite set of subterranean apartments built of pure white limestone blocks all beautifully decorated in low relief and framed in shining faience tiles, made in imitation of the squashy, sweet-smelling rush mats that had surely hung in Djoser's earthly dwellings. In this strange labyrinth deep beneath King Djoser's pyramid, the royal masons built a palace for the royal spirit.

Nowadays, the straggling stairways that take you down beneath the pyramid and deliver you to the roof of Djoser's granite burial chamber are in utter darkness and part-choked with drifts of stone and rubble. Dusty light bulbs illuminate the shaft that soars cathedral-like up to the underside of the pyramid, where the part-disintegration of the ancient scaffolding has produced an uneasy alliance of friction and collapse to fashion an impromptu dome within the pyramid's rough masonry. Tons of stone are suspended precariously above you in the dark warm air. Rattling with falling gravel and undercut with unknown shafts and robbers' tunnels, it is a hot, dangerous and exciting place.

As for Djoser, he is gone. At diverse times, various explorers have taken fragile bits and pieces of a corpse, a foot, a scrap of skull and skin, a gilded sandal, from the granite grave and claimed them to be King Djoser's, though some of these at least appear to date from later ages.[8]

King Djoser's masons made another royal tomb for him some 250 yards south of the Step Pyramid, in a long thin archaic-styled mastaba built of blocks of desert limestone whose high façade of Tura stone, magnificently restored and capped with a splendid frieze of stony cobras, measures out its walls in rectangles of sun and shadow.[9] And at the centre of this mastaba, at the bottom of another enormous shaft, is another burial chamber made from massive blocks of Aswan granite that is virtually identical to the one beneath his pyramid nearby.[10] And all around this chamber as well are yet more corridors and chambers and a second subterranean palace for the royal spirit made of fine white blocks of stone and decorated with images and the hieroglyphic titles of King Djoser, all framed with glistening turquoise tiles! And here as well, archaeologists found further fragments of a body, although the interior of the granite chamber inside this so-called 'Southern Tomb' is smaller than that beneath the pyramid and hardly long enough to hold a full-grown man.

So the archaeological quest to separate archaic tombs from cenotaphs, Abydos from Sakkara, had but little meaning for King Djoser's builders, who set up two tombs side by side at Sakkara, for the burial of a single king. To this extent at least, the people who conceived and built these revolutionary monuments looked back towards the past. Although in earlier centuries Egypt's royal tomb-makers had assumed that the spirits of the kings would move out of their burial chambers to receive their offerings from the living and sail upon the Nile (p. 227 above), now, with the royal funerary arrangements gathered up beside each other, King Djoser's spirit had no need of buried boats.[11]

Nor were these two funerary monuments the only things the pyramid-makers collected up at Sakkara. All around these two grand tombs, upon the dazzling sand, they made a unique stony city inside a great grand funerary enclosure designed in the manner of the archaic mud brick enclosures built at Abydos, although here those crumbling mud-brick walls have been transformed into a huge crisp rectangle of the whitest fine-worked limestone; a desert fortress a third of a mile long enclosing a 40 acre plain.

The full extent and the sheer beauty of this extraordinary funerary palace were revealed in the early years of the twentieth century as egyptologists cleared the ruin fields that lay around his pyramid.[12] Choked in mounds of ancient chip, littered with tumbled stones from buildings broken up by stone robbers, the solution of this 40 acre riddle, King Djoser's resurrection, became the life's work of Jean-Philippe Lauer, an architect who had worked at the Sakkara excavations, and stayed on to study and rebuild King Djoser's monuments.[13] In seventy years of working, Lauer came to know each and every one of the surviving blocks of that most ancient architecture, those splendid blocks of Tura limestone that lie today, row on row, where he laid them out in the Sakkara sand. By their different finishes and edges and their subtle tapers, he

Fig. 122 The Step Pyramid under excavation in the 1920s. The South Tomb is the large part-shadowed structure at the left edge of the enclosure.

Fig. 123 A part of Djoser's funerary architecture, under restoration by Jean Philippe Lauer. Although these solid little buildings were never again made for later pharaohs, their exquisite finish and fine craftsmanship were employed upon the pyramids themselves.

Fig. 124 The tiny and unique entrance of the Step Pyramid's vast enclosure. At the same time that this smooth and perfect finish is being lavished on the traditional forms of archaic mud brick architecture (cf. fig. 101 above), there are the beginnings of that massing claustrophobia that pervades the interiors of all the later pyramids.

could place the best part of them back into a perfect ancient architecture that he had first rebuilt in his imagination. I well remember Lauer in the 1960s, moving excitedly from block to block with a 2 metre rule, tracing out invisible buildings for us in broad gestures and enthusiastic sentences that ended, mostly, in a question. He it was who set the egyptological imagination running freely through King Djoser's spirit city once again.[14]

Many of these elegant stone buildings appear to have been life-sized replicas of the airy accommodations of the living; stone reproductions of structures that were usually constructed from the organic material of the Nile Valley: of wood and mud and palm logs.[15] In the same way that the limestone portraits of King Khufu's nobles caught a passing moment in unchanging stone, so the use of stone inside King Djoser's funerary enclosure has frozen the fragile forms of pretty kiosks and pavilions that long ago dissolved into the Nile-side fields.[16] The wonder of this is that at the same time as his stone masons memorialised the tractable shapes of ancient Egypt's living architecture, they created abstract forms as balanced and as beautiful as anything that humankind has ever made: from its first beginnings, stone architecture and geometry were inextricable.[17]

Lauer's reconstructions have shown that a great part of this funerary architecture was the product of a sort of national stocktaking, a process underlined by the variety of objects and materials that was assembled in the compound; by the assorted hard-stone vases stored beneath his pyramid; by the fine alabaster of the sarcophagi brought from Middle Egypt; by the great granite shafts from Aswan in the south; by the stone setters' desert plaster and white clays carried from the Faiyum; by the enormous quantities of fine white limestone shipped from the Tura hills across the river; and by the huge amount of smelted copper taken from the desert.

This air of national stocktaking, this counting out and gathering up of Egypt's goods and architecture inside a single grand enclosure, is most subtly announced, as Lauer rediscovered, at the first sight of King Djoser's great stone walls. For that 40 acre (16.19 ha) rectangle of white stone is exactly ten times the size of a splendid mud-brick mastaba built three centuries before, at the beginning of the first dynasty of Egyptian kings, in the most ancient heartland of the archaic state at Nagada, 300 miles to the south.[18] Underlining this long tradition of architectural proportion, Nagada's mud mastaba and Djoser's stone enclosure walls also share the same distinctive pattern of the Palace Façade, that same design which also served as the hieroglyphic designation of the royal name.[19]

Here then is hard evidence of the operation of an abstract process of conception and development operating over several centuries, and evidence too of its transportation from one end of Egypt to the other. With their stone-built walls set at a ratio of 1:10 to an older monument, Djoser's masons are announcing in a typically Egyptian manner a new and grander destiny for pharaoh, one based, as it ever would be, on the dual sanctions of tradition and proportion. A century later, that

Fig. 125 This hard-stone vase dug from the royal tombs at Abydos is but one of hundreds of thousands of such vases, large and small and usually with perfect and most expert finishes, that were manufactured over many centuries by craftsmen working at the Egyptian court. With its deep well of expertise, the existence of this royal craft helps to explain the creation of a courtly fine-stone architecture within a single reign.

Fig. 126 Fluted columns in King Djoser's mortuary complex, the first such stone columns in the world. Such forms are common enough in the products of the archaic stone vase workshops; here, however, the vase-makers have applied themselves to architecture.

Fig. 127 Numerous examples of these odd stones are to be found in and around King Djoser's funerary enclosure. They appear to be test pieces, each circular cut displaying the same marks as those produced by the flint drills used by the vase-makers of the archaic period. Their presence at the Step Pyramid, therefore, underlines a continuity of craftsmanship.

same system of design, the same deference to tradition, the same ambition for enlargement and perfection, would be the inspiration and the underpinning of the design of the Great Pyramid at Giza.

By the time that the Great Pyramid was built, however, a conscious decision had been taken to discard all such references to earlier forms of architecture. At Khufu's Pyramid, stone alone is king, the abstraction of the quarry block supreme.

Inside Djoser's stony city these choices have not yet been made. Here, two different uses of stone still sit side by side; the abstract stone block geometries of the burial chambers and the Step Pyramid, next to the petrified organic forms of archaic Egypt's domestic buildings.

Created seemingly without effort, with the abrasive marks of its manufacture visible only in the corners of the sharpest angles of the stone, this eerie funerary city has the same sleek surfaces that the archaic vase-makers had manufactured as they transformed the alfresco forms of rustic platters made from rushes or from fig leaves into marvellously made pots and vases.[20] Here, however, the craftsmen are reproducing wooden gates and doors in stone, and columns made of tied and bundled rushes, and palm-log roofs and reeded cornices and the gentle curve of matting roofs.[21] And all of this organic architecture has been given an unimpassioned stony surface, as smooth as a worn penny and so unobtrusive to modern eyes habituated to the bland precisions of mass production that today its intrinsic quality is largely overlooked. Here, in Djoser's stony city, the ancient masons worked the limestone as carefully as they had for centuries past; as a semi-precious material destined for display. A century on, however, at the Great Pyramid, that myopic archaism eager to reproduce the natural forms of living things has entirely vanished, and that same calm archaic finish has been worked into the abstract forms, the outer surfaces, of Khufu's stone block architecture.

SECTION TWO
The pyramids of Sneferu

28 The Meidum Pyramid

After Djoser's burial within his splendid complex at Sakkara, similarly huge building projects were begun for two of his successors, Sekhemkhet and Khaba, but neither of these was sustained, and it is unlikely that the state undertook more than a few years of work on either one of them.[1] Fifty years later, work started on a pyramid for Khufu's father Sneferu, and this was a new beginning. Over the following half-century, three grand pyramids were built, almost 8 million tons of limestone blocks being quarried, cut and consumed in

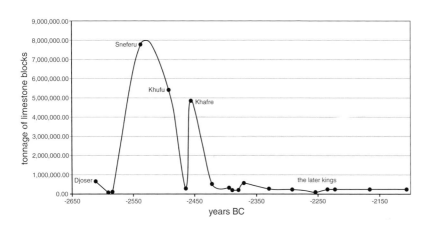

Fig. 128 Graph showing the volumes of cut stone produced in the Old Kingdom. Given the amazing intensity of stone production in the early Fourth Dynasty, the yawning gap between the reigns of Khufu and Khafre probably reflects a gap in modern data.

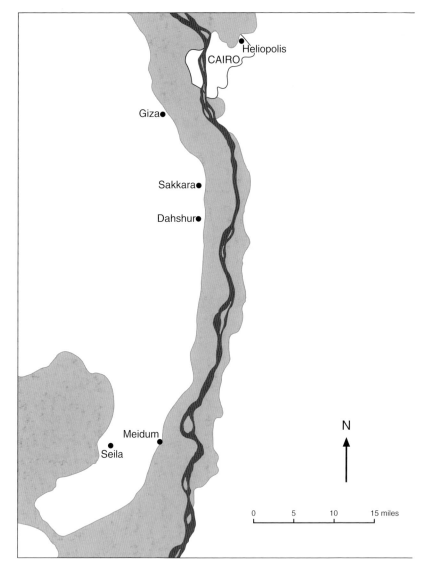

Fig. 129 Map of the section of the Nile Valley in which the great early royal pyramids were built. The white areas are desert; the grey, the cultivated land that stands beside the modern Nile stream. Cairo is indicated to provide a modern reference point; the other names, however, are those generally given to the sites at which these pyramids are found.

their construction; more stone, in fact, than any other workforce on the planet has ever managed to manipulate.[2]

This is what separates ancient Egyptian architecture from all other examples of large-scale building works undertaken in the Bronze Age. After Sneferu, and quite uniquely, stone block construction became a defining millennial activity, an indelible ingredient of pharaonic culture.[3] And the first flowering of this tradition was the Great Pyramid of Giza.

It began modestly enough, with Sneferu's pyramid-makers laying out the base of another stepped pyramid some 35 miles south of Djoser's at the edge of the cultivation. Named after a nearby village, the ruin of this much-altered and much-ruined monument is now known as the Pyramid of Meidum.

There is no obvious reason why the pyramid-makers chose that lonely place for Sneferu's pyramid; why the site of the royal grave was moved so far from the pharaohs' traditional burying grounds. The Meidum Pyramid is amongst the southernmost of all of Egypt's royal funerary pyramids.[4] Away to the west, however, across a 2½ mile plain of clay and gravel that had once been the bed of a prehistoric Nile, upon the high desert and in limestone hills, there stands a little four-stepped pyramid named now after the nearby village of Seila. A small stone stela found close by and inscribed with Sneferu's name suggests that this little monument, a quarter the size of Sneferu's first-planned pyramid at Meidum, was also built for that same king. The Seila pyramid, however, has no internal architecture and is not a funerary monument at all, but one of the group of similarly small stepped pyramids (see p. 250 above), inspired apparently by Djoser's Step Pyramid, that were sprinkled down through Egypt to mark the positions of royal residences or provincial boundaries.[5] This little monument may have marked the position of a royal residence in the plain below; and that in turn may account for the eccentric location of Sneferu's first funerary pyramid.[6]

At all events, the work on the Meidum Pyramid began in the traditional way with the royal tomb-makers digging a large trench into the desert from north to south to give access to the burial chamber – this was a rationalisation of the complicated adjustments that had been made to accommodate the stairway to King Djoser's burial during the

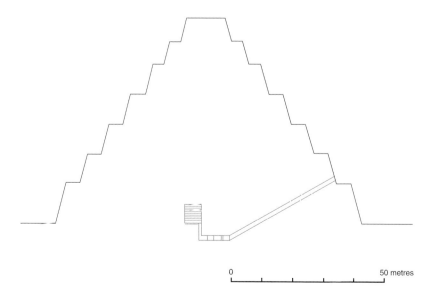

0   50 metres

Fig. 130 A reconstructed section through Sneferu's first-built pyramid at Meidum. The corridor leading to the burial chamber has two side rooms running from it, left and right (see fig. 142).

building of the first step pyramid. Now, the pyramid-makers planned to build their pyramid over and above this trench, and make a monument of slightly smaller volume and dimensions than King Djoser's Pyramid, which would rise more steeply up into the sky.[7]

Already, at the very beginning of this work, Sneferu's government had solved a building problem that had dogged the pyramid-makers ever since the reign of Djoser. Like the Step Pyramid before them, the two unfinished pyramids that were started in the decade after Djoser's death had both been designed, it would appear, to stand at the centre of large stone-walled enclosures.[8] With their massive construction and their elaborately sculpted Palace Façade designs, such enclosures were vast building projects in their own right. At Djoser's pyramid, for example, the volume of cut stone required for the enclosure wall was more than that required for the first low stone tomb – it was equal, indeed, to about a fifth of the volume of stone required for the Step Pyramid itself[9] – whilst the fine stone used in these walls was generally better finished than that used on the pyramids themselves.[10] At Meidum this workload was entirely changed when a decision was taken not to build another of these great grand enclosures nor any other of the elaborate stone buildings that had surrounded Djoser's two great tombs. Now, the pyramid alone was king.

Sneferu's pyramid-makers were off to a flying start. And so successful were they that, just as Djoser's tomb-makers had done before them, they elaborated their first design, enlarging the original pyramid by a third and refacing this second stage of building with more fine stone cladding and crowning the new pyramid with another step, an addition that took its overall height to around 270 feet (82 m), some 70 feet higher than King Djoser's pyramid.[11] At this point after fifteen years of building and with the initial decision not to erect any other architecture than the royal pyramid still holding good, and Sneferu apparently showing few signs of requiring his bright new pyramid for burial, the pyramid-makers, by then a well-established workforce, had little enough to do.[12] Thus, another classic moment for innovation had arrived: the size of the pyramid-makers' workforce was doubled, and they set off to build the king another pyramid.[13]

0   50 metres

Fig. 131 (*top left*) The plain beside the Pyramid of Meidum was explored by several archaeologists in the last decades of the nineteenth century, one of whose excavations is shown in this anonymous photograph. The ruin rising from the rubble of the pyramid's destruction is part of the core of the first pyramid to be built upon the site. The smooth finishes upon its sides, however, show that there were several earlier phases of construction; like those embedded in the fabric of the Step Pyramid, these may be the products of architectural experimentation.

Fig. 132 (*top right*) Many of the architectural complexities of Sneferu's Meidum Pyramid were unravelled in the 1920s by Ludwig Borchardt, who found that it had been composed of three separately finished pyramids enclosed, like Russian dolls, one inside the other. Here, some of his workmen have exposed parts of the fabric of the first and smallest of them.

Fig. 133 (*bottom left*) The remains of the casing on the east face of Sneferu's first pyramid at Meidum. The survey rod held by Borchardt's assistant rests upon the smoothed outer stonework of the pyramid's second step.

Fig. 134 (*bottom right*) Cross section of the second phase of Sneferu's Meidum Pyramid, in which another casing of fine stone was added to the first-built pyramid – which is shown in dotted line.

29 The failed pyramid

. . . the pyramid itself was one of the greatest threats to the royal body that they took such pains to preserve.

Mark Lehner[1]

The site chosen for Sneferu's second pyramid was beside the same dry prehistoric river bed on which his first pyramid had been built; this time, they chose its western edge and a location some 30 miles north of Meidum and well within sight of Djoser's Pyramid. Known now as the Plain of Dahshur, this location too was outside the traditional burying grounds. So Sneferu's new pyramid was again planned to stand on its own, a lone marker on the Western Desert with a spare cemetery of mastabas in attendance.[2]

It has been suggested, although there is no hard evidence to support it, that the new location reflected the relocation of the royal palace from Meidum to Dahshur, for there is a rare record of the relocation of a royal palace in King Sneferu's fifteenth year.[3] A more tangible impetus for the move, however, was that Dahshur, unlike Meidum, may have been closer to a local source of building stone: at Meidum it would appear that, as well as shipping fine Tura limestone for the pyramid's casing and internal architecture, large amounts of its coarser-quality limestone blocks were also brought from similar distances.[4]

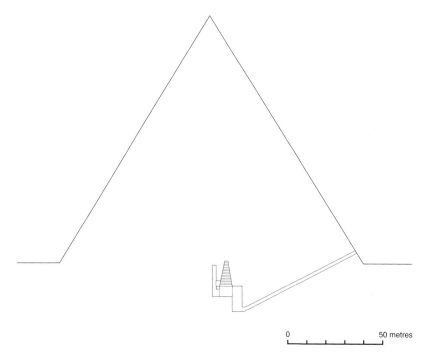

Fig. 135 A reconstruction of the initial phase of Sneferu's first pyramid-building project at Dahshur. If it had been completed – for it appears that it was built to less than half its height – this strange structure would have been somewhat similar in its appearance to the surviving core of Sneferu's Meidum Pyramid.

0   50 metres

Whatever the reason for the move, at Dahshur, and all of a sudden, Sneferu's master builders started work upon a pyramid of revolutionary design: a pyramid whose base at around 515 feet (157 m) gave it a volume almost three times that of their previous pyramid and far and away the largest ever attempted. For the pyramid-makers appear to have planned to set the apex of this pyramid at the heady height of around 405 feet (123.43 m), which meant that it would have risen at an angle of 60°, and stood just 76 feet (23.28 m) short of the Great Pyramid at Giza![5] Yet more remarkable was that this extraordinarily ambitious pyramid was designed as the world's first smooth-sided pyramid: it would have no steps.

What on earth had been the inspiration for abandoning the usual stepped pyramid design, a construction common to several Bronze Age cultures, in favour of the smooth-sided monument that became ancient Egypt's abiding symbol? What had filled Sneferu's builders with the ambition to build another pyramid at all, and plan to build so wide and high that it would require three times the amount of stone than they had previously quarried?[6]

There is no intrinsic profit in building a pyramid, of course, other than the act of building in itself, in which the power of government is made manifest (see ch. 16 above). On these terms Sneferu's second pyramid was made larger because the increasing efficiency of the state building force could make it so; quite simply, the tendency of the early pyramid-makers to build ever larger monuments reflects the growing efficacy of the state's systems of supply; that, and the longevity of a few pharaohs.

As to this pyramid's design; once more, such puzzles cannot be solved by renaming them with labels such as 'evolution' or 'inspiration'. Even in the (unlikely!) event of architectural texts from Sneferu's time coming to light, the writings of an Egyptian Vitruvius or Corbusier, it would be naive to imagine that they would tell us the full story of these pyramids, just as the writings of those later literary architects do not provide us with accounts of the circumstances in which their buildings were designed and made. The real story of this pyramid, and of the Great Pyramid and all the others that followed them, is that they were developed one from another, by generations of anonymous communities of pyramid-makers.

As for the specific reason why the stepped sides of the traditional pyramid were abandoned for a single shining slope, it should first be observed that there was a disposition amongst ancient Egyptian craftsmen of all periods continually to reform earlier designs. Just as Djoser's craftsmen had abstracted, straightened and balanced the organic forms of archaic architecture, the reeds, the mud, the logs and mats, and built elegant architectural equivalents in stone, so by simplifying and smoothing the stepped silhouettes of the earlier pyramids, Sneferu's architects were following the self-same tendency.

This is not to imply that ancient Egyptian designers consciously evolved a set of procedures with which to pare down their forefathers' designs. Pyramid building and design were neither automatic nor mechanical: in the century after Sneferu and Khufu, the design, the scale and the materials of royal funerary architecture all changed in a variety of ways, and one monarch at least was buried in a monument that was not a pyramid.[7] All these building projects, however, were the product of unknown ancient Egyptians consciously exercising choice and free will inside the constraints imposed by the requirements of the royal burial, the resources of the national economy, and the physical limits of the available materials.

So when Sneferu's new smooth-sided pyramid was standing to only half its full height and it started to break down, when the largest mass of stone that humankind had ever gathered up together in one place threatened to implode as the desert underneath began to move, the pyramid-makers were forced to invent a series of immediate practical responses. And eventually, and in their different ways, many of these modifications enabled the successful construction of the Great Pyramid of Giza and affected its design as well.

The crisis at Dahshur was born both of the pyramid-makers' traditional techniques and in the very ground on which the new pyramid had been sited. When they had begun work at Dahshur, the royal builders appear to have prepared the pyramid's foundations in the usual way, laying quarry blocks and a narrow bed of desert plaster and a little sand into four shallow trenches cut into the square shape of the pyramid's intended baselines.[8] At the Step Pyramid, this same procedure had formed a firm bed between the pyramid's stonework and the desert rock on which it sat, and its success is apparent to this day, for the grand old monument has hardly moved.[9] At Meidum too, the pyramid-makers had laid similar foundations to equal effect, setting them into the top of the prehistoric river bed, a 60 foot deep layer of hard compacted clay and gravel.[10] Unlike the Meidum Pyramid, however, the chosen site of the new pyramid at Dahshur had been set right on the western edge of this prehistoric river bed, by strata composed of brittle limestones, shales and sand: a geologic sandwich.[11]

As the stone courses of the huge new pyramid had risen ever higher, its foundations had compressed and shifted, its baselines had wobbled, and the stonework of the interior corridors and rooms had cracked and twisted out of line. And the entire unfinished pyramid, more than 1½ million tons of limestone blocks, began to sink, and sink unevenly.

The evidence suggests that subsidence in the pyramid's building blocks had begun early on in its construction – and this seems to be true of many other pyramids as well.[12] At Dahshur, however, this initial settling did not stop, and indeed appears to have accelerated as the pyramid rose higher and the weight upon its lower courses and the unstable desert beneath rapidly increased.[13]

Buried deep inside the pyramid, the precise mechanics of these processes of movement and destruction are difficult to detect today. Clearly, the massive smooth-sided structure bore down far more heavily upon its foundations than any stepped pyramid had ever done before. Rising at 60°, moreover, its angle was far steeper than the earlier pyramids and this by itself would have led to greater pressure on its baselines and the modest foundation trenches underneath.

The glimpses of the lower sections of this pyramid that can still be seen today between its tumbled stones show that the royal masons made changes to their ways of working as the building rose; these presumably in an attempt to stabilise it. At the beginning, the stone setters appear to have worked in a manner similar to that which they employed upon the earlier pyramids, using rough-shaped and often poor-quality limestone quarry blocks, tilting them down towards the centre of the pyramid, and setting them in large amounts of raw desert mortar and white clay.[14] But the rough finish of these blocks had meant that their weight was not distributed equally over their surfaces and was often borne upon a few irregular protuberances which provoked the splitting and collapse of many individual blocks.[15] Later in the work, with the pyramid still continuing to move, the blocks were more carefully finished, more accurately matched one to another and laid horizontal to the ground, which would have further reduced some of those uneven pressures. Now too, and for the first time in stone architecture, the mortar that the pyramid-builders used to bind these blocks together was kiln dried to make a harder and more compacted bond.[16] A few decades later, exactly these same hard-won lessons in stabilising massive stone constructions would help the Great Pyramid to rise up straight and true and endure through the millennia.

Despite such changes Sneferu's second pyramid continued to twist and move, even as they built it; as one of its surveyors has described, its two interior chambers, which were never finished and were left half-filled with loose stone blocks, are 'of really peculiar shape'.[17] Similarly, the blocks of the corridor that leads down to these two deep chambers had cracked and shifted to produce a 9 inch (23 cm) step which, even after the masons had attempted to smooth it out again by chiselling and adding extra stones, had continued to subside.[18] One might well imagine that in those early years, as the masons went about their work, ominous murmurs, cracks and crunches born in the pyramid's very heart were echoing up and along its entrance corridor, and that at the same time the ever-growing pressures on its masonry were producing alarming cracks in its exterior walls and displacements all along its baselines.

This pyramid was all at sea. Its external building lines and its interior chambers and corridors were moving, and in the days before modern surveying equipment was available, these were the basic reference points by which the pyramid's rising form was controlled and checked.[19]

The situation is best summed up by the present position of a little architectural element built inside this pyramid that appears to have been made precisely for such purposes of control. Although similar in design to the internal layout of Sneferu's earlier pyramid at Meidum, where a single corridor runs down from the pyramid's northern side to a burial chamber underneath the centre of the pyramid, at Dahshur the pyramid-makers had added another chamber on the line of the entrance corridor and a narrow shaft as well, a little over 5 feet (1.6 m) square, set beyond the burial chamber, close to the pyramid's exact centre.

Known now as the Chimney, and rising some 50 feet above the level of the burial chamber's floor and dropping down 16 feet beneath it, this small shaft would have enabled the pyramid-makers to keep a sheltered plumb line at the pyramid's dead centre – a most desirable reference point as the pyramid rose higher and the multiple lines and edges of a stepped pyramid were no longer available to aid in check-ing the architecture of the rising pyramid. Such a shaft would be the first of many similar vertical controls set up inside the early pyra-mids.[20] Today, however, after the slow movement of its stonework, the Chimney no longer stands at the centre of the pyramid.[21]

Working in a continuously distorting environment with no fixed points of measurement other than those that could be taken along the pyramid's sagging foundation lines some 250 feet (77.5 m) out from the pyramid's lost centre line, the masons too would have been lost, their broken pyramid quite stranded.

All at once, Sneferu's state building machine had been placed in an extraordinary predicament. After having spent the best part of thirty years working on two pyramids at Meidum and Dahshur, after cutting and laying the equivalent of three complete Step Pyramid enclosures – more than 2½ million tons of limestone blocks – and laying them at twice the speed at which King Djoser's monuments had been built, the making of ever larger and ever higher pyramids had outstripped their technology. The little deserts of the Nile Valley simply could not support the weight of such vast piles of stone. The more they contin-ued to work upon the Dahshur pyramid, the more unsafe the royal grave, the royal destiny, became. What were they to do?

Their heroic answer to this predicament was to abandon the failing pyramid, to triple the size of the royal workforce and to start to build another and yet larger one.[22] If only for the fact that Sneferu's reign had already been longer than most of his predecessors and the likeli-hood of his builders finishing a third enormous pyramid in time to receive his burial must have appeared remote, it was a truly astonish-ing solution.[23] Equally extraordinary was that they abandoned the failing pyramid when almost three quarters of its stone was already laid,[24] and their scheme to build a third and yet larger funerary mon-ument required previously unattained levels of production both from the royal workforce and from the little state that supported them.[25] National dedication, frenetic effort and all the skill and accuracy the pyramid-makers could muster would be required to make this third pyramid rise up quick and true. Painted on a stone block placed close to the new pyramid's foundation lines, a rough graffito tells us that it was laid in Sneferu's thirtieth year as king: as we have seen in chapter 6, modern calculations have estimated that they built this pyramid in less than eleven years.[26]

30 The jubilee pyramid

Sited on the same plain, and just a mile to the north of the failed pyramid, Sneferu's third great pyramid, the so-called Red Pyramid, was designed and built with that earlier disaster well in view. This time, rather than building upon a rocky outcrop as all previous pyramids had been, on little platforms in the desert, the pyramid-makers chose an area that was flat and undisturbed, an area, one would imagine, where the stable gravels of the ancient river bed ran deep and low.[1]

Fig. 136 The Red Pyramid.

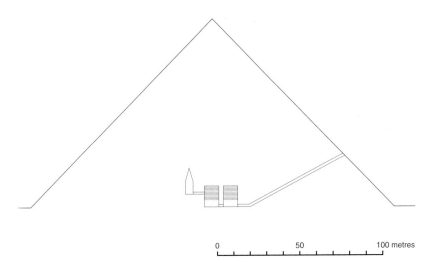

Fig. 137 Cross section of the Red Pyramid.

0   50   100 metres

As for the pyramid itself, from its foundations up, the new construction shows clear evidence of its builders working to new levels of efficiency and consistency, and of a practical and economic engineering too. This time around as well, as far as one can tell, the pyramid's core appears to have been built entirely of relatively well-cut blocks of limestone, set in hard heat-treated mortar and laid in precise horizontal courses. The pyramid's unique reddish hue, moreover, would indicate that a great part of this stone was extracted from a different quarry than that which had provided the poorer-quality stone that had been used for the core of the failed pyramid nearby.[2] At the same time too, the pyramid's overall design was reassessed, its builders returning to a lower slope, which, with a rise of virtually 45°, was much closer to the stepped pyramids of King Djoser and his successors.[3] So even though this new pyramid was designed like its failed predecessor to be smooth-sided, this lower pitch resulted not only in a saving of some 40 per cent in the amount of building stone required, but also in a similar reduction of the weight of stone that would bear down upon the desert.[4]

Despite all this apparent prudence, once more the baselines of the new pyramid were designed to be around a third larger than the previous pyramid, so that its volume would be larger than all of Sneferu's previous projects added up together, requiring no less than 3,800,000 tons of cut limestone for its completion. At previous work rates, this would have required more than thirty years to complete,[5] a prospect that, considering the aging king if nothing else, would have presented a pressing reason for a somewhat swifter rate of working. So, just as one would expect, the graffiti that record the pyramid-makers' progress (see ch. 6 above) show that a swifter construction timetable was built into the project from its beginning,[6] which, in turn, would have required another substantial increase of the royal workforce.

During the first frantic years of work indeed, when the bottom thirty-six courses of this pyramid would have been laid, almost 2 million tons of quarried stone were cut and quarried and transported and set into position, a labour involving, at its maximum, a workforce of unprecedented size and scattered communities of more than 40,000 people, the greater part of whom would have lived close by the pyramid itself.[7] As we have already seen (pp. 72–3 above), however, this enormous enterprise would have dwindled down throughout the decade to a core of around 3000 people as the pyramid's apex was approached, as access was diminished and ever smaller volumes of cut stone were required.

The relative time frame established for all of Sneferu's building projects shows that the workload at the Red Pyramid represents an increase of almost 300 per cent from that of the second failed pyramid.[8] It would appear, therefore, that just as Sneferu's pyramid-builders had doubled their output after the move from Meidum to Dahshur, and so presumably had been doubled in their number, so too when they embarked upon their third pyramid, as the increased workload would suggest, the number of this workforce was precisely trebled.[9]

Here then, in the thirtieth year of the reign of Sneferu, on the bright desert of Dahshur, the greatest concentration of stone workers the world had ever seen was assembled and put to work. Although they would not have known it at the time, it was the Great Pyramid's proving ground. For after the burial of Sneferu, the core of this extraordinary workforce appears to have taken its hard-won knowledge of pyramid logistics and its extraordinary skill in handling blocks of stone to Giza and its Plateau. A direct inheritance of the work at Dahshur, for example, was the perfection of a vaulting system that would appear in an identical if gloriously extended form in the Great Pyramid's Grand Gallery.[10] Here too, at the Red Pyramid, great blocks of Tura stone were used throughout the pyramid's interior. Another direct inheritance was the Great Pyramid's standard block size (pp. 179ff). Like so many of the architectural elements in these early pyramids, it appears to have no ready correspondence with the Egyptian cubit, yet even so such standardisation, of itself, would have allowed Sneferu's master builders a consistent system of calculating the amount of work performed and the volume of stone that was yet required. There is some slight evidence even, although in the haze of numbers that these early pyramids can generate it may be nothing but another pyramidal mirage, that this block size was an element of the pyramid's design; that Sneferu's master builders did not oversee mere blocks of stone arriving from the quarries, but the basic building blocks of the building's final form.[11]

At all events, in all of this, one thing is absolutely certain. Statistics prove that in King Sneferu's day, the state of Egypt and its builders were gripped by a phenomenal absorption in cutting stone and building pyramids: that after thirty years of effort making two great pyramids, another explosion of national energy occurred upon the Plain of Dahshur as work on the Red Pyramid had begun. At the beginning of the work – and in the first two years no fewer than thirty-five courses of the Red Pyramid would have been laid – for a brief while, the workforce would have comprised around a tenth of the adult male population of the ancient Egyptian state.[12]

Similarly urgent assemblies of the state's resources, although usually on a lesser scale, appear to have been undertaken during the first years of the reigns of many pharaohs, as work commenced upon the building of their tombs.[13] And the building of Sneferu's third pyramid appears to have taken place within that same atmosphere, a revisiting of exactly that same detonation of energy and resources. Exactly that same sense of a new beginning that is conjured up by some small fragments of relief sculpture found in a little temple set beside the Red Pyramid, that show King Sneferu wearing the archaic robes of the so-called Sed festival, a ritual of royal revitalisation and renewal traditionally celebrated after a reign of thirty years and echoed to this day by Western monarchs in their ceremonials of jubilee.[14]

This grand old pyramid is silent witness to an explosion of controlled energy in which a monument of vast dimensions was built with incredible speed and accuracy. Just as the building and its temple decoration witness a consolidation of Sneferu's rule on earth and a renewal of his eternal destiny, so too the pyramid is so well built that after four and a half millennia it has hardly moved an inch.

This was Khufu's vast inheritance: the extraordinary machine that made his father's pyramids; the world's greatest stone building enterprise uniquely invested with decades of experience and skill and with the piety, enthusiasm and confidence to contemplate the construction of a Great Pyramid at Giza in the time span of a single reign.

31 The long journey of the spirit

It had taken the state of Egypt half a millennium to arrive at a point where they could construct three huge pyramids in the reign of a single king. Abandoning the archaic complexities of Djoser's spirit city, the last step of that long journey, had consequences well beyond the freeing of the state's stone gangs so that they could concentrate on building pyramids. Alternative arrangements also had to be made to cater for King Sneferu's afterlife. And this, as his funerary architecture shows, led to a majestic reaffirmation of some of the most ancient of all Egyptian beliefs concerning death; those beliefs that saw death as an unending journey and offerings to the spirit of the dead as an aid to this eternal progress. Now, just as the construction of Sneferu's three pyramids had required the mobilisation of national resources on a previously unknown scale, so those same pan-Egyptian mechanisms were brought into the service of King Sneferu's spirit.

King Djoser's pyramid, as we have seen, had been contained within a grandiose enclosure, a spirit city set inside a fortress with a single door, a lonely fortress in a hostile desert. A fortress, however, whose north–south axis and the majority of its buildings, its courts and courtyards and its offering temple, were aligned to the river's flow and to the polar stars.[1] This had been more than a collection of dummy buildings set around a ruler's tomb. Like the Valley of the

Fig. 138 Djoser's mortuary temple under excavation in the 1930s. This novel temple built of stone is set on the archaic locus for an offering place beside a royal tomb (cf. fig. 90). The entrance to the descending stairway that leads to Djoser's burial chamber underneath the pyramid is in the shadowed gouge cutting through the middle of the temple's floor.

Nile itself, King Djoser's spirit city had been set in rhythm with the hourly, daily, monthly, yearly movements of the cosmos, a multifarious network through which the spirit of the dead king would move forever.

As soon as the construction of these grand enclosures was abandoned and the royal tomb was no longer held inside this complex web of architectural and cosmic interrelationships, the effect upon the pyramid itself had been immediate and dramatic. Once, twice and thrice, and with phenomenal exactitude, King Sneferu's stone workers had anchored the baselines of his three great pyramids directly and precisely to the most constant elements of the Egyptian universe: specifically, to that most primeval and enduring set of human orientations, the transit of the polar stars.[2]

In similar fashion, once an offering temple was no longer set up on the north side of the royal grave, the needs of Sneferu's spirit had to be accommodated in quite different ways. Causeways were built from each of Sneferu's three pyramids running down through the desert to the edge of the cultivated land, where quays and canals built for the pyramids' stone barges would have provided access to the river, and thus to all of Egypt and its produce.[3] That this was considered as a genuine architectural alternative to the traditional arrangements by which offerings had been channelled to the spirit of the kings was most beautifully underlined by the exquisite reliefs found in the rare ruin of a small temple set by one of these causeways; reliefs that show images of food offerings being brought to Sneferu from provinces and estates all over Egypt.[4] The focus of this offering cult,

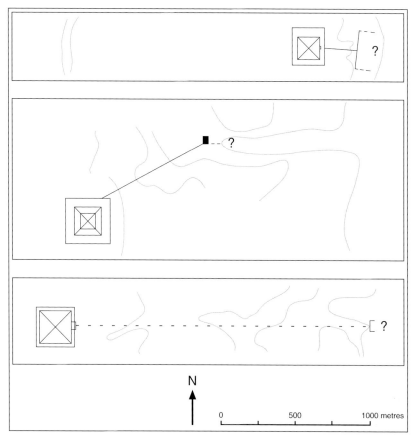

Fig. 139 Sketch maps of the offering temples and the causeways connected to King Sneferu's three pyramids: top, the Meidum Pyramid; centre, the Bent Pyramid – a later version of the first failed pyramid at Dahshur; and bottom, the Red Pyramid. Their joint abandonment of the large high-walled enclosures that surrounded earlier pyramids and their reconnection with the living land of Egypt, in the same manner by which the constructors of these pyramids had been linked to their sources of supply, was a profound change in design.

N

0   500   1000 metres

Fig. 140 The modest ruin of the Bent Pyramid's offering temple: a stone slab and two stout stelae set inside the ruin of a mud brick room.

Fig. 141 The Bent Pyramid and the Meidum Lake. This solitary lake may be the sole survivor of the harbours that provisioned and supplied the pyramid-makers. One would expect, therefore, that the ruins of some temples lie close by, at the ending of the causeways that connected the pyramids in the desert to the living land of Egypt.

and quite literally the direction in which the figures of the offering bearers in these reliefs are headed, appears to be the western end of these three causeways, where modest temples were set up beside each of Sneferu's three pyramids; zones where the world of the living and the dead could intermix. That these novel architectural arrangements were considered to have been entirely successful is shown by the numerous memorials of the cult's officiating priests which were set up over the succeeding centuries, and the decrees of latter kings as well, concerning their extensive and continuing offerings to Sneferu's spirit.[5]

So the archaic ritual of offering to the spirits of the dead had been most gloriously amplified and, with supreme self-confidence, set in a fine stone architecture which physically joined the living lands of Egypt to the royal tomb, and joined as well, by implication, the myriad destinies of the provincial deities, those most ancient gods enshrined in modest temples up and down the Nile, who would appear to have received their daily offerings in the same manner as the spirit of the king.[6]

The royal spirit was on the move again. Djoser's desert fortress, that claustrophobic spirit world, that closed and sacred space entered only by a single narrow door, was burst apart; the new arrangements for the delivery of royal offerings shifting the focus of the royal funerary architecture away from the introspections of a walled domain towards the living valley of the Nile. Now, the royal pyramids were not only coupled to the cosmic elements of the Egyptian universe but, in a model taken from the construction of the royal pyramids themselves, linked to Egypt's farms and fields and temples, to the palaces of pharaoh and the offices of the living government.

The ancient Egypt of King Djoser's day had been a culture in the process of design and definition. Just as his pyramid-builders had made a model state in stone, so working in that stone had provided the foundations of the mature pharaonic state. In the reign of Sneferu, that new economy had found its first fulfilment as his buildings turned all of Egypt into a sacred space, and its inhabitants, both the living and the dead and all its gods, into the citizens of a single sacred kingdom. A new air of assurance and security had liberated Sneferu's funerary architecture, and the land of Egypt of itself had become the royal funerary fortress.[7] The next great pyramid, King Khufu's Pyramid at Giza, would be the perfection and the purification of this extraordinary architectural expression.

Such were the unspoken implications of these extraordinary creations that it took much longer than the reigns of Sneferu and Khufu put together for the Egyptians to appreciate what they had wrought. Centuries on, the Pyramid Texts, the world's first religious writings, were still musing on this grand adventure. Inscribed upon the walls of smaller and far later pyramids, in splendid lines of measured hieroglyphs they meditate on the destinies that Sneferu's and Khufu's pyramid-makers had earlier mapped out in blocks of stone. And in yet later centuries, this magisterial redaction of the archaic forms of funerary ritual would become the model for ancient Egypt's famous tombs and temples, those splendid theatres in which the rituals surrounding life and death within the Nile Valley would be acted out.[8]

32 The dark interior

At the same time as the royal pyramid-makers had stopped building grand enclosures around their pyramids, so too they radically redesigned their dark interiors. The subterranean extravangazas of Djoser's spirit palaces, those mile on mile of corridors and crypts and magazines, the palaces of fine limestone and glistening faience, were all abandoned, and in their place there came a precise preoccupation with the physical accommodation of the dead king; an architectural meditation on the fate of pharaoh.

It was a gradual development. First, the elaborate arrangements of Djoser's huge burial pit where the royal corpse was designed to lie encased in gigantic shafts of granite were discarded, the two unfinished pyramids that followed having rough-hewn burial chambers cut into the crumbling natural rock beneath, that were accessed from the north. Even in Djoser's day such subterranean arrangements had been considered to be potentially unstable, as the contemporary wooden buttresses that still support some of the Step Pyramid's galleries clearly testify.[1] And that, perhaps, is why Sneferu's pyramid-makers set his royal burial chambers inside a stone block architecture similar to the structures of the pyramids that stood above them. At the beginning of their work, however, at Sneferu's first step pyramid at Meidum, the pyramid-builders had started working in the old way,

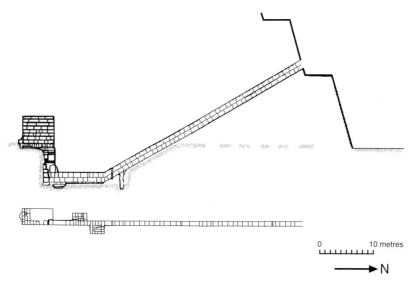

Fig. 142 Plan and cross section of the interior of the Meidum Pyramid, showing how its interior architecture was fitted over and around a pit excavated in the natural surface of the desert. This traditional arrangement would be retained in most of the later royal pyramids, just as would the two chambers set before the burial chamber, which are also a common feature of the archaic tombs.

0   10 metres

➤ N

cutting a pit into the desert rock on which the pyramid would stand, with an access corridor running down from its northern side. Here, and for the first time, they also set an angled entrance corridor into the stonework of the pyramid itself, a corridor that runs from a doorway placed about a quarter of the way up on the pyramid's northern face down through the pyramid's courses to join the original excavation in the natural rock beneath, before turning upwards at its ending to a stone block burial chamber set close to the level of the desert[2] (fig. 142). The rambling accommodations of earlier pyramids had disappeared for ever. The way to the grave had become an abstract architectural journey that changed from a descent to an uprising, a quintessential rendering of the later literary image of the first journey of the royal spirit after death that the texts will describe, in myriad forms, as a rising upward; as a resurrection.[3]

There were other innovations too in the internal architecture of the Meidum Pyramid, an architectural bonus prompted by the placement of the royal burial crypt within the courses of the pyramid itself, which led King Sneferu's masons to develop an elegant high-arching roof that they would later use in all his other pyramids. Enlisting the combined weight and friction – the stiction – of the pyramid's stacked-up building blocks, the master masons re-employed an elementary bonding system used centuries before in archaic mud-brick tombs which, to modern eyes, gives the false impression of being a genuine stressed vault of arched stones, and which in consequence is called a corbel vault.[4] In fact, it is no vault at all, but simply the result of overlapping a succession of the pyramid's massive limestone blocks one above the other in their successive courses until they touch together, high up above the burial chamber's floor.[5]

Soaring and dramatic, this false vault was an entirely novel form of stone block architecture and one that, as the somewhat rough and uneven blocks of the burial chamber at Meidum clearly show, was initially a little hesitant in its execution. Rising up some 20 feet, this first stone corbel vault appears as an irregular acute triangle, a stone tent pitched beneath the centre of the pyramid as if the masons were trying to shape the space of the burial chamber in a series of steps, in something of the same manner as the pyramid's exterior. Here perhaps, a master mason had devised a structure whose shape was intended to do more than support a Damoclesian mass of stone above the royal burial chamber.

By the time of the construction of Sneferu's third pyramid, the essential architectural narrative – a straight descending corridor which rises at its ending to a corbel-vaulted burial chamber – had been developed and enlarged (see figs. 130 and 135). Whereas Sneferu's Meidum Pyramid had but a single chamber, a burial chamber, at the ending of its entrance corridor, the first failed pyramid at Dahshur had an antechamber set before its burial chamber, whilst the third pyramid, the Red Pyramid, had two antechambers, although these were still connected by a single descending corridor which turned upwards to its ending. Now, the pyramid-makers were no longer beginning their work in the traditional way by excavating shafts and trenches in the desert underneath the pyramid. And the corridors and chambers of the royal burial were held within the courses of the stonework of the pyramid itself and in careful and exact relationship to the rest of the pyramid's fine architecture.

Here, the dark heart of the tomb is no longer set at the centre of a crumbling maze of palaces and pits and storerooms; the journey to the grave has become a rational geometrical progression, a single narrative in space and time that, like the pyramid through which it travels, is set in precise conformity with the movements of the heavens and the elements of living Egypt.

As you walk down through the Red Pyramid today, the first two of its three chambers, virtual twins, appear as exquisite, meditative, well-proportioned, finely coffered spaces; the last great chamber, where excavators found the scanty relics of a burial, as an austere, majestic and high-soaring room, a suitable environment for the grave of a pharaoh whose subjects had spent their lives absorbed with pyramids and blocks of stone.[6]

Fig. 143 The splendid corbel vaulting in the first of the Red Pyramid's three chambers, the last being the royal burial chamber.

Here, the pyramid-makers have set a final geometric twist in their crystalline progress through the pyramid. Set beyond the central axis of the pyramid and at right angles to the rest of the interior and with its only access some 28 feet (8.5 m) up in the air, the funeral party must have traversed a special scaffolding, climbing up from the second chamber's floor level on the pyramid's baselines and the horizon of the west, to reach a strange small doorway that opens from the top of the second antechamber's coffered vault, then bowed their heads to pass through the last low portal to the burial chamber that lies beyond. Such then is the substance of the pyramid-builders' last dialogue with royal death before they went to work again upon the cliff at Giza and the pyramid of Sneferu's son, King Khufu.

33 Two last works

After reigning for almost half a century, Sneferu, it appears, was buried in the Red Pyramid at Dahshur in 2491 BC.[1] Like the other early pharaohs, the man remains elusive; only eroded images survive,[2] and certainly we have no knowledge of his role in making pyramids. Clearly, the national adventure of building his three huge pyramids had given the pyramid-makers a sublime self-confidence; specifically, the assurance to conceive and build the Great Pyramid at Giza. Before they started work on Khufu's Pyramid, however, they undertook two other works for Sneferu that would have an indelible effect on the designs of all the later pyramids of Egypt, including the Great Pyramid of Giza.

Even by the matchless standards of King Sneferu's pyramid-making machine, these two late projects were colossal enterprises in their own right, requiring the quarrying of 2 million tons of limestone blocks, almost a quarter of the stone that was quarried in King Sneferu's reign.[3] What, a modern mind might wonder, could possibly be left to build after three decades of furious effort that had culminated in the triumph of the Red Pyramid, that most fine and finished tomb? Why were the royal building works not allowed to run quietly down? A simple reason may have been a reluctance to complete the tomb of someone who yet lived, just as later generations of royal

tomb-makers would leave small parts of the most lavish royal tombs uncompleted, as if the conclusion of their work could only be answered by the death of its intended owner. So there are many funerary complexes in Egypt that sport a few mud-brick walls; even the temple beside Sneferu's Red Pyramid, after all, was finished in mud brick.[4]

A more fundamental reason why Sneferu's enormous building machine was kept hard at work may well have been the perceived value of the act of building in itself, as we have already seen (ch. 16 above). Just as in later ages, when inscriptions tell us that the gods of Egypt are 'well pleased' with their temples – a fact which is hardly surprising, for without them deity would have had no home, and Egypt no settled gods[5] – so in similar fashion the building of pyramids witnessed the power and efficacy and prosperity of the living state. After all, such enormous projects as these pyramids could only have been brought to their conclusion when government was efficient and the nation relatively prosperous.

Nowadays, the Plain of Dahshur is one of Egypt's finest sights, a lustrous desert sprinkled with half-buried mastabas and framed by two of Sneferu's pyramids. Stripped of its fine stone skin and weathered to a rusty brown, the Red Pyramid, the third largest ever built in Egypt, is a stately monument, its deep serenity enhanced by the eccentric bulk of the odd-shaped pyramid that lies a mile to the south of it; this, one of the products of the last years of Sneferu's reign. For as they were finishing the Red Pyramid, the royal builders appear to

Fig. 144 The Plain of Dahshur with Sneferu's two great pyramids, seen from Sakkara.

have returned to the low bulk of their failed and half-finished pyramid and in a virtuoso gesture, reinforced its sides and capped its crest with a near-half-size replica of the Red Pyramid itself.[6] Nor was this enterprise as bizarre or as dangerous as it might at first appear. A decade of working at the Red Pyramid, after all, had proved that the key to building massive yet stable pyramids on Dahshur's sandy plain was to pitch them at a lower angle: they had returned, therefore, to the site of their earlier failure with a proven design.[7]

Work restarted at the failed pyramid by encasing its rump inside a massive well-built buttress, a girdling wall just over 50 feet (15.7 m) in thickness and set at a slightly shallower angle than the steep slope of the original.[8] On top of this, at a height of almost 155 feet (47.1 m), another pyramid was erected with an angle close to 45°, so that when it was completed the apex of this strangely double-angled form would stand within 16 feet of the height of its neighbour.[9] At a stroke, the unique work completed their earlier unfinished pyramid and balanced and harmonised its architecture with that of the Red Pyramid nearby. And it also provided this once-failed pyramid with its modern English nickname: the Bent Pyramid.

The pyramid-makers had returned to their earlier catastrophe with a greatly improved technology, fitting the blocks of this second stage of building with far greater accuracy than they had employed at the beginning of this work. Cut from a hard bluish-white Tura limestone, the finely finished blocks are also set in larger courses than the first phase of building, which would have further aided their stability.[10] Yet though the pyramid-makers did all that, and set six massive courses of the girdling walls' foundation stones some 10 feet down into the gravel of the Dahshur Plain, the pyramid's inherent

Fig. 145 Cross section of the Bent Pyramid, showing the secondary buttresses that encase and support the earlier failed pyramid. Uniquely, this standardised north–south cross section is not adequate to express the outlines of the secondary burial chamber system that was set up inside the pyramid. A more modest version of the pyramid's first three-chambered system, this second system enters the pyramid from high up upon its western face, and was connected to the older lower system after its completion by a tunnel driven through the finished stone work.

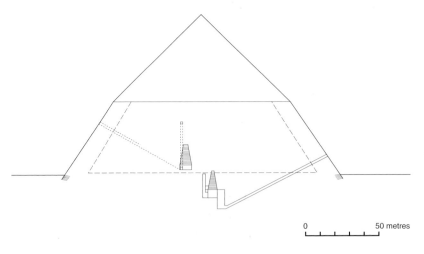

0   50 metres

Fig. 146 Set at an angle in the manner of King Djoser's masons, the Bent Pyramid's beautifully finished casing blocks still serve to buttress the failed lower sections of the earlier pyramid.

Fig. 147 The Bent Pyramid.

instability came back to haunt them, and gaping holes and long vertical cracks once again appeared in their brand-new outer buttress, so that even as they patiently patched the jagged splitting stonework, it separated further as the building grew and threatened new disasters.[11] Inside too, the entrance corridor, which was already skewed through the best part of its length, became displaced at the junction between the girdling wall and the old failed pyramid, producing another unexpected step and a similar disjunction in the ceiling above.[12] This time around, however, like Pisa's Leaning Tower whose architect continued to compensate for the building's movement long after its first lurch out of true,[13] Sneferu's pyramid-makers somehow set up a series of balanced tensions inside the sinking pyramid that served to stress and strengthen it sufficiently to allow them to complete the work, so that today and most ironically, this fragile structure that threatened to collapse even as it was being built is the best-preserved of all Egyptian pyramids.[14]

Another consequence of the second phase of building at the failed pyramid appears to have been the provision of a second burial chamber system inside the pyramid, the original arrangement with its entrance low down on its northern face being replaced by another whose entrance is situated high on the pyramid's western buttress. This was a completely separate arrangement for the royal burial chamber system, as if the work of capping the original failed structure with another pyramid was considered to have been the equivalent of establishing a new pyramid in its own right.[15] If this was true, we may imagine that the second phase of working at the failed pyramid began in the traditional manner, by fashioning a trench to hold part of the new pyramid's burial arrangements; a procedure that in practice, would have entailed the removal of a large quantity of cut stone blocks from the earlier work so that the new burial chamber could dip down close to the level of the desert in the usual way.[16] At all events, the simple plan of this new burial chamber system – an entrance corridor with a single corbel-vaulted burial chamber at its ending – carefully avoided all contact with the earlier interior arrangements of the failed pyramid, this in all probability being the reason for its unique western entrance, set as it is at right angles to the original interior, a twisting of the pyramids' usual orientation that would also represent a fresh start, a new design stage, at the old pyramid.[17]

At the end, these separate burial chamber systems, old and new, were joined together by means of a rough tunnel cut down through the pyramid's stone courses from the western corridor to break into the coffered vault of the original burial chamber. At its finish the Bent Pyramid had no fewer than three interlinking interior chambers lying in a single dramatic sequence, one above the other. Majestically elaborated, the same arrangement, complete with a skew in its axis, would appear again in the next great monument the pyramid-makers built: the Great Pyramid of Giza.

The other and yet more extraordinary task undertaken by King Sneferu's pyramid-builders was a work so closely linked to the Great Pyramid's design that it may well be considered as a prototype. As well as finishing the second failed pyramid, Sneferu's builders also revisited their first-built pyramid at Meidum, enlarging its base and smoothing out its eight great steps in fine-cut blocks of bluish Tura limestone that bear strong resemblance in both size and workmanship to those employed in the final phases of the work at the Bent Pyramid.[18] This time, and most critically, they did not set the angle of their new pyramid at the 45° slope of the Red Pyramid, but at 51° 50', an angle that would be precisely duplicated at the Great Pyramid of Giza. Here at Meidum, ancient Egypt's most distinctive silhouette was born.

It was Petrie who after excavating and surveying the Meidum Pyramid first recognised that these two monuments – the last building phase of Sneferu's Pyramid at Meidum and the Great Pyramid of Giza – were joined in a common system of proportion,[19] part of a sophisticated design tradition that, as we have seen, stretches back beyond the days of Djoser to the beginnings of the First Dynasty of kings.[20] What Petrie did not realise was that this special angle of 51° 50' can be produced by marking the co-ordinates of a six-squared grid set upon the baseline of the Meidum Pyramid and then adding 12½, 25 and 37½ cubits to the consecutive co-ordinates of the grid's first four squares (see fig. 148), just as adding exactly 20, 40 and 60 cubits to the same grid square's co-ordinates at the size of the Great Pyramid produces that same angle and that same familiar silhouette upon the cliff of Giza.[21]

Such mathematical delights are not the overriding experience of a visit to the Meidum Pyramid today. Mined and quarried by Roman

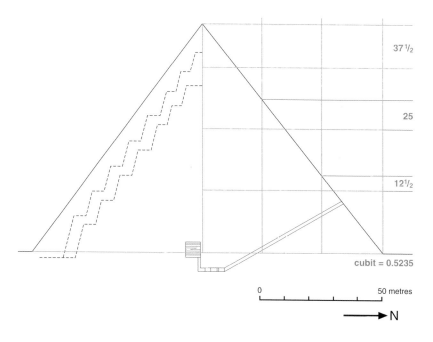

37½

25

12½

cubit = 0.5235

0   50 metres

N

Fig. 148 Cross section of the third and final building phase of the Meidum Pyramid, showing how the angle of its rise may be set by co-ordinates of 12.5 – 25 – 37.5 cubits placed on three grid squares. This same system, although employing co-ordinates of 20 – 40 – 60 cubits (cf. fig. 169), was later used at the Great Pyramid; see also chapters 5 above and 37 and 38 below.

Fig. 149 Borchardt's assistant stands beside the entrance doorway of the third phase of the Dahshur Pyramid. The fine stone casing blocks were set at precisely the same angle as those of the Great Pyramid's; perhaps the doorway, too, is the direct predecessor of the Great Pyramid's now-vanished entrance.

builders like so many of the ancient pyramids,[22] the solitary ruin appears as a steep-sided compendium of successive innovations and interventions, an inadvertent silhouette whose fine stones sink enigmatically into a rolling sea of limestone chip, a high swell of robbers' rubble that shares its tones and colours with the shattered tower-like pyramid above. Here it is difficult to appreciate that the architecture of these great monuments was shaped not by nature, nor by evolution, nor the hand of time, but by a chain of people using numbers and fine craftsmanship, making decision upon decision, generation after generation.

34 Coda: the legacy

When Khufu ascended to the throne of Egypt in about 2491 BC, his kingdom had been building pyramids for about the same length of time as skyscrapers have been erected in our modern cities. All previous pyramids had been innovative both in their construction and in their architectural design, and certainly there was no established model of design. At Giza, the Great Pyramid's design would be decisive; by comparison, all earlier arrangements seem tentative or elementary. The Great Pyramid was conceived on such a scale and built with such passionate intensity that it is as if their previous adventures had led the royal masons to a vision of the perfect pyramid.

Today of course, we can see that Khufu's pyramid-makers followed in their predecessors' footsteps, but at the time that decision was neither automatic nor inevitable. The pyramid of Khufu's immediate successor, for example, would be a far smaller affair with a completely different interior, and part-faced with blocks of Aswan granite.[1] Decades later too, the pyramid-makers would build an enormous oblong funerary monument for King Shepseskaf with a form far closer to that of an archaic mastaba than a regal pyramid.[2] There was always, always, choice. Although 'the Pyramids of Egypt' may appear to be the unthinking products of anonymous labourers, their weathered forms as natural as a canyon, their designs as artless as a

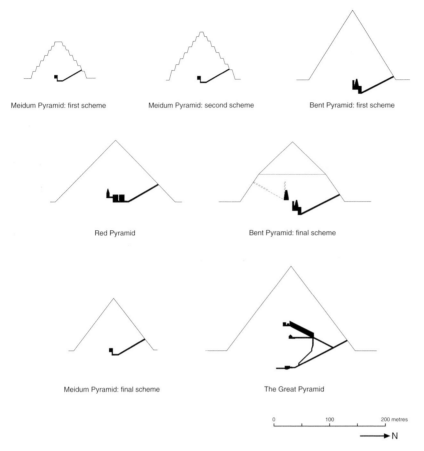

Meidum Pyramid: first scheme

Meidum Pyramid: second scheme

Bent Pyramid: first scheme

Red Pyramid

Bent Pyramid: final scheme

Meidum Pyramid: final scheme

The Great Pyramid

0   100   200 metres

N

Fig. 150 Cross sections of the great pyramid-building projects of the reigns of Sneferu and Khufu. The Bent Pyramid appears as a compendium of forms and shapes from earlier pyramids; the Great Pyramid as a perfect climax.

tree, they owe nothing to nature nor to evolution but are the unique creations of groups of real living human beings faced, as ever, with a wealth of choices.

In the event, King Khufu's pyramid-makers chose to move north to the lonely Giza Plateau and built the world's largest pyramid atop its cliff. And that too was another novel place to build, another choice, just as was their adoption of the integrated geometric plan that underlies the architecture of the Great Pyramid, which tells us that it was conceived as a single unified design from its beginnings.[3] And this too, given that the royal pyramid-makers had spent the previous forty years altering and adapting three great pyramids for Khufu's father, was another major innovation. As was the fact that they planned to build a single pyramid at Giza whose bulk represented almost 70 per cent of the entire tonnage quarried and laid during Sneferu's near-half-century-long building programme; a fact that would suggest that King Khufu's pyramid-makers had planned to build but one pyramid for the new king from the beginning of the work.

Here then at Giza, in the reign of Khufu of the Fourth Egyptian Dynasty, was born the custom of building just one large pyramid for the burial of pharaoh, however long his earthly rule might be.[4] Here too at Giza, the vital choice was made to adopt the distinctive proportions of the Egyptian pyramid's now-standard silhouette; although in this, as we have seen, King Khufu's masons simply copied one of the last great projects of his father's time.[5] With their single pyramid, the various erratic projects of King Sneferu's day that over almost half a century of working had set some seven separate designs over and around three different pyramid cores were purified and extended in a single sure design. At Giza, however, the Great Pyramid's designers planned their monument to be more than half as large again as the earlier design on which it had been based. And the size of this enlargement was in itself exceptional, previous increases in pyramid sizes having multiplied the volume of the stone required for each new project by far less.[6]

As for this vast never to be repeated size: the dynamic held in Sneferu's state machine means that this apparently outrageous scheme, the ambition to build what is still the largest stone block structure ever made by humankind, was one that Khufu's pyramid-makers could reasonably have expected to complete within the lifetime of their king. It was nothing, after all, that they had not done before, and as the ruins of the other elaborate buildings of Khufu's time upon the Giza Plateau show, the Great Pyramid's planners judged their enterprise so well that they had time enough to spend in the latter years of the reign extending the original conception of the royal funerary architecture, just as Djoser's and Sneferu's stone masons had done before them.[7] Rather than the abstract pleasures of mathematics or stone architecture, or theology or architectural whim or inspiration, it was the dynamism of the living state machine, its sheer skills and clever use of live tradition, that was paramount in making Khufu's Pyramid.

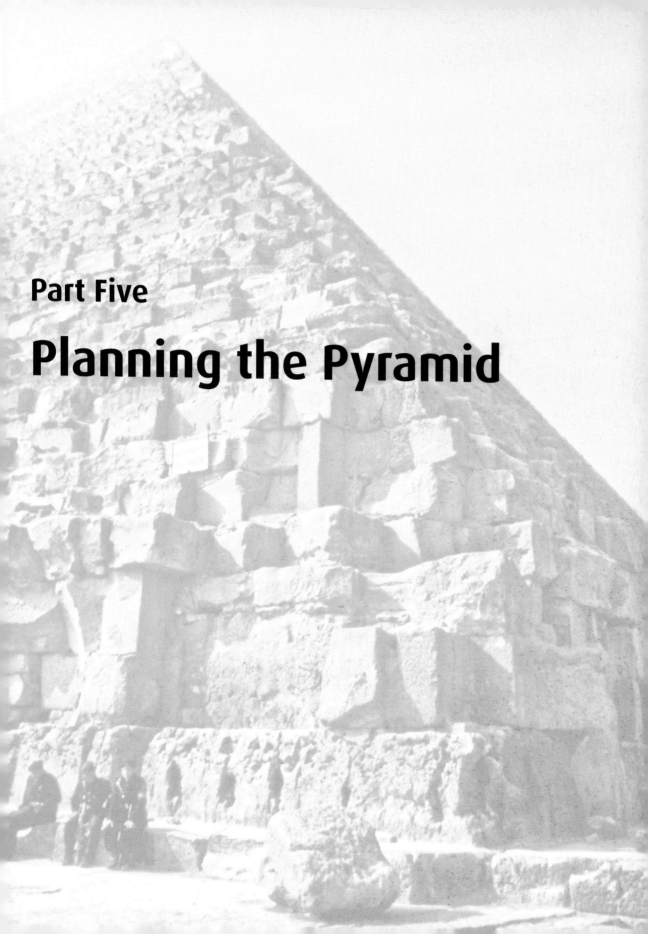

Part Five

Planning the Pyramid

35 Choosing Giza

At first glance, the choice of the Giza Plateau as the site of the Great Pyramid is a surprising one. Unlike the earlier pyramids, it is set high upon a cliff top some 4 miles from the Nile and at the very ending of its valley, where the black earth begins to widen into the delta plains.[1] With the exception of one unfinished royal pyramid, the pyramid-makers never built further north than the Giza Plateau, so that today the Great Pyramid and the Meidum Pyramid, Khufu's and Sneferu's monuments, stand as the alpha and omega spanning a unique strip of desert 40 miles wide on which the best part of Egypt's royal pyramids were placed; a galaxy of monuments eight centuries in the making.[2]

Yet the Giza deserts had been used as cemeteries long before the Great Pyramid was built. A little to the south, opposite King Khufu's quarry and just beyond the sandy valley, there are the modest ruins of a group of archaic mastabas from Djoser's time and earlier.[3] North of Giza too, there are other cemeteries of similar ages, and the remains as well of burials made long before the state of Egypt was invented.[4] Such traces on the Giza Plateau are very rare, most of what may have existed having been swept away, presumably in the huge business of constructing its three mighty pyramids and their attendant cemeteries. In 1904, however, at the foot of the Great Pyramid

Fig. 151 The Giza Pyramids, looking north to Cairo.

itself, the archaeologist Ahmed Kamal excavated four pretty vessels made by the potters of the so-called Ma'adi culture, one of the local communities that had preceded the pharaonic state by more than a millennium.[5] Later discoveries too, some sherds, some sealings and a handful of man-made cutting flints, serve to reinforce the impression that the Giza Plateau had also been a part of that great swathe of archaic and prehistoric cemeteries that had run southwards from this area down both sides of the Nile Valley to beyond the Meidum Pyramid.[6] Nothing has ever been found at Giza to suggest a royal connection with the place from before the time of Khufu. Why then did his pyramid-makers move away from the earlier royal burying grounds and build upon that lonely cliff?

A common explanation treats the Egyptian pyramids as if they were built to stand as markers on the horizon of the west, whose purposes therefore can be divined by drawing lines like arrows through the air, lines to connect the royal pyramids with other ancient tombs or temple sites, or the ancient cities of the area.[7] So for a brief while, until modern surveys proved it to be untrue, King Khufu's burial chamber was thought to be exactly aligned with one of the archaic mastabas that stands nearby, gaining that modest tomb a fifteen-minute fame.[8] In similar fashion, if you stand today upon that well-known stony mound at Giza that forms part of a ridge that runs out from the Great Pyramid towards the Western Desert,[9] and look back down along the angled edges of the three great pyramids – Menkaure, Khafre, Khufu – you will see that they have all been set along a single line.[10] Then, if you extend that line upon a modern map, across the Nile and over Cairo and its suburbs and out towards the Eastern Desert and the sunrise, you will see that this same line passes through the site of ancient Heliopolis, the city where the lost archaic temple of the sun god Re is considered to have stood.[11] Did Giza's pyramid-builders align their mighty monuments to mark the place of sunset as it would have appeared upon specific days of every year, from the most holy temple of the sun god, that ancient site where Djoser's craftsmen built an exquisite shrine of Tura limestone,[12] and where, so later texts affirm, there was a high-set rock on which the first rays of every sunrise have alighted since the beginning of the world?[13] Was this auspicious place of sunset the reason why the Giza Plateau was chosen as the Great Pyramid's location?[14]

The question is of more than geographic interest. Such notions can provide a key to an explanation of the Pyramid itself, its purposes and meaning. Accept the notion that sun worship at Heliopolis was the inspiration for King Khufu's Pyramid, add some suggestive epithets from ancient texts, and you may swiftly concoct a 'scientific' history that moves outward from the Great Pyramid itself to embrace the theology and politics of the age, to characterise the royal courtiers and priests and even volunteer novella portraits of King Khufu and his architects and concubines![15]

Yet there is no shred of contemporary evidence that King Khufu's pyramid-makers intentionally linked their monument to other sites in such a way. Even though the siting of the two later royal pyramids at Giza might suggest that possibility, it may equally well have been the selection of the Giza Plateau as the site of Khufu's Pyramid in the first place that prompted those two later pyramids to fall tidily into line behind it, which leaves the orientation of Khufu's Pyramid as problematical as ever. A similarly unfounded notion is that Giza's pyramids were grouped together on the plateau in imitation of heavenly constellations as they appear on modern star charts; that they were built in ancient Egypt to represent a scientific diagram! If it were true, of course, it would extend the point and purposes of the Great Pyramid way beyond the confines of the ancient East.[16]

Pausing only to wonder how such an ancient pyramid could ever be satisfactorily 'explained' by lines drawn on modern maps, the shortest answer to such theories is that in reality, as recent surveys show, not one of these alleged alignments is nearly accurate enough to prove the case. Checked with modern surveying equipment on the ground in Egypt, those inky lines drawn across a survey map, or for that matter a combination of astronomical charts and maps of the Giza Plateau, hide such errors in them, such a score of yards and miles, that using similarly loose parameters, the Great Pyramid may equally well be aligned with the New York Subway system and entire galaxies of stars. Viewed through the lens of a theodolite, however, even the alleged alignment of the Giza pyramids with the 'lost temples of Heliopolis' – which, it should be emphasised, are well and truly lost – is rather vague. Nor is there a scrap of contemporary Egyptian literature to link the two great sites; or any ancient thing, indeed, that links the site of any royal pyramid to another ancient site. Even those later kings whose very names connect them to the sun god, some of whom built so-called 'sun temples' close to their pyramids, did not physically align their pyramids with Heliopolis and the temple of the gods they so admired, for at the time their pyramids were built the sacred city of the sun god was not visible from the gentle slope of the Gebel of Abusir on which their pyramids stand.[17]

Once again, therefore, only the Great Pyramid itself can inform us of its creation, and show us something at least of why its makers chose this particular rocky outcrop some 40 miles north of Sneferu's first-made pyramid. And once again, the extraordinary national project of creating this man-made mountain holds its own unique imperatives; and for such practical considerations, if for nothing else, the Giza Plateau was a perfect choice.

Look south from the foot of the Great Pyramid, and on a clear day you can see for almost 50 miles, past the pyramid field of Sakkara, down towards the steep ruin of Sneferu's Pyramid at Meidum, until the Nile-side deserts disappear in the greyly shimmering haze where, just out of sight, the valley slowly starts to widen. King Djoser's Pyramid still stands firmly at the centre of this narrow landscape, the local limestone that was used in its construction having been cut from the same formations that provide that pyramid with such a firm foundation. Much of the stone in Djoser's monuments indeed appears to have been quarried very close at hand, from another section of the same rock formation of which the Giza Plateau is composed.[18] As for their fine casing stone, in Djoser's time there was a natural lake to the north of his pyramid's enclosure which could have served as a harbour basin for the necessary barges shipping stone from Tura, whilst the gentle rise that runs up through the desert from this now-vanished lakeside would also have provided a convenient slope on which to set a stone-hauling ramp.[19] Another haulage route that appears to end close by Djoser's 'Southern Tomb' still holds the remains of what may well be part of a stone-hauling ramp (see fig. 106).[20]

In contrast, the locations chosen by several of Djoser's pyramid-building successors did not allow the establishment of such convenient systems of building and supply. King Sneferu's two great Dahshur pyramids, for example, are further away from the Nile and deeper in the desert than any others ever built in Egypt. The desert plain of Dahshur, as we have seen, provided less reliable foundations than those that underpin King Djoser's monuments and appears to have supplied the pyramid-makers with relatively poor-quality local stone, and that perhaps in modest quantities.[21] So though the splendid and distinctive limestone blocks of the Red Pyramid suggest a single source, a single quarry for its stone, they also suggest the grim possibility that, like its Tura facing blocks, these too were hauled or shipped from many miles away.[22]

At Dahshur, the harbour quays appear to have been located by an ancient lake at the edge of the cultivation from which the pyramid-makers would have had to haul the stone up through the desert, along mile-long causeways to their respective pyramids.[23] At Meidum too, where no nearby ancient quarries have been found at all, traces of supply lines and ramps can still be seen running up from the east to the ruins of the pyramid.[24] In Sneferu's time, therefore, it appears that large quantities of building blocks were shipped and hauled considerable distances to his three great pyramids; an exercise that of itself, would have placed considerable pressure on the state machine.

These were the realities of pyramid making at the time when Khufu came to the throne. For more than half a century, the national workforce had struggled with the titanic problem of supplying and constructing a succession of colossal monuments made of cut stone blocks; fifty years of hauling and setting stone and of feeding and supplying a city-sized gathering of pyramid-builders. And at Dahshur as well, the grim experience, the inherited memory, of a near catastrophe.[25] It would hardly be surprising, then, to find that whatever symbolisms or other theological enthusiasms may or may not have led the architects of Khufu's court to Giza and its Plateau, that given their ambition to build a much larger pyramid, the pyramid-makers sought out a location which answered such an extraordinary logistic challenge. At Giza there were plentiful quantities of good-quality local limestone, which curtailed the enormous labour of bulk stone shipping and long-distance rock hauling, a labour-saving decision of

Fig. 152 The hard rock of the Giza Plateau offered a firm platform for King Khufu's Pyramid and the promise of high-quality local quarry stone as well; rounded and polished over the millennia, this is the living rock at the Great Pyramid's north-west corner.

similar magnitude to Sneferu's pyramid-makers' abandonment of building monumental pyramid enclosures. At Giza too, the same strata that provided the pyramid-makers with this local building stone also offered the pyramid itself a firm and equitable foundation.

Although at first glance it might seem to have been less than practical to site a giant pyramid on a lonely cliff two thirds of a mile away from the nearest quarry,[26] in reality the location provided direct answers to the problems previously experienced at Meidum and Dahshur. The Giza Plateau, in fact, offered the pyramid-makers a system of supply that was a virtual mirror image of that of the Step Pyramid.[27] As the Great Pyramid rose into the air, its local quarry would have been but a ramp's length from its baselines.[28] There were ideal locations too for the necessary harbour, offering convenient access to those self-same haulage ramps. And high above this useful landscape, atop the Giza Plateau, a square mile of hard white rock promised the firmest of foundations. So whatever other explanation there may be for the choice of the Giza Plateau for the Great Pyramid, it is undeniable that this enormous enterprise, a holistic product of its ancient landscape and the state that it sustained, was joined to the Giza Plateau by the most practical of considerations: it was, in fact, a perfect place for a Bronze Age workforce to build a giant pyramid.

36 Levelling the site

Work began on building the Great Pyramid by the levelling of the area on which its four baselines were to stand. And from the outset, the expertise with which the work was done tells us that Khufu's pyramid-makers had skills that were the equal of his father's work-force: that they were in fact part of that same rare band of craftsmen, the only people in the whole wide world who could have laid out the mighty Pyramid with such éclat.[1] So very well did those first crafts-men prepare for the work to follow, that avalanche of skill and strain, when month after month thousands of 2½ ton blocks of limestone would be hauled up onto the rising Pyramid in a mass of dust and sweat, that the best part of those great stone blocks still lie precisely in their proper places.

Assuming that the pyramid-makers were still working at the time of Sneferu's death, and given the overwhelming building pro-gramme of his reign that would hardly be surprising, there was probably a standing workforce of several hundred expert masons available at the time of Khufu's succession, with a supporting staff of a few thousand quarrymen and stone handlers along with the necessary auxiliary trades: a small fleet of stone barges for shipping quarried stone from Tura, some working copper miners and all the other necessary elements of the state-wide infrastructure that had supported and supplied the pyramid-makers throughout King Sneferu's reign.[2]

It thus seems likely that in or around 2491 BC, in the first year or so of Khufu's reign, several thousand stone workers shipped north to Giza from their settlements at Dahshur and Meidum; this the key hereditary workforce that would lay the foundations for the work on the new Pyramid. The very pith of the cultural identity of the Egyptian state, these pyramid-makers were the descendants of a community that over the previous half-century had been a permanent adjunct of state government, moving from project to project, pyramid to pyramid.

We may imagine that their journey down to Giza was a minor exodus, a 40 mile voyage of workers, wives and children, their animals and households and their professional equipment, and that in those first days they established their households and their work camps, that they opened the Pyramid's local quarry and set the positions of the first stone-hauling ramps and harbour quays. This, however, would have been a relatively quiet time for Egypt's pyramid-makers, a respite in their unremitting workload between the death and burial of Sneferu and the beginning of work on a new pyramid.

An inadvertent record of a similar removal is implied in that rare text that records the setting up of two palace gates of cedar wood at Dahshur in Sneferu's sixteenth year, shortly after his first pyramid at that site was started, following the work at Meidum.[3] Although no such literary hints have survived from Khufu's day, we might conceive that his court also moved in similar fashion; that following his father's burial in the Red Pyramid at Dahshur, he left the royal residence that he would have known from childhood with its thirty-year-old wooden gates, to live beside the Giza Plateau where his own pyramid would be built.

Assuming that the work rates were the same as those required to build the Red Pyramid, then the pyramid-makers who had shipped to Giza from Sneferu's settlements to the south were joined by a tidal wave of other workers; enough, that is, so that within the first four years of construction over a million 2½ ton blocks of local limestone, more than half the total volume of the Great Pyramid, would have been quarried, delivered and set down upon the pyramid atop the Giza Plateau.[4]

It is difficult now to conjure up the living world that could generate such extravagant statistics. That they reflect a genuine reality, however, is confirmed not only by the Red Pyramid's graffiti but also by the state of other unfinished early pyramids; those, for example, of the two monarchs who reigned briefly after Djoser, and that of the king who followed Khufu. Although these monarchs seem to have ruled but briefly, all of their pyramids have considerable amounts of stone in place.[5] During the first few years of Khufu's rule therefore, all present evidence suggests there was an explosive gathering of people and resources on the Giza Plateau. In the first two years, before work rates diminished, it would have been especially frenetic, with up to 20,000 people working on occasion at the Pyramid itself with thousands in attendance, and thousands more at other sites in Egypt; in all, a company that in the first year of construction would have comprised more than a tenth of the adult male population of the state.[6]

Yet the residue of this extraordinary period does not betray hurry or coercion. From the very first, the stately precision of the Pyramid's stone block courses show nothing other than an intense preoccupation with their accuracy. And year on year, with each and every course set up one upon the other, all of them display the same integrity, that same unbending care that shows that Khufu's masons were absorbed in working out the plan that would produce a pyramid whose four baselines would measure exactly 440 cubits each, and would rise up 280 cubits to a final single point.[7]

Whatever else it may have signified, such a concentration on perfection certainly served as an integral system of control, the stony lines and angles that the pyramid-makers set up inside the continually rising pyramid with such precision acting as a constant check on subsidence and movement and as a buffer for the dust and thrust of thousands upon thousands of workmen hauling hundreds upon hundreds of blocks of stone a day. So successful was the application of this plan that even though the Pyramid's various parts were emplaced ten to fourteen years apart and were thus invisible one to another, being buried in the darkness of the interior, the geometrical interrelationships that had been established at the beginning of the work were held with absolute precision, so that the Pyramid rose pretty well perfectly up into the sky.[8]

Like previous pyramids, the Great Pyramid was also set upon the four points of the compass; although this time the orientation was exalted to previously unattained heights of accuracy. At the beginning of the work, however, all necessary alignments and dimensions could have been established by elementary observations of the passage of the sun and stars and with field surveyors working with posts and cords providing the rough outlines of the four foundation trenches, so that the careful work of levelling their lines around a three-quarter mile strip of open desert could begin.[9]

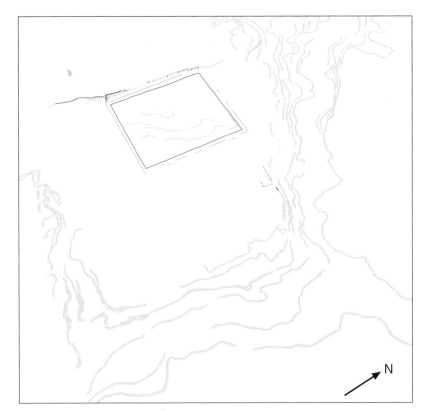

Fig. 153 Reconstruction of the excavation undertaken on the Giza Plateau for the emplacement of the Great Pyramid's baselines.

N

On the good firm limestone of the Giza Plateau, rather than simply digging the pyramid's foundation trenches into the rock and rubble of a desert plain, the work of levelling required considerable excavation into a sloping hillside. This was a labour that required the special skills of quarrymen, the scars of whose work still show that they cut a bright white square into that high headland whose four sides were each around 1000 feet in length and around 100 feet in width. Towards the eastern cliff and at the bottom of the Plateau's slope, the excavation is quite shallow, cutting down just 30 inches (75 cm) to create a level where the living rock would lie just underneath the fine stone pavement of the Pyramid that they would set upon it. Further up the slope, along the western edges of this square, the quarrymen were forced to make a deep cut in the hillside to maintain their level, leaving, in the process, a little man-made cliff that at the Pyramid's south-west corner stands some 35 feet high (see fig. 54).

In a way of building foreign to most modern methods, the central area of living rock that had been isolated by the cutting of these four long trenches was left unexcavated and standing nearly to its natural height, the quarrymen simply trimming its edges down to form an outline of the first stepped courses of the pyramid that was planned to stand above it. It is mostly buried now beneath the Pyramid, but small sections of this squared-off knoll are visible in places amidst the Pyramid's lowest courses, and at those junctures too in its interior architecture where the living rock can be seen to touch the quarry blocks that have been set up on it. Between them, these small signs tell us that King Khufu's quarrymen left some 30 feet of living limestone at the centre of the Pyramid, standing to about the same height as the Pyramid's first seven stone block courses.[10] Such is the huge volume of this Pyramid that, although this Rocky Knoll appears inconsequential on a modern plan, in reality it saved the pyramid-makers the labour of hauling an extra 160,000 tons of quarried limestone up onto the Plateau, some 3 per cent of the Pyramid's total volume. It also served, of course, as the sturdy key on which the first quarried blocks of the Pyramid were laid in careful rows.

So far, so good; the Pyramid itself can show how it rose up from the ground. At this point though, the record stops. After the cutting of the four foundation trenches and the setting of its first few courses, there is no evidence whatever of the order of the Great Pyramid's construction or of the methods used. Nothing other than that which is still held within the architecture of the Pyramid and the pattern of its building blocks.

Yet by itself alone, as we have already seen, this Pyramid can generate a huge amount of information. Most significant perhaps for the story of its own creation is that, as we have already seen, there was a comprehensive building plan in operation from the very beginning of the work: the overarching precision of the relationship between the Pyramid's interior architecture and the smooth white finish of its exterior – a relationship that covers the entire period of construction – simply demands it.

This, then, offers us a brand-new key to an understanding of how this Pyramid was designed and made, for the surviving traces of just such an ancient plan are held at those junctures in the architecture where the hard perfections of its stones precisely match the cool lines of modern analysis; where, as we have already seen (ch. 5 above), modern surveys of the Pyramid have permitted the reconstruction of a basic plan based upon two six-squared grids: grids that inform the main lines of its exterior architecture and govern its interior design. Thanks to the astonishing perfections of the Pyramid's execution, the modern mathematics contained within this lost design can serve to show us how it may have been created; information that, combined with a time line of the Pyramid's building gleaned from the Red Pyramid's graffiti, allows a theoretical restoration of the building programme. Teased from the same old stones, other information can even provide an understanding of how and when the royal builders first set their Pyramid to north, and when therefore the great adventure started.

So whilst all the workaday paraphernalia used by King Khufu's surveyors is entirely lost and virtually all traces of how his Pyramid was built have long been swept away, it is yet possible to paint a picture of the Great Pyramid's creation in the manner of a pointillist painting where a haze of apparently unrelated dots can suddenly resolve into small sharp areas of clarity that give order to the whole and reveal in broad outline how the Pyramid was made.

37 The plan inside the Pyramid

By Petrie's day, an age of industry, the levelled rows of the Great
Pyramid's majestic blocks created the illusion that the making of this
mighty monument had been a matter of logistics, an extended
process of cutting and moving blocks of stone around and setting
them all up in great good order. Yet a study of Bronze Age mechanics,
however ingenious, cannot answer the fundamental questions raised
by this extraordinary monument. Even the discovery of a contemporary papyrus, an eyewitness account of the Great Pyramid under construction, would not necessarily provide an explanation. It is
self-evident, after all, that whatever techniques they used, Khufu's
pyramid-makers knew how to move big stones about and how to set
them down precisely in neat and level rows, and how to angle them
as well. The first stone buildings underneath King Djoser's Pyramid
show similarly skilful if comparatively miniature versions of those
same processes in action, whilst Sneferu's huge building programmes
magnified those techniques to well beyond what King Khufu's
builders would achieve at Giza. The abiding mystery of the Great
Pyramid therefore concerns its inspiration and design, and the purposes of the unique plan that was set so perfectly into its stones.

As with so much to do with the most ancient past, the limit of our
understanding of this Great Pyramid is in direct proportion to the

extent that we can shed our modern notions of how and why such things are made. Essentially, it is an alien thing, so foreign that some of our most basic modern points of reference – the theoretical point, for example, where the Pyramid's central axis bisects its baseline – are but abstractions in themselves. In reality, the much-quoted 481 feet (146.71 m) of the highest pyramid in Egypt, which is the Great Pyramid's theoretical original height of 280 cubits, could never have been measured by its builders, because the theoretical point from which that measurement is taken appears to lie in 30 feet of natural rock beneath the centre of the Pyramid. Nor is there any evidence

Fig. 154 The three guards are sitting on a ledge of natural rock fashioned by Khufu's pyramid-makers at the beginning of their work, as they excavated the positions of the Pyramid's four baselines. Here, however, they also fashioned sections of the living rock into the north-east corner of the Pyramid's first course.

that channels were cut across the Rocky Knoll to reach that vital modern survey point, of accommodations for survey ropes or sighting lines or water channels that in our modern ways of thinking could serve to establish that essential single point.[1]

In similar fashion, the 440 cubits of the Great Pyramid's finished baselines (230.35 m) were only held in its final smoothed and finished casing blocks.[2] Likewise, only the smooth white pavements on which those broken baselines stand, those four pavements cut from Tura limestone that once ran right around the Pyramid and whose ruins still provoke the wonder of surveyors, ever held the exact level of the Pyramid's baseline from which its height is calculated; that same theoretical 280 cubit measurement, the lower point of which lies 400 feet beyond those four fine pavements, deep in solid rock. And all the long smooth lines of the Pyramid's exterior were set years after the body of the Pyramid – whose interior architecture was so precisely linked to those final finished dimensions – had been built.

From the very beginning of the work, therefore, the pyramid-makers had need of much of the information that a modern building plan provides: a plan that described the harmonics of the Pyramid's interior architecture and linked them to the Pyramid's exterior; to its height and width, to the level of its baselines and the position of its central axis. A subtle plan as well, that set a maze of mathematics behind the Pyramid's smooth exterior.

A common modern assumption is that the elaborate harmonics of the Great Pyramid's architecture are merely by-products of the practical geometric systems that were used by the ancient Egyptians to measure and design everything from farms and fields to furniture and paintings.[3] So naturally, the theory goes, as the pyramid-makers employed those self-same methods to lay out the Great Pyramid, so subtle harmonies must inevitably ring throughout its architecture. Yet similar procedures have been used around the world for millennium after millennium, and only Khufu's pyramid-makers ever managed to produce a monument of such precision and sophistication. This is certainly not a product of geometric serendipity.

Yet there is no evidence either that the Pyramid's design was drawn out in a modern way upon a drafting sheet. Not a single scaled architectural drawing has survived from all of ancient Egypt's thirty dynasties[4] – let alone an example of the Euclidean geometric constructions required to produce such harmonies as are contained within King Khufu's Pyramid.[5] Nor has a single drawing table essential for such drafting work been found, no accurate compasses, nor fine-made drawing tools or set squares, and certainly (and of supreme importance for this argument although it is often overlooked) none of the sophisticated equipment required to translate such hypothetical small-scale plans or models into full-sized buildings.

And even if such tools should ever be discovered, such scaled plans as they might have once provided could only ever have allowed the roughest of approximations of the Great Pyramid's precisions. For even the finest-drawn geometrical constructions hide inherent errors in their lines, in-built inaccuracies that, when scaled up to the colossal dimensions of the Great Pyramid, would show up as enormous gaps and overhangs within the finished architecture.[6] Many commonly used geometric constructions also hide intrinsic errors in their very method, errors that, although they are comfortably hidden in the thickness of a painter's line or a chisel-cut, would express themselves in multiples of many yards when scaled to the size of Khufu's Pyramid.[7] And as its surviving architecture shows, the Great Pyramid is accurate on occasion to fractions of a single inch.

This then is a central mystery of this Pyramid. How were its ethereal harmonies obtained? How was its height determined, the angle of its rise, the precise location of its entrance doorway on its northern face, the size of the offset of its six-square grids that set the Great Step in such immediate relationship to the base of the whole Pyramid? How was it made so beautifully; how was it made at all?

By itself alone, the cubit unit used at the Great Pyramid enables us to see how the angle of its rise may have been obtained. As we have already seen (p. 65 above), its angle of 51° 50′ may be precisely calculated by adding 20, 40 and 60 cubits to a diagonal line placed across a grid of three adjacent squares of 73.33 cubits each.

Now as Petrie's measurements inside the Pyramid have shown, the east–west plane of its 280 cubit axis and the centre line of its six-square grids are marked inside the Pyramid by the central angle of the vault in the Queen's Chamber and also by the rise of the Great Step high above it. Set more than 50 feet (15.63 m) apart and separated by tens of thousands of tons of rock and years of building, these points both lie within an inch of absolute abstract perfection.[8]

Without the use of modern surveying equipment, such precision can be maintained with a large-sized version of the plumb bob and string, that modest device which Khufu's stone workers, in common with all other Bronze Age craftsmen, used to trim and set their blocks.[9] Hanging at rest and sheltered from the desert wind and the vibrations common to large building sites, a weighted line, a plummet on a cord, could well have served to mark the plane of the Great Pyramid's central axis and those stones, those vaults and steps that have been so precisely set upon it: there are, indeed, no known alternatives. So the 'mysterious void' that has been detected between the Queen's Chamber and the Great Step and has been touted as a secret treasure chamber would in reality appear to be a gap left at the centre of construction, another shaft, another 'chimney' like the one at Sneferu's Bent Pyramid (pp. 272ff above), to shelter the cord and plummet that marked the essential east–west plane of the Pyramid's central axis on which the six-square grids were set.[10]

In Khufu's day, therefore, it would appear that the plumb bob was not just a craftsman's tool but a major element in the creation of the Pyramid itself. In fact, the Pyramid's architecture shows inaccuracies in exactly those places where a plummet and line could not be effectively employed: at the small vertical displacement, for example, between the plane of the central axis and the doorway of the Subterranean Chamber deep in the natural rock beneath the Pyramid, where the plane of the central axis could only have been re-established by measuring down the length of the descending corridor with the aid of relatively inaccurate devices such as ropes or rods.[11]

First quantified in the nineteenth century with the aid of specialised survey equipment, many of these so-called 'ancient errors' may well have been unmeasurable by the pyramid-makers and would not have been corrected, for they could hardly have repaired errors that they could not detect. This lack of modern surveying equipment on the part of the pyramid-makers is why, by modern standards, the entirety of the Great Pyramid's architecture appears to be inconsistent, although where high levels of precision were achievable such as the vertical relationship of the Great Step to the angle of the vault of the Queen's Chamber, modern building standards are usually surpassed. In fact, the ancient plan of this Great Pyramid, the plan by which the Pyramid was conceived and to which its craftsmen worked, was circumscribed, as it is in every work of architecture, by contemporary methods of building and surveying. At the Great Pyramid, the outline of the ancient plan is held in the near-perfect symmetries that are contained within its architecture.

Now as we have seen (ch. 5 above), the points at which precision and geometry meet inside the Pyramid lie on the planes of the upper six-squared grid, with the single most vital point set one grid square down from the Great Step and the centre line and two squares to its north, at that conjunction in the interior architecture that I have called the Prism Point. This single point was fundamental to the ancient plan. Not only does its height above the level of the baselines mark the size of the offset of the Pyramid's two grids and ultimately, therefore, the level of King Khufu's burial chamber, but it is also the point where the angles of the Pyramid's two great internal corridors join together in near-perfect symmetry (fig. 16).

As all the early pyramids quite clearly show, the pyramid-makers were able to maintain an angle and a level in cut stone architecture as skilfully as they controlled its verticality. Set in a wide-spread A-frame, plumb bobs could be used to measure and control any angle that was required.[12] Unlike the long lines of modern survey work, continual piecemeal measurements with hand-held equipment would have provided a constant check of accuracy on each one of the Pyramid's great stones.[13] However the stone-setters may have measured and controlled their blocks, the fact is that the two long corridors that join at the Prism Point are precisely set on the diagonal across two grid squares and link the Pyramid's entrance with its central axis and the portal of its burial chamber with the entrance to the Pyramid itself.

The Prism Point also marks a critical juncture in that long straight corridor that leads down to the Subterranean Chamber in a mirror image of the corridor that rises up to the Great Step (fig. 26). It also links the Pyramid's baselines and axis with the architecture of the Pyramid's interior. It is not surprising that the Descending Corridor that runs down from the Prism Point into the living rock of the Rocky Knoll was so accurately cut, that it was the only element at the Great Pyramid that defeated Petrie's best efforts to detect an error in its orientation, that it is more perfectly aligned to north than the Pyramid's much-measured eastern baseline:[14] for it was a key element in setting out King Khufu's Pyramid.

Set in fine blocks of Tura stone, the vital Prism Point that extends the line of that Descending Corridor up into the laid stone courses of the Pyramid was built directly on the Rocky Knoll. A year or so later in the Pyramid's construction, when it had been buried under fourteen of the Pyramid's most massive stone block courses, the line of that same small rock-cut corridor would be extended upwards to set the position of the Pyramid's sole entrance, on the eighteenth course of its northern face.

Just as the corbel vaults of Sneferu's Bent Pyramid have been stretched and distorted inside King Khufu's Pyramid into the shape of the Grand Gallery to fit its geometric scheme, so the pyramid-makers have stretched and straightened the lines of the archaic staircases that ran down to the burial chambers of every royal tomb since the beginning of the Egyptian state, to serve as the most vital single unit in this abstract plan. This little corridor and the Prism Point above,

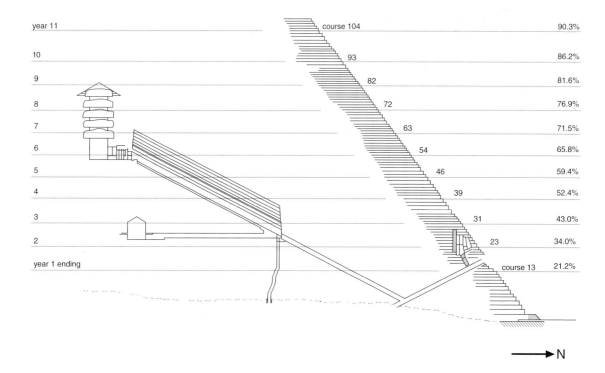

course 104

93

82

72

63

54

46

39

31

23

course 13

90.3%

86.2%

81.6%

76.9%

71.5%

65.8%

59.4%

52.4%

43.0%

34.0%

21.2%

N

therefore, were the fixed lines of the Pyramid's interior architecture that linked them to its baselines and to the very stars of heaven.

Although many of the Pyramid's corridors and shafts are not high enough for a grown person to stand up in, these gem-like elements served as a control within the rising Pyramid, as vital reference points during the first five years of construction when well over half the Pyramid was made. This Pyramid was its own theodolite, the symmetry and accuracy of its interior architecture serving to expose the smallest shifts and errors in its stone work, allowing necessary corrections even as its massive courses rose. With the touch of a finger, the acuteness of the human eye and the skilled manipulation of a few stone-working tools, the building of the world's largest pyramid was expertly maintained without the aid of modern-style survey equipment.

As the Pyramid grew up higher, all the precisions of this gigantic geometric diagram that its makers had set up in its interior would have been slowly buried and could have no longer served as a daily means of accurate control. Even by the time that the pyramid-makers set the Great Step into its position, most of the fixed points inside the Pyramid could no long have served as points of reference; the Great Step itself covers the very place where a chimney could have provided direct access to the line of the Queen's Chamber vault beneath, and

Fig. 155 Cross section of the Great Pyramid's northern stone work with a theoretical construction rate derived from data given in Appendix 5. Although progress appears constant, year on year, in reality the percentage of stone required constantly diminishes (cf. fig. 34).

thus to the central axis of the Pyramid itself. Not only did the setting of the Great Step serve to mark the level of King Khufu's burial chamber and to re-establish the vital level of the grid offset first established at the Prism Point, but it also reset the plane of the Pyramid's central axis. After the lower sections of the Pyramid's architecture had been buried in its rising courses, the Great Step became a vital reference point for the continuing construction and virtually a second baseline. If proof were still required, the sheer precision of the placement of this single step would be further evidence of the value that the pyramid-makers placed on accurate control points within the rising pyramid.

Our modern plan of this ancient Pyramid's interior therefore shows us that, even as it was being built, its architecture was held inside a kind of geometric space frame. Coupled with the Pyramid's alignment to the point of north, that stellar arbiter of any movement in a line of architecture, and with the six sub-divisions of the planes of the Pyramid's east–west grids at the centre of construction, incredible accuracy was achieved. Laid out upon the upper six-square grid, the symmetry of the internal architecture, especially its two long straight corridors, served as a continual check upon its accuracy; over the years, the rooms and corridors of its interior leap-frogged one another, a narrow ruler built inside the Pyramid as it rose up into the sky.

From the very beginning of the work, therefore, it was essential to establish and maintain the precise positions of the squares of the uppermost grid in that narrow north–south envelope inside the

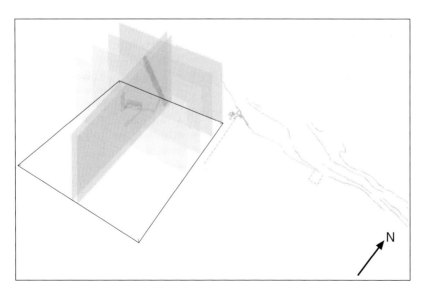

Fig. 156 The planes of the six-square grid projected across the Rocky Knoll and bisected by two alignments to the point of north that contain the Pyramid's interior architecture.

Fig. 157 The west face of the Great Pyramid with the stone-lined grave shaft of Mastaba 4000, the tomb of Hemiunu, in the foreground. The stone work of this shaft is of the same type as that built around the so-called 'Well' inside the Great Pyramid.

Pyramid where its internal architecture would be built. And here it is that modern plan and ancient building methods join together on the Giza Plateau. For the plan demands that with the excavation of the levelled rectangle of the Pyramid's four baselines, the setting of the vertical planes of its two six-squared grids upon the Rocky Knoll would have been amongst the first tasks of work that had to be performed.

The first vertical plane of the six-squared grid, which had been established with the levelling of the Pyramid's northern baseline,

Fig. 158 Part of the walling that rises from the so-called 'Well' within the shaft that runs down from the Great Pyramid's Grand Gallery. Morton Edgar's servant is seated on the living rock of the Plateau. The cave in which he sits was once a naturally formed hollow in the limestone that had been filled with hard conglomerate. At the beginning of the work, when the pyramid-makers cut out their Well, they lined the looser upper section of the excavation, as was the custom, with a stone block wall. The cave that now lies around it, the so-called 'Grotto', was quarried from the conglomerate after the blocks of the Pyramid courses had been laid over and above it.

could have been precisely fixed immediately after the quarrymen had finished that first excavation. The next plane was marked inside the Pyramid with the establishment of the Prism Point. Situated in a fine-cut row of Tura blocks set straight onto the Rocky Knoll, this position too must also have been established at the beginning of the work, along with the precise point where the floor line of the Descending Corridor would be crossed by the as yet unbuilt line of the Ascending Corridor.

In similar fashion, although leaving us rather less exact evidence today, the plane of the adjacent grid plane, the one that lies between the plane of the Pyramid's central axis and the Prism Point (fig. 28), was marked by the north side of a square-cut shaft cut into the Rocky Knoll. This could have served in the manner of the so-called 'chimneys' of King Sneferu's pyramids, accommodating a cord and plummet set right on the plane of the two grids.[15] Made in the same manner as the burial shafts of the tombs of Sneferu's and Khufu's courtiers,[16] lined that is, with courses of odd-sized rough-squared blocks 'from 7¼ to 8 inches (18.4 cm to 20 cm) in height',[17] this square shaft is the only place in Khufu's Pyramid where such modest stonework can be found, a fact that by itself suggests that this was not a work of architecture but built for utilitarian purposes. Dusty, dark and difficult of access, today this shaft forms part of a long and wavering rough-hewn tunnel, a brusque conduit cut down through the finished courses of the Pyramid at the ending of the work, that

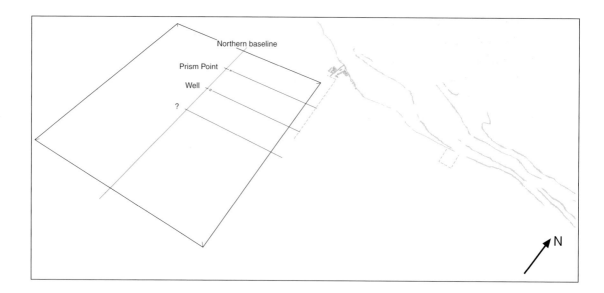

would have provided the burial party with an alternative route to the entrance of the Pyramid after sections of its formal architecture had been blocked with granite plugs.[18] It appears, therefore, that these later tunnellers reused this buried and abandoned shaft to speed their progress through the rock.

Three of the Pyramid's six grid planes, then, were set in hard stone at the Pyramid, and that during the first stages of the work, when the Rocky Knoll still stood in sunlight. Only the original position of the essential central axis on the Rocky Knoll is no longer visible: though most majestically marked by the conjunction of several architectural keystones higher up inside the Pyramid, its origins are a little mystery buried deep inside the Pyramid.

Of more importance to an understanding of this working plan, however, is how the planes of the six-squared grids and the geometric space frames that were built within them were anchored to the baselines of the finished Pyramid. For however accurate the builders may have been in marking the planes of the gridlines upon the Rocky Knoll and in orientating the Descending Corridor to north, such accuracy by itself cannot account for the precision of the Pyramid's final orientation or size. It cannot tell us, for example, how a line of fixed points set up across a rough-cut knoll of rock were related so precisely to the Pyramid's baselines which would be set some 400 feet away and at a lower level. Nor does it explain how the precisions of the Pyramid's interior were connected so precisely with the casing of the Pyramid when virtually all contact between its interior and exterior had been broken.

Fig. 159 The three points known to have been established at the beginning of the Great Pyramid's construction which mark some of the planes of the Pyramid's six-square grid: the Pyramid's northern baseline, the Prism Point and the Well.

Neither indeed can it explain what is perhaps the biggest single mystery held within this Pyramid: how was the exact height from the Pyramid's baseline to the Prism Point established in the first fine blocks set up on the Rocky Knoll? What indeed were the origins of this vital little measurement – the offset of the two related grids – which controls the height of so many elements inside the Pyramid's interior, including that of the Great Step, which it may be recalled has the startling although undeniable property of standing at the exact height where the area of the pyramid above it is precisely half the area of the base of the entire pyramid!

Today of course, the height of the Great Step could be mathematically determined, then set inside a building as required with the aid of modern surveying equipment. Yet the pyramid-makers did not own a theodolite, nor is there a shred of evidence from all of their long history that any ancient Egyptian possessed the expertise or need or inclination to make the necessary calculations to determine the grid offset's exact size.[19] At 8.676768 (!) cubits moreover, the dimension that contains the essential properties required of the grid offset is an awkward measurement to express in ancient Egyptian units; a fact that suggests that it may have been obtained and maintained by other means.[20]

With modern methods ruled right out of court, the only conceivable solution to these and many other mysteries of the Pyramid's construction is that the essential elements of the Pyramid's architecture were established in the same manner as in the construction of Egyptian temples; that is, parts of the Pyramid's plan were laid out full size upon the ground. Centuries before King Khufu's time, after all, just such processes of foundation, of measuring and laying out, were already being represented in scenes of ceremonial, the surveyors' ropes in the hands of the king and the goddess Seshat, a patron of counting and of numeration, both of them busily engaged in staking out their architecture with cords and posts and mallets.[21] Such processes were common enough in later ancient Egyptian history as well, tomb and temple scenes of many different ages showing the self-same techniques of measuring out both fields and buildings.[22] And on the Giza Plateau too, such procedures could have supplied the pyramid-makers with all the angles and dimensions that they required to plan and place the complex architecture of the rising Pyramid: laid out at 1 to 1, such a working diagram would also serve to generate the architecture of the Pyramid with a precision unmatched by any other means.

And with the physical presence of such a plan upon the Giza Plateau, of course, the Pyramid's abstract centre line could remain buried deep within the Rocky Knoll, for the necessary measurements could be held upon the ground outside the area of construction. This method too would provide a solution to the practical problem of applying 20 – 40 – 60 cubits to each of the lower grid squares' co-ordinates to establish the Pyramid's angle of rise at 50° 50′. There is even a hint of the existence of just such a diagram held inside the Great Pyramid itself, for after dropping unerringly down from the bottom of the Grand Gallery, the rough-cut tunnel that runs down through the square shaft that marks one of the vertical planes of the Pyramid's six-square grids suddenly nudges south and east a little before arriving at a position immediately above the shaft, as if sensing its position, before dropping down straight through its centre and then descending once again, nudging south and eastwards as before, before emerging exactly by the side of the Descending Corridor. Such realignments in this tunnelling could only have been possible had there been some kind of basic plan of the Pyramid's interior from which the quarriers could take the necessary measures for their excavation. And in fact there is considerable evidence that parts of this plan yet exist: evidence, that is, of a design field set up beside the Great Pyramid upon the Giza Plateau.

38 The plan beside the Pyramid

As a brisk tour around Khufu's Giza monuments quickly demonstrates, the plain upon the east side of his Pyramid is the only suitable adjacent space where his pyramid-makers could have set up a full-sized design field for the work ahead. The south side of the Pyramid, which slopes gently down towards the royal quarry, would have been encumbered with stone-hauling ramps from the beginning of the work, whilst the north side, which was close to the edges of the cliff, has insufficient space.[1] The west side, although large enough, was also on a natural slope, and one that as we can see today was never levelled; by the middle of the reign, moreover, parts of this hillside were already studded with the stone-block mastabas of some of Khufu's entourage.[2] Apart from a single groove chiselled by an unknown hand upon a paving block close to the centre of the western baseline there is no trace of the presence of a working plan on that side of the Pyramid.[3]

The east side of the Great Pyramid, beyond the basalt pavements of King Khufu's temple, commands attention. Set between the baseline of the Pyramid and the edge of the cliff that swings around it from the north, there yet remains an open area, a near 1000 foot white plain that, judging from the gentle downward slope of the hill above the Pyramid, appears to have been artificially levelled.[4] Shadowed in

Fig. 160 The western baseline of the Great Pyramid. Beyond the narrow levelled strip of rock beside the baseline – half of which is now covered by the modern road – there is a considerable cut excavated by the pyramid-makers as they quarried out the platform for the Pyramid from the slope of the Plateau. By the tenth year of Khufu's reign, tombs were already being built upon the sloping hillside up above the Pyramid, as some of their building graffiti show (see further pp. 412ff below).

Fig. 161 The levelled area to the north of the Great Pyramid was yet narrower when building started on the Pyramid, before hundreds of tons of building debris were tipped down from the cliff top; the hard rock on which the Pyramid is set barely extends beyond the area covered by the shadow in this photograph.

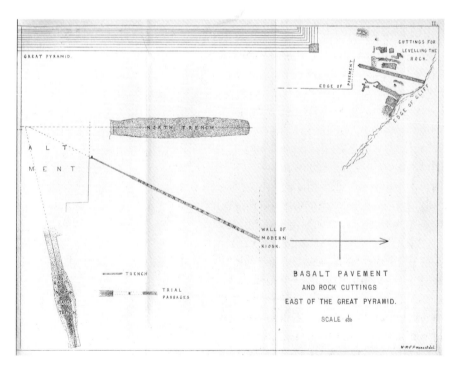

Fig. 162 Petrie's careful plan of the cuttings in the levelled area beside the Great Pyramid's north-eastern baseline, some of which served as survey points in his triangulation of the Giza Plateau. Like Borchardt after him, Petrie considered the Pyramid's eastern baseline to have been the first to have been laid down by the pyramid-makers, hence perhaps his lavish map.

Fig. 163 The levelled area beyond the Great Pyramid's north-eastern baseline, taken in December 1924 from high up on the east face of the Pyramid by one of Reisner's staff photographers. The orientation of Petrie's 'Trial Passages' – the entrances to which stand out as shadowed rectangles – are indicated by an added line. Although part obscured by drifted sand, the line of the 'Trench' that is plotted on Petrie's plan is also faintly visible.

the afternoon by the Pyramid's dark triangle, deep in limestone dust and quite devoid of any natural surface, the raw and much-abraded surface of the little limestone plateau holds considerable evidence of ancient industry.[5] Ever since the days of Petrie and Borchardt most Giza archaeologists have considered that the Great Pyramid's eastern baseline was the first one to be established; indeed, the area all around its foot is pocked with rock-cut holes and grooves that many have supposed to be the scanty remnants of the pyramid-makers' survey work.[6] And even though the bruised and battered area beyond requires much further study, as Mark Lehner, its latest surveyor, has acknowledged, at the same time his work established many links between some of the cuts and excavations in the area and the architecture of the Pyramid above.[7]

The most obvious evidence of the use of this area as a design field is an eccentric arrangement of blank corridors excavated in the living rock and dubbed by Petrie as 'Trial passages'.[8] As he was the first to recognise, this modest and eroded excavation precisely duplicates many of the junctions and the doorways of the Pyramid's internal corridors, most notably the vital Prism Point, where the Pyramid's internal corridors join in near-perfect symmetry and which also holds the vital measurement of the grid offset. As exact as the architecture that it represents, Petrie calculated that the 65 feet of the passages that yet remain match the dimensions and angles of the Great Pyramid's principle corridors to within half an inch (1.27 cm)![9]

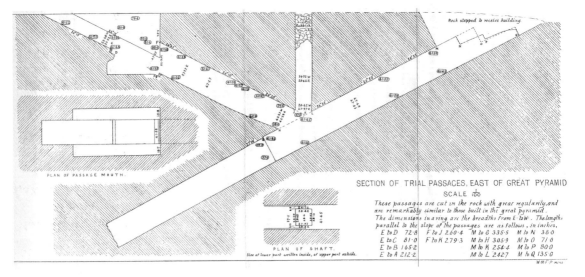

Within the figure:

PLAN OF PASSAGE MOUTH.

Rock stepped to receive building.

SECTION OF TRIAL PASSAGES, EAST OF GREAT PYRAMID
SCALE 1/100

PLAN OF SHAFT.
Size of lower part written inside, of upper part outside.

These passages are cut in the rock with great regularity, and
are remarkably similar to those built in the great pyramid.
The dimensions in a ring are the breadths from E to W. The lengths
parallel to the slope of the passages are as follows, in inches.

E to D 72·8	F to J 260·4	M to G 335·5	M to N 38·0
E to C 81·0	F to K 279·3	M to H 305·9	M to O 71·0
E to B 165·2		M to K 254·4	M to P 80·0
E to A 212·2		M to L 242·7	M to Q 135·0

In many respects, these passages are a typical example of a type of plan that has survived from various epochs of ancient Egyptian history; a plan that can be either drawn out in two dimensions or made as a kind of model, in which many of the elements of the architecture that it describes are drastically contracted so that, as Petrie puts it when comparing his Trial Passages with the architecture inside the Great Pyramid, they are 'shortened in length, but of full size in width and height'.[10] A significant difference between these passages and the other examples of such plans, however, is that the major elements – the doorways and the Prism Point – are made at the same size as their equivalents inside the Pyramid. And this it is that would have allowed their duplication with an accuracy that no small-sized plan could ever match; in the exactness, for example, of the angles of the junction of the corridors and of the architectural arrangements at their endings, even to the extent of a diminishment of some 2 inches (4.95 cm) in the size of one of the corridors, a constriction that inside the Pyramid has served to halt the movement of three massive granite blocks which were cut to the same dimensions as the Ascending Corridor and which were designed to slide down into this tiny taper to plug the way to Khufu's burial chamber (see further, ch. 43 below).[11]

These passages cut into the eastern field appear to be a three-dimensional model of parts of the complex architecture that the royal masons built upon the Rocky Knoll and in the courses of the rising Pyramid. Here in Petrie's Trial Passages, Khufu's stone masons would have been able to visualise and measure out, at full size and in all of their complexity, some of the most vital elements of the

Fig. 164 Petrie's careful plan of the 'Trial Passages', a full-sized if somewhat abridged version of the Prism Point inside the Pyramid in which only the narrow shaft running down into the junction of the Trial Passages' two corridors is not present in the Pyramid itself. Its excavation at the Trial Passages, however, would have enabled the pyramid-makers to establish an exact concordance with a plane of the Pyramid's six-square grid. Inside the Great Pyramid, this point is set exactly on the line of the two corridors' convergence, a line that could have been established earlier at the excavation of the Trial Passages simply by dropping plumb lines down the narrow shaft (see further Appendix 4).

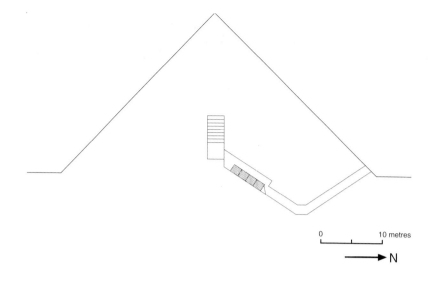

0   10 metres

→ N

Fig. 165 The novel design of this small pyramid of Sneferu's time, built beside the Bent Pyramid at Dahshur, presaged the design of the Trial Passages on the Giza Plateau and, indeed, the mechanisms by which the Great Pyramid's Ascending Corridor were plugged with massive blocks of granite. Within this modest pyramid, however, the granite plugs could have been set on their last journey by the dislodging of a single wooden post.

Such small subsidiary pyramids were often built alongside royal funerary pyramids and are generally considered to have served as secondary ritual tombs.

Pyramid's internal architecture. There is even a small square shaft cut down into them from the surface of the Plateau; the only element which is not present inside the equivalent architecture inside the Pyramid, this would have permitted the masons' plummets direct vertical access to the precise location of the crucial Prism Point, the very tip, that is, of the great triangle of corridors that connects all of the elements of the Pyramid's interior. Here too there are indications that the pyramid-makers may have reconsidered one aspect of the design they excavated at the Trial Passages, for a detail in the shape of the equivalent tapered corridor within the Pyramid itself has been altered slightly from that of the Trial Passages so that the corridor's floor, the crucial skeleton of the Pyramid's geometric plan, has retained a perfect linearity.[12]

Despite this most persuasive kinship, despite the fact that the same distinctive stone cutting techniques are employed both in the Trial Passages and in the lower sections of the Pyramid's own corridors, the Trial Passages are anonymous and certainly they do not hold a written date.[13] There is therefore only circumstantial evidence that they were made before the rooms inside the Pyramid.

Yet there is other evidence that links these Trial Passages directly to the nearby Pyramid and thus suggests that they were both made at the same time. First, the Trial Passages and a well-made trench that lies close by are set precisely parallel to the eastern baseline of the Pyramid; second, as Mark Lehner has observed, a row of post holes that crosses both the Trial Passages and the nearby trench have been precisely aligned to architectural elements within the Pyramid,[14] specifically, as we can now see, with one of the vertical planes of the

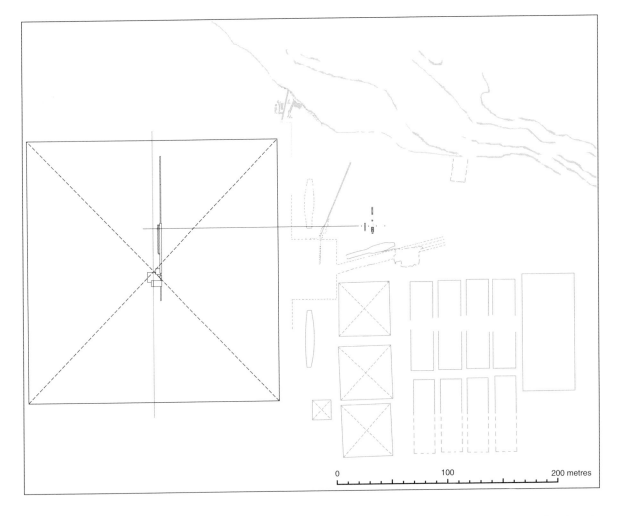

0   100   200 metres

six-square grids on which the Pyramid's interior architecture was set (see figs. 159 and 166).[15] These post holes appear to be a unique surviving trace of the use of sight lines in ancient Egypt, a technique that has often been proposed as a practical and precise method of controlling the angle and linearity of pyramids during their construction, in which the line of the architecture is checked by a row of vertical posts or plumb bobs set up one behind the other, in the manner of a gun sight.[16]

This little group of cuttings has yet more to offer. The distance between the trench and the Trial Passages, for example, is itself related to the Pyramid's six-square grids, being one sixth of their size, a distance reflected in the Pyramid's interior in the width of that thin envelope of space to the east of its central axis, in which all its corridors are set (see fig. 156) and which therefore helped to define the positions of the three great chambers.[17]

Fig. 166 Plan showing the relationship between the architecture of the Great Pyramid and the cuttings upon its eastern side. The Trial Passages and Trench are precisely parallel to the Pyramid's eastern baseline, whilst the plane of the Pyramid's six-square grid established at the Well runs exactly through the Trial Passages at its 'Prism Point'.

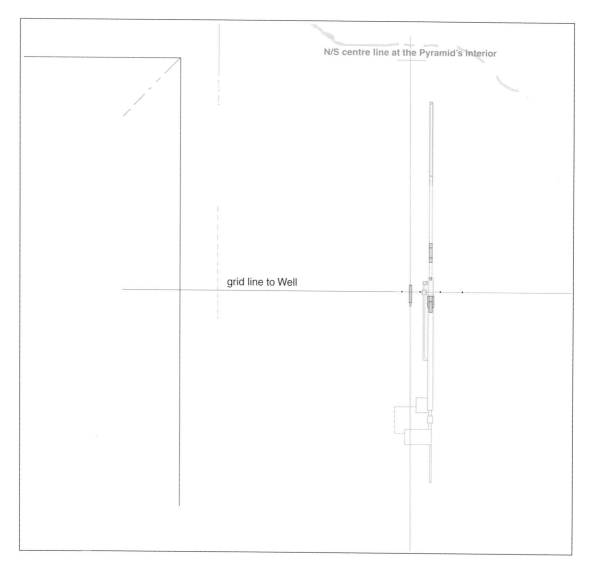

N/S centre line at the Pyramid's interior

grid line to Well

Here in its eastern field, a modest line of post holes is set directly upon one of the six planes of the Great Pyramid's architectural grids, a line that bisects a trench whose distance from the Trial Passages holds a key dimension of the Pyramid's interior architecture, whilst those Trial Passages in themselves are in effect an ancient three-dimensional model of those parts of the Pyramid's internal architecture that hold the very core of its geometry. Surely then, scanty marks and cuttings within the eastern field are the faint traces of the Great Pyramid's design laboratory: that they are indeed the remaining traces of the pyramid-makers at their work is underlined by their distance from the Pyramid, which appears to echo the dimensions of the Pyramid's six-square grids and their offset.

Fig. 167
The superimposition of the plans of the Great Pyramid's interior and the Trench and Trial Passages in the Pyramid's east field establishes a precise relationship.

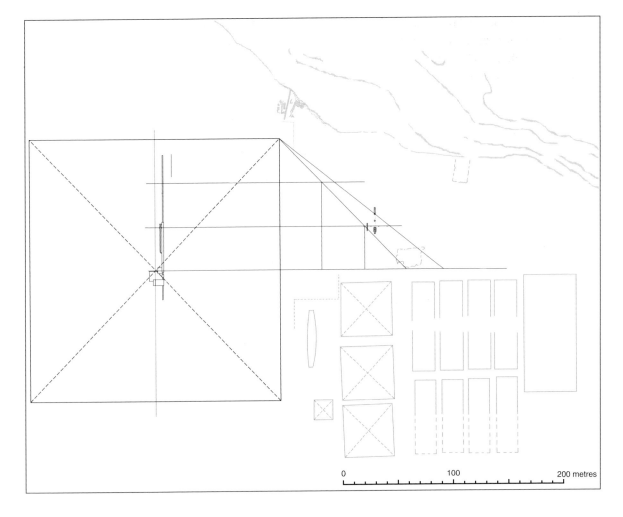

Fig. 168 The system of grid square co-ordinates that control the external angle of the Great Pyramid laid over the cuttings in the Pyramid's east field.

0   100   200 metres

This would appear to be the bones of an ancient diagram in which the Pyramid's eastern baseline represented the central baseline of the Pyramid itself.[18] Certainly, there is room within this levelled eastern field for such a diagram with the height of the Great Pyramid represented at full size (fig. 168): space enough, at least, to lay out the northern half of the Pyramid's six-square grids and thus to set the angle of the Pyramid's rise with the 20 – 40 – 60 cubit additions to the three grid co-ordinates. Another practical advantage of designing the Pyramid's interior upon a similarly sized grid, of course, is that its various elements could also have been set up and measured out on any of the squares laid down within the eastern field, before their transferral to their correct location within the rising architecture.

Such a life-sized diagram set out upon the ground should not be thought of in the modern manner, as if it were a cross-section of the Pyramid that stands above it (see p. 66 above), but rather in the same manner that the ancient Egyptian sculptors made drawings upon the different faces of their blocks of stone before starting on the work of sculpting (see ch. 23). Here then, certain of the Pyramid's key measurements and angles appear to have been established and maintained in linear fashion upon this eastern plain; in a process equivalent to a sculptor moving his chisel from one face of the stone block to another, these relationships were translated from the design field of the levelled plateau up through ninety degrees into the Pyramid above.

This is the answer to the mystery of why the pyramid-makers did not need to level the Rocky Knoll at the beginning of the work to set down the Pyramid's central baseline and the primary dimensions on which its interior architecture depended. The Pyramid's very height and the length of its baselines and the key lines and points of its interior architecture were established and maintained within this design field, with the eastern baseline of the Pyramid serving as the vital hinge that linked this diagram directly to the Pyramid above.

And so powerful, so potent, was the outline of this grand design, these six-squared grids laid out upon the eastern field, that the apexes of a row of three small pyramids that were later built beside King Khufu's Pyramid, were set on one of its co-ordinates (fig. 209).[19]

39 Numbers

By modern lights, King Khufu's pyramid-designers were an idiosyncratic lot; their architecture at once claustrophobic and colossal, grandiose, narrow and constricted. Yet there is a rationality, a logic, in their apparent eccentricity, even if it is one that, as the last two centuries worth of explanations has shown, is not quickly grasped by modern minds. The recovery of the two six-square grids shows us the basis of their way of working and also provides a key to an understanding of their way of using numbers. And this in turn can suggest solutions to some of the remaining mysteries of this Pyramid.

Here then we touch upon the gentle world of ancient mathematics. Less concerned with calculation than with working stone and building ever bigger pyramids, these ancient processes are better described as numerology rather than as arithmetic; a numerology that was concerned with good round numbers and sometimes perhaps with a desire to obfuscate and hide. It is not, therefore, a modern kind of mathematics.

Many of the rare records that have survived from the first few dynasties of ancient Egypt's history emphasise that dimensions set in whole round cubits were a primary specification of things made or donated by the state; everything from mastabas and pyramids, to statues, boats and buildings, land grants, houses, loaves of bread and jugs of beer[1] being listed in quantities or dimensions that could be represented in combinations of the ancient Egyptian hieroglyphs for one, ten and a hundred.[2]

Whilst larger than all other buildings, at 440 cubits wide and 280 cubits high the Great Pyramid's primary dimensions conformed to this general rule. And even though the silhouette of Khufu's Pyramid slopes at an angle that we somewhat awkwardly express today as a gradient of 51° 50′, that same angle may also be obtained, as we have seen, with the use of nice round numbers; that is, by adding 20, 40 and 60 cubits respectively to the points on three grid square co-ordinates crossed by a common diagonal (fig. 30).

In direct contrast, the better part of the Pyramid's interior cannot be counted out in pure round cubits, nor was its architecture established by the addition of pure numbers to irregular numbers like the Pyramid's external angle. This most precise design is in fact a complex product of its commanding six-square grid with the addition of that single small yet vital measurement that offsets it from the Pyramid's baselines.

Now this offset was first set into the architecture of the rising Pyramid at the Prism Point; at the point, as we have already seen, where the living limestone of the Rocky Knoll gives way to those enormous slabs of fine-cut Tura stone that were set down directly on its top. In broad terms, the offset's dimensions approximate the height of the Rocky Knoll above the baselines of the Pyramid. Yet this mysteriously irregular dimension is hardly the serendipitous product of levelling out a section of the Giza Plateau. Not only is it precisely and consistently linked to almost every architectural element of the Pyramid's interior, but it is reflected in the Pyramid's primary dimensions too, in its very height and baselines, for the offset has set the Great Step precisely at the level where the area of the pyramid above it is exactly half the area of the base of the complete monument.

How then was this most critical measurement obtained? From the outset, it should be acknowledged that our enquiry can never prove conclusively how such a thing was done. The traces left by the Pyramid's designers are scanty and ambiguous, and even the massive architectural precisions of the Great Pyramid itself cannot match the exactitude of mathematics to provide an absolute correspondence of ancient measurement and modern calculation. As is usual in this most remarkable of buildings, such 'errors' as its architecture holds within its 5½ million tons of stone are contained in a few inches: the difference, for example, of the measurement of the grid offset at the Prism Point and that at the Great Step some 280 feet away is just 2⅓ inches; a negligible architectural concern perhaps, in the plan of an enormous aged building, but one large enough to deny an absolute surety of proof.[3] Nonetheless, the stones of Khufu's Pyramid are so exact that though we now must deal in a balance of probabilities, in reality the scales are still loaded in our favour.

By modern calculation, as we have already seen, the size of the offset of a six-squared grid required to set a Great Step in a 280 cubit high pyramid precisely at the level where the area of the pyramid above that point would be exactly half the area of the base of a 440 cubit Pyramid would be 8.676768 cubits, which is well within the tolerances of the actual offset in the Great Pyramid as established at the Prism Point and the Great Step. Such mathematical determinations, however, appear to have been beyond the reach of Egypt's pyramid-makers, nor is there any reason to assume that they possessed the need or inclination to set such esoteric feats of numeration in blocks of stone within a pyramid.

Some of the cuttings held within the Pyramid's eastern field, however, suggest a different solution as to how the offset measurement may have been obtained. And at the same time they also provide some tantalising glimpses of how the Pyramid's designers may have gone about their work.

By Khufu's day, as we have seen, there was a long tradition of the use of such co-ordinates as occur within the Great Pyramid's six-square grids: a working drawing from Sneferu's time found by Petrie at Meidum still holds the traces of a similar method used, so it would appear, to establish the angle of the walls of a nearby mastaba.[4] Seen in this light, the stepped pyramids themselves appear as enormous three-dimensional linear grids realised in stone, a process of construction and design whose abandonment for smooth-sided pyramids with the loss of so many of those built-in control points would greatly have increased the builders' difficulties – a problem that Khufu's pyramid-makers solved by setting grid co-ordinates within the architecture of the Pyramid itself.

This was an elaboration of a procedure imported from Meidum and Dahshur. At Dahshur, the angle of the Red Pyramid had been set close to the 45° diagonal;[5] at Meidum, as we have seen (ch. 33 above), the angle of the final smooth-sided phase of Sneferu's pyramid was set by the pyramid-makers adding 12½, 25 and 37½ cubits to a 45° diagonal set upon three of the co-ordinates of the pyramid's six-squared grid.

At Meidum, where the last-built pyramid rose at the same angle as the Great Pyramid, the 275 cubits of its baseline have been divided into six parts of 45.833 cubits each,[6] just as at Giza the same six-part partitioning produced a six-grid square of 73.333 cubits. Given the irregularity of these numbers, it seems highly likely that they were not considered as part of the building's primary specifications, but simply served as part of the pyramids' working diagrams as one might fold a sheet of paper, although here of course using the everyday equipment of stone setters and land surveyors working at full size beside the pyramids' baselines. In similar fashion, we may also infer that the Great Pyramid's interior, which for the most part is set in irregular numbers, was designed with the use of equally practical procedures undertaken with post and cords within the eastern field.

Now the dimensions of the two equal sides of a triangle whose hypotenuse is 12.2 cubits long – that is one sixth of the Pyramid's primary grid dimensions – are 8.6267 cubits each: a measurement within the parameters of the standing offsets inside the Pyramid and equally close as well to the 'ideal' offset established by modern mathematics. In the design field therefore, where the measurement of 12.2 cubits is also the distance between the Trench and the Trial Passages, this offset size of 8.6267 cubits could have easily been set up with cords and posts.

These same scanty traces present an altogether more intriguing possibility, which, though once again lacking modern measurements precise enough for proof, invites us into the wider world of pyramid design. For if, as the present best estimates suggest, the distance between the eastern baseline of the Pyramid and the west side of the Trench is some 152.89 cubits,[7] then this figure is the equivalent of the dimensions of two of the Pyramid's grid squares (2 × 73.333 cubits) plus 6.227 cubits. As the accompanying figure suggests (fig. 169), this shows that the pyramid-makers may have derived their offset measurement from a simple and precise procedure by which they also established and maintained the primary angle of the Pyramid itself. For this provides a size for the grid offset measurement of 8.73 cubits, which once again is well within the existing parameters in the Pyramid, and in fact is identical to the dimension of the grid offset at the Prism Point.

Here then is the outline of a simple route by which the Great Pyramid's primary dimensions were set in three-dimensional harmony with its interior; how, indeed, the widths of its corridors were established and how the height of the grid offset on which their plan was fixed was linked to the 440 cubits of the Great Pyramid's baselines and to the 280 cubits of its height.

It even offers a solution to the mystery that I had innocently set out to solve with a ruler and a set of compasses right at the beginning of this work: the unnerving puzzle as to how the Great Step could have

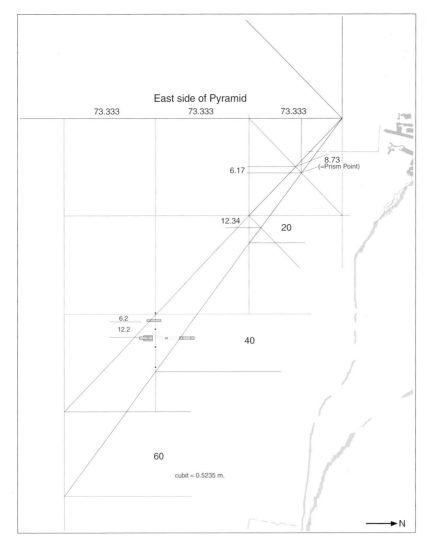

East side of Pyramid

73.333 73.333 73.333

8.73
(=Prism Point)

6.17

12.34

20

6.2

12.2

40

60

cubit = 0.5235 m.

N

Fig. 169 Showing how a system of grid square co-ordinates laid out in the design field may be used to establish the vital link between the Great Pyramid's two design grids that enabled the Great Step to be set precisely at the level at which the area of the base of the pyramid at that level is exactly half the area of the base of the whole Pyramid (see fig. 1 above).

The measurements given on the plan were obtained by calculation, and are well within the levels of accuracy maintained within the Pyramid's own architecture: the offset between the two grids that control the Pyramid's interior and exterior architectures can be precisely established at full size in the gap between the lines set at 45° and 51° by simple procedures traditionally used in building and in field surveys.

been set up by its ancient builders so that the area of the pyramid above it was half the area of the entire Pyramid. For the size of that 'ideal' modern offset is also very close to the size of the small square at the centre of the geometrical construction set between 45° and 51° 50′ and based upon one of the Pyramid's grid squares (fig. 169). Given the intrinsic properties of such constructions when placed inside the Great Pyramid's six-square grids, the inevitable result must be a measurement closely reflecting that unnerving property.[8] Such is the rich potential of grid-based designs, although as the pyramid-makers did not appear to have employed the mechanisms of modern calculation, we may be reasonably assured that this particular abstraction went quite unrecognised.

More work within the eastern field of course, a careful cleaning and survey of its surviving surfaces, would certainly increase our understanding of its graven lines and post holes; and promise too the discovery of more information. Already, the work of Flinders Petrie and Mark Lehner has provided evidence enough to show how a few rough cuttings on the eastern Plateau might well be joined in harmony with the architecture of the Pyramid above: more than enough information to show that the Great Pyramid need not have been designed by shadowy mathematicians, or imaginary architects making scaled plans and working with primitive theodolites, but was made by the core of pyramid-makers who also shaped the Pyramid's fine stones, who planned and built its ramps and harbours, working in the open air, at 1 to 1, with passion, care and giant grids of squares laid out upon the ground beside the Pyramid.

40 Stars

From the very beginning, from the days when the lines of the Great Pyramid were first laid out upon the Giza Plateau, its builders would have required a great deal of Tura limestone. And since that same fine stone was used in quantity right up to the ending of King Sneferu's building projects, it is difficult to imagine that work at the Tura quarries had ceased at the time when Khufu ascended to the throne.[1] At Tura at the beginning of the work on Khufu's Pyramid there could still have been a standing workforce of a hundred men all living with their families on the slopes beside the desert quarries, a community serviced by a little fleet of barges whose crews would ship the quarried blocks across the river.[2]

So as Sneferu's pyramid-making communities were travelling up to Giza from the south and work was beginning on building harbour quays, on opening up the quarry and building stone-hauling ramps up to the Plateau, fresh cut blocks of fine white Tura stone were probably amongst the first to be hauled along the slick new pathways to the cuttings that marked out the base of Khufu's Pyramid.

Many of those blocks of Tura stone still lie beside the Pyramid's ruined baselines, butted hard up against the Rocky Knoll and set precisely to the living rock, a ruined pavement standing on a perfect level platform, each surviving stone cemented down with the finest

kiln-baked mortar. This would be the most accurately levelled
element in all the Pyramid, so exactly set that Petrie used it to establish the Pyramid's original height and width to within a fraction of
an inch.[3] Half-missing now, stripped by stone robbers, only the cloisons of the missing stones still show the pavement's full extent. Once
it must have been a gleaming band of massive oblong slabs running
right around the Pyramid's four sides, with rows of post holes set
along its outer edges, these presumably the surviving traces of the
pyramid-makers' lines of survey and control, the scant marks of the
much-argued-over processes by which the Great Pyramid was sighted
and levelled and provided with this perfect, flat foundation.[4]

Those same surviving cloisons also tell us that the largest block of
this splendid pavement stood at the Pyramid's north-east corner:[5] the
block which held the point that marked the northern ending of the
Pyramid's eastern baseline; that same baseline that, along with the
Descending Corridor upon the Rocky Knoll, was so precisely set to
stellar north. The same block too, it would appear, that marked the
northern ending of that crucial interface between the Pyramid and
its design field; that line on which all the planes and levels and
dimensions of the architecture of the rising Pyramid may have been
generated before they were transferred into the Pyramid above. No
wonder that this line was laid with such precision; it was the Great
Pyramid's ground zero.

Fig. 170 Fitted block by
block into the natural
rock of the Plateau, the
remains of the Great
Pyramid's eastern
pavement, and some
of its eroded casing
stones.

Whatever 'symbolic' significances the exactitude of the Great Pyramid's northern orientation may ever have possessed – if indeed the pyramid-makers were disposed to split such metaphysic hairs – there were sound practical reasons to establish such a high degree of accuracy at the outset of work. The use of an approximated baseline as a reference in a building where measurements were made by dead reckoning would inevitably have resulted in severe building errors high up in the pyramid.[6] Subsidence too, in several of Sneferu's pyramids, had shown the royal pyramid-makers that, left unchecked, even modest movements in such enormous stacks of stone not only threatened a loss of control over the architectural form, but could result in the cracking and collapse of the internal chambers, and even of the pyramid itself.[7]

A carefully established baseline, then, was a vital practical element in the accurate construction of these enormous pyramids. And year on year as well, each one of the Great Pyramid's 200-odd stone block courses was levelled to the high degrees of accuracy that they have maintained down to this day. Beside the constant checks upon the continuing integrity of the Pyramid's interior and baselines, the work of building each and every course also provided further constant checks on the stability and exactitude of the Pyramid's increasing mass – to this extent, the pyramid-makers' resetting of the corridors

Fig. 171 Polished by the tread of its ancient workers and its modern visitors, the north-western corner of the Great Pyramid displays a galaxy of post holes which may have been connected with the Pyramid's stellar orientation and the measuring and levelling of its baselines. Some of these post holes have been convincingly interpreted as providing a means of setting a right angle at the Pyramid's corner. Though the subjects of numerous ingenious but essentially theoretical explanations, the other post holes are of unknown purposes.

displaced by subsidence in Sneferu's Bent Pyramid (see pp. 272ff) may be seen as forlorn attempts to realign its failing building lines.

Even the most sophisticated internal system of control requires a fixed point outside the structure of the pyramid itself to maintain a true precision, a system of external regulation that could have been set up as a series of sight lines, posts and lines placed around the Pyramid like those that still apparently exist (see fig. 166) within its eastern field. Ever since the days of Djoser the royal masons had also set a single externally sighted fixed point into each and every pyramid they built, aligning their baselines to the cardinal points by fixing them upon a straight line drawn from that unique point in the night sky, the point of north, round which the polar stars revolve. Built into their very blocks of stone, this was a solid line of reference that was not subject to movements in the pyramid itself nor in the ground on which it stood. And not surprisingly, as Sneferu's building projects multiplied and the pyramid-makers learned to cope with the slow subsidence that inevitably occurred with the stacking of such huge amounts of stone upon a sandy desert, each pyramid project had not only been better built, but was more carefully aligned to north as well.[8] And so at Giza, just as the accuracy of the Great Pyramid's stonework and the complexity of its internal architecture exceeded all those earlier projects, so Khufu's monument was more carefully aligned to stellar north than any pyramid had ever been before.

Such stellar alignments could have been accomplished with rows of tensioned cords and plummets sighted one behind the other.[9] Drawn in parallel across the Plateau from the western baseline of the Pyramid to the edge of the design field, such sight lines may have been set up along with others on the rising Pyramid itself, so that year on year as the building rose it could have been continuously rechecked.[10] That slight twist, which Petrie measured between the alignment of the courses of the Great Pyramid's quarry blocks and its surviving casing stones, suggests that just such realignments were continually repeated throughout construction as part of the ongoing effort to keep the Pyramid rising straight and true.[11]

The remarkably high level of precision held in various lines of Khufu's Pyramid, however, tokens more than the routine checking of its rising stones. This Pyramid, after all, still holds such a constancy of build within it that 4½ millennia later the equally fastidious Flinders Petrie was able to detect the tiny twist of just 4 inches (average 9.72 cm) between the Pyramid's core and its Tura casing stones;[12] a precision that required the establishment of a single master orientation at the Pyramid to that cosmic abstraction that we now call north.

Most modern specifications of the Great Pyramid assume that its most representative orientation to the point of north is to be found in the alignment of its casing stones: yet there is no way of knowing now if those fine Tura blocks held that same orientation from the beginning of the Pyramid's construction, a product of a grand alignment ceremony as is sometimes postulated.[13] Given the twist in orientation between the courses of the quarry blocks and those of the casing stones, however, one might logically assume, along with Petrie, that those much-measured casing blocks were set in place towards the ending of construction.[14]

This appears to be borne out by the order in which the Pyramid was made. Set deep inside the Pyramid and laid down with unmatched precision, the line of the Descending Corridor down into the Rocky Knoll was surely excavated at the beginning of the work before being completed by the upper sections of that same corridor when they were built in blocks of Tura stone upon the Rocky Knoll.[15] Now as we have already seen, both the horizontal and vertical alignments of this corridor were part of a building diagram based upon the size and orientation of the Pyramid's four baselines; a plan, it would appear, that was established in the eastern design field. It follows, therefore, that from the orientation of the Pyramid's eastern baseline to the setting out of its six-squared grids, the fundamental work of establishing this plan must have been undertaken before the excavation of the Descending Corridor was begun. The alignment of the Descending Corridor and the rest of the Pyramid's internal architecture and even the courses of its quarry blocks differ in their orientation from that of the casing stone along the eastern baseline, which would indicate that they did not share a common orientation and that the pyramid-makers had first established a slightly different line of north than that which is presently preserved in the line of its eastern casing blocks.

It is a commonplace to observe that in their use of the stars the pyramid-makers were developing a knowledge of the movements of the heavens that had been part of human experience from long before the birth of agriculture or the Egyptian state. That the precise stellar alignment used by Khufu's star gazers to set the eastern baseline could be reconstructed by modern archaeologists is, however, a most remarkable testament to the exactitude of the pyramid-makers, both of those who made the necessary observations and of the masons who trapped those astronomical alignments so precisely in the blocks of the Great Pyramid.

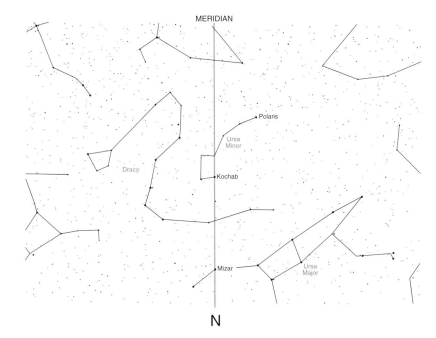

Fig. 172 The northern night sky as seen at midnight at Giza on 20 August 2467 BC. Whilst Polaris, the modern North Star, lies well to the east, Kochab and Mizar stand directly upon the Northern Meridian.

The details of the methods that Khufu's astronomers could have used to make their observations and alignments has been the subject of a deal of speculation over many centuries, a slow progress that quickened with Napoleon's excursion to the Middle East in 1798 and flowered in 2000 in an article in the journal *Nature*, in which Kate Spence, a Cambridge egyptologist, fixed the date of the astronomical observation by which the line of the Pyramid's casing blocks was set to within five years![16] Noting that Sneferu's three monuments deviated from the modern point of north by slightly differing amounts, as do the later pyramids, Spence plotted these deviations and showed that they were not the product of random errors as had previously been supposed, but that they held a pattern in them. Like the blocks of the Great Pyramid itself, they had a constant shift in them that echoed the minute variations that would result from using the movements of specific polar stars at different times to set the point of north – for over time, the position of stellar north is subject to a tiny displacement in the rotation of the earth; that 26,000-year-long polar wobble that astronomers call precession. From these minute discrepancies therefore, Spence estimates that the orientation of the casing stones of the eastern baseline of the Great Pyramid was set in October 2478, ± 5 years, BC.

In re-establishing the exact method Khufu's astronomers used to align the Pyramid using a reconstruction of the ancient sky at Giza, Spence isolated two of the stars that later ancient Egyptian texts describe as the 'imperishables' for their eternal rotation around the dark centre of the ancient sky.[17] Khufu's astronomers, it now appears, had found their north by bisecting the arcs of Kochab and Mizar, two polar stars, as they swung into simultaneous vertical alignment above and below the dark centre of north, such as occurred in the night sky in August 2478 BC, when the single vertical line of a plumb bob passing down through both of them would have provided Khufu's pyramid-makers with the precise point that is set within the Pyramid's great casing blocks.[18]

This might at first appear to have been a simple enough procedure, accomplished with the aid of two plumb bobs one set behind the other, with an accompanying stone mason perhaps, to chisel out the line of north. In reality, the single act that set the birthday of the Great Pyramid within its architecture required patience, skill and practicality along with a familiarity with the problems that arise during such procedures, a detailed knowledge of the movements of the stars and the persistence to check and recheck all results.

The first alignment of the eastern baseline then, the founding of the Great Pyramid, must have been a fastidious undertaking, with the astronomers working on a precisely levelled platform and with perhaps a strip of carefully levelled ground running northwards from the Pyramid's foundation line. The whole area, surely, would have been a veritable observatory, covered with strings and windbreaks and staffed with a variety of people from astronomers to stone masons, and priests perhaps, and scribes and labourers all working together. Sheltered from the desert wind, lines of plumb bobs hanging freely yet completely stilled and set precisely in parallel lines and aligned upon the two polar stars could then have provided the sighting that the masons would have then inscribed, a line upon a levelled stone. Repeated, checked and checked again, the alignment of those two bright stars was narrowed to an 'error' of just 5 seconds of one degree, an error small enough to enable us to reach back in time and fix the vanished pyramid-makers in this specific time and place.

Let us return then to that time, to a starry August night in the first years of Khufu's reign, with the Nile in fresh flood and a group of anonymous Egyptians walking on the soft warm stone of the Tura pavement above the gleaming river plain.[19] There are no written records of this event, nor is there of the cool Hegelian stroll that had surely taken place in this same area some years before when the pyramid-makers' plans were still ambitions and the parameters of national effort throughout the years of Khufu's reign were not yet finalised. On that single night, however, as the hours passed and the reflections of the stars gleamed from the glassy water of the flooded fields and circled round the dark centre in the sky, the astronomers waited for those two special stars to stand one above the other on the self-same line. And at that moment, set by a single living eye, they brought that line down onto a pavement of fine stone, marking their relationship that night, to earth and heaven and to time.

The next step, surely, would have been the establishment of the design field upon the east side of the Pyramid so that the Descending Corridor could be accurately positioned up on the Rocky Knoll. This would have begun with the division of the eastern baseline into two equal halves and continued with the subdivision of the northern half – the half where the better part of the Pyramid's architecture would be situated – into three further sections: those of the east–west grid planes. As Rex Engelbach has written, such extreme precision as would be required for these divisions may be obtained with careful work with wooden measuring poles, but as he also observes,[20] there is no proof of the use of even these simplest of devices, and of course there are many ways of dividing a line into six equal parts. As we have already noticed, however (pp. 340ff), the odd cubit fraction produced by the six-partite division of 440 cubits suggests that rather than employing abstract mathematics and measuring out its product on the ground, the dimension of the six-square grids was set with builders' tools working pragmatically at 1 to 1, directly on the Pyramid's fine stone pavement.

At this same time our modern plan informs us, a number of basic decisions must have already been taken about the architecture of this pyramid. First was that the basic geometrical design of the Pyramid's interior, set from two crossed lines set on the diagonals of four grid squares (fig. 28), would be represented in the hard stone of the Pyramid at the levels of its floors, so as to allow that elegant design to remain intact and so permit, it would transpire, the master builders the freedom to construct an interior architecture over and around this basic framework as circumstances required.

Of necessity, another of these initial tasks would have been to set out the height and the angle of the Pyramid's exterior angle on the co-ordinates of the lower grid, for as we have seen (ch. 39 above), without that basic angle and in all probability at least one of the con-structions that appears to have been preserved within the eastern field, none of the internal architecture could have been set so pre-cisely upon the upper six-square grid. The Pyramid's plan, indeed, insists that the exact location of the Prism Point had been established before the excavation of the Descending Corridor could have begun. At the same time the Trial Passages – that part-full-sized model of the Prism Point which accommodated the exact location of the grid offset within the Pyramid itself – would have been excavated and positioned in the Pyramid's design field and the Pyramid's grid planes projected out from the Pyramid's baseline into the eastern field to serve as the main lines of the plan and to provide sight lines between the plan and the Pyramid itself. So with a simple system of posts and cords, with sighting and aligning, the angles and dimensions and all those measurements that are now so hard to rediscover in our modern plans could have been aligned, designed and set together with a high degree of accuracy within the eastern field.

Then, and only then, could the rush of building up King Khufu's Pyramid with blocks of quarry stone begin. Within two hard years our schedule informs us (ch. 6), a third of its stones could have been set into position. Two years on, with more than half of the Pyramid's bulk in its place, the master builders would have begun the construction of the Grand Gallery. Four years later, with three quarters of the Pyramid in position, they would have been standing on the Great Step itself, at the portal of King Khufu's burial chamber.

41 Coda: considering the architecture

Whilst the Great Pyramid was the quintessence of a millennial tradition of designing for the dead, a novel symmetry has been set up inside it, a unique geometry that redefined the route to royal burial. And then, as if its makers wished to draw a veil over their extraordinary invention, this new itinerary was hidden in a maze of numbers.

King Khufu's burial chamber was also subject to this same strange process. Instead of the royal burial chamber's primary measurements being set in whole cubit numbers in the usual way, one of its dimensions, that of its height, was obtained by setting measurements in whole cubits on the diagonals of its floors and walls. So even though the chamber's length and breadth are laid down in clear round numbers – as 10 and 20 cubits[1] – the 11.163 cubits (5.84 m) of its height is the unlikely product of a sophisticated mix of the diagonals of the chamber's end walls which are 15 cubits (7.84 m) long, and of the diagonals of 25 cubits (13.07 m), which stretch from the corners of the chamber floor to their opposite angles on the chamber's ceiling (fig. 173). Here too a primary element of the Pyramid's identity (see ch. 39), and part of the traditional vocabulary of state architecture, has been encoded.[2] In such a game of camouflage, of course, precision would be essential if the hidden identity of the full round measurements is to be maintained: and of course, the Great Pyramid is as precisely made as anything that the Egyptians ever built.

Whilst on the outside its measurements are crystal clear, the Pyramid's interior is another world, the straightforward six-squared grid inherited from Sneferu's monuments (see ch. 33) having been realigned and offset so that its interior baseline, its architectural horizon, lies 15 feet above ground level. And as if to emphasise the single-mindedness of its designers, even the granite burial chamber, which, as its builders' markings show, was pre-fabricated and then erected inside the half-finished Pyramid block by block (see ch. 44 below), follows the same singular procedure of masking whole numbers.

As is usual with the Great Pyramid, there is no evidence whatever that the complex manoeuvres of its designers were intended to hold an overt religious symbolism: it is characteristic, however, of ancient Egyptian religious texts and images to use complexity in itself, as an expression of the ultimately unfathomable if harmonious order of the universe.[3] Quite uncannily as well, a unique papyrus written centuries later specifically refers to Khufu's 'Horizon' – that is, his tomb – in terms of numbers and of transformation, Papyrus Westcar, telling a tale in which one of Khufu's sons travels upstream to a settlement of Sneferu's to fetch an old man with knowledge of the number of some secret chambers that Khufu wants to replicate within his tomb.[4] And when Khufu asks him for that number, the wise old man replies, 'By your favour, I know not the number therefore, my Lord, but I know the place where the number or the knowledge of the number is.'[5] Replete with pictograms signifying sealing and security, these much-debated lines seem to imply that King Khufu wishes his tomb to be designed in accordance with the 'secret chambers' of Thoth, a god of number and of numeration. In terms of the architecture of the Great Pyramid, however, the text might literally suggest that the old man could not name the irregular number of the grid's offset, but that he had knowledge of how it could be obtained.

Nor was this grid offset the only innovation inside King Khufu's Pyramid. Unlike most of the earlier royal tombs, the Great Pyramid's corridors do not connect its interior chambers one after the other, until the burial chamber is reached: here, and quite uniquely, the Prism Point divides King Khufu's journey to the grave so that the Pyramid's three internal chambers lie one above the other, each one set at the ending of a corridor. The Prism Point, therefore, that innovative knot of corridors where the grid offset is introduced, has changed the route to burial and thus quite literally the royal destiny itself.

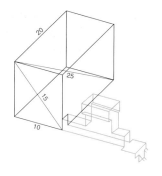

Fig. 173 The Great Pyramid's burial chamber dimensions, given in cubits. Although this granite room has shifted inside the Pyramid and its measurements are now short of perfection, the scheme as given here appears to reflect the pyramid-makers' intentions.

With a height of 11.15 cubits, the 'perfect' measurements of the burial chamber are part hidden; the 15 cubit dimension of the end wall diagonals, however, is repeated in the size of the offset of the Pyramid's main corridors from its north south centreline.

The architectural concept of a prism point, however, was hardly new of itself, being a fundamental element of ancient Egyptian architecture and design.[6] Placed upon a central axis, it governs designs from all periods of ancient Egyptian culture and in a range of works, from tombs and shrines to individual stelae. The ground plans of many Egyptian temples too are based on similar pairs of angles. Set upon the main axis and on a point behind their central shrines the widening angle of such lines controls the ever-enlarging sizes of the temples' halls and courts and colonnades as they approach the temples' main entrances.[7] Although it functioned in reverse, the design of the Great Pyramid's interior is not unlike that of an Egyptian temple.[8] Just as the temples' resident deities were carried straight out of their temples in procession away from the prism point towards the living land and Nile, so at Khufu's Pyramid the burial party came from the living land, and passed right back through its Prism Point to reach the grave.[9]

The snakes and ladders of King Khufu's Pyramid, those narrow-angled spaces more suitable for the progress of a block-shaped coffin than for people, turned death into a symmetric if ultimately unquantifiable progress through the darkness of the rock, a journey

Fig. 174 King Khufu's granite burial chamber and sarcophagus.

in which each leg ends in three separate individual chambers: the lowest and the largest in the Pyramid, rough-quarried like King Djoser's burying place and set deep beneath the surface of the Plateau; the second, the Queen's Chamber, up above it at the ending of a level corridor, a low horizon, like the burial chamber of Sneferu's Red Pyramid; and over and above them both and higher up than any other room in any other pyramid in Egypt, the granite chamber that holds the king's sarcophagus.

And in Khufu's final journey there will be another twist, one last disconnection. For as his burial chamber is approached, as the Pyramid's centre line is crossed at the Great Step, the entire design is turned upon its edge; the tight near-two-dimensionality of its chalky corridors turns sharply towards the west into a booming open space, a shining granite room. Just as in ancient Egyptian reliefs, where a narrow insubstantial slot of space accommodates all aspects of a living head, an eye, a mouth, a nose, an ear, within a single outline, so at the Great Pyramid that same thin envelope, that same astonishing potential, is set to hold the destiny of pharaoh.

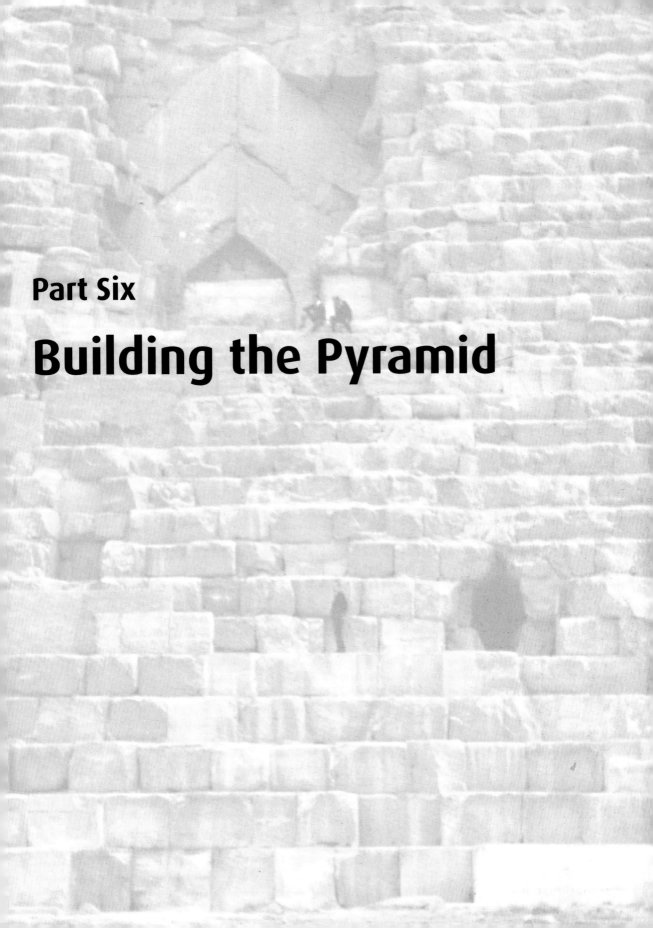

Part Six
Building the Pyramid

42 In the beginning

At the beginning of the Great Pyramid's construction, when the starry precisions of the astronomers and master masons had run their course and the building site had been levelled and readied for the quarry blocks, the area all around the Giza Plateau, both the desert and the plain, would have filled with storerooms and workshops and the various accommodations of King Khufu's pyramid-builders and their attendant households.[1] If building work had proceeded at the same rate that it had at the previous pyramid (ch. 6), then around a fifth of the Pyramid's entire bulk would have been set in place during that first full year of building; some 3700 tons of local stone would have been quarried, cut, hauled and laid in place upon the Pyramid on each and every working day, a labour that would have required some 15,000 stone block haulers and quarrymen working around the Giza Plateau, and 1500 stone setters on the low platform of the Pyramid itself.[2]

Even the amounts of river water that such an enterprise would have required were quite terrific. Not just to slake the workforce and liquefy their building plaster, but to lubricate the slipways of the ramps up which the quarry blocks were hauled. The very substance of those ramps required large amounts of water in their making, for if the remains that stand by the Great Pyramid today are typical, though their substance was composed of dust-dry building debris, the sturdy walls that held that loose mass in position were made of rocks of rough-shaped limestone laid in generous amounts of oozing muddy mortar set straight onto the bone-dry desert (fig. 87).[3] Right from the beginning, the effort needed to support King Khufu's pyramid-makers was an immense undertaking for a Bronze Age economy, with huge amounts of building supplies, provisions and materials flowing into Giza's brand-new harbours to sustain the progress of the endless lines of blocks that were moving up onto the rising Pyramid.

Nor are such images entirely speculative. Now that the method of the Pyramid's design has been re-established along with a practical timetable for its construction, now that the landscapes that provided its materials and shaped its architecture are better known and understood, an outline of the year-by-year construction of this Pyramid can be brought together without the common or garden travesties of 'Ancient Egypt' that colour so many earlier accounts.

It is unlikely, for example, that in the first half of the Pyramid's construction the supply ramps would have resembled those grandiose geometrical constructions that rise, computer-generated, within the popular imagination. Just as the cores of the early pyramids have each been built in different ways, just as the ruins of surviving stone-hauling ramps are built to several different designs, so too the systems of stone delivery during the first years of working on the Giza Plateau could have been as diverse as those that operated in the quarries from which the Great Pyramid's stone blocks were being hauled.[4] In the first two years of work especially, when the workforce was exceptionally large and as many as 150 quarry blocks an hour may have been hauled out of the royal quarries each working day,[5] mass access to the rising Pyramid must have been a primary concern, and so we may imagine there were wide-open delivery systems, a variety of ramps and pathways set right across the Plateau and the Pyramid. At the beginning, with the Rocky Knoll, that stump of natural rock, still standing in the sunlight, we may imagine all sorts of ramps sprawled over the Great Pyramid's construction site, ad hoc arrangements of ever-growing ever-changing inclines built to accommodate the swift emplacement of an ever-rising tide of limestone quarry blocks.

Such a clamorous vision, such a carnival of national power at the beginning of construction, underscores the vital function of that tiny corridor which the master craftsmen cut down through the natural limestone of the Plateau; that simple excavation which is so precisely made that, as Petrie notes, 'in this particular we have not yet gone

within the builder's accuracy'.[6] That this remarkable excavation –
which Petrie observed is as precise as the Pyramid's final baselines –
held more importance for its makers than merely to provide access to
the Subterranean Chamber at its ending is signalled by the fact that
the rough room was never fully excavated (pp. 106ff above).[7] And then
again, as we have already seen, the location and direction of this
perfect little corridor hold most of the parameters that would control
the internal architecture of the rising Pyramid.[8] Together with the
eastern baseline, it was the Pyramid's DNA.

During the first full year of building (fig. 175), the perfect line and
orientation of this rock-cut corridor were extended upwards and outwards in massive blocks of Tura stone onto the Rocky Knoll, towards
the Pyramid's as yet unbuilt northern face. And to this day, those
block-built sections of the corridor rise up through the courses of the
Pyramid with a similar precision to that of its lower rock-cut section.
At its completion, in about the second year of construction, this
perfect line would define the exact position of the Pyramid's single
entrance without the need of mathematical calculation or a single
cubit measure. As in so many architectural elements within this
Pyramid, the placing of the doorway on its northern face was determined by projecting a series of perfect lines and planes in solid stone,
until they met.[9]

Nestled comfortably into the upper surface of the Rocky Knoll, the
first-laid blocks of Tura stone in which the line of the rock-cut corridor was extended, two huge rows of them, were set at right angles to

Fig. 175 Building the
framework of the internal
architecture: a theoretical
cross section of the Great
Pyramid at the ending of
the first year of building.
By establishing the
positions of the Pyramid's
eastern and northern
baselines and the planes
of the six-square grid, the
location of the Pyramid's
entrance may be precisely
fixed without having to
make a single
measurement beyond the
setting of the baselines at
440 cubits.

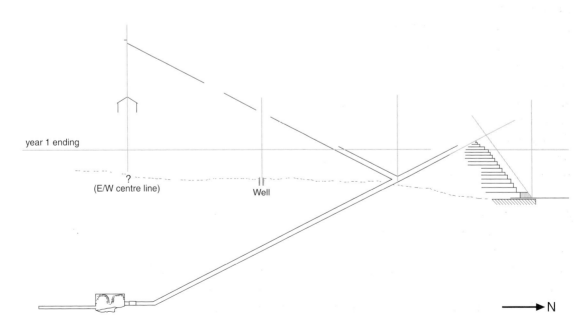

year 1 ending

? (E/W centre line)

Well

N

its downward slope.[10] And in those first-laid blocks, just 6 feet (1.75 m) above the surface of the living rock, King Khufu's masons set the Prism Point, that vital knot of angles, the architectural conjunction between the Ascending and Descending Corridors whose exact location would eventually define the positions of the as yet unbuilt rooms and corridors of the Pyramid's interior.[11]

It follows, then, that even as the master masons cut that perfect little corridor into the Rocky Knoll, the Pyramid's essential plan had already been set up in its design field.[12] And this in turn shows that the outlines of the Pyramid's baselines had also been laid down by that core of master pyramid-makers, astronomers and masons who had worked on the white plain of the design field in that quiet time before the first frantic flood of mass construction had begun. More evidence of this careful long-term architectural planning survives at the Prism Point within the Pyramid itself. For even as the stone masons were setting the first blocks of the Ascending Corridor above it, they were tapering the corridor's height by just two inches in a manner similar to that which can still be seen within the Trial Passages down in the design field.[13] This so that the corridor's walls and ceilings would first slow and then stop the three rectangular shafts of granite that would be slid down into it to plug it up, when the Pyramid was closed.[14]

As the master masons laid the first blocks of the lower sections of the Ascending Corridor on the Rocky Knoll, as well as setting the subtle mechanisms of the Pyramid's final closure they also anticipated that the final scrunching journey of the plugging stones would threaten to displace the corridor's walls and ceiling. So, at regular intervals down through its length, they set six 15 foot long blocks of Tura limestone in the corridor, each one of which having the corridor's rectangular form cut through its centre, so that at the

Fig. 176 A theoretical cross section of the Great Pyramid at the ending of the second year of building. The positions of the girdling blocks in the lower half of the Ascending Corridor are indicated by six pairs of lines.

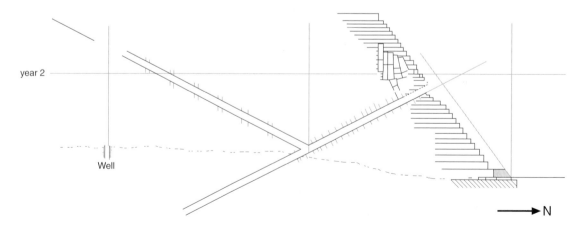

year 2

Well

N

closing of the Pyramid, the granite shafts would slide safely through these solid so-called 'girdle blocks' to their intended destinations (see fig. 176).[15]

Today, of course, there is no way of knowing the full extent of other hidden structures like those massive half-dozen girdle blocks, which the pyramid-makers may have buried in the Pyramid to preserve the integrity of its interior architecture. The ending of another of these huge constructions is, however, visible today upon the north side of the Pyramid, where the stripping of its casing stones has revealed a double vault, a titanic fabrication – one of whose henge-like shafts would bear Dr Lepsius' inscription with the King of Prussia's hiero-glyphic titulary (see fig. 83 above) – set up above the entrance corridor on stacks of building blocks that are double and triple the usual size; a construction conceived, apparently, to direct the Pyramid's weight away from its only entrance.[16]

This enormous inverted v-shaped double arch, four megalithic chamfered shafts, is not to be seen in any earlier pyramid, the only previously known example being a comparatively miniature version erected in a tomb of one of Sneferu's courtiers at Dahshur.[17] At Khufu's Pyramid, however, the same construction would be employed in other locations higher up within the Pyramid in apparent anticipation of the weight of stone that would bear down on its rooms and corridors. First and just a few years later and most beautifully and precisely, the simple vault would be employed to cover and protect the Queen's Chamber, and later in a more utilitarian mode the same construction would cap the elaborately engineered arrangements over Khufu's burial chamber.

So though it is impossible now to discover the full extent of the gigantic vault that stands above the Pyramid's entrance, in all likeli-hood it is but the ending of a long construction built up from the Rocky Knoll to protect the entire length of the entrance corridor down to the Prism Point, and thus ensure that those most vital build-ing lines and points would not shift out of true (fig. 176).

Just as we can know little more about such structures that may be buried in the Pyramid, so too, in similar fashion, our knowledge of the Pyramid's core, its very substance, is very scanty. Apart from a few shallow cracks and holes that have been cut into the Pyramid's four present faces, just a tiny sample of this core is visible today, the merest glimpse of a few hundred quarry blocks revealed by the random excavations that at various times in its long history have been hacked into the body of the Pyramid. Without exception, these holes and tunnels show the Pyramid's substance to be composed of

Fig. 177 The vault above the Great Pyramid's entrance, with traces of an enormous rectangular trench – a 'construction gap' – clearly visible on either side (see further chapters 45 and 46 below). Much of the Pyramid's internal architecture appears to have been constructed inside just such construction gaps left within the rising Pyramid for that specific purpose, the shafts and lintels of the interior vaults and ceilings being dragged into their final positions across the stone work built on either side. After the work's completion, the remaining gaps between the stone work of the interior architecture and the surrounding courses of the Pyramid were filled with plaster and rough stones (see fig. 83).

well-made quarry blocks laid in the same horizontal courses as make up its present façades.[18] Certainly, there is nothing to suggest that the interior is composed of anything other than regular blocks of local quarry stone.[19]

From the very first, however, more care was taken with the setting of the time-yellowed rows of stone that form the Pyramid's four present-day faces, for the greater part of these are the so-called 'backing blocks' to which the all-but-vanished Tura casing stones were

Fig. 178 The intrusive excavation known as 'Caliph Ma'mun's Hole' which opened the sides of the Great Pyramid's Ascending Corridor, and revealed two of the great granite blocks that plug its lower sections. That this enormous rough-cut tunnel resembles a mine shaft cut in living rock shows that the fine cut stone work, the perfect horizontal levels, of the Pyramid's four present faces continues throughout this section of the Pyramid's interior – a fact that is also true in those other places in the Pyramid's interior where further sections of the Pyramid's courses are exposed.

once attached. Such care attended the setting of these backing blocks that the Pyramid's modern surveyors have used them in their various reconstructions of its finished angles and dimensions.[20] As Petrie put it, 'by looking across a face of the Pyramid, either up an edge, across the middle of the face, or even along near the base, the mean optical plane which would touch the most prominent points of all the stones, may be found with an average variation at different times of only 1.0 inch'.[21] That each and every horizontal course of the Pyramid's quarry blocks was precisely levelled and aligned to the stars would have greatly aided the rising Pyramid's precision.

Yet the common assumption that every individual course of the Great Pyramid was levelled and finished before work began on the next layer up is certainly incorrect. During construction, the quarry blocks that lie today in such straight courses and form the substance of the Pyramid also served as building aids. At the centre of the north face, for example, on either side of the gigantic v-shaped vault that stands around the entrance, traces of this process yet remain in the outline of a huge gap in the surrounding courses of the building stones; a gap which after the first two years or so of building stood at around 50 feet (15.3 m) in height and formed two great walls some 40 feet (11.25 m) apart.[22] Inside this narrow slot, the huge stones of the protective vault were pulled into place and the chamfered blocks of the v-shaped vaults slid into their positions over and above them (fig. 83). And afterwards, as can still be seen, the narrow spaces between this immense structure and the edges of the two high walls of the construction gap were filled with odd-shaped stones and plaster (fig. 177).

During the first years of working, with the Pyramid still low and wide, similar temporary gaps within the rising courses could have served to aid the building work in a variety of ways; some perhaps, as Dieter Arnold has suggested, housing internal ramps within the Pyramid for the delivery of building blocks.[23] One may well imagine, then, that a variety of such constructions, both ramps and trenches, built with local quarry blocks, were set up across the Pyramid as local needs required. Despite all this diversity the integrity of the Pyramid's individual courses was so beautifully maintained that still today the golden lines of backing blocks that frame each and every one of them, layer upon layer, are within inches of perfection.[24]

Yet there is also a considerable variation in the sizes of these individual courses that belies the apparent even textures of the Pyramid's four present faces; at 2 feet 4 inches, the height of our standard 2½ ton block is but a convenience for estimation. In reality, the 200-odd courses that still survive vary in their height from 1 foot 7 inches (0.500 m) to 4 feet 4 inches (1.27 m).[25] Within this range, however, there is an overall diminishment of around 4 per cent in the height of each individual course as they rise up to the summit (fig. 179); a reduction so consistent that those few courses that are unusually large stand out today in this gentle diminution, like slubbed wefts in a length of shantung silk.[26] There are a dozen obvious examples of these outstanding courses, each one being followed by far smaller ones that gradually increase again in height until another peak is reached; a gentle rhythm that reaches right up through the Pyramid's full height.

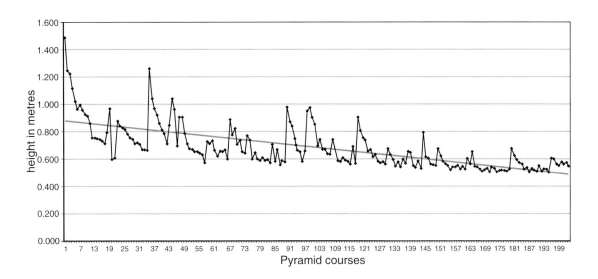

height in metres

Pyramid courses

Some of these changes in course size reflect aspects of the Pyramid's architectural design. Course 19 for example, which marks the height of the lintel above the entrance doorway and is one of the largest in the Pyramid, is followed by two courses that are so small that similarly sized blocks would not be laid for many years to come: this suggests an accommodation in course height that would have enabled the lintel's placement to be used as a horizontal control line right across the Pyramid and its design field.[27] In similar fashion, Petrie's survey also shows that course 24 is set exactly at the level of the sill of the entrance to the Grand Gallery, whilst course 50 is 3½ inches from the height of the rise of the Great Step, a vital element in the Pyramid's construction and design, marking the top of the first square of the upper grid and the level of King Khufu's burial chamber.[28] Similar conjunctions of construction and design also continue to occur in the stonework of the Pyramid well above the levels of its internal architecture: course 99 lies precisely at the height of two of the Pyramid's lower grid squares, and course 105 marks the exact dimension of the grid squares' offset. Here there are clear connections between the Pyramid's abstract plan, the design field, and the hard stones of its rising courses.[29]

These are but the merest traces of building processes that are largely lost to us; it would be interesting, for example, to know if the connections between the Pyramid's plan and the serried courses of its quarry stone were also linked to the logistics of the Pyramid's construction.[30] Fundamentally these horizontal alignments underline how the Pyramid's courses served in the manner of draftsman's graph paper, providing accurate horizontal planes of reference that

Fig. 179 Graph plotting the changing sizes of the Pyramid's individual courses, from its baseline to its present summit. The trend for the courses to decrease in size as the Pyramid rises higher adds illusion to perspective and serves to exaggerate modern perceptions of the Pyramid's true height.

projected the heights of some of the carefully established points of the internal architecture right across the rising Pyramid. Cross-checked by a system of co-ordinates set up in the design field and against the polar stars,[31] such horizontal controls, a series of 200-odd subsidiary baselines, would have provided the pyramid-makers with a constant and immediate control on building movement and inaccuracy; a Nilometer measuring the rising flood of stone.

Such eerie stone-on-stone precision is so out of step with modern building practice and thus with 'common sense', that for the last two centuries it has encouraged pyramidologists and traditional archaeologists alike either to offer symbolical explanations of the Pyramid's accuracy or to ignore, distort or even question its existence.[32] At all events, the precise placement of the Pyramid's building stones clearly had huge utility during its construction. And of course, the pyramid-makers well knew from their previous experience (ch. 29 above) that such enormous stone block structures might move and break apart and thus they could lose control of the enormous building even as they laid its stones. On these terms alone, therefore, the Great Pyramid stands as a perfect product of Bronze Age technology; a work created and constructed with the aid of lines and cords, with craftsmen's hands and builder's squares, with water and the human eye, and with the order of the stars.

43 Setting the lines

The squareness and level of the base of the Pyramid is brilliantly true . . . the Queens Chamber is also very finely fitted.

Paraphrased from Petrie's History of Egypt[1]

By the end of the second full year of building, the Great Pyramid would have been standing to the height of its entrance doorway, and both the Prism Point and the Descending Corridor would have been part-buried in the rising courses of the quarry blocks (fig. 176). During the next six years, as that frantic pace gave way to a gentler and more

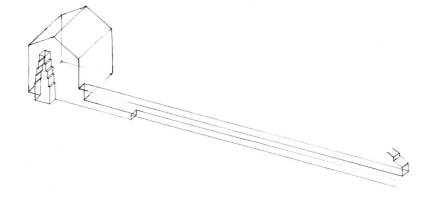

Fig. 180 Sketch showing the form of the Queen's Chamber and its entrance corridor: the Chamber is a little under 20 feet high; its corridor runs from north to south.

Fig. 181 Morton Edgar's photograph of his brother sitting inside the niche in the east wall of the Queen's Chamber.

even progress, the master masons would have set the long line of the Ascending Corridor, that essential element of the Pyramid's interior that rises from the Prism Point to touch the central axis of the Pyramid.[2] And in those same years as well, the Pyramid's two stone-built chambers would be erected and covered over by the courses of the quarry blocks.

Set close to course 23 and at the very centre of the Pyramid, and finished in all probability by the third year of construction, the first of these rooms to be built was the so-called Queen's Chamber. A beauteous nearly 18 feet square white stone cube of a room capped by a massive V-shaped vault, its sophistication, as revealed by Petrie's survey, belies its apparent simplicity.[3] It is also enigmatic; accessed from the Ascending Corridor by a long, straight and stumblingly low corridor, there is nothing other than a corbelled niche set in its eastern wall that appears to give the room a kind of focus, to tell us what role it may or may not have played in Khufu's destiny. Seventy feet above it though, on course 50, and thus begun some five years later in the Pyramid's building programme, the grandiose granite complex of the burial chamber holds clear evidence of its ancient purpose. As the traditional portcullises of the access passage and the dull-red sarcophagus in the room beyond both indicate, this, in all probability, is where Khufu's corpse was set to rest.[4]

That the pyramid-makers viewed the plain unlettered block of this sarcophagus as part of the Pyramid's formal architecture rather than a portable accoutrement of funeral is suggested by its size; though modest in itself, it could not have passed through the burial chamber's doorway and must therefore have been placed within the chamber before its roof was closed.[5] And then again, as if in acknowledgement of its particular significance, this simple stone, a block of granite in a granite room, appears to have been the only element of the Pyramid's internal architecture to have been set in close relationship to its north–south centre line.[6]

In all of the other early pyramids, as we have seen, the internal arrangements had been far simpler; in this, as with so many other aspects of its architecture, the Great Pyramid is unique. No other pyramid in Egypt has such accurately built interiors, nor such rooms and corridors as these set so high up within the body of the pyramid.[7] And from the Subterranean Chamber deep beneath the Rocky Knoll to the granite burial chamber 225 feet above it, all of this unique architecture has been precisely set upon the north–south axis of the Pyramid, inside an envelope of space just 35 feet wide (10.47 m).[8]

During the first eight years of the Great Pyramid's construction, when three quarters of its bulk was set in place,[9] the fine lines of its interior architecture, whose construction must have proceeded in concert with the courses of the Pyramid, would have provided a series of fixed reference points within the rising building,[10] which could themselves have been checked against the bare bones of its plan as set out in the design field.[11] Until the height of the Pyramid's entrance doorway had been reached, at course 19, there would have been two separate fixed points in the internal architecture at each course of the rising Pyramid, these located on the angled floor lines of the Descending and Ascending Corridors that met at the vital Prism Point (fig. 176). After the entrance doorway had been set, however, there was but a single interior fixed point within the Pyramid to aid in its construction, this being the line of the Ascending Corridor (fig. 26).[12]

Rising, so Petrie estimated, at 26° 13′ and aligned to north with the same exactitude as the Pyramid's eastern and western baselines – being so close to them indeed 'that it may be assumed parallel' – the floor line of the Ascending Corridor (fig. 184), which is the longest continuous building line within the Pyramid, would have provided an essential measure of the Pyramid's accuracy and stability during the main years of its construction.[13] At its full extent, however, at course 50 where this corridor crosses the plane of the Pyramid's east–west axis (fig. 182), this near-perfect line comes to its ending at the Great Step, a block emplaced inside the grand old Pyramid with such unearthly accuracy that my curiosity as to its point and purposes served as inspiration for this book.[14]

On paper – in geometric theory – the exact level of the Great Step, as we have already seen (ch. 5), is one of its prime geometric properties in relation to the overall dimensions of the Pyramid. Its position could have been set by fixing the point at which the angle of the floor of the Ascending Corridor rises diagonally through two squares of the Pyramid's upper six-square grid, until it bisected the plane of the

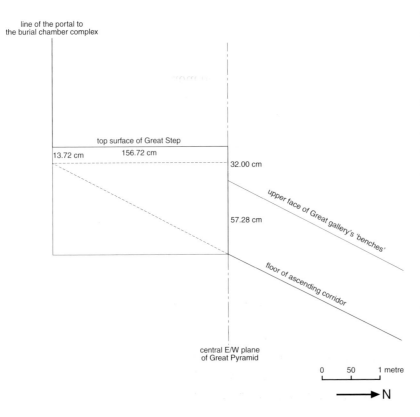

line of the portal to
the burial chamber complex

top surface of Great Step

13.72 cm   156.72 cm

32.00 cm

upper face of Great gallery's 'benches'

57.28 cm

floor of ascending corridor

central E/W plane
of Great Pyramid

0   50   1 metre

N

Fig. 182 Standing almost 3 feet high at the end of the Ascending Corridor, the Great Step's northern face offers majestic proof of the pyramid-makers' use of abstract planes to control the rising architecture of the Great Pyramid. The cross section also shows how the 'erring' line of the Ascending Corridor appears to have been turned back upon itself to be 'contained' within the stone block of the Step. (Note that the plane on which this line turns – where the line of the Ascending Corridor crosses the extended line of the burial chamber's portal – is represented as the spot measurement in Petrie's list described (cf. fig. 19) as 'the ending of the virtual corridor' whose dimensions reflect those of the abstract six-square grid with a precision equal to those of other architectural elements of the Pyramid.)

ridge of the vault of the Queen's Chamber underneath it, which has been set with extraordinary exactitude on the Pyramid's east–west axis (figs. 175 and 223).[15]

Once again even the architectural precisions of the Great Pyramid cannot match the exactitude of trigonometry. Petrie, for example, records that the Great Step is not quite level, and that the joints of the massive blocks surrounding it have opened and appear therefore to have shifted slightly.[16] He also found that the Ascending Corridor rises not at a perfect 30° which is the required angle of the diagonal of two squares, but at 26° 13′, which, if uncorrected, would give rise to an error of more than 10 per cent. And yet, despite all that, remarkably enough, the huge block of the Great Step still stands upon the Pyramid's upper six-square grid within 0.01 per cent of mathematical perfection, and at a point where the difference between the theoretical and physical distance between the Great Step and the Prism Point, some 280 feet away at the other end of the Ascending Corridor, is less than 3 inches![17]

Given the timetable and the equipment available, such enduring precisions are the doughty product of an extraordinary group of master masons working over many years, setting up long straight lines in tons of stone, and then checking and rechecking their positions as the Pyramid rose ever higher up around them. That the Ascending Corridor, for example, was apparently set at a 'wrong' angle has sent the theoretical distance of its ending some 60 inches beyond the plane of the Pyramid's central east–west axis, and more than 20 inches lower than perfection.[18] Yet at the block of the Great Step itself, the stone masons meticulously re-established the correct plane of the Pyramid's central east–west axis by setting the block's northern edge so that it exactly bisects the stone line of the Ascending Corridor with the plane of the vault of the roof of the Queen's Chamber below.[19] The very dimensions of the Great Step's block indeed subsume all of those conflicting measurements and resolve them, turning the low line of the Ascending Corridor back onto the east–west plane of the Queen's Chamber vault against its northern edge (fig. 182). Rising almost 3 feet (0.895 m) at the end of the Ascending Corridor, sheltered by the climax of the great vault of the Grand Gallery, the Great Step's northern face is the most majestic visual evidence of the pyramid-makers' visualisation of abstract planes inside their Pyramid, set down in fine white Tura stone.

The Great Step's precisions, therefore, are the product of a long series of controls. After its position on the rising corridor had been established in relation to the Prism Point below, the accuracy of this result was checked against the plane of the Queen's Chamber vault below. It was a simple process of triangulation. No measurement, no trigonometry whatever was required, only the craftsmanship to build a near-perfect rising corridor, the expert use of a line and plummet and the skill to set the huge block of the Great Step, which weighs at a minimum around 4 tons, into its final position.[20]

This then was a method by which the line and planes of elements within the Pyramid were checked against each other and both could then be rechecked against elements of the Pyramid's plan laid out in the design field. Indeed, the dimensions of the upper six-square grid, its offset from the Pyramid's baseline, and the precise angle of the Pyramid's Ascending Corridor are preserved in the design field down to this day (ch. 38 above).

Now the Trial Passages in the design field are, as we have seen, an entirely accurate, if compressed, version of many elements of the Pyramid's interior. They also hold the errant 26° angle of the Ascending Corridor. Although it is missing now, in all probability they also once held an equivalent of the Great Step within them.[21] This would have stood above the present eroded surface of the levelled Plateau, and was presumably built of blocks of stone, whose use is testified at this location by the rock-cut footings at the Trial Passages' other ending.[22] In this compressed version of the Pyramid's design, which is around a sixth of the length of the full-sized version in the Pyramid, the error produced by the mis-set angle of the Ascending Corridor may simply not have been visible to its makers: inside the full length of the Pyramid, after all, the same angle has still provided a height within a few inches of theoretical perfection (fig. 233)!

This then suggests a solution to the mystery of how the Pyramid's central axis and height were established on the Rocky Knoll. Taking the angle of the Ascending Corridor directly from its model in the Trial Passages, the pyramid-makers could have set the Corridor running up from the Prism Point inside the courses of the Pyramid towards its theoretic central axis without ever having set a fixed point at the beginning of the work upon the Rocky Knoll; that same fixed point which is so essential to our modern plans, yet whose existence deep beneath the Pyramid is yet unproven.[23] In fact, the pyramid-makers set the exact plane of the Pyramid's east–west axis at the centre of the Pyramid in the second year of working when they set the line of the Queen's Chamber vault, and some five years later, the level of the Pyramid's baseline by proxy, at the top of the upper grid's first square, at the Great Step. That the burial chamber itself is at this same level, and not set close to the ground line as in other Egyptian pyramids, is mute acknowledgement that this level was indeed treated as a second baseline.

The success of such a programme, of course, was entirely dependent upon the precise alignment of the line of the vault of the Queen's Chamber roof during the second year of work. Given that the master masons would set and reset their building lines according to the stars time and time again from the beginning of their work upon the Giza Plateau, we should assume that the precise east–west alignment of the Queen's Chamber vault was relatively easy for them to establish. But to set the Great Step in its correct position at the centre of the Pyramid they had to set that east–west alignment exactly upon the central axis of the Pyramid's two six-square grids. And that, in theory, they could have established with a single measurement upon a line drawn due south from the Prism Point.

Up on the rising Pyramid, however, and working without the aid of modern equipment, the use of a single measurement, if such a thing were even practicable, would have allowed no cross-checking or correction, and would therefore have threatened substantial architectural error at the very centre of the rising Pyramid and confusion at every level of its architecture. One would anticipate, therefore, that a similar process of checking and rechecking as that employed at the Great Step was undertaken, and this is exactly what is to be found on the Ascending Corridor, where in a confident line of well-made Tura blocks another perfect corridor, a level line on this occasion, strikes off due south from it – and runs straight into the white cube of the Queen's Chamber.

With its floor line set at the bottom of the portal of the Grand Gallery, at the exact point where the Ascending Corridor opens into that dramatic vault (fig. 192), this junction is treated like all the other changes of angle and direction in the Pyramid's interior corridors – the Prism Point, the Great Step, for example – as a significant element in its formal architectural plan. Unlike the others, however, this junction was not set upon a vertical plane of the Pyramid's six-square grids (fig. 28). Had it been so, the geometry of the internal architecture would have been preserved and could have served to set the central axis of the Pyramid.

It is therefore not surprising that the pyramid-makers appear to have lost interest in the accurate construction of this corridor. Set at its beginning in fine-cut blocks of Tura stone, it suddenly peters out at a strange deep step of 1 foot 7¾ inches (50.038 cm) before continuing on its way in irregular and unfinished stonework so that, at its

ending, the Queen's Chamber's fine-made walls stand directly on rough-cut local quarry blocks whose level appears to have been chopped and changed on at least two separate occasions.[24] Here the pyramid-makers' usual practice of projecting a series of perfect lines and planes in floors of solid stone has lost its way, as if they were all at sea amongst a rising mass of quarry blocks.[25] Yet five years later, the massive block of the Great Step was set in its proper place upon the six-square grids along with the level of the burial chamber floor, and ultimately the full height, the very measure, of the Pyramid itself.

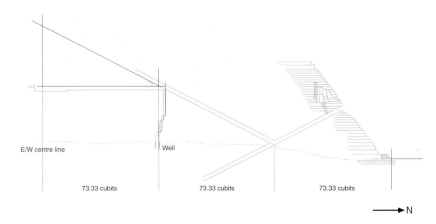

E/W centre line   Well

73.33 cubits   73.33 cubits   73.33 cubits

➤N

Fig. 184 Showing how the pyramid-makers could have regained precise control over the level of the rising Pyramid by resetting a plane of the six-square grid at the level of the floorline of the Ascending Corridor. From this fixed point, a measurement of one grid square along the near-perfect line of the ceiling of the Queen's Chamber corridor would have re-established the Pyramid's east–west central axis.

Clearly, the pyramid-makers had regained control within the rising Pyramid, and most remarkably there is hard evidence that suggests just how they did it. For on the rise of the Ascending Corridor, just inside the portal of the Grand Gallery, a rough square shaft has been cut deep into the fine-finished stonework, a horizontal shaft that runs for 6 feet straight into its fine-made wall before dropping down through fifteen courses of quarry blocks to the buried stone-lined shaft that had been cut into the Rocky Knoll at the beginning of the work, and stands on one of the planes of the Pyramid's six-square grids (see fig. 159 above).

Working with plummets, lines and measuring rods (pp. 320ff), Khufu's master masons could have re-established direct contact with the vertical grid plane that had been set down within the well upon the Giza Plateau at the beginning of the work. This plane could have been indicated by a line drawn upon the walls of the Ascending Corridor, so that the plane of the Pyramid's central axis could have been relocated simply by measuring a grid's length from that line down along the Queen's Chamber corridor. All that would have been required of that little passage would have been a course of levelled stonework and the precise north–south alignment of its walls (fig. 184).

That the pyramid-makers knew that the stone-lined shaft upon the Rocky Knoll – and hence the position of the six-square grid plane that it held – lay to the south of the junction of the Queen's Chamber corridor is shown by the fact that the mouth of their shaft lies inside the portal of the Grand Gallery.[26] Even then they appear to have underestimated its exact position, for after cutting confidently and quite vertically down through ten of the Pyramid's courses, the tunnel nudges further southward to relocate the stone-lined shaft: it is almost as if we are watching the Great Pyramid's surveyors at a vital moment in their work.

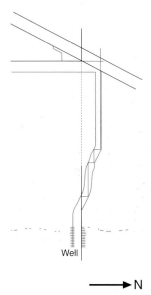

Well

➤N

Fig. 185 Working in the shaft with plummets, lines and measuring rods, Khufu's master masons could have swiftly and precisely re-established the grid plane laid down years earlier upon the Giza Plateau.

Fig. 186 Morton Edgar's sketch of the rough-cut excavation beside the lower portal of the Grand Gallery, the entrance to the shaft that drops down to the Well.

Unfortunately there is no hard evidence to show exactly when this near-vertical shaft was cut. Its *terminus post quem*, however, must be the ending of the second year of working (fig. 176), for it drives straight through the fine stonework of the Grand Gallery's lowest sections, which could only have been constructed, at the earliest, at about that time.[27] And at this same time too – that is to say, when parts of the thirtieth course of the Pyramid's quarry blocks had been laid – the centre line of the angle of the Queen's Chamber vault, a colossal construction of twelve enormous Tura blocks, was also set into position. Slightly off-centre from the Chamber's walls,[28] that last correction, that final flourish, laid down a plane that Petrie describes as being 'exactly in the mid-place of the Pyramid, equidistant from the N. and S. sides; it only varies from this plane by a less amount than the probable error of the determination'.[29] In other words, the accuracy with which the pyramid-makers set down the vital line of this ceiling vault was greater than Petrie's surveying equipment could measure. There can be no greater proof of the quality of this ancient workmanship or of their methods of controlling the construction of such an enormous building.

This is strong circumstantial evidence that the chiselled tunnel running back down through the Pyramid to the stone-lined Well, this 'rough . . . and evidently utilitarian' excavation as Petrie called it, enabled the rechecking of a measurement on which the integrity of the entire Pyramid would eventually depend. And once again, we are brought face to face with the extraordinary difference between ancient Egyptian and modern perceptions of architecture and construction. For archaeologists have invariably assumed this shaft to have been an afterthought, noting that after dropping right down through the stone-lined shaft upon the Rocky Knoll, it straggles southwards through the living rock to join the Descending Corridor deep beneath the Pyramid, suggesting that it was cut for the purposes of providing air to lower sections of the Pyramid and also to serve as an escape hatch for those last workmen who remained inside the Pyramid to send the plugging blocks upon their final journey down into the Prism Point.

Yet the narrowing of the corridor which caught those plug blocks clearly shows the masons had gone to considerable length to leave the width of the Descending Corridor – the last leg of this escape route – open from the first days of working on the Rocky Knoll. And this in turn suggests that the notion of using just such a 'utilitarian' shaft as the last exit of Khufu's Egyptians had been present from the beginning of the work. Cutting through already finished architecture to reset the architecture of the rising Pyramid against its initial building lines moreover had the considerable advantage of annulling the effects of settlement and movement that had certainly occurred within the rising Pyramid, subtle shifts that could send the fixed points of the built architecture astray, just as had occurred in earlier pyramids.

Although the shaft is clearly not a part of the Great Pyramid's formal architecture, it nonetheless appears to have performed several specific purposes within the Pyramid, just as other similarly rough tunnels had in some of the earlier royal pyramids. This shaft therefore is not a bolt hole dug at the last moment (those stupid builders!) for a few fictitious labourers from a Pyramid movie, but a non-formal element of the Pyramid's design that had been envisaged from the beginning of the work, a secondary system vital to both its construction and its closing. So despite the fact that the mouth of this shaft cuts into the finished stonework of the Pyramid and that this to a modern eye appears as a blot upon the presentation of its formal architecture, there is no evidence at all that its makers considered it to be an afterthought.

In exactly similar fashion, though to modern eyes 'there are many indications that work on the Queen's Chamber was abandoned before it was completed',[30] both that Chamber and its access corridor may now be seen to have performed their ancient architectural functions perfectly. Whatever the funereal purposes of this exquisite room – and certainly (ch. 50 below) the Great Pyramid follows both of Sneferu's Dahshur pyramids in having three internal chambers – it has been perfectly finished for its specific purposes, being in the manner of a modern observatory or foundry, accurate where accuracy was required, no more and no less. Although standing on a rough and uneven floor, the Chamber's splendid walls, as Petrie says, are as well made as the finest stonework in the Pyramid, 'with cement no thicker than a sheet of paper'.[31] And when the vault that the pyramid-makers set on those workmanlike walls with such breath-taking skill had had its final check, a last deft reorientation, their quest for absolute precision was done. So it is not surprising that, with that final splendid flourish, all work upon the Queen's Chamber's floor and corridors was stopped, for it had served its purpose in that it would give a near-perfection to one of the cross-hairs on which the Great Step would eventually be set.[32]

44 The miniature shafts

Along with their triumphal return to architectural perfection, the pyramid-makers set another level in the Queen's Chamber, other than the usual floor line, inventing as they did so an intriguing architectural feature unique to the Great Pyramid. Marked within the Chamber by the height of its entrance doorway and also by a pair of corbels within the niche set in its eastern wall, this secondary level is also marked upon its northern and southern walls by the positions of two 8½ inch (0.21 m) square holes[1] – these being the ending of two of the Pyramid's four celebrated so-called 'airshafts'.[2]

Following their discovery in the 1870s – until that time, the ends of these tiny shafts appear to have been closed with little slabs of stone set flush to the surface of the walls[3] – these miniature corridors that extend north and south right up through the body of the Pyramid have excited all kinds of speculation beyond that of serving as mere ventilators, from notions that they had been aligned so as to accommodate the light of specific stars, to the assertion that they were passageways built to accommodate the visitations of aspects of King Khufu's spirit.[4] A partial survey by miniature camera-carrying robots recently disproved the more tangible of these theories by showing that these diminutive passages do not run in smooth straight lines to the surface of the Pyramid as had previously been assumed, but

Fig. 187 The limestone slab that blocks the Queen's Chamber's southern shaft. The two dark objects set into it appear to be copper pins shaped like two handles, whose tops have been secured in bitumen, their lower ends in plaster. In 2002, a spy hole drilled through this modest 8 inch stone revealed but a short gap before it was blocked off again by what appeared to be part of one of the Pyramid's building blocks. It appears, therefore, that this slab marks the ending of the shaft's almost 200 foot run up through the Pyramid and that the two pins had served to secure the ending of the cords which, as other evidence from the shafts also suggests (see figs. 188 and 190), had served as building lines as the little shaft rose up with the courses of the Pyramid.

passed through several different angles, and that neither of them appeared to break the surface of the Pyramid! Journeying up the southern shaft for more than 200 feet, one of these obliging robots also discovered that the pyramid-makers had blocked it off completely with a smooth stone hatch fitted out with what appear to be two bent copper pins![5] The same explorations also showed that both these little shafts had been set into the courses of the Pyramid after the lines of its full-sized internal architecture had already been established, for wherever their upward progress had threatened to collide with the Tura blocks of the Pyramid's more formal architecture, they had been sent on elaborate detours.[6] So the little shafts had been initiated after the plan of the Queen's Chamber and its access corridor had been set down, yet before they had been completed. Like the rough-hewn tunnel cut down to the stone-lined shaft therefore, they were not a part of the Pyramid's formal design.[7]

Two similar shafts run up and away from the granite of King Khufu's burial chamber. Reaching yet higher up into the fabric of the Pyramid, this pair were well known to early explorers, some of whom delighted in discharging their flint-locks into them and sending deafening echoes back down through the Pyramid. Considering that all four of these miniature passageways are set inside the same thin envelope of space as the Pyramid's formal architecture, and that passing as they do through all but the final 10 per cent of the

Pyramid's volume[8] they have far greater spread throughout its mass, it would be reasonable to assume that they performed some of the same services for the builders of the Pyramid's upper sections as the full-sized corridors had performed for its lower and more massy half. Similar in their size to the Trench in the design field (pp. 333ff above), these little corridors, which like their bigger brothers would have laid part-open during the Pyramid's construction, would have pointed up displacements when settlement occurred, whilst at the same time providing fixed lines inside the Pyramid which, with the use of ordinary stonemasons' tools, could have served as a continuous check upon the internal levels of the rising Pyramid. And this time, there is rare specific evidence to bear this out.

Rummaging around inside the Pyramid in the decade before Petrie's survey of the Pyramid, the discoverer of the Queen's Chamber shafts, one Waynman Dixon, a Yorkshire engineer who had travelled to Egypt with his brother to design and build the vessel that would transport 'Cleopatra's Needle' from Alexandria to Charing Cross,[9] managed to dislodge some ancient objects that had been left in one of them by jabbing at them with a long iron rod. Preserved now at the British Museum in a varnished mahogany box,

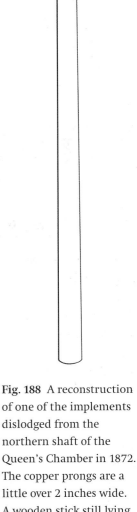

Fig. 188 A reconstruction of one of the implements dislodged from the northern shaft of the Queen's Chamber in 1872. The copper prongs are a little over 2 inches wide. A wooden stick still lying in the shaft may well have served as its handle, which would have been attached to the copper head by two round-headed rivets.

Fig. 189 The Queen's Chamber's southern shaft. The dob of plaster adhering to the shaft's right-hand wall is similar to another on the wall of the Grand Gallery. Both of them appear to show the imprint of a line of cord.

Fig. 190 Bisected by a string line running right up though the shaft, this rough ochre line drawn upon a block set into the Queen's Chamber's southern shaft would have provided an absolute fixed point within the rising Pyramid.

Fig. 191 The end of the line: the present ending of the burial chamber's southern shaft. In common with the Pyramid's full-sized corridors, the blocks of the four miniature shafts appear to have been set at the angle of their rising, and in opposition to the levelled courses of the Pyramid.

his two great prizes were a spherical hard-stone pounder which as we have seen (p. 159, above) could have served the pyramid-makers for a variety of purposes, and a two-pronged copper implement which, given some of the photographs obtained by the robot survey, appears to have been broken from a long wooden haft that still lies within the shaft. Resembling a modern boat hook or a classical implement that served somewhat similar purposes, this forked stick appears to have been used for handling lines of rope or cord.[10] Reinforcing this impression, some of the robot's photographs also appear to show some daubs of plaster upon the walls of these same shafts with traces of cord lines impressed into them. It would appear, therefore, that survey lines were set up inside these minia-ture shafts, just as they would have been in the trenches of the design field or on the upper walls of the Grand Gallery where there are some plaster daubs similar to those within the little shafts.[11] If this were true, then the two bent copper pins set into the slab of stone that blocks one of the lower shafts could well have served to secure those self-same cord lines, as one would lash the rigging of a sail. That the four shafts were intended for some-such utilitarian purpose is underlined by other photographs from the robot survey showing that large quantities of rough-cut local quarry stone were used in their construction, and even on occasion that blocks that had been cut for other purposes were reused in the shafts with a minimum of reshaping to their new function.[12]

As so often with this grand old Pyramid, the surviving traces of its manufacture are ambiguous and scanty. Even though the discoveries in the little shafts appear to have produced unique evidence of the master masons at their work, and indeed they are the only ancient implements ever to have been found within this Pyramid's bare walls, nothing but the roughest outline of their activities remains; some daubs of plaster, a detail on a rock or stone: solely those few traces and the insistent overwhelming undeniable imperative of the mute perfection of the Pyramid itself.

45 The Grand Gallery

It is difficult to imagine how the Great Pyramid would have appeared
as Khufu's masons were installing that enormous block of limestone
now known as the Great Step. Certainly, the Ascending Corridor that
runs right up to it would already have been set in its position, for the
line of its stone was vital to the Step's precise emplacement.
Immediately before that operation, however, the floor of the
Ascending Corridor would have ended in a cliff-like drop, with the
Queen's Chamber vault below lying open and exposed some 50 feet
below it – another of those 'chimneys' perhaps, such as still survive in

Fig. 192 A reconstruction
of the Great Pyramid's
building levels as Khufu's
masons were installing
the Great Step: of
necessity, the line of the
Ascending Corridor must
have been established
and the vault of the
Queen's Chamber's roof
uncovered and accessible.

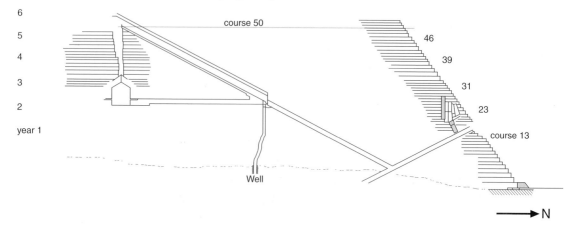

Fig. 193 John Edgar climbs up through the darkness of the Grand Gallery towards the burial chamber; the other figure stands at the entrance to the Queen's Chamber's corridor. The rough slots cut into blocks that line the sides of the Ascending Corridor appear to have held scaffolding or wedges.

the Bent Pyramid (fig. 145 above) – so that the pyramid-makers' cords and plummets could project the precise plane of the vault up to the top of the Corridor and re-establish the central east–west axis of the Pyramid (see pp. 320ff above). Only after that vital level had been established along the edge of what is now the last block of stone in the Ascending Corridor could the Great Step have been manoeuvred into its position, for the act of its emplacement would have closed off all further access to the vault of the Queen's Chamber underneath.[1]

So the Great Step's installation would have first entailed the cutting of the last block of the Ascending Corridor, then the filling of the hole beyond, and finally the installation of the block of the Great

Step, which, as its visible extent shows this Tura block to be at least 3 feet high and 6 feet wide, would represent a considerable labour of hauling and manoeuvre. It would seem unlikely, therefore, that the massive walls that presently close in around the Step were in position at that time. And thus, that most remarkable construction whose culmination soars over and above the Step, that 'corbel vault of unparalleled dimensions', as I. E. S. Edwards has described the Pyramid's Grand Gallery, could hardly have been completed.[2]

An ingenious adaptation of the corbelling developed within Sneferu's three great pyramids, this enormous vault is somewhat different from the rest of the Great Pyramid's internal architecture. Other than the near-perfect line of the Ascending Corridor that it protects, not one of its prime measurements, not the point of its beginning or of its ending, nor its height, conforms to the Pyramid's six-square grids. That it served quite different purposes from the smooth geometries of the other passages within the Pyramid is attested by the purposeful slots and chisel-marks that scar its walls,[3] by the relative imperfection of its workmanship, and by the closing slabs of the corbel vault which, in hooking ingeniously together like gigantic blocks of Lego, employ the same workmanlike technique to cope with stone slippage as that used in sections of the miniature shafts.[4] Despite its apparent grandeur the Grand Gallery has much in common with the little-known utilitarian structures buried deep within the Pyramid's courses; those construction vaults and miniature shafts that were not part of the Pyramid's formal geometrical design, but which were built to cope with some of the practical problems of building such gigantic pyramids.[5]

One of these tasks, as we have already seen, was to provide space enough to house the three granite plugging blocks that would slide down into the Prism Point and shut the Pyramid's interior at the appointed time. The Grand Gallery, in fact, is the only place within the Pyramid where these enormous blocks could have been stored prior to their final slide into position, the two low ledges that lie on either side of the Ascending Corridor providing the necessary room for the positioning of these plugging blocks with beams of wood, just as the chisellings in these ledges and the walls above them would suggest.[6]

The addition of these two ledges, which doubles the width of the central corridor, also provided the necessary room for the development of the enormous corbel vault that rises high above them. And that very vault serves another of the Gallery's practical functions, relieving the pressure of the Pyramid's stonework on the Ascending

Corridor, and also on the ceiling blocks of the Queen's Chamber corridor that runs directly underneath it, and which in consequence does not have sufficient space around it to accommodate a relieving vault of its own.[7] By erecting this 150 foot long Gallery, by setting two side benches in the upper sections of the Ascending Corridor and by raising a high vault above them, the royal masons solved two knotty problems with considerable panache.

Fig. 194 The lower ending of the Grand Gallery's splendid corbel vault. In common with the grooves cut into the side walls of the corridor below, the rough-cut grooves on either side of the third level of the vault appear to be an afterthought.

At the time of the Great Step's emplacement, as we have already seen, this superb construction would probably have been little more than an angled corridor and a mason's plan. During the next two years, however, as the courses of the Pyramid rose up around it, we may well imagine that another so-called 'construction gap' was set up on either side of the upper sections of the Ascending Corridor, one similar to that which still surrounds the Pyramid's doorway (see pp. 365ff above), although narrower and angled, so as to follow the line of the rising corridor beneath.[8] This time, the stone workers did not fill the open space of their construction gap with monolithic blocks of stone as they had done by the Pyramid's small doorway, but vaulted it with a clever corbelled arch, which although it took its inspiration from the simpler rectangular constructions built in Sneferu's pyramids, was most elegantly distorted into an angled rhombus, so as to fit the line of the Ascending Corridor.

46 The burial chamber

The squareness and level of the base of the Pyramid is brilliantly true . . . the Queen's chamber is also very finely fitted . . . above that the work is rougher, the grand gallery has not this superlative fineness, and the construction of the King's chamber is flagrantly out of level.

Paraphrased from Petrie's History of Egypt[1]

Beyond the summit of the Grand Gallery and the Great Step, King Khufu's burial chamber is the climax of the journey through the Pyramid. At the same time this dark shining room with its bizarre acoustic stands apart from the other architecture of the Pyramid.[2] Not only is it made of granite and not of limestone, but its very block sizes are also entirely different, even the cubit unit used to measure out its granite forms being fractionally larger than that employed for the rest of the Great Pyramid.[3] Neither do these differences stop there. For the signs and numbers that the pyramid-makers painted on the burial chamber's granite ceiling blocks not only show that they were numbered and orientated like no others in the Pyramid but also provide evidence of a system of construction that would have ensured that each and every one of them could be set into a previously planned position; that they were, in fact, prefabricated.[4]

All this would suggest that Khufu's burial chamber was made at a remove from the rest of the building work, just as the lack of any traces of red granite dust around the Pyramid would imply, for its telltale stain would be an inevitable and considerable by-product of ancient granite working on such a colossal scale. With the exception of some small evidences of reworking,[5] it is likely that these granite blocks were cut and finished as required at Aswan, as was the common practice during later dynasties,[6] and then shipped to Giza as a largely self-contained architectural unit. That its erection could only have been undertaken after the first fifty courses of the Pyramid had been laid – that is, in about year six of construction[7] – shows another aspect of the nation-wide pre-planning that would have taken place in the early years of Khufu's reign.[8] It also underlines the fact that a comprehensive architectural specification must have existed for the Great Pyramid from the time of its beginning, parts of which appear to have been transmitted in some form or other to Aswan at the southern end of Egypt, and shipped back again to Giza in the form of a hundred or more gigantic building blocks.

And yet, and yet, as Robert Burns has helpfully observed, 'The best laid schemes o' Mice an' Men, Gang aft agley'; for this gigantic prefabricated structure stands so agley, so askew in Khufu's Pyramid, that, as Petrie reflected in his later years, 'they might have done it far better by just looking at the horizon'.[9] Why, after levelling its lower sections with such cool precision, should such obvious error be allowed to creep in and haunt the royal burial chamber?[10] Why this apparent dropping-off in care and accuracy?

Noting that much of the upper sections of the interior held similar imperfections,[11] Petrie had supposed that the Pyramid's original architect, 'a true master of accuracy and fine methods', must have died and that trade unionism had taken over on the Giza Plateau.[12] And still today, whilst the use of expert jargon makes modern speculation appear more circumspect, most explanations of such common tendencies in ancient workmanship hold the same old story at their pith; that for whatever reason, there was a 'decline' as the years went by. Question the use of such novella narrative, however, abandon the notion that structures like the Great Pyramid were made in conformity to modern building specifications, and a different scenario emerges, and the real reasons for the Pyramid's accuracies and inaccuracies can be discovered in the building's antecedents.

Now the primary problem that the early pyramid-makers faced in setting up such mighty piles was as we have seen, that the weight of their stone threatened to crush their interior architecture and the very ground on which they stood. At Sneferu's Bent Pyramid, the royal builders had employed buttresses of limestone blocks and cedar scaffolding to support its failing interior; at the Red Pyramid nearby, they had lessened the angle of its rise and almost halved its weight of stone.[13]

Harbouring the ambition to build a yet larger and far higher monument, Khufu's masons had sited the Great Pyramid's foundation on a good firm cliff, cut their quarry blocks with extra care and set up an architectural scheme of such perfection in its interior that the slightest subsidence or movement that took place during construction would be registered as soon as it occurred. And it has all paid off of course, for those parts of the Pyramid that were set upon its six-square grids appear to have hardly deviated from their original positions.[14] At the same time, however, as its crooked burial chamber attests, there were considerable problems of subsidence at the Great Pyramid and many indications too that such movement may have started early in construction; there are, for example, considerable displacements due to subsidence in both of the Queen's Chamber's miniature shafts.[15]

After the disaster at Dahshur, the pyramid-makers well knew that if left uncorrected the ultimate effects of such movement could multiply disastrously as the pyramid rose higher in the air (ch. 40 above). This may have led them to take extraordinary care to check the mutability of the rising Pyramid and even to correct errors or displacement as they had at the Bent Pyramid (p. 272 above) and indeed, as they had done with their fastidious realignment of the Queen's Chamber roof (p. 377). That this remained a constant preoccupation of the Great Pyramid's builders down to the finish of the work is proven by its perfect silhouette, which, given the visible examples of subsidence inside the pyramid, is the product of careful and prolonged adjustment.

As if to underline the lurking dangers that accompanied the rise of Khufu's Pyramid, just 25 feet away from the limestone perfections of the Great Step and the Ascending Corridor, the stones of the granite burial chamber are not only crooked but badly cracked as well; 'their downfall', Petrie comments gloomily, 'a mere question of time and earthquakes'.[16] Yet as he also acknowledges, some of the underlying stress that caused this damage appears already to have been underway at the time of the Pyramid's construction,[17] and there is dramatic evidence as well that dangerous subsidence was occurring underneath the burial chamber even as the pyramid-makers were still working in the Pyramid.[18]

Just as the pyramid-makers' preoccupation with controlling stress and movement in the Great Pyramid was rooted in previous experience, so too, is the fundamental reason for the burial chamber's tilt from true. In its use of granite, for example, it follows the final versions of King Djoser's twin burial crypts (see ch. 27 above), while the three massive portcullises set up within its entrance corridor are but elaborated versions of more modest arrangements set up centuries earlier in the rock-cut passages of the Sakkara mastabas.[19] King Khufu's granite burial chamber is essentially a re-sorting of the various architectures and materials employed in much earlier royal burial arrangements. Here, as so often at the Great Pyramid, the quality and size of those earlier schemes has been elevated beyond all previous scale. Now all the architecture of the burial chamber, its access corridor and antechamber is made of massive granite blocks and the chamber's flat ceiling, a single 17 foot (5.24 m) horizontal span, a space that in the burial chambers of the early mastabas had been bridged by beams of cedar wood but which limestone could not possibly sustain (see p. 176 above), is composed of nine great shafts, each one of them a 50-odd ton block of perfect even-grained hard stone.

From the beginning of this work, Khufu's pyramid-makers had seen the necessity to protect their daring ceiling by setting a structure up above it to relieve the colossal weight of limestone – close to 160 courses of the Pyramid – that would have eventually borne down on it. Here then, in the first thirty courses that stand above the level of the burial chamber's ceiling, the pyramid-makers built five rough half-sized rooms – those same entresols that have inadvertently preserved King Khufu's names in their graffiti (see p. 31 above). Stacked one above the other, each one of these little rooms is spanned by similarly vast granite ceilings as those of the burial chamber below. And over and above them all, transforming the last of these five low spaces into a tent-shaped pediment, the master masons built another v-shaped arch of enormous blocks of Tura stone, this yet larger than all the other mighty vaults that they had already set up within the Pyramid.[20]

Erecting such a ponderous and elaborate structure at the centre of the Pyramid must have required all of the pyramid-makers' ingenuity and skill. Just as one would expect, they appear to have worked in yet another so-called construction gap,[21] building the 70 foot high monster, storey by storey with rough-faced but precisely levelled blocks of stone so that every single block of its five cumbrous roofs would slide easily into its appointed place.

That this unique construction was built as a separate unit set on independent load-bearing walls within the confines of a construction gap gave the burial chamber an individual integrity within the courses of the Pyramid and has protected it, in great part, from the movements and earthquakes that have occurred at Giza through the ages. At the same time, whilst this independent stack of granite has preserved the burial chamber's integrity, it also appears to have set its floor askew. For rather than the present tilt of its floor being the inadvertent product of rampant trade unionism as Petrie once suggested, his earlier observation that the uppermost of the five low chambers has dropped down some 3 inches, a similar level of subsidence as that which has occurred in the burial chamber's floor far below, suggests that in reality it was the product of building subsidence.[22] That every one of the burial chamber's granite ceiling shafts is cracked right through, and that these cracks are all close to the south wall of the chamber where the floors and walls are also slightly skewed, even tokens a specific and dramatic moment in the history of this Pyramid, when those enormous granite shafts could no longer support the subsidence of the southern wall and cracked; the same moment that Petrie has described, when the architecture of the enormous granite room was 'shaken larger'.[23]

That the granite burial chamber unit is set to the south of all the other elements in the Pyramid's interior and with scant regard for the six-square grids, suggests that Khufu's pyramid-makers may have anticipated the potential danger of erecting this colossal structure – some 6000 tons of granite standing on an area just four quarry blocks in width and eight blocks long – at the very centre of their Pyramid.[24] Nonetheless they did not devote sufficient attention to the problem. Even before the granite entresols were set up, in the first years after the burial chamber was erected and just ten limestone courses had been set up around it, the two lines of the chamber's miniature shafts had already shifted, as the robot's survey clearly shows.[25] Years before the Pyramid stood at its full height, therefore, the weight of the granite burial chamber by itself was causing it to settle. Later on in its construction, with the nine great shafts of the burial chamber's ceiling pinned to the top of the burial chamber walls by the weight of the granite entresols above them (fig. 195), they could no longer take such subtle shift and movement and the brittle blocks split.

That this frightening damage occurred shortly after the construction of the entresols, and certainly before the Pyramid's interior was closed, is proven by the rough-made plaster patches that still obscure sections of those nine dreadful cracks.[26] There is other evidence as well on these same ceiling beams that the pyramid-makers thought that this unwonted subsidence might continue. For as Mark Lehner has recently observed, the symmetric stains that appear on most of them suggest that King Khufu's burial chamber was once filled with wooden buttresses just as some of the earlier pyramid burial chambers had been: that those stains are the marks of resin from cedar logs brought from the mountains of the Anti-Lebanon.[27]

It is hardly surprising that the pyramid-makers appear to have undertaken a close inspection of the burial chamber's nine cracked roofing blocks, cutting another rough passage through the Pyramid's stonework to reopen the lowest of the five half-chambers that stand

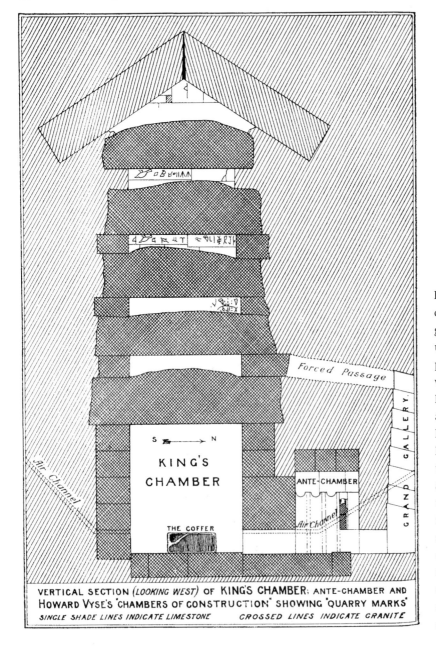

VERTICAL SECTION (*LOOKING WEST*) OF KING'S CHAMBER, ANTE-CHAMBER AND HOWARD VYSE'S 'CHAMBERS OF CONSTRUCTION' SHOWING 'QUARRY MARKS'
SINGLE SHADE LINES INDICATE LIMESTONE   *CROSSED LINES INDICATE GRANITE*

Fig. 195 Piazzi Smyth's careful drawing of the granite burial chamber unit showing the tiny passage cut through the wall of the Grand Gallery. Excavated, it would appear, by people with knowledge of the Pyramid's internal plan, the most likely candidates are the pyramid-makers themselves, anxious to inspect the upper surfaces of the burial chamber's roofing slabs after subsidence had caused them to crack along the chamber's southern side.

above it. By its very exactitude and economy, this tiny tunnel could only have been cut by masons who knew exactly where the half chamber lay within the courses of the pyramid; although this tunnel bears no date, it is therefore almost certainly the work of a few of Khufu's worried pyramid-makers. It would appear that following signs of stress and subsidence within the burial chamber – accompanied perhaps by the noise of the sudden fracture of its ceiling shafts, a sound that must have crackled through the Pyramid's interior like a magazine of bullets – the pyramid-makers undertook an excavation similar to that which their forefathers had cut into a corbel vault in Sneferu's failed pyramid and which they themselves had already undertaken to relocate the Well upon the Rocky Knoll. Chiselling a 20 foot long tunnel southwards from the ending of the east wall of the Grand Gallery's high vault through the laid stone of the Pyramid, they passed directly over the burial chamber's antechamber with its three portcullises, and re-entered the closed half-room above the damaged burial chamber.[28]

Crouching in the self-same place today, on the upper faces of those nine cracked ceiling shafts, you may see how the damage could have been measured and checked along with the condition of the chamber's walls. And surely, the pyramid-makers were pleased with what they saw, for none of the nine shafts had sprung apart, nor did the walls of the half-chamber show any sign of damage. The few inches of subsidence, that slight shift that moved the entire granite structure and cracked the burial chamber's brittle roofing blocks, had been absorbed by the walls and ceilings of the burial chamber itself.[29]

Vertiginous and claustrophobiac, the climb up a high ladder at the very summit of the Grand Gallery, followed by the squeeze from that ladder through the pyramid-makers' tiny dusty tunnel, rewards you at its ending with a unique window on their ancient world. For even though the first entresol appears to have been open since ancient times and despite Mr Davison, one of its modern rediscoverers, having 'left the ladder by which he ascended, for the satisfaction of other travellers' as James Bruce found in 1768, the four half-chambers up above it which had been buried in the Pyramid since Khufu's day were only reopened by Howard Vyse on 24 March 1837 when, as his journal tells us, 'Daoud was sent to blast in Davison's Chamber.'[30]

Following the ancient tomb inspectors and the grand tourists, Daoud had first crawled up the little ancient tunnel to the lowest chamber and, in a series of explosive excavations, blasted a corner of each of the successive chambers' roofs away to reveal first 'Wellington's Chamber', then 'Nelson's Chamber' and 'Lady

Arbuthnot's Chamber' before forcing his way into the v-shaped lime-stone vault up above them all, which the Colonel dubbed 'Campbell's Chamber' after one of his companions on the Giza Plateau;[31] at which point, thankfully, Vyse appears to have run out of powder.

And yet today these entresols are the only places in King Khufu's Pyramid where you may move inside relatively untouched ancient spaces, where visitors are few, the ancient surfaces are still bright and clean and the only major changes that have taken place since Khufu's day have been Vyse's blasting and the recent clearance of the shattered rock that he left behind.[32] Here in these weird low caverns, which can hardly be called rooms for you cannot stand in them, and with the whale-like shapes of the water-worn granite shafts rolling like a rough sea beneath your feet, you may watch King Khufu's builders at their work. Running fresh as milk right down their walls are the marks of the lubricating mortar that Khufu's stone-hauling gangs have used to aid the passage and the placing of the stones. There too, caught between the granite shafts where it had been extruded by the pressure of their impact, a richer mix of desert plaster from the Umm el-Sawwan once hung down in thin white sheets – and you could put your fingers back into the impressions that have been left by a pyramid maker's hand as he flicks away some of that fresh-setting plaster. Those mundane gestures, finger marks in a warm wet paste, have the precision of a cabinet maker's pencil line: in these rough-cut caverns at the very centre of the Pyramid, the unthinking traces of a living craftsman busy at his work.

Here too are the hieroglyphics of the granite gangs. Almost every ceiling block is numbered and marked north and south, left and right, and with a straight line too, precisely drawn across the centre of the dark-red stone with an inch-wide brush in natural desert ochre so that the block could be correctly centred on its walls.[33] And all of these blocks have been most carefully aligned, slid one behind the other, west to east. Judging from the positions of the marks, the master craftsman must have stood at the east end of each one of these five chambers when they had all yet stood in the sunlight. And as the gangs hauled each massive shaft off the mud-slippery ramps and slid it along the levelled edges of their supporting walls, a cord and plummet and the sharp eye of the master craftsman has aligned the centre lines on each and every one of the great stones as they slid upon the liquid plaster, one against the other, into their proper place.

Here too, drawn with that same soft brush and ochre wash, are the casual graffiti recording the names of two, perhaps three, of the gangs who handled the Tura blocks that form some of the upper

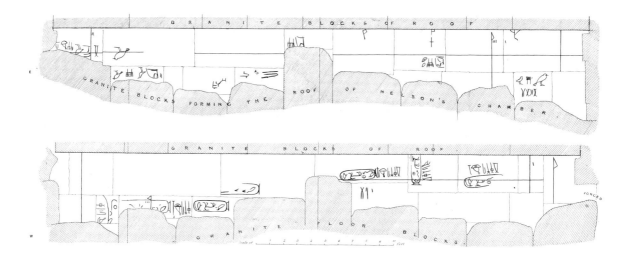

walls and v-shaped vault which covers these strange apartments. Set up in about the year 2484 BC, two thirds through the construction of this Pyramid when more than three quarters of its substance was already in position and the Giza workforce stood at around 6000 souls, they are the only names to have survived that have direct connection with the building of this Pyramid:[34]

May the White Crown of Khufu strengthen the sailing!

Khufu is pure!

Khufu is bright![35]

It is as if, in Khufu's time, building pyramids became an act of worship in itself.

Fig. 196 Vyse's record of some of the graffiti that he found in Nelson's Chamber: the jottings, it appears, of gangs who shipped stone blocks from the Tura quarries. The rough new entrance to this chamber, the second to be opened after its abandonment by the pyramid-makers, was blasted by 'Daoud', Vyse's chief excavator, and can be seen at bottom right.

47 To the top

Despite the myriad reconstructions of its manufacture, the courses of the Great Pyramid would not have risen equitably throughout the first half of its construction, level by level, like water in a bathtub.[1] As we have already seen, great banks of quarry blocks were set up within the rising Pyramid to aid the erection of its internal architecture. From the monoliths around its entrance doorway to the granite shafts of Khufu's burial chamber, these huge constructions were built within the confines of canyon-like construction gaps (see pp. 364ff), a labour that of itself would have required many local changes and adaptations to the Pyramid's stone delivery systems. It is probable, however, that these relatively ad hoc arrangements would have changed after the granite burial chamber and its five protective entresols had been erected, and the Pyramid's courses grew ever narrower.

Up to that point in the work, whatever forms the Pyramid's external supply system may have assumed, we may confidently reconstruct that the best part of them had approached the Pyramid from its southern side, which, as we have seen, is the only practicable route by which that vast mass of building blocks could have been transported from the local quarry, a route that at the same time could also have been used for the delivery of the local quarry stone and for the blocks

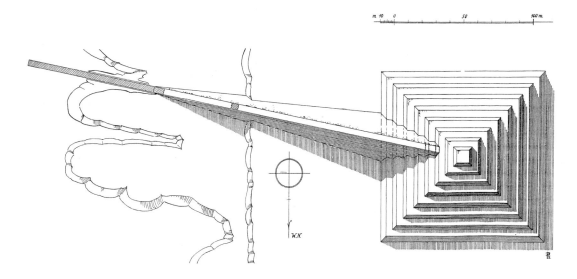

Fig. 197 Borchardt's bird's eye reconstruction of a ramp built to supply stone to the upper sections of the second eight-stepped phase of Sneferu's pyramid at Meidum, based upon the remnants of a low-angled structure he excavated in the pyramid's eastern approach whose vestiges are drawn in diagonally shaded lines. Ramps with similarly sized walkways still exist beside the Great Pyramid (see fig. 86, and pp. 202ff below). Their extension, in the manner of Borchardt's reconstruction, to the full height of the Great Pyramid would appear to offer a contemporary solution to the problem of stone supply to the uppermost parts of the Great Pyramid; the form of this final ramp, however, was probably more makeshift than that of Borchardt's reconstruction.

shipped through the Giza harbours (ch. 22 above).[2] This is supported by the markings on the granite ceiling blocks of the burial chamber unit. For whilst there is no longer any trace of the enormous ramps that delivered those 55 ton shafts up to the centre of the Pyramid, their individual markings show that the order and direction of their emplacement was from west to east across the Pyramid, and thus that their delivery ramps had probably risen in the Pyramid's south-western quadrant.

After ten years of working, with four fifths of the Pyramid's bulk already in position yet whilst it still stood at only half its finished height, the stone-hauling gangs were faced with a different situation: the increasingly dangerous if relatively rudimentary endeavour of delivering quarry blocks to the ever-higher courses of an ever-narrowing Pyramid. We might well expect, therefore, that a single supply ramp was built against the south side of the Pyramid at around that time and that this was perhaps a thin, high – but nonetheless colossal

– ramp such as Borchardt restored from the surviving remains at Meidum (fig. 197), expressly designed to transport the Pyramid's remaining building blocks onto the ever more swiftly rising Pyramid.[3]

In truth, however, there is hardly any evidence of what actually took place during those last years of building, when there was an ever-smaller if increasingly conspicuous section of the Pyramid to be set into position. Whilst the re-excavation of its few surviving casing stones enabled Petrie to restore the time-blunted Pyramid to theoretical perfection in a Hampstead drafting studio, in reality we do not know, and perhaps we never will, how accurately this theoretic geometric form matched the hard reality of the last years of construction, with Khufu's masons working high up on their windy Pyramid. Even the number of its finished courses is presently unknown: 203 of them rise today to the little platform which is the Pyramid's present peak; in Khufu's day, it would have taken around fourteen more to reach a pyramidion.[4]

As many of its surveyors have found to their surprise, the Great Pyramid's present summit, which is the size of a small dining room,

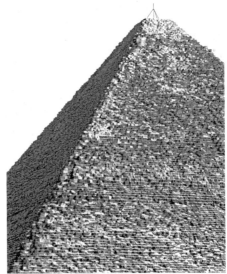

Fig. 198 Edward Lane's drawing of Khafre's pyramid, taken from the top of the Great Pyramid in 1824, in which he has employed a common trick of nineteenth-century illustrators and drawn human figures far smaller than they should be, so that the monuments assume theatrical proportions. None the less, the great Arabist has made a perfect record of the number and condition of the quarry stones upon the summit of the Great Pyramid, and noticed too that, at this height, they no longer form a perfect square.

Fig. 199 The west face of the top of the Great Pyramid. Laid in the last years of construction, when over 80% of the Pyramid's blocks were already in position, the upper courses show an ever increasing use of whiter and finer Tura stone, first for defining the Pyramid's four edges and later for the entire body of the stone work.

Fig. 200 The apex of the smallest of the four pyramids that once stood on the Great Pyramid's east side, discovered and restored during the course of cleaning the east side of the Pyramid in 1992. This is one of three known pyramidions that appear to date from the time of Sneferu and Khufu, all of which are cut from fine white limestone which would suggest that the Great Pyramid's pyramidion was also made from Tura limestone and not, as in the case of the known examples from later pyramids, in other, harder types of stone.

does not form a perfect square.[5] Once more, we appear to have bumped into the physical limitations of Khufu's pyramid-makers; 450 feet (138.46 m) above the ground they were no longer able to maintain the perfection of their work closer to the ground.[6] In those last years, with the masons' working platform shrinking with every course they laid and with the Pyramid's 5 acre (2.147 ha) faces dwindling swiftly to a single abstract point, the tiniest errors of the earlier years were coming home to roost. So from around course 130 a finer Tura-quality limestone was used to set the angle of the Pyramid's four corners to aid, it would appear, the masons' ever-trickier progress to the dwindling summit.[7] After course 190, those whiter dappled blocks of finer stone can be seen to be running right across each course to form the body of the Pyramid, on which the pyramidion and casing stones would have been set.

Standing like broken teeth along its baselines, a few scraps of these now-legendary casing stones yet survive, those same sad excavated fragments that Petrie described as being so well made that a combination of their errors down the length of one side of the Pyramid could be covered over by 'placing one's thumb on them'.[8] Although they are usually seen as but a tiny fraction of a much richer heritage of precision that fills the inner architecture of the Pyramid, they alone are the foundation of the popular belief that once upon a time the Great Pyramid held perfection in its form. In reality, however, we know next to nothing of this now-vanished exterior; neither the extent of the accuracy of its casing blocks nor how and when they were emplaced.

There are indications, however, that some of this lost casing was set up on the Pyramid after the main work of construction was completed.

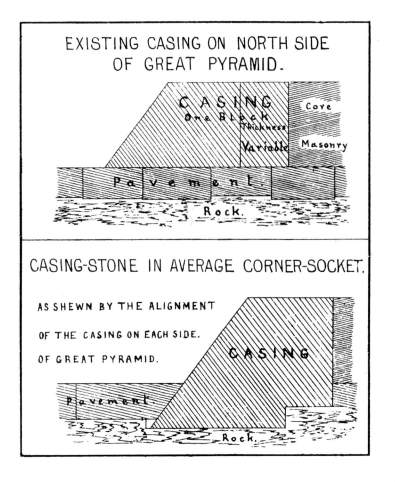

Fig. 201 Petrie's reconstruction of the Pyramid's pavement and corner sockets. The basis of all subsequent theories concerning the markings on the rock around the baseline of the Great Pyramid, his drawings would appear to beg the question of whether the Pyramid's casing was erected at the same time as its courses, or after their completion. The conundrum, however, is best addressed by the recognition that such tasks need not have been separated in the ways of modern building: that the stone could have been laid and relaid in piecemeal fashion; that baselines set down at the beginning of the work could have been replaced by other fresher stones at later stages of the work.

As we have already seen (ch. 40 above), the few surviving examples betray a tiny yet distinct discrepancy in their stellar orientation in comparison with their backing stones; a slight twist that suggests that these fine-cut blocks were set to stand upon the Pyramid's limestone pavement at a later date than the Pyramid's main courses.[9] And this in turn may indicate that these few surviving casing stones were part of a replacement of earlier baselines, from which the vital position of the Prism Point had been derived (ch. 40).[10] That the pyramid-makers' original limestone baselines may have suffered damage during the long years of construction is suggested by the fact that the baselines of succeeding pyramids were made of blocks of Aswan granite.[11]

In similar fashion, the four talismanic sockets that have been cut into the rock beside the Pyramid, those impressive outlying cloisons that led surveyors from Jomard to Piazzi Smyth on such a dance (see pp. 20–36 above), also appear to have been established towards the ending of construction for they all lie outside the baseline of the Pyramid and every one of them is at a different level.[12] They do,

Fig. 202 First excavated by Jomard (fig. 8) and re-cleared by Lepsius, Piazzi Smyth (fig. 15) and Petrie, some of the lines cut into the natural rock beside the Pyramid's north-eastern corner once formed an angle at the point at which the line of the casing of the Pyramid's north-eastern corner touched the rock of the plateau. A block of Tura stone set in this north-eastern corner socket, which would have weighed some 50 tons, could have provided a practical method, in conjunction with the three other corner stones, of maintaining the Pyramid's size and orientation from the beginning of the work.

Fig. 203 The socket at the Pyramid's north-western corner. Below it, at the very bottom of the picture, in an area once covered by the limestone pavement, a post hole which appears to have been anciently filled with plaster and a piece of stone is yet another enigmatic element in the making of the Pyramid.

however, appear to have borne precise relationship to the lines of the Pyramid's four edges as defined by its remaining casing stones, being set at the point at which those vanished edges would have touched the bedrock of the Plateau (fig. 201). These would appear to have been a part of the temporary arrangements that served as a control and check upon the angle of the Pyramid's four corners whilst the casing blocks were set up on the Pyramid.

Tantalising glimpses of the physical processes involved in the finishing of such fine stonework as the Pyramid's remaining casing blocks can still be seen upon the four small near-contemporary satellite pyramids.[13] First, the tough lines of a pointed chisel running across the surface of the stone rough out the angle and flatness of the block; then, the finer flatter marks of more careful chisel work further smooth the surface. Then this in turn is followed by the slower work of producing the far finer final finish, first perhaps with the use of small hard-stone pounders, before a final smoothing with a series of abrasives that produce a shining finish of extraordinary sensitivity; a surface that although quite flat is never mechanical or dead; that same bland surface as is found on Egypt's prehistoric vases. This, of course, is the same quality that is present in the greater part of the internal architecture of the Great Pyramid, which is also built of Tura limestone; that same archaic finish employed at Djoser's funerary monuments (chs. 25 and 27 above). At the Great Pyramid, however, after a century of building gigantic pyramids from enormous blocks of stone, all reference to the forms of nature have entirely disappeared. Beneath the drum-skin finish of its fine white stone only abstract, geometric form remains; the millions upon millions of blocks extracted from the royal quarries had filled the Egyptian imagination.

The seeming parallels between the Great Pyramid's lost casing stones and those that yet survive on its subsidiary pyramids cannot, however, be pushed too far. Just as each one of those modest little pyramids is made in a different way, so we should not assume that the Great Pyramid's craftsmen took up a production line approach in finishing the Great Pyramid, and that the work was done at one time and in one way only. Some of the remaining surfaces of the four small pyramids, for example, have not been completed; this labour, then, was yet continuing after the individual casing blocks had been fitted into position (fig. 206). At the Great Pyramid, however, the remaining casing stones appear to have been well finished before they were set to stand upon the perfect pavement set around the Pyramid.

Fig. 204 top left, Fig. 205 top right, Fig. 206 left. Techniques employed for the finishing of pyramids in the reign of Khufu. The half-worked casing stones that yet remain on the Great Pyramid's attendant pyramids display the marks of a diversity of chisels, pounders and abrasives, precious surfaces mirroring the skills of the craftsmen who created the Great Pyramid's four finished faces.

In common with most of Egypt's other pyramids, therefore, these four satellites of Khufu appear as quick and lively sketches of the grand original in whose shade they stand. They cannot begin to tell us, for example, if the 20 acres of the Great Pyramid's original façades were finished with the same precision as the remaining fragments of its baselines, or if some or all of its casing was made of previously finished blocks set up row by row upon the rising Pyramid, or whether they were finished and polished after they were set into place. Certainly, we know nothing of the timetable of this work, nor even if a single capstone was set up on the Great Pyramid's summit as it appears to have been on some at least of its four small satellites.[14] Neither do we know if the celebrations that appear to have accompanied the placing of such a capstone on royal pyramids of a later dynasty would have occurred in Khufu's day.[15] Just as the topmost courses of the Great Pyramid have vanished into the air, so its casing stones are as illusory as the rest of the assumptions and beliefs that shimmer all around this ancient monument.

So, we may not assume that when the work of setting and finishing the casing stones was done, and the summit of King Khufu's Pyramid rose sharply to a single final finished point, that day in itself was considered to be the climax of the enterprise. Although we might well imagine that such a thing was so, it is a conclusion only in the sense that it fulfils the ambitions of a modern building project. In a society where public works and the identity of the state were bound up together by the royal tomb, it is more likely that the real ending of this enterprise was the placing of the body of the king in its sarcophagus; after Khufu had been taken through the dark corridors of the Pyramid's interior and placed inside the granite box within its granite chamber, and the Pyramid was shut.

48 After the Pyramid

The masons' waste chips were thrown away over the cliffs . . . In one part there will
be a layer of large chips, up to the size of a hand; a foot above that a lot of fine dust
and sweepings; above that perhaps more large chips, and here and there a layer of
desert flints and sand, showing when a piece of desert ground had been cleared to
get more space for working. Among all this rubbish are pieces of the workmen's
water-jars and food vessels, of which I collected a hundred or more fragments, mixed
with chips of wood, bits of charcoal, and even a piece of string, which had probably
been used in patching up a rubbish basket.

W. M. Flinders Petrie, The Pyramids and Temples of Gizeh[1]

One of the tasks that its makers would have undertaken upon
finishing the Great Pyramid would have been the dismantling of its
remaining building ramps. Judging by the fill that still lies within
its stone quarry (ch. 22 above), it is likely that large amounts of
debris from this colossal demolition were simply taken back again
to their beginnings at the bottom of the ramps and buried in that
wide and shallow excavation.[2] As Petrie recognised, however, enormous amounts of building debris were also tipped off the cliff
immediately to the north of the Great Pyramid (p. 139 above);
indeed, the huge screes of rubble that still dominate this landscape
must surely have their beginnings in the time of Khufu, for it was

Fig. 207 Bonfils' beautiful photograph shows the north face of the Pyramid during the inundation of the Nile, with huge soft banks of dust and rubble, a residue of human labour tipped from the top of the Plateau, covering the natural cliff. That these enormous screes were already in position before the Giza archaeologists arrived shows that they are the product of an earlier age; that they have been levelled to the baselines of the Pyramid suggests that this was the work of its ancient makers, a final act of landscaping that set the Pyramid upon an artificial straight horizon.

the only period in history when major building works took place in that immediate vicinity.[3] That both these building tips are mixed with domestic rubbish – this presumably from the demolition of the pyramid-makers' settlements, for not a single trace of workshops, magazines or dwellings has survived in the areas around the Pyramid – suggests that any buildings that had been erected on the Plateau in connection with its construction were also demolished at this time.[4]

Unrecognised in Petrie's survey of the Plateau, the huge quantities of ancient chip and debris that obscured King Khufu's quarry had taken on the natural forms of the Plateau's landscape, an indication of how sensitively the pyramid-makers had performed the task. Similarly, although the Pyramid's baselines would be buried and obscured down through the ages, the top of the great rubble tips that lie to the north of the Great Pyramid stood at the level of the Pyramid's lost baselines, as can be seen in early photographs (see fig. 207).[5] It would appear, therefore, that the pyramid-makers undertook a wide-ranging work of landscaping right across the Plateau with the intention of presenting the Great Pyramid's perfect finished form upon a level cliff-top horizon, with a steep cliff to its north and smooth clean slopes running gently down towards the sandy valley to the south.[6]

Within this carefully re-formed environment, Khufu's masons set a range of monuments which, though more modest in extent than the sparkling Pyramid that loomed above them, were yet a part of that same building programme.[7] Throughout King Khufu's reign – and given that his Pyramid took fourteen years to build, it is likely that he reigned for a decade after it was finished[8] – the area around his Pyramid was changed and changed again as a wide variety of monuments were emplaced, embellished and extended. Given that the materials and the techniques used in these monuments' construction are similar to those used at the Pyramid itself, they would certainly have required state sanction and participation for their construction. It would appear, therefore, that they were undertaken by part of the royal workforce and administration, and may be seen as a direct and purposeful accompaniment to the Great Pyramid itself. Unlike the Pyramid, which holds but a single simple plan within it, these subsidiary works display a diversity of attitudes to death and burial – a special preoccupation, for example, with the refreshment of the spirits of the dead. Between them these monuments contain a spectrum of the funerary beliefs elaborated during Khufu's lifetime and thus they offer the beginnings of an understanding of the interior architecture of the Pyramid itself, which can be seen to represent the fundamental funerary requirements of the pharaoh, set out at the beginning of his reign.

At the time of Khufu's funeral this wide-ranging architectural theatre set around his Pyramid appears to have been comprised of at least five great boat pits, two grand temples with a connecting causeway, four diminutive pyramids and seventy-odd mastabas which were grouped, in turn, in four separate cemeteries. Three of these cemeteries lay on the rise to the west of the Great Pyramid, where courtiers

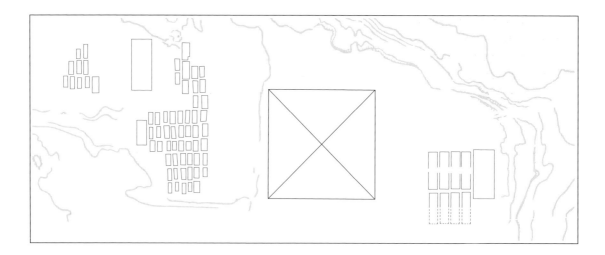

appear to have predominated, and the other to its east, which mostly held the tombs of Khufu's queens and family members (fig. 40).

Unlike the other monuments of Khufu's Giza which had immediate architectural connection with the king and with his Pyramid, these four great cemeteries were simply planned to lie within its shadow, a stony court of tombs beside a royal Pyramid. Given their regularity, it would appear that they were constructed as methodically as the Great Pyramid itself, block by block, row by row, and even perhaps before the names of the occupants of individual mastabas had been determined; an impression underlined by the little portable tablets whose inscriptions appear to have been the only original evidence of the identity of their intended owners.[9] With the exception of three enormous mastabas that are much larger than the others, all of these tombs once shared the same design; they were conceived as a stripped-down version of earlier monuments built in the similar though sparser cemeteries of King Sneferu's courtiers.[10] Some 75 feet in length and around 24 feet in height (22 m × 7.5 m)[11] and built of massive blocks of local quarry stone whose combined bulk would represent some 2 per cent of the Pyramid's building stone, they were set on simple grids like those used in planning the Great Pyramid, so that the battered sides and flat tops of the individual tombs would have made the four cemeteries appear like bars of chocolate lying in the sand.

As to their date, it is certain that at least one section of these cemeteries' gridded plan was already under construction in the middle years of the building of Khufu's Pyramid, for one of the rare stone workers' graffiti on the foundations of the mastaba of Hemiunu (ch. 8 above) – would that there be such a thing inside the Pyramid itself! –

Fig. 208 Map showing the relationship between the Great Pyramid and the mastabas of Khufu's courtiers. Set 400 feet back from the Great Pyramid's baselines, the positioning of the mastaba cemeteries would have allowed the pyramid-makers ample access to the rising Pyramid – and also to its design field.

refs to the winter of year ten of the reign.[12] With the royal work-force at its most inflated and the national resources focussed hard upon establishing the royal tomb (ch. 42 above), it would seem unlikely that work upon these subsidiary monuments began at the same time as the Pyramid itself.[13] This indeed is reinforced by the subsidiary monuments that stand beside the earlier unfinished royal pyramids, where though several years of construction had clearly been undertaken on the royal pyramids themselves, there is but scant evidence of noble cemeteries, and work upon the royal temples when they exist at all is hurried or incomplete.[14]

Given that the first big drop in the Great Pyramid's building rates appears to have occurred around year five of its construction, it would seem likely that the first major phase of secondary building on the Giza Plateau would have begun at that same time. This broadly concurs with the situation of the splendid eastern cemetery, which, though it contains no unequivocal graffiti like that of Hemiunu's tomb, is sited immediately to the south of the area that would have been used during the earlier years of the Great Pyramid's construction as the design field: indeed the very layout of this cemetery derives from elements set up in the Pyramid's design field (fig. 209), which must therefore already have been established at the time of the cemetery's foundation.[15]

At the other end of this secondary building programme, the two huge boat pits on the south side of the Great Pyramid could only have been cut and covered with their rows of massive limestone blocks after the Great Pyramid itself had been finished and the Plateau had been levelled, for up until that time parts of the Pyramid's south side (pp. 400ff) would have been covered by construction ramps.[16] This reasoning is borne out by a graffito found on the roof of one of these boat pits that informs us that its closing was undertaken in the reign of Khufu's successor, Djedefre (ch. 21): the last-known building work connected to King Khufu's Pyramid, in all probability, it was a part of his funerary rites.

The same logic also suggests that the reason why the mastaba cemeteries were set at least 400 feet (125 m) back from the Great Pyramid's baselines was because that narrow strip of land was still in use by the Pyramid's constructors at the time of the cemeteries' foundation. This in turn shows that the minor pyramids, the boat pits and the royal temple that all stand within that narrow strip of land upon the Pyramid's east side were constructed after the pyramid-makers had no further need of it, neither for construction purposes nor for access to the Pyramid's design field. That the open courtyard of the

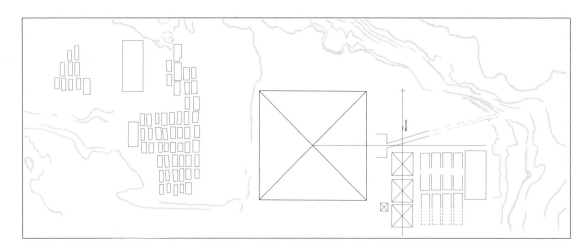

temple at the centre of the Pyramid's east face – the temple sometimes called the Mortuary Temple, and here called the Pyramid
Temple[17] – shares its footprint with the nearby row of little pyramids
(fig. 209) shows a commonality of design. That the apexes of three of
these small pyramids are all set upon the line of the little Trench that
itself echoes the height of the Great Step on the central axis of the
Pyramid points up the architectural unity within this group of monuments which, as we have already seen, shows remarkable connection
to the Pyramid's interior design as well![18] All this points to a secondary plan of building initiated, at the earliest, after year six of the
Great Pyramid's construction, when the Great Step would have been
set in place and the primary purposes of the design field had been
accomplished.[19] This again is borne out by the condition of the
temples built near other early royal pyramids, which show that
although the pyramids themselves may well have been completed,
their associated temples were sometimes still in the process of construction when all work was stopped.[20]

Fig. 209 The Giza
monuments at the time
of Khufu's death, showing
the range of monuments
fitted into the strip
between the Pyramid and
the mastabas upon its
eastern side. The three
minor pyramids appear
to have been set into the
Pyramid's six-square grid
as laid out in its design
field; their common
footprints would appear
to be the same as that of
the Pyramid's temple.

Fig. 210 The ruin of the
Pyramid temple – of
which only a splendid
basalt pavement is
preserved – and the four
small pyramids built in
the gap between the
eastern cemetery and the
Great Pyramid's eastern
baseline.

Fig. 211 A limestone block bearing Khufu's names, and the broken phrase 'building the sanctuaries of the gods'. Recovered from the interior of a later pyramid where it had been re-employed as building stone, the block appears to come from one of Khufu's Giza temples, and may be dated, by following the construction timetable established for Khufu's monuments upon the Giza Plateau, to that period of his reign after his Pyramid was finished, that is, after 2476 BC. Another broken phrase upon this stone, 'in the [horizon of] Khufu', records one of the first-known occurrences of the ancient name of the Great Pyramid itself.

This circumstantial evidence for the founding of King Khufu's Giza temples years after the founding of the Pyramid itself is inadvertently confirmed by some of the rare loose fragments of their decorations to have survived, one of which appears to name King Khufu's funerary monuments as 'Akhet Khufu' – the 'Horizon of Khufu'[21] – which would indicate that the Great Pyramid was well established at the time when that relief was made.[22] Another fragment, excavated at the site of the Pyramid Temple, shows King Khufu at a jubilee, which strongly suggests that the decoration of that temple was undertaken in the latter stages of the reign, just as was a similar jubilee fragment of relief found by the temple of the Red Pyramid, where construction had begun in around the thirtieth year of Sneferu's rule.[23]

It would appear, therefore, that after the main bulk of the Great Pyramid had been completed, a secondary building phase took place upon the Giza Plateau, and that this was a period of architectural

Fig. 212 below Part of a long thin block of fine white limestone found by Selim Hassan in the winter of 1938–9, during his excavation of King Khufu's Pyramid temple. This section of relief, which is about 1 foot 8 inches wide, shows Khufu, who is identified by a broken cartouche, enthroned within a booth and decked out in robes traditionally worn by kings at the ceremonial of their jubilee. That this scene may represent a genuine royal jubilee is born out by the date of the foundation of the Pyramid temple, which, following the construction timetable established for Khufu's monuments upon the Giza Plateau, could only have taken place in the second decade of Khufu's reign.

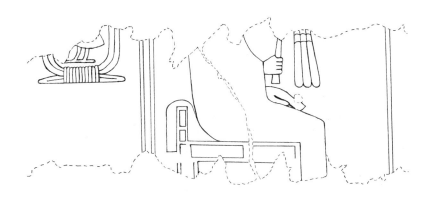

innovation; one similar to the later years of the reigns of Djoser and of Sneferu when their first-made funerary monuments had also neared completion (Part Four, and pp. 246–7). In Khufu's reign, just as a secondary phase of construction in his nobles' cemeteries saw little chapels, statue rooms and offering places built onto the mastabas (ch. 10 above), so this secondary phase of royal architecture saw a temple added to the east side of his Pyramid as well: a temple connected to a great long causeway that ran right down into the plain.

Little remains to ascertain this temple's purposes. Although its traces are impressive, they are fragmented and obscure;[24] that it once housed royal statues and offering chapels are but reasonable inferences from other similar royal temples of earlier and later dates where this may be seen to be true.[25] Of Khufu's so-called Valley Temple which, by similar comparisons, may once have stood amidst the fields of the river's floodplain, not the merest hint exists. The spare ruin of the Pyramid Temple, however, is still connected to the shadow of a causeway, a lost processional that, if parallels with other pyramid temples are pursued, would have connected with that yet mistier construction, the Valley Temple, which may have stood by a canal down in the river's valley. For centuries past, so it is said, local villagers living by the faint lines of this ruined causeway have built

Fig. 213 The Great Pyramid and its causeway, which appears as a ruined roadway running up the cliff, at left of centre in the photograph. Taken in the 1870s, Antonio Beato's photograph shows the causeway little changed since the 1840s, when it had been drawn by Lepsius' topographers (Hassan 1960, pl. 1). Over the following century, however, it would be greatly denuded by local villagers who, following the enormous increase in the tourist trade, used it as a source of building stone.

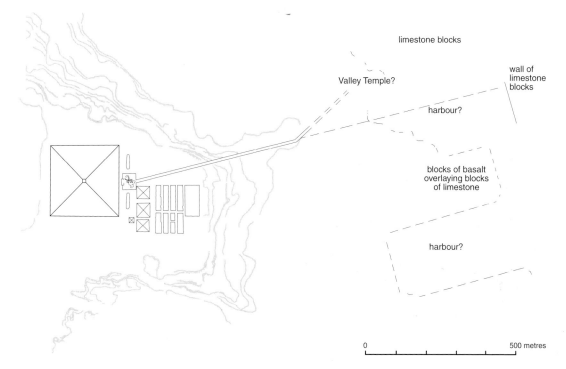

limestone blocks

Valley Temple?

wall of limestone blocks

harbour?

blocks of basalt overlaying blocks of limestone

harbour?

0   500 metres

their houses from its shattered stonework, breaking the pyramid-makers' quarry blocks into bite-sized pieces suitable for the walls and steps of village houses. More than a mile in length and some 18 feet in width, Khufu's causeway once rose up from the floodplain in the manner of a narrow stone-hauling ramp, gaining the top of the Plateau, so its ruin shows, by ascending the 130 foot (40 m) cliff face and ending its progress, as we have already seen, at the central eastern doorway of the Pyramid Temple.[26]

The making of this causeway, so the Greek Herodotus informs us, was by itself alone a labour equal to that of building the Great Pyramid, and certainly, as its surviving quarry blocks still show, it was indeed a labour equal to the making of a minor pyramid.[27] Yet both the causeway and its two ghostly temples were robbed of their fine limestone long before Herodotus took a tour of Egypt. Five centuries after the Great Pyramid had been plugged and sealed, some of the beautiful reliefs from this extended complex had already been carried off some 30 miles southwards up the Nile and set into the interior of a later and far lesser pyramid, where they were reused as bulking building blocks.[28]

There are shadows too down in the plain of more mysterious constructions, hints of enormous structures that may also have connection to King Khufu's Pyramid. Local legends from the 1900s tell of

Fig. 214 Modern contractors working in the plain below the Great Pyramid have occasionally uncovered traces of massive walls and pavements, the shattered relics of vast building projects. Set well to the north of the other Giza monuments and causeways, they appear to be orientated to the direction of the causeway of the Great Pyramid, and may therefore echo unknown elements of Khufu's building programme. Zahi Hawass' subtle restoration joins these diverse fragments to the lines of old canals that are rapidly disappearing under urban development.

Fig. 215 Rescued from a building contractor's trench, these broken basalt blocks heaped in the central reservation of a modern highway may well be the relics of a pavement similar to that which still lies beside the Great Pyramid. These broken blocks, some of which still bear the cuts of a massive saw (cf. pp. 164ff), may therefore be remnants of a temple built at the far ending of King Khufu's ruined causeway that, so it may be estimated, lay beneath some of the houses in this photograph.

village gardens that were watered from wells whose brackish depths, when plumbed by iron buckets, would fill with echoes ringing through deep-buried halls of dark hard stone.[29] And well beyond the causeway's known extent, laid bare occasionally by earth-moving machinery and caught up now within a net of modern roads and drainage systems, are buried blocks of ancient stones all set into colossal rows; fragments, perhaps, of unknown harbour walls or even other temples, other causeways. Despite the heroic efforts of the archaeologists, little sense can be made of these far-flung fragments that are now buried once again, beneath Giza's growing city.[30]

All that remains of these colossal wrecks are some brief reports in scientific publications and a substantial pile of basalt fragments, some still bearing the marks of Khufu's gigantic copper saw (fig. 71 above), lying on the central reservation of a four-lane highway. That, and the splendid pavements of the Pyramid Temple that still lie beside the Great Pyramid itself; blocks of the finest basalt rolled down from the twin peaks of the Widan el-Faras, along distant desert quarry tracks, and shipped to Giza and the Pyramid (p. 162 above). Blocks that are some 3 feet thick which have been levelled and smoothed and set in fine white plaster upon foundations of the finest Tura limestone. Huge, tough and beautifully finished, they yet allow a partial reconstruction of the lost architecture that stood upon them.

Set on the Pyramid's east–west axis, King Khufu's Pyramid Temple was centred on a grave and simple courtyard, a bruise-black pavement open to the sun and so hot that you could not stand upon it barefoot at midday. Dominated by the dazzling triangle of the Pyramid above, this dramatic open space was succeeded by a shadowed hall lined with dull-red granite columns, and on its western side by a row of small dark rooms set back to touch the baseline of the Pyramid itself. Judging by the remains of other temples built in similar locations, this austere monument once housed a cult that tended to King Khufu's spirit; that same spirit which, in the times before the state of Egypt had been born, was thought to stay close to the place where a person's body was entombed.[31]

Fig. 216 Selim Hassan's excavation in the winter of 1935–6 on the east face, photographed by Mohammedani Ibrahim as the remains of the Great Pyramid's temple were coming to light. The black blocks are stones from the temple's basalt pavements, which have been overturned by ancient robbers.

49 The rites of death

Not only, Sir, has the great pyramid been coated, and finished on the outside, but it was shut, and has been Forcibly opened. This I take upon me to establish, so as to leave no doubt of the fact.

Savary's Letters on Egypt, London, 1786

There is no contemporary literature, not a single document, a single word, describing Khufu's interment in the Great Pyramid and it would be but sleight of hand to break this ancient silence and concoct a bogus ceremonial out of later texts, a process as circular as ransacking the writings of the Fathers of the Church to concoct a funeral for Jesus. By themselves alone, however, the logistics and the architecture of that stupendous tomb tell a great deal about the state that Khufu ruled and of its relationship to its king both alive and dead, and these same factors surely also shaped the physical event of Khufu's interment.

The building schedule shows that the primary aim of Khufu's funerary architecture was the construction of a substantial and robust grave and that this was followed by the building of the Pyramid Temple with ritual facilities for the maintenance of the royal spirit. In that all these funerary monuments hold an implicit journey in their separate parts, an upward progress through the Pyramid's rooms and corridors and also in its exterior, through its temples and its causeway, Khufu's monuments took their cue from those of his father Sneferu. So, whilst the ritual function of the Great Pyramid's interior is utterly unknown and the plan of Khufu's Valley Temple is lost and both the Pyramid Temple and its mile-long causeway are reduced to their foundations, the clear precedent of his father's temples, which yet have some surviving words and images in them, allows a glimpse at least of other aspects of contemporary ideas connected with state monuments, with royal tombs and with the rituals of offering.

Unlike the anagraphic emptiness of Djoser's standing monuments, Sneferu's names were written large in great grand hieroglyphs on two pairs of bulky stelae set up before the offering tables in the little temples built upon the east sides of the Pyramid at Meidum and the Bent Pyramid at Dahshur (fig. 139).[1] This, then, was a return to the archaic ways of Abydos (ch. 24 above), where the spirits of individual kings are given clear identity as well as sustenance. At Sneferu's Bent Pyramid an elaboration of this traditional view of the requirements of the royal dead was introduced in the shape of a unique temple set on the Pyramid's causeway.[2] About half the size of Khufu's Pyramid Temple, this temple also had an open courtyard and, set behind two rows of pillars in the darkness, six large statues of King Sneferu set up in six small rooms, an arrangement echoed, so it would appear, in Khufu's Pyramid Temple, which had five similarly shaped rooms set in a shadowed row behind the open court.[3]

The stone walls of this causeway temple had also held a series of elegant reliefs: rows of female figures, personifications of Sneferu's estates. Many of these provinces and farms were colonies established in previously unoccupied areas of the river's floodplain, and all of them were assembled here from all over ancient Egypt to provide the spirit of the king with offerings.[4] Here too, carved upon its four-square pillars, were scenes of Sneferu himself bringing the products of the river and the desert to his temple.[5] And there were other images as well, of the royal jubilee, and Nile deities, and of the King embraced by gods – the last being amongst the first-known occurrences of a pose that would become the standard fare of pharaonic mortuary reliefs throughout the following millennia.

Now some of the loose blocks of relief with Khufu's names upon them that were reused inside another later pyramid (p. 415, above) hold fragments of these self-same images. One of them at least shows a female figure bearing the name of one of Khufu's estates (fig. 218); another bears images of three fine fat cattle from his farms.[6] These latter, in all probability, would have been accompanied by a herds-man, and certainly they formed a part of that immemorial procession that runs through a great part of ancient Egyptian wall decoration, in which great numbers of different people, functionaries of households and estates, move in a single direction along a wall within a tomb or chapel, bearing the produce and product of the deserts, fields and river towards an offering place.

Many similarly sculpted blocks reused in that same pyramid hold other scraps of these same activities: splendid images of servants carrying sunshades, sailors with cordage from a boat, domestic animals and fishermen upon the Nile, a woodsman cutting trees.[7] Yet other fragments are from scenes that showed the age-old rituals of jubilee;[8] and there are pieces too of long-lost scenes that had shown pharaoh in the company of the gods[9] and even one that celebrated Khufu as the founder of other temples, for its broken inscription describes him as 'building the sanctuaries of the gods'.[10]

All together these blocks are kaleidoscopic images of the systems of supply and ritual operating in King Khufu's kingdom and they embrace virtually every aspect of his state. Centuries after Khufu's time similar scenes in other pyramid temples would celebrate these same state systems which were collecting extraordinary amounts of Egypt's produce as offerings for the spirits of the dead kings;[11] vast quantities of cereals, of bread and beer, and live oxen too, that were slaughtered in special butcheries attached to the royal pyramid temples and which it has been speculated were a major source of red meat for the entire state.[12]

Just as the living governments of Sneferu and Khufu had funnelled the wealth and riches of their state into the harbours by their pyramids, so, their funerary monuments inform us, the same state system of supply continued after they were buried, to cater for their spirits. In life, the building of their pyramids had defined the role of the early pharaohs on earth and provided national purpose and identity; in death, their temples served as an interface between the living state and the spirit of the dead king, as theatres to accommodate the rituals that were a continuance and a codification of the processes that had defined their living state.[13]

In this sense King Khufu's funerary monuments can be seen as an architectural diagram of the order of his state machine. From the beginning of the work, Khufu was destined to lie at their centre. And just as his funerary monuments were connected throughout the long years of their construction to stone-hauling ramps and harbours and canals, and through them to a national network of provision and

Fig. 217 An offerer at the cult of Sneferu: a fragment from a series of reliefs cut into the limestone walls of a temple set on the Bent Pyramid's causeway. Like many other figures that appear in these royal processionals, this woman is a personification of one of the royal estates that were spread throughout the land of Egypt. The name of her particular estate, however, is largely lost, having been spelled out in hieroglyphs set to the left of the rectangular sign above the woman's head. In the time-honoured way, she has been sheltered from the sun by a well-balanced palm branch.

Fig. 218 A fragmentary relief bearing Khufu's name, excavated from the
filling of a later pyramid. Though from the north wall of a royal temple and
thus facing in the opposite direction to her counterpart in Sneferu's relief
(see fig. 217), this woman is another personification of a royal estate – named
here as 'Khufu is beautiful'. And in the manner of her predecessor, she too
has been sheltered from the sun by a trimmed palm branch. The cartouche
she carries on her head holds a fine drawing of a stout loop of rope such as
would have been used to pull the stones of the Great Pyramid into place. In
all probability, this beauteous stone once decorated one of Khufu's Giza
monuments.

supply, so too the physical forms of these systems of supply – from the
sloping corridors inside the Pyramid to the ramp-like walls of its great
grand causeway (fig. 214) – were echoed in the finished architecture
whose construction they had supported. So when Khufu died and was
taken to his grave, it was much as it had been at Giza when he was
alive, when the Pyramid's building stone was brought up from the
living land of Egypt, up from the riverside and the canals and harbours,
up the hauling ramps onto the horizon of the Giza cliff, and up onto
the rising Pyramid. Khufu's interment was the last act of a physical progression from the activities of the living present to the rhythms of the
ritual. His tomb, both threshold and accommodation, was the locus
where he crossed the boundaries between the living and the dead.

The very name of the Great Pyramid – and the only contemporary
evidence of how this greatest of all Egyptian buildings may have been

regarded by its makers – is 'Akhet Khufu'; the Akhet being defined as the horizon, where sky and heaven meet, the threshold between sky and earth and underground.[14] Thus, King Khufu's Pyramid is often described as the place from where he rises up, in the manner of the sun. This, however, seems to take a modern point of view of things, a viewer's role, for 'Akhet Khufu' might equally well describe the place where Khufu's body lies transformed, and the order of his state is physically manifested.[15]

As for the offices that may have accompanied King Khufu's journey from his death bed to the Pyramid, the order of his wake and funeral, nothing has survived: not of words that may have been said, nor of the ceremonials that may have been enacted.[16] Was he even mummified? Was Khufu prepared so as not to show the processes of his decomposition, was he turned into a sort of stone so that the visible suspension of the effects of death would serve to bridge that gap between flesh and statue, real and ritual? Some of the courtiers buried in his cemeteries certainly were,[17] and whilst his mother's cadaver was mysteriously absent from her Giza tomb, her guts were found, some of them still submerged in liquid, placed in four alabaster compartments in the approved manner, which would suggest that her missing corpse was also turned into a kind of statue.[18] So it would seem an apt fate for Khufu too.[19]

And yet the cult has gone, and its prayers have all been said, so we no longer know where Khufu may have been embalmed or if he was taken for a last trip on the Nile in one of the splendid cedar sailing boats that were buried beside his Pyramid (ch. 21 above) or if his corpse was carried in grand procession to his temples or to his tomb or any of the other places in which his funerary rites might have taken place.[20]

There yet remains, however, a valid and dynamic timeline inside the Great Pyramid itself that tells us of the real-time process of its final closing. That tells us too that the final acts of Khufu's burial were every bit as lively as was the work of the Pyramid's creation, for in the corridors of Khufu's grave the pyramid-makers set up mechanisms as precise as the cocking of a gun. First then, from around halfway through the Pyramid's construction, the granite plugging blocks had been loaded in the dark breech of the Grand Gallery; the great stones readied for their tremendous slide down into the Prism Point at the heart of the Pyramid's design, to jam that strange geometry for ever. A little later, the slabs of the three portcullises were set up in their slots within the low granite corridor that leads to the royal burial chamber, a process painstakingly outlined in Borchardt's convincing restoration.[21] And before the final closure, a long deep shaft was excavated down into the Rocky Knoll, the so-called escape hatch that would have enabled the last members of the royal burial party to leave the Pyramid.

So one fine day in around the year 2464 BC, Khufu's encoffined corpse would have been carried through the dark interior of the greatest pyramid the human race would ever build, the burial party carrying that plain rectangular wooden box over the granite blocking plugs in the Grand Gallery and under the portcullises, poised now to slide into their planned positions in the finished Pyramid.[22] Yet this was not a grand procession, all stereo flutes and sistra, in the way of Hollywood. Most of the Pyramid's corridors, after all, are just a little larger than the dimensions of a wooden coffin that would fit inside King Khufu's stone sarcophagus, and certainly they are far too small for humans, who cannot even stand up straight in them.[23] In modern terms, therefore, we might well view the progress of King Khufu's journey to the grave as utilitarian. The very volume of his coffin, indeed, would have equalled that of one of the Pyramid's building blocks,[24] and with the slopes of the Pyramid's two main corridors set like stone-hauling ramps, its progress would have appeared about the same as that of a limestone block being hauled up from the local quarry.[25]

That Khufu was interred by officers of the court of his successor is suggested, as we have already seen, by the fact that King Djedefre's name is found on the covering blocks of the Great Pyramid's buried boats (p. 413, above); that they really did release those six poised blocking stones is shown by the substantial portions of them that yet remain in their pre-ordained positions. We do not, however, know the route they took. If, for example, they passed up through the temples and the causeway, or how they gained the doorway of the Pyramid, some 70 slithering feet up on the gleaming casing of its eastern face. Nor do we know if, once inside the Pyramid's interior, they took the royal corpse to the two lower chambers before setting it within its blank sarcophagus. Yet the Subterranean Chamber was unfinished and still part-filled with unquarried rock, so it would seem unlikely that the burial party would have ventured down its perfect little corridor to visit what is still today a murky work in progress (see pp. 106ff). It is equally unlikely too that the burial party could have visited the Queen's Chamber at all, for its entrance passage is situated at the bottom of the Grand Gallery and would have been stoutly closed with specially angled blocks of stone, so that the three great granite plugging blocks could slide straight over them and down into the Prism Point.[26]

As to the purposes of those two other chambers, we can do little more than guess; as our modern theories are derived from parallels with later texts and monuments they are ultimately unprovable, and somewhat unconvincing too. Outside the usual run of ancient architecture, the Great Pyramid was also a great original, and thus not amenable to generalising theories of its ritual purpose.[27] Just as its makers took over and transformed selected parts of earlier royal monuments, so many aspects of its architecture were never built again (ch. 50 below).

At all events, it is unlikely that in a prequel of the peroxide flash of King Tut's treasure, King Khufu's burial party carried tons of gold into his Pyramid. Judging by his mother's burial equipment, his funerary fittings would have been restrained and elegant in the manner of the time: a superb attenuated cedar furniture with proportions set in the same fine units that governed the architecture of his Pyramid, and whose lines were drawn in gold and ebony and studded with jewel-like hieroglyphs.[28] A thinly gleaming canopy covered with a finely woven sun-bleached linen cloth was perhaps set over the sarcophagus, and the burial party may have left some of the common residues of ancient burial, a scattering of reeds or broken pottery upon the chamber floor.

And at the ending of the work, after the deposition, after the three portcullises were closed and those shining blocks of granite had rumbled down the Ascending Corridor and lay fixed for ever in their massive girdling blocks, the last of Khufu's pyramid-makers could have climbed into the shaft at the bottom of the Grand Gallery and

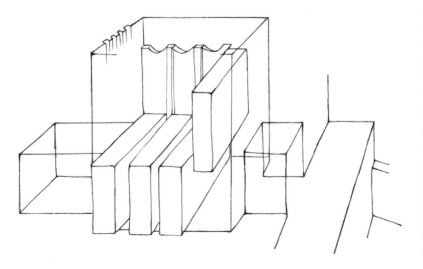

Fig. 219 The Great Pyramid's portcullises shut down. The burial chamber's entrance lies to the left; the Great Step is at the right. Such stone portcullises had blocked the entrances to royal tombs since the days of mud brick mastabas. The means of their closing inside the Great Pyramid is generally assumed to have been that proposed by Ludwig Borchardt: that the three portcullises in their little granite antechamber were lowered by means of ropes wound around three wooden beams whose ends lay in the three scalloped slots cut high up on the chamber's walls.

Fig. 220 The Descending Corridor in the Great Pyramid, showing the rough mouth of the passage that gives access to the ending of the shaft that runs down from the Grand Gallery: the sole exit by which the pyramid-makers and burial parties could have left the Pyramid after the blocking of its interior architecture.

dropped down a rope to pass right through the stone-lined pit that a quarter of a century earlier the pyramid-makers had cut in sunshine on the Rocky Knoll. Then, far further down in the wandering darkness of their tiny tunnel, they would have reached at last that diamond-sharp Descending Corridor and walked up and out of it into the light.[29] All that remained was for the pyramid-makers to close the entrance, and the Pyramid was complete.[30]

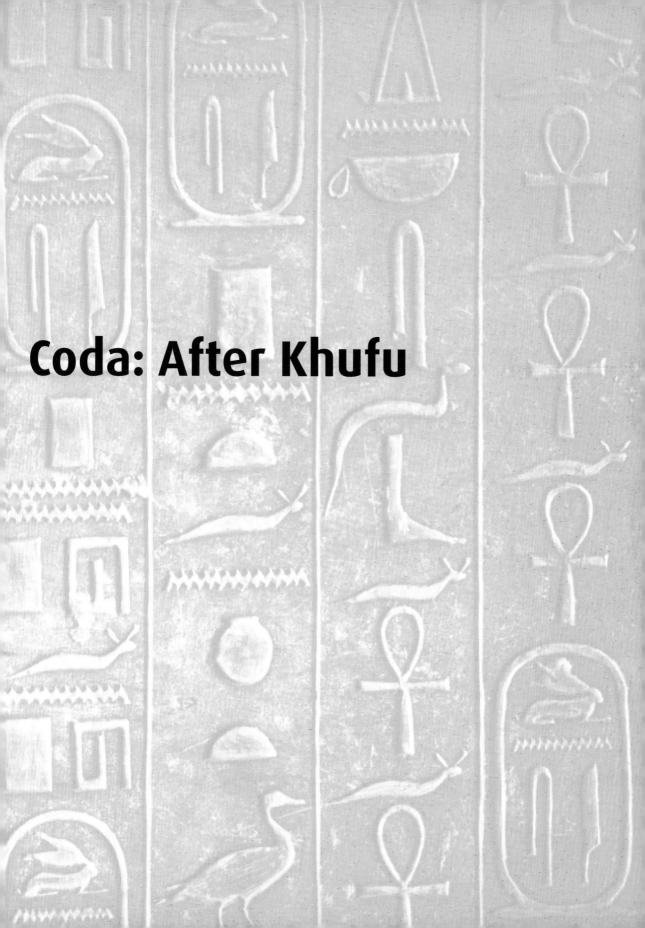

Coda: After Khufu

50 Stone

After they had buried Khufu, the pyramid-makers moved 5 miles to the north of the Giza Plateau, where they set up another pyramid for Khufu's son, the pharaoh Djedefre. Even in its present dilapidation, which was wrought by stone robbers in Roman times, this new pyramid, which was connected to the Valley of the Nile by an enormous causeway that ran for miles,[1] tokens another considerable labour.[2] Yet it was radically different from its predecessors. For the first time, there was little originality in its design and no attempt whatever to match the earlier pyramids in their excellence of construction. The only surviving chamber in the pyramid's present ruin was set at the bottom of an enormous deep-cut pit and trench in the manner of the Step Pyramid's burial chamber; and the pyramid's foundations too were laid in a similarly antique manner, the stone setters reverting to the use of angled blocks (ch. 26 above).[3] It seemed that the astonishing ambition of the previous century to make ever yet more colossal pyramids had run its course, for the pyramid of Djedefre was planned to be less than half the size of the Great Pyramid.[4]

Djedefre ruled for but a brief few years, and his modest pyramid seems not to have been completed.[5] The next king, the pharaoh Khafre, another of Khufu's sons, ruled for a similarly long length of

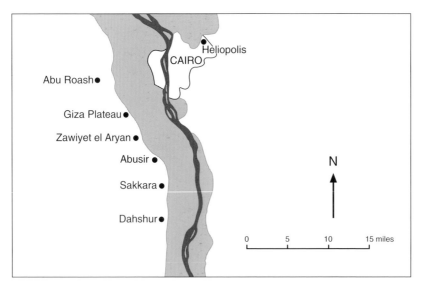

Fig. 221 Map showing the locations of some of the pyramid-building projects undertaken after the reign of Khufu. Cairo is indicated to provide a modern reference point; the other names, however, are those generally given to the sites at which these pyramids are to be found.

Fig. 222 The burial pit and entrance corridor excavated to contain the burial chamber underneath the pyramid of Djedefre. After setting the Great Pyramid's burial arrangements within the courses of its quarried stone, a man-made burial pit, the pyramid-makers returned the royal burial to its traditional setting within the rock of the Egyptian desert. This form of pit and staircase, which had been a common feature of archaic royal tombs (cf. fig. 100), was maintained to the end of the Old Kingdom.

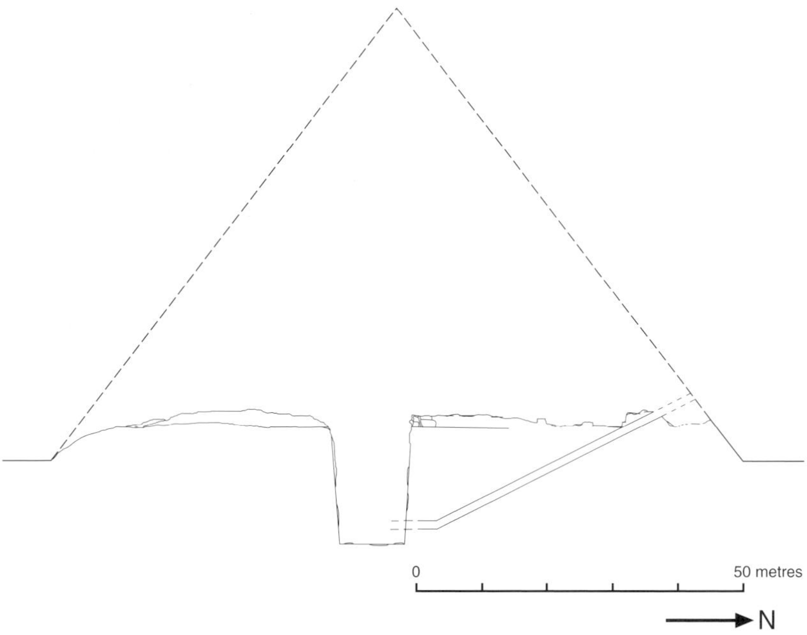

Fig. 223 Cross section of Djedefre's pyramid at Abu Roash.

0   50 metres

N

Fig. 224 The north side of the pyramid at Abu Roash, stripped to its foundations by Roman stone workers. After Khufu's, this pyramid appears modest in its size, archaic in its construction, and crude in its execution.

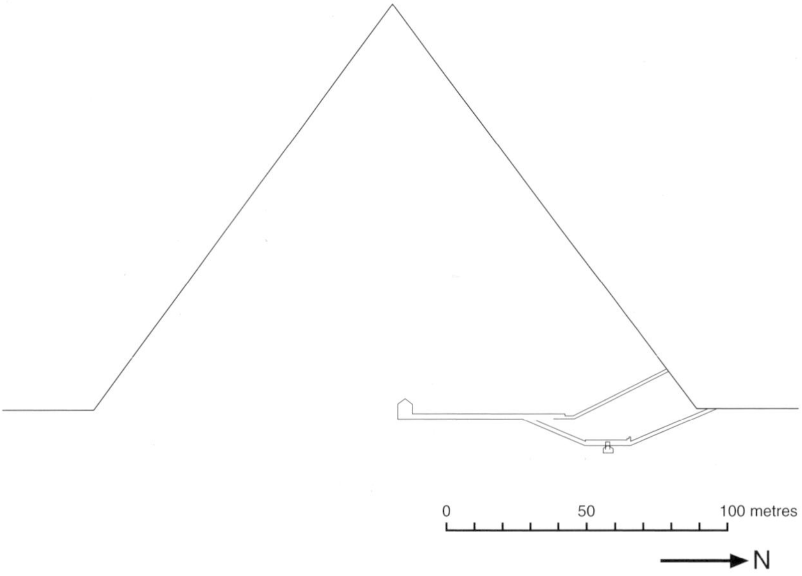

Fig. 225 Cross section of Khafre's pyramid.

0   50   100 metres

→ N

time as his father, and thus the pyramid-makers were able to make a finished monument for him, ending their sojourn in the desert to return to the Giza Plateau and build the last great pyramid in Egyptian history. Less than 10 feet smaller (2.84 m) than his father's monument and standing in its morning shadow, Khafre's pyramid is better preserved today than its great companion, and in its ruin it is perhaps more picturesque.[6] At the beginning of this work, King Khafre's pyramid-makers employed similar procedures as those of his father's, setting fastidiously accurate baselines – in granite casing

Fig. 226 Whilst Khafre's pyramid displays a return to the great pyramid-building tradition of his forefathers, it also shows the application of lessons hard-earned in the construction of the Great Pyramid close by. By levelling a steeper part of the Plateau, Khafre's masons were able to utilise the natural rock for several of the pyramid's lower courses, a considerable economy of stone. The royal burial chamber was excavated in time-honoured fashion, in the natural rock of the Plateau, and granite blocks rather than the vulnerable limestone used at his father's monument were used for the pyramid's four baselines.

Fig. 227 Khafre's pyramid boasts parts of its original casing stones and is more photogenic than its neighbour. Yet the monument owes its form and present perfections to the innovations held within King Khufu's Pyramid, and has very little of its architectural subtlety.

stones on this occasion – along the pyramid's lower courses, and employing other blocks of the same hard stone to line its entrance corridor which was as precisely set as the Descending Corridor in Khufu's Pyramid.[7] Yet they appear to have built the bulk of this new pyramid from a more friable limestone and with smaller and more irregular blocks than had been used for Khufu's Pyramid.[8] Its interior too is far less ambitious than that of the Great Pyramid, with the burial chamber's walls cut from the living rock and set in the way of older monuments, at the level of the pyramid's baselines, so there is no upward progress to its burial chamber. It would appear therefore that the extreme accuracy and control that had been built into the very heart of Khufu's Pyramid were no longer thought to be necessary; that the pyramid-makers considered it sufficient for the pyramid to be set upon the same firm strata as the Great Pyramid and for the key controls of its baselines and its entrance corridor to have been accurately established at the beginning of the work. And in this they were correct, for their pyramid still stands straight and true.

The last of the great grand pyramid-building projects in all of Egyptian history was initiated, it appears, for Khafre's shadowy successor, a virtually unknown pharaoh, known today as Nebka II. Sited some 3 miles to the south of the Giza Plateau at a site now known as Zawiyet el-ʿAryan and set like Khafre's Pyramid upon the desert's edge, it was a colossal if somewhat old-fashioned scheme with another enormous burial pit and trench cut down through the living rock in the manner of King Djedefre's, yet with the pyramid above conceived at a similar size to its two largest predecessors.[9] The work,

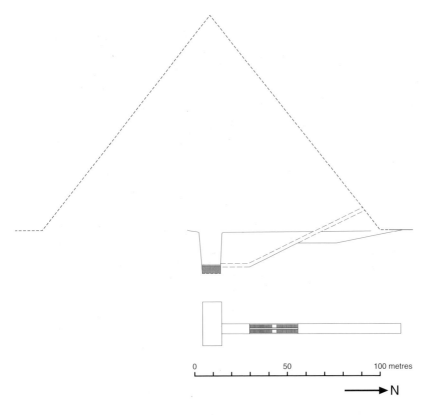

Fig. 228 Reconstruction of the 'unfinished pyramid' at Zawiyet el-'Aryan, the last great pyramid-building project in ancient Egyptian history.

Though its massive burial trench was most beautifully excavated, there are no known traces of the pyramid's baselines. This restoration has been made by analogy to the similarly shaped burial pit at Abu Roash (see fig. 223 above), whose connected pyramid suggests that this 'unfinished pyramid' would have had baselines some 600 feet in length; just a 100 feet smaller, that is, than those of the Great Pyramid at Giza.

however, appears to have hardly progressed beyond the cutting of the outline of the pyramid's foundations in the living rock. Nevertheless the chasm-like burial trench had already been furnished with some colossal foundation blocks and an enormous and bizarre sarcophagus of Aswan granite – here, as at the Great Pyramid, its makers evidently anticipated that the interior corridors of Nebka's pyramid would not be large enough to enable the sarcophagus to be hauled into position after the burial chamber was completed. That, however, is the burden of our present knowledge of this ill-fated project, which is so sunk in sand today that even its prime dimensions are uncertain.

Whilst that mysterious cutting at Zawiyet el-'Aryan signals the ending of ancient Egypt's colossal pyramid-building projects, pyramid building of itself was far from finished. Of the following eighteen-odd monarchs whose combined reigns stretched through the next three centuries to the ending of the Old Kingdom, no less than ten of them ruled long enough for their builders to make finished monuments for them, creating in the process pyramid clusters running south and north along the desert ridge of Sakkara.[10] These pyramids, however, were but a third of the size of those of their illustrious ancestors, and certainly they were nothing like as well built nor were their

Fig. 229 The burial pit of the 'unfinished pyramid' of Zawiyet el-'Aryan. The surviving sections of the last great pyramid-building project, photographed by Jean Capart in the 1920s, when they were freshly cleared of windblown sand. The horizontal lines are striations in the desert limestone; the broad white stripe on the burial pit's back wall is one of a series of sight lines drawn to control the excavation of the pit and trench (Arnold 1991, p. 18 and figs. 1.15–16).

foundations so carefully situated; today many of them are in ruin. As to their design, with silhouettes virtually indistinguishable from that of the Great Pyramid,[11] and interiors that were relatively modest and quite similar one to the other, they were neither as innovative nor as ambitious as the earlier colossal pyramids.[12]

The enormous cut of Nebka's burial trench, therefore, marked the ending of the single most creative, most imaginative and most influential phase of all pharaonic history. Before the great early pyramids were built, the surviving relics of the early pharaonic state show little coherence or consistency beyond that which you may find in the relics of many other ancient cultures: a few fine buildings and some memorable works of art. The time when ancient Egypt's high state culture was fully realised, however, when the style and repertoire of that vast body of material that in its millennial coherence and self-confidence we recognise today as 'ancient Egyptian' was established and canonised, was at the same time that the early pyramids were built.

In this, as we have already seen, the act of building with blocks of quarried stone played the decisive role: this, as Jan Assmann has described, was 'ethnogenesis by means of building'.[13] So though there are no surviving literary ruminations on the subject – nor in ancient Egypt is this to be expected – there are signs that many ancient Egyptians of later ages recognised its significance. Many texts describe the state's creation, that is, they recognise a time before Egypt was in existence;[14] others invoke the early pyramids as images of its permanence.[15] Some pyramid graffiti at Sakkara (see p. 246 above) also appear to acknowledge that the foundations of their state were laid with the beginning of architecture and the 'opening of stone',[16] whilst others imply that the age of pyramid building had established the ancient Egyptian expectations of an afterlife.[17] And right throughout the span of ancient Egypt's history, stone block architecture was hardly used for anything other than for tombs and temples; it was at once a state resource and a dimension of the spiritual and of the dead.

The age of the early pyramids also appears to have provided a model for the society of the living. The ideal social order described in many later literary texts, one whose citizens inhabit a virtually feudal hierarchy that is at the same time genuinely harmonious and interdependent,[18] could also be a recipe for that rare society that cut and set the stone blocks of the Great Pyramid with such individual integrity and in such great good order. In this world, the hieroglyphic feather of the Goddess Ma'at, a personification of that ideal social order, provides a perfect metaphor.[19] At Giza, it had been the pyramid-makers' feather touch that had set each and every one of the huge stone blocks of Khufu's Pyramid, the product of thousands of Egyptians up and down the Nile, into its individual place, whilst his father Sneferu had been labelled as a man of Ma'at and some of his courtiers had incorporated the goddess' name within their own.[20]

More than a thousand stone block buildings would be erected throughout the land of Egypt throughout the following millennia, and although a few of them were pyramids, most of them were temples whose designs were elaborations of those first few temples built beside the early pyramids.[21] Just as the early pyramids were testament to the integrity and good order of the state, so the ritual in these later temples was also seen as the means of guarding the integrity of that same state and the universe that it inhabited.[22] It is hardly surprising then that later literary descriptions of the gods emerging from these temples in procession, and muddling earth and heaven as they do so, should read like a description of the building of a royal pyramid on the horizon of the west.[23]

Nor perhaps is it surprising that as ancient Egypt neared its ending and was coming under increasing pressure from the cultures of the Mediterranean, there was a reassertion of its most basic values, with a return to massive stone block building in its ancient heartland. At Egyptian Thebes, at Karnak Temple, the largest religious complex in the Nile Valley, the final doorway of that temple is its largest single element: two massive pylons made of fine-cut blocks laid, most untypically for pharaonic monuments, in careful horizontal rows of well-made ashlars in the manner of the early pyramids.[24] And in the centuries that followed, whilst Greek and Roman pharaohs lived and died, the making of yet more massive monuments in this same technique continued inexorably. Whilst their stone was sandstone, coarse and thinly cut with hard iron chisels, the workmanship in these last temples was frequently as accurate as it had been in the first century of stone block architecture,[25] as if their makers were insisting on the basic virtues of their ancient culture that 3000 years before had made King Khufu's Pyramid.

51 Spirit

Hindsight: perception gained by looking backward.

Oxford English Dictionary

O King, raise yourself upon your iron bones and golden members, for this body of yours belongs to a god; it will not grow mouldy, it will not be destroyed, it will not putrefy. The warmth which is on your mouth is the breath which issued from the nostrils of Seth, and the winds of the sky will be destroyed if the warmth which is on your mouth be destroyed; the sky will be deprived of its stars if the warmth which is on your mouth be lacking. May your flesh be born to life, and may your life be more than the life of the stars.

Pyramid Text, Utterance 723[1]

Halfway through the procession of pyramids built in the centuries after Khufu, their stones began to speak. Quite suddenly, from one monument to the next, columns of handsome hieroglyphics were engraved into the fine white walls of their interiors that talk of life and death, of rituals, stars and gods, and even royal pyramids.

O all you gods who shall cause this pyramid and this construction of the King to be fair and endure: You shall be effective, you shall be strong, you shall have your souls, you shall have power, you shall have given to you a boon which the king grants.[2]

Known now as the Pyramid Texts, the oldest extant examples of these writings cover a great part of the rooms and corridors in the pyramid of King Unis, who reigned from about 2257 BC, two centuries after the Great Pyramid was built.[3] The discoverers and early decipherers of these writings – which yet remain the most venerable body of religious writings in the world – were nineteenth-century scholars, the most influential of whom had studied under the successors of Professor Richard Lepsius at Berlin (see above, pp. 29ff).[4] Intractable and elusive, and salted with the ancient Egyptians' predilection for puns and word plays,[5] many of the Texts' early explicators cut through the dense forest of their meaning and interpretation with the assumption that they were products of a 'primitive' society and that the texts were 'spells' which contained all kinds of encoded information, from quasi-histories of Egypt's origins to symbolical explanations of how the pyramid-makers had chosen building stone and why they had invented pyramids.[6] The same assumptions still cast spells of confusion around the Great Pyramid today.

In essence, the Pyramid Texts are an anthology of short texts concerned with the rites of royal funeral and the destiny of kings. From their first appearance in the pyramid of Unis, the corpus virtually trebled in the number of its verses, from pyramid to pyramid. In that some of them appear to refer to simple burials in sand, they would appear to have been preserved from archaic times. Others, which seem to describe graves of stone – and record ritual verses apparently intended to accompany the carrying of a sarcophagus and recitations to be performed as the lid was lowered into position – were certainly composed in the age of the pyramids themselves.[7] Yet underneath them all, there is the single theme of death as the beginning of a journey, a recurring destiny that sets the dead king back into the endless powers and rhythms of the Egyptian universe. For without this resurrection, 'the winds of the sky will be destroyed . . . the sky will be deprived of its stars'.[8]

Despite their frequent impenetrability, their stubborn awkwardness, the verses' sheer energy and anxiety are brilliant foils to the silent architecture of the pyramids themselves, filling those smooth interiors with vivid images of death and dying, and above all with an urgent overwhelming need for cosmic resurrection.

Some verses are shot through with the ageless emotions generated by the physical realities of death, in those moments when that drama is playing out before your eyes and the panoply of culture is dwindling down to the commonality of humankind. There are screams of grief, of mourning from within the royal palace at the passing of a

Fig. 230 He lives – this Unis lives!
          he is not dead, this Unis is not dead;
          he is not gone down, this Unis is not gone down.

Engraved in Tura limestone on the south wall of the burial chamber of King Unis' pyramid; part of Utterance 219 of the Pyramid Texts, where Pharaoh is appearing before the Gods.

king, descriptions of the smell of a rotting corpse, evocations of the flight of the royal spirit. There are records too of rites of death and burial. And there are hundreds of tiny narratives that with enormous energy and extraordinary ingenuity of metaphor aid the progress of the royal spirit to resurrection. Voyages through fields of reeds, on lakes and winding waterways, over the desert and the sown, through night and day and through the seasons of the year. And texts that arm the voyager with instructions upon how to speak to demons and to ferrymen, how to dispose of desert snakes and evil demons, how to prove regality and avoid the stinging scorpion. Heaven is the dead king's destination – a heaven which includes the clouds and the sky and the realms of space in which the heavenly bodies move, a heaven that is the celestial abode of spirits and of gods. Like lightning bolts and grasshoppers, birds and beetles, the pharaohs spring, and jump and plunge and fly to heaven. They flower like lotuses upon the Nile, they climb ladders of wood and rope, they shin up the legs of the gods that hold up the corners of the sky, and they hunt and kill and eat the gods as well.[9] In that they describe different stages of a transition from death to rebirth – as will so many Christian writers and artists – they are a series of physical definitions.

Nor, in all of this, is the pyramid itself forgotten. In several verses, the king appears to offer much the same contract to his pyramid's creators as those contained in the brief inscriptions set up in some of the tombs of Khufu's nobles (see ch. 10 above): 'O all you gods who shall cause this pyramid and this construction of the King to be fair and endure . . . you shall have given to you a boon which the king grants of bread and beer, oxen and fowl, clothing and alabaster; you shall receive your god's offerings, you shall choose for yourselves your choice joints, you shall have your oblations made to you.'[10]

Given egyptology's traditional insistence upon the primacy of text and writing in the development of ancient Egypt,[11] it is hardly surprising that these vivid verses are often used as explanation of the architecture of the pyramids in which they were inscribed.[12] And of course, as the architecture of the later pyramids was derived from the pyramids of Sneferu and Khufu, such explanations are easily extended to the Great Pyramid itself, decorating its architecture with fine verses and filling its interior with casts of gods and priests performing rituals.[13]

Yet as we have already seen, the Great Pyramid and the entire sequence of colossal pyramids of which Khufu's was the climax were designed and built in what was effectively a pre-literary world (pp. 50ff above). There are firm indications too that the initial compilation of the Pyramid Texts took place long after the Great Pyramid's construction.[14]

It is especially telling, for example, that the kings for whom the Pyramid Texts were inscribed are identified on hundreds of occasions with the god Osiris, the ruler of the Underworld,[15] of whom no trace has yet been found before the time of the first-known Pyramid Texts, yet whose role in the afterlife that these texts describe is absolutely critical.[16] As to the date of their creation, the Texts' fastidious conservatism and their extraordinary longevity – the version in King Unis' pyramid was precisely duplicated five centuries afterwards in a private tomb, whilst some of the same verses were still quoted in burials of the Roman Period – suggests they owe their origin to a single point in time.[17] Verses threatening those who would damage the royal pyramid may suggest that this first recension, in common with many other religious compilations, was compiled at a time of cultural pressure.[18] At all events, given the present state of knowledge, the Pyramid Texts can only be considered to be as old as the first-known monument in which they are inscribed; that is, the pyramid of Unis.

There are, however, clear correspondences between the Pyramid Texts and the architecture of the colossal early pyramids. Both, after all, are elaborate and original responses to one of the deepest problems that ancient Egypt would ever face: the crisis of the inevitable yet essentially random circumstance of the royal death. Just as later texts give graphic descriptions of what threatened when the kingship and the offices of state ceased within the land of Egypt – that there was no order, no monuments were built, and people starved[19] – so too the initiation of a new pyramid after the death of a king may be seen as a physical response to that same threat, a literal reaffirmation of royal power and order, an attempt to absorb potential chaos, whilst the long years of construction kept the random event of the royal death in carefully ordered suspense. In that they provided a commentary rather than a solution to the ever-present threat of the death of the king, the building of the colossal early pyramids and the offerings in the pyramid temples may be said to have performed the functions of a myth.[20] A myth whose living literary narrative would only be developed later, within the verses of the Pyramid Texts.

Just as the Great Pyramid's architecture holds a cat's-cradle of geometries in its every turn, so too the Pyramid Texts provide a numbing multiplicity of solutions to the crisis of the royal death. Yet underneath these common traits of elusiveness and complexity, the route, the narrative, which text and tomb hold out for pharaoh is simple and straightforward; the most common exhortation of the Pyramid Texts, that pharaoh should 'rise up!' is laid out in blocks of stone in the climb to Khufu's burial chamber.[21]

Nor do these formal similarities end there. Just as the endless journey of the royal spirit from death to rebirth is a tripartite excursion – from the grave, through resurrection to re-establishment in heaven – so too King Khufu's Pyramid also holds three separate parts within it. This is specific to the Great Pyramid. Whilst a three-roomed scheme was first realised within his father's pyramids,[22] it is only in the Great Pyramid that those three destinations were characterised in such a distinctive way, and although the later smaller pyramids still hold three separate rooms within them, Khufu's Pyramid remains exceptional in that it divides the way to those three chambers in three different corridors set one above the other.

Now the pivotal point of this unique architecture is the Prism Point at the bottom of the Great Pyramid's Ascending Corridor, and this is paralleled, as we have already seen, in many later temples, where their prism points are the crux of their designs as well (ch. 41 above). In these temples, the prism point marks the back wall of the sanctuary from which the god was carried in procession from the darkness out into the land of Egypt.[23] In the Great Pyramid, however, instead of opening outwards from the darkness towards the living land, the prism is reversed: at this juncture in his physical progress to the grave, Khufu was provided with three separate alternatives.

So if the Great Pyramid's interior had been designed to accommodate three different aspects of King Khufu's afterlife, if the architecture of the royal tomb had been geometrically resolved so that its rooms and corridors housed different aspects of the royal destiny, then those three rooms may well have housed the stages of the literary journey that the Pyramid Texts so vigorously describe. Nor are hints of such conjunctions difficult to discover. Rough and unfinished and cut from the living rock, the Subterranean Chamber shares its position with the burial chambers of the earlier pyramids, and indeed with all the earlier burials in the Valley of the Nile. As for the granite burial chamber high up above it, as Djoser's burial chambers in some of their various manifestations appear to have had rows of stars painted on their ceilings, it is clear that such royal burial chambers had been long identified with the sky.[24] In similar fashion, that the unfinished floor of the Queen's Chamber lies roughly halfway between the Pyramid's two grids[25] suggests a median between earth and heaven, a place of transience and disjunction; an aspect of the royal destiny that later on the Pyramid Texts will fill with a host of transitive verbs.

If this were true, of course, the act of building and designing the Great Pyramid not only created the mature Egyptian state in a social and political sense, but outlined a national theology as well, a process that Jan Assmann has described as the 'anteriority of action to sacramental explanation'.[26] And here, and most remarkably, we are on firm ground again. There is an exact contemporary example of just such a transition from abstraction to literary image in the figure of Osiris, god of the Egyptian Underworld. For Osiris, who down through the ages will become the saviour god of all ancient Egyptians, makes his historical debut in the Pyramid Texts on the walls of Unis' pyramid.[27]

This is exceptional. Unlike the other gods of the Egyptian state, who first appear as shadowy figures aiding and accompanying the figure of the king, and only later, over the millennia, are individuated as they gain more titles and temples of their own, Osiris appears suddenly, fully fledged, complete with a family history and elaborate allusions to the well-known stories that the Greeks and Romans would later transform into literary myth. So whilst in the literature the myth of Osiris has watery beginnings like many modern theories of creation, the great green-faced god of the Egyptian Underworld appears to have been a theological invention.[28]

The most fundamental of Osiris' qualities, and the one that inspires the Pyramid Texts' most vivid images, is that of god of the dead. But he is also a god of resurrection. And in this second role he takes on specific attributes that had been developing since earliest times and were born of the observation of phenomena in the Nile Valley. For example, as in the fifth millennium BC when the occupants of the prehistoric village of Merimda Beni Salama sprinkled their dead with grains of wheat, so later in pharaonic history those same seeds were sometimes planted in beds shaped in the form of Osiris and left to sprout in the darkness of a tomb chamber.[29]

In similar fashion, many of the ritual practices described in the Pyramid Texts – mummification and offering, for example – which had been celebrated throughout the Nile Valley before the state of Egypt came into existence were also absorbed into the central story of the god Osiris, in which Horus, his living son, performs a series of actions that provide his dead father with eternal life. Long before Osiris had been born, of course, the altars and the offering rites of the pyramid temples of Djoser, of Sneferu and of Khufu too, whose basalt pavements show them to have been larger and more elaborate than the earlier examples, had been a monumental exemplar of the living king caring for his dead father and thus ensuring his continuing existence.[30] In the Pyramid Texts, therefore, aspects of the dead pharaoh that had been previously accommodated in the plain architecture of the pyramid temple were personified in a family of deities disposed around the central figure of Osiris.

In the absence of any traces of the god himself, the architecture built to accommodate the body and the spirit of King Khufu could be said to be an architectural prefiguration of Osiris and his rites, just as the rites and rituals that may have accompanied King Khufu's progress to the grave would have been derived from those celebrated at far older burials, where their ultimate intention was to suffuse the dead with the abstract forces that had sustained the Nile Valley in ages long before the state of Egypt and certainly Osiris had been born: the rising river, the sprouting grain, the soaring falcon and the rising sun.[31]

Clearly, the implications of the invention of this dying and resurrecting god are immense. Osiris is the original embodiment of a concept so fundamental that if he really is prefigured in the Great Pyramid's interior, then that three-chambered tomb may be considered in Christian terms as the burial in the darkness of the rock-cut tomb followed by that 'triumphant expedition', as a nineteenth-century divine described the journey from death through resurrection to establishment in heaven, a progress mapped in the 'rising up!' through the Subterranean Chamber through the Queen's Chamber to the burial chamber up above.

If then the rigorous geometry of the Great Pyramid's interior played a key role in the differentiation of the destiny of the ancient Egyptian dead, if those three chambers that were set together with such accuracy and clarity had prefigured the three stages of Osiris' everlasting journey, then the physical act of interring Khufu's body into the Great Pyramid's sarcophagus would have quite literally placed him amongst the stars of heaven.[32] Just as theologians require paper and a pen, so the pyramid-makers needed a fine strong platform, chisels, ramps and nation-wide supply lines to build their Pyramid. And like a notch cut in a palm reed, that classic ancient Egyptian way of measuring out the years, they marked a moment in our history, too.

Appendices

Since the implications of the data are great, a higher level analysis is warranted, but the reader is forewarned that none of the numerical data are to be taken literally.

Butzer 1976

. . . we do not have to explain everything in order to explain something.

Lewis-Williams 2002

Appendix 1 A chronology of the Egyptian Old Kingdom

	Regnal years	Length of reign
First Dynasty	2928–2738	
Second Dynasty	2738–2611	
(Khasekhemui	2638–2611	27)
Third Dynasty		
Djoser	2611–2591	20
Sekhemkhet	2591–2584	7
Khaba	2584–2578	6
Nebka	2578–2561	17
Huni	2561–2537	24
Fourth Dynasty		
Sneferu	2537–2491	46
Khufu	2491–2464	27
Djedefre	2464–2455	9
Khafre	2455–2429	26
Nebka II	2429–2422	7
Menkaure	2422–2394	28
Shepseskaf	2394–2389	5
Djedefptah	2389–2387	2
Fifth Dynasty	2387–2237	
(Unis	2257–2237	20)
Sixth Dynasty	2237–2117	

All regnal dates have been calculated from the reign of Khufu using the year 2478 BC ± 5 years, as established in Spence 2000. The relationship of that year to the order of the Great Pyramid's construction, however, has been qualified by my observations in ch. 47 concerning the date of the orientation of its baselines and by my calculations given in Appendix 5, Table 1 below, concerning the length of time that the Great Pyramid took to build.

Other data for this chronology have been derived from Stadelmann 1987, von Beckerath 1997, Dreyer 1998b, Wilkinson 1999, and Kuper and Förster 2003; see further, my comments in the Apparatus, pp. 7–8 above.

Appendix 2 Dimensions, volumes and plans of the great pyramid-building projects of the early Old Kingdom

Reference	Pyramid projects	Base in metres	Height in metres	Volume in m³	Approximate tonnage of finished project
Lauer 1962	**Step Pyramid's final form**	121 × 109	60	263,780.00	574,887.26
Lauer 1962	**Sekhemkhet's Pyramid**	120	60	263,780.00	574,887.26
Lauer 1962	**Khaba's Pyramid**	84	40	175,853.33	383,258.17
Borchardt 1928	**Meidum Pyramid 1 (first scheme)**	100	72	240,000.00	523,060.66
Borchardt 1928	**Meidum Pyramid 2 (enlargement)**	120	82	393,600.00	334,758.82
Dorner 1986	**Bent Pyramid 1 (first scheme)**	156.99	123.43	1,014,012.84	2,209,959.28
Dorner 1998	**Red Pyramid**	219.08	109.54	1,752,495.64	3,819,423.05
Dorner 1986	**Bent Pyramid 2 (second scheme)**	189.43	136	1,626,728.86	3,545,324.49
Dorner 1986	**Bent Pyramid 3 (upper part, as completed)**	123.58	57.56	293,019.09	638,611.49
Borchardt 1928	**Meidum Pyramid 3 (final version)**	144.32	123.43	856,944.14	1,009,821.23
Petrie 1883	**Great Pyramid**	230.35	146.71	2,594,816.96	540,769.93[1]
Valloggia 2003	**Djedefre's Pyramid**	106.20	66.00	248,125.68	540,769.93
Petrie 1883	**Khafre's Pyramid**	215.26	143.87	2,222,161.71	4,843,022.42

Additional data concerning the dimensions and volume of the Great Pyramid

Petrie's mean measurement of the Great Pyramid's baseline was 9068.8 inches (755 feet 8.76 inches), or 230.3475 m.[2] Joseph Dorner's, taken a century later, is 230.336 m.[3] The two measurements, therefore, contain a discrepancy of 0.01152 m, or 0.454 of an inch.

In keeping with my extensive use of dimensions taken from Petrie's internal survey of the Great Pyramid (Petrie 1883), I have also employed Petrie's exact estimations of the Great Pyramid's restored height and baseline lengths for my calculations, these being 146.7104 m x 230.3475 m.

Petrie (1883, pl. ix) shows the Rocky Knoll, an attenuated stump of natural rock on which the Great Pyramid was built,[4] reaching to the height of the first seven of the Pyramid's courses for approximately half the length of its baselines, and continuing upwards for a further two courses for approximately one third of the baselines' length. Total volume of the Rocky Knoll, therefore, may be estimated at around 74,418.70 m³.[5]

[1] In common with the other pyramids in this list, this figure does not take into account the living rock that forms part of the body of the Pyramid (see further above and note 4 below).

[2] Petrie 1883, p. 39.

[3] Dorner 1981.

[4] See p. 314, and fig. 153.

[5] Calculated from Petrie's course sizes (Petrie 1883, pl. viii), this figure represents the sum of 66,034.14 m³, derived from the volume of the first seven courses, and 8,384.56 m³, from the two courses above.

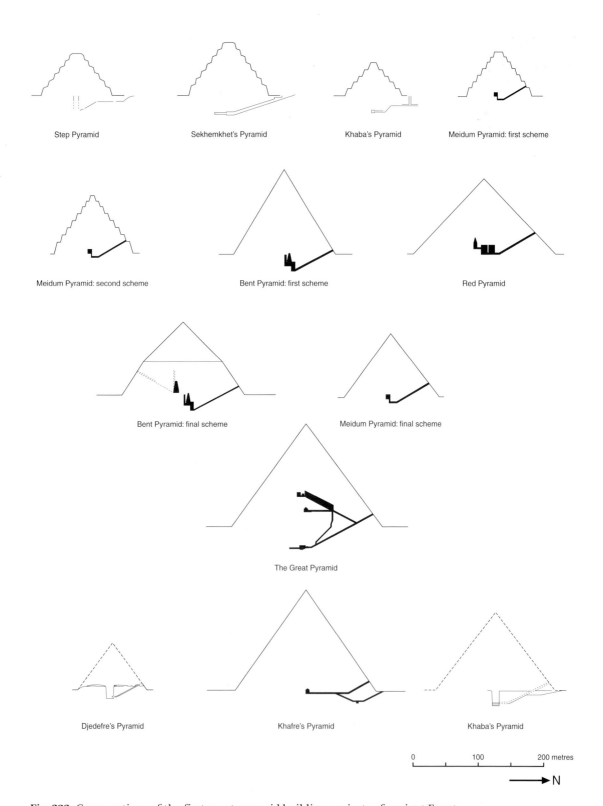

Step Pyramid

Sekhemkhet's Pyramid

Khaba's Pyramid

Meidum Pyramid: first scheme

Meidum Pyramid: second scheme

Bent Pyramid: first scheme

Red Pyramid

Bent Pyramid: final scheme

Meidum Pyramid: final scheme

The Great Pyramid

Djedefre's Pyramid

Khafre's Pyramid

Khaba's Pyramid

0   100   200 metres

N

Fig. 232 Cross sections of the first great pyramid-building projects of ancient Egypt.

Appendix 3 A timeline for Sneferu's major pyramid-building projects

Years BC	Regnal years	Meidum Pyramid	Dahshur Bent Pyramid	Dahshur Red Pyramid
2537				
		Project 1		
2535		begun in year 2?		
		Project 2?		
		completed before		
		move to Dahshur?		
2521	**14**	Move to Dahshur	**Pyramid project 1?**	
			Two Thirds of first project completed?	
				Pyramid begun
2507	**30**			'fifteenth count' (graffito)
		return for project 3?	**Project 2?**	
		?		
	41		**Project 3?**	**10.6 year completion**
		?		
		?	? .	
2491	**46**	'twenty-third count' (graffito)	?	**Sneferu buried?**

Data derived from Appendix 1, Appendix 5 below, and Stadelmann 1987.

Appendix 4 Petrie's spot measurements in the Great
Pyramid's interior compared with the theoretical
positions of the elements of a six-square grid

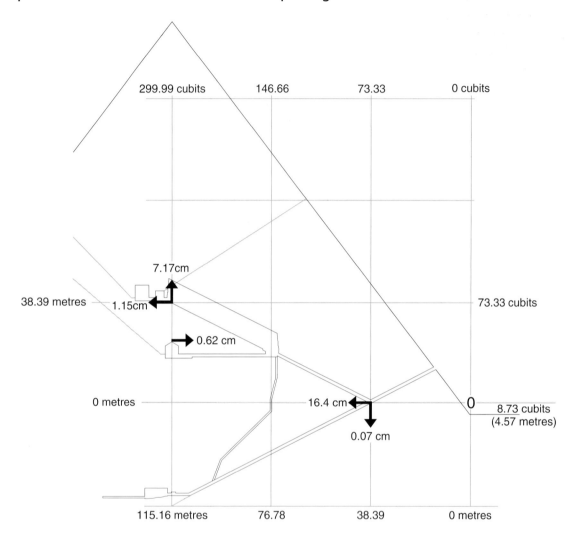

Fig. 233 Graphic concordance between Petrie's spot measurements and the positions of a theoretical grid of 73.33 cubit squares.

The locations chosen for this analysis are (1) the Prism Point, (2) the groin of the Queen's Chamber vault and (3) the top edge of the north face of the Great Step. In Petrie's 'General Summary of the Positions inside the Great Pyramid' (given in fig. 19 above) these locations are identified as (1) 'Beginning Ascending Passage', (2) 'Queen's Chamber mid. W roof' and (3) 'Gallery, top of step face'.

The black arrows indicate the differences between Petrie's spot measurements and the 'ideal grid'. Taken together, the mean error between them is 2 inches, which is similar, in Petrie's estimation, to that between the Pyramid's four baselines (Petrie 1883, p. 39).

Note that this 'ideal grid' is set 8.73 cubits above the Pyramid's baselines (see further fig. 28 above). That the pyramid-makers were aware of this displacement is indicated by the fact that they appear to have accommodated its dimensions in other aspects of the Pyramid's internal plan. The spot measurement named 'End of Ascending passage' in Petries' 'General Summary', for example, shows that the level of the floor of the first section of the corridor that leads to the Queen's Chamber – which is also the level of the portal of the Grand Gallery – is close to the theoretical measurement of half of the size of a theoretical grid square plus half the size of the two grids' displacement.

Appendix 5 A construction schedule for the Great Pyramid of Giza and an estimate of the sizes of the workforce required for its completion

Table 1 *A theoretical construction schedule for the Great Pyramid of Giza based upon that of an earlier pyramid built in the previous reign*

The Red Pyramid's build rates

years	% of volume	volume in m³	years	m³ per annum
0.60	20	350,499.13	1	512,759.14
1.80	40	700,998.26	2	814,382.16
3.50	60	1,051,497.38	3	993,795.86
6.40	80	1,401,996.51	4	1,149,807.76
8.10	90	1,577,246.08	5	1,282,417.89
9.30	95	1,664,870.86	6	1,403,327.11
10.60	100	**1,752,495.64**	7	1,516,435.75
			8	1,599,853.36
			9	1,678,540.00
			10	**1,752,495.64**

The Great Pyramid's build rates

years	% of volume	volume in m³	years	m³ per annum
0.85	20	496,827.03	1	540,496.12
2.55	40	993,654.07	2	830,910.78
4.96	60	1,490,481.10	3	1,067,062.51
9.07	80	1,987,308.14	4	1,292,345.89
11.48	90	2,235,721.65	5	1,477,742.68
13.18	95	2,359,928.41	6	1,639,657.96
14.03	100	**2,484,135.17**	7	1,778,091.73
			8	1,907,078.41
			9	2,026,618.01
			10	2,144,693.87
			11	2,244,917.47
			12	2,328,554.54
			13	2,406,932.79
			14	**2,484,136.24**

The annual volumes of laid stone are calculated on the basis of the percentual build rate established for the Red Pyramid (Krauss 1996). For charts of this common build rate, see figs. 33 and 34 above.

The m³ per annum of the Great Pyramid used in these estimates differs from that given in Appendix 1 in that the volume of natural rock levels at the Giza Plateau and stone brought from other quarries have been taken into account.

Table 2 *Estimation of the annual requirement of the quarry stone used in the Great Pyramid's construction, based upon the m³ totals given in Table 1, expressed as units of 1.1471 m³, which is the size of a 'standard' 2½ ton limestone block; see further pp. 116–18*

year	m³ %	Standard units	Giza	Tura	Aswan
1	21.22%	471,187.10	451,631.87	19,173.65	289.99
2	33.90%	253,174.14	242,490.34	10,302.22	289.99
3	42.96%	205,869.47	197,110.60	8,377.29	289.99
4	52.42%	196,394.79	188,021.47	7,991.74	289.99
5	59.42%	161,622.95	154,664.57	6,576.80	289.99
6	65.80%	141,152.52	135,027.13	5,743.81	289.99
7	71.49%	120,682.10	115,389.70	4,910.82	289.99
8	76.92%	112,446.43	107,489.16	4,575.70	289.99
9	81.55%	104,210.77	99,970.20	4,240.57	
10	86.23%	102,934.73	98,746.09	4,188.64	
11	90.34%	87,371.70	83,816.35	3,555.35	
12	93.76%	72,912.10	69,945.14	2,966.96	
13	96.89%	68,327.64	65,547.24	2,780.40	
14	100.00%	67,303.48	64,564.75	2,738.73	

This theoretical unit has been employed to facilitate the calculation of the annual sizes of the Great Pyramid's workforce; see further below, Table 3 of this Appendix.

The total volume of Aswan granite used within the Great Pyramid has been apportioned equally to the years when that stone was used by the Great Pyramid's constructors; see further ch. 19.

The volumes of Tura limestone have been assessed at 4.1 per cent of the total yearly volumes listed in Table 1 above; see further ch. 20 and p. 183 note 5. However, as Tura limestone was employed in all stages of the Great Pyramid's construction, I have assumed that it was not shipped to Giza at the rate of the Pyramid's construction, but according to the availability of the stone barges; see further, ch. 21 and p. 195, and Table 3 below.

Table 3 An estimation of the size of the workforce required for the construction of the Great Pyramid of Giza (with fig. 234 providing a chart of these same workforce numbers for the full fourteen-year period of the Great Pyramid's construction)

Giza Plateau	Year one	Year eight	Year twelve
Hourly number of 'standard' Giza quarry blocks required to have been set upon the Pyramid each day, assuming a 300-day working year[1]	**150.57**	**35.86**	**23.32**
List of personnel required, working ten-hour days:			
Block haulers in gangs of 20 hauling a block per hour	3,011.49	717.20	466.30
Stone setters in gangs of ten setting a block per hour	1,505.74	358.60	233.15
Ramp builders, estimated at stone setters' rates	1,505.74	358.60	233.15
Quarrymen, estimated at block haulers' rates x 4, cutting a block per hour	12,043.96	2,868.82	1,865.20
Plasterers, tool makers, water carriers etc., estimated at block haulers' rates	3,011.49	717.20	466.30
Giza workforce totals	**21,080.43**	**5,020.43**	**3,264.11**
Workforce x 2 for estimated settlement population living around the Giza Plateau	42,160.86	10,040.87	6,528.21

Tura quarries	Year one	Year eight	Year twelve
Hourly requirement of 'standard' Tura blocks to be quarried and shipped to Giza, assuming a 300-day working year	**6.39**	**1.53**	**0.99**
List of personnel required, working ten-hour days:			
Block haulers in gangs of 20 hauling a block per hour	127.82	30.50	19.78
Quarrymen, estimated at block haulers' rates x 4, cutting a block per hour	511.30	122.02	79.12
Tura workforce totals	**639.12**	**152.52**	**98.90**
Workforce x 2 for estimated settlement population living at the Tura Quarries	1,278.24	305.05	197.80

Aswan quarries	Year one	Year eight	Year twelve
Theoretical hourly work rate expressed in 'standard' units, at 300 working days per year, and ending in year 8 of construction	0.97	0.97	0.00

Table 3 (continued)

Aswan quarries	Year one	Year eight	Year twelve
List of personnel required, working ten-hour days:			
Block haulers in gangs of 20 hauling a unit per hour	1.93	1.93	0.00
Quarrymen, at Giza/Tura rates x 50, cutting a unit per hour	96.66	96.66	0.00
Aswan workforce totals	**98.60**	**98.60**	**0.00**
Workforce x 2 for estimated settlement population at Aswan quarries	197.19	197.19	0.00

Other quarries, supplies, copper mines, etc.	Year one	Year eight	Year twelve
Workforce and transporters at x 2 Tura settlement sizes	1,278.24	610.09	197.80
Quarrymen, plaster makers, woodworkers/rope makers, etc., at the same size as the Tura settlement	639.12	305.05	98.90
Tura/Aswan boat crews, chandlers, fitters	400	400	0.00
×2 for sailors' communities	800	800	0.00
Total workforce sizes	**24,135.51**	**6,129.12**	**4,059.70**
Pyramid-makers' communities	46,992.78	11,953.20	7,921.60

[1] The figures are modelled upon the annual requirements of quarried stone as established in table 2, and the rate of construction as given in table 1. The listed work tasks are discussed throughout the text; especially chs. 11–12, 18–22; the 300-day year on p. 75 note 20; the shipping rates are detailed on pp. 194–5.

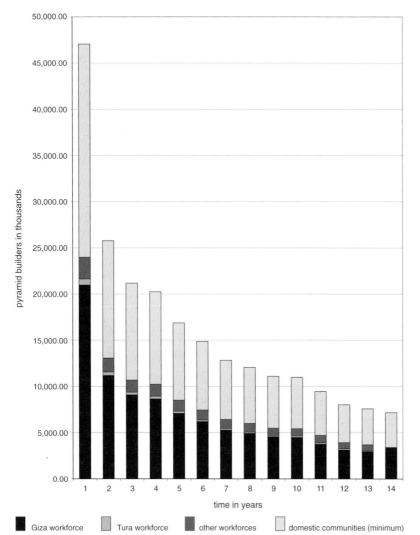

Fig. 234 Chart showing the numbers of people required for the building of the Great Pyramid, based upon the construction rates established for the Red Pyramid.

Notes

Prologue

1 Pound 1938, p. 196.
2 Even indeed to make a fair stab at designing a tomb for a fictional Ramesses XII: Romer (1976) describes the origins of the scheme that underlines New Kingdom royal tomb design.
3 From a *Times* book review (Ray 2003).
4 Literary, that is, as opposed to literate; the first examples of writing in ancient Egypt precede the so-called Pyramid Texts, the first known body of ancient Egyptian literature, by almost a millennium.
5 Recently and most cogently, in the opening chapters of Assmann 2002. For an alternative view, see Trigger 1993, pp. 6ff.
6 Lehner 1997; Stadelmann 1997a; Arnold 1991.
7 Petrie 1883.
8 Petrie 1883 and Dorner 1981 for the later surveys; and see ch. 3, p. 42 below. Note that the second edition of Petrie 1883 (Petrie 1885) lacks some of the data and plans of the first edition and has a greatly attenuated text (see further ch. 2).
9 *EAAP* and Daniel 1975, p. 376. The reference to 'Gombrich' refers to his *Story of Art* (1959), a long-celebrated standard textbook.
10 Lehner 1985b.
11 Baines and Málek 1980.
12 See Jeffreys and Tavares 1994, pp. 154–7 and fig. 15.

13 Von Beckerath 1997, with two minor updates of reign lengths; following recent discoveries in the Western Desert (Kuper and Förster 2003, p. 26, reporting Kuhlmann's preliminary translation) I have extended Khufu's reign by four years; following Lehner's recent review of the step pyramid at Zawiyet el-'Aryan (Lehner 1996; 1997, p. 95), I have also provided the shadowy King Khaba of the Third Dynasty, who appears to have been the likely owner of that large anonymous pyramid, with a six-year reign of his own.

14 Spence 2000.

15 The 46-year reign attributed to Khufu follows Stadelmann (1987), whose arguments, along with those of many others, are reviewed and extended by Krauss (1996). Whilst I have made extensive use of Krauss' clever calculations (see pp. 71ff below), I cannot see that his figure of a 10.6-year construction period for the Red Pyramid greatly affects Stadelmann's earlier argument concerning the length of Sneferu's reign. I have therefore left things as they were in 1987.

16 Briefly: von Beckerath's so-called 'lower' chronology (1997) proposes 2554–2531 BC as the provisional dates of Khufu's reign. Spence's astronomical observations (2000), however, have led her to propose the period of 2480 BC ± 5 years for the alignment of the casing stones of Khufu's Pyramid. See further below, chs. 35 and 49, and Appendix 1.

17 From Allen 1999 and see David's useful outline of this problem on the previous page (David 1999).

18 For further elaboration of Khufu's names see the quotation from Leclant (1999), given on pp. 81–2 below.

19 Baines and Málek 1980.

20 I have changed Petrie's terminology, so that the Ascending Corridor runs from the junction at the Descending Corridor to pass up through the Grand Gallery to the Great Step; 'for the angle of the passage, and its straightness, it will be well to consider it all in one with the gallery floor, as they were gauged together all in one length' (Petrie 1883, pp. 64–5).

21 *LÄ* IV, col. 1021 for 'Pharaoh'. *OED* 'Pharaoh' for an Anglo-Saxon Pharaoh, and for the fourteenth-century 'Pharaones tyme'; *Piers Ploughman* A, viii, 150.

1 Introduction

1 The oldest-known examples of free-standing architecture in Egypt made of blocks of stone are the monuments of Djoser at Sakkara, built around a century before the reign of Khufu. Whilst blocks of bonded stone were indeed used in structures built in the century before King Djoser, most of these appear to have served as wall facings and pit linings (Arnold 1991, p. 174; Wood 1987); nor is it yet clear if the walls of the Gisr el-Mudir enclosure at Sakkara, which may well be older than Djoser's

monuments (Mathieson et al. 1997), were free-standing or indeed if they are properly described as architecture! See further, Part Four below.

2 Bober (1980) provides a rare account of medieval and early modern European attitudes to the Great Pyramid; Romer and Romer (1995, part 7) set these in a broader context.

3 More's *Antidote against Atheism* 1653, i, vii. §5.

4 The Oxford professor was John Greaves, who published his *Pyramidographia*, with a plan of the 'the first and fairest Pyramid', in 1646. Newton is quoted from the Preface of his *Chronology of Ancient Kingdoms Amended* (Iverson 1961, p. 102); White (1997) outlines the scientist's esoteric interests.

5 Hornung (2001, p. 157) attributes this saying, which is quoted by al-Maqrizi (Khitat 1, 121), to Ibn Fadallah al-'Umari (died 1343).

6 Anciently attributed to the god Hermes Trismegistos, these Wisdom Texts are generally thought to date from the first to third centuries after Christ; Hornung (2001, chs. 2–8) provides an overview of the Alexandrian literature.

7 Recent claims (as described in Lawton and Ogilvie-Herald 1999, pp. 94ff) that these texts are fakes are quite unfounded. Painted in chambers sealed by the Great Pyramid's builders, they were rediscovered in the early nineteenth century by explorers who could not read hieroglyphic, whilst the uncertainty of the egyptologist first asked to decipher them (Vyse 1840, pp. 256–85) shows the difficulty of their translation in the early days of the decipherment; they could hardly, therefore, have been forged. Such bureaucratic jottings moreover have since proved to be a typical residue of early pyramid construction, and hundreds more have now been recorded (see, for example, Stadelmann and Sourouzian 1982, pp. 387–93; Posener-Kriéger 1991).

8 Haas 1987, for the C14 dating of Egyptian pyramids; Spence 2000 and below, ch. 40, for the Great Pyramid's stellar orientation.

9 See further Part Two below.

10 Lehner (1997) provides an excellent compendium of these discoveries.

11 Volney 1787, I, p. 278.

12 Assmann 2002, p. 121.

13 Arnold 1991, p. 84.

2 Making the mystery

1 From Moreh 1975.

2 From Starobinski 1964, p. 183.

3 19 September 1798. For this and the following paragraphs: Denon 1802, pp. 61–3 and pl. XVIII, 4, XIX–XX; Wilkinson 1847, p. 173; Beaucour et al. 1990, pp. 149 and 261; Gillispie and Dewachter 1987, pp. 12–13.

4 Sherer 1825, p. 150.

5 Denon 1802, pl. XX, 1.

6 Beaucour et al. (1990) provide a handsome modern reference of these artists' works.

7 'Great thoughts stir within me at the sight of ruins. Everything gradually crumbles and vanishes. Only the world remains. Only time endures. And how old the world is! I am walking between two eternities. Whichever way I turn my eyes, I see objects that have perished – and am reconciled to my own end. What is my own ephemeral existence in comparison with the age of this valley scooped out between the walls of crumbling rock, this quivering forest, or these trembling masses swaying above my head? The very marble of the tombs falls away into dust; and I do not want to die . . . A torrent hurls nations in tangled disarray into the depths of a common abyss, while I, and I alone, have the presumption to halt on the brink and cleave the waters flowing by me!' (from Starobinski 1964, p. 183).

8 This (mistaken!) reconstruction is illustrated in *Description* V, pl. 1.

9 Diodorus Siculus I, 63. Strabo XVIII, 818.

10 The metre was defined by the French Academy of Sciences in 1791 as 1/10,000,000 of the quadrant of the Earth's circumference running from the North Pole on the meridian of Paris to the equator ('Metric System' in *Encyclopaedia Britannica*, 11th edn, 1910).

11 Gillispie and Dewachter 1987, p. 1; Beaucour et al. 1990, pp. 133–5 and 210.

12 Gillispie and Dewachter (1987, pp. 23–9) provide a brief account of the *Description*'s compilation and production.

13 Iverson 1961, pp. 131–2. Jomard's commentaries are in the quarto *Mémoires* that accompanied the *Description*'s folios; his writings on the pyramids, in vol. II, ch. 18 and pp. 163–236.

14 *Description* V, pls. 1, 6–15, 19(4).

15 Quoted by Beaucour et al. 1990, pp. 200–1.

16 Iverson 1961, ch. V, and for the following paragraphs.

17 Starobinski 1964, p. 151. 'Before Gibbon, and after him the "antiquarians", scholars and archaeologists of the eighteenth century questioned the old remains and tried to reconstruct a credible picture of the past. Even Piranesi's imaginative monuments were taken to be systematic accounts; works of the imagination began to appear scientific. When men reached the stage of deciphering the names of the forgotten gods, of unearthing ancient vases, it was the end of the ambiguous poetry of the ruins.'

18 Iverson 1961, ch. IV; Hornung 2001, chs. 2–8.

19 Iverson 1961, pp. 132–3.

20 Hartleben 1909, p. 123. Champollion's sentiments find echo in the tale of an eminent egyptologist of the following century, who, whilst working in a Cairo library on a Sunday afternoon, refused his students' offer of a trip to the Giza Plateau which he had not visited, with the comment that the 'pyramids are published'.

21 Pliny, *Nat. Hist.* xxxvi, 16.

22 Vyse 1840, I, pp. 1–2.

23 The Colonel seems to have put great store in high explosive: 'May 20th. Foremen 9, men 126, children 132; Great Pyramid – excavation in northern front [of Great Pyramid] . . . the wedding of a Sheikh's son took place in an adjoining village . . . I gave them a few piastres, and a pound of English gunpowder': Vyse 1840, I, pp. 266–7.

24 Perring (1839, pl. I) shows that two trenches were cut through the outlying debris towards the Great Pyramid's northern face – one of them towards its centre, the other half way down its eastern half – whilst a third trench was cut in a line towards the centre of the southern face. Perring's illustrations show that at their full extent these dangerous trenches were around 10 feet wide and 40 feet in depth.

25 Vyse 1840, I, pp. 261–2.

26 The first of these chambers had been entered earlier; see p. 397 below.

27 Along with Vyse 1840, an enormous folio of plans published by one of his assistants, 'The Pyramids of Giza from actual survey and admeasurment by J. S. Perring Esq. civil engineer' (Perring 1839), forms the foundations of modern study of the Egyptian Pyramids.

28 Ebers 1887; Hari 1972.

29 Lepsius 1852, pp. 25–6.

30 The colourful folio volumes of Champollion's expedition had appeared under the auspices of a French government ministry, whilst those of his Italian co-director were dedicated to the Grand Duke of Tuscany. Lepsius' *Denkmaeler*, however, is the largest and heaviest of all of these monumental works; Mariette is reported to have said that it required the services of a corporal and four men just to turn its pages (Hari 1972, p. 1).

31 *LD* II, pl. 1.

32 Gliddon 1849, p. xix.

33 Capart (1930, fig. 50) shows the lower sections of Lepsius' text.

34 'The inscription composed in commemoration of the birthday festival of His Majesty has become a stone tablet, after the manner of the ancient steles and proscynemata': Lepsius 1852, pp. 32–3.

35 Reid 2002, ch. 2.

36 Vyse 1840, II, pp. 105–8.

37 Hale (1925) provides a partial account of pyramidal observations made, so it is said, by the pioneering egyptologist Auguste Mariette which are apparently otherwise unpublished: he is reported to have used the Pyramid's shadow to calculate accurately the timing of the Equinox. The 'sun to shade' effect upon the other hand, a trick of light by which, on an appointed day in every year, one face of the Great Pyramid changed from shade to sunlight upon the stroke of noon, appears like the Indian Rope Trick to have been reported often but never actually observed; Isler (2001, p. 133) discounts it entirely. Tompkins (1973) provides a lengthy, if uncritical, digest of many of these theories.

38 Black 1963, pp. 436–7.

39 Tompkins (1973) provides an overly enthusiastic sketch of some of these pyramidological activities; Drower (1985, ch. 2) a more accurate, though much narrower, one.

40 The survey, Smyth recalled, was 'earnestly as well as formally urged upon me by the late John Taylor during the last few months of his useful and laborious Life': Smyth 1867, I, p. vii.

41 Petrie (1883, pp. 3–6) gives Smyth's list 'Of the Practical Work still necessary for the Recovery of the Great Pyramid's ancient, from its modern, dimensions'.

42 Tompkins 1973, ch. VII.

43 This culled from Smyth's first manifesto of his aims: *Our Inheritance at the Great Pyramid* (London, 1864).

3 Surveying Giza

1 Petrie 1883, p. 182.

2 Drower (1985) provides the outlines of Petrie's astonishing career although the flavour of the man is perhaps better conveyed in his own words (Petrie 1933), and, most appreciatively, in Sir Mortimer Wheeler's essay (1966).

3 Drower 1985, pp. 26–7.

4 Wilkinson 1847, p. 172.

5 Drower 1985, p. 31.

6 Petrie 1883, p. 2.

7 Drower 1985, p. 31. Edgar and Edgar (1923, p. 103) record that though 'Ali Gabry's descendants still aided their investigations at the Great Pyramid in 1909, the old man had died in December 1904.

8 Petrie 1933 and Drower 1985.

9 Petrie 1924, p. 59.

10 Petrie 1883, p. 44. This 'cement' is the remnants of the lubricant by which the huge stones were manoeuvred into their positions (Arnold 1991, pp. 291–3).

11 Petrie 1893, p. 14.

12 Petrie 1883, p. 59.

13 The preface to Petrie 1883, observing that the work is 'supplementary to the previous descriptions' recommending both Piazzi Smyth and Vyse. Petrie also employed many of the graphic conventions of his two predecessors in his drawings of the Great Pyramid. It should be noted, however, that though these are commonly redrawn in modern treatments of the Pyramid, in hard reality the shape of many of the Pyramid's physical components – the 'Rocky Knoll' for example (see pp. 313–14 below), and the form of the better part of the granite blocks of which the burial chamber unit is constructed (see ch. 46) – are as yet buried and unknown.

14 *Scientific American* 1976/2, October.

15 Dorner 1981. The presently accepted mean of the Pyramid's four base-lines is 755 feet 8.35 inches (230.336 m); see for example Stadelmann 1997a and Lehner 1997.

16 Smyth's confusion arose, perhaps, because Vyse gives both the measurements between the corner sockets, the 'former base' as he calls it, and the dimensions provided by the casing blocks that he had found, which he calls the 'present base' (Vyse 1840, II, p. 109). At all events, both of Vyse's measurements were inaccurate.

17 Petrie 1883, p. xvi.

18 Badawy 1965, pp. 53–7. The Golden Mean is the point at which a line is divided so that the proportion of its smaller part to the larger is the same as the larger part to the entire line; the Fibonacci series is a sequence of numbers in which each number is the sum of the previous two. These two systems of proportion are related, and both of them also approximate to the value of pi: the ratio of the circumference of a circle to its diameter. The alleged detection of the deliberate use of such proportions in works of art and architecture should be treated with great caution, as some kind of 'almost factor' is almost always a component of the argument.

19 Petrie 1883, p. 183.

20 See further pp. 372ff below.

21 Petrie 1883, p. 74. Chapters 43 and 45 below contain a full description of the Great Step's dimensions and location, and its role in the Pyramid's construction.

22 Drower 1985, p. 46.

23 From a review of Amelia Edwards, quoted by Drower 1985, p. 70.

24 Drower 1985, p. 70.

25 Petrie 1885, p. xi.

26 'Dig Days, The Giza Conspiracy', on Dr Hawass' web site.

27 Petrie 1933, pp. 34–5.

28 Whilst sometimes citing the 1883 edition in their bibliographies, in practice most modern commentators use the abbreviated second edition of 1885, as their citation of the page numbers shows (cf. Lehner 1985b; Verner 2002).

4 Excavating Giza

1 Nothing if not photogenic, the Giza pyramids had long been a favourite subject of early photographers, the French artist Horace Vernet and the Parisian photographer Frédéric Goupil-Fesquet exposing the first plates on the Giza Plateau in 1839, within months of the communication of Daguerre's invention to the French Academy of Sciences (D'Hooghe 2000, pp. 16–17 and pl. p. 39). Ironically enough, whilst that dramatic event had included a specific advertisement of photography's potential use to egyptology, it took the profession some seventy years to utilise it as a

regular aid in excavation, the work of the US expedition at Giza being a notable trailblazer (Der Manuelian 1992).

2 Petrie 1883, p. 30.

3 Der Manuelian 1999, p. 142.

4 Following in the footsteps of the New Kingdom pharaohs who had hunted on the Giza Plateau (Zivie 1976, ch. 4), 'Mena House' was founded by the Khedive Ismaeil in the 1860s. Set a half-mile from the Great Pyramid and surrounded by sparkling desert gardens, the little hunting lodge was transformed into a 'first class English establishment' in the Arab style following the British Invasion of Egypt in 1881 (Ward 1900, pp. 27–8; Reid 2002, p. 73). With its swimming pools, dairies and kitchen gardens, some considered the Mena House to be 'the best hotel in the world'; and certainly it soon became an integral part of almost every enterprise involving the Great Pyramid. Unfortunately, the international hotel that stands on this same site today retains but few parts of the original; the historic wooden veranda was demolished in the 1970s. The old Mena House's long-time function as a magnet of expatriate Cairene social life is, however, brilliantly encapsulated in two sparkling photographs of the 1940s, in D'Hooghe 2000, pp. 82 and 129.

5 Quoted from Der Manuelian (1999, p. 142), who also provides a splendid summary of excavation on the Giza Plateau.

6 Hawass 1999, pp. 156–7.

7 For an account of this remarkable transformation by its instigator and director, see Hawass 2003, ch. 3.

8 *PM* III, Part I provides a detailed listing of the texts and monuments recovered in these excavations. Jánosi (1997) gives a flavour of the Austrian-German expeditions; the splendid Giza Archive Project at the Boston Museum of Fine Arts web site an extraordinary account of the daily work of the US archaeologists.

9 As the half-century of editions and revisions of Edwards (1993) clearly testifies.

10 Borchardt awaits his biographer; see, however, Roemer 1982 and Dawson et al. 1995. Reisner's remarkable career, if not his formidable personal reputation, is outlined by Wilson (1964, ch. 8); see also Thomas 1995, pp. 50ff.

11 Petrie 1883, ch. IV; Saleh 1974, and further ch. 13 below.

12 Petrie 1883, ch. XIX.

13 Reisner (1936) provides a summary of this work.

14 J. H. Cole, the Government Survey of Egypt's main surveyor, found that Petrie's measurements were within an inch of his own measurements (Cole 1925), a process of refinement repeated in the 1970s by Joseph Dorner (Dorner 1981).

15 *Gegen die Zahlenmystic an der grossen Pyramide bei Gise* (Borchardt 1922).

16 It thrives spasmodically, however, amongst architects and designers – most notably, Lauer (1960) and Badawy (1965). These works have virtually

no impact upon the egyptological explication of the Great Pyramid, as a glance through reference volumes by for example Lehner (1997) and Stadelmann (1997a) will confirm.

17 The cultural historian Fritz Saxl has provided an interesting commentary on the rise of this phenomenon in Germany, which he regarded with alarm (Saxl 1957, I, pp. 73–84).

18 Borchardt is said to have rebuked the archaeologist J.-P. Lauer, who had just excavated and surveyed a monument that contradicted one of his dictums of ancient Egyptian design, with the phrase 'Young man, do not try to teach me archaeology!' This tale, which I recall Lauer relating to me in the 1960s, is also recorded by Verner (2002, p. 117).

19 Lepsius wrote upon the accretion theory whilst still in Egypt, though as his translator notes (Lepsius 1852, p. 44) the idea is yet older. Edwards (1993, p. 280) dismisses it entirely; Arnold (1991, p. 159) offers an oblique appraisal.

20 That this theory was taught in Berlin seminars well before Borchardt's extensive archaeological examination of the Great Pyramid is indicated by comments in Breasted's *History*, which was written in the first years of the new century and a decade after his studies in Berlin (Breasted 1907, p. 118).

21 Steindorff 1905, pp. 23ff; Erman 1905, p. 6.

22 '"Do you know who made you?" "Nobody, as I knows on", said the child . . . "I spect I grow'd".' From Harriet Beecher Stowe's *Uncle Tom's Cabin* (New York, 1851).

23 Reisner (1936 and 1942), for example, unhesitatingly follows Borchardt's thesis.

24 For example Baines and Málek 1980, pp. 158–60, Smith/Simpson 1981, p. 98, and Verner 2002, p. 204.

25 'His prestige no doubt gave the movement in search of mystery a powerful impetus which, after a century of theory and counter theory, shows no sign of reaching exhaustion' (Edwards 1993, p. 296).

26 Lehner 1997; Stadelmann 1997a.

27 A functionalist approach exquisitely if unconsciously caricatured by Michel Serres in his Fable of the Termites: 'Consider a colony of termites, whose motion, at first apparently Brownian, will much later appear to be directed toward the construction of a termitarium. It is a gargantuan task compared to the size of these individuals, and quite ordered compared to the disorder of their comings-and-goings. Every termite, or almost every one, is a carrier, let's say, of a ball of clay. It does not bring it anywhere; it positions it somewhere in the space under consideration. This particular space is only the ensemble of balls' (Serres 1981, p. 1).

28 As Arnold (1991, p. 15) has observed.

29 Spence 2004.

30 Lawton and Ogilvie-Herald (1999) provide a gruesome account of some of these shenanigans.

31 Mention should be made here of the pioneering work of Karl Kromer and Hans Goedicke, who investigated various aspects of ancient transport and housing on the Giza Plateau in the 1970s.

32 Hawass 1998, pp. 57–9.

33 Lehner (1997) provides an overview of these developments.

34 See further, ch. 6 below.

35 The seminal publication in the reassessment of the Giza Plateau was Mark Lehner's 1985 essay, 'The Development of the Giza Necropolis: The Khufu Project', this following a wealth of articles upon various aspects of Egyptian pyramids by Dieter Arnold also in *MDAIK* (especially Arnold 1981), which appears to have been the first modern publication to consider aspects of the construction of individual pyramids in their specific environments.

36 For example Schenkel 1963; Kemp 1989; Assmann 2001.

5 The Pyramid's plan

1 Petrie n.d., p. 24.

2 Arnold 1991, p. 15. None of the Great Pyramid's subsequent surveyors (cf. Dorner 1981) have detected major errors in Petrie's external survey of the Pyramid. We may reasonably assume therefore – especially as surveying error was a subject with which he was particularly preoccupied (cf. Petrie 1883, Appendix, pp. 226ff) – that Petrie's interior survey contains similar if not yet smaller errors than his exterior work, which was technically far more demanding.

3 Cf. note above.

4 Tompkins (1973) provides numerous examples of what can be called the 'almost principle' in action.

5 The large-scale drawings of Maragioglio and Rinaldi (*MRA* IV) and the many computer-generated plans that they have for the most part inspired are all based, as some of their authors acknowledge, on the surveys of Petrie and Piazzi Smyth and some of the other pyramidologists.

6 Using the dimensions given above, the area of the Pyramid's base would be 53,051.91 m²; its half base, 26,525.95 m². The theoretical height of this half base above the baseline is therefore 162.87 m. By comparison, Petrie's spot measurements at the Pyramid show that the physical height of the Great Step above the pavement is 162.72 m, a difference between abstraction and the Pyramid's stones of 15 cm!

7 The following description is confirmed by Petrie's spot measurements, given in Appendix 4. The use of grids in ancient Egyptian design is discussed further, pp. 213ff below.

8 Precisely, 14.993 feet; see further, ch. 37 below.

9 The cubit was the unit of measurement most commonly used in ancient Egyptian architecture (Arnold 2003, p. 61). Between early, royal

monuments, as Joseph Dorner has established (1986, 1991, 1998), its physical size could vary by some 2 cm. At the Great Pyramid, a cubit of precisely 0.5235 m may be obtained by dividing the nominal length of its four baselines – 230.33 m – into 440 units (Dorner 1998, pp. 26–7), which in turn produces six-grid squares of 73.33 cubits. Arnold (1991, pp. 10–11) provides an overview of how such units may have been measured out. With the exception of its height and baselines, the use of cubit sizes at the Great Pyramid is limited to the relatively modest dimensions of its three chambers and the width and height of their connecting corridors.

10 The *OED*'s first reference to a 'cross section' is from 1835. In regard to the architecture of Egyptian pyramids, however, their use may easily effect an illusion, for by showing the full extent of their corridor systems – which are usually displaced from the pyramids' central axes – the typical cross-sections given in archaeological textbooks cannot also show them at their full height!

11 Arnold (1991, Part 1) provides a recent overview of ancient Egyptian architectural plans, and surveying and measuring equipment.

6 The Pyramid's timetable

1 Lewis-Williams 2002, p. 8.

2 Rawlinson 1848, pp. 199ff, with minor changes. Herodotus' claim that the Great Pyramid's height was the same as the length of its baselines is not correct.

3 Romer and Romer (1995, Part 7) provide an outline of classical attitudes to the Great Pyramid. They do not, however, examine the vexed relationship of Herodotus – 'that consummate carpenter of tales' (Buxton 1994, p. 10) – and other classical writings on ancient Egypt to modern history writing. Turning traditional egyptological attitudes to such ancient informants upon their head, however, Richard Buxton remarks that 'to get behind literary constructions like . . . Herodotean history . . . is methodologically problematic' (p. 11) and that 'to mark Herodotus out of 10 by confronting him with the real truth . . . is a simplistic procedure which risks many points in, perhaps even the point of, the narrative' (p. 77).

4 For this now-traditional etymology, see for example Rawlinson 1848, II, p. 201 note 7 and Dickerman 1893. The term obelisk, derived from the word for a Greek meat skewer, appears to have an exactly similar role in its Egyptian applications. Such attitudes are also part of our cultural inheritance. Many of the photographs in D'Hooghe 2000, for example, show the same basic shot, the mid-tone of the Great Pyramid juxtaposed with local ephemera: a horse, a stone, a signpost, the debris of the tourist trade; pyramis, pyramis, pyramis; the same old chestnut.

5 Briefly, Old Kingdom Egyptians lived in a Bronze Age – a 'soft tool' –

economy without large-scale slavery; classical society was an Iron Age, 'hard tool' economy in which slavery played an important and ever-increasing role.

6 Von Beckerath (1997), superseded now by Kuper and Förster (2003), who report a text which they date to regnal year 27.

7 For a further explanation of these work rates and the amount of stone required for the Great Pyramid, see pp. 118ff and Appendix 5 below.

8 Stadelmann and Sourouzian 1982; Stadelmann 1983. (Although scholars once doubted that Sneferu should have three such grand pyramids attributed to his reign, the issue now seems resolved; see for example Lehner 1997; Stadelmann 1997a; Verner 2002.)

9 Although Stadelmann states that one at least of these graffiti 'provided us with the date of the placing of the cornerstone'(Stadelmann 1997b, p. 5), could it not be argued that the graffiti might equally well refer to the date of the blocks' quarrying or transportation? The difference, however, would not greatly affect the overall time frame that the graffiti have provided.

10 Assuming that the Great Pyramid was begun shortly after Khufu's accession, even Stadelmann's generous estimation of the building time for the Red Pyramid (Stadelmann 1987) would only allow a maximum of twenty-three years between the foundation of these two great monuments.

11 My assumptions here follow those of Krauss' ingenious extrapolation (Krauss 1996) of the graffiti's data into a building process, specifically his theoretical 'rate of deceleration', as outlined in pp. 49–50. Modification of these figures would not greatly affect my broad historical conclusions: failing fresh evidence, therefore, I recommend the adoption of David Lewis-Williams' maxim given at the beginning of this chapter.

12 Krauss 1996, p. 50.

13 The pyramids of Sekhemkhet (fig. 232 and ch. 28 note 1) and Djedefre (fig. 223, ch. 50), for example; Lehner (1997) provides an overview of several such early and unfinished monuments.

14 The Red Pyramid was a late project in Sneferu's long and profligate building programme that, in total, was a labour larger than the construction of the Great Pyramid itself (see further Part Four below, and Appendix 3).

15 The facts and figures quoted below are derived from Appendix 5. Please note, however, that in the absence of any contemporary documents, these tables contain data derived from a variety of sources, as indicated in the Appendix. They are best regarded, therefore, as a spreadsheet subject to recalculation when better data become available: at this stage, once again, I recommend the adoption of Professor Lewis-Williams' saw.

16 To provide this outline of the various volumes of laid stone that this timetable supplies, I have assumed that the Pyramid was built up layer upon horizontal layer. In reality, however, large parts of the Pyramid were built irregularly; see further, Part Six below. The extraordinary

spurt in height at the beginning of the work is partly explained by the rocky outcrop on which the Great Pyramid's blocks were set. See further, ch. 36 below.

17 Broadly speaking, the most conservative estimates are as follows; in the first year of construction some 11,000 stone cutters would have been working in the Giza quarries, with 2750 hauling these blocks up onto the Great Pyramid where something of the order of 1400 stone setters waited to emplace them. The remaining numbers of my estimate are made up of those engaged in supplying and sustaining this core work-force: plaster and tool makers, water carriers, etc., with a modest dou-bling of these workforce numbers to account for householders, etc., living with the pyramid-builders. See further and for what follows, Appendixes 2 and 5.

18 This paragraph outlines the contents of Part Three below.

19 These figures do not include any other people – support staff, family members, etc. – who may have inhabited the pyramid-makers' settle-ments. Evidence from similar though mostly later settlements has led me to double the numbers of some of the pyramid-makers' settlements; see further Appendix 5.

20 It is unlikely that the intense labour of pyramid making could have been undertaken without the provision of regular rest periods. Records from later periods of Egyptian history show that the ancient Egyptian week was of ten days, of which at least one may have been set aside for rest (*LÄ* I, cols. 1035–6, *LÄ* II, cols. 145–6). The same records also show that many and various festivals and holidays were celebrated; some of the workers who made the royal tombs at Thebes, for example, appear to have been absent from work for at least one third of each and every year! I have assumed that Khufu's men were less fortunate, and that they attended for 300 days each year and, for the sake of calculation, worked a ten-hour day – a workload not uncommon in non-industrial societies where labour is governed by the passage of the sun. Ammar (1954, p. 27) calcu-lates that twentieth-century Egyptian villagers, whose labour, he reports, was similar to the pyramid-makers in that it lacked industrial-style con-formity, worked on average an eight-hour day.

21 That is, if the deliveries of Khufu's stone gangs dropped from ten to five blocks each day – for an elaboration of this overview, see Appendix 5. Utilising data from Butzer (1976, Table 4, p. 83) and given in chart form in fig. 35, there would have been some 1,600,000 people in Egypt at the beginning of Khufu's reign.

22 The adult male population is estimated at one third of the total popula-tion. I am well aware that such a bald statistic begs many questions con-cerning the nature and the sex of pyramid-makers. Given the present lack of data, however, closer estimation seems impractical.

Concerning the numbers of people involved in food production in the time of Sneferu and Khufu, various ingenious estimations have been made and some of them are outlined by Butzer (1976). Both O'Connor (1979) and Katary (1989, p. 72) estimate that around 40 per cent of the professions listed in the Wilbour Papyrus were directly involved in food production, which given the extremely conservative nature of agricultural technology in Egypt and with the exception of the introduction of the shaduf (Butzer 1976, chs. 5 and 7) may well reflect a similar situation in earlier periods. On the other hand, several overviews of the economies of non-industrial towns and cities in agrarian societies (Sjoberg 1960, for example) provide a rule of thumb that requires the labour of around ten agriculturists to support one non-food producer, this figure being dependent upon unmechanised agricultural production and contemporary methods of food preservation, storage and transport (see too Hassan 1993, pp. 560ff). None of these data conflict with my general observations concerning the potentially devastating effect of slow pyramid building upon the Egyptian population.

23 These figures are calculated on the basis of the pyramid-makers' settlement populations, rather than the numbers of the workforce. See further, Appendix 5.

24 Reisner 1932; *LÄ* IV, cols. 302–5 'Naga (Nag')-ed-Dêr' (Edward Brovarski). The contrast is especially great between the huge mastabas of the 'headmen' of Dynasty III and the modest 'headman' tomb N 739, that contained a diorite bowl bearing one of Sneferu's names.

25 From one of the graffiti painted upon a block in the Great Pyramid (cf. p. 29 above), with a translation kindly provided by Hans Goedicke.

7 At the court of the king

1 William Faulkner's lines are quoted from memory, I'm afraid – but who could make them up? 'I like this the least of my films', said Howard Hawks in an interview with Peter Bogdanovich (Cameron 1962, p. 11). 'I don't know how a Pharaoh talks. And Faulkner didn't know either . . . but I really wanted to understand how the Egyptians had built that pyramid.'

2 Petrie 1903, pls. xiii and xiv. Stadelmann (1997a, pl. 38) provides an excellent colour photograph. The statue is probably made of African elephant ivory (cf. Krzyszkowska and Morkot 2000; van Haarlem 2002).

3 Kemp 1989, pp. 77ff.

4 Gardiner 1957, p. 75.

5 Guralnick 1976.

6 *EAAP*, catalogue nos. 21, 34, 57, argues the case for some of these *ci-devant* Khufus.

7 As the on-going process of redating Old Kingdom sculpture has served to reinforce greatly (cf. Arnold and Ziegler 1999).

8 Jan Assmann has characterised this period as 'Ethnogenesis by means of building' (Assmann 2002, p. 53).

9 For Khufu in the quarries, see Anthes 1928, pl. IV; at the mines, Gardiner et al. 1952–5, p. 26.

10 Excerpted from Leclant 1999.

11 Bann 1984, ch. 1.

12 A recent catalogue of Old Kingdom titles (Jones 2000) has more than a thousand pages!

13 These examples were culled from *PM* III, I. Some of their detail has been changed to conform to the style of this book.

14 The *OED*'s earliest use of an astronomical 'companion', in 1782, is given to Sir John Herschel's father.

15 Whether Khufu knew such women by 'direct experience' or simply by 'knowledge-about', to employ William James' distinction is, like most things to do with his reign, utterly unknown. As Lévi-Strauss observes, where 'positive knowledge fell well short of the imagination, it was the task of myth to fill the gap' (Lévi-Strauss 1995, p. xii).

16 Arnold (1985) provides an egyptological commentary upon nineteenth-century European libretti with ancient Egyptian settings; Said (1993, pp. 133ff) an account of *Aida*'s splendid synthesis of Verdian taste and the 'ancient Orient'. The standard contemporary syntheses of egyptological research with historical narrative yet await similarly perceptive analyses.

17 Lepsius 1852, p. 33.

18 Grzymski 1999; previous lines: 'The king was the key element of society . . . Without a king there would be no society to speak of, no state, no order; there would be only chaos.'

8 The adventures of the vizier

1 *OED* quoting Robert Whittinton's *Vulgaria* fol. 14r (1520).

2 *EAAP* (p. 231) shows two fine photographs of the statue's discovery. The impression that it is similar to a portrait in the modern meaning of this word is emphasised by a fragmentary relief from the same tomb bearing an image of Hemiunu's face, for the noses of both statue and relief share the same distinctive profile. Smith 1949, pp. 22–3 and 303–4, and *EAAP*, catalogue no. 44 (Marsha Hill) and 45 (Dorothea Arnold).

3 Translation by James P. Allen, *EAAP*, pp. 229–30.

4 *LÄ* II, col. 1117, 'Hemiunu'; Strudwick 1985, p. 117.

5 Not in informal usage; as for example, the affectionate vernacular ''ullo, ma sun!'

6 Faulkner 1955, pp. 28–9, and *LÄ* VI, cols. 1227ff, 'Wesir'.

7 Cf. *LÄ* I, col. 654, 'Bauleiter'.

8 The *OED*'s further characterisation of an architect as a creative genius in the European manner seems yet more remote from ancient reality; 'No person who is not a great sculptor or painter can be an architect. If he is not a sculptor or painter, he can only be a builder' (Ruskin's architectural

lectures of 1854 (Add. 113) and virtually repeated in the preface to the *Seven Lamps of Architecture*.

9 Assmann 2002, p. 103.

10 *Burke's Peerage* was published annually from 1847, gaining in bulk and in complexity in each edition until the First World War. See also Hobsbawm 1983.

11 Cf. Rouse 1972, p. 139: Cannadine 1983.

12 See for example the excellent maps of Khufu's cemeteries by Der Manuelian (1999, figs. 80 and 83), where Hemiunu's tomb is number 4000. The illusion of an automatic relationship between tomb size and social position may be easily dispelled by a trip around a nineteenth-century Western burial ground.

13 This subject, of course, is vast. For a brief introduction to a great deal of modern thinking upon non-Western modes of thought, and the underly-ing inspiration of a great diversity of later work, see Lévi-Strauss (1966).

14 The implausibility of the notion that the builders of the Great Pyramid were somehow preoccupied with modern economic values is nicely underscored by the fact that the ancient Egyptian language appears to have had no separate verbs for 'buy' and 'sell', only terms for barter and exchange; Peet 1929, p. 275 and Janssen 1975, p. 495.

9 The new Egyptians

1 Roehrig (1999) provides a crisp account of current data and opinion con-cerning this group of sculptures.

2 Millet 1999, p. 233.

3 I owe this attribution to Don Grant.

4 The head from Giza tomb 2110, now in Boston's Museum of Fine Arts (06.1886), appears to have been cut down so that the profile of its nose matches the profile of the reliefs of 'Treasurer Nofer', the owner of the tomb (see Smith 1949, p. 27 (no. 22), and pl. 48d and 48e; and Smith 1960, pp. 36–7). Note too that the lengths of the two sideburns on the statue's head appear to have been changed at the same time as the nose and with the use of a similarly wide flat chisel.

5 Cf. Smith 1949, pp. 23–8, and Assmann 1996, p. 60. (The mask of Assmann's fig. 8 is part of a plaster encasement, now in the Boston Museum no. 39.828, that probably covered the entire corpse.)

6 The first question was posed by Lorenz Hart in 1937, the last by George Andrew Reisner (1915, pp. 32–5); the one in the middle, following Smith (1949), by a variety of art historians.

7 Leek (1980 and 1986), though it may not be prudent now to concur with Leek's more sanguine observations on the social status enjoyed by the original proprietors of all of the Vienna skulls.

8 Assmann (1996) enjoins us to view such sculptures as creations of their patrons rather than the stone masons.

9 The similarities shared by Hemiunu's images in sculpture and relief (see ch. 8, note 2, above) are not common. Smith (1949, p. 301) lists and discusses the discrepancies between figures shown in portrait and relief, observations now partly re-emphasised by Christiane Ziegler (1999, p. 242).

10 This intense concern with physical appearance became a preoccupation of much later Egyptian sculpture: plaster casts of human faces apparently taken from subjects both alive and dead have survived from all periods of ancient Egyptian history; Tacke (1996) presents a remarkable corpus of Old Kingdom examples.

10 The social contract

1 From *The Social Contract* II, ch. 4.

2 Der Manuelian (1998, fig. 2) locates the known positions of Slab Stelae and the find spots of the Reserve Heads in Khufu's northern cemeteries.

3 For archaic examples of this same common pose, see for example, Smith/Simpson (1981, figs. 33–4, 36, 56, 80). Der Manuelian (1998) provides a thoroughgoing description and overview of the Slab Stelae and their various interpretations.

4 *PM* III, Part I, index II, p. 391, 'Slab Stela', and Der Manuelian 1998, pp. 122–3.

5 Convenient pictorial reference for these stelae and their original locations can be found in *EAAP*, catalogue nos. 51–3 (Christiane Ziegler) and fig. 47, p. 76, along with the basic references: see also Smith 1949, pp. 159–61.

6 There are examples of similar offering scenes from all the first three dynasties, see for example Smith/Simpson 1981, figs. 21, 31, 32 and 47.

7 Franke (2003) provides a recent overview of this egyptological perennial. Following Gardiner's remarks concerning the evolution of this formula, (Gardiner 1915, pp. 79–93, esp. p. 81), I have adopted his archaising 'boon' to the more commonly employed 'offering' on the basis that during the reign of Khufu the pharaonic gift was not exclusively composed of food and drink.

8 Kemp (1989, p. 136) characterises this workforce as inhabiting a proto-welfare state 'as yet innocent of social ideology'.

9 Assmann (2001, pp. 152ff) inadvertently provides a wider range of religious possibility for the earlier phases of Egyptian history. Eliade (1964, p. 374, n. 116) sketches the basis for a study of African shamanism that, unlike much later work in the same vein, is not restricted to hunter-gatherer communities. Málek (1997, pp. 90–5) offers a splendid antidote to common though misplaced assumptions concerning our present state of knowledge about archaic Memphis and its 'White Walls'.

10 See further, Part Five below, from p. 310.

11 Hawass (1997, fig. 1) shows the path of the causeway through the modern town; Lehner (1985a, pp. 118–20, B6 and B7) provides a bibliographic

discussion before the discoveries of 1990. See ch. 43 below for a discussion of the timetable of this causeway's construction.

12 Arnold (1997) and Stadelmann (1997a) propose two recent though very different readings of the function and accommodations of this temple, traditionally called a 'mortuary temple'; see also ch. 48 below.

13 Hassan (1960, fig. 13) where the causeway underpass is indicated as lying 300 yards (185 m) from the eastern baseline of the Great Pyramid.

11 Working the stone

1 From E. P. Wright's translation. (Nummulites are fossils found in Tertiary strata.)

2 Lehner 1985a, pp. 119–2 (B10).

3 Stadelmann (1980, p. 438) estimates the amounts of building stone used during the Fourth Dynasty; Lehner (1985a, pp. 121–2 (B1–B13 and fig. 3B)) describes the Giza quarry and the quantities of stone removed.

4 With the possible exception of Sneferu's Red Pyramid at Dahshur, all the royal funerary monuments from Dynasty 0 to the ending of the Old Kingdom have pits or trenches excavated underneath their architecture. On the order of working at the Great Pyramid, see further Part Five below.

5 This reconstruction presupposes that Khufu's architects began this excavation at a point in the bedrock of the Plateau that would later be covered by the Great Pyramid, a procedure that would require careful planning, and this in fact is my contention in Part Five below.

6 Petrie 1883, pp. 58ff.

7 Petrie (1883, pp. 58 and 39) records an error of -3.44 inches ± 10 for the Descending Corridor's axis and -3.43 inches ± 12 for the Pyramid's baselines. (Quoting Dorner (1981), Spence (2000) gives -2.8 inches for the eastern baseline, -3.4 inches for the western.)

8 These fossils, which are also known as 'Pharaoh's pence' and 'Pharaoh's beans', are a genus of primeval shellfish, *Nummulites gizehensis*. For an excellent introduction to the geology and topography of the Giza Plateau and their relationship to its monuments, see Lehner (1985a, pp. 112–17).

9 *LÄ* III, cols. 301–3, 'Kalkstein', where Claude Traunecker hails it as the Egyptian stone *'de luxe'*.

10 Aston et al. 2000, figs. 2.1 and 2.2, and pp. 40–2.

11 In the 1970s, I watched two men excavate a garage in the cliffs of Thebes in a single day of working. I also visited working limestone quarries in the north-west of Thebes on many separate occasions where, in those last years before modernisation, the technology employed was similar to that of the Greco-Roman period: the rock struck with iron chisels or alternatively simply levered from the fissured cliff with crow bars. Unlike the carefully excavated blocks of ancient quarrymen, the product of these labours, generally small irregular chunks of rock, was tractored from the

quarries to be used for the most part in the foundations of domestic architecture.

12 This process was endlessly repeated down through the dynasties in the tombs and quarries of ancient Egypt and is well documented: Arnold (1991, pp. 27–36) provides an overview; Owen and Kemp (1994) a microcosm, albeit of New Kingdom material.

13 Cf. Černý 1973, pp. 101–3.

14 Arnold (1991, fig. 2.5 upper) shows just such a 'stairway' in an open quarry; fig. 2.1 shows the visual appearance of this method of extraction when the work is finished.

15 Lehner 1997, pl. pp. 111–12.

16 For a useful selection of Fourth Dynasty chisel types (models?), see D'Amicone (1988, pl. 91), who shows four 'flats' and two 'points'. (Although the date of the tomb in which these chisels were found is sometimes given as being of either the Fourth or the Fifth Dynasty, Professor Roccati has kindly informed me that he considers the unpublished hieratic inscription from the tomb – this, barely visible in D'Amicone (1994, p. 71 pl. bottom right) – to have been written during the middle to late Fourth Dynasty.) Arnold (1991, pp. 257–9) provides an overview of ancient Egyptian chisel types. This, however, includes a variety of implements – engravers and mortises, for example – that were used for purposes other than the shaping and setting of limestone blocks. (The apparent scarcity of Egyptian chisels in museum collections should not be considered as evidence that they were not widely used as is sometimes implied; nor should that assumption lead to the unwarranted conclusion that stone picks were commonly used for working soft rock such as limestone; see further below pp. 110–11.)

17 These comments upon the use of 'points' and 'flats' are generalised and not invariable; as with most craft-based activities, one should allow for a wide spectrum of techniques and individual preference.

18 Donadoni Roveri and Tiradritti (1998, pl. 274) show a rare example from the era of the early pyramids (see note 16 above for this attribution). Fischer (1988, p. 44, U22) provides a common alternative shape to the 'balloon-headed' variety, with an Old Kingdom exemplar from the Tomb of Ty (PM III, Part II, p. 476 (46, I–II)), as does Arnold (1991, fig. 6.19).

The balloon-headed mallet pictured by Arnold (1991, pl. 6.18) is similar in form to those still used in English academic sculpture studios for hard-wood carving. There are differences, however, between the ancient and modern examples. Unlike the ancient ones which all appear to be made from a single piece of cedar(?) wood, the modern variety is made in two separate pieces and two different woods, the balloon head fitted upon its circular central handle where it is held in place with a wooden wedge, in the manner of a modern hammer head. With wear, modern mallets obtain a circular groove identical to those seen in both ancient mallet types, this being produced by the contact with the chisel's head upon repeated impact as Arnold (1991, pp. 264–5) surmises, the practised sculptor being habituated to shifting the circular-handled mallet in his hand after every blow so that it wears evenly and its overall balance is maintained – the deeply abraded example shown by Donadoni Roveri and Tiradritti (1998, pl. 274) is at the end of its working life; the groove, however, would have allowed a fine level of control over the angle of the strike. Both balance and control would have been entirely lost if Arnold's suggestion that such abraded grooves had accommodated a metal band should prove correct.

19 For example, Anderson (1999, pp. 118–19); Winlock (1955, Model J) offers a unique vision of a Middle Kingdom carpenter's shop with many of these same tools in active use.

20 Arnold 1991, pp. 257–67.

21 See for example Ziegler 1999, pp. 280ff.

22 Ogden 2000, pp. 148ff; and further, Part Three below.

23 Such was not the case just a century ago. My grandfather recalled that in the years before the First World War every one of the masons engaged in cutting a slot for a previously forgotten damp course into the Aberdeen granite foundations of Sir John Burnet's extension to the British Museum required several chisel sharpeners working full time at their grindstones to keep them actively employed.

24 Forbes (1950, pp. 323ff) comments that copper hardened by cold hammering 'brings a Brinell hardness from 87 to 134, that is more than is achieved by the alloying with the normal 10 per cent of tin to make bronze and it approaches the hardness of mild steel'. Ogden (2000, pp. 152–3) notes that the alloying of a small percentage of arsenic with copper provides a 'far greater hardness' and certain benefits of ductibility as well, but he also observes that it is naturally present in many copper ores and can find no evidence of its deliberate employment.

25 As Arnold (1991, p. 33) has observed (although his observation upon the chisels shown in his fig. 6.10 appears unjustified, for such chisels could certainly have been used as 'points' as the slight pattern of their wear suggests). Other chisels in his list, moreover, such as Cairo 68754 (shown in the excellent plate of Drioton (1949, pl. 21), and fig. 72), do have fairly pronounced points.

26 See for example Arnold (1991, p. 257 fig. 6.10, the right-hand chisel), and Pendlebury (1951, pl. lxxix, 3.30) where, judging by the pattern of their wear, two flat chisels have been used in the manner of a point – a technique preferred by many Italian masons to this day (cf. Giusti and Godoli 1997, pl. on p. 307).

27 Noted at Giza by Hawass and Lehner (1992), and from personal observation, in chippings from tomb quarrying in the Valley of the Kings, many of which often carry the same distinctive mark, a smear of copper at their 'bulb of percussion', i.e. at the point of the strike. Clearly the quar-

rying of such stones, which typically weigh up to 10 lb or so, would rapidly waste the most substantial copper chisels.

28 Cf. Petrie 1901, p. 13; Arnold 1991, pp. 258–64.

29 Vachala and Sroboda (1989) describe the large quantities of flint recovered from the Fifth Dynasty freestone workshops beside the pyramids of Abusir. By comparison, the size of the flint workshop excavated at Dahshur (Eger 1994), the site of one of the pyramid-makers' last projects before the move to Giza, would suggest that this material was not a major component in the manufacture of King Sneferu's pyramids, and this is borne out by the relative scarcity of flint around the pyramids themselves.

30 Eger (1994) describes some of the hammer stones collected around the Red Pyramid.

31 Such pounders may still be seen trapped between the limestone blocks of Menkaure's Pyramid Temple.

32 Arnold (1991, fig. 6.14) shows a surviving Middle Kingdom example of just such a tool; from earlier periods only the stone hammer heads survive. The springy handle of this tool – and similar ones are pictured in several Old Kingdom tombs – would greatly increase the tool's efficiency, allowing a regular rhythm of work in a manner similar to that of a blacksmith hammering upon an anvil. Judging by the surviving marks of their use, masons became extremely skilful in such techniques.

33 Egyptological epigraphers are frequently faced with this type of stone bruising where secondary random fracturing of limestone inscriptions has been employed by their would-be erasers to devastating effect; see for example Epigraphic Survey 1980, pls. 18–19.

12 The Giza quarry

1 Mawe's *Minerals of Derbyshire* (1802), p. 207.

2 Lucas/Harris (1962, pp. 53–4) has a basic discussion of Giza's quarries and the Great Pyramid's limestone, though petrographic identification of any of the quarries that supplied the Great Pyramid's stone is still lacking; see Aston et al. (2000, p. 69) for an overview of this ongoing process.

3 Hume 1925, pp. 88ff, pls. XLI and LXIV; Aston et al. 2000, pp. 40ff.

4 Isler 2001, pp. 223ff; Hume 1925, pp. 11–28.

5 *PM* III, Part I, pp. 230 ff, 'Central Field'. Reisner (1942, p. 12) recognised the general area as that of the 'Cheops-Chephren Quarry'; similarly, his descriptions (1931, pp. 67–70) of quarrying in this same area are the foundations of later observations on these activities.

6 *PM* III, Part I, pp. 230ff, 'Central Field'; for example LG 86, 'Nebemakhet'; LG 88, 'Per[sonet]'; LG 89, 'Sekhemkare'.

7 Lehner (1985a, fig. 3B, nos. 9 and 24, and fig. 2), where the northernmost part of the quarry is indicated as 'FILL' behind the Sphinx. It should be

noticed, however, that this part of the quarry has not yet been dated with the same degree of certitude as the so-called 'Central Field'.

8 Lehner (1985a, pp. 128ff and fig. 3C, no. 16) presents compelling topographic evidence that the site of this quarry lies at the centre of the only practical route available for hauling blocks of stone onto the Pyramid. See further Part Five below.

9 These comments describe the most exposed sections of the quarry to the west, which are those shown in *PM III*, Part I, plans xx–xxiii; in plan xx the lines of the tombs' façades follow the west face of the quarry.

10 Some of these hard-stone spheres are still in place beneath some of the massive foundation blocks of King Khafre's Giza temples where they appear to have been employed in the manner of loose ball bearings; it would not therefore be surprising if this seemingly unlikely technique was also employed at the Great Pyramid. See also Arnold 1991, pp. 270–80.

11 Eloquently described by Lehner (1997, pp. 206–7).

12 Petrie 1883, p. 210.

13 Arnold (1991, pp. 58–66) provides an overview of ancient Egyptian techniques of stone moving.

14 Roth (1991) has collected and discussed the available data on the organisation of the so-called 'phyles' in ancient Egypt – the structures on which the workforces that built the Egyptian pyramids appear to have been based. Whilst early Fourth Dynasty material is thin compared with later periods, the fact that Roth has traced the existence of these phyles back to the First Dynasty suggests that such work groups may have been in operation during Khufu's reign as well.

15 Whilst the day registers of the craftsmen working upon the royal tombs of Thebes can hardly serve as explanation of the practices of their most distant ancestors, the seemingly erratic behaviour of many of these later royal tomb-makers – see for, example, Botti and Peet (1928) – serves to remind us that ancient Egypt was never an industrial society.

16 See Appendix 5. We have no proof, of course, that the stone at the centre of the pyramid is cut into blocks of this same size; see, however, pp. 365ff below.

17 See Appendix 5.

13 Fire and the Pyramid

1 Petrie 1883, p. 102.

2 Saleh 1974. Kemp (1989, pp. 134–5) and Saleh (1996) provide further discussions of this same material.

3 Kemp 1989, pp. 134–5.

4 These comments and those of the following paragraphs are based upon a wealth of comparative material derived from both archaeological and pictorial sources. For a basic bibliography of ancient Egyptian domestic

architecture see *LÄ* II, cols. 1055–61, 'Haus'; for the proposal that some similarly sized structures recently excavated at Giza may have served as dormitories, see the opening paragraphs of Lehner 1991–2002 for 2001-2, and section 'Gallery III-4'; for a thoughtful review of a broad range of ancient Egypt's utilitarian architecture, see Kemp 1989, especially chs. 4, 5 and 7.

5 Ziermann (2003, III) provides a digest of just such adaptations in Old Kingdom civil architecture.

6 Kemp 1989, pp. 134–5; Ziermann 2003, pp. 88ff.

7 Wetterstrom 1993, pp. 210ff.

8 Murray 2000, p. 505.

9 From the published plans and personal observation, it seems likely that these four lines of plinths were originally contained within two long halls about the same size as the five warehouses to the north. Samuel (2000, pp. 537–8) lists scenes of bread production in Egyptian tombs and provides an extensive comparison with archaeological realities.

10 Saleh 1974, p. 145.

11 To my knowledge, there are no parallels for such a large mill in ancient Egypt although they are not uncommon in other near-contemporary Middle Eastern cultures such as that of Ebla, for example (Matthiae et al. 1995, pp. 107 and 173); for a recent overview of this material, see Curtis 2001, pp. 199–203. Tomb models such as those of Mekhet-ra's, however, those animated systems diagrams, show ancient Egyptian women using quern stones placed close together side by side in just this way, and Winlock remarks (1955, p. 28, and see Kemp 1989, p. 120 fig. 42) upon the distinctive mud colour of the models' plinths which are of the same material as the Giza plinths; this seems also to have been the usual material of Egyptian quern installations, as the recent researches at Tell el-Amarna have underlined (Samuel 2000, p. 562, 22.12).

12 Kemp 1994, pp. 146–7, though given the apparent absence of bread moulds at the Giza kilns, my estimate may fall well short of the ancient reality. (Note that though this estimate is based upon evidence gathered from later sites, the outlines of the technologies employed at large-scale ancient Egyptian bakeries do not appear to have undergone radical change, as Kemp (1994, p. 148) and Samuel (2000, pp. 539–42 and 565–9) underline.

13 Using later examples as a model, it might also be suggested that the product of only one of these two grinding halls was for the use of bakers; the other may have been destined for the related technology of brewing, as for example the model from the tomb of Mekhet-ra suggests (Winlock 1955, pp. 25ff; Kemp 1989, p. 120 fig. 42). What appears to be a large quantity of brewing or storage jars, moreover, is pictured under excavation, by Saleh (1974 pl. 33 a–b), and they appear to have been uncovered a short distance from the rows of plinths.

14 For ceramics, see for example Bourriau et al. 2000, pp. 122–4, fig. 5.2; for metals, Ogden 2000, pp. 149–55.

15 Kemp 1978, pp. 7–12.

16 For a glimpse of these tiny workshops, see Arnold and Bourriau 1993, pp. 66–74.

17 Ancient Egyptian arrangements for drying freshly made pottery are not much considered in the literature; these plinths, however, resemble similar structures used by Egyptian village potters to this day. See Arnold and Bourriau 1993, p. 84 for an overview, and p. 67 fig. 80C for an example of a modern drying bench.

18 Hope 1993, p. 121 (Type 1). My comparison has been made from personal observation at the site; one of these kilns, however, is pictured by Saleh (1974, pl. 30a), and see this volume fig. 73, p. 167. In its section, at least one of these now-ruined kilns strongly resembles 'Holthoer's Type I or II', as discussed by Arnold and Bourriau (1993, pp. 107–10).

19 Emery 1963. After inspecting the newly published plans of these three Nubian ovens, some scholars claimed that they had not been furnaces at all, but kilns (Shinnie in Adams 1977, pp. 170–3 and n. 20; Arnold and Bourriau 1993, p. 109). A re-examination of some slag found beside these ovens proved that, just as their excavator had described, they had been used as furnaces for smelting copper ore (El Gayar and Jones 1989).

20 Rothenberg 1990, pp. 9ff.

21 Rothenberg 1990, p. 14. There is a world-wide variety of recipes for dishes cooked at potters' kilns. At Impruneta, close to Florence, the *fornacini* on night watch made *peposo*, a stew of beef, garlic and black peppercorns slow-cooked beside the doorway of the kiln; the same dish, so it is told, that had been hauled up along with bricks still hot from their firing, to Brunelleschi as he worked upon the dome of Florence Cathedral.

22 Bourriau et al. 2000, p. 127; Ogden 2000, pp. 151–5.

23 Forbes (1950, p. 323) notes that hammer-hardened copper requires constant maintenance by annealing and rehammering, a process that eventually causes embrittlement, which then requires the chisels to be recast.

24 Data upon utilitarian ancient Egyptian casting moulds is sparse: for a recent general overview of copper working see Ogden (2000, pp. 155–60).

25 Ogden 2000, pp. 148ff.

26 Emery 1963, facing p. 118.

27 Rothenberg 1990, p. 78 fig. 107, and see ch. 18 below.

28 Saleh 1974, p. 146. The excavator of the splendid Dahshur ovens has speculated that they may have been employed as furnaces for copper smelting; see Stadelmann 1983, p. 228 and figs. 2 and 3.

29 Faltings (1989, p. 152) reports the discovery of pieces of pure charcoal beside one of the Dahshur kilns, the use of which in desert conditions would offer considerable advantages over heavier and less efficient wood. She also speculates upon the use of the Dahshur ovens for cooking food,

though a lack of excavated bread moulds leads her to deny their use as a bakery.

30 Petrie 1883, p. 102. Following excavations in the 1980s, at least parts of this unit are considered to have comprised specialised royal workshops. Apart from Conard (2000), who discusses the flint artefacts, the results of these new excavations are not published; see Hawass 1996a, pp. 54–5 and Lehner 1997, pp. 238–9 for the excavators' overviews.

31 Murray 2000, p. 512.

14 Entrepôt and accommodation

1 See Lehner 1991–2002 for 2000–1, 'Environmental history of site', which outlines the results of Karl Butzer's fieldwork.

2 Lehner 1985a, p. 133 (C18) and Hawass 1997, pp. 245–8, although the exact location of this first harbour yet remains uncertain.

3 *LÄ* II, cols. 926–8, 'Hafen' (Wolfgang Schenkel).

4 The pharaoh known as 'Scorpion': Millet 1990/91, fig 2.

5 Engelbach (1938) provides a vivid anthropological reconstruction of the process of canal digging; in his account, the basket man worked beside the digger lifting basket loads of excavated earth up onto the backs of a line of basket carriers.

6 As far as Western perceptions were concerned, the classic oriental *levée en masse* was that employed during the first years of excavation of the Suez Canal, which annually engaged some 20,000 workers who suffered an annual death rate of around 1.75 per cent. Before the nineteenth century, however, and the Viceroyalty of Mohammed Ali, the Egyptian corvée had been largely localised and concerned with the self-help of local populations. For a vivid account of this shameful development, see Willcocks and Craig 1913, ch. XV.

7 Goyon 1977 and Lehner 1985a, pp. 137–9 (C28 and C29) and pp. 122–3 (B17 and B18).

8 These speculations owe their origins to Lehner's acute remarks (1985a, pp. 137ff).

9 Jeffreys and Tavares 1994, pp. 155–7 and fig. 15, for the Nile's drift; Jones 1995, pp. 88–92, for the extent of Nile silt lying on the valley plain at a site a little to the north of Giza.

10 Butzer 1976, chs. 5 and 6.

11 See further p. 139.

12 Butzer 1976, ch. 3.

13 Butzer's estimates of Egypt's total population in 2500 BC are 1,040,000 living in the Nile Valley, 9000 in the Faiyum, 540,000 in the Delta, and 25,000 in the deserts (Butzer 1976, p. 84, table 4, and ch. 7), and see pp. 75–6. In Khufu's day, Butzer estimates that cultivated land had a population density of 130 people per square hectare – much higher than it had ever been before in Egypt.

14 Zivie 1976, chs. 4 and 5.

15 Lehner 1991–2002 for 1991–2, 'Probing the Wall of Crow . . .' and 2000–1, 'Inside the Great Gate'.

16 As a relief map of the Giza Plateau will confirm; and see Lehner 1991–2002 for 2000–1, fig. 1, and section 'Environmental history of site', outlining the results of Karl Butzer's geophysical survey.

17 Kemp (1989, ch. 4) provides a convenient overview of the other 'pyramid towns'. See Lehner (1991–2002) for the annual reports of the ongoing Giza excavations, with section 2001–2, fig. 1, presently providing the most up-to-date site plan.

18 Curtis 2001, p. 122 for bread and beer; Lehner 1991–2002 for 2000–1, 'East end of Wall of Crow' and following, for the sculptors' workshops.

19 Lehner 1991–2002 for 2001–2, 'Conclusions'.

20 *EAAP*, pp. 386–95 (Marsha Hill) provides an overview of these 'servant statuettes'.

21 *LÄ* VI, cols. 773– 7, 'Trunkenheit' (Helmut Brunner), and Lehner 1997, p. 225.

22 Samuel 2000, pp. 537ff.

23 Hawass 1996a, pp. 62ff.

24 Lehner 1991–2002 for 2000–1, 'Under granite dust' and 'Environmental history of site', and Hawass 1996a, pp. 59–62.

25 Arnold 1991, pp. 60–1 (Menkaure) and *PM* III, Part I, p. 20, 'Mortuary Temple (Khafre)'; Stadelmann (1981) and Goyon (1977) would also date this great stone wall to the reign of Khafre.

26 See ch. 12 above

27 Lehner 1991–2002 for 2000–1, 'WCE Deep Probe'; Kemp (1989, chs. 2 and 4) provides valuable discussions of such formalising processes; for a splendid later parallel at Deir el Medina, see Bonnet and Valbelle 1975.

28 Stadelmann 1997a, fig. 23.

29 Butzer 1976, ch. 7.

30 For this paragraph see Jones 1995 and Hawass 1996a, pp. 56–9.

31 Kromer 1978; and see Butzer 1982 and Hawass 1996a, p. 56, for brief accounts of current opinion regarding these interesting excavations.

32 Five sealings bearing Khufu's name, thirty-eight with Khafre's; Kromer 1978, pp. 90–3.

33 Petrie 1883, p. 213 and Lehner 1985a, p. 124 (B24), p. 121 (B 10).

15 The living city

1 *LÄ* V, cols. 9–14, 'Pyramidenstadt' (Rainer Stadelmann); for Lehner's reconstruction of Khufu's Giza, Lehner 1985a, pp. 139–40 (C31). Both share the belief that Khufu had a main residence at Giza, beside his rising pyramid.

2 Hawass 1996a, pp. 56–9.

3 Please note that my estimation of the sizes of the pyramid-makers'

various communities, which has been achieved by the simple expedient of doubling the numbers of pyramid-builders working within the Nile Valley, is not intended to imply any specific kind of domestic arrangements, but merely to provide a bare minimum estimation of the number of people which Khufu's state would have been obliged to support.

4 See fig. 35 above.

5 Assmann 2002, p. 51.

6 The state's provincial organisation in this period, as discussed by Seidlmayer (1996), is outlined on p. 250 below.

7 Petrie 1883, pp. 209–10.

8 Butzer 1976, pp. 45–6.

9 Reisner and Smith (1955) provide a remarkable glimpse of the beauteous accoutrements of courtly life in the time of Khufu; *EAAP*, Catalogue nos. 31–3, a taste of a few of these same objects in modern photographs.

10 Smith (1949, pls. 31–6) shows a variety of noble costumes and accoutrements as worn: *EAAP*, catalogue nos. 17, 18, 23, etc., modern photographs of similar images.

11 An observation recently underlined in a specifically Egyptian context by the discovery of Tomb U–j at Abydos (Dreyer et al. 1998).

12 Taking a broader view than der Manuelian (1998); and see ch. 10 above and ch. 24 below.

13 The subject of the final paragraphs of this chapter is enormous; my generalisations are sweeping. Of the tomb inscriptions, Jones (2000) provides a recent bibliography; Franke (2003) an overview. Of their putative sociology, Sjoberg (1960) introduced much of the vocabulary of this discussion; Trigger (1993) provides some updated and alternative viewpoints.

14 Speculatively, could this circumstance have found reflection in the later literature's Good King Sneferu? (Gunn 1926, pp. 250–1; Wildung 1969, pp. 104–52.)

16 Coda: thinking with stone

1 Known as the 'Tomba degli Ignoti', this vault was opened and cleared by Virginio Rosa, the assistant of Ernesto Schiaparelli, in 1911. Presently, the best accounts of the excavation and the finds are by D'Amicone (1988 and 1994).

2 D'Amicone 1988, pls. 76, 79–81; 1994, pls. 16–18.

3 D'Amicone 1988, pls. 88, 92.

4 D'Amicone 1988, pl. 93, upper.

5 For example *PM* V, p. 26 (Nag el-Deir), p. 36 (El-Raqaqna), p. 39 (El-Mahasna).

6 *LÄ* II, cols. 483–501, 'Gefäße' (Dorothea Arnold). For a recent overview of this subject see Arnold and Pischikova 1999; for the early exploitation of desert amethysts and porphyries, see Aston et al. 2000, pp. 48–52.

7 Lauer 1962, pl. XI, and further pp. 238ff below. Although the age of Sneferu and Khufu saw a decline in the variety of shapes and the types of stone used to make these vases, a genuine fascination with the exuberance of antique vases yet remained inside the court, hundreds of fragments of these so-called 'antiques' having been excavated from the pyramid temples of the Giza Plateau (Arnold and Pischikova 1999, pp. 121–5).

8 Gardiner 1961, pp. 97–9.

9 Although Kozloff et al. (1992, pp. 138ff) were unconvinced by the geological analysis of Klemm et al. (1984) and largely concurred with the traditional argument outlined by Stadelmann (1984) that the stone of both statues had come from the northern quarry, the geologists' attribution seems to have been widely accepted by their peers; see for example Aston et al. 2000, pp. 53 and 69.

10 Arnold 1991, p. 60.

11 These reliefs are presently unpublished; Stadelmann and Sourouzian (2001), however, report an ongoing photogrammetric survey of both statues. Lange and Hirmer (1967, pl. 163) show the south side of the southern colossus in good light.

12 Schäfer (1974, pp. 155–6) outlines the history of the so-called 'sema-towy' device and provides other references to this neglected subject. The drawing of Khufu enthroned is given by Anthes (1928), and reproduced by Smith (1949, p. 145 fig. 54, where on p. 36 other Old Kingdom examples of this same motif are discussed).

13 See note 9 above.

14 Camden's *Remembrances*, 1634, p. 146.

15 Roth (1993a, p. 33) provides an inadvertent overview of some of these proposals in relation to the Old Kingdom pyramids.

17 Prospecting Egypt

1 As an indication of the scale of previous desert activity, Mallory-Greenough (2002) provides an analysis of prehistoric and early dynastic basalt vase production and an estimate of that industry's size, whilst Aston et al. (2000, pp. 60–2) and Harrell (2004) indicate the modest extent of some of these earlier forays into desert quarrying.

2 Aston et al. 2000, pp. 21–2.

3 This stone, which is a form of calcium sulphate, is similar to the greyish-white alabaster that medieval sculptors mined in the English Midlands and used for funerary effigies and religious sculptures. It should not, however, be confused with the more common so-called 'Egyptian' alabaster, a water-deposited carbonate of lime which was specifically employed throughout ancient Egyptian history for objects connected with purification and death (Lucas/Harris 1962, pp. 59–61; *LÄ* I, cols.129–30, 'alabaster').

4 This is the so-called Dahshur Road, a cleared desert strip some 60 feet
   (23 m) in width and 12 miles long (Aston et al. 2000, p. 19). Although its
   origins are uncertain, its route makes it an ideal supply line for the
   desert materials used in many pyramids of differing ages and other royal
   building works as well. De Morgan (1897a, pls. 5 and 6) shows its present
   ending at the Mastabat Phara'on in South Sakkara; Arnold (1981,
   pp. 15–17 and fig. 1 A and B) shows what appears to be an earlier ending
   of the same road at Dahshur and C and D, possible routes from this road
   down to Sneferu's old harbours.

5 This is the ancient ancestor of the modern lake known as the Birket
   Qarun. Bloxam and Storemyr (2002, p. 29) provide an overview of the literature upon this quarry road; Hoffmeier (1993, p. 120) suggests that the
   northern 'Dahshur Road' once joined it.

6 Caton-Thompson and Gardner 1934, p. 134, and Ginter et al. 1980, p. 136.

7 Whilst the last archaeological survey at Qasr el-Sagha (Ginter et al. 1980,
   pp. 107ff) casts doubt upon the age of a lake-side quay that had previously been identified as being in use during the Old Kingdom, the
   random scattering of Old Kingdom ceramics throughout the area and
   the fact that large quantities of quarried basalt certainly were transported along this celebrated Fourth Dynasty desert road during Khufu's
   reign (Bloxam and Storemyr 2002) shows that the necessary port facilities of that period were located somewhere close by.

8 Lucas/Harris 1962, pp. 74–79 and p. 469–72; this remains the best
   account of the Great Pyramid's plaster and mortar mixes.

9 The walls of the so-called 'Relieving Chambers' for example, above the
   Great Pyramid's burial chamber, are streaked with this lubricating
   plaster. These streaks, however, are hardly visible in published photographs; Lehner's illustration (1997, p. 51 left) shows faint evidence of
   one of these fine veils of plaster upon a chamber wall.

10 Kemp (1989, p. 247, fig. 83) provides a useful summation of our present
   knowledge of these quarries.

11 Arnold (1991, pp. 268–9) provides an overview of this subject; Teeter
   (1987) discusses the processes of rope making as they appear in scenes in
   later private tombs. For evocative photographs of hauling ropes that date
   from Khufu's times and which were buried beside the Great Pyramid, see
   Nour et al. 1960, pls. LXIII and LXIV; pls. XIXff show their modern successors at work.

12 Section V of Gardiner's sign list (1957, pp. 521ff) shows a wide variety of
   ropes and knots and usages.

13 LÄ III, cols. 610–26, 'Königsring' (Peter Kaplony); Gardiner 1957, pp. 73–4;
   Seidlmayer 1996, pp. 120–1.

14 Arnold 1991, pp. 258–64.

15 Some hard-stone pounders may be seen still supporting some of the
   foundation blocks of the northern sections of the temple adjacent to the
   pyramid of Menkaure.

16 Anthes 1928, pl. IV, *PM* IV, pp. 237–9 and Aston et al. 2000, pp. 59–60, where we are invited to replace the egyptologists' traditional usage of the term 'Egyptian alabaster' with 'travertine', an equally traditional term of classical scholarship employed to describe the celebrated product of some quarries outside Rome. Etymologically, as the *OED* informs us, alabaster is 'said to be from the name of a town in Egypt' and 'Travertine' 'of the [river] Tiber'. Whilst petrologically the equivalence may be appropriate, in truth Roman travertine and Hat-nub alabaster are as chalk and cheese. This usurpation, I would suggest, denies the first purpose of naming things, one of the tasks of which, as Petrie specified in relationship to stone, was to distinguish one from another by 'obvious appearances' (Petrie 1901, p. 43).

17 Saleh (1974, p. 131) records the excavation of a substantial deposit of unworked blocks of Egyptian alabaster in a Giza settlement, most of them in a similar condition to those that modern quarrymen deliver to Upper Egyptian alabaster workshops today.

18 Reisner and Smith 1955.

19 Aston et al. 2000, p. 19. If some of the Third Dynasty sarcophagi that have been identified as Egyptian alabaster prove to have been quarried in the vicinity of Hat-nub, however, this quarry track may well predate the reign of Khufu.

20 Aston et al. 2000, pp. 32–3; Shaw 2000 and 2003.

21 *PM* VII, p. 275.

22 Engelbach (1938, pls. lv and lvi) records that the full extent of this remote site took years to establish; see also Shaw 2000, p. 29.

23 Seidlmayer (1996, p. 120), however, prefers 'The fishing net of king Kheops'.

24 This stone formerly known as 'diorite', or more precisely 'Chephren diorite' after a celebrated statue of that king, is now labelled (Aston et al. 2000, pp. 33–5) under the geologically accurate though less specific designation of 'diorite – or gabbro – gneiss'.

25 'All these pieces [of "diorite"] . . . seem exactly as if some small construction, or object, in diorite, had been smashed up in one spot; but there are no foundations or traces of a building on the bare rock, for hundreds of feet on either side of it. The site of these fragments is exactly opposite the entrance to the Great Pyramid' (Petrie 1883, pp. 136–7).

26 In later dynasties, some of the royal stone boats that had to pass through this natural barrier were known as 'August' barges (Breasted 1906, 105 and 326 n.); that is, they were intended to ride upon the Nile's flood during the first month of the annual inundation.

27 Bloxam and Storemyr 2002, fig. 1.

28 Bloxam and Storemyr 2002, table 2. Hawass (1997, pp. 248–51) provides a sense of the scale of these as yet unexcavated building works.

29 Bloxam and Storemyr (2002) provide an overview of my description of this quarry and its stone.

30 Figures extrapolated from Hume (1925, pp. 14–24).

18 Desert copper

1 Bloxam and Storemyr 2002, p. 35.

2 Arnold 1991, pp. 266–7.

3 Moores (1991) provides the fundamental data upon Khufu's basalt saw.

4 The details of this find spot are recalled from the text and photograph of an old Cairo Museum label written apparently by Reginald Engelbach, the first archaeologist to visit and describe the Gebel el-Asr quarries. See also Engelbach 1938.

Arnold (1991, table 6.1) shows the Gebel el-Asr chisel, designated as the 'Abusimbel' chisel, and accepts the Khufu dating. In comments upon the chisel's inscriptions, however, Sourouzian (in Stadelmann and Sourouzian 1982, p. 390) suggests the possibility of a dating in the reign of Sneferu. Yet diorite gneiss does not appear to have been much used in Sneferu's time and it seems unlikely that such well-equipped stone workers would have visited these quarries during his reign.

5 Drioton 1949, pl. 21.

6 Roth 1991, pp. 120–1.

7 Following Lucas/Harris (1962, p. 208), Ogden (2000, p. 151) notes evidence that the importation of foreign copper into Egypt first appears in the Eighteenth Dynasty, some thirteen centuries after the reign of Khufu.

8 And see p. 110 above.

9 See, for example, Peter Green's discussion of the technological conservatism of Hellenistic culture (1990, ch. 27).

10 Gardiner 1957, Sign List, U 23 'chisel'.

11 Valbelle 1985, pp. 71–2; Wente 1990, 312 (LRL 50) and 314 (LRL 16).

12 Ogden 2000, pp. 149–61.

13 Rothenberg (1990) provides a detailed account of the archaeology of ancient smelting sites and reconstructions of the technology employed; Petrie (1906, pp. 51 ff) has a description of some of the Sinai mining settlements.

14 Ramesses II, for example, called the 'Great' not one imagines in deference to his military record but on account of his numerous, widespread, impressive monuments.

15 Appendix 1.

16 Lucas/Harris 1962, pp. 206–8, and Lucas 1927, pp. 166–7, where he notes that the Sinai production figure only represents the period now estimated to have been between 3000 and 1800 BC.

17 Engelbach 1938, pl. LIX. Though Arnold's table (1991, pp. 238–9) shows the Gebel el-Asr tool to be one of the largest of the type, this would appear to reflect the extent of these chisels' usage rather than their original size. Note too that for stone working at the scale of pyramid making, practical considerations alone discount the use of the smaller thinner chisel types listed in Arnold's table.

18 I have not included other copper building implements and chisel types in this broadest of calculations, and my estimate of five chisels per annum, which is based upon later records such as Valbelle (1985, pp. 71–2), is somewhat arbitrary. The estimate of the numbers of copper chisels used in Khufu's reign was derived by assuming that at any one time, 90 per cent of the quarrymen were using heavy copper chisels like that found on the Gebel el-Asr, as were 40 per cent – four members – of each stone setting gang and an equal percentage of workers in the ancillary trades. This provides a ratio of copper to cut stone at the Great Pyramid of 1 to 190,000; a ratio which admittedly is crude and probably rather generous. Yet halving the total numbers of these chisels would not in itself affect the main thrust of my argument: that an exceptionally high percentage of the total amount of ancient Egyptian copper production was employed in the construction of the early pyramids.

19 See further ch. 48 below, for an account of the pyramid-makers' timetable.

20 Ziegler (1999, pp. 58–63) observes that limestone – and hence the use of copper chisels – first came into use for private statuary as late as the reign of Sneferu.

21 Ziegler 1999, pp. 63ff.

22 See ch. 11 above.

23 The apparent reservations expressed in Lucas/Harris (1962, pp. 202–3) concerning the Wadi Maghara's ancient exploitation for copper mining – which for the greater part were based on lexigraphic confusions rather than the clear archaeological evidence presented by Lucas (1927) – should surely now be laid to rest: see, for example, Stos-Gale et al. 1995, pp. 127–8 and Ogden 2000, p. 149, with Aston et al. 2000, pp. 62–3. (Note too, that as Wilkinson (1999, p. 97) indicates, the mining of the Wadi Maghara on a substantial scale began at the same time as the adoption of stone architecture in Egypt.)

24 Gardiner et al. 1952–5.

25 The colour and texture of the Wadi Maghara's stone is well described in the plate of Schulz and Seidel (1998, p. 40), which shows one of King Sneferu's stelae.

26 Petrie 1906, ch. V, and C. T. Currelly's account of their removal in ch. XVII.

27 Petrie (1906, pls. 40–55) shows the surviving reliefs *in situ*, before their removal to the Cairo Museum.

28 Swan Hall (1986) provides an overview of the 'Pharaoh Smiting' pose, though her study may now be extended by the recent discoveries at Abydos. My quotation is from the vivid account of Palmer (1871, p. 196).

29 Swan Hall 1986, p. 9.

30 Palmer 1871, p. 205.

31 Appendix 5.

32 Forbes 1950, p. 334.

33 Aston et al. 2000, pp. 62–3.

34 Petrie 1906, pp. 38ff and 48ff.

35 For a careful account of early smelting practices and the excavation of ancient furnaces in the northern Sinai, see Rothenberg 1990.

36 Extract from Graeme Barker's paper 'Coping with Desertification' delivered at the World Archaeology Congress, 2000: 'One of the most exciting results of our project is geochemical evidence from sediments sampled near Tell Wadi Faynan and Khirbet Faynan [some 80 miles north of ancient Egyptian copper mines at Timna] and analyzed by EDMA (Energy Dispersive X-ray Micro-Analysis) that appears to record changing levels of heavy-metal pollution in the atmosphere caused by the copper smelting. The initial results suggest that this pollution was small-scale in the Chalcolithic and the Early Bronze Age, significantly greater in iron age and Nabatean times, and enormous (lethal in terms of modern pollution criteria) in Roman/Byzantine times, with further smaller impacts later.' This is perhaps the first-known example of toxic industrial pollution in human history.

37 Lucas/Harris 1962, p. 210.

38 *LÄ* V, cols. 866–70, 'Serabit el Chadim' (Raphael Giveon).

39 The following sentences are based upon Ventura (1985, pp. 281-2).

19 Aswan granite

1 This site has been investigated by the German Archaeological Institute since the 1970s. For an overview of these excavations and earlier work at Elephantine, see Kaiser et al. 1999; for the early settlement of the island, Ziermann 2003.

2 Aston et al. 2000, pp. 35ff; Dreyer et al. 1998, pp. 141–5.

3 'Elephant Land' being in turn a translation of the ancient Egyptian name (*LÄ* I, col. 1217) (Labib Habashi).

4 Engelbach 1922, pp. 11–13, still the most informative account.

5 Estimates of the speed of cut with granite pounders vary according to their individual size and shape; two examples of many such: Engelbach (1922, p. 13) reported that, reworking an ancient cutting at Aswan, he was able 'after an hour's hard work' to cut one tenth of an inch (5 mm), and found his effort to be well within the range of ancient records that describe the cutting of a granite obelisk: Lehner (1997, p. 207), working at 'the grimmest of the pyramid builders' tasks', took five hours to pound down a 12 inch square by four fifths of an inch (2 cm).

6 The use of emery is explicitly denied by Lucas/Harris (1962, pp. 42–3), though specifically included in the ancient repertoire by others without further comment; see for example, Aston et al. 2000, p. 65.

7 A précis of these techniques obtained from material dated a half-century after the Great Pyramid was made, for Khufu's reign offers few surviving examples of unfinished sculptures: *EAAP* catalogue no. 73 shows the earlier parts of the process and *EAAP*, figs. 36 and 37 the later stages of smoothing and polishing. *EAAP*, catalogue no. 54, the well-known head of Khufu's son King Djedefre, shows how skilful combinations of these techniques allowed the slightest touch of a copper chisel at the very ending of the work to control the precise aspect of the face.

8 Aston et al. 2000, fig. 2.3; Baines and Málek 1980, p. 72.

9 Engelbach 1922, pp. 13–15.

10 Petrie 1883, p. 64.

11 Reisner (1931, p. 71) asserts that the granite at Giza was 'not quarried in the modern way, nor in the manner of the obelisks of the New Kingdom, but was taken directly from the piled masses of boulders at Aswan in which the blocks lay already separated by internal splitting and weathering'. Bloxam and Storemyr (2002, p. 35) describe the mechanics of these natural processes.

12 *PM* V, p. 43.

13 Arnold 1991, p. 60, table 3.1.

14 A rule of thumb estimate obtained in discussion with modern quarrymen at Tura and Aswan.

15 This corresponds closely to independently produced figures concerning the rate and practices of working in such hard-stone quarries. See Bloxam and Storemyr (2002, pp. 28–9) on the work routines of the basalt quarries of the Widan el-Faras and Engelbach (1922, pp. 13–15), who calculates the size of quarry gangs at Aswan quarries for a later age than that of Khufu. Employing the same work patterns as Engelbach describes – that is with rows of workmen pounding side by side along the edges of the blocks required, forty-man gangs pounding out the two long sides of a 55 ton block could easily be accommodated within the workloads I have calculated. Allied to the fact that Khufu's quarrymen also extracted smaller blocks of stone and worked in locations closer to the river than the later quarry gangs (see previous paragraphs), my estimates of gang numbers err on the side of generosity.

16 Broadly estimated at seventy-five blocks for the burial chamber, fifty-six for the entresols above, and four for the plugging blocks, etc.

17 See Appendix 3.

18 These figures are estimations based upon the maximum length of time available; that is, with the work schedules established in ch. 6 above, the granite corridors and chambers were in place by the eighth year of the Great Pyramid's construction. If the numbers of quarriers at Aswan were higher, of course, this work could have been finished in a shorter time frame.

19 Appendix 5, which also quantifies the numbers of the barges and sailors required to carry the quarry blocks to Giza.

20 As well as several granite sarcophagi in the Giza cemeteries dating from the time of Khufu, odd blocks bearing Khufu's names have also been found at several Delta sites (see for example, *PM* IV, p. 28, 45).

21 Lauer 1962, pl. vii, and pl. xx: table des plans, pls. xii and xx.

20 Tura limestone

1 Whilst no scientific tests have yet proved that the Great Pyramid's fine limestone is from Tura (Aston et al. 2000, p. 40), the assumption, which has a long scholarly history (see for example Lauer 1962, p. 241; Lucas/Harris 1962, p. 54; Lehner 1997, p. 207), is founded in the Greek tradition and ultimately upon the occurrence of the quarry's ancient name in large numbers of hieroglyphic texts (*LÄ* VI, cols. 807–9, nn. 10–12). It should be noted also that the term 'Tura' is taken here to include the adjacent quarries of Ma'sara which have a similar quality of stone. These, however, presently appear to have been opened later in Egyptian history (*LÄ* III, col. 1196).

2 The 'Meidum bowl' being a good example of this; see for example Hendrickx et al. 2002.

3 Petrie, 1883, p. 44.

4 See p. 44 above.

5 Lehner (1997, p. 207) estimates that some 67,390 m³ – that is, some 46,000 tons of Tura limestone – were needed to sheath the Great Pyramid, to which an extra 50 per cent may be added to account for extensive stone trimming and substantial additional architectural requirements. This figure represents 4.1 per cent of the Pyramid's total volume.

6 Appendix 5.

7 Although written two centuries after Khufu's time, a single letter replete with references to Tura's work gangs, the stone barges and some officials of their administration provides a unique glimpse of the established community of royal quarrymen at Tura; Cairo Papyrus 49623; *LÄ* IV, col. 716, C4. Appendix 5 also indicates the heavy workloads involved in shipping the Tura blocks to Giza.

8 The *OED*'s equation of 'Tura' with a Tougra, an Imperial Ottoman seal, must be rejected as the origin of the quarry's modern name, which appears to be a corruption of the ancient Egyptian (*LÄ* VI, cols. 807–9).

9 Baedeker's *Egypt*, 1929, p. 180. Page May (1901) has a useful near-contemporary map of south Tura and its surroundings, surveyed by Georg Schweinfurth.

10 *PM* IV, p. 74.

11 Charlton 1978.

12 Lucas/Harris (1962, p. 135) describes these enormous ropes as having a careful and elaborate technology of three separate strands, each one of which had forty yarns of seven separate fibres.

13 I have observed both diagonal and herring bone patterns of cutting at random locations throughout the Tura quarries, these latter, it is now generally accepted (Aston et al. 2000, p. 7), deriving from the New Kingdom period or later.

21 The river

1 Bass 1972, Introduction.

2 Vinson's observations about freight charges on Nile cargo boats during Ramesside and Greco-Roman times (1998, pp. 65–6) – the earliest such records that exist – underline a general truth of non-motorised river traffic that, as Vinson puts it, 'the longer the trip was, the lower was the cargo unit cost per unit of distance', i.e. the greatest effort/cost was in loading and unloading the cargo.

3 As Manfred Bietak once observed (1979), archaeologists have yet to locate an ancient Egyptian metropolis. Nothing within the Nile Valley has yet been uncovered that resembles a 'town' or 'city' in the modern sense at all, the character of those ancient Egyptian settlements that have been investigated being best characterised, perhaps, either as state-supported purpose-built housing systems or as strings of self-sustaining villages, or as conurbations of the two. For a useful overview of the 'town problem', see O'Connor 1993.

4 Pyramid Text Utterance 325; Faulkner 1969, pp. 104–5.

5 *PM* III, p. 14 ('Thrust-relieving chambers').

6 Appendix 2.

7 *LÄ* VI, col. 1107 and Valbelle (1985, pp. 197–8), for example, record the details of stone-gathering expeditions to Wadi Hammamat in the reign of Ramesses IV that appear to have engaged the royal tomb-makers of the day in a variety of roles.

8 Calmed now by the High Dam, the changing patterns of silty islands in the Nile have been variously chronicled from the Abbott Papyrus to Robert Bruce's Journals and the Napoleonic survey.

9 See pp. 82–3 above.

10 Lehner 1997, p. 225; Roth 1991.

11 Černý 1973, p. 99.

12 Vinson 1998, pp. 84ff.

13 *LÄ* IV, col. 1044; Černý 1973, pp. 99–103.

14 Winkler (1938, pls. xxxiii–xli) provides an overview of images of complex prehistoric river craft in Egypt – the earliest of which appear to date from early Nagada II – and shows their essential bilateral symmetry under a single organising principle.

15 *LÄ* IV, col. 1044, 'Phyle'.

16 A glance at most of Hornung's figures (1999), underlines the universality and longevity of the image of a voyage on a crewed ship in the literature of the ancient Egyptian afterlife.

17 This of course is another Methuselian metaphor; 'Full ahead with skipper Ted!' as the novelist John Wain once exhorted those reluctant to re-elect Prime Minister Edward Heath. Whilst the bipartition of the Egyptian government is first attested some 250 years after the reign of Khufu, in the reign of Pepi II (*LÄ* VI, cols. 1227–35, 'Visir' (Eva Martin-Pardey)), it follows a fundamental element of life in the ancient Egyptian state, echoing, so Assmann (2002, p. 46) observes, 'remnants of the semantic system of the Archaic period, when the boat was the most important instrument of rule'.

18 The rediscovery and rebuilding of this beautiful boat is described by Nour et al. (1960) and Lipke (1984).

19 Appendix 5.

20 These scenes are listed by Aston et al. (2000, p. 18).

21 Arnold 1991, p. 60.

22 These apportionments are based upon the data given by Arnold (1991, pp. 58ff).

23 Calculations of the draft and size required show that the accommodation of the largest of these cargoes would have required a 230 foot barge with a beam of 80 feet (70 m × 24 m), a figure gleaned from Cheryl Ward's painstaking examination of the surviving evidence (2000, p. 128), from which a great part of the information contained in the following paragraphs has been derived.

24 Gale et al. 2000, pp. 367–8.

25 Arnold 1991, pp. 85–90.

26 The best-preserved and best-studied of these ships' timbers are those found during recent excavations at the Pyramid of Senwosret I, 1965–1911 BC; see Ward 2000, ch. X.

27 Ward 2000, fig. 70.

28 Similar techniques of lashing were also used on early land-bound structures such as beds and coffins – see for example D'Amicone 1988, pls. 76 and 96, and Ward 2000, pp. 32ff.

29 Ward 2000, p. 30.

30 Ward 2000, pp. 15–24.

31 Meiggs 1982, chs. 2 and 3.

32 Arnold 1991, pp. 234–5, and see further below.

33 Hartung 2001, pp. 313–16; Dreyer et al. 1998, pp. 141–5; Dreyer 1998a, pp. 4–7, and pp. 189–92 (Feindt and Fischer).

34 Meiggs (1982) provides a thoughtful account of the cedar forests of Syria and Lebanon. A unique scene at Karnak Temple shows the armies of King Seti I engaged in logging in the Lebanon (Epigraphic Survey 1968, pl. 10), whilst a later document (*LÄ* VI, cols. 1215–18, 'Wenamun') tells of the adventures of an Egyptian priest sent to the Lebanon to obtain wood for the shrines of the Theban gods. The potential effect of this trade on the ancient Egyptians elicited this typical musing from Fernand Braudel: 'Timber forced a breach in Egypt's economic isolation, and through this

breach, many other things would flood in. A comparable example is northern China, another zone of muddy terrain, as barren as the moon, and obliged to look to the south or far south for timber' (Braudel 2001, p. 74).

35 Ward 2000, p. 43.

36 *PM* V, p. 190.

37 Breasted 1906 I § 146–8.

38 See further pp. 395–6 below.

39 *PM* VII, pp. 386–91.

40 Of the five boat-shaped pits clustered around the Great Pyramid, three are empty, one has been cleared of its contents which after twenty years of study have been reassembled into a splendid boat, whilst the last pit is still filled with the dismantled elements of another river craft, and yet awaits its archaeologists and conservators (Ward 2000, pp. 61–8).

41 Landström (1970) provides clever reconstructions of several of these boats, though with some much-debated detail.

42 See Appendix 5.

43 Appendix 5 provides an explanation of these estimates. Naturally, the use of bigger boats, such as are pictured in the reliefs of later ages, would affect the numbers of journeys that were required, though not the total tonnage that they had to carry.

44 Adapting the remarks of Arnold (1987, pp. 73ff and 1991, pp. 59ff), I have estimated that the 110 ton barge would have operated with a crew of 150 who, on occasion, would have to tow the loaded barge with cables from the bank. By similar estimation, the smaller transports capable of holding eight or nine 2½ ton Tura blocks would have required crews of thirty-three.

22 The Giza ramps

1 A fact that the ancient Egyptians of later ages well understood: as several creation texts describe, there had been a time before Egypt had existed (cf. *LÄ* V, cols. 677–90, 'Schöpfung' (Jan Assmann)).

2 For these calculations and for those of the following sentences, see ch. 6 above.

3 Arnold 1991, pp. 79–95, and see for example chs. 17 and 20 above.

4 Arnold 1991, pp. 61–3.

5 Arnold 1991, pp. 98–101.

6 Modern accounts of this basic technique (Arnold 1991, p. 63; Lehner 1997, pp. 224–5) follow the report of Borchardt and Croon on his Meidum excavation of 1897 (Borchardt 1928, pp. 27 ff), and an essay by Henri Chevrier (1970), a French engineer. Although quite brief, the latter paper represents the fruits of long experience of reconstruction at Karnak Temple (1926–54), both on his own account and following the pioneering work of Georges Legrain, whose extraordinary reconstruction of the

Great Hypostyle Hall employing ancient methods such as rope hauling and ramps is documented in a remarkable series of photographs (Legrain 1929, ch. VII).

7　Gunn and Peet (1929, pp. 176–85) discuss the mathematical text, whilst Robins and Shute (1987, p. 48) provide a recent commentary. The Karnak ramp is described by Arnold (1991, pp. 95–8) and Legrain (1929, ch. II).

8　Arnold 1991, pp. 83–4.

9　Saleh 1974, p. 137.

10　Hawass 1997, pp. 57–8.

11　For an excellent introduction to the geology and topography of the Giza Plateau see Lehner 1985a, pp. 112–17.

12　See fig. 54 above.

13　Lehner 1985a, pp. 114–15, A8 and A10. See also figs. 54–5 and 88–9.

14　Standing on this headland, it is amusing to reflect that the number of tourists who visit the Great Pyramid on an average day is about the same as the gangs of stone workers who built it. These tourists, whose taxis and buses appear as rows of matchboxes lined up beside the Pyramid, have more mechanical power at their disposal than ever was available to King Khufu's workforce: the Great Pyramid indeed was built with less horsepower than that of a dozen Land Rovers.

15　The first archaeologist since the 1920s to consider Giza as the site of the Great Pyramid's construction and write a commentary upon it appears to have been Dieter Arnold (1981). The archaeologists Zahi Hawass and Mark Lehner of the joint US/Egyptian Sphinx Conservation Project were the first to undertake detailed groundwork right across the Giza Plateau concerning virtually all aspects of pyramid building, the results of these pioneering studies being summarised in Lehner 1985a and Hawass 1990.

16　Lucas/Harris (1962, p. 54), following Reisner (1931, p. 69), states that there are quarries 'south east of Menkaure's Pyramid'.

17　Lehner 1985a, pp. 121–2, B10–B12.

18　For a timetable of Khufu's building programme at Giza, see Appendix 5.

19　Hawass 1998, pp. 55–6; *PM* III, Part I, p. 122, 'Masons' graffiti with dates'.

20　See ch. 48 below for a discussion of the construction dates of these two temples. Like the west side of the Great Pyramid, the extensive cemeteries built for Khufu's courtiers to its east whilst the Pyramid itself was still under construction show that this area too must also have been free of massive ramps or other building works.

21　Another major objection to the Great Pyramid causeway having served for stone delivery during its construction is that it crosses the flat area at the Pyramid's base from where its design and accuracy were controlled during construction: see further Part Four below.

22　See p. 197 above. A ramp, perhaps, whose maximum size is suggested by the present distance between the edge of the quarry and the foot of the Great Pyramid: that is, a slope of around 2:1, a proportion much favoured by King Khufu's pyramid-makers; see fig. 28 above.

23 Any number of ideal ramp systems have been proposed by engineers and archaeologists, their relative value to Khufu's pyramid-makers based upon assessments of their efficiency in enabling the transportation of stone blocks (Lehner 1997, pp. 215–18 and 222–3). Most of these systems, however, postulate that whilst under construction the Great Pyramid was a regular four-sided solid standing in a flat plain and growing tidily course by course. The specific terrain of the Giza Plateau is not taken into account nor the elaborate arrangements made to accommodate the architecture of the Pyramid's interior (see further Part Six below).

24 Petrie 1883, p. 209.

25 Petrie 1883, p. 213.

26 Although the bulk of the filling in this quarry may be dated circumstantially to Khufu's time, proof, such as appears to have been found during the clearance of the eastern ramp beside the Pyramid (Saleh 1974, p. 137), is lacking.

27 This identification of these deposits as marl clay is based on personal observation and a rule-of-thumb comparison of their grain size. Not naturally present on the Giza Plateau, the raw material would be readily obtainable as shale, from the strata of the nearby Heit el-Gurob (see fig. 86), which shows considerable signs of ancient mining. Whilst I could find no general accounts of the physical properties of such Egyptian shales, their employment as a basis for pottery clays has been widely discussed, and such descriptions (e.g. Arnold and Bourriau 1993, pp. 160ff 'marls', and p. 12, figs. 2A and B) provide tangential information. Curtis (1979), also makes the following helpful observation: 'Pieces of the shale placed in water began to decrepitate at once into small fragments and in a few minutes, a 50 gram sample is completely disaggregated. The disaggregated fragments absorb almost 50 per cent of water by weight. In its moistened condition, the shale feels unctuous.' A perfect medium to lubricate the surfaces of the Pyramid's stone-hauling ramps, with a conveniently located source close by.

28 Quoted in Beer 1983, p. 117.

29 See further Part Four, below.

30 Kemp (1989, ch. 3) discusses the surviving literary relics of just such micro-management in ancient Egypt; Kadish (1996) uses similar notions to conjure up an early modern state beside the Nile.

31 This vision of Gothic art and cathedral building has a literary history spanning Ruskin's Letters of 1854 on the Oxford Museum, the *fin de siècle* writings of Émile Mâle and, latterly, the popularisations of Jean Gimpel.

23 Coda: the commanding landscape

1 Butzer 1976, pp. 18–21.

2 This description of ancient Egypt is based largely upon the Valley of the Nile; see further note 12 below.

3 Von Beckerath 1997, ch. 3.

4 Stars are first found in Egyptian literature in the Pyramid Texts (Utterance 513 (Faulkner 1969, p. 189), where the constellation of Ursa Major is identified (Roth 1993b, p. 70)), and certain hieroglyphs bespeak an observation of the phases of the moon (Gardiner 1957, Sign List, N 9–13). The precise positioning of the Great Pyramid, however, shows a practical excellence of stellar observation in Khufu's reign well beyond all literary references; see further below, Parts 5 and 6, and for example, Spence 2000.

5 Spence (2000, figs. 2 and 3) provides diagrams of the night sky at the time of the building of the Great Pyramid.

6 Corpus Hermeticum, Aesclepius III (Scott 1924, p. 136).

7 Goedicke 1961. Could the vertical line between the wings at the centre of the composition on which the barge is balanced mark the river at the centre of the valley and its orientation to the north?

8 Assmann (2001, ch. 3), though set in a different context, provides convenient references to the textual origins of many of the statements in this paragraph.

9 This beautiful passage is quoted from Assmann (2001, p. 62).

10 Houlihan 1986; Brewer and Friedman 1989.

11 Robins (1994, ch. 10) describes the various discreet adjustments to this basic grid introduced over three millennia.

12 The following discussion assumes that the roots of ancient Egyptian art and style are products of cultures living in the Nile Valley, the long-promised re-evaluation concerning the Delta's contribution to the formation of ancient Egypt's cultural identity having not progressed beyond a re-evaluation of the spread and scope of the predynastic cultures (see for example Midant-Reynes 2000). As represented at the Delta sites, indeed, the classical pharaonic style appears as transplanted as the stones and statues in its dusty mounds.

13 This, however, is rarely true of modern images of the Egyptian landscape, which are mostly products of a modern inclination to asymmetry; specifically, the continuing influence of post-Renaissance romantic landscape painting.

14 Based upon personal observation during the last decade of Egypt's inundations.

15 These observations are not intended to question standard explanations of why Egyptian drawing appears the way it does to many modern viewers, as epitomised by Schäfer (1974), which, according to E. H. Gombrich's Foreword (p. ix), 'constitutes the only attempt ever made of analysing an artistic style as a mapping procedure'. My purpose here is simply to move the space in which the 'viewer' stands from Greece to Egypt – though surely Schäfer's Greece was more a product of German literary neo-classicism than a study of the original material.

16 Robins (1994, pp. 176–81) describes the graphics of this process using an example from the Ptolemaic period; Schäfer (1974, Part 7, and esp. from

pp. 326ff) gives other examples and provides the intellectual pedigree of this paragraph. Unequivocal evidence of the use of this technique in the Fourth Dynasty is found in a variety of unfinished sculptures excavated at Giza and dating to the reign of Menkaure, which between them show various stages of the processes of cutting down and smoothing; see *EAAP*, catalogue no. 74 (Christiane Ziegler) and Reisner (1931, pp. 112–14), who describes this same technique in practical detail. Unfinished Third Dynasty sculptures too show stages of this process; see for example Sourouzian 1995, pl. 54. The use of this method is self-evident in virtually all ancient Egyptian stone sculpture, in the characteristic poses and in the forms of the statues' bases and back-pieces.

17 Davis 1989, pp. 15–18.

18 Giedion 1964, fig. 308.

19 Gardiner 1957, Sign List, O 24; the stela Cairo Museum. JE 72273 (*PM* III, Part I, p. 43), for example, holds a drawing of two of the Giza pyramids.

24 The spirit and the tomb

1 Midant-Reynes 2000, p. 43.

2 Midant-Reynes 2000, pp. 116ff and ch. 7.

3 And see Prologue, p. 9 above.

4 Midant-Reynes 2000, pp. 234ff, and widely of course through modern archaeology; see for example Hodder 1992, pp. 101ff.

5 Cf. Kemp 1989, figs. 9 and 11.

6 The notion that the architecture of some of these great archaic tombs were representations of a living royal household is half a century old; Stadelmann (1996) provides a brief account of its history; see also, Dreyer 1998a; Emery 1939 and *GT* II, pl. xxxix and 'The Model Estate'; *GT* I, Tomb 3038; Dreyer et al. 1996, pp. 57–81.

7 Wilkinson 1999, fig. 7.1.

8 Hartung (2001, Part 2) provides a recent discussion of imported goods in the earlier examples of these great tombs; Petrie (1900, p.14) describes archaic perfume scenting his excavation.

9 Whilst many coffin fragments have survived, the scanty evidence of the bodies buried in the central chambers of these great tombs was not adequately reported, a century-old exception being the splendid linen-wrapped and desiccated arm from the tomb of Djer at Abydos laden with fine jewellery (Petrie 1901, pl. 1 and pp. 16–19). A similar care for the dead, including their wrapping in cloth and burial in coffins, has recently been reported from far older cemeteries (Midant-Reynes 2000, pp. 187ff; Friedman et al. 1999, pp. 3–11), and many of the modest subsidiary burials near some of the great dynastic tombs also show evidence of body wrapping and the use of wooden coffins (see for example Quibell 1923, pl. xxix).

10 Stadelmann 1996, pp. 794–7; Dreyer 1998a, pp. 4–7.

11 *GT* III, Tomb 3505; Dreyer et al. 1996, pp. 57–66 (Tomb of Qa'a); Dreyer
   et al. 2003, pp. 94–8 (Tomb of Den). The north–south orientation of these
   offering places echoes the positions of the bodies in most prehistoric
   graves; Debono and Mortensen (1988, pp. 45–6) provide a check list and
   commentary upon the orientation of these burials; Kemp (1989,
   pp. 112ff) an account of the role of the mortuary cult in dynastic Egypt.

12 *GT* III, Tomb 3505, and pl. 27. The find spots of the large statue fragments
   found at other tombs (for example Petrie 1901, pp. 28 and 39) are
   unrecorded. Dreyer et al. (1990, pp. 76–7) suggest the existence of a base
   of a royal statue in the tomb of Den at Abydos.

13 Assmann (2002, pp. 66–70) discusses the role of the tomb in ancient
   Egypt, and on pp. 91–101 describes the mentalities of some individuals
   based upon their tomb inscriptions.

14 Wilkinson 1999, pp. 220–2; Assmann 2002, pp. 46ff.

15 A convenient visual compendium of the plans of many of these tombs is
   given by Kaiser and Dreyer (1982, fig. 13); and see 'Kenotaph' in *LÄ* III,
   cols. 387–91 (William Kelly Simpson).

16 Baines and Málek 1980, p. 14, map.

17 *LÄ* VI, cols. 475–93, 'Thinis' (Edward Brovarski) and 'Thinitenzeit'.

18 Málek 1997, pp. 90–5; Wilkinson 1999, pp. 359 ff.

19 This has been the standard reconstruction of the superstructures of
   these tombs, since Petrie's excavations in the first years of the twentieth
   century; whilst greatly elaborating the detail of its construction, the ongoing re-excavation of the site by the German Archaeological Institute
   has provided further evidence of its basic soundness (Dreyer 1991; and
   further Dreyer et al. 1996, pp. 58–61 and Dreyer et al. 2003, pp. 108–11
   and pl. 17).

20 O'Connor 1989.

21 Kemp 1989, pp. 53–5.

22 Gardiner 1957, pp. 72 and 75; Wilkinson 1999, pp. 224–9. (That the Horus
   name sometimes pictures a palace rather than a tomb is suggested by
   the door bolts which are shown occasionally at the centre of the design,
   for tombs with 'Palace Façades' did not have such doors in them.)

23 Stadelmann (1996, pp. 728–9) and Wilkinson (1999, pp. 238–40) provide
   discussions of these so-called Talbezirke. If they had housed buildings
   made of reeds, however, as Kuhlmann (1996) suggests, they would have
   left very little trace upon the enclosures' earthen floors.

24 Ward 2000, p. 40.

25 Abydos boat burials: O'Connor 1995, pp. 3–7. Sakkara boat burials: *GT* I,
   Tomb 3036; *GT* II, Tomb 3503 and 'Model Estate' of Tomb 3357; *GT* III,
   Tomb 3506.

26 *LÄ* III, cols. 1214–31, 'Mastaba' (Jürgen Brinks).

27 *GT* II, pls. VI and VII; *GT* III, pls. 6–8 and 16.

28 The plans of the largest of these mastabas are given by Kaiser and Dreyer
   (1982, fig. 13); *LÄ* III, cols. 1216ff, lists them all.

29 For example, *GT* II, pp. 1–4, and Kemp (1966) who provides an overview of these literary debates and the beginning of their resolution too. Stadelmann (1997a, pp. 10–35) and Wilkinson (1999, pp. 259–60) offer recent syntheses.

30 For example Bard 2000, pp. 69–76. This continuing discourse on owner-ship and exclusivity has a curiously modern air; in common with many later pharaohs (cf. *LÄ* III, cols. 387–91), and choirs of Christian saints, several dynasties of European monarchs have also been provided with more than one funerary monument, separate entombments being made on occasion, for various parts of the royal corpse which was divided after death; see for example, Panofsky 1992, pp. 77–8.

25 Mud to stone

1 Galdieri (1982) provides a global compendium of mud-brick architecture.
2 Kemp 2000; Rosen 1986, ch. 5.
3 Fathy 1969, p. 242.
4 Galdieri 1982.
5 Kemp 2000, p. 82, quoting Borkowski and Majcherek.
6 Kemp 2000, p. 82.
7 The largest of all Egyptian mud-brick mastabas, one of several similar structures built in the time of Djoser, is 280.5 feet by 151.6 feet, and 38.3 feet high (85.5 m $\times$ 46.2 m $\times$ 11.66 m) (Garstang 1902, pp. 8–11).
8 Dreyer et al. (2003, pp. 108–14) substantially revises Petrie's earlier sug-gestion (1900, p. 14) that these walls had been built with bricks that were not properly dried.
9 The tomb of King Qa'a, for example (Petrie 1900, p. 14).
10 *GT* III, p. 37.
11 Emery (1961, pp. 128–64 and 180–91) provides a broad outline of these architectural changes, although his account has been greatly amplified by the on-going excavations at the royal cemetery of Abydos; for the work so far, see Dreyer et al. 1990, 1996, 1998, 2003 and Dreyer 1998a.
12 Jeffreys and Tavares (1994, pp. 147ff). and Smith (1997, pp. 379–84) have reviewed and discussed the archaeological context of the surviving Second Dynasty royal monuments at Sakkara; Stadelmann (1996) and Wilkinson (1999, pp. 240–3) discuss some of the speculation that this has inspired.
13 See, for example, Stadelmann 1997a, pp. 30ff.
14 Mathieson et al. 1999, pp. 22–3.
15 Jeffreys (1998, p. 64) endorses the prevailing opinion that the so-called Gisr al-Mudir was erected in the reign of Khasekhemui. For the recent survey of several of these enclosures see Mathieson and Tavares 1997 and Mathieson et al. 1997. It is not clear, however, whether these long walls were free standing – nor indeed if they are to be counted as independent architectural structures!

16 Mathieson et al. 1999, pp. 36–8.

17 Dreyer et al. 1998, pp. 164–5; 2000, pp. 122–5; 2003, pp. 108–14.

18 Petrie 1901, p. 13.

19 Petrie 1901, pl. LVII, 4, 5 and 6. There must remain the slight possibility that this rebuilding of Khasekhemui's burial chamber was undertaken in the reign of Djoser, when stone block production was already under-way; cf. Dreyer 1998b, pp. 31–4 and Dreyer et al. 1998, pp. 164–6.

20 This a personal observation in Tomb 3505.

21 Wilkinson 1999, p. 97.

22 See also ch.18 above. Officials of Djoser's predecessor, Khasekhemui, in whose reign stone block building is first attested, also appear to have visited many of the regions around Egypt where copper was mined. The use of copper in Khasekhemui's time is celebrated too, in a rare inscription (see Wilkinson 1999, pp. 91–4 and 97).

23 Petrie 1900, p. 18.

24 Lucas/Harris 1962, pp. 421–2, from which all the figures in this para-graph are drawn. See also *EAAP*, catalogue no. 5 (Sophie Labbé-Toutée, who puts the total number of vases so far discovered underneath the Step Pyramid at 'about forty thousand') and Arnold and Pischikova 1999, p. 121, n. 1.

25 Reisner 1931, pp. 139–40 and 180.

26 By rule of thumb, I have estimated the working of hard stone as requir-ing ten times the labour of soft stones such as limestone; this would rep-resent a broad equivalence between the relative tonnages of the vases and the limestone used in the king's first tomb.

27 Lauer 1962, figs. 19 and 20; pp. 69–70 and 245–8. His identification of the fine limestone as 'calcaire fin de Tourah' (p. 69) appears to have been based upon experience. The nub is not the scientific exactitude of Lauer's identification, but that he recognised that Djoser's tomb-makers had selected, quarried and transported a fine-grade Tura-type limestone to use in this building; it might also be observed that no sources for this distinctive quality of limestone (Aston et al. 2000, p. 42) have been found upon the west side of the Nile Valley in the vicinity of Memphis (Lucas/Harris 1962, pp. 52–5).

Similar quality stone worked in the reign of Djoser or his immediate predecessors was shipped to other sites as well, fine-quality architectural blocks bearing scenes and inscriptions of the period having been found at the site of two provincial centres. Their fragmentary nature, however, allows no indication of the shape or size of the buildings from which they came. See Donadoni Roveri and Tiradritti 1998, catalogue nos. 236, 239–41 (Valeria Cortese) and Wilkinson 1999, pp. 96–7.

28 Dreyer 1991, and p. 227 note 19 above.

29 See, for example, Stadelmann 1997a, pp. 37–40ff.

30 The precise order and number of the Step Pyramid's various building phases remain a subject of debate, as does the building programme of

the complex that surrounds it; see for example Stadelmann 1997a, pp. 44ff. and Lehner 1997, pp. 84–93. None of these interpretations, however, substantially affects the order of construction that I outline below.

26 To make a pyramid

1 Lauer 1962, pls. IV–VI and plans 10 and 11.
2 This is visible at the bottom of the lower photograph in Lauer 1962, pl. IV (see also Stadelmann 1997a, fig. 3a). For the 'bench', as Emery called it, on the Sakkara mastabas, see for example GT II, Sakkara Mastaba 3504.
3 Lauer 1962, pl. V.
4 Lauer 1962, p. 250 and pls. V and VI. Note too that the angle of these rectangular foundations blocks is the reverse angle of the rise of the Pyramid's six steps.
5 See ch. 18 above. It seems prudent in the case of ancient and archaic peoples to modify the OED's definition of a generation, 'usually computed at thirty years, or three generations to a century', to twenty years.
6 For Coleridge's Serpent, see p. 208 above.
7 This translation from Lauer 1999, p. 13; see also Lauer 1996.
8 Amusingly revisited in Gombrich 1969, pp. 6ff.
9 LÄ III, cols. 145–18, 'Imhotep' (Dietrich Wildung).
10 By its nature, building with large blocks of stone was a dangerous affair; no wonder, then, that Imhotep was later worshipped as a god of medicine! Although compiled in periods much later than the great pyramids, the surviving medical papyri (LÄ III, cols. 1273–6, 'Medizin' (Wolfhart Westendorf)), contain remedies for misfortunes that agricultural workers were unlikely to suffer: as well as war wounds, there are remedies for fractures and trauma caused by strain and crushing, common enough events one might imagine, on the ramps and quarries of state stone building projects.
11 That some ancient craftsmen appear to have placed their names in hieroglyphic inscriptions beside their handiwork is hardly evidence of an intention to 'sign' it in the post-Renaissance manner, as is sometimes assumed (cf. Smith 1949, pp. 351ff; LÄ V, cols. 938-9, 'Signaturen').
12 Lévi-Strauss outlined some of the implications of these discoveries for Western cultural history in the 1960s – most graphically in a celebrated set of interviews with Georges Charbonnier (Charbonnier 1969).
13 Wilkinson 1999, pp. 94ff.
14 KRI III, 90, 193, 195, 196ᐧWilkinson 1999, pp. 95–8.
15 LÄ VI cols. 809–10, 'Turiner Königspapyrus' (Alessandro Roccati).
16 Appendix 1.
17 Stadelmann 1997a, pp. 44ff and Lehner 1997, pp. 84–93.
18 For novel or elaborated architectures built late in the reigns of various pharaohs see, for example, the pyramid complexes of Pepi II and

Amenemhet III, and the wide diversity of buildings made during the reigns of Amenhotep III and Ramesses II.

19 Von Beckerath (1997, pp. 160–3) apportions nineteen years to Djoser, though his reign may have been far longer, as many have speculated (Lehner 1997, p. 84; Wilkinson 1999, pp. 94–8).

20 Dreyer 1991, fig. 7. This so-called 'Russian doll' system of enclosure (Arnold 2003, p. 205) is a common element of ancient Egyptian design.

21 Cf. Jeffreys and Tavares 1994, figs. 7 and 9, where the wash runs down north towards Abusir, and Hartung 2001, fig. 1, where a similar wash runs out of the gorge in the western cliff.

   That the disposition of the huge rectangular enclosures in the Sakkara desert appears similar to the earlier examples at Abydos suggests that the subterranean burial chambers of the now-vanished tombs of that same period were also part of a similar architectural scheme as the tombs at Abydos (Arnold 2003, p. 97, 'Gallery tomb' and Wilkinson 1999, pp. 240–3 and fig. 7.2). (The plan of Lauer (1962, 14b) appears to have prompted the suggestion that the subterranean remains of Second Dynasty tombs outside the walls of the Step Pyramid's enclosure were once part of a larger necropolis that was enveloped by Djoser's building schemes.)

22 One of the two model courtyards beside Sakkara Mastaba 3357 (*GT* II The 'Model Estate') has exactly the same proportions of half of Djoser's so-called 'Heb-Sed Court' (Lauer 1962, pp. 144–8).

23 Clarke and Engelbach (1930, pp. 52–4), suggest that this incomplete sketch once showed six co-ordinates.

24 Lauer (1962, Table des Plans, pl. 10) shows a theoretical 20 – 40 – 60 cubit co-ordinate controlling the Step Pyramid's three bottom steps, just as these same figures will later control the angle of the Great Pyramid at Giza; cf. p. 65 above.

25 Lauer 1962, Table des Plans, pls. 10 and 11, though the hypothetical 'Pyramide I', drawn in these plans has not been widely accepted.

26 See p. 505 note 27.

27 Jeffreys 1998.

28 Seidlmayer 1996, pp. 122–4.

27 Accommodating Djoser

1 My interpretation of these changes broadly follows that of Kaiser (1997, pp. 197–200). (Note that although Lehner's isometric plan (1997, pp. 88–9) allows a useful overview of these jumbled rooms and corridors, it does not hold the significant details of Lauer 1962, Table des Plans, pls. 10 and 11.)

2 Lauer 1962, pp. 82–98. The impression that these shafts were originally part of a subsidiary cemetery that had been buried during the later phases of the work is reinforced by a series of inscriptions naming

members of Djoser's family found on the surface of the Step Pyramid's enclosure (Wilkinson 1996, p. 96; *EAAP*, Catalogue. no 4 (Christiane Ziegler)).

3 Lauer 1962, pp. 83–98, and pls. 10 and 11.

4 Part of these earlier arrangements appear to survive and can be seen in the upper sections of the shaft, see for example, Lauer 1962, pls. 10 and 12.

5 Lauer 1962, pl. 7 and Table des Plans, pl. 12.

6 Lauer 1962, pp. 74–6 and pl. 7.

7 The largest of the remaining flooring blocks in King Den's tomb at Abydos, for example, is some 9 feet long (2.75 m) and 10 inches thick (25.5 cm) (Petrie 1901, pp. 9–10, and Dreyer et al. 1998, p. 144). Rifat Farag (*MDAIK* 36, pp. 77–9) lists six known examples of the architectural use of granite during the later reign of Khasekhemui.

8 Strouhal et al. 1994.

9 Lauer 1962, pls. XX–XXIV.

10 Lauer 1962, Table des Plans, pl. 20

11 It is now accepted that the other large monuments of the time, the colossal mud-brick mastabas at Beit Khallaf, were not made for Djoser but for either provincial 'headmen' (*LÄ* IV, col. 303 (Brovarski, quoting Reisner)) or members of the royal family (Wilkinson 1999, p. 97).

12 Many earlier egyptologists, of course, had explored around the Step Pyramid, most notably Richard Lepsius, who dismantled a part of one of Djoser's subterranean palaces and shipped it off to Berlin (Lepsius 1852, pp. 375ff for a general account of these activities). Remarkably the full extent of Djoser's epoch-making architecture has yet to be uncovered; the largest complex inside the enclosure walls – containing structures almost 600 yards (547 m) long and 100 yards wide and threaded with unmapped subterranean galleries – is still buried in the sand (Lauer 1962, pp. 142–4).

13 *EJ-PL*, Préface and Bibliographie.

14 Lauer 1962, Table des Plans, pls. 16ff.

15 The best account of these vegetal forms is by Edwards (1993, ch. 2).

16 Inside Djoser's stone enclosure, however, it appears to be the very offices of the Egyptian state that have been made 'eternal', for rare archaic drawings show earlier kings enthroned amidst such buildings, performing courtly ceremonial. Kemp (1989, figs. 19 and 20) neatly encapsulates these graphical interrelationships. The notion of building such replicas beside a royal tomb appears to have its origins in the First Dynasty, see for example *GT* II Tomb 3503 and 'Model Estate' of Tomb 3357.

17 Here, Laugier's pretty rococo conceit of 'la petite cabane rustique' – that the architectural orders had their origin in pastoral shelters made of wood and wattle – appears to have been true (Abbé Laugier's *Essai sur l'architecture*, Paris, 1753; Chambers' *Treatise on Civil Architecture*, London, 1759).

18 The Step Pyramid enclosure is 544 m × 277 m; the Nagada Mastaba 54 m × 27 m (1785 feet × 909 feet and 177 feet × 89 feet, respectively) (Lauer

1962, p. 109; De Morgan 1897b, p. 154). (Note that the measurements usually given for the Nagada Mastaba are those of Ludwig Borchardt (Borchardt 1898, pls. XIV and XV and pp. 104ff; Dorner 1991, p. 82 n. 3), who appears to have taken them at the bottom of the mastaba's walls. Here, however, I have used its discoverer's original measurements, which as his plan shows (De Morgan 1897b, p. 154), were taken at the bottom of the 'bench' on which the mastaba's walls were situated.) Published decades before the Step Pyramid's enclosure walls were excavated or surveyed, the demonstrated relationship between the two monuments is striking.

19 See p. 228 above.

20 Precise photographs of this finish are provided in Donadoni Roveri and Tiradritti 1998, catalogue no. 165, which also has excellent photographs of a broad selection of predynastic and archaic objects made in stone.

21 Lauer 1962, pp. 144ff.

28 The Meidum Pyramid

1 The stepped pyramid made for Sekhemkhet was set behind King Djoser's at Sakkara; the other, the so-called 'Layer Pyramid', which appears to have been made for the little-known King Khaba, is 9 miles northwards at Zawiyet el-ʿAryan and set upon the same desert escarpment (Lehner 1997, pp. 9–10). Apart from making the base of both these pyramids a perfect square as Djoser's first stone mastaba – although not his pyramid – had been, they show few changes to the Step Pyramid's design and these were practical in nature. Applying statistics derived from later pyramid construction (see Appendix 5 below), the work on both these pyramids would have taken just a few short years, which coincides with our present information on the lengths of these kings' reigns (Wilkinson 1999, pp. 98–101). The plans of these two pyramids are given in Appendix 2.

2 This is ten times the volume of the stone used in Djoser's monuments, and a third as much again as the volume of the Great Pyramid of Giza, see Appendix 2.

3 Some other large-scale Bronze Age stone building projects: the European megaliths, and the later monuments of Central and South America.

4 Sandford and Arkell (1929) provide a general geological account of this area, and on pp. 17 and 32ff descriptions of the specific geology at the Meidum Pyramid. (Note too that in the older literature doubts are frequently expressed as to the ownership of the Meidum Pyramid, these based largely upon the fact that two other huge pyramids are also ascribed to Sneferu. Stadelmann's reconstruction of building activity during Sneferu's reign (1980; 1987; 1997a, pp. 80ff), which I have generally followed, discusses the inscriptional evidence, and demonstrates the plausibility of three great pyramids having been built for this one king.)

5 Seidlmayer 1996, p. 122.

6 Stadelmann 1981, pp. 77ff.

7 *MRA* III, pp. 16ff; Stadelmann 1997a, pp. 80–6.

8 Lehner (1996, pp. 508–10) and *MRA* (II, p. 49) both suggest that the largely unexcavated Layer Pyramid at Zawiyet el-'Aryan was to have been set inside an enclosure.

9 See ch. 18 above.

10 Lauer 1962, cf. pls. VI, XIII, XXXVII.

11 The base, however, was almost the same size as the two longer sides of Djoser's pyramid (Stadelmann 1997a, p. 86).

12 Both the dates and the identities of many of the buildings in the vicinity of the Meidum Pyramid have yet to be determined. It appears, however, that the only features which may have survived the stripping away of a Djoser-like pyramid complex are a modest enclosing wall and a second royal tomb, which may have been represented at Meidum, as elsewhere, by a small stepped pyramid (see further ch. 46 below).

13 This notion of the doubling of the workforce assumes that some fifteen years were spent upon the first building phase of the Meidum Pyramid, and that the following fifteen years were spent building the next pyramid. Cf. Appendixes 2 and 3.

29 The failed pyramid

1 Lehner 1998, p. 113.

2 Stadelmann and Alexanian 1998, figs. 1 and 2.

3 (Year 15) 'Making the doors of the king's palace of cedar wood' (Breasted 1906 1, §148); Stadelmann 1980, p. 440.

4 Unlike Dahshur, where quarry tracks run towards the desert hills behind the pyramids and presumably to as yet undiscovered quarries (Stadelmann 1983, pp. 225–6; Stadelmann and Alexanian 1998, fig. 2), at Meidum no roads or tracks have been located running west across the 3 mile wide desert plain towards the hills beyond; nor have any quarries been located in them. The remains of at least one enormous stone delivery ramp, however, run up from the river to the Meidum Pyramid (Arnold 1981, p. 19).

5 Dorner 1986, figs. 4 and 5.

6 Appendix 2.

7 Cf. Lehner 1997, pp. 16–17.

8 Arnold 1991, pp. 109–10, fig. 4.1; Dorner 1986, p. 44, figs. 1 and 4.

9 Lauer 1962, pp. 245ff.

10 Sandford and Arkell 1929, p. 32; *MRA* III, p. 36.

11 Sandford and Arkell 1929, pp. 6–7. This is the same rock series as the Heit el-Gurob beside the Giza Plateau (see ch. 22, above), where it has been described as 'a sequence of soft marly limestones and sandy marls with some intercalated shell beds and sandstones' (Lehner 1985a, p. 114, quoting Aigner).

12 Petrie (1883, pp. 213ff), for example, notes that the granite units of the Great Pyramid's interior are considerably less accurate than the rest: here the ancient masons did not correct such subsidence as must inevitably occur when erecting a stone block structure of such vast dimensions.

13 This deduction is based upon the continued movement at the pyramid after building work was restarted late in Sneferu's reign. See further ch. 32 below.

14 See ch. 26 above.

15 *MRA* III, pp. 58 and 94.

16 Whilst calcined plaster had been used in domestic contexts since pre-dynastic times (Aston et al. 2000, p. 22), its appearance in this pyramid appears to have been a genuine innovation in stone block architecture. That some of it was over-fired at temperatures above 200°C, which has the effect of hardening the calcium carbonate to a point where it is no longer capable of absorbing water, might indicate the pyramid-makers' inexperience at the kilns, especially as the plaster used in other sections of the pyramid is more accurately cured (*MRA* III, p. 92), and that used decades later at the Great Pyramid at Giza appears to have been made perfectly (Iskander, in *MRA* III, p. 92; cf. Nour et al. 1960, pp. 32–3).

17 *MRA* III, p. 64.

18 *MRA* III, p. 98.

19 See further on this subject, ch. 37 and Part Six below.

20 See further chs. 41–43 below. Arnold (1991, figs. 1.8 and 1.16) provides examples of the use of similar vertical controls in other contexts.

21 Although earlier surveys considered this chimney to have been set upon the pyramid's central axis, both *MRA* (III, p. 66) and Dorner (1986, fig. 4) place it slightly north of centre.

22 Appendix 3.

23 Appendix 1.

24 Standing at around a third of its height, the pyramid would have had some 70 per cent of its stone in place: Appendix 2.

25 Stadelmann's extended observations upon the cult arrangements at Sneferu's three pyramids (summarised in Stadelmann 1997b) convincingly argue that this third pyramid was his ultimate intended place of burial, and that his other two great pyramids were adapted to serve as cult centres.

26 Stadelmann 1987, pp. 233ff; Krauss 1996.

30 The jubilee pyramid

1 Cf. Stadelmann and Alexanian 1998, figs. 1 and 2. Sandford and Arkell (1929, p. 32) estimate this river bed to have been fully 60 feet thick'. For previous pyramid locations see Jeffreys and Tavares 1994, fig. 7 (Djoser

and Sekhemkhet), Lehner 1996, fig. 1 (Khaba), and Borchardt 1928, fig. 1 (Meidum).

2 *MRA* III, p. 126 notes this difference in the quality of the limestones used at the two adjacent pyramids. Whilst we await the full report of Stadelmann's investigation of the Red Pyramid's materials, Stadelmann and Sourouzian (1982, pp. 381–2) provide some preliminary observations; see also p. 307 note 22 below.

3 Dorner 1998, p. 25. The overall angle of rise of the three large stepped pyramids may be approximated as; Djoser 47° 30'; Sekhemkhet: 52° and Khaba 47°.

4 Appendix 2.

5 Appendix 5; 'previous work rates' assumes that the failed pyramid was the product of 15 years of building, that work had started in Sneferu's fifteenth year of rule and was abandoned around year 30, when work on the next project began.

6 Stadelmann 1987.

7 Appendixes 2 and 3.

8 Appendix 3.

9 As in all these calculations, this is but a rule of thumb and does not take into account the possibility of variable workloads during the various phases of these pyramids' construction.

10 *MRA* III, p. 128.

11 At the Great Pyramid, there are indications that this may have been true; at 4¼ feet × 4¼ feet × 2¼ feet high (1.3 m × 1.3 m × 0.7 m), the block size fits neatly into the division of its baselines into eight and sixteen parts, as well as having connection with the pyramid's height. Thus, the block size adopted at the Red Pyramid may have had an influence on the Great Pyramid's design.

12 See pp. 75–6 above.

13 See p. 263 note 1 above.

14 *LÄ* V, cols. 782–90 'Sed fest' (Karl Martin); Stadelmann 1983, pp. 233–4, and pl. 73. *EAAP* catalogue no. 23 (Dorothea Arnold) assigns a group of the so-called Lisht blocks to the Red Pyramid's temple; cf. Goedicke 1971, catalogue nos. 10–22.

31 The long journey of the spirit

1 Djoser's pyramid, 3 degrees east of north; Sekhemkhet's pyramid, 11 degrees west of north (Lauer 1960, p. 99); Layer Pyramid 8 to 9 degrees west of north (Lehner 1996, p. 510).

2 Spence 2000, table 1 and fig. 1.

3 *LÄ* I, cols. 555–6, 'Aufweg' (Rosemarie Drenkhahn).

4 *PM* III, 2, pp. 877–8; Edel 1996; *LÄ* II, cols. 919–21, 'Güterprozession' (Helen Jacquet-Gordon).

5 *PM* III, 2, pp. 878ff.

6 See, for example, Kemp 1989, pp. 65–83.

7 That the traditional maintenance of the spirit of the king with offerings was not abandoned is emphasised by the plans of the three temples that were built beside his pyramids (Arnold 1997, pp. 45ff).

8 This is not to deny the possibility of cosmic references in the royal tombs of earlier reigns than Sneferu's. Nor would it be surprising in this context if the early pyramid-building kings became increasingly identified with Re, as several commentators have observed (Hawass 1987, pp. 84ff; Stadelmann 1997a, pp. 124ff).

32 The dark interior

1 Firth and Quibell 1935, pls. 36, 46 and 108.

2 *MRA* III, pls. 2–7.

3 'Generally speaking, the [Pyramid] texts were supposed to be of special service to the deceased king in his ascent to the sky and his reception in the divine realm. In this regard, every suitable means of assistance was included: a ladder or ramp leading up to the sky, clouds, storms, hail, incense, sunlight, and animal forms such as a bird, a beetle, or a locust' (Hornung 1999, p. 5 (cf. Assmann 2002, p. 58, 'The central topic of these [Pyramid] texts is the idea of ascent to heaven').

4 Reisner (1932, p. 42) provides an example of early mud-brick corbelling.

5 Arnold 1991, pp. 184ff.

6 Although the age and identity of these fragmentary mummified remains are still uncertain (see most recently Ikram and Dodson 1998 pp. 111 and 320), other burial arrangements such as the placing of royal sarcophagi, indicate that the last large chambers in these pyramids were intended to serve as the burial chamber. Stadelmann (1983, pls. 76–8) shows fine views of the Red Pyramid's interiors.

33 Two last works

1 A persuasive reason for the Red Pyramid being Sneferu's burying place is that it is the only one of his three pyramids whose adjacent temple is similar in style to – and is the predecessor of – the later royal pyramid temples, including that of the Great Pyramid at Giza (Stadelmann 1997b). Another, of course, is that the decision to build a third pyramid for Sneferu was taken precisely because the earlier pyramids, the stepped pyramid at Meidum and the failed pyramid at south Dahshur, were deemed to have been insufficient.

2 Stadelmann 1995.

3 Appendix 2.

4 Stadelmann 1997b, p. 5. This apparent hastiness need not necessarily signal that the state stone workers had been taken by surprise at the king's death, merely that they had moved to another project.

5 See for example Meeks and Favard-Meeks 1996, pp. 122ff.

6 The girth of the Bent Pyramid at the bend in its exterior angle is 123.58 m (Dorner 1986, fig. 5), which is 56 per cent of the size of the Red Pyramid's baselines (219.08 m) (Dorner 1998, pp. 25–6).

7 Whilst the sequence of building work at the Bent Pyramid is clear enough, its time frame is not. Following Stadelmann (1997a, pp. 80ff) I have assumed that the lower girdling wall was made immediately before the low-sloped pyramid above, which shares the same distinctive stone work. There may, however, have been a gap of unknown length between these two building phases.

8 Dorner 1986, fig. 5.

9 Bent Pyramid height 343.54 feet (104.71 m); Red Pyramid height, 359.38 feet (109.54 m).

10 This high-quality stone work (cf. Arnold 1991, fig. 4.56; Stadelmann 1997a, pls. 26 and 33) is typical of the second phase of construction and is evident in Sneferu's reign after year 30 (Stadelmann 1987).

11 Arnold 1991, figs. 5.32 and 5.34.

12 *MRA* III, p. 98. In common with a deal of patching and repair work undertaken at the pyramid during this second stage of building, an attempt was also made to reset the line of this descending corridor, the drop in its roof being shaved down, and extra stones set into the floor below to level it. Even these adjustments show that the ruinous processes of subsidence had not yet run their course, for these realignments have subsequently cracked and shifted out of true.

13 Conant 1978, p. 381.

14 Note in this connection that an interior chamber added at this time was half-filled with stone and fitted with extensive cedar buttressing, which has preserved the chamber's shape down to this day (Arnold 1991, pp. 234–5).

15 *MRA* III, p. 92, quoting Varille, notes that at the Bent Pyramid 'everything is double . . . two entrances and corridors, two closings, two apartments, two portcullises'.

16 The equivalent of manufacturing a so-called 'construction gap' (Arnold 1991, pp. 179–82) within the body of the pyramid.

17 Chapter 23 discusses the ancient Egyptian conception of architectural design within pyramids, which conceives their interiors as being situated in a narrow envelope of space.

18 This quality of stone working is typical of the second phase of stone working of Sneferu's reign (see note 10 above), and indicates the commonality of these two building projects. As Stadelmann has noted (1987, pp. 236ff), however, there are indications that work on the last phase of building was already underway at Meidum by about year 30 of Sneferu's rule; at the same time, that is, as work on the Red Pyramid was beginning, so the relative timetables of these two restarted building projects must remain uncertain.

19 Petrie 1924, pp. 57–8.

20 Ch. 27 above.

21 For reasons already outlined in the Introduction, I have not included the ancient Egyptian unit of the 'seked' in this account of the angle of the slope of these early pyramids. It is not attested for the period of their construction nor indeed for centuries afterwards (Gunn and Peet 1929, p. 176, n. 1), whilst compared with the known use of numbered co-ordinates (ch. 26, and further below) the 'seked' appears a clumsy and imprecise unit with which to describe such precisions (cf. for example, the table given in Arnold 1991, p. 12, with Robins and Shute 1987, p. 15). I would suggest, therefore that, rather than the 'seked' having been the theoretical unit in which the silhouettes of the great early pyramids were specified as it is often claimed to be, its main function was in matters of practical estimation 'for grasping the meanings of things and knowing everything that is', just as the title of the Rhind Mathematical Papyrus, that scribal ready reckoner in which the 'seked' first appears, describes (Robins and Shute 1987, p. 11; and see also pp. 44–9 and 58–9).

22 Petrie 1892, p. 3; Stadelmann 1983, pp. 230–4.

34 Coda: the legacy

1 Valloggia 1997.

2 Jéquier 1928.

3 This plan is described and considered in Part Five below.

4 This is not to deny the so-called 'satellite' pyramids; see ch. 44 below.

5 See ch. 32 above.

6 See Appendix 3.

7 Chapters 44 and 45 below outline the construction timetable of Khufu's monuments at Giza; chapter 26 above comments upon the role of long-lived kings in forwarding ancient Egyptian architectural design.

35 Choosing Giza

1 Jeffreys (1998) provides an illuminating discussion of pyramid topography in the area of Memphis and Heliopolis.

2 Lehner 1997, pp. 10–11.

3 Martin 1997; see also Brovarski 1996, pp. 118ff.

4 LÄ I, cols. 24–5, 'Abu-Roach' (Adolf Klasens).

5 Mortensen 1985.

6 Jeffreys 1998, pp. 69–70; Wilkinson 1999, p. 339.

7 Jeffreys (1998) provides an overview of this subject.

8 This, in fact, was a century-old observation (see for example Martin 1997, fig. 1), and has been disproved following modern survey work (Lehner 1985a, p. 115, A 12).

9 Lehner 1997, pp. 106–7. (The 'stony mound' lies approximately at the point where the contour line crosses the 'back sight' line on the plan, p. 107.)

10 Jeffreys 1998 and Goedicke 2000.

11 *LÄ* II, cols. 1111–13, 'Heliopolis' (Lászlo Kákosy); Kees 1961, pp. 155ff.

12 Donadoni Roveri and Tiradritti 1998, catalogue nos. 239–41 (Valeria Cortese).

13 *LÄ* I, cols. 694–5, 'Benben' and 'Benben-Haus' (Eberhard Otto).

14 A sentiment shared by cultures all around the world: 'At the going down of the sun . . .' The majority of ancient Egyptian cemeteries are on the west bank of the Nile, which many later texts describe as the realm of the dead (see for example Piankoff 1972, pp. 33ff, esp. p. 5).

15 See chs. 7 and 8 above.

16 The theory was amusingly refuted in a BBC television documentary. See ch. 35 for a further discussion of scaled maps and plans in ancient Egypt.

17 Jeffreys 1998, fig. 3. (Note that the assertion in Verner (2002, pp. 302–3) that the pyramids of Giza and Abusir were both aligned with Heliopolis is simply a translation of the text of the first edition, published in 1997.)

18 Aston et al. 2000, p. 12 ('Soft-stone Quarries 3'); Sandford and Arkell 1929, end map; Lehner 1985a, pp. 112–14.

19 Jeffreys and Tavares 1994, pp. 149ff and figs. 7 and 9; Málek 1997, pp. 92–5.

20 Jeffreys and Tavares 1994, p. 151 and fig. 7, no. 10.

21 See ch. 29 above. Sandford and Arkell (1929, end map) also show that the limestone hills that run south from Dahshur to Lahun are composed of lower-level Middle Eocene formations than those at Giza and Sakkara: that these would yield a lesser-quality building stone than that of the Giza Plateau or Sakkara is precisely reflected in the map of quarries (fig. 21 1 in Aston et al. 2000), which shows no ancient quarries in the area at all.

22 The ancient supply tracks that run westward from the Red Pyramid into the desert head towards the same Upper Eocene formation (Sandford and Arkell 1929, end map) that is represented at Giza by the Heit el-Gurob (see chs. 22ff and note 27 above). Whilst it is these newer limestones rather than those of Giza or Sakkara that occasionally obtain the same distinctive colour as the Red Pyramid's blocks, no quarries have yet been located in this area, a major source of this unusual limestone in antiquity being the upper sections of the quarries in the Mokkatam Hills to the east of Cairo, some 20 miles away (Abu Al-Izz 1971, pp. 29–30 and 121; Aston et al. 2000, p. 12, '5').

23 Stadelmann and Alexanian 1998, figs. 1 and 2. (This assuming that, in Sneferu's day, the present lake at Dahshur had extended northward.)

24 Arnold 1991, pp. 81–3. The Meidum Pyramid, however, is presently a little more than half a mile from the riverbank, close to the present line of cultivation (Lehner 1997, p. 10). Given the general eastward shift of the Nile since ancient times, this distance would have been less in Sneferu's day.

25 See ch. 29 above.

26 The base of the Great Pyramid is approximately 190 feet above sea level, the quarry bottom about 125 feet below it.

27 That is, both sites offer a building position on a knoll of high-quality local rock with locations for nearby harbours.

28 A line drawn down from the top of the Pyramid to the quarry's nearest edge runs at a slope of about 26 degrees, a strenuous but not impossible angle up which to drag the Pyramid's last blocks, and incidentally an angle similar to those of the internal corridors of the Pyramid itself.

36 Levelling the site

1 See pp. 310–11 above. Similar though less precise levelling was undertaken on the third and final stage of the pyramid of Meidum, and also for the Red Pyramid at Dahshur (Arnold 1991, p. 23, n. 35).

2 Appendix 5. (Chapter 18 note 4 observes that, like the royal workforce, the great copper chisel found on the Gebel el-Asr also seems to have found employment under both Sneferu and Khufu.)

3 Breasted 1906, I, §148, and see p. 268 above.

4 See ch. 6 above and Appendix 3.

5 Appendices 1 and 2.

6 Appendix 5.

7 See above, ch. 5, note 2.

8 Arnold (1991, p. 13 and n. 35) notes that similar though less precise levelling was undertaken at Meidum on the Pyramid's third and final stage, and at Dahshur for the Red Pyramid.

9 Arnold 1991, pp. 10ff.

10 There is no evidence that the real form of the Rocky Knoll conforms to the symmetrical low-stepped shape shown in most modern plans, which simply echo the drawings of Smyth (1867).

37 The plan inside the Pyramid

1 The presence of the Rocky Knoll haunts many theoretical explanations of how the Pyramid's central axis was established and maintained; see recently, for example, Lehner 1983; Isler 2001, chs. 8 and 9. Working without the benefit of modern surveying equipment or mathematics, however, there would have been little practical advantage in the ability to view the positions of the Pyramid's four corners across a flat foundation platform.

2 Even the four right-angled sockets that the pyramid-makers cut so carefully into the natural rock by the Pyramid's four corners are set at different levels and placed outside the perimeter of its pavements as Petrie has established (1883, pp. 37–40 and pl. 10); this, it would appear, to aid the placing of the Pyramid's casing stones; see further ch. 47 below.

3 For example: '[ancient Egyptian] designers employed simple constructional procedures. These, rather than mysterious "systems", are responsi-
ble for the interplay of proportions' (Baines and Málek 1980, p. 63).

4 Arnold 1991, p. 7: 'no true building plan as executed by an architect for
construction purposes has been preserved'. This is not to deny the existence of a variety of ancient Egyptian diagrams and models that describe
a wide range of architecture; Arnold (1991, pp. 7ff) provides a selection
and discussion of some of these; see also, the following chapter of this
book, pp. 318ff.

5 Robins and Shute 1987, pp. 44–9.

6 Cf. ch. 35 above.

7 Badawy (1965, pp. 60–2) provides a fine example; although it is theoreti-
cally impossible to draft a perfect heptagon, a method that provides a
close approximation was widely used by ancient craftsmen. By connecting three of this fake heptagon's points, moreover, one may construct a
triangle whose angles resemble those of the Great Pyramid; this,
however, would show considerable error when rendered at full size. Nor
is such geometrical fuzziness restricted to works of art. Many writings on
the Golden Mean, and proportion theories, including many explicators
of the Great Pyramid's harmonics, conjure similar illusions, as did Le
Corbusier with his celebrated 'Modulor', which in similar fashion is not
sustained by calculation or geometry.

8 Petrie gives a displacement of 0.3 ± 0.8 inches for the Queen's Chamber
vault and 0.4 ± 0.9 inches for the Great Step's top edge (Petrie 1883,
pp. 74 and 95); the building schedule in Appendix 3 shows that the Great
Step would have been emplaced at least two years after the blocks of the
Queen's Chamber vault.

9 Arnold 1991, pp. 253ff. Boning rods, of course, must be used in connection with plumb lines to achieve verticality. A wide variety of ancient
Egyptian lines and plummets of various ages have been preserved. They
are also reproduced on occasion, in jewellery for the dead (Badawy 1965,
figs. 11 and 12), this perhaps with connotations of balance and correct-
ness, cf. Gardiner 1957, Sign List, U 41.

10 Dolphin and Moussa 1977, pp. 134ff and fig. 109.

11 Whilst both the angle of the Descending Corridor and the exact point of
its commencement are precisely set into the geometry of the Pyramid's
six-square grid system, as are most other major elements of the
Pyramid's interior architecture, the 3 feet 8 inch (1.2 m) displacement of
the Subterranean Chamber's doorway from the central axis appears to be
quite random.

12 Arnold (1991, pp. 253–5) describes how such tools may have been
employed.

13 As noted by Arnold (1991, pp. 13–14) and reinforced by Dorner's observation recorded in fn. 38, on p. 24 of that same work.

14 Petrie 1883, p. 59 and see above, ch. 11, note 7.

15 See p. 273 above, for 'chimneys'; Lehner (1985b, p. 60) provides a résumé of present knowledge and opinion concerning this shaft.

16 This being similar to Arnold's classification of free-standing wall masonry (Arnold 1991, fig. 4.82, 4).

17 Petrie 1881, p. 74.

18 Petrie 1883, p. 214, and see further pp. 377ff below.

19 Toomer (1971, pp. 27–41) provides an apposite résumé of ancient Egyptian mathematics in this respect.

20 This ideal measurement, however, is close to 8⅔ cubits, a fraction which was a common-enough ancient expression (Toomer 1971, p. 28), and is an equivalence that is contained within the limits of the physical measurements of the offset's various occurrences at the Pyramid – which are within ± 1.2 inches of each other (0.0562 cubits). See further ch. 38 below.

21 Badawy 1965, pp. 58–60; *LÄ* II, cols. 912–14, 'Gründungszeremonien' (Bernadette Letellier) and *LÄ* V, cols. 884–8, 'Sechat' (Wolfgang Helck).

22 Arnold 1991, pp. 252–3.

38 The plan beside the Pyramid

1 Lehner 1985a, figs. 2 and 3C.

2 *EAAP*, fig. 47. Note that the 150 m gap between the base of the Pyramid and the mastabas of the plan's '4th building phase' would also allow the possibility that a low stone-hauling ramp was set against the Pyramid's west face during the first years of its construction.

3 *MRA* III, p. 96, observes that this survey line was first noted by Borchardt.

4 Lehner (1985b, Part II) provides the only modern account of this area.

5 Lehner (1985b, figs. 21–5) provides an overview of the area's general appearance.

6 Petrie 1883, pp. 44ff and pl. II; Borchardt 1926, pp. 4ff and fig. 3; Lehner 1985b, pp. 54–9; 1997, pp. 212–13; Spence 2000, p. 320, table 1.

7 Lehner 1985b, Part II, from which I have derived a great deal of information and insight. (In the interests of clarity, please note, however, that Lehner (1998, p. 112 n. 45) has since modified some of his conclusions.)

8 Petrie 1883, pp. 50–1 and pl. III.

9 Petrie 1883, p. 50. The most extensive description of this fascinating oddity is to be found in Lehner 1985b, Part II, especially pp. 45–50, where it is termed 'replica passages'. Here I have reverted to the name that Petrie gave these passages, as I have reinterpreted their purposes as proposed by Lehner (1985b, pp. 45ff) and sustained in Edward's review of that work by the belief (Edwards 1989, p. 264), derived from Borchardt's theory (see pp. 54–5 above), that the Great Pyramid had been designed in three separate stages.

10 For further examples of this type see Arnold (1987, pp. 86–8 and pls. 36 and 66–8), who describes the interior architecture of a royal pyramid; and Carter and Gardiner (1917, p. 132), where the celebrated plan of the

tomb of Ramesses IV is described as aiming 'at nothing so ambitious as drawing to scale; for [the Egyptian architect] it sufficed if his chambers were displayed in the correct order and with a rough approximation to the real shape and proportions', a comment frequently repeated in other accounts of ancient Egyptian architectural plans and models, and which has obvious connection too with representations of buildings in ancient Egyptian wall scenes; cf. for example Schäfer 1974, pp. 129–37.

11 Petrie 1883, pp. 61–4.

12 Petrie 1883, pp. 63–4.

13 See pp. 104 and 111–12 above for a description of the finish of the Descending Corridor.

14 Lehner 1985b, pp. 51–2 and figs. 9 and 12.

15 Although Lehner (1985b, fig. 9 and p. 49) describes four of these post holes, his measurements, if I have understood them correctly, would provide for five; in a superficial inspection in January 2002 I could find the traces of but three of them. For a description of the six-squared grid, see ch. 5 above.

16 Outlined by Clarke and Engelbach (1930, pp. 125ff) and ingeniously elaborated by Isler (2001, chs. 11 and 12).

17 Lehner 1985b, pp. 51–2 and figs. 9 and 12. This measurement, from the west edge of the Trench to the west edge of the Trial Passages, is of 12.2 cubits. (Although this Trench displays rough edges, I have assumed that a line would have been set along its western side in the manner that other control lines were set up within the Great Pyramid itself in somewhat similar locations; for a further account of these control lines inside the Pyramid, see ch. 44 below.)

18 See further ch. 39 below.

19 Lehner 1985b, pp. 51–2, and figs. 9 and 12.

39 Numbers

1 Dorner 1991; Breasted 1906, I, § 146ff ('Palermo Stone') and 173 ('Biography of Methen').

2 Gardiner 1957, pp. 191ff.

3 Petrie's spot measurement of the offset at the Great Step is 8.6163 cubits; that at the Prism Point 8.7287, the difference between them being 0.1124 cubits, or 0.0588 m (2⅓ inches).

4 Arnold (1991, pp. 12–13) cites evidence of a similar procedure at a small pyramid of Khufu's day, upon the Giza Plateau.

5 Dorner (1998, p. 25) provides a mean of 44° 44′ for the pyramid's angle; Arnold (2003, p. 199) simply 45°.

6 Arnold (2003, pp. 145–6) gives 144.32 m $\times$ 92, which with a 0.5248 m cubit provides the pyramid with primary dimensions of 275 $\times$ 175 cubits.

7 This being the mean, with the necessary adjustments, of Lehner's 'about 87.5m' (1985b, p. 45) and measurements taken from Petrie's map (1883, pl. II), which would appear to differ by about 4½ inches (0.115 m).

8 Robins and Shute (1987, pp. 48–9) provide a useful commentary upon
these properties.

40 Stars

1 The last two pyramid projects undertaken at Dahshur and Meidum in
Sneferu's reign were sheathed in blocks of Tura-quality limestone
(Arnold 1991, pp. 164ff).
2 See Appendix 3.
3 Petrie 1883, pp. 42–5.
4 Petrie 1883, pl. 6; Lehner 1985b, pp. 56ff and figs. 26–7; Lehner 1997,
pp. 212–13. Isler (2001, ch. 8) provides a lively digest of the speculations
that these holes and cuttings have inspired.
5 Lehner 1997, pp. 212–13.
6 Kurt Mendelssohn (1974, p. 207), for example, calculated that a two
degree error at the base of a 'great Giza Pyramid' would result in a 15 m
error at its pyramidion!
7 See ch. 29 above.
8 Spence 2000, table 1 and fig. 1.
9 Arnold 1991, pp. 15–16; Isler 2001, ch. 7.
10 Arnold 1991, pp. 13–14 and n. 38.
11 Petrie 1883, pp. 41, 125–6 and pl. VI: 'showing that the orientation of the
pyramid was slightly altered'.
12 Petrie 1883, pl. VI.
13 For example Spence 2000, p. 320; see, however, Arnold's caveat (1991, p. 15).
14 Petrie 1883, p. 126.
15 Petrie 1883, pp. 57–9 and pl. V.
16 Spence 2000.
17 *LÄ* I, cols. 511–14, 'Astronomie und Astrologie' (Jürgen von Beckerath),
provides an overview of the few known facts concerning ancient
Egyptian astronomy; *LÄ* VI, cols. 11–14, 'Stern' (Horst Beinlich), discusses
the known named stars.
18 Kochab and Mizar –β-Ursae Minoris and ζ-Ursae Majoris respectively – are
components of the Little Dipper and the Plough (Gingerich 2000, p. 297).
(Both Borchardt (1926, pp. 10ff) and Žába (1953, *passim*) had previously
drawn attention to the potential of these two stars in the determination of
the orientation of the Great Pyramid's baselines, although neither of them
took their observations as far as Spence's (2000) convincing resolution.)
19 Ross' account of basin irrigation in Egypt (Willcocks and Craig 1913,
pp. 303ff, esp. p. 306) suggests that August, the most dramatic month of
the Egyptian agricultural year, may have been chosen as the moment of
the Pyramid's foundation to correspond with the flood's arrival or even
the opening of the basin irrigation channels.
20 Clarke and Engelbach 1930, p. 66.

41 Coda: considering the architecture

1 As for example in the Red Pyramid (Dorner 1998, p. 27).

2 That there is 'a remarkable diagonal drafted line across the immense block of granite over the [burial] chamber doorway' (Petrie 1883, p. 83) shows the conscious use of diagonals by the makers of this chamber, though Petrie describes the line as serving as a control for the work of finishing the stone.

3 First identified, it appears, by Henri Frankfort and encapsulated in his term a 'multiplicity of approaches'; cf. Hornung 1982, p. 252 n. 1 for a First Dynasty example.

4 Berlin 3033; Papyrus Westcar 7, 1–9, 20 (Simpson et al. 1972, pp. 22–6).

5 Adapted from Gardiner 1925, p. 4, from which my following observations are derived.

6 Badawy 1965, Part II.

7 Badawy (1965, pp. 57–8) discusses the ancient name for this vital architectural point which he calls the 'pillar' (*iwn*; Gardiner 1957, Sign List, O 28). (Note that the drawings of Papyri Abbott cited in this connection by Badawy (cf. Robins and Shute 1987, pls. 16 and 17) also make clear distinction between triangular designs laid out upon the ground, which are horizontal, and those which stand upright, and are drawn like the hieroglyphic determinative for 'pyramid' (Gardiner 1957, Sign List, O 24).)

8 Assmann (2001, pp. 30ff) provides an apposite description of the common functions of the Egyptian temple.

9 The unique verticality of this common geometrical design, as used at the Great Pyramid, would suggest that its origins are to be found in a more usual horizontal application that was first laid out in the Pyramid's east field.

42 In the beginning

1 See ch. 14.

2 See chs. 5, 6 and 36.

3 See ch. 22. From personal observation, it appears that the mud cement used in these ramps is very 'sharp'; that is to say, it has been mixed with much larger quantities of sand than the mud mortars commonly employed in other contexts upon the Giza Plateau, such as the settlement discussed in ch. 13 above. This would make it harder, and more brittle too.

4 Arnold 1991, pp. 98ff.

5 See ch. 6 and Appendix 5.

6 This corridor, it may be recalled, is accurate to within one fiftieth of an inch in a descent of nearly 100 feet, and its alignment to the point of north is equal in its precision to that of the eastern baseline (Petrie 1881, p. 59). See chs. 11 and 36.

7 There is no firm information about when work upon this chamber was
started or suspended; that the chisels used for its quarrying display far
larger width of cut than those used in the Descending Corridor probably
reflects the fact that work within the chamber did not progress beyond
its roughing out.

8 See chs. 11 and 37.

9 A reconstruction underlined by the irregularity of the theoretical measurements of this doorway's location on the Pyramid's now-vanished
casing; measurements are not capable of exact expression in any known
system of Egyptian metrics.

10 Petrie 1883, pl. IX.

11 See chs. 5 and 37–8.

12 See ch. 38.

13 Petrie 1883, pp. 63–4, and ch. 38.

14 Further evidence of this advanced planning is to be found in the dimensions of the Grand Gallery, which is the only element in the Pyramid
large enough to have accommodated those great rectangular plugging
stones before their final slide down the Ascending Corridor. At the
height it stands within the Pyramid, this gallery would not have been
constructed until half the work of building was completed.

15 Petrie 1883, p. 64. This massive engineering project at the heart of the
rising Pyramid not only re-emphasises the existence of a master plan
during the first full year of construction, but also suggests that the quarries at Aswan that would eventually supply the granite plugging blocks
were already a part of the Pyramid's specification (see Appendix 5). Given
that the burial chamber complex would have been erected from around
year five and that it employed large quantities of similarly sized blocks of
granite, it seems most likely that the Aswan quarries were in operation
from the first years of work upon the Pyramid (cf. Appendix 5).

16 Whilst archaeological textbooks seem reticent to use the term (Arnold
(1991, p. 191) dubs this vault, which is similar to a Late Gothic form, a
'Saddle Roof'), the *OED*'s definition of a vault as 'A structure of stones or
bricks so combined as to support each other' would seem to serve for its
description.

17 Arnold 1991, p. 191 (the Mastaba of Iynufer). Interestingly, several other
construction devices used in the great early pyramids were derived from
smaller examples in older funerary structures; the so-called satellite
pyramid of Sneferu's Bent Pyramid for example (Arnold 1991, pp. 220–1;
Stadelmann 1997a, pp. 95–6 and fig. 165 above), which appears to have
served a similar function to the South Tomb of Djoser (ch. 27), had a
closing mechanism of three blocks of Aswan granite that anticipates the
arrangement inside the Great Pyramid at Giza.

18 These interior courses are primarily revealed in the Queen's Chamber
and corridor, in the shaft (Petrie 1883, pp. 67 and 214–15), and in the
forced passage that now serves as the Pyramid's tourist entrance and

which, by Egyptian tradition, was cut in the ninth century by the workmen of the Caliph Ma'amun. (The literary sources that provide this attribution are conveniently collected in Vyse 1840, II, pp. 319ff.)

19 The 'voids' and 'anomalies' detected in the Pyramid by various scientific surveys in the last few decades are all at locations where one would expect construction gaps and chimneys (see for example fig. 192) to have occurred and can hardly be considered as typical of the Pyramid's interior as a whole.

20 See chs. 2 and 3 above.

21 Petrie 1883, p. 37.

22 Arnold 1991, 'Construction Gaps', pp. 179–82 and fig. 4.113.

23 Arnold 1991, p. 101, and fig. 3.53 (4).

24 The continuing horizontal accuracy of these courses is detailed in Petrie 1883, pl. VIII.

25 Petrie 1883, pl. VIII; see also, Tarrell and Petrie 1925.

26 This analysis does not include the first step of the Pyramid which is part-cut into the Rocky Knoll and which, at 4 feet 10½ inches (1.488 m), is exceptionally large.

27 Petrie suggests that the larger size of this course was determined by the need to place a thicker lintel stone above the Pyramid's doorway (1883, p. 52). But this does not take into account the existence of the construction gap and vaulting around the entrance doorway (cf. ch. 43 below), which shows that this structure was set up in the same manner as the burial chamber (ch. 46 below), as a semi-independent entity inside the body of the Pyramid.

28 The conjunction of the Pyramid's courses and its interior architecture is further discussed in the next chapter. Excepting the Pyramid's first course, which is partly composed of the living stone of the Rocky Knoll, course 35 is the widest in the Pyramid, though it is impossible to know if it is connected to any internal features. In all likelihood its presence echoes the height of the Queen's Chamber vault which, as the following chapters will suggest, was a vital component of the Pyramid's design and construction.

29 Appendix 4.

30 It has been suggested, for example, that these variations in the Pyramid's course sizes represent changes in ancient work patterns and/or work at various quarries (Tarrell and Petrie 1925; Clarke and Engelbach 1930, pp. 128–9), or even that they are the product of techniques of construction found at other pyramids that have yet to be detected in the fabric of the Great Pyramid itself (Arnold 1991, pp. 167–8).

31 See chs. 38 and 40.

32 See chs. 3 and 4.

43 Setting the lines

1 Petrie 1924, p. 59.

2 Appendix 5.

3 In broad terms, the chamber may be said to measure around 17 feet 1¾ inches north–south (5.23 m) by 18 feet 10½ inches east–west (5.75 m) and 20 feet 5 inches (6.23 m) to the top of the gable. Although the chamber's floor measurements are close to 10 × 11 cubits, the precision of its stone work, which is as fine as any in the Pyramid, does not permit the claim of an exact concordance.

4 See further, ch. 44 below.

5 Petrie 1883, p. 216. This sarcophagus is one of the oldest known royal sarcophagi, though it shares a commonality of design with others of the same period that were placed in non-royal mastabas. (LÄ V, cols. 471–2 'Sarkophag' (Edward Brovarski)). It appears to be unfinished, and it is impossible to discern if this plain form was derived from earlier wooden examples or simply from the granite block itself.

6 All known records show the sarcophagus lying at a distance from the chamber's doorway, at the western end of the room, and thus close to the Pyramid's north–south central axis. Petrie, incidentally, appears to have been especially affected by the Great Pyramid's sarcophagus during his survey: 'The only time I put my name on a monument, was when chalking on the bottom of the sarcophagus the date of raising it. Ellis [a co-worker] put his name on the floor, before we let it down again; those may last a few thousand years' (Petrie 1933, pp. 30–1; cf. Petrie 1883, p. 8).

7 Any tabular diagram of the Egyptian pyramid interiors (e.g. Lehner 1997, p. 16) brings home this fundamental point.

8 Chapter 23 offers explanation for this strangely two-dimensional architecture.

9 Appendix 3.

10 Chapter 26 holds an earlier discussion of the use of co-ordinates in pyramid construction, whilst Badawy (1965, pp. 55–6) discusses their use from the days of Djoser to the New Kingdom.

11 Chapter 29 contains an account of the effects of subsidence and displacement during the construction of a colossal early pyramid.

12 Petrie 1883, pp. 64–5: 'For the angle of the passage, and its straightness, it will be well to consider it all in one with the gallery floor, as they were gauged together all in one length.'

13 Petrie's calculation places this corridor to within 1¼ inches (3 cm) of the Pyramid's theoretical east–west axis (Petrie 1883, p. 65). As we have seen, the technical detail of how the stone masons achieved such levels of precision is but speculation in relation to the Great Pyramid. In skilful hands, however, the simplest of ancient masons' tools would certainly permit such accuracy; Clarke and Engelbach (1930, p. 126) provide

pertinent remarks upon the use of lines and plumb-bobs; Badawy (1965, pp. 40–4), discusses ancient Egyptian masons' tools, including the all-important A-frame which measures angles with precision; Arnold (1991, pp. 253–5) describes surviving examples; Isler (2001, pp. 179–83) theorises on their potential for pyramid surveying. (Remarkably enough, A-frames identical to those used by the ancient Egyptians were still a standard tool of Egyptian masons at the time of Napoleon's invasion, as Nicolas Conté's elegant watercolours attest (Beaucour et al. 1990, p. 72).)

14 See chs. 1 and 5.

15 I have assumed, for there would appear to be no other rational explanation, that the line of the vault's groin with the chamber is the product of a vertical joint as is common with such vaults, and thus that its orientation is repeated on the upper surfaces of the blocks (cf. Arnold 1991, pp. 191ff).

16 Petrie 1883, p. 75.

17 See ch. 5. and Appendix 4.

18 This is the line of Petrie's 'virtual floor end': 'where the general floor slope, if carried through the [Great] step would intersect the plane of the S. wall' (Petrie 1883, p. 75); and see Appendix 4.

19 Given the absence of modern surveying equipment, the relative positions of the groin of the Queen's Chamber vault and the eastern face of the Great Step some 50 feet above it – although 50 feet apart, their two planes lie, so Petrie calculates (1883, p. 74), within a tenth of an inch of each other – could only have been determined by physical connection, that is, with a cord and plummet.

20 The Great Step's visible surfaces show that it must weigh a minimum of 4 tons.

21 As we have already seen (pp. 341–2 and fig. 169 above), the angle held within the Trial Passages could have been generated by setting the relevant line between the grid squares and the Trench, at full size in the design field.

22 Petrie 1883, pp. 50–1 and pl. III.

23 See chs. 5 and 37.

24 Petrie 1883, pp. 68 and 215. (Petrie, as ever, was the first to recognise and quantify this seeming disarray within the lower central sections of the Pyramid's interior architecture, noting that the floor lines of both the Queen's Chamber and part of the little corridor that leads to it appear muddled and confused.)

25 There is no knowing now why the Queen's Chamber was sited at this level and why the precise relationship between the clean clear lines of the Pyramid's interior architecture and its six-square grid had been abandoned. That the line of the floor of the corridor leading to the Queen's Chamber is within 5 inches of the halfway point between the level of the Great Step and the Pyramid's baseline, rather than the Prism Point where the baseline of the six-square grid is situated, might suggest some kind of planning confusion.

26 Petrie 1883, p. 74.

27 Petrie 1883, pp. 214–15 and 74. (Detailed if highly stylised drawings of this crude shaft are to be found, along with several useful photographs, in Edgar and Edgar 1923, I).

28 Petrie 1883, p. 67.

29 Petrie 1883, p. 66.

30 Edwards 1993, p. 123.

31 Petrie 1893, p. 20.

32 The work of finishing may also have been brought to a halt because of the pressure of the rising courses of the quarry stone, which would already have been at least halfway up the Ascending Corridor by the time that work on the Queen's Chamber corridor had begun, as the stone work in the Grand Gallery shows. In similar fashion, the sarcophagus may also have been installed in an unfinished condition (Petrie 1883, p. 84) owing to pressure of the building work (see further ch. 46 below).

44 The miniature shafts

1 Petrie 1883, p. 70.

2 The term 'airshaft', however, is inappropriate as neither of these miniature corridors appears to have reached to the surface of the Pyramid and thus provided ventilation to the Pyramid's interior as has sometimes been assumed. See further below.

3 Despite claims that the ends of these two hidden shafts were left uncut at their point of entrance into the chamber – which probably owe their origin to Petrie's ambiguous description of them (1883, p. 70) – practicalities of stone cutting make it more likely that the two square holes were closed with two well-made 'flickstein' which had been rendered invisible by the copious deposits of soot and salt which, prior to their recent conservation, had long obscured the chamber's walls (Hawass 1990, p. 103, Section 2).

4 Lehner 1997, pp. 114 and 248–9; Stadelmann 1994 and 1997a, pp. 282–4.

5 Stadelmann (1994) gives an overview of the findings of the robot researches undertaken during 1992–3, whilst www.cheops.org provides further documentation and a lively account of how the data were obtained. Set up by Rudolph Gantenbrink, the robot's engineer, this website also provides excellent three-dimensional graphics which, if due allowance is made for the seductions of the false perfections inherent in CAD drafting, offer novel views of the Great Pyramid's interior.

6 Gantenbrink at www.cheops.org provides a detailed account of these miniature shafts with a unique description of sections of their interiors. The detail of the accompanying drawings, however, should be treated with reserve; short of demolishing the Pyramid, we can know next to nothing of the sizes or proportions of the blocks in which the shafts are cut.

7 That the miniature shafts may have been set up, in part, to indicate subsidence at the centre of the Pyramid is suggested by the fact that they registered exactly this problem within a few years of their installation. See further ch. 47 below.

8 Offering a correction of the standard printed sources, Gantenbrink reports that the two miniature shafts that rise up from the King's Chamber reach the outside of the Great Pyramid at courses 101 (southern face) and 102 (northern face) (www.cheops.org).

9 Cooper 1877, pp. 140ff.

10 *EAAP* Catalogue nos. 36 and 37 (Christiane Ziegler), has a recent discussion of these two objects; Gantenbrink provides additional information (www.cheops.org).

11 Gantenbrink (www.cheops.org) Borchardt 1932, p. 12, fig. 3 and pl. 2.

12 Gantenbrink (www.cheops.org).

45 The Grand Gallery

1 Petrie (1883, p. 75) details errors of up to an inch in the stone work around the Great Step and in the level of the Step itself; these perhaps token minor subsidence following the filling of the opening to the vault below.

2 Edwards 1993, p. 124.

3 These chisellings are reviewed in Lehner 1998.

4 Petrie (1883, pp. 71–5) provides the most accurate description of this corbel vault.

5 Engraved for Napoleon's *Description* (V, pl. 13), Cécile's splendid drawings of the Grand Gallery yet remain the best views of this eccentric and ultimately unphotographable interior.

6 Lehner (1998), discusses the extensive literature that speculates upon the detail of how the plugging blocks may have been stored.

7 The enormous construction that the pyramid-makers set up around the Pyramid's entrance (ch. 43) protects a similarly small-sized corridor.

8 The use of granite in the Pyramid's interior can further serve to aid an understanding of the order of this work: that the plugging blocks must have been placed within the Grand Gallery before its vault was built, for example, shows that large blocks of granite were being shipped to Giza before the Grand Gallery was closed, and that in turn would support a timetable in which the Grand Gallery and the granite burial chamber unit beyond were constructed simultaneously.

46 The burial chamber

1 Petrie 1924, p. 59.

2 A division sensed by some of its modern visitors who, after struggling up to the top of the Grand Gallery, turn back down the wooden staircase when confronted with the low granite corridor ahead.

3 The cubit size employed consistently throughout the burial chamber appears to have been 52.41 cm (Petrie 1883, p. 81); that of the rest of the Pyramid 52.35 cm (Dorner 1998, and see p. 65 note 9 above). Although this difference of less than a quarter of an inch may appear to be a frivolous distinction, at the size of the Great Pyramid baselines its use would have resulted in errors five to ten times larger that those that Petrie recorded in his survey (1883, p. 39).

4 From the graffiti visible on the limestone and granite blocks in the five entresols, almost all of the granite blocks are separately numbered and marked by the pyramid-makers with cardinal points and centre lines, whilst the graffiti on the limestone wall blocks appear to name the gangs that moved them, and those of the limestone vaulting blocks are cubit numbers (PM III, Part I, p. 14). These invaluable graffiti yet await full publication. See especially Vyse (1840, plates by pp. 279 and 284) who provides general views of some of the work gangs' graffiti, and Petrie (1883, pp. 91–4), with an overview of the masons' markings on the granite shafts. Arnold (1991, p. 17) provides a general account of the purposes of many of these markings.

5 There is considerable variation in the quality of finish and cut amongst these granite blocks, as Petrie details (1883, pp. 77–83). Whilst most of the larger surfaces have been part-polished, some still show saw marks (see also Arnold 2003, p. 210) and other evidences of the methods of their working, whilst many handling bosses (Arnold 1991, p. 135) have also been left in place.

6 Arnold 1991, pp. 58ff.

7 As appears to have been the case in most periods of ancient Egyptian history (Arnold 1991, pp. 36ff and 58ff).

8 The granite plugging blocks at least must have been planned from the first full year of full construction (see p. 390 note 8 above, and Petrie 1883, p. 21).

9 Robert Burns, 'To a mouse', in *Poems*, 1786; Petrie 1893, p. 20.

10 Petrie 1883, p. 82. The slope down to the burial chamber's south-eastern corner is of some 2 inches (5.82 cm).

11 Petrie 1883, p. 214.

12 Petrie 1893, p. 21. Petrie returned to the theme of organisation throughout his career; in a splendid unpublished essay from the 1930s preserved in the Brooklyn Museum Library, he attributes Europe's 'Dark Ages' to an over-organised Roman bureaucracy.

13 See chs. 29 and 30.

14 Even perhaps corrected in the manner of some of the corridors in Sneferu's pyramids, see ch. 29 above.

15 Their investigator surmises that this was caused by pressure exerted by the roof beams of the Queen's Chamber (Gantenbrink, www.cheops.org, 'lower southern shaft').

16 Petrie 1883, p. 80.

17 Petrie 1883, p. 82: 'The crack across the Eastern roof-beam has been also daubed with cement [i.e. gypsum plaster], looking therefore as if it had cracked before the chamber was finished.'

18 See further pp. 395ff below.

19 Arnold 1991, pp. 223ff.

20 These five utilitarian spaces are usually described, rather inelegantly, as 'relieving chambers'.

21 Petrie (1883, p. 82) notes that these granite chambers stand between two independent walls of limestone.

22 Petrie 1883, p. 86.

23 Petrie 1883, p. 80.

24 Appendix 5.

25 Gantenbrink www.cheops.org.

26 Petrie 1883, p. 82.

27 Arnold 1991, p. 234; Lehner 1998, pp. 108 ff.

28 Petrie 1883, p. 91.

29 Petrie 1883, pp. 79–80.

30 Vyse 1840, I, pp. 200ff. The same valiant 'Daoud' also appears to have excavated the deep shaft in the Subterranean Chamber. As the Colonel describes him, he was 'an excellent workman, extremely zealous and active and possessed of great strength, although he was said to live entirely on spirits, and Hhasheésh (an intoxicating preparation of hemp)' (Vyse 1840, I, p. 199 n.).

31 Along with Vyse and the British vice-consul, Colonel Patrick Campbell was the holder and sustainer of the firman under which these investigations of the Great Pyramid were conducted (Vyse 1840, I, p. 13).

32 Bruce 1813, p. 114, where Nathaniel Davison is called 'Davidson' (Vyse 1840, I, p. 200). Vyse also notes (p. 276) that other travellers had reported the existence of the tunnel before Davison's exploration.

33 Other than the elaborate description by Petrie (1883, pp. 91–4) these granite shafts and their markings have not been studied or recorded.

34 Vyse 1840, I, pp. 279 and 284. Stadelmann (1997a, pl. 35) shows the quality of these graffiti.

35 Hans Goedicke kindly informs me that the last of these names employs a royal titulary – Mededju, or 'straight of eye' – that would appear to be a reference to archery: an approximation of 'dead-eye Dick', and an apt appellation for a king whose subjects worked with such precision.

47 To the top

1 See ch. 42.

2 See ch. 22. Had the pyramid-makers employed Dieter Arnold's theoretical 'interior ramps', their slopes would also have been part-contained inside the Pyramid's baselines (Arnold 1991, p. 101 and fig. 3.53 (4)).

3 Borchardt 1928, pp. 20–4; Arnold 1991, p. 99 and fig. 3.53 (1B).

4 Petrie gives the surviving height of the Great Pyramid in 1881 at 138.48 m and the average height of the last surviving courses – courses 193 to 203 – at 0.56 m (Petrie 1883, pl. VIII). Given that his estimated finished height for the Pyramid is 146.71 m (1883, p. 43), there would be room for another 14.7 courses, which I have rounded to 14, to allow for the setting of a larger pyramidion at course 217.

5 For example Petrie 1883, p. 43.

6 Cf. pp. 42ff.

7 Lehner 1997, p. 222.

8 Petrie 1893, p. 19. There are also several blocks in European museums; both Howard Vyse and Piazzi Smyth, for example, helped themselves to substantial souvenirs; see for example, *EAAP*, catalogue no. 35 (Christiane Ziegler).

9 Petrie 1883, p. 45.

10 Petrie's observation (1883, p. 212) that the surviving stones appear to have been cut before being placed into their positions on the finished pavement would add to the impression that these are indeed replacements of the original eastern baseline, set up towards the ending of the work.

11 Arnold 1991, p. 169; Valloggia 1997, fig. 6.

12 Petrie 1883, pp. 37–8, pl. X. A somewhat similar arrangement is also to be seen at the Bent Pyramid, where the foundation stones at its corners mark out a larger footprint than the baseline of the pyramid itself (see Dorner 1986, fig. 1 and pl. 5a).

13 These are the three so-called Queen's Pyramids (*PM* III, Part I, pp. 16–17; Lehner 1997, p. 116), and a fourth recently discovered pyramid, set between the line of three and the baseline of the Great Pyramid (Hawass 1996b).

14 Hawass 1996b, pp. 385–6; Rossi 1999, p. 221.

15 Hawass and Verner 1996, p. 181 and pl. 54.

48 After the Pyramid

1 Petrie 1883, p. 213.

2 Lehner 1985a, p. 124 (B24).

3 Just as Perring had recognised in the 1830s: 'stone cuttings and rubbish were thrown over the front of the rock, where they still remain in prodigious quantities' (Perring 1839, introduction to the plates).

4 Petrie (1883, p. 213) (as quoted at the beginning of this chapter) gives the only description of the northern tips known to me; evidence of the plentiful amounts of ancient domestic rubbish deposited in Khufu's quarry can be seen in figs. 6 and 93 above.

5 The site plan (Perring 1838) shows the natural rock of the Giza Plateau extending but 100 feet (30.3 m) beyond the Great Pyramid's north-eastern corner and only 220 feet (67.0 m) beyond its north-western corner. This

would suggest that the levelled area that presently lies beyond those two points, and which is approximately twice as wide, is composed of ancient debris. See also Lehner 1985a, p. 124 (B24).

6 Lehner 1985a, fig. 3B and pp. 118–24.

7 Lehner (1985b, fig. 3B) provides an overview of the Giza Plateau late in Khufu's reign; Jánosi (1999, fig. 13) strips away the present confusions of Khufu's cemeteries, which were altered and extended down through following centuries. I regret that I was unable to use Peter Jánosi's full treatment of this subject, which appeared too late for inclusion in this book, and I trust that his outline of the cemeteries' history given in *EAAP* will not have greatly changed.

8 Appendix 1.

9 Jánosi 1999, pp. 29–32; and see chs. 9 and 10 above.

10 See, for example, the plan in Arnold 2003, 'Dahshur', p. 65.

11 Jánosi 1999, fig. 14.

12 Junker 1929, pp. 157–61.

13 The limestone used for the construction of the four mastaba cemeteries was the equivalent of about 2 per cent of the Great Pyramid's quarry blocks.

14 The pyramids, for example, of Khaba and Nebka II at Zawiyet el-ʿAryan (pp. 263 and 435), and Djedefre at Abu Roash (p. 431).

15 Mark Lehner's painstaking re-examination of the circumstances surrounding the entombment of Hetep-heres' funerary equipment (1985b, pp. 1–44 and 72–4) shows that its deposition on the Giza Plateau predated the laying-out of Khufu's eastern cemetery as it now appears, and this in turn suggests a construction phase at Khufu's Giza that is earlier than the first phase that I describe. Unfortunately, the ancient circumstances of the deposition of that golden cache are so ambiguous, I would suggest, that the present data are insufficient to prove what actually occurred. At all events, this should not affect the general outline that I propose here. Apart from the improbable notion that the position of the Great Pyramid was itself decided by the location of the tomb of Khufu's mother, the only role which the entombment of Hetep-heres' funerary equipment could play within my scheme of building is that of an architectural false start – for as all its commentators have agreed (Lehner 1985b, pp. 1–44 and 72–4), the caching of Hetep-heres' funerary equipment was but partially completed then buried and obscured in Khufu's lifetime, beneath Reisner's so-called 'Queen's Street'.

16 Nour et al. 1960, p. 7, and pl. XI A. That the design of these two southern boat pits differs from those upon the east side of the Pyramid may indicate that they were made during a different phase of work, see further below.

17 Given the present level of our understanding of the purposes of this building, the old term 'Mortuary Temple' is tendentious. I have therefore adopted Arnold's neutral term of Pyramid Temple, along with the term Valley Temple for the lost temple that is generally believed to have stood

upon the Giza Plain (see, for example, Arnold 2002, p. 187, 'Pyramid temple', and p. 252, 'Valley temple').

18 Lehner (1985b, fig. 12) indicates the alignment of these three Pyramids with the Trench in the design field.

19 An alternative date would be around years 12–13 of construction, when work upon the last pair of miniature shafts – the last elements within the Pyramid whose lines could have been usefully checked against elements set up in the design field – would have been completed.

20 The recently excavated temple by the Red Pyramid may be added to the examples given earlier (see, for example, Stadelmann 1997b, pp. 4–5).

21 See further pp. 423–4 below.

22 Goedicke 1971, pp. 19–20 (5).

23 Hassan 1960, p. 23 and pl. VI B, and the ending of ch. 29 above. Note too that unless the quarry teams at Aswan working in the first years of Khufu's reign were considerably larger than my present estimate (see pp. 178–9 above) the fact that all the granite blocks used within the Great Pyramid were installed before the ending of the eighth year of its construction could provide a shadowy indication of the date of the Pyramid Temple's construction, in which considerable quantities of granite blocks were employed (Arnold 1997, pp. 49–51).

24 In similar fashion too, the four pyramids nearby, both the majestic row of three which appear to have housed the graves of queens and their diminutive neighbour, are now largely ruined, the fourth being so reduced that its very existence was only detected in 1991, in the course of restoration work (Hawass 1996b).

25 See, for example, Arnold 1997, pp. 49–50 and fig. 13.

26 Lehner 1985a, pp. 118–20 (B6).

27 Herodotus, Book, 2, ch. 24. To assume, like Herodotus, that this stone causeway was used 'for the conveyance of the [Great Pyramid's] stones' (Rawlinson 1848, II, p. 201), is to propose that after cutting their blocks from the Giza quarries, Khufu's pyramid-makers then slid them for half a mile down to the desert's edge then another half a mile through the soggy cultivation and up again upon this narrow causeway, over the Plateau's 130 foot cliff to the foot of the Great Pyramid! And even after this astonishing peregrination, the patient stone haulers would have had to elevate their quarry blocks from the area of the Pyramid Temple to the heights of the Pyramid above. In reality, of course, the situation was the reverse. With its battered walls, the very form of Khufu's great stone causeway appears to owe its origin to the enormous ramps of mud and broken rock that served to carry quarry stone up onto the early pyramids (cf. p. 401 above).

28 The attribution of the Old Kingdom blocks found within the pyramid of Amenemhat I at Lisht have been widely discussed; see Goedicke (1971) and Dorothea Arnold, in *EAAP* catalogue, nos. 23, 38–43 for a recent

partial re-evaluation. Goedicke (1971, pp. 9–10) also lists other fragments of relief from Khufu's funerary monuments.

29 Hassan 1960, pp. 17–18.

30 Briefly in Lehner 1997, p. 232; Hawass (1997) provides maps and further details of these dislocated elements.

31 Two recent, authoritative though rather different readings of the functions and accommodations of this temple are proposed by Arnold (1997, pp. 47–59) and Stadelmann (1997a).

49 The rites of death

1 Arnold (1997, pp. 45ff) provides a recent synopsis of the material discussed in the following paragraphs.

2 *PM* III, Part II, pp. 877–8.

3 Fakhry 1961, I, pp. 106ff, pl. 49; Arnold 1997, p. 49.

4 Fakhry 1961, II, part 2; *LÄ* II, cols. 919–20, 'Güterprozession' (Helen Jacquet-Gordon).

5 *PM* III, Part II, pp. 877–8; Edel 1996.

6 Goedicke 1971, pp. 16–19 (nos. 3 and 4); *EAAP* catalogue nos. 41 and 38 (Dorothea Arnold). A small fragment of a man leading an ox was also excavated by Khufu's Pyramid Temple (see Reisner and Smith 1955, p. 5 and fig. 7).

7 The greater part of these loose blocks lack inscriptions and thus may be ascribed to different kings and different monuments. The consensus is that some of these pieces date to the reigns of either Sneferu or Khufu (see Goedicke 1971, nos. 1–7, 10–22, 29–30, 53); *EAAP*, catalogue nos. 23 and 38–43 (Dorothea Arnold).

8 Goedicke 1971, pp. 9–10 and 31–41, nos. 11–18, and *EAAP*, catalogue no. 23 (Dorothea Arnold).

9 Goedicke 1971, pp. 42–5, nos. 19–20.

10 Goedicke 1971, pp. 19–20, no. 5.

11 Arnold (1999b) summarises this material.

12 Kemp 1989, pp. 112–17; Verner 1986, p. 187; Ikram 2000, p. 669.

13 'The royal mortuary cult of the Old Kingdom systematically established a mythic world of meaning' (Assmann 2001, p. 51).

14 Hans Goedicke's restoration (Goedicke 1971, pp. 19–20, block 5) would make this name contemporary with the Pyramid itself.

15 Paraphrased from Assmann (2002, pp. 57–8), who offers an account of this expression, although I am reluctant to share his opinion that the act of building the early pyramids was, of itself, the 'realisation of a symbolic purpose', preferring to believe that these pyramids, in common with the founding acts of many religions, were endowed with their 'symbolic purpose' at a later date; an order of events borne out on this occasion, as in so many other instances, by the relative age of the texts and the events and/or the monuments that they describe.

16 Arnold (1981) questioned the roles that the Valley and Pyramid temples had long played in the archaeological imagination; the popular media, however, have yet to abandon such Victorian 'reconstructions'.

17 See ch. 10. D'Auria (1992, catalogue entry 6 and figs. 4 and 36) has a fine description of a Giza mummy.

18 Reisner and Smith 1955, pp. 21–2.

19 And in the tight bindings of these hypothetical shrouds may we not detect the same anxieties, the same protective claustrophobias, that placed his corpse within a wooden box, fitted it into a stone sarcophagus and set it in the oppressive bulk of the world's most monumental tomb?

20 Here we are at the nub of the so-called 'mystery' that has grown up around this Pyramid, for a great part of our modern world asks not what function its construction may have performed – which was, as we have seen, fundamental to that ancient state – but what purpose the building could have served on its completion. The best part of these 'mysteries', then, are but the product of the gap in time and in mentality between ourselves and those who made King Khufu's tomb; between its ancient makers and the expectations of the modern world.

21 Arnold 1991, p. 223, and fig. 5.15.

22 I have assumed that Khufu's body was enclosed in the rectangular wooden coffin that was typical of the period, and with proportions similar to those of his sarcophagus (*LÄ* V, cols. 430–4, 'Sarg' (Günther Lapp)). Anne Macy Roth's fine description of a noble's coffin from the Giza cemeteries serves to show the manner of the day: 'The outer surfaces of the coffin were perfectly flat and uninscribed, though the whole was beautifully crafted of cedar boards fitted together with round wooden pegs; knotholes were carefully patched with better wood. The interior was equally unadorned, as was the lid, which was recessed to fit the top edge of the coffin' (D'Auria 1992, pp. 76–7).

23 Petrie's remark (1883, p. 216) that the sarcophagus 'is nearly an inch wider than the beginning of the ascending passage' may be set against his interior measurements of the sarcophagus (1883, p. 86), which are around 5½ inches smaller!

24 At $1.98 \text{ m} \times 0.68 \text{ m} \times 0.87 \text{ m}$ (adapted from Petrie 1883, p. 86) the interior volume of this sarcophagus would be 1.17 m^3, which is identical to the volume of the Pyramid's ideal block size, as given on pp. 116ff above.

25 Later in Egyptian history, images of the progress of the dead on just such ramp-like corridors as those of the Great Pyramid's became a popular illustration to the funerary texts – see for example the illustrations of the third to the sixth hour of the Am Duat (cf. Hornung 1999, pp. 44–6, figs. 16–18).

26 Petrie notes that for the plugging blocks 'to be slid down the passage, it was necessary that the opening to the Queen's Chamber should be completely covered with a continuous floor. The traces of this floor may still be seen, in the holes for beams of stone, across the passage; and in

fragments of stone and cement ["plaster"] still sticking on the floor of the Queen's Chamber passage at that point. It is certain, then, that the Queen's Chamber was closed and concealed before the ascending passage was closed' (Petrie 1883, p. 216). (Modern reconstructions of the detail of this closure, however, follow that of Borchardt (1932).)

27 Some have suggested (Edwards 1993, pp. 123–4; Verner 2002, pp. 197ff) that one or both of these rooms were built as alternative burial chambers: a notion that derives from Borchardt's mistaken three-stage theory of the Great Pyramid's construction (Borchardt 1932); others that the Subterranean Chamber was a place where aspects of King Khufu's spirit mixed with the gods, and that the Queen's Chamber served as a ceremonial hall, and that the great niche in its eastern wall was designed to hold a statue of the king (Stadelmann 1997a, pp. 118–21; Lehner 1997, p. 111).

28 Reisner and Smith 1955; *EAAP*, Catalogue no. 33 (Julie Anderson).

29 This theory has a considerable pedigree: 'It was also by this way certainly that the attendants of the funeral penetrated even to the interior of the building, and returned from it after rendering the last duties to the prince, and depositing his corpse in the mausoleum he himself had chosen' (Savary 1786, letter 18).

30 There is no way of knowing, of course, how the Pyramid's entrance was set into its now-vanished casing. Comparing a passage on the Great Pyramid's door from the Greek writer Strabo, to the 'traces of a stone flap door, or turning block, in the mouth of the South Pyramid of Dahshur [a small satellite pyramid to the Bent Pyramid]', Petrie's suggestion was a single casing stone set upon a swinging hinge (Petrie 1883, p. 168 and pl. XII); a solution that preceded Arnold's somewhat unconvincing reconsideration of the problem at Dahshur (Arnold 1991, pp. 220ff), and taken up again at Giza by Stadelmann (1997a, p. 111), and reprinted by Lehner (1997, p. 39).

50 Stone

1 Capart (1930, fig. 44) provides an impressive image of this causeway.

2 Valloggia 2003.

3 Valloggia 1997, fig. 6.

4 The baselines of the so-called Abu Roash pyramid are less than 350 feet (106.20 m) (Valloggia 1997, p. 418).

5 Although its current excavators have suggested that Djedefre's reign may have been far longer (Valloggia 1997, p. 419).

6 *MRA* V, pls. 14–16; Stadelmann 1997a, pp. 130ff; Lehner 1997, pp. 122–6.

7 Petrie says that '[the corridor's] azimuth is almost exactly the mean azimuth of the sides . . . This is much the same arrangement as in the Great Pyramid' (Petrie 1883, p. 104); Spence (2000) underlines the extreme accuracy of the Pyramid's baseline orientation.

8 Lehner 1997, pp. 122–3.

9 Lehner 1997, pp. 139 and 248; Stadelmann 1997a, p. 140 and fig. 41, for a reconstruction of the pyramid's intended plan. Capart's photographs (Capart 1930, figs. 18–24) provide the best views of the extent of this enormous project, which has been buried once again in drifted sand.

10 Lehner 1997, pp. 10–11.

11 Seven of these pyramids measure about 78.75 m (some 150 cubits) at their baselines (Lehner 1997, p. 17).

12 Lehner 1997, p. 16; Verner 2002, pp. 265ff. All these pyramids have their entrance corridors set low upon their northern sides, followed by a corridor that, typically, runs down through two small rooms until, at around the level of the pyramid's baselines and directly underneath its central apex, it gives access to the burial chamber, an oblong room covered by a massive limestone vault made in the manner of the Queen's Chamber of the Great Pyramid (Arnold 1991, pp. 191–2).

13 Assmann 2002, p. 53.

14 Assmann 2001, pp. 119ff.

15 See, for example, 'The Song of the Harper' (Simpson et al. 1972, pp. 306ff).

16 For an outline of later ancient Egyptian belief concerning building in King Djoser's reign, see *LÄ III*, cols. 145–8, 'Imhotep' (Dietrich Wildung).

17 'Year 47, 2nd month of Winter, Day 25 [January, 1232 BC], the Treasury Scribe Hadnakht, son of Tjenro and Tewosret, came to take a stroll and enjoy himself in the West of Memphis, along with his brother Panakht, Scribe of the Vizier. He said: "O all you Gods of the West of Memphis . . . and glorified dead . . . grant a full lifetime in serving your good pleasure, a goodly burial after a happy old age, like yourself!" ' (*KRI* III, 148: 5–10).

18 Simpson et al. 1972, pp. 159ff.

19 Assmann 2002, pp. 131–4 and 237ff.

20 *LÄ* III, cols. 1110ff 'Maat' (Wolfgang Helck).

21 *LÄ* I, cols. 145–9, 'Altar' (Rainer Stadelmann) and Arnold 1997, pp. 45ff; Assmann 2001, pp. 47ff, esp. p. 51.

22 Assmann 2001, p. 79.

23 Assmann 2001, pp. 32–3.

24 Arnold 1999a, pp. 97 and 115.

25 Arnold 1999a, pp. 152ff.

51 Spirit

1 Translated by Raymond Faulkner (Faulkner 1969, p. 311).

2 Faulkner 1969, p. 246, extracted from Utterance 599 (1650–1).

3 Hornung (1999, pp. 3–6) provides a brief description of these texts; see also *LÄ* IV, cols. 14–23, 'Pyramidentexte' (Hartwig Altenmüller).

4 The Pyramid Texts were discovered at Sakkara in 1880 by Émile Brugsch of the Cairo Museum; their first publication, in *Recueil de Travaux* 1881, was by the French egyptologist Gaston Maspero.

5 The Prefaces of Piankoff (1968) and Faulkner (1969) provide useful accounts of the progress and pitfalls in the process of the Pyramid Texts' translations. See also Assmann 2001, pp. 83ff.

6 Although Sethe's synoptic treatment of the Texts was surely derived from German nineteenth-century biblical analysis, the use of the Pyramid Texts as a 'symbolic' explanation of the pyramids is founded upon more traditional modes of biblical exegesis (see, for example, *CHB*, chs. 7 and 8).

7 *LÄ* V, cols. 18–20, 'Pyramidentexte' (Hartwig Altenmüller); Utterances 427–34 (777–85).

8 Taken from Utterance 723, given above.

9 Piankoff (1968) provides a translation of the texts within the pyramid of Unis; Faulkner (1969) a translation and extension of Sethe's synoptic edition.

10 Faulkner 1969, p. 246, extracted from Utterance 599 (1650–1).

11 See ch. 2, and more recently, for example, Assmann 2001, pp. 94–5.

12 Allen (1994) provides a recent overview.

13 Cf. ch. 49.

14 An elementary observation, for example, is that Khufu's sarcophagus could not have been carried through the Great Pyramid's corridors at the time of funeral as the Pyramid Texts apparently describe (see p. 371 above).

15 'The identification of the king with Osiris . . . is especially stressed in Spell 219 and the many allusions to the myth of Osiris take on even greater weight, and we have here the earliest texts in which Osiris appears as ruler of the netherworld. Practically all the important motifs of the Osiris myth are found' (Hornung 1999, p. 6).

16 *LÄ* IV, 'Osiris' (John Gwyn Griffiths); cols. 623–5 provide a list of speculations on the elusive origins of this god.

17 Hornung 1999, p. 1; *LÄ* V, col. 20, 'Pyramidentexte' (Hartwig Altenmüller).

18 'As for anyone who shall lay a finger on this pyramid and this temple which belong to me and to my double, he will have laid his finger on the Mansion of Horus in the firmament, he will have offended the Lady of the Mansion everywhere . . . his affair will be judged by the Ennead [of Gods] and he will be nowhere and his house will be nowhere; he will be one proscribed, one who eats himself' (Faulkner 1969, p. 202, extracted from Utterance 354 (1278–9)).

19 Simpson et al. 1972, pp. 211ff.

20 'Mythologising may be as much a way of keeping problems in suspense as of solving them. It makes endurable the contemplation of irreconcilable contraries' (Beer 1983, p. 114).

21 'Arise!' 'Stand Up!' 'Lift yourself!' (Assmann 2001, pp. 127–8).

22 Stadelmann 1991; 1997a, pp. 120–2. The three rooms in the Bent Pyramid, evidently the first with this number, are a collocation of two stages of building work (see ch. 33).

23 Rather than accommodating the ministrations of the priests, the temples were designed to facilitate the god's progress out into the world, as Assmann notes (2001, pp. 32ff).

24 Firth and Quibell 1935, I, pp. 46–7; Kaiser 1997, pp. 196ff.

25 The discrepancy is some 8 inches (0.21 m), see Appendix 4.

26 Assmann 2001, p. 185.

27 *LÄ* VI, cols. 623–33, 'Osiris' (John Gwyn Griffiths), provides a splendid general reference for the god.

28 Goedicke 2000, pp. 408–9, n. 55; Assmann 2001, pp. 96–7.

29 *LÄ* III, cols. 744–5, 'Kornosiris' (Christine Seeber); *LÄ* VI, col. 628, 'Osiris' (John Gwyn Griffiths).

30 Assmann (2001, p. 77): 'form and meaning' in the god Osiris and the Sun. In similar fashion, all of the elements of Osiris' distinctive costume appear in images far older than that god's first-known appearance in the pyramid of Unis. The typical iconography of Osiris, indeed, is already assembling by the beginning of the pyramid age in the funerary images of the kings themselves; statues found in Djoser's and Sneferu's funerary complexes, for example, show those kings standing in a typically Osirian pose, with legs together and arms crossed and holding sceptres.

31 By such reasoning, the time of Khufu's funeral may be set to August, to that dramatic month when, as we now know, the northern alignment of the Great Pyramid's baselines was fixed, a time that also corresponded to the opening of the irrigation channels, and thus to the transformation of the dead land of Egypt into fertile fields (Willcocks and Craig 1913, pp. 306ff).

32 Rainer Stadelmann's observation (1990, pp. 126ff) that Djedefre and Khafre, both sons of Khufu, were the first Egyptian kings to bear the epithet 'son of Re' may be another reflection of Khufu's unique place in the formation of Egyptian kingship, just as his pyramid would show; another such reflection may be the untypical name of the Great Pyramid itself, see pp. 423–4 above.

Bibliography

ABBREVIATIONS

AA	*The Archaeology of Africa: Food, Metals and Towns*, ed. Thurstan Shaw, Paul Sinclair, Bassey Andah and Alex Okpoko, London, 1993
AEMT	*Ancient Egyptian Materials and Technology*, ed. Paul T. Nicholson and Ian Shaw, Cambridge, 2000
Ann.Serv.	*Annales du service des antiquités de l'Égypte*
BdE	*Bibliothèque d'étude, Institut français d'archéologie orientale*, Cairo
BIE	*Bulletin de l'institut d'Égypte*
BIFAO	*Bulletin de l'institut français d'archéologie orientale*, Cairo
CAJ	*Cambridge Archaeological Journal*
CHB	*The Cambridge History of the Bible*, III, ed. S. L. Greenslade, Cambridge, 1963
Description	*Description de l'Égypte, ou Recueil des observations et des recherches qui ont été faites en Égypte pendant l'expédition de l'armée française*, Paris, 1809–28
EA	*Egyptian Archaeology, the Bulletin of the Egypt Exploration Society*
EAAP	*Egyptian Art in the Age of the Pyramids* (Metropolitan Museum Exhibition Catalogue), New York, 1999
EJ-PL	*Études sur l'Ancien Empire et la nécropole de Saqqâra dédiées à Jean-Philippe Lauer*, ed. Catherine Berger and Bernard Mathieu, Montpellier, 1997

GT	W. B. Emery, *Great Tombs of the First Dynasty* (3 vols.), I, Cairo, 1949; II, London, 1954; III, London, 1958
HUPAÄ	*Haus und Palast im Alten Ägypten* (Papers from a symposium held in Cairo, April 1992, ed. Manfred Bietak), Vienna, 1996
JARCE	*Journal of the American Research Centre in Egypt*
JEA	*Journal of Egyptian Archaeology*
JNES	*Journal of Near Eastern Studies*
KRI III	*Ramesside Inscriptions* III, translated and annotated by K. A. Kitchen, Oxford, 2000
LÄ	*Lexikon der Ägyptologie*, ed. Wolfgang Helck, Eberhard Otto and Wolfhart Westendorf (7 vols.), Wiesbaden, 1975–92
LD	Karl Richard Lepsius. *Denkmäler aus Aegypten und Aethiopien*, Berlin and Leipzig, 1849–1913
MDAIK	*Mitteilungen des Deutschen Archäologischen Instituts Abteilung Kairo*
MRA	Vito Maragioglio and Celeste Ambrogio Rinaldi, *L'architettura delle Piramidi Menfite* (8 vols), Turin and Rapallo, 1963–75
OED	*Oxford English Dictionary*, Oxford, 1989
PM	Bertha Porter and Rosalind L. B. Moss, *Topographical Bibliography of Ancient Egyptian Hieroglyphic Texts, Reliefs and Paintings*, Oxford, 1927–
RdE	*Revue d'égyptologie*
STAT	*Stationen. Beiträge zur Kulturgeschichte Ägyptens: Rainer Stadelmann Gewidmet*, ed. Heike Guksch and Daniel Polz, Mainz, 1998
SWKS	*Studies in Honor of William Kelly Simpson*, ed. Peter der Manuelian (2 vols.), Boston, 1996
TAE	*The Temple in Ancient Egypt*, ed. Stephen Quirke, London, 1997
ZÄS	*Zeitschrift für Ägyptische Sprache und Altertumskunde*

References

Abu Al-Izz, M. S. 1971. *Landforms of Egypt*, trans. Yūsuf A. Fāyid, Cairo

Adams, William Y. 1977. *Nubia*, London

Allen, James P. 1994. 'Reading a Pyramid', *BdE* 106, pp. 5–28

    1999. 'Dynastic and Regnal Dates', in *EAAP*, p. xx

    2004. Review of Catherine Berger-el Naggar et al., 'Les textes de la pyramide de Pépy Ier', *JEA* 90 (Reviews Supplement), pp. 12–16

D'Amicone, Elvira 1988. 'The Religious Buildings and the Necropolis of Gebelein in the Third Millennium B.C.', in *Egyptian Civilization: Religious Beliefs*, ed. Anna Maria Donadoni Roveri, pp. 62–80, Milan

    1994. 'La necropoli', in *Gebelein il villaggio e la necropoli*, ed. Anna Maria Donadoni Roveri, pp. 19–39, Turin

Anderson, Julie 1999. 'Furniture of the Old Kingdom', in *EAAP*, pp. 117–19

Anthes, Rudolf 1928. *Die Felseninschriften von Hatnub*, Leipzig

Ammar, Hamed 1954. *Growing up in an Egyptian Village*, London

Arnold, Dieter 1981. 'Überlegungen zum Problem des Pyramidenbaues',
     MDAIK 37, pp. 15–28
     1985. 'Moses und Aida: Das Alte Ägypten in der Oper', in *Ägypten – Dauer
     und Wandel*, Mainz
     1987. *Der Pyramidenbezirk des Königs Amenemhet III. in Dahschur*, Mainz
     1991. *Building in Egypt*, New York
     1997. 'Royal Cult Complexes of the Old and Middle Kingdoms', in *Temples of
     Ancient Egypt*, ed. Byron E. Shafer, Ithaca, NY
     1999. *Temples of the Last Pharaohs*, New York
     2003. *The Encyclopaedia of Ancient Egyptian Architecture*, ed. Nigel and Helen
     Strudwick, London
Arnold, Dorothea 1999. 'Royal Reliefs', in *EAAP*, pp. 83–101
Arnold, Dorothea and Bourriau, Janine (eds.) 1993. *An Introduction to Ancient
     Egyptian Pottery*, Mainz
Arnold, Dorothea and Pischikova, Elena 1999. 'Stone Vessels: Luxury Items
     with Manifold Implications', in *EAAP*, pp. 121–32
Arnold, Dorothea and Ziegler, Christiane 1999. 'Introduction', in *EAAP*,
     pp. xxi–xxiii
Assmann, Jan 1996. 'Preservation and Presentation of Self in Ancient
     Egyptian Portraiture', in *SWKS* I, p. 55–81
     2001. *The Search for God in Ancient Egypt* (David Lorton's translation of
     Ägypten: Theologie und Frömmigkeit einer frühen Hochkultur, Munich, 1984),
     Ithaca, NY
     2002. *The Mind of Egypt* (Andrew Jenkins' translation of *Ägypten. Eine
     Sinngeschichte*, Munich, 1996), New York
Aston, Barbara G., Harrell, James A. and Shaw, Ian 2000. 'Stone', in *AEMT*,
     pp. 5–77
D'Auria, Sue, Lacovara, Peter and Roehrig, Catherine H. (eds.) 1992. *Mummies
     and Magic: The Funerary Arts of Ancient Egypt*, Boston
Badawy, Alexander 1965. *Ancient Egyptian Architectural Design*, Berkeley
Baines, John and Málek, Jaromír 1980. *Atlas of Ancient Egypt*, Oxford
Bann, Stephen 1984. *The Clothing of Clio*, Cambridge
Bard, Katherine A. 2000. 'The Emergence of the Egyptian State', in *The Oxford
     History of Ancient Egypt*, ed. Ian Shaw, pp. 61–88, Oxford
Bass, George (ed.) 1972. *A History of Seafaring*, London
Beaucour, Fernand, Laissus, Yves and Orgogozo, Chantal 1990. *The Discovery of
     Egypt*, Paris
von Beckerath, Jürgen 1997. *Chronologie des pharaonischen Ägypten: die
     Zeitbestimmung der ägyptischen Geschichte von der Vorzeit bis 332 v. Chr.* Mainz
Beer, Gillian 1983. *Darwin's Plots*, London
Bietak, Manfred 1979. 'Urban Archaeology and the "Town Problem" in
     Ancient Egypt', in *Egyptology and the Social Sciences*, ed. Kent Weeks, Cairo
Black, H. M. 1963. 'The Printed Bible', in *CHB*, pp. 408–75
Bloxam, Elizabeth and Storemyr, Per 2002. 'Old Kingdom Basalt Quarrying
     Activities at Widan el-Faras, Northern Faiyum Desert', *JEA* 88, pp. 23–36

Bober, Harry 1980. 'The Eclipse of the Pyramids in the Middle Ages', in *Pyramidal Influence in Art*, ed. P. Berg and M. Jones, Dayton, Ohio

Bonnet, Charles and Valbelle, Dominique 1975. 'Le village de Deir el-Médineh: reprise de l'étude archéologique', *BIFAO* 75, pp. 430–46

— 1997. 'The Middle Kingdom Temple of Hathor at Serabit el-Khadim', in *TAE*, pp. 82–9

Borchardt, Ludwig 1898. 'Das Grab des Menes', *ZÄS* 36, pp. 87–105

— 1922. *Gegen die Zahlenmystik an der grossen Pyramide bei Gise*, Berlin

— 1926. *Längen und Richtungen der vier Grundkanten der grossen Pyramide bei Gise*, Berlin

— 1928. *Die Entstehung der Pyramide, an der Baugeschichte der Pyramide bei Mejdum nachgewiesen*, Berlin

— 1932. *Einiges zur dritten Bauperiode der grossen Pyramide bei Gise*, Berlin

Botti, Giuseppe and Peet, T. Eric 1928. *Il Giornale della Necropoli Di Tebe*, Turin

Bourriau, Janine D., Nicholson, Paul T. and Rose, Pamela J. 2000. 'Pottery', in *AEMT*, pp. 121–48

Breasted, James Henry 1906. *Ancient Records of Egypt* (6 vols.), New York

— 1907. *A History of Egypt* (2nd edn), New York (1st edn New York, 1905)

Brewer, Douglas J. and Friedman, Renée F. 1989. *Fish and Fishing in Ancient Egypt*, Warminster

Brovarski, Edward 1996. 'An Inventory List from "Covington's Tomb" etc.', in *SWKS*, pp. 117–55

Bruce, James 1813. *Travels to Discover the Source of the Nile* (3rd edn), Edinburgh

Butzer, Karl W. 1976. *Early Hydraulic Civilization in Egypt*, Chicago

— 1982. Review of Karl Kromer '*Siedlungsfunde aus dem frühen Alten Reich in Giseh*', *JNES* 41.2, pp. 93–5

Buxton, Richard 1994. *Imaginary Greece: The Contexts of Mythology*, Cambridge

Cameron, Ian (ed.) 1962. *Howard Hawks* (National Film Theatre programme notes), London

Cannadine, David 1983. 'The Context, Performance and Meaning of Ritual: The British Monarchy etc.', in *The Invention of Tradition*, ed. Eric Hobsbawm and Terence Ranger, Cambridge

Capart, Jean 1930. *Memphis à l'ombre des pyramides*, Brussels

Carter, Howard and Gardiner, Alan H. 1917. 'The Tomb of Ramesses IV etc.', *JEA* 4, pp. 130–58

Caton-Thompson, G. and Gardner, E. W. 1934. *The Desert Fayum*, London

Černý, Jaroslav 1973. *A Community of Workmen at Thebes in the Ramesside Period*, Cairo

Champollion, Jean-François 1909. *Lettres et Journaux Écrits pendant le Voyage d'Égypte*, cd. H. Hartleben, Paris

Charbonnier, Georges 1969. *Conversations with Claude Lévi-Strauss*, London (trans. of French edn 1961)

Charlton, Nial 1978. 'The Tura Caves', *JEA* 64, p. 128

Chevrier, Henri 1970. 'Technique de la construction dans l'Ancienne Égypte', *RdE* 22, pp. 15–39

Childe, V. Gordon 1954. *What Happened in History*, Harmondsworth

Clarke, Somers and Engelbach, Reginald 1930. *Ancient Egyptian Masonry: The Building Craft*, Oxford

Cole, J. H. 1925. *The Determination of the Exact Size and Orientation of the Great Pyramid of Giza*, Cairo

Conant, Kenneth John 1978. *Carolingian and Romanesque Architecture*, Harmondsworth

Conard, Nicholas J. 2000. 'Flint Artefacts from the 1988/1989 Excavations at Giza', *MDAIK* 56, pp. 21–41

Cooper. W. R. 1877. *A Short History of the Egyptian Obelisks*, London

Curtis, Garniss H. 1979. 'The Geology of the Valley of the Kings, Thebes, Egypt', in *Theban Royal Tomb Project*, ed. John Romer, p. 21, San Francisco

Curtis, Robert I. 2001. *Ancient Food Technology*, Leiden

D'Hooghe, Alain and Bruwier, Marie-Cecile 2000. *The Great Pyramids of Giza*, Paris

Daniel, Glyn 1975. *150 Years of Archaeology*, London

David, Élisabeth 1999. 'A Note on Egyptian Chronology', in *EAAP*, p. xix

Davis, Whitney 1989. *The Canonical Tradition in Ancient Egyptian Art*, Cambridge

Dawson, W. R., Uphill, E. and Bierbrier, M. L. 1995. *Who Was Who in Egyptology* (3rd edn), London

Debono, Fernand and Mortensen, Bodil 1988. *The Predynastic Cemetery at Heliopolis*, Mainz

Denon, Vivant 1802. *Voyage dans la Basse et la Haute Égypte*, Paris

Dickerman, Lysander 1893. 'On the Etymology and Synonyms of the Word Pyramid', *Journal of the American Oriental Society* 15, pp. xxv–xxxi

Dolphin, Lambert and Moussa, Ali Helmi 1977. *Applications of Modern Sensing Techniques to Egyptology*, Menlo Park, CA

Donadoni Roveri, Anna Maria and Tiradritti, Francesco (eds.) 1998. *Kemet: alle sorgenti del tempo*, Milan

Dorner, Joseph 1981. 'Die Absteckung und astronomische Orientierung ägyptischer Pyramiden', PhD thesis, University of Innsbruck

    1986. 'Form und Ausmasse der Knickpyramide', *MDAIK* 42, pp. 43–58

    1991. 'Überlegungen zur Fassadengliederung der grossen Mastabagräbern aus der 1. Dynastie', *MDAIK* 47, pp. 81–92

    1998. 'Neue Messungen an der Roten Pyramide', *STAT*, pp. 23–30

Dreyer, Günter 1991. 'Zur Rekonstruktion der Oberbauten der Königsgräber der 1. Dynastie in Abydos', *MDAIK* 47, pp. 93–104

    1998a. *Umm El-Qaab I, Das Prädynastische Königsgrab U-j und seine frühen Schriftzeugnisse*, Mainz

    1998b. 'Der erste König der 3. Dynastie', in *STAT*, pp. 31–4

Dreyer, Günter et al. 1990. 'Umm el-Qaab: Nachuntersuchungen im frühzeitlichen Königsfriedhof 3./4. Vorbericht', *MDAIK* 46, pp. 53–90

    1996. 'Umm el-Qaab. Nachuntersuchungen im frühzeitlichen Königsfriedhof 7./8. Vorbericht', *MDAIK* 52, pp. 11–81

1998. 'Umm el-Qaab. Nachuntersuchungen im frühzeitlichen Königsfriedhof 9./10. Vorbericht', *MDAIK* 54, pp. 77–167

2003. 'Umm el-Qaab. Nachuntersuchungen im Frühzeitlichen Königsfriedhof 13./14./15 Vorbericht', *MDAIK* 59, pp. 67–138

Drioton, Etienne 1949. *Le Musée du Caire*, Cairo and Paris

Drower, Margaret S. 1985. *Flinders Petrie: A Life in Archaeology*, London

Ebers, Georg 1887. *Richard Lepsius*, trans. Zoe Underhill, New York

Edel, Elmar 1996. 'Studien zu den Relieffragmenten aus dem Taltempel des Königs Snofru', in *SWKS* I, pp. 199–208

Edgar, John and Edgar, Morton 1923. *The Great Pyramid Passages and Chambers*, Glasgow

Edwards, I. E. S. 1989. Review of Lehner 1985b, *JEA* 75, pp. 261–5

1993. *The Pyramids of Egypt*, Harmondsworth; with various subsequent editions and three major revisions, 1961, 1985 and 1993

Eger, Christophe 1994. 'Steingeräte aus dem Umfeld der Roten Pyramide in Dahschur', *MDAIK* 50, pp. 35–42

Eliade, Mircea 1964. *Shamanism: Archaic Techniques of Ecstasy*, Washington, DC

Emery, W. B. 1939. *Hor-aha*, Cairo

1961. *Archaic Egypt*, Harmondsworth

1963. 'Preliminary Report on the Excavations at Buhen, 1962', *Kush* 11, pp. 116–20

Engelbach, Reginald 1922. *The Aswân Obelisk*, Cairo

1938. 'The Quarries of the Western Nubian Desert', in *Ann.Serv.* XXXIII, pp. 369–89

Engelbach, Reginald and Macaldin, J. W. 1938. 'The Great Lake of Amenophis III at Medînet Habu', *BIE* 20, pp. 51–61

Epigraphic Survey of the Oriental Institute of the University of Chicago 1980. *The Tomb of Kheruef*, Chicago

1986. *The Battle Reliefs of Sety I*, Chicago

Erman, Adolf 1905. *Die ägyptische Religion*, Berlin (trans. *A Handbook of Egyptian Religion*, London, 1907)

Fakhry, Ahmed 1959–61. *Monuments of Sneferu at Dahshur* (2 vols.), Cairo

Faltings, Dina 1989. 'Die Keramik aus den Grabungen an der nördlichen Pyramide des Snofru in Dahschur', *MDAIK* 45, pp. 133–54

Fathy, Hassan 1969. *Gourna: A Tale of Two Villages*, Cairo

Faulkner, R. O. 1955. 'The Installation of the Vizier', *JEA* 41, pp. 18–29

1969. *The Ancient Egyptian Pyramid Texts*, Oxford

Firth, Cecil Mallaby and Quibell, James E. 1935. *The Step Pyramid* (2 vols.), Cairo

Fischer, Henry 1988. *Ancient Egyptian Calligraphy* (3rd edn), New York

Forbes, R. J. 1950. *Metallurgy in Antiquity*, Leiden

Franke, Detlef 2003. 'The Middle Kingdom Offering Formulas – a Challenge', *JEA* 89, pp. 39–57

Friedman, Florence Dunn 1996. 'Notions of Cosmos in the Step Pyramid Complex', in *SWKS*, pp. 337–51

Friedman, Renée, et al. 1999. 'Preliminary Report on Field Work at Hierakonpolis, 1996–1998', *JARCE* 36, pp. 1–35

Galdieri, Eugenio 1982. *Le meraviglie dell'architettura in terra cruda*, Rome

Gale, Rowena, Gasson, Peter, Hepper, Nigel and Killen, Geoffrey 2000. 'Wood', in *AEMT*, pp. 334–71

Gamble, Clive 1986. *The Palaeolithic Settlement of Europe*, Cambridge

Gardiner, Alan H. 1915. *The Tomb of Amenemhēt* (no. 82), London

　1925. 'The Secret Chambers of the Sanctuary of Thoth', *JEA* 11, pp. 2–5

　1957. *Egyptian Grammar* (3rd edn), Oxford

　1961. 'The Egyptian Memnon', *JEA* 47, pp. 91–9

Gardiner, Alan H., with Peet, T. Eric and Černý, Jaroslav 1952–5. *The Inscriptions of Sinai* (2 vols.), London

Garstang, J. 1902. *Mahâsna and Bêt Khallâf*, London

El Gayar, El Sayed and Jones, M. P. 1989. 'A Possible Source of Copper Ore Fragments Found at the Old Kingdom Town of Buhen', *JEA* 75, pp. 31–40

Giedion, Sigfried 1964. *The Eternal Present*, London

Gillispie, Charles and Dewachter, Michel 1987. Introduction to *Monuments of Egypt*, Princeton

Gingerich, Owen 2000. 'Plotting the Pyramids', *Nature* 408, November

Ginter, Boleslaw, Heflik, Wieslaw, Kozlowski, Janusz and Śliwa, Joachim 1980. 'Excavations in the Region of Qasr el-Sagha 1979', *MDAIK* 36, pp. 105–69

Gliddon, George 1849. *Otia Ægyptiaca*, London

Goedicke, Hans 1961. 'Unity and Diversity in the Oldest Religion of Ancient Egypt', in *The Bible and the Ancient Near East: Essays in Honor of William Foxwell Albright*, ed. G. Ernest Wright, New York

　1971. *Re-used Blocks from the Pyramid of Amenemhet I at Lisht*, New York

　2000. 'Abusir – Saqqara – Giza', *Archiví Orientální*, suppl. ix, Prague

Gombrich, E. H. 1959. *The Story of Art* London (15th edn 2002)

　1969. *In Search of Cultural History*, Oxford

Görsdorf, Jochen, et al. 1998. '14C Dating Results of the Archaic Royal Necropolis Umm el-Qaab at Abydos', *MDAIK* 54, pp. 169–75

Goyon, Georges 1969. 'La chaussée monumentale et le temple de la vallée de la pyramide de Khéops', *BIFAO* 67, pp. 49–69

　1977. *Le secret des bâtisseurs des grandes pyramides*, Paris

Green, Peter 1990. *Alexander to Actium*, Berkeley

Groenewegen-Frankfort, A. 1951. *Arrest and Movement*, London

Grzymski, Krzysztof 1999. 'Royal Statuary', in *EAAP*, pp. 51–5

Giusti, Maria Adriana and Godoli, Ezio (eds.) 1997. *L'Orientalismo nell'architettura Italiana etc.*, Viareggio

Gunn, Battiscombe 1926. 'Notes on Two Egyptian Kings', *JEA* 12, pp. 250–3

Gunn, Battiscombe and Peet, T. Eric 1929. 'Four Geometrical Problems from the Moscow Mathematical Papyrus', *JEA* 15, pp. 167–85

Guralnick, Eleanor 1976. 'The Proportions of Some Archaic Greek Sculptured Figures: A Computer Analysis', *Computers and the Humanities* 10, pp. 153–69 van Haarlem, Willem M. 2002. 'The Ivory Objects from Tell Ibrahim Awad', *EA* 20, pp. 16–17

Haas, Hans, et al. 1987. 'Radiocarbon Chronology and the Historical Calendar in Egypt', in *Chronologies in the Near East* (BAR International Series 379 (II)), Oxford, pp. 585–605

Hale, George Ellery 1925. 'The Oriental Ancestry of the Telescope', *Scribners Magazine* April

Hari, Robert 1972. 'Avertissement' to a reprint of *LD*, Geneva

Harrell, James 2004. 'A Stone Vessel Quarry at Gebel Umm Naqqat', *EA* 24, pp. 34–6

Hartung, Ulrich, et al. 2001. *Umm el-Qaab II*, Mainz

Hassan, Fekri A. 1993. 'Town and Village in Ancient Egypt', in *AA*, pp. 551–69

Hassan, Selim 1960. *Excavations at Giza*, vol. X: *The Great Pyramid of Khufu and Its Mortuary Chapel*, Cairo

Hawass, Zahi 1987. *The Funerary Establishments of Khufu, Khafre and Menkaura during the Old Kingdom* (University Microfilms), Ann Arbor

    1990. 'The Pyramids and Temples of Egypt, an Update,' an appendix to a reprint of Petrie 1885, London

    1996a. 'The Workmen's Community at Giza', in *HUPAÄ*, pp. 53–67

    1996b. 'The Discovery of the Satellite Pyramid of Khufu (GI-d)', in *SWKS*, pp. 379–98

    1997. 'The Discovery of the Harbors of Khufu and Khafre at Gîza', in *EJ-PL* I, pp. 245–56

    1998. 'Pyramid Construction. New Evidence Discovered in Giza', in *STAT*, pp. 53–62

    1999. 'Excavating the Old Kingdom: The Egyptian Archaeologists', in *EAAP*, pp. 155–65

    2003. *Secrets from the Sand: My Search for Egypt's Past*, London

Hawass, Zahi and Lehner, Mark 1994. 'The Sphinx: Who Built It, and Why?', *Archaeology* 47, no. 5, pp. 30–47

Hawass, Zahi and Verner, Miroslav 1996. 'Newly Discovered Blocks from the Causeway of Sahure', *MDAIK* 52, pp. 177–86

Hendrickx, Stan, Faltings, Dina, Op de Beek, Lies, Raue, Dietrich and Michiels, Chris 2002. 'Milk, Beer and Bread Technology during the Early Dynastic Period', *MDAIK* 58, pp. 277–304

Hobsbawm, Eric 1983. 'Introduction', in *The Invention of Tradition*, ed. Eric Hobsbawm and Terence Ranger, Cambridge

Hodder, Ian 1992. *Theory and Practice in Archaeology*, London

Hoffmeier, James K. 1993. 'The Use of Basalt in Floors of Old Kingdom Pyramid Temples', *JARCE* 30, pp. 117–23

Hope, Colin 1993. 'Pottery Kilns from the Oasis of el-Dakhla', in Arnold and Bourriau 1993, pp. 121–7

Hornung, Erik 1983. *Conceptions of God in Ancient Egypt*, trans. John Baines, London

    1999. *The Ancient Egyptian Books of the Afterlife*, trans. David Lorton, New York

2001. *The Secret Lore of Egypt: Its Impact on the West*, trans. David Lorton, Ithaca, NY

Houlihan, Patrick F. 1986. *The Birds of Ancient Egypt*, Warminster

Hume, W. F. 1925. *Geology of Egypt*, vol. I, Cairo

Ikram, Salima 2000. 'Meat Processing', in *AEMT*, pp. 656–71

Ikram, Salima and Dodson, Aidan 1998. *The Mummy in Ancient Egypt*, London

Isler, Martin 1983. 'Concerning the Concave Faces on the Great Pyramid', *JARCE* 20, pp. 27–32

2001. *Sticks, Stones and Shadows: Building the Egyptian Pyramids*, Norman, OK

Iverson, Erik 1961. *The Myth of Egypt and Its Hieroglyphs*, Copenhagen

Jánosi, Peter 1997. *Österreich vor den Pyramiden*, Vienna

1999. 'The Tombs of Officials', in *EAAP*, pp. 27–39

Janssen, Jac J. 1975. *Commodity Prices from the Ramessid Period*, Leiden

Jeffreys, David 1998. 'The Topography of Heliopolis and Memphis: Some Cognitive Aspects', in *STAT*, pp. 63–71

Jeffreys, David and Tavares, Ana 1994. 'The Historic Landscape of Early Dynastic Memphis', *MDAIK* 50, pp. 143–73

Jéquier, Gustave 1928. *Le Mastabat Faraoun*, Cairo

Jones, Dilwyn 2000. *An Index of Ancient Egyptian Titles, Epithets and Phrases of the Old Kingdom*, Oxford

Jones, Michael 1995. 'A New Old Kingdom Settlement near Ausim, etc.', *MDAIK* 51, pp. 85–98

Junker, Hermann 1929. *Giza I: Die Mastabas der IV. Dynasty auf dem Westfriedhof*, Vienna

Kadish, Gerald E. 1996. 'Observations on Time and Work-Discipline in Ancient Egypt', in *SWKS*, pp. 439–49

Kaiser, Werner 1994. 'Zu den Königsgräbern der 2. Dynastie in Sakkara und Abydos', in *Essays in Egyptology in Honor of Hans Goedicke*, ed. Betsy M. Bryan and David Lorton, San Antonio, CA

1997. 'Zu den Granitkammern und ihren Vorgängerbauten unter der Stufenpyramide und im Südgrab von Djoser', *MDAIK* 53, pp. 195–207

Kaiser, Werner and Dreyer, Günter 1982. 'Umm el-Qaab. Nachuntersuchungen im frühzeitlichen Königsfriedhof (Zweiter Vorbericht)', *MDAIK* 38, pp. 211–69

Kaiser, Werner, et al. 1999. 'Stadt und Tempel von Elephantine. 25./26./27. Grabungsbericht', *MDAIK* 55, pp. 63–236

Katary, Sally L. D. 1989. *Land Tenure in the Ramesside Period*, London

Kees, Herman 1961. *Ancient Egypt: A Cultural Topography*, ed. T. G. H. James, London

Kemp, Barry J. 1966. 'Abydos and the Royal Tombs of the First Dynasty', *JEA* 52, pp. 13–22

1978. 'Preliminary Report on the el 'Amarna Survey, 1978', *JEA* 65, pp. 5–12

1989. *Ancient Egypt: Anatomy of a Civilisation*, London

1994. 'Food for an Egyptian City', in *Whither Environmental Archaeology?* ed. Rosemary Luff and Peter Rowley-Conwy, Oxford, pp. 133–53

2000. 'Soil (including Mud-brick Architecture)', in *AEMT*, pp. 78–103

Klemm, D. D., Klemm, R. and Steclaci, L. 1984. 'Die pharaonischen
    Steinbrüche des Silifizierten Sandsteins in Ägypten und die Herkunft der
    Memnon-Kolosse', *MDAIK* 40, pp. 207–20

Kozloff, Arielle P., Bryan, Betsy M. and Berman, Lawrence M. 1992. *Egypt's
    Dazzling Sun: Amenhotep III and his World*, Cleveland

Krauss, Rolf 1996. 'The Length of Sneferu's Reign and How Long It Took to
    Build the "Red Pyramid"', *JEA* 82, pp. 43–50

Kromer, Karl 1978. *Siedlungsfunde aus dem frühen Alten Reich in Giseh: Öste-
    reichische Ausgrabungen*, Vienna

Krzyszkowska, Olga K. and Morkot, Robert 2000. 'Ivory and Related Materials',
    in *AEMT*, pp. 320–31

Kuhlmann, Klaus Peter 1996. 'Serif-style Architecture and the Design of the
    Archaic Egyptian Palace ("Königszelt")', in *HUPAÄ*, pp. 117–38

Kuper, Rudolph and Förster, Frank 2003. 'Khufu's "Mefat" Expeditions into
    the Libyan Desert', *EA* 23, pp. 25–8

Landström, Björn 1970. *Ships of the Pharaohs*, London

Lange, Kurt and Hirmer, Max 1961. *Egypt* (3rd revised edn), London

Lauer, Jean-Philippe 1960. *Observations sur les pyramides*, Cairo

   1962. *Histoire monumentale des pyramides d'Égypte*, vol. I: *Les pyramides à Degrés*,
       Cairo

   1989. 'Le problème de la construction de la Grande Pyramide', *RdE* 40,
       pp. 91–111

   1996. 'Remarques concernant l'inscription d'Imhotep gravée sur le socle de
       statue de l'Horus Neteri-khet (roi Djoser)', in *SWKS* II, pp. 493–8

   1999. 'The Step Pyramid Precinct of King Djoser', in *EAAP*, pp. 13–19

Lawton, Ian and Ogilvie-Herald, Chris 1999. *Gîza: The Truth*, London

Leclant, Jean 1999. 'A Brief History of the Old Kingdom', in *EAAP*, pp. 3–11

Leek, Frank Filce 1980. 'Observations on a Collection of Crania from the
    Mastabas of the Reign of Cheops at Gîza', *JEA* 66, pp. 36–45

   1986. 'Cheops' Courtiers: Their Skeletal Remains', in *Science in Egyptology*,
       ed. A. R. David, Manchester

Legrain, Georges 1929. *Les temples de Karnak*, Brussels

Lehner, Mark 1983. 'Some Observations on the Layout of the Khufu and
    Khafre Pyramids', *JARCE* 20, pp. 7–25

   1985a. 'The Development of the Giza Necropolis: The Khufu Project', *MDAIK*
       41, pp. 109–43

   1985b. *The Pyramid Tomb of Hetep-heres and the Satellite Pyramid of Khufu*, Mainz

   1991–2002. *The Giza Mapping Project Annual Report*, in seven parts, 1991–2,
       1993–4, 1995–6, 1998–9, 1999–2000, 2000–1, 2001–2, at the Oriental
       Institute of the University of Chicago's web site

   1996. 'Z500 and the Layer Pyramid of Zawiyet el-Aryan', in *SWKS* II,
       pp. 507–22

   1997. *The Complete Pyramids*, London

   1998. 'Niches, Slots, Grooves and Stains: Internal Frameworks in the Khufu
       Pyramid?', in *STAT*, pp. 101–13

Lepsius, Richard 1852. *Discoveries in Egypt, Ethiopia and the Peninsula of Sinai*, trans. Kenneth Mackenzie, London

Lévi-Strauss, Claude 1963. *Structural Anthropology*, trans. Claire Jacobson and Brooke Schoepf, New York

1966. *The Savage Mind*, London

1995. *The Story of Lynx*, trans. Catherine Tihanyi, Chicago

Lewis-Williams, David 2002. *The Mind in the Cave*, London

Lipke, Paul 1984. *The Royal Ship of Cheops*, Oxford

Lucas, Alfred 1927. 'Copper in Ancient Egypt', *JEA* 13, pp. 162–70

Lucas, Alfred, revised Harris, J. R. 1962. *Ancient Egyptian Materials and Industries*, London

Málek, Jaromír 1997. 'The Temples at Memphis. Problems Highlighted by the EES Survey', in *TAE*, pp. 90–101

Mallory-Greenough, Leanne M. 2002. 'The Geographical, Spatial and Temporal Distribution of Predynastic and First Dynasty Basalt Vessels', *JEA* 88, pp. 67–93

Der Manuelian, Peter (ed.) 1992. 'George Andrew Reisner on Archaeological Photography', *JARCE* 29, pp. 1–34

1998. 'The Problem of the Giza Slab Stelae', in *STAT*, pp. 115–34

1999. 'Excavating the Old Kingdom: The Giza Necropolis and Other Mastaba Fields', in *EAAP*, pp. 139–54

Martin, Geoffrey T. 1997. ' "Covington's Tomb" and Related Early Monuments at Gîza', in *EJ-PL* II, pp. 279–88

Mathieson, Ian and Tavares, Ana 1997. 'Preliminary Report of the National Museums of Scotland Saqqara Survey Project 1990–1991', *JEA* 79, pp. 17–31

Mathieson, Ian, et al. 1997. 'The National Museums of Scotland Saqqara Survey Project 1993–1995', *JEA* 83, pp. 17–54

1999. 'The National Museums of Scotland Saqqara Survey Project, Earth Sciences 1990–1998', *JEA* 85, pp. 21–43

Matthiae, Paolo, Pinnock, Frances and Matthiae, Gabriella la Scandone 1995. *Ebla: alle origini della civiltà urbana*, Milan

Meeks, Dimitri and Favard-Meeks, Christine 1996. *Daily Life of the Egyptian Gods*, trans G. M. Goshgarian, London

Meiggs, Russell 1982. *Trees and Timber in the Ancient Mediterranean World*, Oxford

Mendelssohn, Kurt 1974. *The Riddle of the Pyramids*, London

Midant-Reynes, Béatrix 2000. *The Prehistory of Egypt*, trans. Ian Shaw, Oxford

Millet, Nicholas B. 1990/91. 'The Narmer Macehead and Related Objects', *JARCE* 27, pp. 53–9, with reversed plate correction, *JARCE* 28, pp. 223–5

1999. 'The Reserve Heads of the Old Kingdom: A Theory', in *EAAP*, pp. 233–4

Momigliano, Arnaldo 1990. *The Classical Foundations of Modern Historiography*, Berkeley

Moores, Robert G., Jr. 1991. 'Evidence for Use of a Stone-cutting Drag Saw by the Fourth Dynasty Egyptians', *JARCE* 28, pp. 139–47

Moreh, Shmuel 1975. *Al-Jabartī's Chronicle of the First Seven Months of the French Occupation of Egypt: Muharram rajab 1213, 15 June–December 1798. Tarikh muddat al faransis bi misr*, trans. Shmuel Moreh, Leiden

De Morgan, Jacques 1897a. *Carte de la nécropole memphite*, Cairo
  1897b. *Recherches sur les origines de l'Égypte*, II, Paris

Mortensen, Bodil 1985. 'Four Jars from the Maadi Culture found in Giza', *MDAIK* 41, pp. 145–8

Murray, Mary Anne 2000. 'Cereal Production and Processing', in *AEMT*, pp. 505–36

Nour, Mohammad Zaki, Iskander, Zaky, Osman, Mohammad Salah and Moustafa, Ahmad Youssof 1960. *The Cheops Boats*, Cairo

O'Connor, David 1979. 'The Geography of Settlement in Ancient Egypt', *Man, Settlement and Urbanism*, ed. Peter J. Ucko, Ruth Tringham and G. W. Dimbleby, London, pp. 681–98
  1989. 'New Funerary Enclosures (*Talbezirke*) of the Early Dynastic Period at Abydos', *JARCE* 26, pp. 51–86
  1993. 'Urbanism in Bronze Age Egypt and Northeast Africa', in *AA*, pp. 570–87
  1995. 'The Earliest Royal Boat Graves', *EA* 6, pp. 3–7

Ogden, Jack 2000. 'Metals', in *AEMT*, pp. 148–76

Owen, Gwil and Kemp, Barry 1994. 'Craftsmen's Work Patterns in Unfinished Tombs at Amarna', *CAJ* 4.1, pp. 121–9

Page May, W. 1901. *Helwan and the Egyptian Desert*, London

Palmer, E. H. 1871. *The Desert of the Exodus*, London

Panofsky, Erwin 1992. *Tomb Sculpture*, London

Peden, Alexander J. 2001. *The Graffiti of Pharaonic Egypt*, Leiden

Peet, T. Eric 1929. Review, *JEA* 15, p. 275

Pendlebury, J. D. S., et al. 1951. *The City of Akhenaten, Part III*, London

Perring, John Shea 1839. *The Pyramids of Giza*, vol. I, London

Petrie, W. M. Flinders 1883. *The Pyramids & Temples of Gizeh*, London
  1885. *The Pyramids & Temples of Gizeh* (revised edn), London (reprinted, with update by Zahi Hawass, London 1990)
  1892. *Medum*, London
  1893. *Ten Years Digging in Egypt*, London
  1900. *The Royal Tombs of the First Dynasty, Part I*, London
  1901. *The Royal Tombs of the Earliest Dynasties, Part II*, London
  1903. *Abydos, Part 2*, London
  1906. *Researches in Sinai*, London
  1924. *A History of Egypt* I (11th edn), London
  1933. *Seventy Years in Archaeology*, London
  n.d. 'The Egyptians', in *Hutchinson's Story of the Nations*, London (*c.* 1925)

Piankoff, Alexandre 1968. *The Pyramid of Unas*, Princeton, NJ
  1972. *The Wandering of the Soul* (completed by Helen Jacquet-Gordon), Princeton, NJ

Posener-Kriéger, Paule 1991. 'Graffiti on the Revetment Blocks of the Pyramid', in Ali el-Khouli et al., *Meidum*, Sydney

Pound, Ezra 1938. *Guide to Kulchur*, London

Quibell, J. E. 1923. *Excavations at Saqqara (1912 –1914)*, Cairo

Rawlinson, George (trans.) 1858–60. *The History of Herodotus* (4 vols.), London, 1858

Ray, John 2003. 'Fact, Fantasy and "Pyramididiots" ', *The Times*, London, 23 July

Reid, Donald M. 2002. *Whose Pharaohs?* Berkeley, CA

Reisner, George Andrew 1915. 'Accessions to the Egyptian Department during 1914', *Bulletin of the Museum of Fine Arts* (Boston), 13, pp. 29–36

   1931. *Mycerinus*, Cambridge, MA

   1932. *A Provincial Cemetery of the Pyramid Age, Naga-ed-Dêr*, Berkeley

   1936. *The Development of the Egyptian Tomb down to the Accession of Cheops*, Cambridge, MA

   1942. *A History of the Giza Necropolis*, Cambridge, MA

Reisner, George Andrew and Smith, William Stevenson 1955. *The Tomb of Hetep-heres, the Mother of Cheops*, Cambridge, MA

Ridley, Ronald T. n.d. *Napoleon's Proconsul in Egypt*, London (c. 2000)

Robins, Gay 1994. *Proportion and Style in Ancient Egyptian Art*, London

Robins, Gay and Shute, Charles 1987. *The Rhind Mathematical Papyrus*, London

Roehrig, Catharine H. 1999. 'Reserve Heads: An Enigma of Old Kingdom Sculpture', in *EAAP*, pp. 73–81

Roemer, Hans Robert 1982. 'Relations in the Humanities between Germany and Egypt', in *Ägypten – Dauer und Wandel*, Mainz, pp. 1–6

Romer, John 1976. 'Royal Tombs of the Early Eighteenth Dynasty', *MDAIK* 32, pp. 191–206

   1988. *Testament, the Bible and History*, London

Romer, John and Romer, Elizabeth 1995. *The Seven Wonders of the World*, London

Rosen, Arlene Miller 1986. *Cities of Clay*, Chicago

Rossi, Corinna 1999. 'Note on the Pyramidion found at Dahshur', *JEA* 85, pp. 219–22

Roth, Anne Macy 1991. *Egyptian Phyles in the Old Kingdom*, Chicago

   1993a. 'Social Change in the Fourth Dynasty: The Spatial Organisation of Pyramids, Tombs, and Cemeteries', *JARCE* 30, pp. 33–55

   1993b. 'Fingers, Stars and the "Opening of the Mouth" ', *JEA* 79, pp. 57–79

Rothenberg, Beno (ed.) 1990. *The Ancient Metallurgy of Copper*, London

Rouse, A. L. 1972. 'The Abbey in the History of the Nation', in *Westminster Abbey*, Radnor, PA, pp. 37–145

Said, Edward W. 1993. *Culture and Imperialism*, London

Saleh, A. A. 1974. 'Excavations around Mycerinus Pyramid Complex', *MDAIK* 30.1, pp. 131–54

   1996. 'Ancient Egyptian House and Palace at Giza and Heliopolis', in *HUPAÄ*, pp. 185–93

Samuel, Delwen 2000. 'Brewing and Baking', in *AEMT*, pp. 537–76

Sandford, K. S. and Arkell, W. J. 1929. *Paleolithic Man and the Nile-Faiyum Divide*, Chicago

Savary, Claude É. 1786. *Letters on Egypt*, London

Saxl, Fritz 1957. 'The Revival of Late Antique Astrology', in *Lectures* (2 vols.), London

Schäfer, Heinrich 1974. *Principles of Egyptian Art*, trans. and ed. John Baines, Oxford

Schenkel, Wolfgang 1963. 'Die Farben in Ägyptischer Kunst und Sprache', *ZÄS* 88, pp. 131–47

Schulz, Regine and Seidel, Matthias (eds.) 1998. *Egypt, the World of the Pharaohs*, Cologne

Scott, Walter 1924. *Hermetica* I, Oxford

Seidlmayer, Stephan 1996. 'Town and State in the Early Old Kingdom: A View from Elephantine', in *Aspects of Early Egypt*, ed. Jeffrey Spencer, London, pp. 108–27

Serres, Michel 1981. *Rome, the Book of Foundations*, trans. Felicia McCarren, Stanford

Shaw, Ian 2000. 'Khafra's Quarries in the Sahara', *EA* 16, pp. 28–30

Shaw, Ian and Heldal, Tom 2003. 'Rescue Work in the Khafra Quarries at Gebel el-Asr', *EA* 23, pp. 14–16

Sherer, Moyle 1825. *Scenes and Impressions in Egypt*, London (published anonymously)

Simpson, William Kelly, Faulkner, R. O. and Wente, Edward F., Jr. 1972. *The Literature of Ancient Egypt*, Yale

Sjoberg, Gideon 1960. *The Preindustrial City, Past and Present*, Glencoe

Smith, Harry S. 1997. 'Uncharted Saqqâra: An Essay', in *EJ-PL* II, pp. 379–93

Smith, William Stevenson 1949. *A History of Egyptian Sculpture and Painting in the Old Kingdom*, London

1960. *Ancient Egypt as Represented in the Museum of Fine Arts* (6th edn), Boston

Smith, W. Stevenson, revised Simpson, W. Kelly 1981. *The Art and Architecture of Ancient Egypt*, Harmondsworth

Smyth, Charles Piazzi 1867. *Life and Work at the Great Pyramid* (3 vols.), Edinburgh

Sourouzian, Hourig 1995. 'L'iconographie du roi dans la statuaire des trois premières dynasties', in *Kunst des Alten Reiches*, Mainz, pp. 133–54

Spence, Kate 2000. 'Ancient Egyptian Chronology and the Astronomical Orientation of Pyramids', *Nature* 408, November

2004. 'Bookshelf', *EA* 24, p. 42

Stadelmann, Rainer 1980. 'Snofru und die Pyramiden von Meidum und Dahschur', *MDAIK* 36, pp. 437–49

1981. 'La ville de pyramides à l'Ancien Empire', *RdE* 33, pp. 67–77

1983. 'Die Pyramiden des Snofru in Dahschur Zweiter Bericht über die Ausgrabungen an der nördlichen Steinpyramide', *MDAIK* 39, pp. 225–41

1984. 'Die Herkunft der Memnon-Kolosse: Heliopolis oder Aswan?' *MDAIK* 40, pp. 291–6

1987. 'Beiträge zur Geschichte des Alten Reiches. Die Länge der Regierung des Snofru', *MDAIK* 43, pp. 229–39

1990. *Die grossen Pyramiden von Giza*, Graz

1991. 'Das Dreikammersystem der Königsgräber der Frühzeit und des Alten Reiches', *MDAIK* 47, pp. 373–87

1994. 'Die sogenannten Luftkanäle der Cheopspyramide: Modellkorridore für den Aufstieg des Königs zum Himmel' (with an additional note by Rudolf Gantenbrink), *MDAIK* 50, pp. 285–94

1995. 'Der Strenge Stil der frühen Vierten Dynastie', *Kunst des Alten Reiches*, Mainz, pp. 155–66

1996. 'Origins and Development of the Funerary Complex of Djoser', in *SWKS* II, pp. 787–800

1997a. *Die ägyptischen Pyramiden, vom Ziegelbau zum Weltwunder* (3rd edn), Mainz

1997b. 'The Development of the Pyramid Temple in the Fourth Dynasty', in *TAE*, pp. 1–16

1998. 'Royal Tombs from the Age of the Pyramids', in *Egypt: The World of the Pharaohs*, ed. Regine Schulz and Matthias Seidel, Cologne, pp. 46–77

Stadelmann, Rainer and Alexanian, Nicole 1998. 'Die Friedhöfe des Alten und Mittleren Reiches in Dahschur', *MDAIK* 54, pp. 293–317

Stadelmann, Rainer and Sourouzian, Hourig 1982. 'Die Pyramiden des Snofru in Dahschur. Erster Bericht über die Ausgrabungen an der nördlichen Steinpyramide', *MDAIK* 38, pp. 379–93

2001. 'Der Totentempel Amenophis' III. in Theben Grabungen und Restaurierung am Kom el-Hettân', *MDAIK* 57, pp. 271–80

Starobinski, Jean 1964. *The Invention of Liberty 1700–1789*, Geneva

Steindorff, Georg 1905. *The Religion of the Ancient Egyptians*, New York

Stos-Gale, Zofia, Gale, Noel and Houghton, Judy 1995. 'The Origins of Egyptian Copper', in *Egypt, the Aegean and the Levant*, ed. W. Vivian Davies and Louise Schofield, London, pp. 127–35

Strouhal, Eugene, et al 1994. 'Re-investigation of the Remains Thought To Be of King Djoser and Those of an Unidentified Female from the Step Pyramid at Saqqara', *Anthropologie* 32.3, pp. 225–42

Strudwick, Nigel 1985. *The Administration of Egypt in the Old Kingdom*, London

Swan Hall, Emma 1986. *The Pharaoh Smites His Enemies*, Berlin

Tacke, Nikolaus 1996. 'Die Entwicklung der Mumienmaske im Alten Reich', *MDAIK* 52, pp. 307–36

Tarrell, J. and Petrie, W. M. Flinders 1925. 'The Great Pyramid Courses', *Ancient Egypt* 1925, Part II, June, pp. 36–9

Teeter, Emily 1987. 'Techniques and Terminology of Rope-making in Ancient Egypt', *JEA* 73, pp. 71–7

Thomas, Nancy 1995. *The American Discovery of Ancient Egypt*, Los Angeles

Tompkins, Peter 1973. *Secrets of the Great Pyramid*, London

Toomer, G. J. 1971. 'Mathematics and Astronomy', in *The Legacy of Egypt*, ed. J. R. Harris (2nd edn), Oxford

Trigger, Bruce G. 1993. *Early Civilizations, Ancient Egypt in Context*, Cairo

Vachala, B. and Sroboda, J. 1989. 'Die Steinmesser aus Abusir', *ZÄS* 116, pp. 174–81

Valbelle, Dominique 1985. *'Les ouvriers de la tombe': Deir el-Médineh à l'époque Ramesside*, Cairo

Valloggia, Michel 1997. 'La descenderie de la pyramide de Radjedef à Abu Rawash', in *EJ-PL* II, pp. 417–28

 2003. 'Radjedef's Pyramid Complex at Abu Rawash', *EA* 23, pp. 10–13

Ventura, Raphael 1985. 'Snefru in Sinai and Amenophis I at Deir el-Medinah', in *Pharaonic Egypt*, ed. Sarah Israelit-Groll, Jerusalem, pp. 278–88

Vernant, Jean-Pierre 1991. *Mortals and Immortals: Collected Essays*, ed. Froma I. Zeitlin, Princeton

Verner, Miroslav 1986. 'A Slaughterhouse from the Old Kingdom', *MDAIK* 42, pp. 181–9

 2002. *The Pyramids: Their Archaeology and History*, London

Vinson, Steve 1998. *The Nile Boatman at Work*, Mainz

Volney, C. F. de Chassebœuf 1787. *Travels through Syria and Egypt* (2 vols.), London

Vyse, Colonel Howard 1840. *Operations Carried on at the Pyramids of Gizeh* (3 vols.), London

Ward, Cheryl A. 2000. *Sacred and Secular: Ancient Egyptian Ships and Boats*, Philadelphia

Ward, John 1900. *Pyramids and Progress*, London

Wente, Edward 1990. *Letters From Ancient Egypt*, Atlanta

Wetterstrom, Wilma 1993. 'Foraging and Farming in Egypt', in *AA*, pp. 165–226

Wheeler, Mortimer 1966. *Alms for Oblivion: An Antiquary's Scrapbook*, London

White, Michael 1997. *Isaac Newton: The Last Sorcerer*, London

Wildung, Dietrich 1969. *Die Rolle ägyptischer Könige im Bewusstsein ihrer Nachwelt*, Berlin

Wilkinson, Sir Gardner 1847. *Murray's Hand-Book for Travellers in Egypt*, London

Wilkinson, Toby A. H. 1999. *Early Dynastic Egypt*, London

Willcocks, W. and Craig, J. I. 1913. *Egyptian Irrigation* (2 vols.), London

Wilson, Charles W. 1880. *Picturesque Palestine*, vol. I: *Sinai and Egypt*, London

Wilson, John 1964. *Signs and Wonders upon Pharaoh*, Chicago

Winkler, Hans A. 1938. *Rock-Drawings of Southern Upper Egypt* I, London

Winlock, H. E. 1955. *Models of Daily Life in Ancient Egypt from the Tomb of Meket-Rēʿ at Thebes*, New York

Wood, Wendy 1987. 'The Archaic Stone Tombs at Helwan', *JEA* 73, pp. 59–70

Žába, Zybněk 1953. *L'orientation astronomique dans l'ancienne Égypte et la précession de l'axe du monde*, Prague

Ziegler, Christiane 1999. 'Nonroyal Statuary', in *EAAP*, pp. 57–71, and 'Sculptor's Tools', p. 280

Ziermann, Martin 2003. *Elephantine XXVIII. Die Baustrukturen der älteren Stadt etc.*, Mainz

Zivie, Christiane 1976. *Giza au deuxième millénaire*, Cairo

Acknowledgements

I would like to express my sincere gratitude to those who in diverse ways have helped to bring this book to its fruition.

First, to the many skilled stone cutters I have known; from my grandfather James Simpson who worked with almost every type of building stone used in Edwardian London, to Mohammed 'Ednein' of Tarif village in Upper Egypt who showed me how to cut and open Theban limestone and guided me around his local quarries, and to those Italian masons who, in the course of various domestic adventures, helped me understand the nature of *pietra serena* and other local building stones, especially Massimo Mazzi of Arezzo, and Silvio and Virgilio Guidi of Morra, in Umbria.

To John Ross, who entrusted me with many of the books and essays listed in the bibliography and who has lately showered me with a plethora of assorted images of the Great Pyramid, from the rarest nineteenth-century plates to his own splendid photographs taken over fifty years of working in the land of Egypt.

To Dr Zahi Hawass, Secretary General of the Supreme Council of Egyptian Antiquities, whose friendly staff have welcomed me to the Great Pyramid and the other Giza monuments in the course of a variety of projects. I hope that in some small manner this book may aid his patient discourse with those silly foreigners who yet pretend that Egypt's ancient monuments were not made by Egyptians.

To Hans Goedicke, my first guide to Giza and Sakkara and indeed to ancient Egypt, for his learned passion for the pyramids, and more specifically for his most generous and careful reading of my typescript over these past months.

To Elizabeth my wife, who forty years ago, on our first trip to the Giza Plateau, sat beside me on the slatted seat of a number 8 Cairo tram and later, after an exhausting trudge around the monuments, stood with me on the wooden balcony of Mena House watching the Pyramid above dissolve into a silky, starry, perfumed desert darkness. With a sharp eye and most loving care, she has read, corrected and improved this text in all its manifestations. Without her, I would not have seen that Pyramid at all.

Last, but by no means the least of these pleasurable acknowledgements, I should like to thank Michael Sharp and his Cambridge colleagues for making such a splendid volume from a plain paper typescript, some photographs and scans, and a handful of rough sketches.

John Romer, Arezzo, 2006

Index